Places in the Parasha
Biblical Geography and Its Meaning

Michael Scharf Publication Trust
Yeshiva University Press

MAGGID

Yoel Elitzur

Places in the Parasha

Biblical Geography and Its Meaning

Translated by
Daniel Landman

Yeshiva University Press
Maggid Books

Places in the Parasha
Biblical Geography and Its Meaning

First English Edition, 2020

Maggid Books
An imprint of Koren Publishers Jerusalem Ltd.

POB 8531, New Milford, CT 06776-8531, USA
& POB 4044, Jerusalem 9104001, Israel
www.maggidbooks.com

The publication of this book was made possible
through the generous support of *The Jewish Book Trust.*

ISBN 978-1-59264-486-5, *hardcover*

A CIP catalogue record for this title is
available from the British Library

Printed and bound in the United States

Dedicated in loving memory of
John Alexander Franks, z"l
יעקב בן משה ז"ל
Husband, father, grandfather,
solicitor, collector, scholar, writer

Contents

Leviticus

Numbers

Shabbat Ḥol HaMoed Pesaḥ

Seventh Day of Pesaḥ

Shavuot

Foreword

> If you seek it as you do silver and search for it as for [buried] treasures, then you will understand the fear of the Lord and attain knowledge of God. (Prov. 2:4–5)

When learning Tanakh with the literary-theological method,[1] certain elements become primary. Others lend themselves less to this type of analysis and religious exploration. To cite a familiar example, one learning the Book of Joshua likely will focus on the gripping narratives of chapters 1–12 and then skip to chapters 22–24. Joshua's role as leader and his relationship to Moses' leadership, the balance between God's intervention and human efforts, the reenactment of the covenant, the thorny question of war against the Canaanites, and many other vital religious and human issues dominate the discussion. The lengthy city lists in chapters 13–21 would receive scant attention at best, perhaps a few scattered bullet points. Further, the classical commentators do not offer extensive help expanding the middle chapters, since they generally were unaware of the geography of the Land of Israel.

1. See especially Shalom Carmy, "A Room with a View, but a Room of Our Own," in *Modern Scholarship in the Study of Torah: Contributions and Limitations*, ed. Shalom Carmy (Northvale, NJ: Jason Aronson, 1996), 1–38; Hayyim Angel, "The Literary-Theological Study of Tanakh," afterword to Moshe Sokolow, *Tanakh: An Owner's Manual: Authorship, Canonization, Masoretic Text, Exegesis, Modern Scholarship and Pedagogy* (Brooklyn, NY: Ktav, 2015), 192–207.

Now imagine an entire book about those city list chapters, written by an expert in both the text of Tanakh and contemporary historical and archaeological scholarship. Imagine that book teaching a rigorous methodology in a clear accessible way that enlightens our understanding of Tanakh and strengthens our religious connection to the Land of Israel. Such a book would fill a monumental void in our learning. You are holding that book.

Professor Yoel Elitzur has made a remarkable contribution to religious Tanakh study precisely by focusing on the oft-neglected biblical places and names. Prof. Elitzur, who taught Tanakh for many years at Herzog College of Yeshivat Har Etzion and at Hebrew University, not only believes in the sanctity of Tanakh. He takes its historical relevance seriously.[2] Following in the venerable footsteps of his father and teacher, Professor Yehuda Elitzur, *z"l* (1911–1997), Prof. Yoel Elitzur combines cutting-edge academic research with careful text analysis, bringing both together with rigor and religious passion.

One must wait until page 431 of this volume to hear Prof. Elitzur's assessment of his contribution:

> This is a lonely task, as the classical commentators were not familiar with the land or with the extrabiblical sources, and many God-fearing students today who take interest in these matters believe that they should not pursue information or sources that were beyond the purview of the classical commentators. On the other hand, most scholars of biblical geography and history do not pay attention to what the Tanakh says about itself…We will read the Tanakh as it is written and attempt to understand what exactly it is saying, with the help of all the historical, geographical, archaeological, and linguistic tools available to us.

2. For a particularly instructive example, Prof. Elitzur insists that the Pharaoh at the time of the Exodus was not Ramesses II, based on his acceptance of the chronological signpost in I Kings 6:1, which states that Solomon built the Temple 480 years from the Exodus (pp. 143–55).

This volume provides the serious religious student of Tanakh with information and methodology that impact on many aspects of learning. In this foreword, I cite several representative examples of the types of contributions he makes.

In his study of *Parashat Bereshit*, Prof. Elitzur explores the role of the Euphrates River in Tanakh (pp. 6–10). One noteworthy point is his analysis of I Kings 5:4, which states that King Solomon "controlled the whole region beyond the River, from Tiphsah to Gaza." In this verse, "beyond the River" clearly refers to the west of the Euphrates, where Israel is located. This verse, argues Prof. Elitzur, reflects a later geographical perspective introduced by the Assyrians (first evidenced in the writings of Sargon II, 722–705 BCE), who referred to the western nations of the Assyrian Empire as *eber nari*. Prior to the rise of the Assyrian Empire, Israel's original perspective is that we are "here," and "beyond the River" refers to nations *east* of the Euphrates (see Josh. 24:2–15; II Sam. 10:16). After the rise of the Assyrian Empire, Israel adopted the Assyrian-centric perspective and referred to the Land of Israel as "beyond the River," that is, *west* of the Euphrates.[3] This later point of reference appears thirteen times in the Book of Ezra. Returning to the verse pertaining to King Solomon's reign, it appears that this perspective reflects the time of the later prophetic author (traditionally Jeremiah; see Bava Batra 15a), rather than the time of Solomon, who ruled prior to the eighth century BCE. In Solomon's time, the Israelites would not yet have referred to the Land of Israel as "beyond the River."

Prof. Elitzur does not often engage in direct "know how to answer the heretic" (Mishna Avot 2:14) polemic. On occasion, however, he brings biblical and archaeological evidence to bear when there are popular misconceptions based on a misunderstanding of either the biblical text or archaeology. In his analysis of the proper identification of the Ai (pp. 18–36), for example, Prof. Elitzur surveys the biblical evidence for clues on locating the city vis-à-vis Bethel. It

3. Prof. Elitzur notes the parallel to contemporary people living in the "Middle East" (synonymous with the "Near East") also referring to their lands as the Middle East, adopting the Eurocentric perspective of that term.

should be located just east of Bethel. And indeed, just over one mile east of Bethel's probable location, a large tell was discovered. Known by Arabs as Khirbet et-Tell (the ruins of the tell), it appeared to be the perfect location to unearth Ai. In the 1930s, analysis of archaeological findings suggested that et-Tell was a highly fortified city that was destroyed by fire in approximately 2100 BCE, long before Abraham. After that, the city lay in ruins except for a brief period prior to the founding of Israel's monarchy when an unfortified village was settled on top of the destroyed city. The scholarly conclusion, therefore, was that Joshua would have found an uninhabited city in ruins. Although this conclusion cast doubt on the veracity of the battle account in the Book of Joshua (chs. 7–8), Prof. Elitzur argues that even a superficial reading of the biblical passages illustrates that the Ai was a tiny town. Et-Tell, in contrast, reveals a large city. In all likelihood, et-Tell is *not* the location of the biblical Ai. The biblical Ai would be somewhere else in the vicinity of Khirbet et-Tell, and has not yet been unearthed in archaeological digs. Thus, there is no conflict between the biblical account and the current state of archaeological scholarship.

In his essay on *Parashat Vayishlaḥ* (pp. 84–95), Prof. Elitzur weighs in on a controversy surrounding the traditional site of Joseph's tomb in Shechem, which was vandalized by Arabs in 1996 and again in 2000. In the 1980s and '90s, several Israelis, often motivated by their political viewpoints, asserted through various media that this gravesite was merely a tomb of a Muslim Sheikh named Yusuf who lived some two hundred years ago. Prof. Elitzur responds that the site has been known and venerated for thousands of years. He surveys ancient and medieval writings that identify the site, and couples that with an analysis of archaeological findings to support his conclusion.

Prof. Elitzur is equally equipped to debunk unfounded folk traditions. A recent Jewish tradition marks two graves near Zorah as those of Samson and his father Manoah. This identification, however, is specious (p. 422). Samson was buried "*between* Zorah and Eshtaol" (Judges 16:31), whereas these two graves are adjacent to Zorah itself.

Prof. Elitzur even ventures occasionally into the realm of halakha. For example, cities surrounded by walls at the time of Joshua must observe Purim on the fifteenth day of Adar. What cities were surrounded by walls at that time? Prof. Elitzur provides archaeological evidence to contribute to this discussion (pp. 373–85).

In his study on *Parashat Masei* (pp. 531–52), Prof. Elitzur examines a halakhic debate between Rambam and Ramban. Rambam follows the talmudic ruling that all forty-eight Levite cities served as cities of refuge. Ramban adopts the plain sense of the texts of the Torah and the Book of Joshua and insists that only six Levite cities served as cities of refuge.

Rather than simply concluding that Ramban is closer to the plain sense of the Torah and Joshua, Prof. Elitzur observes that in the parallel list of Levite cities in I Chronicles 6, there is a different formulation from the list in Joshua. For example, the Book of Joshua lists Hebron as a Levite city that became a city of refuge: "But to the descendants of Aaron the priest they assigned Hebron – the city of refuge for manslayers – together with its pastures, Libnah with its pastures, Jattir with its pastures, Eshtemoa with its pastures..." (Josh. 21:13–14). It is clear that Hebron is the city of refuge, and the other Levite cities are not cities of refuge. Ramban has *peshat*.

Contrast the parallel passage in Chronicles: "To the sons of Aaron they gave the cities of refuge: Hebron and Libnah with its pasturelands, Jattir and Eshtemoa with its pasturelands..." (I Chr. 6:42). This passage uses the term *cities* of refuge, suggesting that *all* of these Levite cities served as cities of refuge. Rambam has *peshat*!

The same contrast between city and cities occurs with Shechem:

> They were given, in the hill country of Ephraim, Shechem – the *city* of refuge for manslayers – with its pastures, Gezer with its pastures... (Josh. 21:21)

> They gave them the *cities* of refuge: Shechem with its pasturelands in the hill country of Ephraim, Gezer with its pasturelands... (I Chr. 6:52)

Prof. Elitzur suggests that Chronicles reflects the reality in a later period, when all Levite cities served as cities of refuge based on a special enactment or custom. He quotes several relevant rabbinic and other ancient sources to support this thesis. In the final analysis, Ramban reflects *peshat* in the Torah and Joshua, which was likely the original law. Rambam reflects *peshat* in Chronicles, which was likely the law followed some generations later.

My favorite analyses encompass several essays that explore the correlation between enthusiastic desire to inherit the Land of Israel and the inheritance of that land. In his essay on *Parashat Pinḥas* (pp. 502–14), Prof. Elitzur explores a curious feature regarding the inheritance of the daughters of Tzlofhad. Because Manasseh and Ephraim were born in Egypt, we do not learn of their family branches until the census in the fortieth year of the wilderness:

> These were the descendants of Gilead: [Of] Iezer, the clan of the Iezerites; of Helek, the clan of the Helekites; [of] Asriel, the clan of the Asrielites; [of] Shechem, the clan of the Shechemites; [of] Shemida, the clan of the Shemidaites; [of] Hepher, the clan of the Hepherites. (Num. 26:31–33)

In sum, there are six family branches in Manasseh. The daughters of Tzlofhad are the granddaughters of Hepher, and presumably would split the portion that would have been assigned to Tzlofhad son of Hepher.

When the Book of Joshua describes the tribal inheritance of Manasseh, however, it identifies ten districts instead of the expected six:

> And this is the portion that fell by lot to the tribe of Manasseh… The descendants of Abiezer, Helek, Asriel, Shechem, Hepher, and Shemida…Now Tzlofhad son of Hepher son of Gilead son of Machir son of Manasseh had no sons, but only daughters… So, in accordance with the Lord's instructions, they were granted a portion among their father's kinsmen. *Ten districts* fell to Manasseh… as Manasseh's daughters inherited a portion together with his sons, while the land of Gilead was assigned to the rest of Manasseh's descendants. (Josh. 17:1–6)

From the simple reading of these verses, the five daughters of Tzlofhad each became independent districts in Manasseh, instead of simply all becoming part of Hepher's district! Why should they become their own districts, equal to those of their grandfather's generation? Prof. Elitzur quotes a midrashic resolution, that Tzlofhad amassed a total of five portions that he then bequeathed to his daughters. Alternatively, Malbim proposes that the ten districts in Manasseh are actually ten geographic portions not connected to the family tree.

However, it is far smoother to say that the daughters of Tzlofhad became independent districts. To support his reading, Prof. Elitzur quotes from the Samaria Ostraca that were discovered in 1910 in the treasury of the palace of the kings of Israel in ancient Samaria. Fifteen place names and seven clans appear in these documents. The seven clans are Shemida, Abiezer, Helek, [A]sriel, Shechem, Hoglah, and Noah. Hoglah and Noah were two of Tzlofhad's daughters. These districts were named after the family members, just as reported in Joshua 17. Evidently, the singular enthusiasm to inherit land displayed by the daughters of Tzlofhad elevated their rank within their tribe so that they ultimately received their own districts, unlike any of their male cousins from that generation.

In his essay on *Parashat Matot* (pp. 515–30), Prof. Elitzur continues the theme of the special enthusiasm to inherit the land exhibited by the tribe of Manasseh. He asks two basic questions: (1) Why does the half-tribe of Manasseh appear in Numbers 32 only as an afterthought? Why were they not included with Reuben and Gad from the beginning of their request of the eastern lands of Sihon and Og? (2) After the Israelites defeated Sihon, why did they then march north to confront Og in the Bashan (Num. 21:33)? They already had a clear entry path into the Land of Israel!

While yet in Egypt, the tribe of Manasseh named some of its children Gilead, Hepher, Shechem, and Tirzah. These are place-names in Manasseh's territory on both sides of the Jordan. These names expressed the wish of the tribe to return to their homeland, and evidently Manasseh considered territory on both sides of the Jordan home already during the nation's sojourn in Egypt.[4]

Building on the medieval rabbinic suggestions of a student of Rabbi Saadia Gaon and Rabbi Yehuda the Pious, Prof. Elitzur proposes that while the nation was still in Egypt, certain families from Manasseh settled parts of the Bashan. Throughout Israel's enslavement in Egypt, these Manassites remained in that territory and were there when Moses and the majority of the nation returned from Egypt. This hypothesis also accounts for the population explosion in Manasseh from the first year (32,200; see Num. 1:35) to the fortieth year (52,700; see Num. 26:34). Those who had left Egypt were joined by those living in Bashan.

Moses and the nation therefore marched north to Bashan, to greet and liberate their "sabra" brethren of Manasseh from the rule of Og. These Manassites also had nothing to do with Moses' deal with Reuben and Gad, since this land belonged to them from beforehand. The tribe of Manasseh earned this additional territory as a consequence of their enthusiasm to inherit the land.

Unlike the exceptional enthusiasm to inherit the land exhibited by the tribe of Manasseh, the tribe of Dan represents the opposite extreme. In his study of *Parashat Naso* (pp. 421–38), Prof. Elitzur explains that the tribe of Dan was lax in taking possession of the land, thereby squandering their assigned territory and forcing many of their members to find additional land to the north of Israel.

To support this thesis, Prof. Elitzur observes that the cities of Zorah and Eshtaol typically are associated with Dan. Samson, who hailed from the tribe of Dan, was active between these towns (Judges 13:25) and later was buried between these towns (16:31). Members of the tribe of Dan ventured from there to find new territory for Dan to occupy, and eventually conquered Laish in the north (18:2, 8, 11).

---

4. In a similar vein, Prof. Elitzur (p. 165) observes that Moses' father Amram had a brother named Hebron (Ex. 6:18). Evidently, Hebron was named in Egypt after the city to express a profound longing for the people to return to the land of the Patriarchs. Once Joshua and the people entered Israel, this dream was fulfilled as Hebron became a Levite city and a city of refuge.

In the Book of Joshua, however, Zorah and Eshtaol are identified *both* with Judah and with Dan. With Judah: "In the Lowland: Eshtaol, Zorah, Ashnah…" (Josh. 15:33). With Dan: "Their allotted territory comprised: Zorah, Eshtaol, Ir-shemesh…" (19:41). To whom did these towns belong?

Although Dan was a large tribe, it was unable to conquer or hold land:

> But the territory of the Danites slipped from their grasp. So the Danites migrated and made war on Leshem. They captured it and put it to the sword; they took possession of it and settled in it. And they changed the name of Leshem to Dan, after their ancestor Dan. (Josh. 19:47)

> The Amorites pressed the Danites into the hill country; they would not let them come down to the plain. (Judges 1:34)

Further, the description of Dan's portion in Joshua chapter 19 is a list of cities, with no clearly defined borders. Prof. Elitzur explains this phenomenon by noting that the tribes of Judah, Ephraim, and Manasseh were quick to inherit their land and also dispossessed Canaanites from the surrounding regions. Consequently, they obtained this additional land.

Joshua supported the expansion of the tribes of Judah and Joseph, and encouraged the less active tribes to follow their lead:

> But there remained seven tribes of the Israelites which had not yet received their portions. So Joshua said to the Israelites, "How long will you be slack about going and taking possession of the land which the Lord, the God of your fathers, has assigned to you? Appoint three men of each tribe; I will send them out to go oposes of apportionment, and then come back to me. They shall divide it into seven parts – Judah shall remain by its territory in the south, and the house of Joseph shall remain by its territory in the north." (Josh. 18:2–5)

By the time the tribe of Dan decided to become active, there was little territory left available for them. The tribes of Judah and Ephraim therefore allotted cities to them, without any contiguous land borders. We see a similar phenomenon with the tribe of Simeon, which occupied cities within the boundaries of Judah.

To round out this discussion, Prof. Elitzur surveys the varying accounts of the borders of the Land of Israel in his study on *Parashat Mishpatim* (pp. 208–19). There appear to be two different sets of borders enumerated. One border stretches all the way from the Euphrates to the River of Egypt or the Red Sea (e.g., Gen. 15:18; Ex. 23:31), and other borders that are smaller and do not stretch to the Euphrates or the Red Sea (e.g., Num. ch. 34). The history of Israel is based on the smaller borders, since the people are not considered to be in Israel immediately after crossing the Red Sea.

The smaller borders represent the first stage of the biblical program, as Israel's population would not have been large enough to settle in the greater borders. Joshua was tasked with conquering a territorial nucleus so that the nation could begin its life in the Land of Israel. The larger borders represent "potential holiness," that a religious and enthusiastic nation would be able to settle and sanctify over time.

Prof. Elitzur shines his spotlight on the oft-neglected areas of Tanakh. His approach calls to mind Ramban's words in his commentary on Genesis 35:16. The verse reads, "They set out from Bethel; but when they were still some distance short of Ephrath (*vayhi od kivrat haaretz lavo Efrata*), Rachel was in childbirth, and she had hard labor." Ramban composed his commentary in Spain, and he adopted Radak's interpretation of "when they were still some distance short" to mean the distance one may walk from morning until mealtime.

Toward the end of his life, however, Ramban moved to *Eretz Yisrael,* and updated this comment:

> That is what I wrote initially [while still in Spain – HA]. But now that I have merited coming to Jerusalem ... I saw with my eyes that the distance between Rachel's tomb and Bethlehem is not even one *mil.* Therefore [my original] interpretation is refuted ... But [the term means] a unit of distance, as Rashi had interpreted.

Prof. Elitzur is as uncompromising in his research as he is enthusiastic regarding his subject matter, which is holy in addition to being academically rigorous. Prof. Elitzur has given us the opportunity to upgrade our understanding of many elements in Tanakh, rabbinic teachings, and even folk traditions. This volume enlightens our learning, and will foster a more profound love of the Land of Israel through intimate knowledge of the settings for the eternal prophetic narratives in Tanakh.

Rabbi Hayyim Angel
Bible Faculty, Yeshiva University
National Scholar, Institute for Jewish Ideas and Ideals

Preface

This book is the English version of my Hebrew *Makom baParasha,* published in 2014. The credit for this book belongs first and foremost to Yedidya Tanami, editor in chief of the Reshet Moreshet radio station of the Israel Broadcasting Authority. He had invited me to host a weekly program, bearing the same name, which aired every Friday afternoon before Shabbat. In these broadcasts, usually no more than ten minutes long, I presented a short summary of a topic that held professional interest but was also accessible to the layperson. I tried to avoid the most well-worn topics, preferring to focus on the unusual and unfamiliar. This gave me the opportunity to present my own and others' original ideas on biblical geography without the burdensome requirements of academic writing – which compel one to spend months reviewing the body of existing research before writing a single original sentence, and sink every fresh idea into a quagmire of citations and analysis of dissenting or similar opinions. The limited time frame of the radio program forced me to focus and present the main idea clearly and concisely.

When I collected the recordings of most of these segments, I realized that I was in possession of a treasure that would be a shame to lose. I decided to publish them in written form, along with some additional material. As someone who has been immersed in the fields of Hebrew language, biblical and historical realia, and geography, I had here been given an opportunity to present numerous subjects that I had heard and read about, and ideas that I had developed, in brief and plain language. The structure of this book – the cycle of the year and the weekly *parasha* – allowed and indeed obligated me to weave in some reflections on conceptual aspects of the Torah and Jewish thought, which lead from time to time to a style reminiscent of traditional homiletics as well as to discussion of current events.

In writing this book, my guiding light was the fascinating work *Words and Their History* (Heb.), written by the greatest of the previous generation's scholars of the Hebrew language, Prof. Yechezkel Kutscher, *z"l*. This short book was described by its author as "a book for reading, not for study," in which he presented, charmingly and without the weightiness of academic writing, a variety of topics at the intersections of language, history, and realia that were uniformly fascinating to read. Thanks to the professionalism and broad range of knowledge reflected in the book – and contrary to the author's assertions – the book is considered a legitimate source for academic citation, which goes to show that thoughtful professionalism and lighthearted brevity are not necessarily mutually exclusive. Thank God, I have realized that my attempt to emulate his style turned out to be successful and found an audience beyond the "weekly *parasha* sheets."

My greatest and most esteemed teacher was my father, Prof. Yehuda Elitzur, *zt"l*. My late father truly united faith and science and was an extraordinary source of original ideas and interpretation. However, much of his work remains unpublished, passed down in manuscripts or as an oral inheritance. In this book, as in much of my other writing, I frequently cite his work and ideas, both published and unpublished; sometimes his influence is evident even when I do not mention him by name.

I have also quoted in a number of places my other teachers and friends with whom I clarified certain issues through methodical study, tours of the relevant area, or casual conversation. I spent formative years working in the Ofra Field School in the 1970s and '80s. Israel was generally a quiet place back then, and the staff of the field school – young, talented, hungry for knowledge – wandered the land freely and guided tours through the cities of our Patriarchs and in villages in the Benjamin region and Samaria, talking with Arabs and Samaritans, making discoveries, and creating a fertile ground for the study of concrete findings from the field through the lens of the Bible and other Jewish sources. Prominent people from this group include Hanan Eshel *z"l*, Amos Frumkin, Ze'ev Erlich, and especially Rabbi Yoel Bin-Nun – a man from whom I have learned a great deal about understanding the Bible, even if I do not always agree with his understanding of the present.

My son-in-law, Shlomi Samet, was the one who encouraged me to work quickly and publish a book that is aesthetically pleasing and includes maps and pictures that elucidate the content. In the current volume, I attempt to continue in the same line. My daughter Rivka helped me prepare some of the sketches. The maps were created with the utmost professionalism by Studio Waldman in Ofra. More than one hundred images are included in this book. I would like to thank all of the people who helped me collect them, some of whom did so with no expectation of reward. Their names appear in the captions alongside the pictures.

The English version of this book started out in the form of chapters that were serialized on the Israel Koschitzky Virtual Beit Midrash website of Yeshivat Har Etzion in Alon Shevut, Israel, expertly translated by Daniel Landman, under the supervision of Rabbi Reuven Ziegler, who kindly recommended the next stage of publishing it at Maggid Books. I extend my heartfelt thanks first and foremost to the editorial director of Maggid Books, Rabbi Ziegler, without whom this English publication would neither have commenced nor been completed, and to Mr. Matthew Miller, publisher of Koren. It was a pleasure to work day-to-day with Shira Finson, Ita Olesker, and Caryn Meltz, who managed the editing of the book. I would also like to express my thanks to the wonderful editing team of Avigayil Steiglitz and Sorelle Spitzer, for their careful review and contributions, and to Kuti Teper and Shlomit Partok for their help in compiling the indexes.

Yoel Elitzur
Iyar 5780 / May 2020

Genesis

Parashat Bereshit

The Garden and the Euphrates River

Where Is the Garden of Eden?

As we begin the yearlong cycle of Torah reading with *Parashat Bereshit*, we find ourselves in the midst of a narrative that centers around a unique setting: the Garden of Eden. Where is this mysterious place? Is it some supernatural realm that does not truly exist in the world as we know it, or can we actually pinpoint its location on a map?

The Torah describes the Garden of Eden using concrete geographical terminology:

> A river issues from Eden to water the garden, and it then divides and becomes four branches. The name of the first is the Pishon, the one that winds through the whole land of Havilah, where the gold is... bdellium is there, and lapis lazuli. The name of the second river is the Gihon, the one that winds through the whole land of Cush. The name of the third river is Tigris, the one that flows east of Asshur. And the fourth river is the Euphrates. (Gen 2:10–14)

Two of these four rivers are well known to us: the Tigris and the Euphrates. In contrast, we are unfamiliar with the identities of the first two rivers listed here, and, what is more, they are not mentioned thereafter in all of Tanakh. The verses provide us with hints as to their locations, but these serve only to confuse us further: the Pishon surrounds the land of Havilah, while the Gihon surrounds the land of Cush. Cush can ostensibly be found somewhere in Africa. The land of Havilah, "where the gold is," is most likely connected to the "Havilah" listed as one of the sons of Yoktan (a descendant of Shem, son of Noah). Yoktan's sons and their descendants were tribal people who settled in the southern end of the Arabian Peninsula.[1] The problem is that there are no significant rivers in South Arabia, and all attempts to link the Pishon to one of the torrents of that region have been unconvincing. In light of this difficulty, perhaps we must conclude that the information presented to us in these verses does not actually reflect real-world geography. Yet the Tigris and the Euphrates are quite real, and furthermore, the descriptions of the Pishon and the Gihon are written in a realistic, geographic style, not in the abstract terminology that characterizes descriptions of otherworldly locations and entities.

What are the major rivers of the Eastern Mediterranean, the home of our forefathers? Undoubtedly these are the Tigris and the Euphrates in the north and the Nile in the southwest. Since the tributaries of the Nile originate in "the land of Cush," which is in central Africa, there may actually be some justification in identifying them as the Pishon and the Gihon, and their meandering course may fit the phrase, "the one that winds through." Indeed, following the lead of William F. Albright, many believe that the Pishon and the Gihon are what we refer to today as the Blue Nile and the White Nile, the two major tributaries of the Nile River.

But this theory creates a new, fundamental problem: the Blue Nile and the White Nile are located far to the south of the so-called Fertile Crescent, while the sources of the Tigris and the Euphrates are located far to the north. Because of this difficulty, there is a wide range of other

1. Genesis 10:26–30. Arabs trace the lineage of these southern tribes to an ancient forefather named Qaḥṭān, apparently equivalent to the biblical Yoktan.

opinions about the identity of the Pishon and the Gihon. According to an ancient Jewish interpretation,[2] the Pishon is the Ganges and the land of Havilah is India. Still others maintain that the Pishon and the Gihon are located in Asia Minor, and other opinions abound. In order to square these interpretations with the biblical text, some invoke a possible alternative location for the land of Cush: what we know today as the mountainous Hindu Kush region in Afghanistan and northern Pakistan. This discrepancy is reflected in the Talmud (Megilla 11a): "One said that Hoddu [India] is at one end of the world and Cush is at the other, and the other said that Hoddu and Cush adjoin one another."

Dov Ashbel placed the Garden of Eden in the vicinity of Mount Ararat in Eastern Anatolia, the region in which both the Tigris and the Euphrates originate. Ashbel maintained that the Pishon and the Gihon are additional rivers local to that region that drain into the Caspian Sea and the Black Sea, forcing him into some creative interpretations of "the land of Havilah" and "the land of Cush."

German scholar Friedrich Delitzsch, who dedicated an entire book to the question of the Garden of Eden's location, maintained that the Garden of Eden was in Babylonia, specifically its fertile southern region adjacent to the Persian coast. Delitzsch identified the Pishon and the Gihon as canals running from the Euphrates (which may originally have been natural streams) and Cush as the land known as kašši, or northern Babylonia. Others placed the Garden of Eden in modern-day southern Iraq and identified the Pishon and the Gihon as the Karun and Karkheh Rivers, which originate in the mountains of Iran (the Karkheh flows through the ruins of Susa, ancient Shushan).

Hermann Gunkel took his analysis of this question to an entirely different dimension – quite literally to outer space. The river that "issues from Eden," according to Gunkel, refers to the Milky Way and its four spiral "arms" visible to the naked eye. The names the Torah gives these arms are borrowed from the names of four famous rivers throughout the world.

---

2. See Josephus, *Antiquities* 1:38, *Targum Neofiti, Targum Pseudo-Jonathan,* and even Jerome, the Church Father, apparently following his Jewish teachers, in his book *Hebraicae Quaestiones in Libro Geneseos.*

Ultimately, it seems unlikely that we will be able to pinpoint the precise location of the Garden of Eden. All we know is where we are today – exiled from its borders, with the "fiery, ever-turning sword" barring us from entering again.

The Euphrates River

The Euphrates is the fourth river listed in the geographical description of the Garden of Eden, and we would be remiss if we did not discuss its great importance in the region. The Torah often refers to the Euphrates as "the Great River." It is longer than the Tigris, and unlike the Tigris, all of its water originates in the northern mountains and no tributaries augment its flow in its course through Iraq, the more significant section of its overall course. As a result, the flow of the Euphrates in its southern part is generally serene, and the water level decreases gradually.[3] The area of the Tigris-Euphrates river system is known as Mesopotamia, Greek for "between the rivers," and is often termed "the cradle of civilization."[4] The land between the Euphrates and the Tigris was home to Assyria in the northeast, Mari and Aram in the northwest, and Sumer, Babylonia, and Akkadia in the south.

Ḥazal interpreted "the Great River" as a reference to its role as the border of the Land of Israel. However, it is worth noting that throughout Tanakh, the term "the River" is a reference to the Euphrates as well. In his farewell speech to the nation, Joshua reminds the people of Israel of their roots: "In olden times, your forefathers lived beyond the River" (Josh. 24:2). Aḥiya the Shilonite later warns the people of the exile that will drive the nation back to that region: "And [He] will scatter them beyond the River" (I Kings 14:15). In addition to the mention of the Euphrates's role as a border in God's promise to Abraham – "from the river of Egypt to the Great River, the Euphrates River" (Gen. 15:18) – we find another mention in God's promise to Abraham's descendants

3. See *Sifrei Deuteronomy* 7 and Genesis Rabba 16:3, Ed. Theodor-Albeck.
4. There is some debate over whether this was the meaning of "Mesopotamia" in the original Greek. Jacob J. Finkelstein argued that the word, along with the Hebrew name "Aram Naharayim" that preceded the Greek, actually referred solely to the Euphrates.

at Sinai: "I will set your borders from the Sea of Reeds to the Sea of Philistia, and from the wilderness to the River" (Ex. 23:31).

A well-known characteristic of biblical poetry is the lack of the definite article. Because of this, in the poetic portions of Tanakh, the Euphrates is often referred to simply as "River," and not "the River." For example, Jeremiah rebukes, "What, then, is the good of your going to Egypt to drink the waters of the Nile? And what is the good of your going to Assyria to drink the waters of River?" (Jer. 2:18). Similarly, we find in Psalms: "Let him (King Solomon) rule from sea to sea, and from River to the ends of the earth" (Ps. 72:8), an abbreviated version of the promised borders we read of in Exodus 23.[5]

Ever Ha-nahar – Beyond the Euphrates

At a certain point during the biblical period, the meaning of the expression "beyond the River (Euphrates)" seems to have changed. We have already noted the usage of the phrase in both Joshua's farewell address and in Aḥiya's ominous prophecy, where they mean "beyond" quite literally: Joshua is speaking about our forefathers who lived on the "other side" of the Euphrates, with respect to the Land of Israel – meaning beyond its eastern banks – and Aḥiya is threatening that the people of Israel would later be exiled to that same far-flung region. The same usage can be found in the description of David's wars: "Hadadezer sent for and brought out the Arameans from across the River (Euphrates)" (II Sam. 10:16).

However, in the beginning of I Kings we read that Solomon "controlled the whole region beyond the River – all the kings beyond the River, from Tiphsah to Gaza" (5:4). In this verse, it seems clear that "beyond the River" refers not to the eastern side of the river, but to its western side, where the people of Israel actually lived. If so, why is this region called "beyond the River"?

The answer to this question can be found by examining the Book of Ezra-Nehemiah. The expression "*ever ha-nahar*" (or *avar nahara* in the Aramaic part of Ezra) appears thirteen times throughout the book, each time referring to the area within the boundaries of the greater Land

5. In Zech. 9:10 the same phrase is used concerning the prospective king.

of Israel – from the Euphrates to the Egyptian border. This usage can be traced back to the time of Sargon II, king of the Assyrian Empire, when it was written in Assyrian texts as *eber nāri*. In a royal inscription of Esarhaddon (680-669 BCE), the kings of Tyre, Judah, Edom, Moab, Gaza, Ashkelon, Ekron, Byblos, Arwad, Shamshiruna (?), Ammon, and Ashdod are listed as the kings of *ḫatti and eber nāri*, the former being the Akkadian name for Syria. From here the usage passed to the Babylonians and the Persians, who minted coins bearing the Aramaic version of the name: *avar nahara*. The same phrase was also found in a Greek inscription, written as *peran Euphratou*, literally "beyond the Euphrates."

The fundamental question here is where the true geographical center of gravity lies. The earlier occurrences of the expression "beyond the River" were based naturally on the perspective of the Land of Israel: We are "here" and they – Assyria, Babylonia, and Haran – are "beyond the Euphrates." Only much later do we find sources that unintentionally take the opposite approach, identifying ourselves as the "other": Assyria, Babylonia, and Susa represent the epicenter of the world, while we in the Land of Israel are resigned to the region "beyond the Euphrates."

We can draw an analogy here to the modern usage of the expression "Middle East" (synonymous with "Near East"), a term used even by those who live in the region, despite its Eurocentric implications. From the perspective of the Europeans who coined the phrase, Israel and its neighbors lie, literally, to the near east, while China and Japan comprise the Far East based on similar logic.

The watershed moment at which "beyond the Euphrates" reversed its meaning was, in all likelihood, the rise of the Assyrian Empire. The only difficulty with this explanation is the verse in I Kings describing Solomon, who predated the rise of the Assyrians by many years. The answer, quite simply, is that the verse "For he controlled the whole region beyond the Euphrates – all the kings beyond the Euphrates" reflects the mindset of the author of the Book of Kings and not that of Solomon or the people of his time.

Appearances in the Targumim

It is worth noting that Onkelos and Jonathan, in their respective Aramaic translations of the Torah and the Prophets, render the Hebrew word *nahar* as *perat* (Euphrates) even when the term is plainly used in the general sense. Balaam's laudatory description of the people of Israel upon seeing their encampment – "like gardens beside a river" (Num. 24:6) – was translated by Onkelos as: "like watered gardens by the Euphrates." The same phenomenon can be seen in the final chapter of Isaiah: "I will extend to her prosperity like a river" (66:12), translated by Jonathan as: "I will bring to her prosperity like the floods of the Euphrates River." The first example may, to some extent, reflect the speaker's background. After all, Balaam lived in the vicinity of the Euphrates,[6] and it stands to reason that river imagery, whether consciously or subconsciously, would enter into his poetic lexicon.

Kerei and *Ketiv*

One notable example of the interplay between "the River" and "the Euphrates River" in Tanakh can be found in the description of David's battle with Hadadezer: "David defeated Hadadezer son of Rehob, king of Zobah, who was then on his way to recover his border at the Euphrates River" (II Sam. 8:3).[7] The commentators dispute exactly what series of events led to David's victory: Did David ambush Hadadezer while the king of Zobah was en route to the Euphrates? Or was it David himself who was traveling to the river to restore his own monument, stopping along the way to defeat Hadadezer? The answer to this question does not interest us here; instead we will focus on a quirk in the wording of the verse. According to Masoretic tradition, the word "Euphrates" is an example of *kerei velo ketiv*, a word that is read along with the rest of the verse but not actually written in the traditional text. Thus, the *ketiv* of the verse reads simply: "to restore his monument at the River." Which version we accept – the *ketiv* or the *kerei* – is irrelevant; the two traditions are equivalent in meaning. Whether we read "the River" or "the Euphrates River," the identity of the river here is never in question.

The Euphrates as a Border of the Land of Israel

Before we conclude, we must emphasize the most important function of the Euphrates River as its role as one of the borders of the greater Land of Israel. The Euphrates plays a part in each of the Torah's repetitions of

6. See Num. 22:5, 23:7, and Deut. 23:5.
7. See the parallel verse in I Chronicles 18:3, where the verse reads, "to set up his monument."

the borders of the Land of Israel in its broad, promised form. The river is mentioned as a border in God's original promise to Abraham at the Covenant of the Pieces: "To your offspring I assign this land, from the river of Egypt to the great river, the river Euphrates" (Gen. 15:18). This pledge is repeated at the covenant at Sinai (Ex. 23:31) and three times in the plains of Moab (Deut. 1:7; 11:24; Josh. 1:4).

We will close with a remarkable commentary from an unlikely source. In several interviews, Yasser Arafat made a startling claim regarding the modern Israeli flag: The two broad blue stripes represent the Nile and the Euphrates Rivers, and the Star of David between the stripes represents the Jewish people. Thus, argued Arafat, the flag symbolizes Israel's intent to expand its territory to the entire area between the two major rivers. Arafat's theory angered many Israelis at the time, but the truth is that his take on the flag was merely a visual representation of what can be found explicitly in the words of the Torah. Instead of reacting to Arafat's commentary as if it were a kind of blood libel, we should instead see it as a message of well-wishing for the realization of our national destiny.

For further study:

Albright, W. F. "The Location of the Garden of Eden." *AJSL* 39 (1922): 15–31.

Ashbel, D. "*Arba'a Neharot Hayotze'im MeEden.*" *Beit Mikra* 40 (1970): 100–104.

Bagg, A.M. "*Die Orts und Gewässernamen der neuassyrischen Zeit.*" *Teil 1: Die Levante* (RGTC 7/1), Wiesbaden, 2007, 64.

Cassuto, U. *A Commentary on the Book of Genesis*. Illinois, 2005, 114–121.

Delitzsch, F. *Wo lag das Paradies*. Leipzig, 1881.

Elitzur, Y., and Y. Kil. *Atlas Daat Mikra*. Jerusalem, 1993, 20–21 (Hebrew).

Finkelstein, J. J. "Mesopotamia." *JNES* 21 (1962): 73–92.

Fischer, A., and A. K. Irvine, "Ḳaḥṭān." In *Encyclopaedia of Islam, Second Edition*, edited by P. Bearman et al. Online Edition <http://dx.doi.org/10.1163/1573-3912_islam_SIM_3790>

Grintz, Y.M. *Studies in Early Biblical Ethnology and History*. Jerusalem, 1969, 35–50 (Hebrew).

Müller, W.W. "Pishon." In *The Anchor Bible Dictionary*, 5, 282.

Radai, Y.T. "*Arba'a Neharot,*" in Y. T. Radai et al., eds., *LaAteret Tzevi: A Token of Friendship in Honor of Rabbi Professor Zvi A. Kurzweil*. Haifa, 1980, 25–30 (Hebrew).

Rainey, A. F. "*Ever HaNahar, Ever Nahara, Avar Nahara.*" In *Encyclopaedia Biblica* 6, 43–48 (Hebrew).

The Garden and the Euphrates River

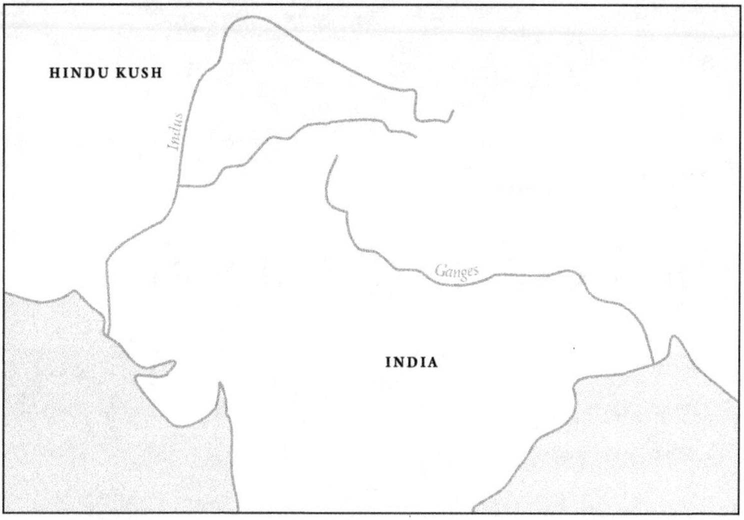

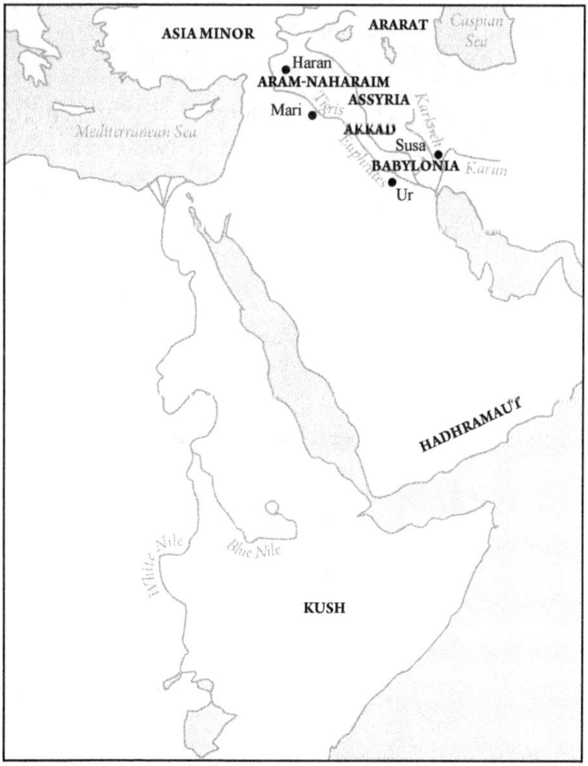

Parashat Noaḥ

The Borders of Canaan

Parashat Noaḥ: An International Story

When reading *Parashat Noaḥ*, the Jewish reader might feel some confusion and strangeness, as if he has suddenly been thrust into an alien environment, like a visitor in a foreign country with no familiar face in sight. *Parashat Noaḥ* describes a world without the Jewish people. We begin with the Flood – pairs of animals enter the Ark and exit once the flood has abated – continue with the story of Noah getting drunk, enduring humiliation and cursing his grandson, and then we become lost in a tangle of Pathrusim and Casluhim, the great warrior Nimrod, and a tower "with its top in the sky." Only at the end of the *parasha* do we return to the comfort of the known, when we meet an old friend: "When Terah had lived seventy years, he begot Abram, Nahor and Haran…Abram and Nahor took to themselves wives, the name of Abram's wife being Sarai…Terah took his son Abram, his grandson Lot the son of Haran… and they set out together from Ur of the Chaldeans for the land of Canaan" (11:26–31). We encounter Canaan and Abraham and begin to feel more at home.

From a geographic perspective as well, the *parasha* makes it clear that our characters inhabit a vast world, home to seventy nations with strange, exotic names like Ashkenaz, Riphath, Togarmah, Elishah, Tarshish, Kittim, and Dodanim. Only at the very end, when the rest of the ancient world has seemingly been mapped out completely, do we arrive at the land of Canaan.

The Canaanite Nations and Their Land

There are two groups of people listed in *Parashat Noaḥ*, the borders of whose respective geographical regions are described. The first is the children of Yoktan: "Their settlements extended from Mesha as far as Sephar, the hill country to the east" (Gen. 10:30). More interesting to us is the second group – the Canaanites. It is noteworthy that the list of Canaanite families described here is markedly different from the "seven Canaanite nations" that we find later in Tanakh. In fact, this is an earlier list, one that places greater emphasis on the northern Canaanite nations. Alongside the Jebusites, Amorites, and Girgashites, we find a host of "northern" names: Hivites,[1] Arkites, Sinites, Arvadites, Zemarites, and Hamathites.

The Torah proceeds with the borders of the land of Canaan: "The Canaanite territory extended from Sidon as far as Gerar, toward Gaza, and as far as Sodom, Gomorrah, Admah, and Zeboiim, toward Lasha" (Gen. 10:19). The inclusion of these geographic details is no coincidence. It clearly serves to prepare the reader for what is in store: the entry of Abram, and eventually the nation of Israel, into the land of Canaan. However, it must be noted that the land described here is not identical to the land of Canaan described later in the Torah. The Samaritans, who have a tendency to emend biblical verses creatively in order to avoid internal contradictions, suggest a textual change here. In the Samaritan version of the Torah, the verse reads, "The Canaanite territory extended from the river of Egypt to the great river, the Euphrates River, to the Western Sea."[2] This substituted text is borrowed from God's promise to Abraham in Genesis 15, as well as a parallel promise in Deuteronomy 11. In any case, the Masoretic text and all the other versions of this verse are unlike any other description of the borders of

1. See Josh. 11:3: "And to the Hivites at the foot of Hermon, in the land of Mizpah."
2. A similar emendation can be found in the Samaritan Pentateuch in Moses's surveillance of the Promised Land from Mount Nebo, supplanting our text in Deuteronomy 34:1–3.

the land of Canaan mentioned in the Bible. Instead, we are confronted with several place-names that we do not generally think of as borders of the Holy Land. These locations delineate the pre-Abrahamic borders of the land of Canaan.

Where Is "Lasha" and What Is the Geographical Logic Behind the "Canaanite Territory"?

The first thing we need to do in order to make some sense of these borders is to identify each one geographically. We already know the locations of Sidon and Gaza; conveniently, these ancient sites roughly correspond to their modern-day equivalents. The location of Gerar is disputed,[3] but it is unquestionably in the vicinity of Gaza. Sodom, Gomorrah, Admah, and Zeboiim are generally assumed to be located in the southern Dead Sea region,[4] but the location of Lasha is problematic. The name cannot be found in any other source outside of Genesis 10:19.

Some have suggested that Lasha might be connected to Leshem (Josh. 19:47), the ancient name of Dan, a northern city near the headwaters of the Jordan. If this theory were true, a symmetrical picture would have emerged from the list of borders: Sidon in the northwest; Gaza and Gerar in the southwest; Sodom, Gomorrah, Admah, and Zeboiim in the southeast; and Lasha/Leshem in the northeast. There is only one problem: "Lasha" is not "Leshem," and the two cannot be equated simply because they share two of three letters.

Others have attempted to link Lasha with La'ash, a city near the ancient Aramean capital of Hamath, in modern-day Syria, mentioned in an early Aramaic inscription found between Hamath and Aleppo. However, this identification is equally problematic: while letter transmutations do occur in Biblical Hebrew – prominent examples include *kesev/keves*, *salma/simla*, and the place-name Timnath Serah/Timnath Heres – they are rare. More importantly, the Lasha-La'ash connection is geographically problematic as well: La'ash should be situated at a line of latitude approximately one hundred miles north of that of Sidon, creating an asymmetrical – and thus unlikely – border scheme.

3. We will discuss this question in depth later, in *Parashat Toledot*.
4. See the discussion in *Parashat Vayera*.

Various imaginative (and improbable) textual emendations have also been suggested: "Lasha" becomes "Bela," or even "Lashon." Intriguingly, Genesis Rabba 37:6, *Targum Yerushalmi* (MS *Neofiti*) and *Targum Pseudo-Jonathan* translate "Lasha" as "Kalrahi,"[5] referring to Kalliroē, the Greek name for a group of hot springs in the northeast Dead Sea region.[6] This translation is based not on an interpretation of the words of the verse, but rather on a traditional identification presumably known among the inhabitants of the region. Seemingly, this identification of Lasha is difficult to accept as well, as it excludes the entire northeast corner of the land of Canaan.

One particularly illuminating explanation for our verse was suggested by Yehoshua Meir Grintz in his article *Eretz HaYi'ud*. Grintz emphasizes that the verse speaks of "the Canaanite (*HaKena'ani*) territory" rather than "the land of Canaan (*Kena'an*)." In other words, the locations listed in the verse are not the borders of Canaan as we know it, but those of the land inhabited by the Canaanite nation, the most eminent nation among the various peoples of Canaan. With regard to the identity of Lasha, Grintz accepts the local tradition reflected in the *Targum Yerushalmi* and the Midrash – "Kalrahi." Furthermore, he explains that the "Sidon" listed here is actually a general territorial term for the entire region of what is now southern Lebanon. Grintz marshals several biblical sources that support this usage of "Sidon." First, the people of Laish, a city by the headwaters of the Jordan River, are described as "dwelling carefree, after the manner of the Sidonians" (Judges 18:7). On the other hand, the city itself is "distant from Sidon" (18:28), implying that Laish and the other cities of that region were governed from afar by Sidon. Another example is the description of Mount Hermon found in Deuteronomy: "Sidonians called Hermon Sirion, and the Amorites call it Senir" (Deut. 3:9). How a person would refer to Mount Hermon depended on geography; those to the west of the mountain would call it Sirion, while those to the south would call it Senir.

5. Jerome, probably following his Jewish teachers, also mentions this identification as fact in his *Hebraicae Questiones in Libro Geneseos*.

6. Καλλιρ(ρ)όη, meaning "beautiful flow," is also the name of a spring located near Athens, as well as several figures in Greek mythology.

Once again, we see that "Sidon" is used in the territorial sense – it is the region that abuts Mount Hermon.

Now that we understand "the Canaanite territory" in its more limited meaning, we can begin to make sense of the borders. The northern border is the territory of Sidon, or southern Lebanon. From there, two strips emerge; the western one is stretched southward along the coastal plain, "as far as Gerar, toward Gaza," and the eastern one stretches across the Jordan Rift Valley, "as far as Sodom, Gomorrah, Admah, and Zeboiim, toward Lasha."[7] This understanding seems to correspond with the two places in Tanakh where the geographic division of the land of Canaan between the Canaanite nations is described. The first instance is in the report of the twelve spies: "Amalekites dwell in the Negeb region; Hittites, Jebusites, and Amorites inhabit the hill country; and Canaanites dwell by the Sea and along the Jordan" (Num. 13:29). The second can be found in Joshua; it is a description of the northern Canaanite nations that joined forces to battle the people of Israel: "To the Canaanites in the east and in the west; to the Amorites, Hittites, Perizzites, and Jebusites in the hill country" (Josh. 11:3).

In conclusion, it is clear that the description of the borders of "the Canaanite territory" found in our *parasha* serves to prepare the reader for the encounter with the land of Canaan, which would later be promised to the Patriarchs and then given to their descendants. However, note the delicate terminology used in the verse, seemingly written with a careful eye on the geographic realities of that period. Indeed, at the time there was no land of Canaan as we know it from later biblical narratives. Accordingly, it is not described in *Parashat Noaḥ* as one unified bloc of land, but rather as a sprawl of individual territories, in which the northern Canaanite tribes asserted their dominance over the region. Despite this sensitivity to relating an accurate account of history, there is still an underlying tone of purpose and preparation for the next series of narratives – the story of Abraham and the Israelite inheritance of the land of Canaan.

---

7. According to Grintz, the word *bo'akha* ("as far as") signifies a distant point that the borderline seems to lead to but does not actually reach. Thus, in his opinion, the city of Gerar must be located somewhere in the western Negev, south of Gaza. However, it is noteworthy that the whole interpretation of the verse, in which Grintz's suggestion is conceivable, does not necessarily depend on this less convincing detail. See the chapter on *Parashat Toledot.*

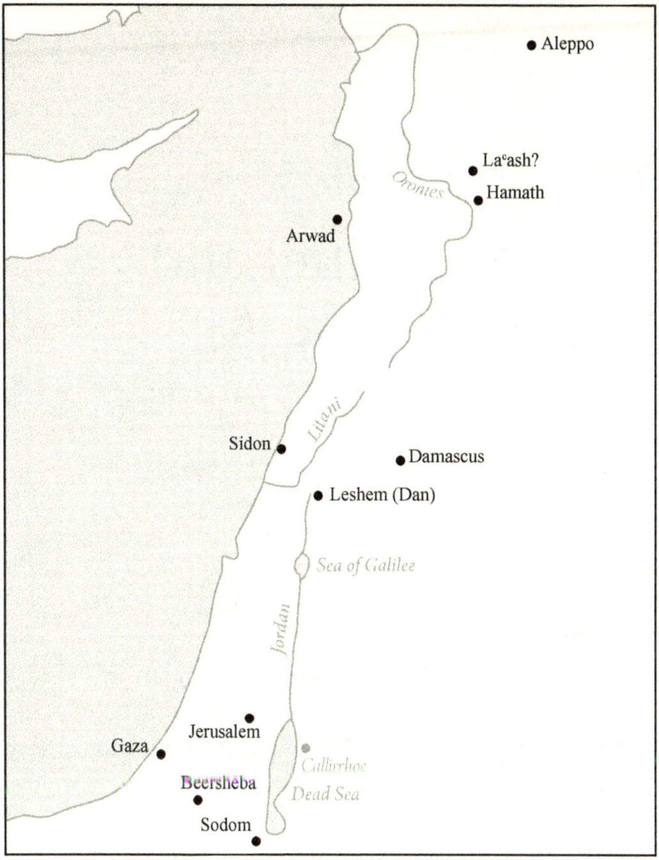

For further study:

Clamer, C. "The Hot Springs of Kallirhoe and Baarou." In: Piccirillo, M. and Alliata, E. *The Madaba Map Centenary*, Jerusalem, 1999, 221–225.

Ginsberg, H. L. *Lasha. Encyclopaedia Biblica* 4, 532 (Hebrew).

Grintz, Y. M. *Motza'ei Dorot*. Tel-Aviv, 1969, 141–142 (Hebrew).

Hayward, C. T. R. *Saint Jerome's Hebrew Questions on Genesis*. Oxford, 1995, 42.

Parashat Lekh Lekha

"Between Bethel and Ai": Identifying Ai

The Linkage

There are five contexts in Tanakh where Bethel and Ai are linked.

- Abraham's tent: "Between Bethel and Ai" is mentioned as the location of Abraham's tent and the place in which he first "invoked the Lord by name." This phrase appears twice in *Parashat Lekh Lekha,* the first instance of which occurs shortly after Abraham enters the land of Canaan:

> Go forth from your native land … Abram passed through the land as far as the site of Shechem, at Elon Moreh … From there he moved on to the hill east of Bethel and pitched his tent, with Bethel on the west and Ai on the east; and he built there an altar to the Lord and invoked the Lord by name. (Gen. 12:1–8)

The second instance occurs upon Abraham's return from Egypt:

> And he proceeded by stages from the Negeb as far as Bethel, to the place where his tent had been formerly, between Bethel and

Ai, the site of the altar that he had built there at first; and there Abram invoked the Lord by name.[1] (Gen. 13:3–4)

- The conquest of Ai: Ai is described in the Book of Joshua at the start of the story of the land's conquest: "Joshua sent men from Jericho to Ai, which lies close to Beth-aven – east of Bethel" (Josh. 7:2). Joshua set an ambush of thirty thousand warriors, followed by a second ambush of five thousand, strategically placed "between Bethel and Ai – west of Ai."[2] When Joshua and his men feigned retreat, the armies of both cities emptied out in pursuit of their fleeing Israelite foes, leaving the cities defenseless against the hidden ambush: "Not a man was left in Ai or in Bethel who did not go out after Israel; they left the city open while they pursued Israel" (8:17).
- The thirty-one Canaanite kings: One of the kings listed is "the king of Ai, near Bethel" (Josh. 12:9).
- The returnees from exile in Zerubbabel's time: In the second half of the list of those "who returned to Jerusalem and Judah, each to his own city" (Ezra 2:1; repeated in Nehemiah 7:6), the returnees are organized by point of origin. There we find: "The men of Bethel and Ai – two hundred twenty and three" (Ezra 2:28; in Nehemiah 7:32 the number is given as 123).
- The final geo-demographic listing of the people of Israel in Tanakh: "The Benjaminites: from Geba, Michmas, Aija [Ai], and Bethel and its outlying towns" (Neh. 11:31).

Bethel is mentioned numerous times on its own throughout Tanakh, but Ai is only once mentioned alone, without connection to

1. Since Hebrew does not have a past perfect pattern, this sequence can be interpreted in two ways: either that Abraham traveled to the place where he had invoked the Lord by name earlier, or that he invoked the Lord by name anew in that very same place (Rashi).
2. That Joshua was able to hide such a vast number of troops between the two cities is a result of the uniquely wooded topography of the region, referenced in the story of Elisha and the bears (II Kings 2:23–25).

Bethel. Isaiah describes the route that the Assyrians took (or could have taken) in their march on Jerusalem, a roughly diagonal eastern path, presumably from the fords of the Jordan, that did not pass through Bethel: "He advanced upon Aiath [Ai], he proceeded to Migron, at Michmas he deposited his baggage" (Is. 10:28).

Identifying Bethel

Most scholars agree that ancient Bethel was located in what is now the village of Beitin (a rough preservation of the ancient name), just southeast of modern-day Beit El; Bethel was a well-known village even as late as the Roman-Byzantine period. The site fits the biblical description for the most part. First, it is the point of intersection between the Benjamin-Ephraim border (a line running east-west) and the Way of the Patriarchs (a line running north-south). Second, according to *Ḥazal,* Bethel was unique in that its fruits would ripen later than in any other place in the Benjamin region. This observation fits Beitin, as it is the highest town in the region (approximately three thousand feet above sea level). Third, early Christian sources note that Bethel lay twelve Roman miles from Jerusalem and twenty-eight Roman miles from Shechem, numbers that are consistent with the distance of Beitin from those two cities.

Archaeological excavations in Beitin have revealed a walled city sitting near a spring and containing an ancient ritual site. The city's origins date back to approximately 2000 BCE, shortly before the Patriarchal Age, and it continued to be inhabited until the end of the Byzantine era.

Identifying Ai: The Story of Et-Tell

According to the biblical account, Ai should be located just east of Bethel. Sure enough, just over one mile east of Beitin, a large tell was discovered atop a tall rise. It is the largest of its kind in the Benjamin region, and the Arabs there call it "Khirbet et-Tell," or "the ruins of the tell." In addition, there is a tall peak located between the site and Beitin, which fits the description of "the hill east of Bethel" (Gen. 12:8). The excellent view provided by this hill makes it the perfect lookout point for Lot in the narrative of the following chapter: "Lot looked about him and saw how well watered was the whole plain of the Jordan" (13:10).

In 1928, British archaeologist and Bible scholar John Garstang visited the site and, upon preliminary inspection, determined that the architectural style was characteristic of the Middle Bronze Age. He also argued that he found pottery sherds from the Early, Middle and Late Bronze Age, dating up to 1400 BCE. The findings spanned from before the Patriarchal Age through to the conquest of Canaan.[3]

1. - La grande salle vue du nord.

From Judith Marquet-Krause's findings at et-Tell: the floor of the central chamber of the fortified palace from the Bronze Age found at the top of the tell. On the floor, one can make out the bases of the pillars that supported the ceiling. (*Syria*, 1935)

These findings, which seemed to positively identify the ancient city of Ai – famously featured in connection with both Abraham and Joshua – generated a great deal of excitement worldwide. Baron Edmond de Rothschild sponsored further, more intensive investigations of et-Tell,

3. This reckoning follows an early chronological system that dates the Exodus circa 1450 BCE and the conquest of Canaan circa 1400 BCE. This chronology, which was accepted by Garstang and others, was rejected by most scholars. According to the common position among Bible scholars, the Exodus and Conquest actually took place nearly two hundred years later than this. However, this latter position is inconsistent with the biblical text. We shall discuss this when we reach *Parashat Shemot*.

culminating in a new, systematic excavation of the site in 1933. The lead excavator was a young archaeologist by the name of Judith Marquet-Krause, the daughter of agronomist Eliyahu Krause, the longtime headmaster of the famed Mikveh Israel agricultural school and close friend of Rothschild.

What happened next shocked the world of biblical archaeology. Marquet-Krause's findings, published in 1935, were dramatically different from what most had anticipated. As it turned out, et-Tell was a highly fortified city in the Early Bronze Age, long before our forefathers lived. The site contained a fortified temple-palace compound, a municipal reservoir and a double line of walls and gates. The city was destroyed by fire in approximately 2100 BCE and since then only ruins remain. On top of these ruins, in one section of the tell, an unfortified village was established at some point during the Iron Age I (pre-monarchic Israelite period). The village was inhabited for 150–200 years until it was abandoned. No evidence of activity from other periods of history was found.

What this meant, as people immediately realized, was that the large, fortified city had already been destroyed before Abraham arrived in the land of Canaan, and the small, unfortified village was built only after Joshua's conquest of Ai. Instead of helping to solve some of the Bible's mysteries, Marquet-Krause's archaeological findings only generated more of them.

It may be difficult to appreciate today the extent of the uproar that these findings caused, particularly in the scientific community of pre-state Israel. Much of this community was dedicated wholeheartedly to the cause of unearthing biblical and national roots in the Land of Israel, in the hopes of reinforcing the Zionist claims on the land.

A fascinating correspondence demonstrating this acute sentiment has come into my possession, and I am publicizing it here for the first time in a non-Hebrew publication. My late uncle, Professor Samuel Klein, was then the head of the Land of Israel Studies department at the Hebrew University, as well as of the Jewish Palestine Exploration Society and editor of the prestigious Hebrew journal *Yedi'ot Hachevra Lachakirat Eretz Yisrael Va'atikoteha* (*Bulletin of the Jewish-Palestinian Exploration Society*). Judith Marquet-Krause sent a report of the findings

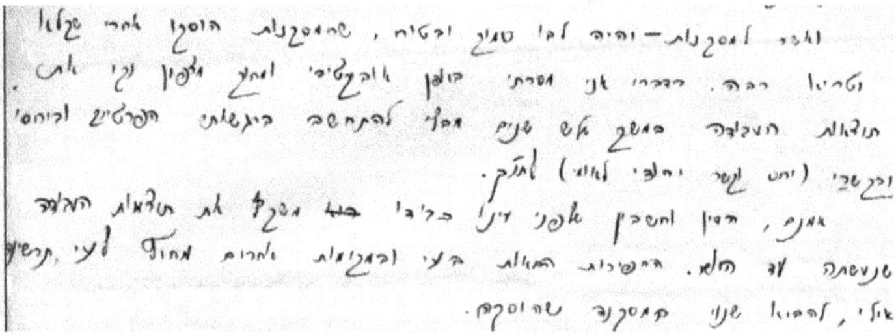

From Judith Marquet-Krause's letter to Samuel Klein

"Rest assured that the conclusions were reached only after extensive debate...without the involvement of my personal emotions..."

from her excavation for publication in *Yedi'ot,* along with an attached request that the journal refrain from changing any details from the report. When Marquet-Krause was informed that her article was not in the hands of an anonymous editorial board, but rather was being overseen by the eminent Professor Klein himself, she immediately retracted her request. In a letter to Professor Klein dated Sunday, December 1, 1935, Marquet-Krause writes:

> ...As to the findings – rest assured that the conclusions were reached only after extensive debate. I have submitted, objectively and with a clear conscience, the results of my work over the course of three years, without the involvement of my personal emotions or of my attitudes or connections (Jewish national attitudes and connections) to the Tanakh.
>
> Indeed, the report that sits before your honor's eyes represents the findings of the work that has been done until today. Future excavations in Ai and in other locations outside of Ai may allow us to arrive at different conclusions from those that were reached.
>
> In a few days, an exhibition will take place at Mikveh Israel at which all of the findings of the Ai excavation will be displayed (you are invited in advance to this exhibition, the opening date of which I will inform you of personally), and I am certain that in light of what will be presented there you will undoubtedly come

to the same conclusion as I have, or to a similar one. But for the time being I hope that you will allow me to present before you in writing the reasons that caused me to express the position that I took in my article.

Over the course of three years in Ai, we excavated several locations within the tell, and we were unable to find any remains of settlement during the period between 2000 BCE and 1450 BCE, as the Early Bronze Age city was completely destroyed by 2000 BCE. You will certainly agree that in order to prove the existence of a small kingdom at the time of Joshua's conquest, it would have been necessary to produce some remains of settlement from around 1450 BCE. Some remains of this kingdom, however negligible, should have been discovered at one of the excavation points. But we only found remains from two periods: the Early Bronze Age (3000–2000) and the Iron Age (1200–1000). This indicates that the city was destroyed long before Joshua arrived and remained abandoned for approximately eight hundred years.

In light of this, we may propose several hypotheses: (a) though the tell fits the general topographical description in the Book of Joshua, it is not, in fact, Ai (no one supports this hypothesis); (b) a different city was conquered, whose name was switched with the name of the city of Ai (in which case we should not be using the biblical descriptions to identify the location of Ai); and (c) the great importance that Ai possessed until its destruction in 2000 BCE (and its ruins were important as well, as the name "Ai" [literally, heap of ruins] testifies) gave rise to the story of its conquest as recorded in the Book of Joshua.

It can also be assumed that the upcoming excavations will lead to a change in our conclusions: In due time we may find, in some corner of the tell, remains of settlement from the Middle and Late Bronze Age (remains from these periods, as you know, have been found in many tells throughout the land: Gezer, Jericho, Bethel, etc.).

These conclusions, which I have detailed in my article, are drawn from the results of the excavations conducted to date. As God is my witness, I hope to find evidence that corroborates the biblical narrative in the upcoming excavations.

I would be delighted to learn that I have succeeded, even slightly, in explaining to you the reasons that led me to the conclusion that is expressed in my article. When you visit Mikveh Israel you will find corroboration for my position in light of the findings. However, if you decide that this position should not be publicized for religious or national reasons, I will take your view into consideration and will not object to concluding my article with a broad summary of the findings.

It would be my pleasure to read your opinion regarding this matter.

With great respect and with great admiration,
Judith Krause

Professor Klein responded briefly, writing:

> ... As to the heart of the matter, I am certain that your intentions are good, and I too hope that, in the upcoming period you will find the proofs – and I am almost certain you will – that this is truly Ai and that there was settlement there before the period of the conquest, in a location that has not been excavated to date.
>
> Due to my heavy workload, I must be brief, but I would like to express my thanks for the invitation to the exhibition at Mikveh Israel. Of course, I will make an effort to attend.
>
> With great respect and endearment,
> S. K.

Prof. Samuel Klein (1886–1940)

Klein's hopes were dashed twofold: Judith Marquet-Krause died suddenly a few months after their correspondence, and the archaeologists who followed her in excavating the tell found remains from neither the Patriarchal Age (Middle Bronze Age) nor the period of the Conquest (Late Bronze Age). In a letter of condolence sent by Klein to the Krause family on July 7, 1936, he mentioned Judith's letter, calling it "a letter full of both scientific and Jewish insight."

How Can We Reconcile the Tanakh and the Archaeological Findings?

In light of the findings, a variety of critical views on the story of Joshua's conquest of Ai have been accepted by historians. The renowned scholar William F. Albright posited that the biblical narrative originally described the conquest of Bethel, rather than Ai, but over the course of time the details of the story changed. Other scholars, such as Martin Noth, took a more extreme position, seeing the story of Ai's conquest as part of an Israelite corpus of fictional, etiological myths. In other words, these are legendary stories that serve to explain the origins and characteristics of significant geographic locations.

According to Noth, "Ai" did not refer to any particular location – it was a common noun, simply meaning "ruins," similar to the later Arabic name "Khirbet et-Tell," which was named for the ruins of the ancient city that lay abandoned a thousand years before the Israelites arrived. When they did arrive, Israelite children from a neighboring village would ask their fathers how this formerly great city became the ruins that they now beheld. Not knowing the true history, the fathers would respond by connecting the destruction of the ruin with Joshua, the legendary Israelite warrior.[4] Other scholars claimed that the identification with Joshua's Ai stems from a kind of "transference" from the story of the battle between the Israelites and the Benjaminites at Gibeah, found in Judges 20.

Other writers, particularly those who took a more traditional approach, began to search for Ai in various other unlikely locations. One scholar placed Ai in the vicinity of Jericho, one declared that the ancient city could be found further south, near Michmas, while another placed it further north, in the vicinity of 'Ain Samiya, north

4. Scholars who adopted this theory evidently overlooked the fact that the Ai narrative in Joshua is not a story of miracles and bravery. Rather, it is one of initial military failure and, following this, of a planned war featuring superior forces and escaping tactics.

of Kochav HaShahar. Unfortunately, none of these theories fits the description of the biblical text, which states plainly: "Ai, near Bethel" and "Not a man was left in Ai or in Bethel who did not go out after Israel." Recently, Bryant G. Wood raised the possibility that throughout history, the name "Ai" was never associated with one distinct location. Rather, the name bounced about from place to place, and each of these places was known as "Ai" at one period of time.[5]

Grintz's Analysis

At this juncture, I will present the brilliant analysis of Professor Yehoshua Meir Grintz. Grintz was a Bible scholar and Jewish historian who possessed broad knowledge in the areas of both Ancient Near Eastern languages and culture and the classical world. His innovative interpretations demonstrated a keen eye for detail and a tendency to accept the biblical narrative as it is, rejecting both historical and literary biblical criticism. I quoted Grintz approvingly in the previous chapter, and here too I find his position very compelling.

One of the guiding principles in Grintz's methodology is his insistence on separating the respective roles of the archaeologist and the historian. The archaeologist's role is to uncover and present new information, while the role of the historian is to analyze that information in light of the existing sources. With this in mind, let us return our attention to the question of Ai: What geographical information can be gleaned from Tanakh?

The opening verse of the Ai narrative in the Book of Joshua mentions three adjacent locations: "Joshua sent men from Jericho to Ai, which lies close to Beth-aven – east of Bethel" (Josh. 7:2). What does Tanakh tell us about each of these three places?

- Bethel: Bethel is mentioned during the time of Abraham and Jacob, several times in the books of Joshua and Judges, and through the time of Samuel and Saul. From the time of the post-Solomonic schism until the reign of Josiah, Bethel was home to

5. Wood invokes the view of the late David Livingston, who assigned the same phenomenon to the city of Bethel as well.

a *bama* ("high place" used for sacrifice) that served as a central location in the Kingdom of Israel. In the time of Zerubbabel, some exiles returned to their former home in Bethel: "Who returned each to his own city" (Ezra 2; Nehemiah 7). Toward the end of the biblical period, Bethel is mentioned in the latest geographical listing in Tanakh, in Nehemiah 11.

It seems clear from this wealth of information that Bethel was a continuously inhabited city throughout the entire biblical period, from the beginning of the Patriarchal Age until the time of Nehemiah.

- Ai: Ai is mentioned during the time of Abraham and thereafter only in the Book of Joshua. Following the conquest of Ai, its utter destruction is described vividly: "Then Joshua burned down Ai, and turned it into a mound of ruins for all time, a desolation to this day" (Josh. 8:28). In other words, the city lay desolate for a significant period of time, at least until the final redaction of the Book of Joshua. However, Ai seems to return in the time of Isaiah, its name altered slightly: "He advanced upon Aiath, he proceeded to Migron, at Michmas he deposited his baggage" (Is. 10:28). Finally, Ai is among the destinations of the returning exiles listed in Ezra-Nehemiah, and it is mentioned one last time in Nehemiah: "The Benjaminites: from Geba, Michmash, Aija [Ai] and Bethel and its outlying hamlets" (Neh. 11:31).

This seems to indicate that Ai was an inhabited city at the beginning of the biblical period, was destroyed by Joshua and his army, and lay desolate for several generations until it was resettled at some point no later than the period of the Judean Kings.

- Beth-aven: The Torah makes no mention of Beth-aven during its account of the Patriarchs. However, some of Abraham's activities took place at the location known as "between Bethel and Ai": This was the second place he visited in the Promised Land, and he travels there again after his return from Egypt; the conflict between his shepherds and

> Lot's took place there; it is there that he and Lot agreed to part ways; there Lot "looked about him and saw how well watered was the whole plain of the Jordan" (Gen. 13:10); and it is there that God asked Abraham to look out upon the land and know that it would all belong to him and his descendants.

Since we learn in Joshua that Ai "lies close to Beth-aven," it is curious that Beth-aven is not mentioned in any of these stories. A similar, yet more critical question can be asked regarding the story of the Battle of Ai in the Book of Joshua. The text of the narrative is extremely thorough; not even the smallest details are omitted regarding the forces involved on both sides of the battle, the two different ambushes that Joshua set up between Bethel and Ai, and the staged retreat: "Not a man was left in Ai or in Bethel who did not go out after Israel" (Josh. 8:17). But in the midst of all this military maneuvering, where were the people of Beth-aven? Did they participate in the battle? Did they sign a treaty with Joshua in order to avoid confrontation? We learn that Ai was conquered (12:9) and that Bethel was conquered (Judges 1:22–26), but what happened to Beth-aven?

The most straightforward answer to these questions, writes Grintz, is that Beth-aven was uninhabited during the periods of both Abraham and Joshua. However, by the time the Book of Joshua was finally redacted, this reality must have changed, as the book uses Beth-aven as a reference point for the location of Ai – "Ai, which lies close to Beth-aven" – meaning that by then Beth-aven was inhabited, and was thus a significant place on the map. The same conclusion can be reached by reading the description of the Benjaminites' territory in Joshua 18:12. Beth-aven is mentioned two more times in I Samuel 13–14, in the story of Saul's war with the Philistines: "They encamped at Michmas, east of Beth-aven" (I Sam. 13:5); "The fighting passed beyond Beth-aven" (14:23) – indicating that Beth-aven was still inhabited at that point.

From this point on, Beth-aven is not mentioned explicitly in Tanakh, at least not in the sense of a distinct location. The name does appear in the prophecies of Hosea and Amos, but there it is used as a derogatory reference to Bethel and its history of calf worship: "For Gilgal shall go into exile, and Bethel shall become a delusion (*le-aven*)" (Amos 5:5); "The inhabitants of Samaria fear the calf of Beth-aven" (Hosea 10:5). Grintz explains that the name "Beth-aven" took on this new role because, since the actual town known as Beth-aven had been deserted by the time of Hosea and Amos, its name became available for use as a derogatory nickname for nearby Bethel.

It seems, therefore, that Ai and Beth-aven maintained a kind of inverse relationship throughout history, evoking *Ḥazal*'s statement on the relationship between Jerusalem and ancient Caesarea: "If one says to you that both are destroyed, do not believe him; if he says that both are flourishing, do not believe him... if this one is inhabited, that one is destroyed, and if that one is inhabited, this one is destroyed" (Megilla 6a). From the Patriarchal Age to Joshua's conquest of the land, Ai was inhabited and Beth-aven was abandoned. Then, during the time of the tribal allotments of the land and the redaction of the Book of Joshua, through the time of Samuel and Saul, the converse was true: Beth-aven was inhabited and Ai was destroyed. Finally, during the time of Hosea, Amos, Isaiah, and seemingly thereafter until the end of the biblical period, Ai once again became inhabited and Beth-aven returned to its former state of desolation.

What could be the explanation for this inverse relationship between Ai and Beth-aven? As the two towns were clearly located in close proximity to each other ("Ai, which lies close to Beth-aven") and likely supported themselves by farming the same agricultural area, it may be that there was simply not enough room for two towns to survive on one shared tract of land. Because of this, only one of the two towns was able to exist at any given point in time, creating a kind of historical rotation.

Now that we have established a working biblical chronology for Bethel, Ai, and Beth-aven, our next step is to translate this chronology from biblical periods to archaeological periods. Without getting too entangled in the intricacies and points of debate that are inherent in this task, we can present the following basic timeline: David and Solomon reigned during the tenth century BCE, David's reign having begun in approximately 1000 BCE.[6] According to I Kings 6:1, Solomon built the First Temple in the 480th year following the Exodus from Egypt, meaning that the Exodus took place in approximately 1450 BCE.[7] About four hundred years passed between the time of Abraham and the Exodus, meaning that the events involving Abraham in the land of Canaan took place in 1900–1800 BCE. In the world of archaeology, the last two centuries before the reign of David are known as the Israelite Period I, or alternatively, the Iron Age I. The period during which the Exodus and the conquest of Canaan took place is known as the Late Canaanite Period or the Late Bronze Age (LB). Finally, the Patriarchal Age is known as the Middle Canaanite Period or the Middle Bronze Age (MB).

The following table may help illustrate how the information we collected regarding Bethel, Ai, and Beth-aven fits into the archaeological timeline we just established:

	Bethel	*Ai*	*Beth-aven*
Patriarchal Age (MB: 1900–1800 BCE)	inhabited	inhabited	uninhabited
Conquest of Canaan (LB: c. 1400 BCE)	inhabited	inhabited	uninhabited
Redaction of Joshua, Judges and Samuel (Iron I to 1000 BCE)	inhabited	uninhabited	inhabited
Kingdoms of Israel (Iron II–III: 1000–586 BCE)	inhabited	inhabited	uninhabited
Return to Zion (Persian period: 5th–4th century BCE)	inhabited	inhabited	uninhabited

6. Some place the beginning of David's reign in 1010 BCE. This calculus factored into Israel's decision to celebrate the trimillenial anniversary of the city of Jerusalem in 1997.
7. See above, note 4.

Now let us build a parallel table for the archaeological findings from the two relevant sites in the region: Beitin and et-Tell. Note the addition of a new first row representing the Early Bronze Age (EB).

	Beitin	***Et-Tell***
Early Bronze Age until 2000 BCE	uninhabited	inhabited (large, fortified city)
Middle Bronze Age: 2000–1550 BCE	inhabited	uninhabited
Late Bronze Age: c. 1400 BCE	inhabited	uninhabited
Tribal allotments to David's reign (Iron I to 1000 BCE)	inhabited	inhabited (small, unfortified town)
Kingdoms of Israel (Iron II–III: 1000–586 BCE)	inhabited	uninhabited
Return to Zion (Persian period: 5th–4th century BCE)	inhabited	uninhabited

The first row in this table (Early Bronze Age) is irrelevant for our purposes, as it describes the period before Abraham arrived in the land of Canaan. But contained in the remainder of the table is a startlingly clear solution to the problem of Ai. As we expected, the Beitin findings are completely consistent with the biblical account of Bethel. The shocking revelation here is that not only are the et-Tell findings the absolute converse of the biblical account of Ai, they are in perfect accord with that of Beth-aven! Indeed, it seems clear from this analysis that et-Tell is not Ai at all, but Beth-aven, a small, unfortified Israelite town built on part of the ruins of a huge, fortified, ancient Canaanite city. This Canaanite city existed only in the pre-Abrahamic period, and thus bears no connection to the history of the people of Israel.

Now that we have successfully located Beth-Aven, we are still left with one problem: Where is Ai? According to the biblical sources, it must be located in close enough proximity to Beth-aven that it was necessary to share farmland with its neighbor. In fact, it is likely that the ruins of Ai can simply be found in a section of et-Tell that has not yet been excavated, perhaps buried beneath part of the adjacent town of Deir Dibwan.

It is critical to stress that the mere lack of archaeological evidence for this claim is no proof of its illegitimacy. Many important sites appear completely innocuous – like unremarkable open areas – before they are excavated. Take, for instance, Tel Muqanna' (Miqne) in the Shefela lowlands, which scholars today unanimously identify with the ancient Philistine city of Ekron. This tell is one of the largest in the country, but before it was excavated one would have had great difficulty discerning the site from the rest of the landscape. The same is true of Tel Ashtara in the Bashan region: Early researchers refused to identify it with the city of Ashtaroth, due to the area's "wretched appearance." Then archaeologists excavated the site and the findings reflected the existence of a large, fortified tell. This same phenomenon transpired even at et-Tell itself: when Edward Robinson visited in 1838, he suggested that the tell was not an ancient site at all! Whether the tell is Ai or not, it is clear that Robinson erred in this particular claim.

A retrospective analysis of the attempts of scholars throughout modern history to locate Ai enables us to focus on a fundamental failing on the part of many of them. Scholars recognized Ai from its repeated mention in Abraham's narrative and from its role in the long, dramatic battle story in the Book of Joshua. When a large, impressive tell was found in the Benjamin region, these scholars rushed to find evidence of Ai therein (and many then proceeded to deny the veracity of the biblical narrative when the expected findings did not materialize). However, if these scholars had analyzed the biblical texts more closely beforehand, they could have easily rejected the possibility that Ai was located at et-Tell without the use of a single shovel or hoe. As it turns out, there is not always a correlation between how long or memorable a city's narrative is and the city's actual size. In the case of Ai, the Book of Joshua implies that it was not a particularly large city, stating that Gibeon was a larger city than Ai (Josh. 10:2). The location of ancient Gibeon is known to us, and the area of its ruins spans approximately fifty dunams, less than half the size of et-Tell.

Finally, it may not be necessary to reject Noth's position – that "Ai" was a generic expression meaning "ruins" – in its entirety. In fact, it seems very likely that the location known as "Ai" in Abraham's time was named for the ruins of the large Canaanite city that had been destroyed years earlier. Whether Ai was built directly atop these ruins or in their general vicinity, they were undoubtedly one of the defining geographical landmarks of the region, providing a compelling explanation for the choice of the name "Ai."

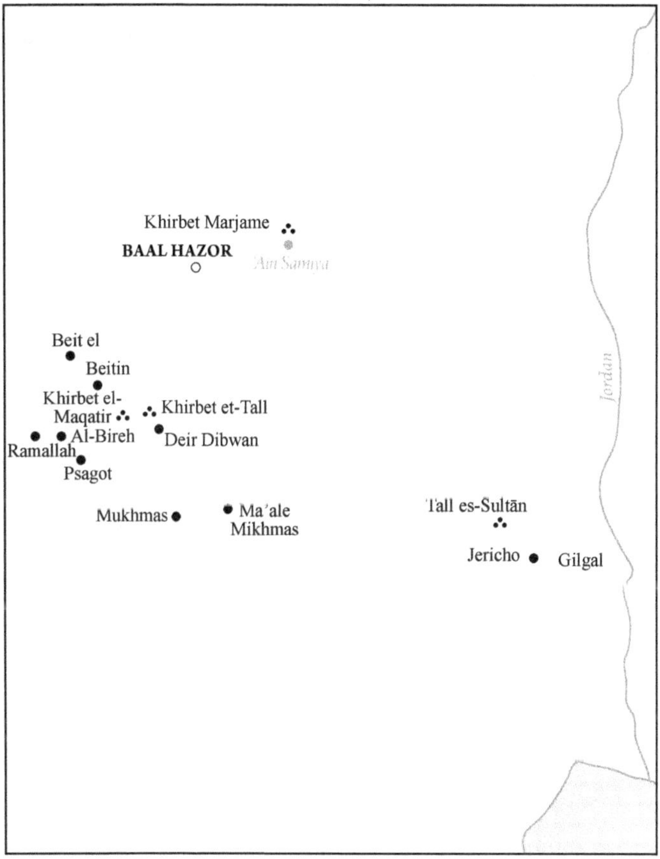

For further study:

Bin-Nun, Y. "'*Ba al Aiat' – Pitaron Ḥadash Lezihui HaAi.*" *Judea and Samaria Research Studies* 2, Kedumim-Ariel, 1993, 43–63 [Hebrew].

Callaway, J. A. "Ai." In *The Anchor Bible Dictionary*, 1, 125–130.

Elitzur, Y. "*Madua' I Efshar Lezahot et HaAi BeEin Samiya? Hasagot Lehatza'ato shel Harav Yoel Bin-Nun.*" *Judea and Samaria Research Studies* 2, Kedumim-Ariel, 1993, 63–64 (also see 64, "*Teshuvat Yoel Bin-Nun Lehe'arat Yoel Elitzur*") [Hebrew].

Garstang, J. *Joshua Judges*. London, 1931, 149–161, 355–356.
Grintz, Y. M. "Ai which is beside Beth Aven." *Biblica* 42 (1961), 201–216.
Livingston, D. "One Last Word of Bethel and Ai." *BAR* 15 (1989): 18–30.
Luria, B. Z. "*Mekomah shel HaAi*": *Iyunim Besefer Yehoshua: Diyunei Haḥug Lemikra Beveit David Ben-Gurion*. Jerusalem, 1971, 12–41 (note the responses of scholars therein!) [Hebrew].
Riklin, S. "A New Proposal for the Identification of the City Ha'Ai near Ma'aleh Michmash." *Judea and Samaria Research Studies* 5, Kedumim-Ariel, 1996, 27–32 [Hebrew].
Wood, B. G. "The Search for Joshua's Ai." *Critical Issues in Early Israelite History*, edited by R. Hess, G. A.Klingbeil, and P. J. Ray, Winona Lake, 2008, 205–240.

Parashat Vayera

Sodom and Gomorrah

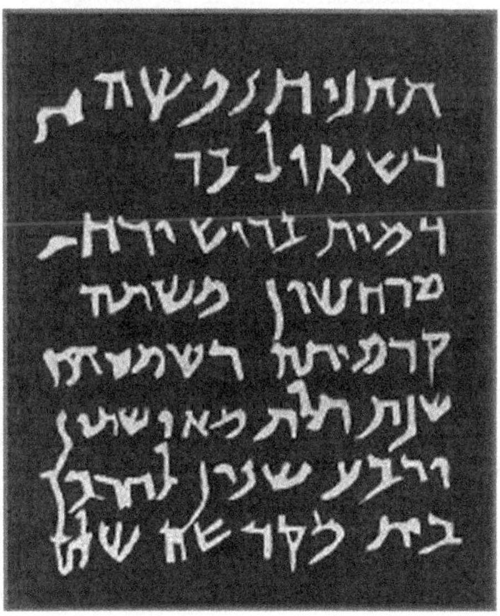

(E. Cowley, PEFQst, 1925)

Jewish tombstone from Zoar, talmudic period: "Rest in peace the soul of Saul son of... who died on Rosh Chodesh Marcheshvan of the first year of Shemitta, three hundred sixty-four years from the destruction of the Temple. Shalom."

Parashat Vayera contains the Torah's account of the cataclysmic destruction of Sodom, Gomorrah, Admah, and Zeboiim, four of the five major "cities of the Plain." Following their annihilation, these cities became synonymous with extreme sinfulness and corruption, both throughout Tanakh and in today's parlance. Similarly, the destruction of the cities became synonymous with utter desolation and ruin.

Where Are Sodom and Gomorrah?

The cities of the Plain are traditionally identified in the southern Dead Sea region. This identification is generally accepted today, as evidenced by the appearance of the names Sodom and Zoar on today's maps. Modern Sodom is rich in phosphate and potash, and it is not far from a large hotel and resort complex. Mount Sodom looms over the area, a remarkable peak made up almost entirely of salt. Zoar, the only city of the Plain that survived destruction, is commonly identified as the modern-day Jordanian town of Safi in the southeast Dead Sea region. Remains have been found in Safi that shed light on Jewish life in the talmudic period, including tombstones inscribed with dates reckoned from the destruction of the Second Temple and with the year of the *shemitta* cycle.

In order to determine where the destruction of Sodom and Gomorrah took place, we must ask : How did the destruction of Sodom and Gomorra take place? The Torah's description – "the Lord rained upon Sodom and Gomorrah sulfurous fire" (Gen. 19:24) and "the smoke of the land rose like the smoke of a kiln" (19:28) – gives the impression of a kind of volcanic eruption. The eastern Dead Sea region does, in fact, contain deposits of volcanic ash, but experts have said that these are prehistoric in origin and thus irrelevant to our current discussion.

A more feasible claim is that the destruction of Sodom was the result of a powerful earthquake that featured "sulfurous fire" as a secondary effect. Accounts describing the flooding of the cities of the Plain can be found in both non-Jewish second Temple-era sources and in several passing remarks by *Ḥazal*, and some modern scholars considered the possibility that these ancient sites were flooded by the southern basin of the Dead Sea. To date, however, no remains of any cities have been found either beneath the waters of the Dead Sea or in its southern basin, which is now dry due to the sea's receding water level (excluding areas that have been inundated artificially). To be sure, there is a rapid rate of sediment accumulation in the Dead Sea, and it is certainly possible that the lost cities were covered in multiple layers of sediment and simply have yet to be dug out.

Some scholars connected the story of Sodom's destruction with several fortified towns in the southeast Dead Sea region that existed in the Early Bronze Age and were destroyed in approximately 2300 BCE. These scholars point to a large cemetery found in Bāb edh-Dhrā^{c} on the eastern coast of the Dead Sea, on the Lisan Peninsula,[1] which seems isolated from any significant settlements of the same time period. The problem with this theory is that all of the findings at Bāb edh-Dhrā^{c} predate Abraham's arrival in the region according to the biblical account. In order to deal with this obstacle, some claimed that the Torah's chronology is inaccurate, while others suggested that the chronology presented by archaeologists is at fault.

The Northern Theory

Many authors suggested that the five cities of the Plain are not to be located in the southern Dead Sea region, but rather they could actually be found in the northern Dead Sea region, near the Jordan River estuary into the sea, not far from Jericho. Scholars who support this theory have based themselves on several considerations:

- The term "cities of the Plain" refers to the plain of the Jordan. The Torah states: "So Lot chose for himself the whole plain of the Jordan," later summarizing, "Abram remained in the land of Canaan, while Lot settled in the cities of the Plain" (Gen. 13:11–12). If so, Sodom and Gomorrah should be located near the Jordan River, rather than in the southern Dead Sea region.

1. *Lisan* is Arabic for both "tongue" and "cape," due to their similar shape. Compare to the Modern Hebrew *lashon*, which functions in the same way. However, in Biblical Hebrew, *lashon* meant the opposite – an elongated body of water projecting into the land (see Josh. 15:2, 15:5, 18:19, and Is. 11:15).

- Abraham and Lot stood between Bethel and Ai, overlooking the plain of the Jordan: "Lot looked about him and saw how well watered was the whole plain of the Jordan, all of it – this was before the Lord had destroyed Sodom and Gomorrah ... so Lot chose for himself the whole plain of the Jordan ... and he moved his tents near Sodom" (13:10–12). According to this account, Sodom and the Plain are apparently visible from the Bethel region, a claim that is only possible if they are located in the northern Dead Sea region – the southern Dead Sea region is simply too far away.[2]
- The narrative of Lot's daughters and the subsequent births of Ammon and Moab took place on the heels of Lot and his family's dramatic escape from the destruction of Sodom. Some have argued, based on this fact, that Sodom must be located near the ancient lands of both Ammon and Moab, which were inhabited by the descendants of Lot. While Moab was situated along the entire eastern coast of the Dead Sea, Ammon was located to its northeast. Therefore, Sodom could only have been somewhere in the northern Dead Sea region, in relative proximity to both Ammon and Moab.
- The city of Zoar is mentioned as one of the places that Moses viewed from atop Mount Nebo: "Moses went up from the steppes of Moab to Mount Nebo ... and the Lord showed him the whole land: Gilead as far as Dan; all Naphtali; the land of Ephraim and Manasseh; the whole land of Judah as far as the Western Sea, and the Negeb; and the Plain – the Valley of Jericho, the city of palm trees – as far as Zoar" (Deut. 34:1–3). The verses essentially sketch out for us a large circle on the map, beginning with Mount Nebo and continuing counterclockwise, arcing north, west, south, and finally returning to Mount Nebo – to Jericho and Zoar. The verse seems to imply that Jericho and Zoar are close to each other on the map, meaning that Zoar and

2. The fact that Abraham was able to view the ruins of Sodom and Gomorrah from the area east of Hebron is not a proof in either direction, as Hebron lies at about the midpoint of the Dead Sea.

the other cities of the Plain are in the northern Dead Sea region rather than the southern Dead Sea region.[3]

In light of these considerations, proponents of the northern theory have identified various sites throughout the northern Dead Sea region as candidates for the ruins of Sodom, Gomorrah, and the other cities of the Plain.

In recent years, archaeologist Steven Collins excavated in Tall el-Ḥammām in the eastern Jordan Valley, northeast of the Dead Sea, and discovered a huge fortified city in terms of ancient times (about 250 dunams within the walls of the city and another settlement outside the walls of about 150 dunams; its massive stone wall was surrounded by a rampart made up of milions of mudbricks), which was destroyed in a fierce fire in the Middle Bronze Age. Nearby were cities and smaller settlements that were also destroyed in time. The entire region, which is rich in water and has the potential for large agricultural productivity, was destroyed during the Middle Bronze Age and remained in its desolation for 600-700 years. The researcher reports on the discovery of ceramic remains that were melted in a huge heat and have a glass cover as a result of the heat. Collins suggests identifying Sodom and the Cities of the Plain in this and other nearby towns.

Based on several cases of collision of huge meteors on Earth in the modern era, he proposes to explain the destruction of Sodom and Gomorrah. According to him, the crush of the meteor with the earth caused a tectonic shock that raised the Dead Sea and caused salinity of soil that could not be processed for hundreds of years.

Considerations in Favor of the Southern Theory

Despite the above considerations, there remain many significant indications that the cities of the Plain are located in the southern Dead Sea region, in accordance with the traditional identification:

- There is a well-documented ancient tradition placing the five cities in the south. Jerome, the famous early Church Father, wrote in

3. This argument is not foolproof, as it may be that the verse considered the entire Dead Sea region, both the north and the south, as one region.

approximately 400 CE that Zoar is the southern border of the land of Moab. The Madaba Map, commonly dated to the sixth century CE, features a fortified town called "Zoora" in the southeast Dead Sea region. In addition, in the late 1980s, a monastery was discovered built atop a natural cave that early Christians apparently identified with Lot's place of refuge after leaving Zoar.[4] This monastery was also noted on the Madaba Map east of Zoora.

- Tanakh contains several detailed lists of the cities in the northeast Dead Sea region. These include the cities conquered from Sihon (Num. 32:3), the cities settled by the tribes of Gad and Reuben (32:34–38), the cities in the region occupied by the people of Israel when they encamped in the plains of Moab (33:48–49), the cities that were given to the tribe of Reuben (Josh. 13:15–23) and the cities that the tribe of Reuben ceded to the Levites (I Chr. 6:63–64). Tellingly, Zoar is not mentioned in any of these lists. Even in the Mesha Stele of King Mesha of Moab, which contains an extraordinary number of place-names in northern Moab, Zoar is nowhere to be found. Zoar is mentioned, however, in Isaiah's "burden of Moab" prophecy (Is. 15:5) and in Jeremiah's Moab prophecy (Jer. 48:34), both of which include southern Moabite cities.
- The Torah says that Lot "moved his tents near Sodom" (Gen. 13:12), and the same language is used for Abram – "And Abram moved his tent, and came to dwell at the Eloney of Mamre, which are in Hebron" (13:18). The word for "moving" one's tent – *vaye'ehal* – refers to the slow pace characteristic of nomadic shepherds, whose progress is limited by that of their flocks, and who pitch tents anew for themselves and for their cattle after each incremental move. When Abraham "moved his tent," we learn the extent of such a move – from Bethel to Hebron, a distance of over thirty miles. If we assume that Lot "moved his tents" in a similar way, then he would still have had to travel a significant distance upon reaching the

4. It is noteworthy that significant remnants from the Middle Bronze Age (which coincided with the Patriarchal Age) were also found in this cave below the Byzantine pavement made by the builders of the monastery.

plain of Jordan before arriving in Sodom. Thus, Abraham's view from where he stood "between Bethel and Ai" did not include Sodom.[5]

- There is one place in Tanakh that seems to explicitly corroborate the southern theory. Much of the first half of the Book of Ezekiel contains harsh admonition directed at Judah and Jerusalem. In chapter 16, Ezekiel accuses Jerusalem of being worse than both Samaria and Sodom: "Your elder sister was Samaria, who lived with her daughters to the north of you; your younger sister was Sodom, who lived with her daughters to the south of you. Did you not walk in their ways and practice their abominations? You were almost more corrupt than they in all your ways" (Ezek. 16:46–47). The prophet places Samaria north of Jerusalem and Sodom south of Jerusalem,[6] proving that even as early as Ezekiel's time it was accepted that Sodom lay to the south.

I will conclude with the words of Ezekiel from later in chapter 16. He relays an extraordinary prophecy, one that is unique in all of Tanakh:

> I will restore their fortunes – the fortunes of Sodom and her daughters and the fortunes of Samaria and her daughters – and your fortunes along with theirs...Then your sister Sodom and her daughters shall return to their former state, and Samaria and her daughters shall return to their former state, and you and your daughters shall return to your former state. (53–55)

Amazingly, the prophecy speaks of redemption and return, not just for Jerusalem and Samaria, but also for "Sodom and her daughters." I believe that this trifold promise has been fulfilled in our generation: we have witnessed the return of Jerusalem to Jewish hands, along with its resurgence and expansion. Samaria too, while it is certainly far from its former glory, is beginning to grow and regain some of its lost stature.

---

5. I am indebted to Dr. Arye Bornstein for this consideration.
6. The Scripture uses here the words *yamin* ("right") and *smol* ("left") for north and south respectively. For the background to this terminology see the chapter on *Parashat Vayikra*.

(Provided through the generosity of the Tamar Regional Council)

Hotel complex in the modern city of Sodom, which transformed from a desert to a flowering garden.

Finally, modern Sodom is a flourishing hub of tourism and industry, bearing little resemblance to the ruin of its ancient namesake. May we merit to see the return of all the cities of Israel to a state of lasting peace and economic and cultural prosperity.

For further study:

Bin-Nun, Y. "*Arei Hakikar Mitzafon Leyam Hamelaḥ?!*" In Z. Ehrlich (ed.), *Shomron UBinyamin*, 2, Jerusalem, 1991, 34–45 [Hebrew].

Ginzburg, D. "*Hafichat Sedom VaAmora: Re'idat Adama o Tofa'a Ga'ashit.*" *Midrash Uma'as* 1 (1982): 31–35 [Hebrew].

MacDonald, B. *East of the Jordan*. Boston, 2000, 45–61.

Mulder, M. J. "Sodom and Gomorrah." In *The Anchor Bible Dictionary*, 6:99–103.

Politis, K. D. "The Monastery of Aghios Lot at Deir 'Ain 'Abata in Jordan." In *Bizanz – das Römerreich im Mittelalter* = Byzantium – the Roman Empire in the Middle Ages, edited by F. Daim and J. Drauschke, 1–24. Mainz, 2011.

Rast, W. E. "Bab edh-Dhra and the Origin of the Sodom Sage." *Archaeology and Biblical Interpretation*, edited by L. E. Toombs and G. L. Johnson, 185–201. Atlanta, 1987.

Simons, J. J. *The Geographical and Topographical Texts of the Old Testament*. Leiden, 1959, 222–229.

Le Strange, G. *Palestine under the Moslems*, Beirut, 1965, 286–292.

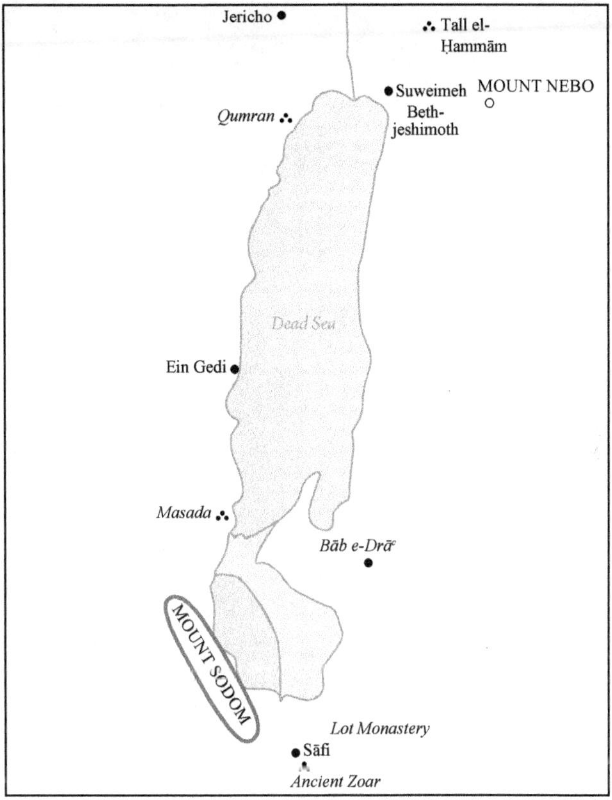

Jericho
Tall el-
Ḥammām
Suweimeh
MOUNT NEBO
Beth-
jeshimoth
Qumran
Dead Sea
Ein Gedi
Masada
Bāb e-Drāʿ
MOUNT SODOM
Lot Monastery
Sāfi
Ancient Zoar

Parashat Ḥayei Sara

The Field of Machpelah

Instead of adding one more chapter to the already vast literature on the cave of Machpelah, discussing and debating the finer points of its location, history, and significance to the Jewish people, I would like to focus on a place that has garnered far less attention: the field of Machpelah.

What Does "Machpelah" Mean?

Our *parasha* mentions not only the storied cave of Machpelah, but also the surrounding field of Machpelah. Rashi comments on the verse, "Let him give me the cave of Machpelah that he owns" (Gen. 23:9): "A structure with an upper story over it. Another interpretation: [It was called this] because it was doubled with couples." Rashi presents here an abridged version of a passage that appears in the Talmud:

> The cave of Machpelah – Rav and Shmuel differ as to its meaning. One holds that the cave consisted of two chambers, one behind the other; and the other holds that it consisted of a

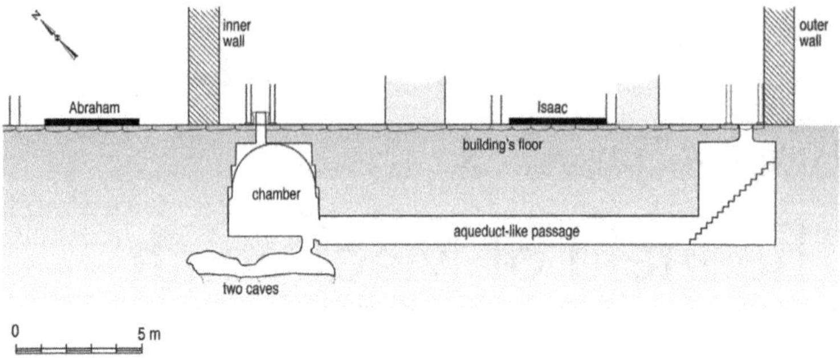

(Image courtesy of Prof. B. Z. Kedar)

The subterranean passage, chambers, and caves in the Machpelah structure: "Two chambers, one behind the other" and "a lower and upper chamber."

> lower and upper chamber. According to him who holds that the chambers were one above the other, the term "Machpelah" is justified. But according to him who holds that it consisted of two chambers, one behind the other, what could be the meaning of *Machpelah*? [The answer is] that it had multiples of couples. (Eiruvin 53a)

Nahmanides, in his commentary on this verse, was troubled by this interpretation, and allowed himself to voice a sharp critique on the approach of Rashi (and in truth, on the Talmud as well):

> But this is not true, as the verse states, "Ephron's land in Machpelah" (Gen. 23:17), indicating that this was the name of the place where the field was located, and it is not necessary to seek explanations for names of places.

In other words, "Machpelah" is not the name of the cave, nor is it the name of the field surrounding the cave. It is, in fact, the name for the entire area, an area that happens to contain a field and a cave within it. If one is still curious as to the meaning of the name, Nahmanides determines that one simply cannot know. Just as we do not know the meaning of "Lachish" and "Ziklag," or even "Jerusalem" or "Hebron," so too do not bother trying to understand the meaning of "Machpelah." It is a Canaanite place-name, no more and no less, without any special significance to the history of our people.[1]

Those who, in recent years, have taken the opportunity to visit and inspect the underground cavities at the cave of Machpelah will be able to confirm both talmudic interpretations. First, beneath the floor of the monumental Second Temple-era structure lie two ancient burial caves, one located behind the other. Second, above these caves is an underground chamber – a structure that fits with the approaches of both Rav and Shmuel. Thus, both interpretations of *Ḥazal* are supported by examining the actual layout of the site, which was probably accessible in the period of our sages.

It is worth noting that the area surrounding the cave is littered with similar burial caves, all built in a style typical of the Middle Bronze Age, the Patriarchal Age.[2] Despite this, the name "Machpelah" as it is used in chapter 23 still clearly refers to the overall area, which includes within it both the field and the caves in question.

The Field and the Caves

It is important to emphasize that the Torah gives equal significance to the field of Machpelah and the cave of Machpelah. Later in the same chapter we find explicit evidence of this perspective:

> So Ephron's land in Machpelah, near Mamre – the field with its cave and all the trees anywhere within the confines of that field — passed to Abraham as his possession, in the presence of the Hittites, of all who entered the gate of his town. (Gen. 23:17–18)

We see from this that, for the Torah, the purchase of the cave itself is not the main point of the narrative here. Rather, it is the purchase of "the field…and all the trees anywhere within the confines of that field"

1. In this statement, Ramban follows Ibn Ezra (his commentary to Genesis 10:8) and Radak (his commentary to Genesis 2:20). I am indebted to Yael Gwili and Itamar Haddad (respectively) for these references.
2. The abundance of burial sites in the vicinity of the cave of Machpelah calls to mind the Hittites' statement to Abraham, "Bury your dead in the choicest of our burial places" (Gen. 23:6).

that is the crux of the matter. What this means, on a fundamental level, is that *Parashat Ḥayei Sara* is less concerned with Sarah's burial and the events surrounding it and more concerned with the story of the first formal acquisition of land in *Eretz Yisrael* by the first Hebrew.

My late father, Professor Yehuda Elitzur, demonstrated how to read *Parashat Ḥayei Sara* properly, and the following interpretation is based on one of his articles, with minor changes. If one reads this *parasha* on a superficial level, it may seem that the conversation between Abraham and Ephron is a polite, amicable dialogue between two friends. Ephron uses the phrase "My lord, hear me" repeatedly, while Abraham bows humbly twice before the Hittites. Abraham demeans himself, saying, "I am a resident alien among you" (Gen. 23:4), while the Hittites glorify him, saying, "You are the elect of God among us" (23:6). It seems almost as if this is a kind of lovers' quarrel: Abraham wants to pay for the burial plot, while Ephron and the Hittites refuse (at first) to accept his money, insisting that Abraham take the site as a gift. Each party is exceedingly courteous to the other, almost cloyingly so.

But if we analyze further the language of these interactions, we find that the truth is quite different from what it seems. In fact, what we perceive as polite conversation is actually a trademark of the Middle Eastern marketplace, where vendors and buyers use friendly language to mask cutthroat bargaining tactics.

In light of this, what is actually going on behind the scenes in the story of Abraham and Ephron? In all ancient societies, the sale of land to foreigners was a serious taboo. This can be seen several times in Tanakh, such as in the narrative of the daughters of Tzlofhad: "No inheritance shall pass over from one tribe to another" (Num. 36:9); and later in Navot the Jezreelite's narrative: "The Lord forbid that I should give up to you what I have inherited from my fathers" (I Kings 21:3). This reluctance to sell land to outsiders features prominently throughout Ancient Near Eastern history, and, as we know all too well, in the geopolitics of today's Middle East as well.

In 1925–1931, a series of excavations of the ancient city of Nuzi in northern Iraq unearthed thousands of clay tablets dating from the fifteenth to fourteenth centuries BCE. These tablets contained a wide variety of documents, including those detailing a complex adoption system.

Apparently, adoption was a very common phenomenon in that society. What surprised scholars, however, is that some of these adoption records depicted a scenario in which a relatively young man would adopt an older, well-off man – an arrangement that seems odd to our sensibilities and in light of our modern notion of adoption. According to the Nuzi tablets, the adoptee would give his adopter a sizeable gift, at which point the adopter would designate a portion of his property as an inheritance for the adoptee. Sometimes, multiple people would adopt the same person simultaneously.

What is the meaning of this strange form of "adoption"? Scholars explain that this procedure is essentially a business arrangement that effectively allowed for the sale of land to foreigners without breaking the social taboo against such a transaction. The parties involved exploit a legal loophole that states that an adopted son may inherit his father's property. While a landowner cannot sell his property to a foreigner outright, if that potential buyer becomes his "son" there could be no legal objection to his eventual acquisition of the land by way of inheritance.

Let us now return to Abraham in the Land of Canaan. Abraham had already been living in the land for many years, but had not yet been able to acquire land for himself, his family, and his descendants. God had promised him that "to your offspring I will assign this land" (Gen. 15:18), and "I assign the land you sojourn in to you and your offspring to come" (17:8). But despite this promise, the great wealth that Abraham had amassed, and his sterling reputation and stature among the Canaanites, he was still essentially a stranger in a strange land. Abraham first lived between Bethel and Ai. When he then moved to Elonei Mamre in Hebron, he became a tenant farmer on land belonging to his "ally" Mamre the Amorite, kinsman of Eshkol and Aner. This meant that Mamre gave Abraham permission to live on his estate land, raise his flocks, and support his growing household, which included hundreds of apprentices and servants. Abraham was given free rein to build his fortune of cattle, gold, and silver, but not a speck of the land belonged to him.

The Canaanites greatly respected Abraham and probably even the new monotheistic religion that he discovered and represented. We read in *Parashat Lekh Lekha* that some of the native people even shared his views. King Melchizedek of Salem "brought out bread and wine"

(Gen. 14:18) in Abraham's honor, blessing him in the name of the one God: "Blessed be Abram of God Most High, Creator of heaven and earth" (14:19). The people clearly held Abraham in great esteem, even, in the case of the Hittites, going so far as to call him "the elect of God among us" (23:6). But despite this respectful relationship, the people of Canaan would not, under any circumstances, sell Abraham land.

When Sarah dies, Abraham decides to take advantage of the opportunity to realize God's promise of "I assign the land you sojourn in to you and your offspring to come, all the land of Canaan, as an everlasting holding" (Gen. 17:8), by making his first real attempt at acquiring land from the Canaanites. He begins his appeal while the people of the land are gathered around Sarah's bier, mourning the death of a woman they had come to love, and honoring her respected husband. Abraham faces the crowd, saying, "I am a resident alien among you." This introduction is not simply a display of modesty. Rather, Abraham is pointing out the frustration inherent in his current situation: I have been living in your midst now for decades, but I am still considered a resident alien. Abraham continues, "Give me a burial site among you, that I may remove my dead for burial." In other words, Abraham is announcing that he will not bury Sarah until he is sold a burial site *as an inheritance.*

It may be that Abraham's request takes the Hittites aback – here is an old man whom they know as an honorable idealist who is now exploiting the personal tragedy of his wife's death in order to acquire property. But Abraham alone knows the truth: This is not just a plot of land, but a manifestation of his entire life's purpose – "Go forth ... to the land that I will show you"; "To your offspring I will assign this land." It is for this reason alone that Abraham makes his brazen request of the Hittites.

The negotiation process that follows Abraham's plea constitutes a shrewd battle of wits. The Hittites present their first offer – *permission* to bury Sarah in *their* cave: "You are the elect of God among us. Bury your dead in the choicest of *our* burial places; none of us will withhold *his* burial place from you for burying your dead" (Gen. 23:6). But Abraham is not interested in this kind of arrangement. Knowing that he is about to make a highly irregular request, Abraham bows to the Hittites and focuses his language, letting them know exactly what he wants:

> You must agree to intercede for me with Ephron son of Zohar. Let him give me the cave of Machpelah that he owns, which is at the edge of his land. Let him give it to me, *at the full price*, for a *burial estate* in your midst. (23:8–9)

The extreme public nature of this exchange certainly added to the drama of the situation. The crowd that had gathered simply to attend Sarah's funeral and burial was now rapt with attention, hundreds of eyes alternately fixating on Abraham and Ephron, waiting for each figure to make his next strategic move. Abraham may have been counting on the psychological pressure of the moment to influence the outcome of the negotiation. Perhaps the public nature of the scene has an additional role: to certify the deal. The exceptional permission to sell a piece of ground to a stranger needs public verification.[3] Note that at this stage, all Abraham is requesting is the right to purchase the cave – a mere burial site. In response, Ephron acts as if he does not understand the request, repeating, with the same magnanimous language, the first offer that the Hittites made – permission to bury Sarah in the cave, which would continue to be owned by Ephron.

There is a subtle linguistic nuance at play here. Ephron recognizes that Abraham consistently uses the verb root N-T-N, meaning "give": "Give me a burial site"; "Let him give me the cave of Machpelah"; "Let him give it to me, at the full price." Because of this, Ephron mirrors that language, using the words "I give" three times in succession: "I give you the field and I give you the cave that is in it; I give it to you in the presence of my people" (Gen. 23:11). In Ephron's usage, however, "giving" refers not to a sale of property, but to giving permission, thus bending Abraham's phrasing to his own goals. This explains Ephron's sudden addition of "the field" to the transaction: He is not offering the field for sale, but only giving Abraham permission to use *his* cave, which happens to be located within *his* field.

3. Note the final summing up in the last verse of the chapter: "So Abraham secured the field and the cave that was in it as a burial site *from the sons of Heth*." The sellers here are the whole congregation of the sons of Heth. I have to thank Elitzur Segal for this insight.

In response to Ephron's continuing refusal to sell him land, Abraham bows once more and again makes a point to address Ephron in public, "before the people of the land" (Gen. 23:12). He digs in further, taking his terminology to a new level: "Let me give the price of the land;[4] accept it from me!" (23:13). In response, Ephron changes the scope of the land in question; instead of selling just the cave, as Abraham requested, Ephron is now speaking about the field surrounding it as well. Ephron then sets a price for the transaction that is astronomically high,[5] masking this unreasonable sum with faux-courteous pleasantries: "My lord, do hear me! A piece of land worth four hundred shekels of silver – what is that between you and me?" (23:15). At that point, Ephron may have expected Abraham to back down from the deal, a sensible move from a pure business perspective. Instead, Abraham accepted Ephron's terms: "Abraham paid out to Ephron the money that he had named in the hearing of the Hittites – four hundred shekels of silver at the going merchants' rate" (23:16).

The deal was done, but on a much larger scale than Abraham had ever anticipated, and with the public acknowledgment of the people. The Torah concludes solemnly:

> So Ephron's land in Machpelah, near Mamre – the field with its cave and all the trees anywhere within the confines of that field – passed to Abraham as his possession, in the presence of the Hittites, of all who entered the gate of his town. (Gen. 23:17–18)

Abraham finally achieved his goal: he became a legitimate landowner in the Promised Land. Then, and only then, was he able to take the final step in cementing his ownership of the land: "And then Abraham buried his wife Sarah in the cave of the field of Machpelah" (Gen. 23:19).

---

4. Literally: *I have given* the price of the land; the act is already done.
5. According to Judges 17:10, a year's salary was ten shekels. Leviticus 27:16 notes that the value of a field is fifty shekels per *chomer* of barley seed required to plant it, which is approximately fifty shekels per 4.5 acres of land.

(Genesis 23:17–18; photo courtesy of David Wilder, Hebron)

"So Ephron's land in Machpelah…and all the trees anywhere within the confines of that field – passed to Abraham as his possession."

3,800 Years Later

In the wake of the Six-Day War of 1967, we merited to return to Hebron, and with it, to the cave of Machpelah. Jewish families returned to Hebron as well, in a slow and politically complicated process. Every step forward in the growth of the Jewish communities in Kiryat Arba and Hebron was a result of the great dedication of the individual settlers, and in particular the women among them.

One incident that truly brings to mind Abraham's purchase of the cave of Machpelah is the story of the burial of Avraham Yedidya Nachshon, the infant son of Baruch and Sarah Nachshon. Avraham Yedidya was born on March 11, 1975 in a clinic in Kiryat Arba. He was the first Jewish boy to be circumcised in the cave of Machpelah and was named for Abraham – beloved (*yedid*) of God. One night, when Avraham Yedidya was four months old, he died suddenly in his crib, without any clear medical cause. His parents decided to bury their son in the old Jewish cemetery in Hebron. When their car was blocked from entering by IDF officers, Sarah took her son's corpse, wrapped in burial shrouds, in her arms and strode toward the cemetery. Sarah's

(Photo courtesy of Noam Arnon, Hebron)

Tombstone of Avraham Yedidya Nahshon, the first to be buried in the old Jewish cemetery of Hebron after the Six-Day War.

determination paid off, and her son became the first Jew to be buried in Hebron since the Hebron Massacre of 1929.

This incident paved the way for a resurgence of Jewish life in Hebron. Today, despite political agreements that have placed control over most of the city in Arab hands, the heart of the city – Tel Hebron of antiquity and the Jewish Quarter of the past few centuries – is currently populated by Jews, the descendants of Abraham, Isaac, and Jacob.

Furthermore, Jews from Israel and from around the world regularly visit the cave of Machpelah, something that was not always possible even in recent memory.

The cave of Machpelah is not the only site in Hebron that is bustling with Jewish life at all hours of the day; the field of Machpelah fits this description as well. Today, the field of Machpelah consists of a large, landscaped area to the west, south, and east of the magnificent Second Temple-era structure built directly atop the cave. At the southeast corner of that structure,[6] Jews would pray and light candles opposite a small opening that led to an underground system of passages. These passages, in turn, led to the area adjacent to the actual tombs of the Patriarchs. Jewish weddings and other celebrations are occasionally held in the field of Machpelah, and an enormous sukka is erected there every year for the festival of Sukkot. On all the festivals, and on *Shabbat Ḥayei Sara* as well, thousands of the descendants of Abraham, Isaac, and Jacob converge on the cave of Machpelah to celebrate together at the very site where their ancestors rest. On those occasions, the field of Machpelah brims with prayer and joyous dancing.

The freedom to visit the cave of Machpelah that we enjoy today should not be taken for granted. Years ago, the area surrounding the cave was a crowded Arab neighborhood known as Ḥārat al-Akrad (the Kurdish Quarter), and contained a "qal[c]a" (a large structure, partially in ruins, understood to be a kind of citadel; it was used for military purposes during the Ottoman Period), a small pool used for water storage (really an ancient cave that had been plastered over and converted to a pool), and homes for members of the Muslim waqf. Attached to the southern corner of the area was the stairway that later became known for its "seventh step," the closest that Jews were allowed to approach the cave.

In Jerusalem, where a similar situation arose following the Six-Day War with regard to the area surrounding the Western Wall, the Israeli government had the fortitude to convert the crowded Moroccan Quarter into what we know today as the Western Wall Plaza. It is doubtful that Israel would have been capable of implementing a similar solution in

6. This was the location of the notorious "seventh step," the closest that Jews were allowed to approach the cave of Machpelah for hundreds of years.

Hebron – but such an operation was never necessary. King Hussein of Jordan, in an attempt to promote the cave of Machpelah as a tourist site, cleared out the area on his own in the early 1960s, evicting its residents and bulldozing their homes.[7] Little did he know that his actions made it much simpler for Israel to access the field of Machpelah following its return to the city in 1967. Some say that Hussein razed the area in the context of infighting with radical Muslim groups, calling to mind the Talmud's assertion that "Ammon and Moab became purified through Sihon" (Gittin 38a) – the occupation of Ammon and Moab by the Amorite king Sihon was what enabled the Israelites to capture their land, as the Torah (Deut. 2:9, 19) forbids direct conflict with Ammon and Moab. Similarly here, one could say that the field of Machpelah was "purified through Hussein."

But the person who deserves the most credit for reinforcing the ability of Jewish people to access the field and cave of Machpelah is Rechavam "Gandhi" Ze'evi, the legendary general and politician who was assassinated by an Arab terrorist in 2001. Ze'evi recounted that once, when he was a small child in the early 1930s, his father took him to visit Hebron. The senior Ze'evi climbed the steps, going as far as the permissible seventh step. Young Rechavam decided to try to continue to the eighth step. Just as his foot reached the forbidden eighth step, an Arab guard jumped out at him and kicked him all the way down to the bottom of the stairway. Rechavam swore never to forget this incident, resolving to someday destroy that stairway and rid the site of its Arab guards. Years later, Ze'evi made good on his vow. Following the Six-Day War, Ze'evi was appointed head of the IDF's Central Command, and one of his first directives was the removal of that degrading stairway.

The daily presence of crowds of Jews at the field and cave of Machpelah is what truly connects us to our roots. On a personal level, I feel a unique happiness when I visit the site and see trees growing in the area surrounding the cave. I like to think that, in a way, these are the very same trees that Abraham might have gazed upon when he

7. The electrical generator that Hussein installed in the area is still in operation to this day.

(H. B. Tristram, *The Lcnd of Israel*, 1865)

The Cave of Machpelah and its surroundings in the ninteenth century

purchased his land from Ephron the Hittite: "And all the trees anywhere within the confines of that field – passed to Abraham as his possession" (Gen. 23:17–18).[8]

8. I would like to thank Hebron residents Noam Arnon, Aryeh Klein, Shalom Elkobi, and Gershon Bar-Kochba, who shared much of their vast knowledge with me.

For further study:

Arnon, N. "The Cave of Machpelah." *Niqrot Zurim* 18 (1992): 27–36 [Hebrew].
Arnon, N. *HaMe'arah*, Jerusalem 2017, 253 [Hebrew].
Avissar O., ed. *Sefer Ḥevron*, Jerusalem, 1970, 466–495 [Hebrew].
Chen, D. "Measuring the Cave of Abraham in Hebron." *Liber Annuus* 37 (1987): 291–294.
Elitzur, Yehuda. *Israel and the Bible*. Ramat Gan, 2000, 37–39 [Hebrew].
Kedar, B. Z and H. Barbé. "Dating of the Subterranean Passage at the Patriarchs' Cave, Hebron." *Israel's Land*. Edited by J. Geiger, H. M. Cotton, and G. Stiebel. Raanana, 2009, 179*–184*.
Klein, A. "*Me'arat Sde haMakhpela*." *Meḥqerey Ḥevron* 1 (2012): 95–123 [Hebrew].
Pritchard, J. B. *Ancient Near Eastern Texts Relating to the Old Testament*. Princeton, 1950, 219–220.
Yeivin, Z. "The Machpelah Cave Subterranean Complex." *Israel: People and Land*. Edited by R. Ze'evi. 2–3 (1985–1986), 53–62 [Hebrew].

Parashat Toledot

Gerar

Gerar and the wadi of Gerar are the central locations of Isaac's narrative, where he consistently reinforces his connection to the Promised Land. It was there that he dug his wells, there that he returned to re-dig his father's wells, which the Philistines had stopped up, and there that he "sowed in that land and reaped a hundredfold" (Gen. 26:12). One of the two times Isaac experienced divine revelation was while he lived in Gerar. What is more, that revelation itself concerned Gerar:

> Stay in the land that I point out to you. Sojourn in this land, and I will be with you and bless you; I will assign all these lands to you and to your heirs, fulfilling the oath that I swore to your father Abraham. (26:2–3)

The phrase "all these lands" hints at the land of Gerar and the area surrounding it.

This is not the first time we learn of Gerar's significance in Genesis. It is mentioned in the Torah's description of the "Canaanite territory" in chapter 10 and is noted as the seat of the king of the Philistines during the time of Abraham and Isaac. During Joshua's conquest and apportionment of the land, Gerar does not appear, nor can the name be found in any other place in Tanakh, aside from one appearance in II Chronicles.[1] Gerar is absent from extra-biblical sources of the biblical period as well (suggestions connecting Gerar with a location found in Egyptian sources are unconvincing). It is only during the talmudic era that Gerar returns to prominence, appearing in both Jewish and non-Jewish sources.

Where Was Gerar?

Before we proceed, we must clarify that the "land of the Philistines" that appears in Genesis bears no geographical connection to the "land of the Philistines" that appears in Judges and Samuel. Yehoshua Meir Grintz, and subsequently his mentor Umberto Cassuto as well, demonstrated convincingly that the Philistines of the Torah are a completely different people from the Philistines of the Early Prophets.[2] The Philistines who served as frequent antagonists in Judges and Samuel were a cruel, warlike nation that continuously terrorized the neighboring Israelites. They lived all along the Mediterranean coast in a pentapolis of five city-states: Gaza, Ashkelon, Ashdod, Ekron, and Gath. Each city-state was governed by its own lord, known as a *seren,* a word whose Greek parallel[3] reflects the foreign elements that influenced Philistine language and culture.

In contrast, the Philistines of Genesis were much less aggressive people, shepherds and farmers whose lifestyle resembled that of Abraham and Isaac. These Philistines had one city – Gerar – and wells along the wadi of Gerar; the conflict between them and our Patriarchs over these disputed wells ended peaceably, with a pact signed between the two parties. Their ruler was called a *melekh* (king), and he bore a

1. In the account of King Asa's defeat of Zerah the Cushite in II Chronicles 14:12. The name Gerar also appears in the Septuagint's translation of the description of the Simeonites' expansion in the time of Hezekiah (in contrast to the Masoretic text, which reads "Gedor" (I Chr. 4:39).
2. It is noteworthy that the Septuagint distinguishes between two types of Philistines. In the Torah they are called *Phylistiim,* while in the Prophets they are called *allophyloi* ("strangers").
3. *Tyrannos,* meaning "tyrant" (in Greek, "s" and "t" are often exchanged). Other examples of foreign words adopted by the Philistines are *argaz* and the name *Akhish.*

distinctly Semitic name: Abimelech. Genesis makes no mention at all of a connection to the Mediterranean coast. In Genesis, the Philistines have Hamitic-Egyptian ancestry (Gen. 10:14), whereas the rest of Tanakh speaks of Caphtor, where the Cherethites resided (modern-day Crete), as the ancestral home of the Philistines.

In light of this, it seems unlikely that Gerar was located in the coastal region, and certainly not in the vicinity of Ashdod or Ashkelon. If so, what information can we find in Tanakh to help us identify the location of Gerar?

Let us begin in Genesis. According to chapter 10, Gerar was apparently not far from Gaza: "The Canaanite territory extended from Sidon as far as Gerar, near Gaza" (Gen. 10:19).[4] On the other hand, we read later: "Abraham journeyed from there to the region of the Negeb and settled between Kadesh and Shur. He sojourned in Gerar" (20:1). This verse seems to point to a location much farther to the south: Kadesh is identified as northwest of Makhtesh Ramon in the Negeb and Shur is what we know today as the northern Sinai Peninsula.[5] This southern location fits well with the identification of biblical Rehoboth with the ruin at Ruheibeh (known in Israel today as Rehovot Ba-Negev), about twenty miles southwest of Beersheba. It also fits in light of the verse describing Asa's war with the Cushites: "All the cities in the vicinity of Gerar were defeated… All the cities were plundered… They also ravaged the encampment of herdsmen, capturing many sheep and camels" (II Chron. 14:13–14).

The two major Christian sources from the Byzantine period on the historical geography of the Land of Israel – Eusebius's *Onomasticon* and the Madaba Map – contain important information for our discussion. The *Onomasticon* (early fourth century CE) states that the entire region surrounding Gerar was known as "Geraritike," and is located twenty-five Roman miles (twenty-three miles) south of Eleutheropolis (Beit Guvrin). In the entry devoted to Beersheba he says that it is "in Geraritike." The Madaba Map (sixth century CE) notes the town of

4. In this context, the verse refers presumably to the *land* of Gerar and the *city* of Gaza.

5. See the discussion in *Parashat Behaalotekha*.

Gerara between Beersheba and Gaza and labels the area surrounding it "Geraritikon Salton."[6]

R. Saadia Gaon, in his Arabic translation of the Torah, renders Gerar as "al-Khalūṣ," modern-day Haluza – some fifteen miles southwest of Beersheba and about thirty miles southeast of Gaza!

The scholarly literature has yielded a variety of opinions on the matter of Gerar's location. Grintz argued forcefully for a southern location based on the information outlined above, rendering the phrase *bo'akha Gerara ad Azza* not "as far as Gerar, near Gaza," but "near Gaza, on the route that eventually leads to Gerar." According to Grintz, the only reason that Gerar is mentioned in this context is that it features prominently in the later stories of the Patriarchs. In contrast to Grintz, most scholars maintain that Gerar is a general term for the western Negeb region, between Beersheba and Gaza. The information provided by both Eusebius and the Madaba Map spells out this interpretation almost explicitly.

Proponents of this approach must then explain the above verse: "[Abraham] settled between Kadesh and Shur. He sojourned in Gerar" (Gen. 20:1), in a new light. They note the use of two distinct verbs: *vayeshev* (he settled) and *vayagor* (he sojourned). In contrast to Modern Hebrew, the word *lagur* in its various forms always refers to a temporary dwelling, while *lashevet* always refers to a permanent dwelling. With this in mind, it seems the Torah is conveying that Abraham settled down for several years in the southern region between Kadesh and Shur (home to Beer-lahai-roi, where Isaac lived and Sarah's tent stood), and for a separate, shorter period he sojourned in Gerar – a completely different location.[7]

This region between Beersheba and the Gaza Strip contains four large archaeological tells: Tell esh-Shari'a (Tell Shera' on Hebrew maps), Tell Abu Hureyra (Tell Haror), Tell el-Far'ah (Tell Sharuhen, based on Albright's identification) and Tell Jemmeh (Tell Gama or Tell Re'im). The last tell in this list may be familiar to some from the period before the

6. "Salton" here indicates that the region is Caesarean territory.

7. The phrase *Vayagor biGerar* is also a play on the similarity of the two words, but this does not detract from the normal linguistic meaning of the word.

so-called "disengagement" from Gush Katif, as it is situated just before the Kissufim crossing. Each of these archaeological sites has been suggested by scholars as a candidate for the identification of Gerar.

The identification with Tell el-Far'ah, suggested by several early scholars, was rejected after the academic world became convinced of its identification with the ancient town of Sharuhen. Many scholars do still support the identification of Gerar with Tell esh-Shari'a or with Tell Abu Hureyra on the banks of Wadi esh-Shari'a, as it fits well with the distance measurements found in the *Onomasticon*. Based on these identifications, Israel's naming department called Wadi esh-Shari'a "Naḥal Gerar."

From an archaeological standpoint, Tell Haror (suggested by Yoḥanan Aharoni) seems to be the most likely candidate of the four. It is a large tell, most of whose settlement activity occurred during the Middle Bronze Age, which corresponds to the Patriarchal Age. Few remains of settlement have been found from the late Canaanite period and the first Israelite period, but more significant remains were found from the latter half of the Israelite period, which may be reflected in Gerar's appearance in Chronicles.

Despite this, my late father, Professor Yehuda Elitzur, concurred with the assessment of W. J. Phythian-Adams and Sir Flinders Petrie, who identified Gerar with Tell Gama on the southern bank of Naḥal Ha-Besor (Wadi Gaza), about ten miles west of Tell Haror and about three miles east of Kissufim. This identification is supported by the persistence of the name Gerar throughout history: A large Byzantine-era ruin called Khirbet Umm-Jarrar (Ḥorvat Gerarit in Hebrew) is located two miles north of the tell.[8] Its distance from Beit Guvrin is greater than the twenty-five Roman miles described in the *Onomasticon*, but it may be that Eusebius was referring to the region he called Geraritike and not to one precise location.

8. It is noteworthy that some seven kilometers west of Tell Gama, north-east of Khan Yunes, south of the now-ruined Kfar Darom, there is a district called al-Qarāra (in the local pronunciation, al-Garāra). In Arabic it may mean "the plain," "permanent inhabitants," "circular reservoir for rainwater," or "preserved garden." On an Israeli map I found the name spelled Jarāra, probably a mistake. Perhaps one might connect it to Gerar or the district of Gerar. I thank Mota Grinblatt, formerly a resident of Neve Dekalim, who informed me of this name. I confirmed it on Musil's map and in Arab sources.

In my father's opinion, eastern and southern identifications of Gerar do not fit the Torah's formulations well enough to pass muster. For example, *Parashat Toledot* relates that when famine struck the land of Canaan, Gerar – with its many wells – was flourishing agriculturally. In light of this, Gerar must have been closer to the coast, not in the central Negeb, and certainly not in areas further to the south. The phrase "as far as Gerar, near Gaza" indicates that Gerar must have been located somewhere in the western Negeb and not in its central region. According to this identification, "the wadi of Gerar" mentioned in our *parasha* is not Wadi esh-Shari'a – Naḥal Gerar on Israeli maps – but the wadi we know today as Naḥal Ha-Besor.

"A Bad Climate" and the Holiness of the Land

Ḥazal's description of Gerar (Y. Shevi'it 6:1 and Genesis Rabba, 52, 64) is of utmost importance for our analysis here. The Midrash provides an explicit identification for Gerar: "'He sojourned in Gerar' – in Gerarike"; "'And Isaac went to Abimelech, the king of the Philistines, in Gerar' (Gen. 26:1) – to Gerarike."[9] The Midrash then goes on to discuss Gerarike:

> Why did they obligate (*gazeru*) the region of Gerarike [in commandments that only apply in the Land of Israel]? Because it has a bad climate. And until where did they obligate them?[10] R. Ḥanin said in the name of R. Shemuel b. R. Yitzḥak: Until the wadi of Egypt.

The Yerushalmi has a slightly different text:

> Why *didn't* they obligate (*lo gazeru*) the region of [Gerarike]? R. Simon said in the name of R. Yehoshua b Levi: Because its climate is bad. Until where? R. Ḥanin said in the name of R. Shemuel b. Yitzḥak: Until the wadi of Egypt.

9. This is according to the text found in MS Vatican 60, p. 283. Other versions read "Gerdike."

10. *Ḥiyyevu*. So in the reliable manuscripts; the word is missing from the printed editions.

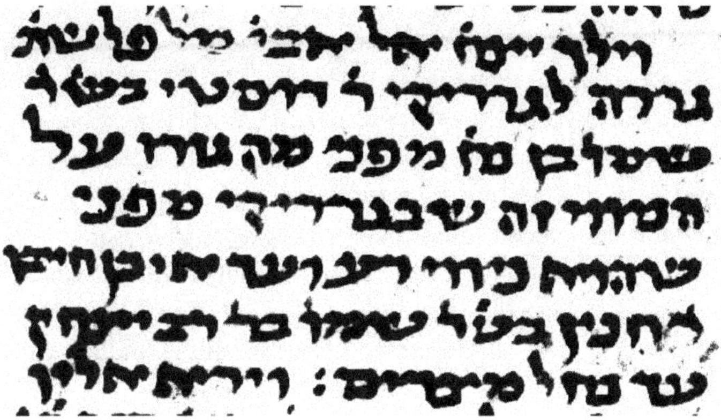

(Image courtesy of the Vatican Library)

Genesis Rabba 64, as it appears in MS Vatican 60: "to Gerarike"; "and until where did they obligate them."

My father *z"l*, Professor Yehuda Elitzur, explained the seemingly contradictory passages as follows: Despite the fact that Gerarike lay well to the south of Ashkelon, which is generally considered the southern border of the territory of the "returnees from the Babylonian exile," it was nevertheless considered part of the Land of Israel. This includes its obligation (*gazeru*) in *terumot*, tithes and *shemitta*, and, on the other hand, the fact that the region was not considered "impure" (*lo gazeru*) like most areas outside the Land of Israel. Even though more non-Jews than Jews lived there at that time (similar to Beit She'an and Ashkelon), and this factor was generally enough to exclude even a place within the borders of the Land from land-based commandments and holiness, Gerar was still considered part of the Land for those purposes.

The reason for Gerar's anomalous inclusion, according to the Midrash and the Yerushalmi, is that its region has "a bad climate" and is thus unsuitable for farming due to its relative aridity and abundance of sand dunes. These conditions made it very difficult for the region's residents to make a living, so it was only sparsely settled, with no large population of non-Jews to preclude the presence of the holiness of the Land.[11] In

11. *Ḥazal* considered the semi-desert of Geraritike similar to the Mediterranean Sea, in that the consideration of population is irrelevant and therefore it did not interfere

contrast, concludes the Yerushalmi, Gaza itself possesses "a good climate," and thus it is exempt from tithes and *shemitta*.

In conclusion, even if we cannot be absolutely certain of the precise identification of Gerar, we can still be fairly sure of its general whereabouts. The relatively arid swaths of land in the western Negeb, the region that contains the tributaries of Naḥal Ha-Besor, including Gush Katif and the Yamit region, as far as Wadi el-Arish, is what God was referring to when He promised "all these lands" to Isaac in our *parasha*. These lands are included in the "Gerarike" of the Midrash and the Yerushalmi and the "Geraritike" of the *Onomasticon*.

Gush Katif and Yamit were located in a sandy, arid region, which, until the establishment of Jewish settlements there, was almost completely desolate. It seems that our sages had precisely this desolation in mind when they considered the region surrounding Gerar "a bad climate" – and, as a result, obligated its residents in land-based commandments. The fact that we, the children of Abraham, Isaac, and Jacob, were able to transform this same Gerar into a thriving paradise is a testament to the ever-present hand of God guiding our undertakings, fulfilling the promise made to Isaac – the man of the field – in this very location.

The crime of the destruction of Gush Katif and the expulsion of its inhabitants, like the wells of Abraham that were stopped up by the Philistines and filled with earth, can only be atoned for when the children of Isaac can once again return to their rightful place. Then can we merit the blessing of our Patriarchs: "The Lord has granted us ample space to increase in the land" (Gen. 26:22).

For further study:

Cassuto, U. *A Commentary on the Book of Genesis*. Translated by I. Abrahams. 2, Jerusalem, 1964, 206–208.

Dabbāgh, M. *Bilādunā Filasṭīn* II/1. Kafr Qara' 1991, 428 [Arabic].

with the original borders of the Torah. According to Gittin 8a and Yerushalmi Shevi'it 6:1, the inland border of the Land of Israel ends in the north at Acre or Achzib, while the seaward border stretches from *Turey Amanon/Amanas*, the Nur Mountains in modern-day Turkey, which *Ḥazal* identify with the northern Hor Hahar of Numbers (34:7–8) to "the wadi of Egypt" (34:5) – Wadi el-Arish.

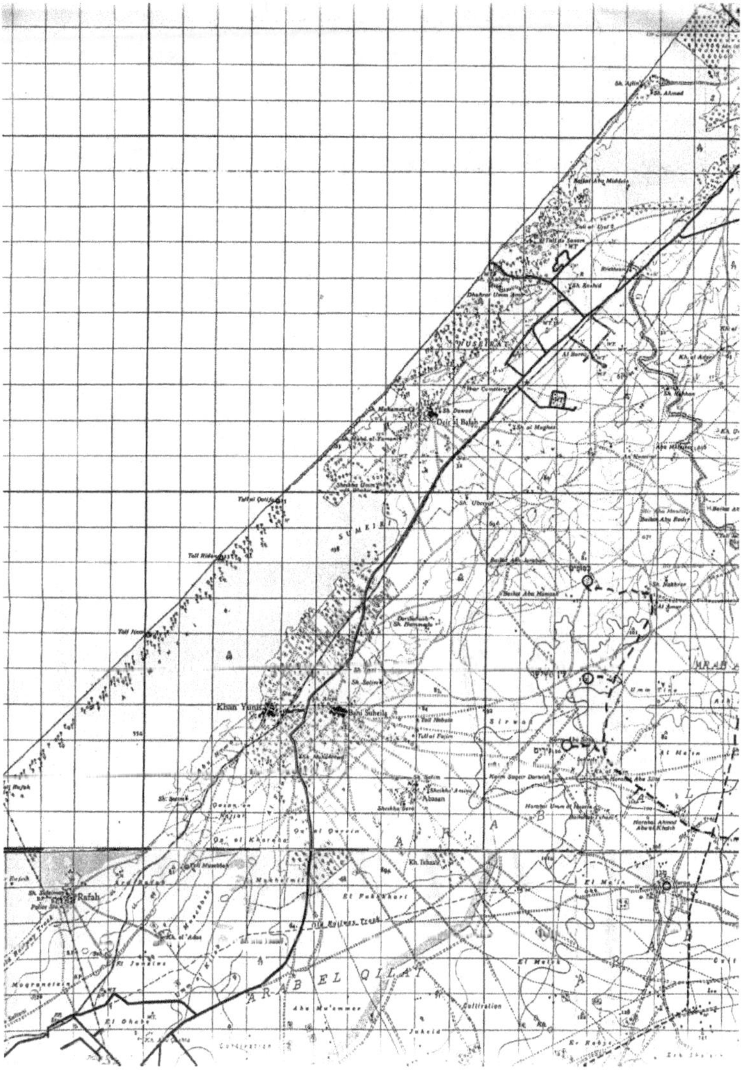

(Image courtesy of the Survey of Israel)

British map of the Gaza Strip with Israeli emendations (1955). Note the sandy empty space in the southwest: "a bad climate."

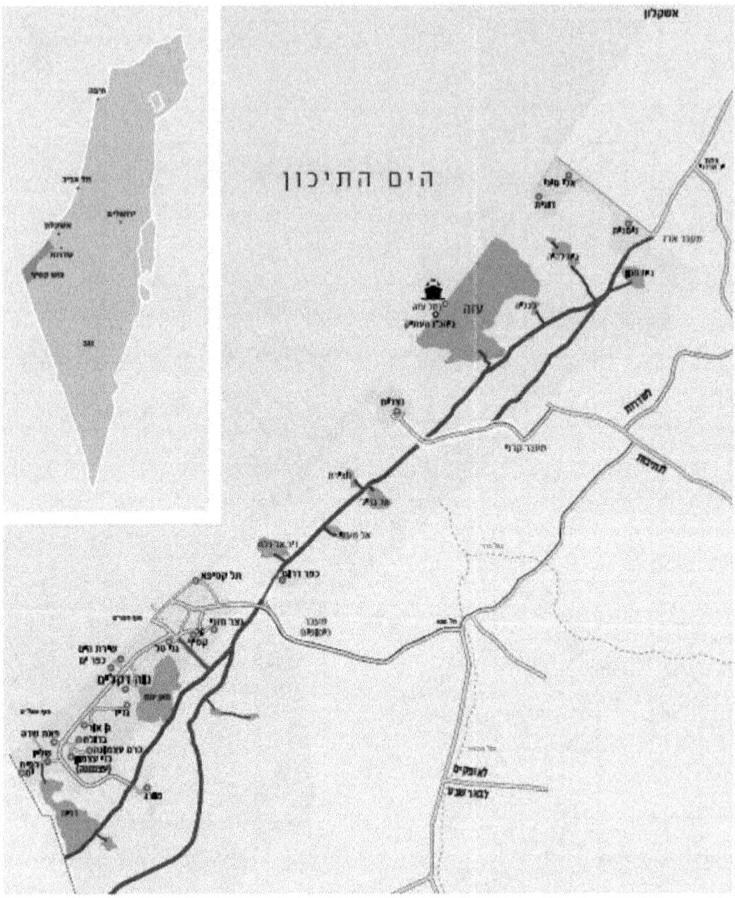

(Image courtesy of the Gush Katif and Northern Samaria Commemoration Center)

Map of Gush Katif. The Jewish settlements in the Gush fill the desolate sandy area of the British map above.

Elitzur, Yehuda. *"Eretz Gerar." Israel and the Bible.* Ramat-Gan, 2000, 352–356 [Hebrew].

Grintz, J. M. *"HaPelishtim Harishonim."* In *Studies in Early Biblical Ethnology and History*, 99–129. Tel-Aviv, 1969, [Hebrew].

Oren, E. D. "Gerar." In *The Anchor Bible Dictionary*, 2, 989–990.

Oren, E. D. "Haror, Tel." In *The New Encyclopedia of Archaeological Excavations in the Holy Land*, 580–584.

Van Beek, G. W. "Jemmeh, Tell." In *The New Encyclopedia of Archaeological Excavations in the Holy Land*, 667–674.

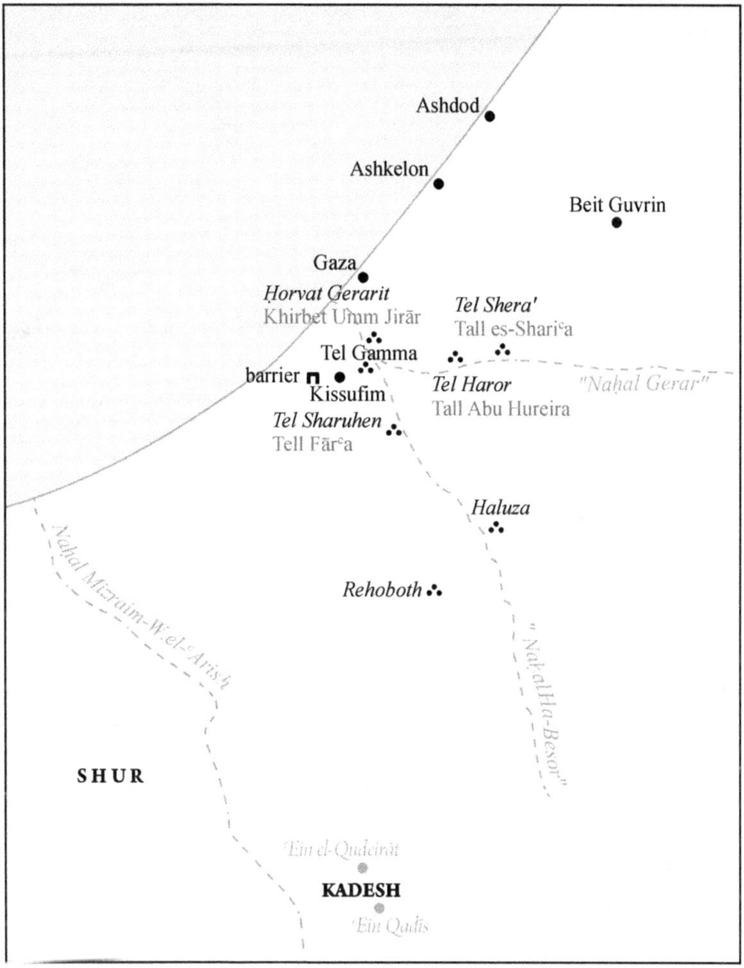
Ashdod
Ashkelon
Beit Guvrin
Gaza
Ḥorvat Gerarit
Khirbet Umm Jirār
Tel Shera'
Tall es-Shariʿa
Tel Gamma
barrier
Kissufim
Tel Haror
Tall Abu Hureira
"Naḥal Gerar"
Tel Sharuhen
Tell Fārʿa
Haluza
Naḥal Mizraim-W.el-ʿArish
Rehoboth
"NaḥalHa-Besor"
SHUR
ʿEin el-Qudeirāt
KADESH
ʿEin Qadīs

Parashat Vayetzeh

Assigning Names

Parashat Vayetzeh opens with a naming – "Jacob named that site Bethel" (Gen. 28:19) – and closes with a naming – "So he named that place Mahanaim" (32:3). Indeed, a host of new names is given throughout the *parasha*, including people (all of Jacob's sons) and places (Gal'ed and Mizpah). Each new name is generally accompanied by an explanation that clarifies why the name was given, usually a reflection on an incident that occurred or on the emotional state of the person giving the name.

The phenomenon of naming people and places and concurrently including an explanation for the name can be found throughout the Torah and the books of Joshua, Judges, and Samuel; it is a central fixture of the biblical narrative.

The Problems

Those familiar with this biblical naming procedure will note several problems that arise.

- Multiple namings: In our *parasha*, Jacob names Bethel on his way to Haran, but to our surprise, names it Bethel again upon his return from Haran in *Parashat Vayishlaḥ*: "There he ... named the site El-bethel, for it was there that God had revealed Himself to him when he was fleeing from his brother" (Gen. 35:7). Several verses later, he names the same place yet again: "Jacob gave the site, where God had spoken to him, the name of Bethel" (35:15). Why did Jacob name the same location three times?

The Vilna Gaon (Rabbi Elijah of Vilna), in his commentary on Joshua 16, proposes a brilliant solution. According to him, Jacob actually visited three different places and gave each place a distinct name. The first place (Gen. 28:19) was named "Bethel," the second place (35:7) was named "El-bethel" and the third place (35:15) was named "Elohim-bethel."[1] What makes this interpretation especially significant is that it comes as an explanation for a problematic verse in Joshua: "From Bethel it ran to Luz" (Josh. 16:2), implying that these are two different locations, and not two names for the same location, as the plain meaning in Genesis 28 indicates. Additionally, the Vilna Gaon bolsters his argument for the name "Elohim-bethel" with a novel interpretation of a phrase in Samuel: *Shelosha anashim olim el HaElohim Beit-El*" (I Sam. 10:3). While the common translation is "three men making a pilgrimage to God at Bethel," the Vilna Gaon translates it as "three men making a pilgrimage at Ha-Elohim-Bethel."

While the Vilna Gaon's interpretation is certainly clever, the actual language of the text makes it difficult to accept. Why would Jacob have given three adjacent locations names that are almost identical to one another? Also, if the location mentioned in Joshua was not actually Bethel but "El-bethel" or "Elohim-bethel," then why would the text have used the inaccurate, misleading name Bethel? Furthermore, the Masoretic cantillation marks in both Genesis and Samuel suggest a pause between

1. The idea of more than one Bethel in the Torah is found in the works of previous commentators (see Rashi on Josh. 18:13, Rashbam and Ibn-Ezra on Gen. 26:23, Radak on Josh. 16:2, and *Kaftor Vaferaḥ* 296–297, who removes one of the Bethels toward the Jordan valley).

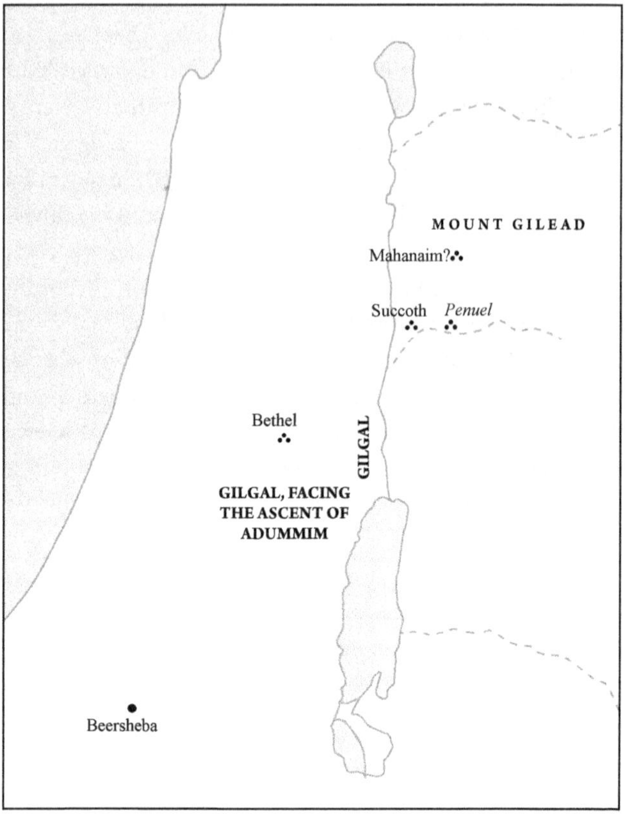

"Elohim" and "bethel," indicating that "Elohim-bethel" is not a discrete phrase, let alone the name of a unique location, and the Targumim on Genesis and Samuel indicate the same. Most importantly, the Torah explicitly states in *Parashat Vayishlaḥ* that Jacob was commanded to return to the location where "God had revealed Himself to him when he was fleeing from his brother" (Gen. 35:7), meaning that Bethel and El-bethel are clearly one and the same. In light of all these difficulties, it seems that the Vilna Gaon's innovative approach only accentuates the problem.

- Different explanations for the same name: This phenomenon can be seen in the naming of Beersheba. First, the problem of multiple namings occurs in the case of Beersheba as well: Abraham gives it this name in *Parashat Vayera* (Gen. 21:31) and Isaac does the same in *Parashat Toledot* – "Isaac's servants came and told him about the well they had dug... He named it Shibah; therefore the name of the city is Beersheba to this day" (26:32–33).

But the case of Beersheba poses a new difficulty. The Torah relates:

> Abraham then set seven (*sheva*) ewes of the flock by themselves, and Abimelech said to Abraham, "What mean these seven ewes which you have set apart?" He replied, "You are to accept these seven ewes from me as proof that I dug this well." Hence that place was called Beersheba. (Gen. 21:28–31)

Noting in particular the repetition of the number seven in the Torah's account, it may seem clear that Beersheba was named for the seven ewes that Abraham gave to Abimelech as part of their pact. However, the sequence concludes, "For there the two of them swore an oath (*nishbe'u*)" (21:31), meaning that the place was named for the oath, not the ewes.

Thus, we have two different explanations for Beersheba's name in one passage – one at the beginning and one at the end. There is a syntactic subtlety here as well. One can begin reading from verse 28 – "Abraham then set...'What mean these seven ewes?'...'You are to accept these seven ewes from me'... Hence that place was called Beersheba" – and stop at that point, satisfied with the Torah's explanation. Alternatively, one can begin reading from verse 31 – "Hence that place was called Beersheba, for there the two of them swore an oath" – and be equally satisfied with that explanation. Each reading can be taken as a distinct textual unit, and each tells a different story about the etymological history of Beersheba.[2]

2. An innovative but unsatisfactory and also unconvincing solution was offered by Sforno (Gen. 26:33), who distinguished between Be'er Sheva with a *segol* and Be'er

Our *parasha* contains a similar contradiction, not relating to the name of a place but to the name of a person: "She conceived and bore a son, and said, 'God has taken away (*asaf*) my disgrace.' So she named him Joseph, which is to say, 'May the Lord add another (*yosef*) son for me'" (Gen. 30:23–24). What is the explanation for the name Joseph? Again, one can read the first section of the passage as a distinct unit – "[She] said, 'God has taken away my disgrace.' So she named him Joseph" – and one can read the second section of the passage as a distinct unit as well – "So she named him Joseph, which is to say, 'May the Lord add another son for me.'" According to the first version, "Joseph" is a kind of shortened version of "Yehoasaf," whereas according to the second version, "Joseph" is a verb conjugated in the future tense from the root Y-S-P.

- The name exists already in a different place: Often, a name is explained in one place in Tanakh, but the same name exists already, referring to an entirely different location. One example of this is Gilgal:

> After the circumcising of the whole nation was completed, they remained where they were, in the camp, until they recovered. And the Lord said to Joshua, "Today I have rolled away (*galloti*) from you the disgrace of Egypt." So that place was called Gilgal, as it still is. (Josh. 5:8-9)

But if we read through the Book of Joshua thoroughly, we will find two other Gilgals, one in the list of the kings of Canaan – "the king of Goiim in Gilgal" (12:23) – and the other on the northern border of the tribe of Judah – "Gilgal, facing the Ascent of Adummim which is south of the wadi" (15:7). Sources outside the Book of Joshua, not to mention sources outside Tanakh entirely, feature still other Gilgals, but only the Gilgal of Joshua 5 comes with an explanation.

Shava with a *kamatz*, claiming that the former referred both to the oath and the number seven, whereas the latter referred only to the oath.

We find this same phenomenon in the cases of some people's names in Tanakh as well. For example, the explanation given in our *parasha* for the name Reuben is: "The Lord has seen (*ra'a*) my affliction (*be'onyi*), that now my husband will love me (*ye'ehavani*)" (Gen. 29:32). However, the Book of Joshua lists a place on the border of the territories of Judah and Benjamin known as "the Stone of Bohan, son of Reuben" (Josh. 15:6; 18:17), seemingly referring to a Canaanite who preceded the Israelites' arrival in the Land.[3] Clearly, there is no reason to connect this Canaanite Reuben to the Israelite tribe of Reuben, whose territory lay entirely in Transjordan.

- The name preceded its explanation: Continuing with the example of Gilgal, the Book of Joshua mentions Gilgal well before the name is explained in chapter 5: "The people came up from the Jordan… and encamped at Gilgal on the eastern border of Jericho" (Josh. 4:19). At that point, the people erected a monument out of twelve stones, the nation was circumcised and they named the place Gilgal. The same is true of Bethel: Abraham moved his tent "between Bethel and Ai" years before his grandson Jacob named the site Bethel – and other examples of this abound. The suggestion that each of these places was named for events that would only occur much later in history is difficult to accept, as the text usually indicates explicitly when it uses the future as a point of reference.[4]
- The explanation does not fit well linguistically: Many explanations for names that we find in Tanakh seem to ascribe homiletical meaning to names that are easily explained in a much more simplistic manner. These interpretations often eschew the basic and simple meaning of the name in favor of a deeper, more sophisticated approach. In these explanations, the linguistic connection to the name is often tenuous and awkward, sometimes using

3. Similarly, we read of "Ben-hinnom" (Josh. 18:16), probably a Jebusite through whose valley the continuation of that same Judah-Benjamin border passes.
4. See, for example: "the Valley of Siddim, now the Dead Sea" (Gen. 14:3) and, "For the prophet of today was formerly called a seer" (I Sam. 9:9).

artificial phrases and *hapax legomena.*[5] For example, according to the Book of Joshua, Gilgal was named for the national circumcision that took place there. However, a person visiting the site two hundred years later would certainly not be able to guess that explanation from simply hearing the name "Gilgal."

Similarly, we read: "'This is God's camp (*maḥaneh Elohim*).' So he named that place Mahanaim" (Gen. 32:3). The use of the term *maḥaneh* seems out of place for a description of angels, which is what Jacob is referring to here. *Maḥaneh* usually denotes a cluster of tents in which a nomadic people or an army in the field dwells.

We also find: "And [Jacob] built a house for himself and made stalls (*sukkot*) for his cattle; that is why the place was called Succoth" (Gen. 33:17). Why would Jacob name the place for the stalls that he built for his cattle and not for what he built for himself and for his family? In addition, the word *sukkot* in Biblical Hebrew usually refers to temporary living structures for people, whereas stalls for animals are generally called *gidrot tzon.*[6] On the other hand, it would be very reasonable for a place that began as a group of temporary houses to take on the name "Succoth," as we find in the case of the other Succoth, on the Egyptian border: "The Israelites journeyed from Raamses to Succoth" (Ex. 12:37).[7]

This phenomenon is especially striking in the names of Jacob's sons. There is no simpler name to understand than Reuben: "*Re'u, ben!*" – "Look, a son!" Jacob's wife Leah has just given birth to a firstborn son. She is overjoyed, and the choice of the name Reuben is simply her way of inviting the world to come look at her beautiful baby boy. But according to the Torah, Leah was saying something completely different. She says, "The Lord has seen (*ra'a*) my affliction (*be'onyi*), that now my husband

5. Words that do not appear elsewhere in Tanakh.
6. See, for example, Numbers 32:16.
7. A modern equivalent of Succoth is the city of el-Arish in North Sinai, *ᶜarīsh* or *ᶜarīshe* meaning "hut" or "arbor" in Arabic.

will love me (*ye'ehavani*)" (Gen. 29:32). The first portion of the name Reuben is taken from *ra'a,* while the letters *beit* and *nun* of the latter section of the name are taken from the words "*be-onyi*" and "*ye'ehavani.*" There is no natural linguistic connection between these words and the common word *ben* – the final element of the name Reuben.

The same can be seen in the case of Naphtali: "'A fateful contest I waged [literally: twisted ropes (*naftulim*) I was entangled (*niftalti*)] with my sister; yes, and I have prevailed.' So she named him Naphtali" (Gen. 30:8). Nowhere else in Tanakh, or in any ancient Hebrew source, does the term *naftulim* appear. Its meaning may be understood based on verbs and nouns that share the same linguistic root, but the word *naftulim* itself is unique in the Hebrew of Tanakh and is not known in either the Hebrew of Qumran or *Ḥazal* or in any other Semitic language.

Regarding Zebulun, we read: "'God has given me (*zevadani*) a choice gift (*zeved*); this time my husband will exalt me, (or will dwell with me) (*yizbeleni*), for I have borne him six sons.' So she named him Zebulun" (Gen. 30:20). Based on several similar words and names, we might be able to infer the meaning of the words *zevadani* and *yizbeleni.* However, the root Z-B-D only appears a handful of times, all in biblical names, and the root Z-B-L only appears in one noun and one other person's name, but never in verb form.

In all of these cases, it seems clear that the name is what led to the explanation, and not that the explanation led to the name![8]

Rabbi Obadiah Seforno's Approach

Parashat Vayetzeh provides an uplifting, spiritual explanation for Leah's choice of the name "Judah" for her fourth son: "This time I will praise (*odeh*) the Lord" (Gen. 29:35). Rabbi Obadiah Seforno comments on

8. With the exception of cases in which the place in question was located in an unoccupied area so that it had no name. In such cases the given name was clear and natural, such as Taberah ("Burning") (Num. 11:3), Kibroth Hattaavah ("Graves of Craving") (Num. 11:34), Perez Uzzah ("Outbreak Against Uzzah") (II Sam. 6:8).

this verse, "This name contains both the letters of God's distinguished name and the language of praise." However, he also points out that the name of Judah's aunt by marriage to Esau – "Judith daughter of Beeri the Hittite" (26:34) – shared these characteristics. Was it Beeri the Hittite's intention to praise God when he named his daughter as well? Similarly, Seforno notes that the famed prophet Samuel was preceded by several centuries by Samuel son of Ammihud (Num. 34:20), the tribal chieftain of the Simeonites. In contrast to the better-known Samuel, in all likelihood, Samuel son of Ammihud's conception and birth did not share the drama described in the first chapter of I Samuel:

> [Elkanah] had two wives... Peninnah had children, but Hannah was childless... [Peninnah] would taunt [Hannah] that the Lord had closed her womb... In her wretchedness, [Hannah] prayed to the Lord, weeping all the while. And she made this vow... and the Lord remembered her. Hannah conceived, and at the turn of the year bore a son. She named him Samuel, meaning, "I asked the Lord for him (*me'Hashem she'iltiv*)."

Samuel son of Ammihud was most likely born under normal circumstances, without any taunting, weeping, or vows. He was named Samuel – a beautiful name whose simple meaning is "the name of God," as we read: "The name of the Lord is a tower of strength, to which the righteous man runs and is safe" (Prov. 18:10).

Seforno addresses this problem and comes to the conclusion that "all of these were names that were common among the ancients... and they would choose from these ancient names a name that would play upon the events of the present." If this is true, the whole naming phenomenon that we are analyzing here is not a process of *creating* new names, but of *homilizing* on existing names.

The same is true regarding names of places. People would travel to a place that already had a name from ancient times, and place their stamp upon the place by giving its name a novel interpretation that reflected their ideas and values. In our *parasha* this idea can be found explicitly: "And Mizpah, as he said, 'May the Lord watch (*yitzef*) between me and you'" (Gen. 31:49). The verse does not say, "And he called the place Mizpah," but "And [concerning the name] Mizpah, he said…"; he pointed to Mizpah and expounded upon its name.

Rabbi Matityahu Strashun's Incredible Discovery

Those who have spent time studying the Talmud extensively are undoubtedly familiar with Rabbi Samuel Strashun of Vilna, better known as the Rashash, whose illuminating commentary on almost every page of the Talmud is hard to overlook. But Rabbi Samuel's son, Rabbi Matityahu, was also an eminent Torah scholar, as well as a prominent expert in many languages and fields of research. Rabbi Matityahu was famous for his personal library that contained a vast collection of Jewish books. A part of this library survived the Holocaust and eventually found its way to the Heichal Shlomo library in Jerusalem.

In the Rashash's commentary on Genesis Rabba 71, he quotes his son, Rabbi Matityahu, who had managed to solve a puzzling textual difficulty. The text of the Midrash, according to the common printed version, reads: "R. Jose b. R. Ḥanina said: 'The names of the tribes are not foul (*akhur*) for them, but rather hemmed (*ḥafut*)[9] for them.'" The meaning of this line is difficult to understand, and the commentaries struggled with it.[10] Based on the Amsterdam print, Rabbi Matityahu proposed emending the word *akhur* to *avud*, meaning "made" (following the Aramaic *avad*), rendering the line as "The names of the tribes are not made for them, but rather hemmed for them."[11] What does this mean?

Rabbi Matityahu explained as follows: When a person goes to buy a suit, he has two options: He can go to a tailor, who will take careful measurements and prepare a new suit that will fit him precisely. On the other hand, if he does not have the time or money for a custom-made suit, he can go to a large clothing store and buy a suit there. Since it is unlikely that he will be able to find a suit that will immediately fit his

9. Compare to *ubechefet chaluko*" (Mishna Shabbat 10:3).

10. See for instance the curious translation of Jacob Neusner (Genesis Rabbah: The Judaic Commentary to the Book of Genesis: A New American Translation, 2, Atlanta, 1985, p. 46): "The names of the tribes are not meant to stir up the recollection of their shortcomings but to cover them up."

11. This version is corroborated by MS Vatican 60, one of the most reliable Genesis Rabba texts that we possess, which was not available to the Rashash or to his son.

exact dimensions, a store employee will have to alter the closest-fitting suit to his precise measurements, perhaps taking in the waist or letting out the cuffs.

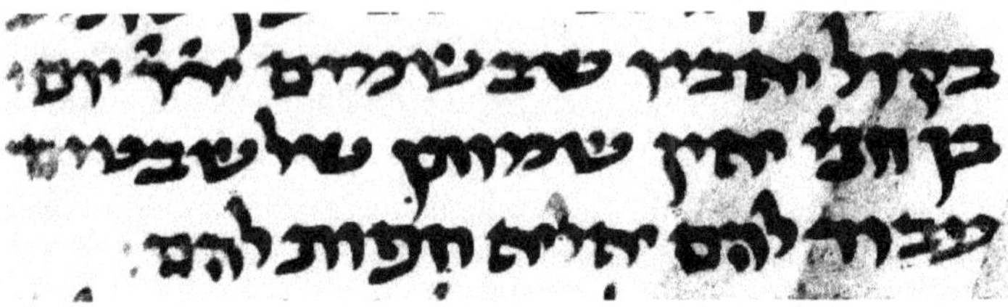

MS Vatican 60: "The names of the tribes are not made for them, but rather hemmed for them."

The names of the tribes can be thus compared to a store-bought suit. Our Matriarchs took names that already existed and "altered" those names to the current situation or to their current emotions by giving them novel explanations. Clearly, this notion was not innovated by Seforno, but was accepted long before his time, as early as the time of the Midrash.

To take this idea one step further, we may explain that the concept of injecting new meaning into existing names is intrinsically connected to the way in which the Jewish people relates to the world around it. Devotees of other religions and cultures often preach separation from the world and its vices. Some dream of destroying the old world and building a new, better world in its place. Not so the faith of the Torah and the Jewish people, which has always worked under the assumption that the world that the God of Israel created is meant to exist. It is our responsibility as the Chosen People to perfect the world, sanctifying it with holiness, faith, and mitzvot. This is why the first commandment in the Torah is to "be fertile and increase" (Gen. 1:28). We sow in the world and we harvest in the world, and through the grains that we reap we fulfill the commandments that sanctify them – "You shall appoint magistrates and officials for your tribes" (Deut 16:18), "You shall be free to set a king over yourself" (17:15), and "Army commanders shall assume command of the troops" (20:9). The concept of assigning names ties into this idea. We do not create our own separate framework, full of new names. We take the naming system that already exists, which arose naturally in the course of the world's cultural and linguistic development, and inject within it new meaning.

For further study:

Elitzur, Y. "*Anashim Venaḥalot BiMenasheh Uveshivtei Yisrael.*" *Al Atar* 4–5 (1999): 243–249 [Hebrew].

Garsiel, M. *Biblical Names: A Literary Study of Midrashic Derivations and Puns.* Translated by P. Hackett. Ramat Gan, 1991.

Parashat Vayishlaḥ

The Parcel of Land in Shechem

"The Parcel of Land" in Genesis and Joshua

The second place in the Land of Israel, following the cave of Machpelah, to have been purchased by one of our Patriarchs, and the first place where Jacob built an altar and invoked the name of God, is the "parcel of land" in Shechem:

> Jacob arrived safe in the city of Shechem which is in the land of Canaan – having come thus from Paddan-aram – and he encamped before the city. The parcel of land where he pitched his tent he purchased from the children of Hamor, Shechem's father, for a hundred kesitas. He set up an altar there, and called it El-elohe-yisrael. (Gen. 33:18–20)

Centuries later, in the time of Joshua, the parcel of land is revisited:

> The bones of Joseph, which the Israelites had brought up from Egypt, were buried at Shechem, in the parcel of land which Jacob had bought for a hundred kesitas from the children of Hamor, Shechem's father, and which had become a heritage of the Josephites. (Josh. 24:32)

This verse is part of the Book of Joshua's epilogue. Most of the book tells the story of the conquest and apportionment of the land, but the final verses list the burial sites of three luminaries: Joshua, the nation's leader; Eleazar, the high priest; and Joseph, whose burial symbolizes the connection between the Patriarchs and their descendants, who are now settling the Promised Land. Note how the text describes Joseph's burial site: it is known primarily as the "parcel of land" that Jacob purchased, to which the people of Israel later added Joseph's remains.

Joseph's Tomb in the Last Decades

It is impossible to speak today about Joseph's burial site without getting into a bit of politics. Joseph's Tomb in Shechem is the historical site that is perhaps the most apt microcosm of the sociopolitical events of the past three decades in Israel. First, the site was attacked on two separate occasions by a violent Arab mob, in September 1996 and in September 2000. In each instance, the Israeli government refused to act like a sovereign nation that protects its property and its people, turning instead to the Palestinian Authority to free our trapped soldiers. In each instance, the result of that decision was a loss of lives and severe property damage; all in all, these were degrading incidents and desecrations of God's name.

In the first attack, six Israeli soldiers were killed, seven others were injured, and several military vehicles were burned. In the second attack, Madḥat Yusef, a member of the Israel Border Police from the Druze village of Beit Jann, was killed. He died from loss of blood as a result of his wounds on the second day of Rosh HaShana, after four hours during which the Arab mob prevented his rescue. On the night of *Shabbat Shuva*, the IDF abandoned Joseph's Tomb, while the Arabs, despite their assurances to the contrary, shot at the vehicles making their retreat. The Arab mob then stormed the site, burning it and destroying it. Hillel Lieberman of Elon Moreh, who had rushed to the Tomb wrapped in a *tallit*, was murdered. When his bullet-ridden body was finally found and taken for burial in the neighboring settlement of Yitzhar, the funeral was interrupted by gunfire from rioting Arabs.

Ever since then, Joseph's Tomb has not been in Israeli hands. However, many still return to the site intermittently, usually in coordinated night visits under army guard, but sometimes in unauthorized visits as well. On April 24, 2011, Palestinian Authority police officers shot at and murdered twenty-four-year-old Ben-Yosef Livnat, who came to pray at Joseph's Tomb.

Through the 1980s and 1990s, some in Israel voiced doubts as to the authenticity of Joseph's Tomb. Shulamit Aloni, then Israel's minister of education, asserted in several media interviews that, based on the research of archaeologist Meir Ben-Dov, the site is merely a late Arab grave of a certain Sheikh Yusuf, who lived only two hundred years ago. In an issue of *Haaretz* from 1986, in connection with its coverage of the events at Joseph's Tomb, a short background piece was published – with no attribution – with the headline: "Archaeologists: Joseph's Tomb in Shechem Belongs to Muslim Sheikh." The article contained an authoritative declaration:

רקע

ארכיאולוגים: קבר יוסף בשכם של שייח' מוסלמי

האתר המכונה "קבר יוסף" ליד שכם הוא מבנה, שהוקם כנראה בתקופה הממלוכית (בין המאה ה־14 למאה ה־16) כקבר של שיח' מוסלמי. נוסעים יהודים, שעברו באזור שכם בימי הביניים, והכירו את המסורת הגורסת שעצמותיו של יוסף נטמנו באזור שכם, ייחסו לאתר את מקום קבורתו של יוסף.

על פי המקרא, חי יוסף ומת במצרים. בעת שבני ישראל יצאו ממצרים, הם נטלו עמם את עצמותיו. לפי המסורת היו אלה בני שבט אפרים, שבירתם היתה העיר שכם. טמנו את העצמות בסביבת העיר.

לדברי הארכיאולוג, מאיר בן דב, מבנה הקבר תואם את הדפוס המובהק של קברי השייחים המוסלמים, שנבנו באזור ארץ־ישראל בתקופה הממלוכית והעותמאנית. הקהילה היהודית הקטנה, שהתקיימה באזור שכם במאה הקודמת ובראשית המאה הנוכחית, שמרה על המסורת בדבר מקום קבורתו של יוסף באתר. הוא ציין כי באורח דומה נוצרו מסורות רבות בימי הביניים, בדבר מקום קבורתם של דמויות אחרות מההיסטוריה היהודית.

Haaretz (10/15/86)

"A tomb for a Muslim sheikh"

> The site known as "Joseph's Tomb" near Shechem is a structure that was apparently erected during the Mamluk Period as a tomb for a Muslim sheikh… According to archaeologist Meir Ben-Dov, the structure of the tomb fits the distinctive style of the tombs of Muslim sheikhs that were built in the country during the Mamluk and Ottoman Periods. It was the local tradition of the small Jewish community, which existed in the Shechem region during the last century and at the start of the present century, that identified the tomb of Joseph with this site. He noted that many traditions were created in a similar manner in the Middle Ages, by identifying the burial sites of various other characters from Jewish history.

On May 4, 1990, a *Hakhnasat Sefer Torah* took place at Joseph's Tomb, celebrating the addition of a new Torah scroll to the yeshiva located there. Following this event, which was attended by ministers and senior members of the Likud Party, an even more extreme article on the matter appeared in *Haaretz*, this time penned by Ben-Dov himself. He wrote:

> The *Hakhnasat Sefer Torah* at the yeshiva at Joseph's Tomb that took place yesterday is based on an error. Anyone who thought that he was entering the tomb of Joseph, son of Jacob, was actually entering the opening to the tomb of a Muslim sheikh, a domed structure that was built two hundred years ago. There is not even a hint of a connection between this site and the tomb of Joseph. Not one iota of information exists as to the location of Joseph's Tomb, to which, according to tradition, Joseph's remains were brought from Egypt. The veneration of holy burial sites in Judaism is a later phenomenon that did not exist when the nation of Israel still lived in the Land.

In this vein, countless newspaper articles from that period – even, to some extent, in more right-leaning venues – gave the impression that the "scientific truth" is that the traditional location of Joseph's Tomb is actually a marginal Muslim site; any belief in its significance to the Jewish people is rooted in religious folklore, like the countless "holy burial sites" in the Galilee and in other regions around the country. The religious journalist Michael Shashar wrote in *Maariv* on December 21, 1993:

> Moreover, anyone who is familiar with the history of the Land of Israel and the history of burial sites in the Land of Israel knows that it is absolutely clear that what is presented today as Joseph's Tomb is not Joseph's Tomb…

Echoing Shashar, orientalist Yehoshua Porat wrote in *Maariv* on October 16, 1996:

יהושע פורת

שני קברים – שני עולמות

קבר רחל וקבר יוסף, למרות הדמיון בטרמינולוגיה, אין דינם שווה

Prof. Yehoshua Porat in Maariv (10/16/96)

"The belief that Joseph is buried there is an Islamic folk tradition."

> Joseph's Tomb and Rachel's Tomb – how little they have in common, despite the linguistic similarity…the belief that Joseph is buried there is an Islamic folk tradition. The religious folklore of the Muslims in this land consecrates many sites as, according to folk tradition, burial sites of biblical characters who are considered prophets in Islam, or of various Islamic personalities.

> Until 1967, Joseph's Tomb did not exist in the Jewish historical consciousness. No one went there on a pilgrimage, it was not customary to pray at the site, it was not listed in descriptions of Jewish travelers and pilgrims, and it was not a symbol of national identity... only after 1967 came the turning point. As a result of zealots among us, who thought that we needed to seize a stronghold in the heart of Samaria, within a crowded town of hundreds of thousands of Arabs, they turned Joseph's Tomb into a Jewish place of worship and pilgrimage and established a yeshiva alongside it...

It may very well be that the Israeli government's lack of desire to protect Joseph's Tomb during the events leading up to the army's humiliating abandonment of the site was significantly influenced by this version of reality depicted in the Israeli media.

In truth, anyone who is even slightly familiar with the geography and history of the Land of Israel knows that the statements presented above contradict both the facts on the ground and the historical sources, and simply represent wishful thinking on the part of their writers. It is truly regrettable that, at the time those statements were made, no clear voice of protest from the experts in the field – outside the political framework – was heard. All that would have been required to debunk the claims of inauthenticity is to present some basic information and sources regarding Joseph's Tomb. In this essay, I will try, albeit belatedly, to do just that – to provide a small, concentrated amount of material about the site and its origins. I will also quote early accounts from individuals who described the location, demonstrating that the site we know today as Joseph's Tomb was known and venerated by the inhabitants of the Land of Israel for thousands of years. I will trace the connection to the site that the Muslims claim to possess, and will close with considerations in analyzing the region in light of the biblical text.

Selected Accounts of the Site from the Roman-Byzantine Period

- John 4:4–6:

"Now, he had to go through Samaria. So he came to a town in Samaria called Sychar, near the parcel of land Jacob had given to his son Joseph. Jacob's well was there."

The significance of this New Testament source is, first, the indication that the "parcel of land" was a well-known place at the time the Gospel of John was written (toward the end of the first century CE or a little later), used as a point of reference to identify the location of the city of Sychar. In addition, the description of the geography here is quite rich in detail. The source does not mention Shechem, which was destroyed at the time, nor does it mention Neapolis, which was only founded in 72 CE. Sychar has been identified with great certainty as the village of Askar (based on many sources, in particular the Samaritan chronicles), whose ancient center is located about two thousand feet northeast of the modern Joseph's Tomb. "Jacob's well" apparently refers to the deep (100 feet) ancient well about 1,700 feet south of Joseph's Tomb (located today within the grounds of an Eastern Orthodox monastery).

- Genesis Rabba 79:19:

"The parcel of land...he purchased..." (Gen. 33:19). R. Yuda b. R. Simon [early fourth century CE] said, "This is one of the three places of which the nations of the world cannot defraud Israel, saying that we stole them from them. They are: the cave of Machpelah, the Temple and the tomb of Joseph. The cave of Machpelah – 'Abraham paid out to Ephron' (23:16). The Temple – 'So David paid Ornan' (I Chr. 21:25). The tomb of Joseph – 'The parcel of land...he purchased.'"

Clearly, Rabbi Yuda's statement is only possible if a distinct location exists, by which it is possible to defend an ancient Jewish claim of ownership.

- Eusebius's *Onomasticon* (early fourth century CE) 150:1: "Sychem – City of Jacob now deserted. The place is pointed out in the suburb of Neapolis. There the tomb of Joseph is pointed out nearby."

Neapolis, or Nablus, refers to today's "qasba" (the ancient part of Shechem), about 1.5 miles west of Joseph's Tomb. Eusebius was still able to recognize the ancient, ruined tell of Shechem, noting its location in relation to Neapolis, and was aware of Joseph's Tomb nearby. This description is entirely congruous with Joseph's Tomb as we know it today, at the foot of the ancient tell to the east.

- "Theodosius" (Christian pilgrim, 518–520 CE), *De Situ Terrae Sanctae* (On the Topography of the Holy Land): "There [near Neapolis] is the well which Jacob made. There are the bones of Joseph the holy."

Accounts from the Middle Ages

There exist numerous accounts of the site in the various writings of travelers in the land during this period. The accounts that are particularly important for our discussion are those that describe the gravestone itself as flanked by two short pillars, a piece of information that is not mentioned anywhere else in descriptions of other gravestones and is a trademark of Joseph's Tomb even today.

- Menachem ben Peretz of Hebron (1215 CE)[1]: "And from there I walked to Shechem, and I saw the tomb of Joseph the Righteous, son of Jacob our Father, between two marble pillars, one at his head and one at his feet."
- "These are the Journeys" and "Avenues in the Land of Israel" (1270–1290 CE):[2] "And here in Shechem is the tomb of Joseph the Righteous, and on it are two marble pillars, one at his head and one at his feet, and a short stone wall surrounding the tomb."

1. Recent research indicates that there is no reason to dispute the authenticity of this work.
2. Two very similar works whose authorship is unknown. The question which of them is the source for the other is a matter of dispute.

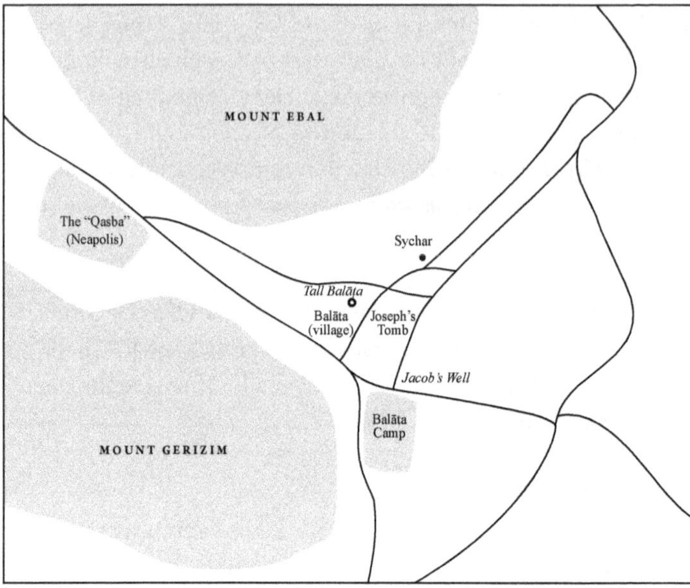

- Rabbi Ishtori HaParchi, the great Jewish topographer of the Land of Israel during the Middle Ages:[3]

  Shechem can be found between two mountains, Mount Gerizim and Mount Ebal, and it is, I believe, the village known as Balata, not the city about a *techum Shabbat*-distance (two thousand cubits, about three-fifths of a mile) to the west of it, which is called Nablus. And what forced me to say this (i.e. that ancient Shechem is located at Balata and not in Nablus) is the gravestone of Joseph the Righteous, which is about fifty cubits (about seventy-five feet) north of Balata, in the field that Jacob purchased, as explained at the end of the Book of Joshua, and it is located in front of Shechem and Nablus, at a distance from there. And it is that field where Joseph, *a"h,* lies, that from the day I began to study the Land of Israel, I have refrained from entering. The area of the grave is fenced with stones, due to the holiness of the site, for there was an altar there.

3. His work *Kaftor Vaferaḥ* on the Land of Israel and its unique laws was completed in 1322 CE; the quote here is taken from chapter 11, based on MS Milano.

Joseph's Tomb (David Roberts, 1839); note the two pillars on either side of the gravestone.

Lack of Muslim Connection to the Site

Muslims generally identify the tomb of Joseph with a site next to the cave of Machpelah in Hebron, whereas what we call Joseph's Tomb in Shechem they occasionally mention in their literature as a marginally significant site. This Muslim tradition, which stands in contradiction to the Tanakh and to the solid evidence found in the early sources, has its roots in the apocryphal book "Testaments of the Twelve Patriarchs" 20:6 and in the itinerary of the sixth-century pilgrim Antoninus of Piacenza.

Authentic Tradition vs. Folk Tradition

Joseph's Tomb is located at the foot of the eastern gate of ancient Shechem, which was discovered in the twentieth century in the course of archaeological excavations. The area around the tomb is flat and lower than the area surrounding it, in contrast to the style typical of the folkloric "burial sites" of Muslim sheikhs and prophets, which are generally situated atop mountains. The tomb's location east of the ancient Tell Balata, which was unknown throughout the Byzantine Period and the Middle Ages, and not within the later Neapolis/Nablus complex, demonstrates the antiquity of the tradition. It also proves the

Joseph's Tomb (photograph taken c. 1900); the two pillars are still a prominent feature of the site

Joseph's Tomb after its destruction by Arab rioters (March 2003); the two pillars are still visible.

tradition's congruity with the Torah's account of Jacob's arrival in Shechem, east of the Jordan: "And he encamped *before the city.* The parcel of land where he pitched his tent he purchased..." (Gen. 33:18–19); "The bones of Joseph... were buried at Shechem, in the parcel of land which Jacob had bought" (Josh. 24:32). If someone were to have created a new, false tradition regarding the parcel of land and Joseph's Tomb later in history, he would undoubtedly have situated the tomb within Neapolis, and not in the remote Platanus-Balata. Sure enough, there developed a folk tradition among the Samaritans that places the "parcel of land" precisely where they likely imagined it would be – at the entrance to Neapolis ("the site of Jacob's mourning").

For further study:

Ben-Ḥaim, Z. *Teivat Markeh: Asufat Midrashim Shomroniyim.* Jerusalem, 1988, 335 [Hebrew].

Dabbagh, M. *Biladuna Filastin* II/2. Kefar Qara, 1991, 277–279 [Arabic].

Ehrlich, Z. H. "*Kever Yosef Vehamivne She'alav.*" *Shomron Ubinyamin* 1, 1987, 153–162 [Hebrew].

Ish Shalom, M. *Kivrei Avot.* Jerusalem, (1948) 2001, 79–82 [Hebrew].

Le Strange, G. *Palestine under the Moslems.* (1890), Beirut, 1965, 314, 319, 325, 512.

Tailor J. E., ed. *The Onomasticon by Eusebius of Caesarea.* Jerusalem, 2003, 83.

"Theodosius." Latin source: *Itineraria et alia geographica* (CCSL 175), Turnholt 1965, Par. 2. English translation: *Theodosius* (PPTS, translated by J. H. Bernard), London 1893, 7.

Wilkinson, J. *Egeria's Travels to the Holy Land,* Jerusalem-Warminster, 1981, 193.

Wikipedia entries: "Joseph's Tomb" [English]; "*Mehumot Minharat Ha-kotel*" and "*Kever Yosef*" [Hebrew].

Parashat Vayeshev

"He Was at Chezib When She Bore Him"

Chezib/Achzib

Parashat Vayeshev states: "Judah left his brothers and camped near a certain Adullamite whose name was Ḥirah" (Gen. 38:1). He then married and had three sons: Er, Onan, and Shela. In its description of Shela's birth, the Torah says, "Once again she bore a son, and named him Shela; he (or it) was at Chezib when she bore him" (38:5).

Before we go further, we must note that there are two different places known as Chezib, or Achzib,[1] in Israel. The first is an ancient town on the northern coast, now home to a well-known national park near the city of Nahariya. The second is located in the heart of the Shephelah region in south-central Israel, and it is to this latter location that our *parasha* refers.

Achzib is also mentioned in the list of cities in the Shephelah found in Joshua (15:44), and later in the beginning of Micah in the list of Judean cities conquered by the Assyrians (1:14). Our *parasha* mentions

1. The two names are functionally identical; the letter *aleph* at the beginning of "Achzib" merely eases the pronunciation of "Chezib," which begins with a consonant cluster ("prosthetic *aleph*").

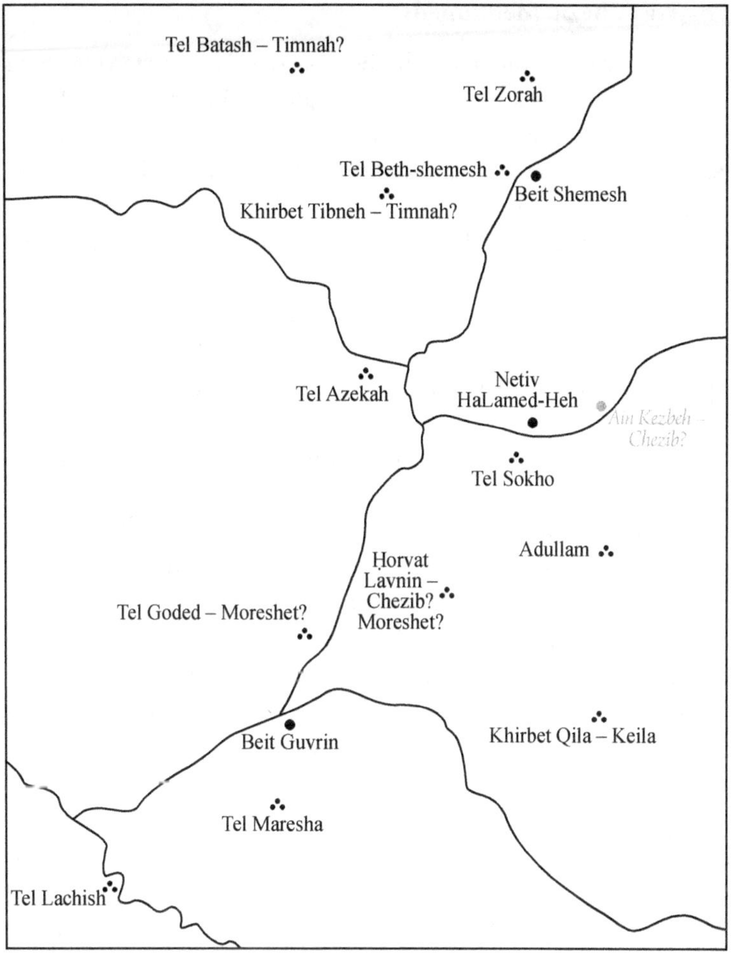

Chezib alongside places like Adullam, Enaim, and Timna; in Joshua it can be found near Keilah and Maresha; and in Micah it follows Lachish and Moresheth-gath, while preceding Maresha and Adullam. Most of these locations have been identified with a great degree of certainty (see the map above). Achzib itself has not been positively identified, but the region where it was located is clear. In the fourth century CE, Eusebius (*Onomasticon* 172:6–7) described it as a ruin in the vicinity of Adullam, and modern researchers have suggested two locations for this ancient city. (See map.)

Why Was Chezib Mentioned?

The obvious question on this biblical passage is why the verse mentions Chezib. Translators and commentators alike have debated even the simple meaning of the verse: Who was in Chezib? Some explain that the verse refers to Judah, and the verse mentions this to tell the reader that Judah was not home when Shela was born. According to the Septuagint, it was Judah's wife, the daughter of Shua, who was in Chezib. Still others explain that the verse refers not to a person, but to the birth itself (either of Shela or of both him and his brothers) that took place in Chezib. In any case, the detail of Chezib seems superfluous; it is difficult to understand why the verse needed to include it.

According to an interpretation found in several ancient translations,[2] the word Chezib here does not refer to an actual location at all. Instead, the verse is simply saying that after this point, Judah's wife stopped having children. In this interpretation, the word *bikhziv* is used in the sense of a *ma'ayan akhzav*, an intermittent spring whose flow of water is characterized by periodically stopping entirely. However, this explanation is difficult from a linguistic perspective, and also cannot be accepted since Achzib is evidently the name of a city in the Shephelah, found in the lists of cities in Joshua and Micah. In light of this, it is unlikely that this is the simple meaning of the verse.[3]

Radak suggests that according to ancient custom, the father would name the first and third children, while the mother would name the second and fourth children. When Shela was born, Judah was not home but in Chezib, and as a result Shela was named by his mother despite being the third child. Nahmanides cites this explanation only to forcefully reject it. Some scholars have claimed that Chezib was, for a certain period of time, home to Shela's descendants, and because of this the Torah mentioned

2. These include Aquila, the Palestinian Targumim, and a translation cited in Genesis Rabba, as well as the Peshitta and the Vulgate.
3. Rashi tried to connect this interpretation to the simple meaning of the verse by explaining that the city was named Chezib because it was the place where Judah's wife stopped having children. Nahmanides rejected this proposal.

the city in connection with Shela's birth.[4] Ultimately, it seems that the question is better than the answers.

Hidden Interpretations of Biblical Names

As we mentioned earlier, in the chapter on *Parashat Vayetzeh*, the interpretations given throughout Tanakh of names of people and places generally do not account for how these names were first created. Instead, they serve to inject new homiletical meaning, based on our ancestors' experiences, into names that already existed. To add a new dimension to this concept, very often these interpretations are not found explicitly in the text, but are hidden or subtly implied.

Several examples of this phenomenon can be found in Genesis alone. In *Parashat Vayetzeh*, an explicit interpretation for the name Machanaim is found in the text: "'This is God's camp (*maḥaneh*).' So he named that place Machanaim" (Gen. 32:3). But there is also a hidden interpretation for the name, hinted at multiple times throughout the narrative: "He divided the people… into two camps" (32:8); "If Esau comes to the one camp and attacks it, the other camp may yet escape" (32:9); "and now I have become two camps" (32:11).[5]

Another similar example is the name Penuel. The Torah says, "So Jacob named the place Peniel, meaning, 'I have seen a divine being face to face (*panim el panim*)'" (Gen. 32:31). But less explicitly, the word *panim* and its linguistic relatives appear countless times in the narrative – "Go on ahead (*lefanai*)" (32:17); "'If I propitiate him (*akhapera panav*) with presents in advance (*lefanai*), and then face him (*er'eh panav*), perhaps he will show me favor (*yisa panai*).' And so the gift went on

4. According to Aaron Demsky, Chezib was named for Shela's son, Cozeba, who is mentioned in I Chronicles 4:22.

5. It is noteworthy that, in this case, the hidden interpretation of the name has two advantages that the explicit interpretation lacks: (a) According to the explicit understanding – "this is God's camp" – the word "camp" is metaphorical, while in the hidden interpretation it refers to a real camp; (b) the hidden interpretation explains well not only the name itself, but also its dual ending *-ayim* (*maḥanayim*) – ostensibly meaning "two camps." For more on the dual-like suffixes of place-names, and in particular the case of Maḥanaim, see the discussion in my *Ancient Place Names*, referred to in the bibliography.

ahead (*al panav*) ..." (32:21–22); "For to see your face (*panekha*) is like seeing the face of God (*penei Elohim*), and you have received me favorably" (33:10).

In other instances, there is only implicit interpretation. For example, after Jacob crosses the ford of the Jabbok, we immediately read that "a man wrestled (*vaye'avek*) with him until the break of dawn" (Gen. 32:25). Tellingly, this is the only place in the Tanakh that the verb *vaye'avek* appears, most probably due to its similarity to the name Jabbok. In the course of Jacob's stay in Laban's house, we read that "Jacob then got fresh shoots of poplar (*livneh*), and of almond and plane, and peeled white (*levanot*) stripes in them, laying bare the white (*halavan*) of the shoots" (30:37). Even the shoots of almond mentioned in that verse – *luz* in Hebrew, another word that appears nowhere else in Tanakh in this context – is perhaps a reference to Bethel, formerly known as Luz (28:19), where Jacob visited prior to arriving in Haran. Finally, when Jacob leaves Laban's house, we find a hint of his impending meeting with Esau in Laban's accusation: "It was a foolish thing for you to do (*aso*)" (31:28). Another striking case of the same type from the narrative of Jacob and the angel was presented by Jonathan Grossman: "Jacob said, 'Please tell me your name' (*haggida-na shmekha*) ... Therefore to this day the Israelites do not eat the tendon (*gid hanashe*) attached to the socket of the hip" (Gen. 32:30–33). Grossman also cited Stanley Gevirtz, who had revealed the interesting resemblance between *gid hanashe* and the two tribes whose border passed near Mahanaim and the Jabbok: Gad and Menasheh.

The Importance of Names and Their Connection to Events

It is clear that the Torah considers the interpretations given for names extremely significant. In a sense, these interpretations serve to establish the true essence of the people and places that bear the corresponding names, not unlike a blessing or a curse. Names and their interpretations are not always mere ancillary elements in a story, but can often propel the plot forward, giving it the proper narrative emphases.

For example, the word *tzeḥok* – laughter – is not only the linguistic root given for Isaac's name, but it is also a motif that runs through his entire life. Before Isaac was born, his father Abraham laughed in joy, while his mother Sarah laughed derisively, leading to her being reprimanded. When he was born, his mother said, "God has brought me laughter; everyone who hears will laugh with me" (Gen. 21:6). Sarah witnessed Isaac's rival Ishmael "playing (*metzaḥek*)" (21:9), and years later, Abimelech witnessed Isaac "jesting (*metzaḥek*) with his wife Rebekah" (26:8). The verse purposely leaves vague the exact nature of Ishmael and Isaac's actions; the important message from the Torah's perspective is the disproportionate use of the linguistic root that can be found within the name of the protagonist.

It is doubtful that the Torah would have found it necessary to mention the exact nature of the food with which Jacob purchased the birthright from his brother in *Parashat Toledot*, if not for the linguistic connection to Esau: "'Give me some of that red stuff (*adom*) to gulp down'...which is why he was called Edom" (Gen. 25:30). Once again, in addition to this explicit interpretation of the name Edom, we find another hidden connection: "Red (*admoni*), like a hairy mantle (*ke'aderet sei'ar*) all over" (25:25), which clearly hints at the land of Edom and Mount Seir.[6]

Shela and Chezib

Let us now return to *Parashat Vayeshev*, and the verse, "[She] named him Shela; he (or it) was at Chezib when she bore him" (Gen. 38:5). The style in which the verse is written suggests that it is an interpretation of Shela's name, but there is seemingly no connection between Shela, son of Judah, and the place called Chezib. A solution to this problem can be found in an early commentary on the Book of Chronicles ascribed by the Tosafists to "a student of Rav Saadia Gaon" (Yoma 9a). This answer is cited in the *Daat Mikra* commentary on I Chronicles 2:3, and Nahmanides suggests the same idea in his own commentary. The answer is that this is a case where the interpretation of the name is hidden within a synonym. This kind of interpretation can only be appreciated by individuals who possess a deep understanding of the Hebrew language.

6. Also compare "But my brother Esau is a hairy man and I am smooth-skinned (*ḥalak*)" (Gen. 27:11) to the description of the southern border of the Land of Israel, which it shares with the land of Edom: "Mount Chalak, which ascends to Seir" (Josh. 11:17).

In the Book of Kings, Elisha promises the Shunammite woman that "At this season next year, you will be embracing a son." She responds, "Please, my lord, man of God, do not delude (*tekhazev*) your maidservant" (II Kings 4:16). When her son dies, his mother runs back to Elisha, accusing, "Did I ask my lord for a son? Didn't I say, 'Don't mislead (*tashle*) me'?" (4:28). This episode teaches us that in Hebrew, the words *tekhazev* and *tashle* are synonymous, since in verse 28, the Shunammite woman is actually quoting her own earlier statement substituting *tashleh* for *tekhazev*. In light of this, the implied linguistic connection in our *parasha* between Shela and Chezib suddenly makes perfect sense.

There may have been an additional connection between Shela and Chezib, relating to the meaning of the word *akhzav*: Shela's life was characterized by disappointment. In Tanakh, the verb *lekhazev* and the expression *akhzav* are used to describe things that disappoint, that do not realize the potential that is associated with them. Some examples include: "Like a spring whose waters do not fail (*yekhazevu*)" (Is. 58:11); "You have been to me like a spring that fails (*akhzav*), like waters that cannot be relied on" (Jer. 15:18); "Behold, any hope [of capturing him] must be disappointed (*nikhzava*)" (Job 41:1); and "All men are false (*kozev*)" (Ps. 116:11). In the story of Judah and Tamar, it had been expected that Tamar would marry Shela, but Judah was afraid to proceed with the match, "for he thought, 'He too might die like his brothers'" (Gen. 38:11). Thus, Shela was indeed a disappointment, and the name Chezib hints at this disappointment that would later be the hallmark of Shela's life. Once we accept this explanation, whether the birth took place in Chezib or whether Shela's father was in Chezib at the time matters little – either way, the Torah conveys the connection to Chezib and probably also to the theme of disappointment.

Name Interpretation Through Synonyms in Other Texts

The notion of interpreting the meaning of a name through the use of a synonym is found in other sources as well. Yair Zakovitch wrote on this topic, citing several examples, some of which are more convincing than others. The following is a compelling example brought by Zakovitch in his article.

In Judges 15, we read the story of Samson at "the cave of the rock of Etam," where the men of Judah handed him over to the Philistines:

> When he reached Lehi, the Philistines came shouting to meet him. Thereupon the spirit of the Lord gripped him, and the ropes on his arms became like flax that catches fire... He came upon a fresh jawbone (*leḥi*) of an ass and he picked it up; and with it he killed a thousand men. Then Samson said: "With the jaw of an ass, mass upon mass! With the jaw of an ass I have slain a thousand men." As he finished speaking, he threw the jawbone away; hence that place was called Ramath-lehi. (Judges 15:14–17)

The level of detail in the final verse of this passage is curious. Why do we need to know that Samson discarded the jawbone at the conclusion of his declaration? Would we have thought otherwise that the jawbone remained in his hand until today? It is obvious that he threw the jawbone away, and to state explicitly that he did so seems superfluous.

Furthermore, the very use of the word *leḥi* to refer to a jawbone is slightly odd. The word *leḥi* generally refers to the cheek and not to the jaw itself, even in Biblical Hebrew.[7] It may be that if the incident with Samson and the Philistines had not taken place in Lehi, a different word may have been preferred over *leḥi* in this context. The location may have been named Lehi because of a raised plateau (*rama*) whose topographical form resembled a person's cheek.[8] Since the incident occurred in a place called Lehi or Ramath-lehi, the author of Judges chose the word *leḥi* specifically.

But how can we explain the verse, "he threw the jawbone away"? Zakowitz answers convincingly that the full name of the location was Ramath-lehi (verse 17). The Hebrew word *rama* means "plateau" here, but taken as a verb, it can also mean "threw away," as in the verse, "Horse and driver He has hurled (*rama*) into the sea" (Ex. 15:1). The word has a similar meaning in its Aramaic and Arabic cognates. For the sole purpose of interpreting the name Ramath-lehi, the Book of Judges added

7. The word for jawbone in Rabbinic Hebrew and Modern Hebrew is *leset*.
8. As it is common in the field of topographical items in Biblical Hebrew; see the chapter on *Parashat Bemidbar*.

this seemingly superfluous detail of Samson throwing away the jawbone: "As he finished speaking, he threw the jawbone away; hence that place was called Ramath-lehi" (Judges 15:17).

With this in mind, let us return to *Parashat Vayeshev* to analyze an additional name. The city of Dothan (or Dothain) is mentioned only twice in all of Tanakh, once in the story of Joseph and his brothers (Gen. 37) and a second time in the time of Elisha (II Kings 6). The name Dothan appears to derive from the word *dut* and the suffix *-an* or *-ain*. What is the meaning of the word *dut*? In the Hebrew of the tannaitic period, the word *dut* often accompanies the word *bor*,[9] in connection to different types of storage in one's house. What is the difference between a *bor* and a *dut*? The Talmud states: "Both *bor* and *dut* are excavations in the soil, only a *bor* is merely dug out, whereas a *dut* is faced with stone" (Bava Batra 64a). The Rashbam explains: "Dug out – in hard soil ... Faced with stone – they dig a well in soft dirt, and then build a stone wall within it; this is called a *dut*." The word *dut* exists in Akkadian as well (*dûtu*). The Proto-Semitic form of the word was apparently **dawt*, and it is likely, as we stated above, that the name Dothan was derived from this form.

It is reasonable to ask why the Torah mentions Dothan in the story of the sale of Joseph. The detail that the brothers were in Dothan at the time is not necessary for the story, and there is no further mention of Dothan in the narrative. Considering all that we have discussed above, it may be that the Torah mentions Dothan in this context in order to hint at the role of the location in the story – it is home to the pit (*bor*) into which the brothers threw Joseph.[10]

For further study:

Demsky, A. "The Houses of Achzib." *Israel Exploration Journal* 16 (1966): 211–215.

Elitzur, Yoel. *Ancient Place Names in the Holy Land: Preservation and History.* Jerusalem-Winona Lake, 2004, 283–290, 335.

9. The phrase *bor vadut* appears five times throughout the Babylonian version of the Mishna, and it appears in the Tosefta as well. Other versions of the Mishna read instead *bor veḥadut* and the Yerushalmi reads *ḥarut*. See my articles devoted to this topic in the bibliography at the end of this chapter.
10. At this point, I would like to thank my close friend Professor Yoḥanan Breuer; this last idea took shape as a result of a conversation with him.

(Image courtesy of Prof. Adam Zertal, Haifa University)

Tel Dothan

Elitzur, Yoel. "דות and חדות." *Lešonenu* 48–49 (1985): 132–141 [Hebrew].

Elitzur, Yoel. "*Od He'ara al Dut-Dotan.*" *Lešonenu* 50 (1986): 75–76 [Hebrew].

Gevirtz, S. "Of Patriarchs and Puns: Joseph at the Fountain, Jacob at the Ford." *HUCA* 66 (1975): 33–54.

Grossman, J. *Ambiguity in the Biblical Narrative and Its Contribution to the Literary Formation* (PhD Thesis), Ramat Gan, 2006, 89 [Hebrew].

Prausnitz, M. W. "Achzib 1." In *The Anchor Bible Dictionary*, 1:57.

Zakovitch, Y. "The Synonymous Word and Synonymous Name in Name-Midrashim." *Shnaton – An Annual for Biblical and Ancient Near-Eastern Studies* 2 (1977): 100–115 [Hebrew].

Zissu, B. "The identification of biblical Achzib at 'Khirbet 'En el-Kizbe' in the Judean Shephela, and the origins of Shimon Bar Kokhba." *Go Out and Study the Land: Studies in Honor of Ḥanan Eshal.* Edited by A. M. Maeir, J. Magness, and L. W. Schiffman), Leiden, 2012, 377–426.

Parashat Miketz – Ḥanukka

Modi'in

"In those days arose Mattathias the son of John, the son of Simeon, a priest of the sons of Joarib, from Jerusalem, and dwelt in Modein" (I Maccabees 2:1).

Modein, in Hebrew sources Modi'in, Modi'im or Moda'it, is well known as the town in which the Hasmonean family dwelt and were buried in an ancestral tomb. But where is Modi'in?

Today, it seems strange to even ask such a question. There is a large city in Israel known as Modi'in, in whose vicinity lie towns with names like Matityahu, Hashmonaim, and Maccabim, as well as a historical site known as the Tombs of the Maccabees. Seemingly it is obvious that this region is where ancient Modi'in was located. But is this actually true? What is the source of this identification?

In reality, the connection between ancient Modi'in and its modern-day counterpart is not so simple. The identification is based on several sources.

Sources that Seem to Place Modi'in in the Eastern Part of Shephelat Lod

Let us begin with the Book of Maccabees. Following the death of the High Priest Jonathan, who had been betrayed and captured by the Seleucid ruler Diodotus Tryphon, we read:

> Then sent Simon, and took the bones of Jonathan his brother, and buried them in Modein, the city of his fathers... Simon also built a monument upon the tomb of his father and his brothers, and raised it aloft for all to see, of hewn stone behind and before. Moreover he set up seven pyramids, one against another, for his father, and his mother, and his four brothers. And in these he made cunning devices, about which he set great pillars, and upon the pillars he made all their armor for a perpetual memory, and by the armor ships carved, that they might be seen by all who sail on the sea. This is the tomb that he made at Modein, and it stands yet until this day. (I Maccabees 13:25–30)

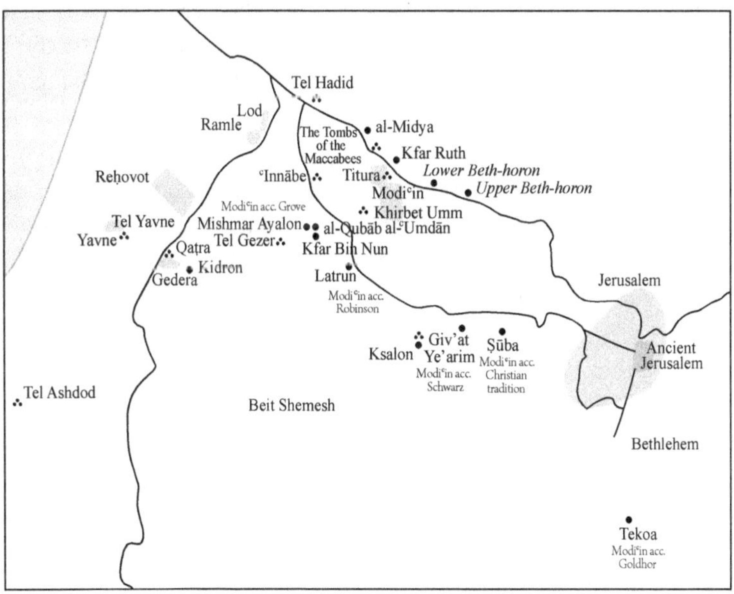

According to Maccabees, Simon built a magnificent burial complex, with seven pyramids atop the tombs and carved pillars depicting weapons, armor, and ships. But the interesting part of this passage for our purposes is the ending: "that they might be seen by all who sail on the sea" and "until this day."

The words "until this day" refer to the time when I Maccabees was written, namely, several decades following the events recounted in the book. But later authors also seem to be familiar with the location. In Josephus's *Antiquities of the Jews*, he writes: "Moreover, he built seven pyramids also for his parents and his brothers, one for each of them, which were made remarkably, both for their size and beauty, and which have been preserved to this day" (13:211). Apparently even in Josephus's time – in other words, after the destruction of the Second Temple – Simon's burial complex at Modi'in was still well known.

To date, we have not found any remnants of these seven adjacent pyramids anywhere in Israel. A nineteenth-century scholar, George Grove, suggested that a vestige of these Maccabean tombs could be found in the name of the Arab village of al-Qubāb (just east of Mishmar Ayalon and Kfar Bin Nun, abandoned in 1948). The word *qubāb* is a plural form of *qubba*, "dome," which can be used to refer to a burial structure for an important person. Victor Guérin rightfully rejected this highly dubious theory.

The expression "that they might be seen by all who sail on the sea" perhaps hints at a location that is not far from the sea. This would also fit with an elevated location within the inner Shephelah. To be fair, though, there is no solid proof for this speculation; some explain that the reference to "all who sail on the sea" simply means that the intricately carved pillars, which depicted ships, tended to attract sailors.

An additional, more explicit source supporting the inner Shephelah location can be found at the end of I Maccabees. In chapters 15–16, we read that Antiochus VII (Sidetes) demanded that Simon return to Seleucid hands Jaffa, Gezer, and the Acra, a Jerusalem fortress built by Antiochus IV (Epiphanes). Simon refused, relaying the famous message to Antiochus's envoy:

> We have neither taken other men's land, nor held that which belongs to others, but the inheritance of our fathers, which our enemies had conquered wrongfully at a certain time. And we, having opportunity, hold the inheritance of our fathers. (I Maccabees 15:33–34)

In response, Antiochus appointed the military leader Cendebeus, commander of the coastal region, and sent him to attack Judea.

In the course of the war narrative, the names Jamnia (Yavne in Hebrew, today an Israeli city) and Cedron appear in connection with the Seleucids, and Gezer and Modi'in in connection with the Jews. John Hyrcanus and Judah, the sons of Simon, led the fight against Cendebeus:

> They rested that night at Modein. And when they rose in the morning, and went into the plain, behold, a mighty host both of footmen and horsemen came against them, and a brook was between them…and Cendebeus and his host were put to flight, so that many of them were slain, and the remnant fled to the stronghold…but John still followed after them, until he came to Cedron…So they fled to the towers in the fields of Azotus [Ashdod] where he burned it with fire. (16:4–10)

The location of Cedron is not known with certainty. Many believe that Qaṭra, an Arab village that lay at the northern edge of Gedera before it was destroyed in 1948, preserved a remnant of Cedron in its name. A similar name – Gedrus (variants: Kedus, Cedrus) – appears in Eusebius's *Onomasticon* (circa 320 CE): "There is now a large village [called] Gedrus ten miles from Diospolis [Lod] on the road to Eleutheropolis [Beit Guvrin]" (*Onomasticon* 68:22–23). Based on this identification, a moshav established in 1949 just east of that site was named Kidron.

Whether or not there is actually a connection between Kidron and Qaṭra, it is clear from the geographical context that Cedron, the site mentioned in I Maccabees, was located in this general region. In light of this, we can reasonably assume that Modi'in was not far from there as well. The details of the narrative point to a location that borders on the plains but is itself located on the Judean hillsides.

In the *Onomasticon*'s entry for Modi'in, Eusebius writes: "Village near Diospolis. Home of the Maccabees where their tomb is pointed out even now" (*Onomasticon* 132:16–17). We see from here that even centuries after the destruction of the Second Temple, the tombs of the Maccabees were still plainly visible in a village near Lod.

The most important piece of information in support of this identification of Modi'in is the Madaba Map. In this ancient mosaic map, dated to the sixth or seventh century CE, the village of Modi'in is accompanied by the following label in Greek: "Mōdeeim which is now Mōditha, whence were the Maccabees." West of the village lies the city of "Lōd"; to the east lies the village of "Bethōrōn"; to the south lies "Bētoannaba"; to the northeast lies "[Kaph]eruta"; and to the northwest lies "Aditha." All of these locations are familiar to us. Lod and Beth-horon (today Beit 'Ūr at-Taḥta) are well-known places. Bētoannaba refers to 'Innābe, an Arab village that was destroyed in the War of Independence. Its name is preserved today in the form of Naḥal Anava and the Anava Interchange. Kapheruta apparently refers to Khirbet Kafr Lūṭ, located east of Kfar Ruth. Finally, Aditha refers to al-Ḥadītha, an Arab village, now known as the archaeological site Tel Hadid, inhabited until 1948. All of this information essentially corroborates the notion that ancient Modi'in and modern Modi'in are located in the same region.

Thirteenth-century theologian and bishop Jacques de Vitry and fifteenth-century pilgrim Bernhard von Breidenbach both identified Modi'in with Latrun. Edward Robinson wrote in 1841 that this was a reasonable identification. Despite this, it is difficult to accept such a theory, as Latrun is neither "east of Lod" nor in the vicinity of either Hadid or Kfar Ruth. The information in the sources points very clearly further north, toward modern Modi'in.

Scholars have found a preservation of the name Modi'in in the name of the Arab village of al-Midya, located near the town of Hashmonaim.[1]

1. This identification was first suggested by the Franciscan monk Emmanuel Forner in 1866.

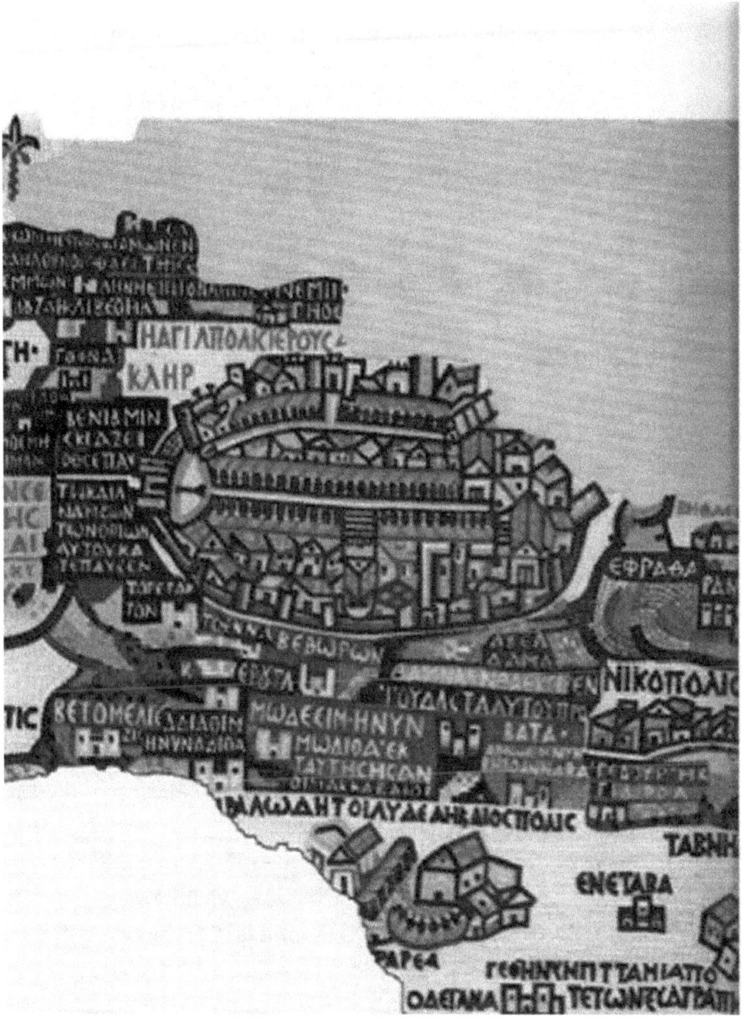

A portion of the Madaba Map. The map faces east. In the upper part of the image, the walled city of Jerusalem is visible. Below Jerusalem – the village of ΒΕΘWPWN (Beth-horon). Below it – the village of K[ ]ERሄTA (K[ap]eruta/Kfar Ruth). Below it – the village of ΜΟΔΕΕΙΜ · Η ΝΥΝ ΜWΔΙΘΑ ˙ ΕΚ ΤΑΥΤΗC HCAN ΟΙ ΜΑΚΚΑΒΑΑΙΟΙ (Modi'im, which is today Moditha; home of the Maccabees). Below it, a large, unwalled city with the label ΛWΔ Η ΤΟΙ ΛΥΔΕΑ Η Κ ΔΙΟCΠΟΛΙC (Lod, which is Lydea, also known as Diospolis). Left (north) of Modi'im – the village of ΑΔΙΑΘΙΜ Η ΝΥΝ ΑΔΙΘΑ (Adiathim, which today is Aditha). Right (south) of Modi'im – the village of ANWB H NYN BETOANNABA = (Anob, which today is Betoannaba).

Several locations have been suggested as the precise location of ancient Modi'in. Adjacent to the residential area in al-Midya, there is a tell that many have identified with Modi'in, but this is questionable; the remnants of city life found at the tell date back to the biblical period, while there are relatively few remnants from the Second Temple period. Some suggested Titura Hill, formerly known as Qal'at Ṭanṭūra,[2] or Khirbet al-Burj,[3] a large ruin on a hilltop where findings from throughout history have been unearthed, located at the edge of modern Modi'in, near Maccabim-Re'ut junction.[4]

In recent decades, two new theories have been suggested. In 2004, it was suggested that ancient Modi'in might be identified with Khirbet Umm al-'Umdān – "the ruin of the pillars" – on the southern edge of modern Modi'in. This site was excavated in 2001, when remnants were found of a town that existed mostly during the Hellenistic period and the Hasmonean period, and lasted until the Bar Kokhba revolt. A public building at the heart of the site was identified by the excavators as an ancient synagogue from the Hasmonean period, perhaps the oldest known synagogue today. According to the excavators, while the name "'Umdān" has a very feasible interpretation – indeed, pillars were found at the site – it may still be that the name represents some kind of evolution from the name Modi'in.[5] In 2008, the location of ancient Modi'in was debated further in the research of Boaz Zissu and Lior Perry. Zissu and Perry rejected the earlier identifications based on both archaeological reasons and methodological reasons. In the end, the pair opted to identify Modi'in with Khirbet Ḥammām, also known as Khirbet al-Midya, in the vicinity of the "Tombs of the Maccabees." Numerous burial caves, built in the typical Jewish style,

2. The word *qal'a* means "fortress," referring to a prominent fortress at the top of the hill that existed during the Middle Ages. A *ṭanṭūr*, in colloquial Arabic, is a pointed hat; it can also refer to a conical hill.
3. *Burj* is another word for "fortress."
4. Thanks to the work of advocates for the preservation of nature and antiquities, in particular Professor Yair Parag, this hill was saved from the clutches of building developers and converted into a nature park.
5. Lending credence to this theory is the existence of other locations in the Land of Israel where the ancient name evolved and took on a new meaning in Arabic. Examples were detailed by the excavators in their article; see bibliography below.

were found at the foot of the ruin. On one of the ossuaries found with the caves (in a series of salvage digs conducted in 1995 by Shimon Riklin), the names "Simon" and "Eleazar" were inscribed.

Let us summarize what we have established until this point:

Two separate passages in I Maccabees seem to indicate that Modi'in was located in the inner Shephelah, on the border of the hillsides and the plains, not far from the latitude of Yavne and Ashdod. The tombs of the Maccabees were a prominent site, visible even from afar. In the Byzantine period, Modi'in and the tombs of the Maccabees were known to be located east of Lod, in the vicinity of modern Modi'in. It is reasonable to assume that the information we have gleaned from the Byzantine-era sources is reliable, and that it is based on an authentic tradition. The precise location of ancient Modi'in within the greater Modi'in area has not been determined conclusively.

Complications Arise

Modi'in is mentioned in the Mishna on two separate occasions as a name for the outermost reaches of Jerusalem's borders. The Mishna states: "What is 'a far-off journey'?[6] From Modi'im and beyond, and the same distance on all sides [of Jerusalem]; this is R. Akiva's opinion" (Mishna Pesaḥim 9:2). Elsewhere we find: "From Modi'im inward [the potters] are trusted in regard to earthenware vessels" (Mishna Ḥagiga 3:5). In other words, from Modi'in inward one may purchase earthenware from any merchant, even if he is an *am haaretz* (one who is ignorant of the laws of ritual purity). The purpose of this leniency was to allow the entire nation to celebrate the festivals together in Jerusalem.

It seems from these examples that Modi'in refers to the border of Jerusalem. But where is this border located? The Gemara, following the mishna cited above (Pesaḥim 93b), explains, in a position ascribed to the Palestinian *Amora* Ulla, that "from Modi'im to Jerusalem is fifteen miles (*mil*)." The problem with this is that fifteen miles is a much shorter distance than the distance between Jerusalem and the Modi'in

6. The question concerns the distance beyond which a person is exempt from bringing the Passover sacrifice on its usual date, and must instead do so one month later on *Pesaḥ Sheni*.

we have been discussing until this point, on the border of Shephelat Lod. How can we deal with this discrepancy? As a result of these talmudic sources, some authors ignored the evidence in Maccabees and the Greek sources and suggested identifying ancient Modi'in with a point located much closer to Jerusalem, in the mountainous region surrounding the city. Thus Rabbi Joseph Schwarz in 1845 chose the Giv'at Ye'arim-Ksalon ridge, while Yitzḥak Goldhor in 1913 chose the desert of Tekoa. Additionally, some Christian and Muslim traditions identified Modi'in with Ṣūba (as reported by Victor Guérin). However, once again, Modi'in's proximity to the Shephelah is practically proven by the account in I Maccabees, and moreover, it is difficult to question the authenticity of the early Christian traditions that seem to fundamentally match both the Modi'in of I Maccabees and the Modi'in of modern Israel.

Talmudic geography scholar Samuel Klein proposed a compromise. He saw the name "Modi'in" as a territorial term, parallel to the phrase *Har Hamoda'i* that appears in one of the later sources, and suggested that the sources referred to two examples of ancient Modi'in: First, there was the "city" at the eastern end of the larger region of Modi'in, which, being closer to Jerusalem, fits Ulla's statement in Pesaḥim. Second, there was the "village" at its western end, which fits Eusebius's description and the Madaba Map. But with all due respect to Professor Klein, this theory seems farfetched.

The Solution

I believe that the following solution provides the answer to all the questions raised above: Upon analyzing the Gemara in Pesaḥim, a careful reader will note that Ulla's position is emphatically rejected, using the strong language, *teyuvta deUlla teyuvta*.[7] Ulla's position was his attempt at quantifying the distance of a "far-off journey" mentioned in the mishna. In his opinion, this term refers to the distance a person generally covers in a half-day's walk,[8] and Ulla calculated that this distance is fifteen miles.

7. Literally, "the refutation of Ulla stands as a refutation."
8. According to Rashi, the half day here refers to the hours during which the *korban Pesaḥ* is slaughtered, i.e., from midday to sunset. In contrast, Maimonides writes that the half day refers to the hours leading up to the time when the *korban Pesaḥ* is slaughtered, i.e., from sunrise to midday.

However, it becomes clear by the end of the Gemara's discussion, in light of the commentaries of the main *Rishonim*, that the accepted interpretation of a half-day's walk is twenty miles – not fifteen miles as Ulla claimed.

Maimonides adds a fascinating variable to the discussion. He writes:

> One who was, on the 14th [of Nisan] at sunrise, at a distance of fifteen miles or more from Jerusalem, this is considered a far-off journey. One who was at a shorter distance than that is not on a far-off journey, because he can reach Jerusalem after midday *if he walks at a leisurely pace.* (*Hilkhot Korban Pesaḥ* 5:9)

The commentators on Maimonides did not seem to notice anything out of the ordinary in the language of this ruling. But something is indeed out of the ordinary here. In general, measurements of this nature that are based on a person's physical ability are defined using an average person as a point of reference. Accordingly, we would have expected that the pace used to determine the distance of a half-day's walk would be a normal walking pace, not a "leisurely pace," as Maimonides states.

It seems to me that Maimonides intentionally used this language in order to resolve the discrepancy between the accepted position in the Gemara – that a half-day's walk is twenty miles[9] – and Ulla's position – that it is only fifteen. Perhaps Maimonides was reluctant to reject Ulla's position outright because Ulla actually lived in the Land of Israel, making his position a kind of eyewitness account.[10] Because of this, Maimonides proposed a novel explanation: In the case of the "far-off journey," we measure distance based on a leisurely pace rather than a normal walking pace.[11] In Maimonides' reckoning, then, a fifteen-mile

9. Maimonides' support of the twenty-miles view can be deduced from his commentary to Mishna Berakhot 1:1.
10. In Maimonides' halakhic methodology, he tended to defend rulings based on the eyewitness accounts of *Ḥazal*, even when they went against the accepted halakha. See *Hilkhot Kelei Mikdash* 9:1 for comparison.
11. In order to accept this approach, it is necessary to find a logical or text-based explanation for why here, unlike other areas of halakha, a leisurely pace is used.

walk at a leisurely pace takes the same amount of time as a twenty-mile walk at a normal pace – half a day.

Now that it has become clear to us that "Modi'im" is located more than fifteen miles away from Jerusalem, perhaps we can beg Maimonides' forgiveness and admit that Ulla's position was most likely based on interpretive speculation rather than his personal experience.[12] In light of this, we can accept that the Gemara's conclusion – *teyuvta deUlla teyuvta* –actually means that "a far-off journey" is twenty miles and not fifteen miles.

Before we actually measure the distance between Jerusalem and Modi'in, I would like to note that, in contrast to the commonly held view of the *Rishonim*, *Aḥaronim*, and even many contemporary Talmud scholars, I believe that when *Ḥazal* used the term *mil*, they were referring to the Roman mile, not their own independent measure of distance. This is a complicated issue that requires its own comprehensive discussion, far beyond the scope of this chapter. I will just mention that the word *mil* is, in essence, a Roman noun (the Latin phrase *mille passuum* means "a thousand double paces"), and the Romans who then ruled the land erected milestones all along the major roads. It is reasonable to assume, then, that the Roman mile was the same mile that *Ḥazal* used.[13]

If we accept that the *mil* found in the Talmud is the Roman mile, which is approximately 4,800 feet, twenty Roman miles comes out to about eighteen English miles. This is the precise distance between Jerusalem and modern-day Modi'in. I believe this is the best solution to the contradiction between the two groups of sources that we outlined above.[14]

---

12. Modi'im was located in the region known as Har Hamelekh (King's Mount), which was inhabited solely by non-Jews during the amoraic period. Visiting the area at the time often proved deadly for Jews; see Y. Shabbat 1:4 (3d). No synagogue remnants have been found in this region from the Byzantine period, while many churches from that era have in fact been found.
13. We will elaborate on this topic later, in the chapter on Yom Kippur.
14. J. J. Ajdler suggested a similar solution in his article, though his proposal contains several flaws and unnecessary complications.

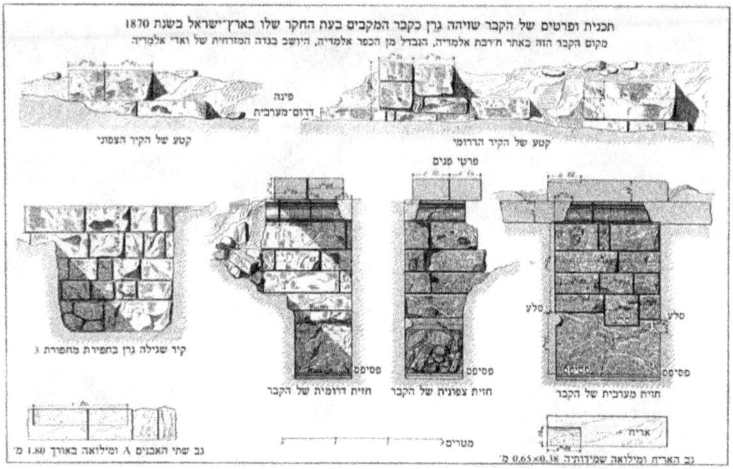

(Yad Ben Zvi)

Detailed schematics of the tomb identified by Guérin as the tomb of the Maccabees in his expedition to the Holy Land in 1870. This tomb is located in Khirbet al-Midya, which is distinct from the village of al-Midya on the eastern bank of Wadi al-Midya.

As for the site known today as "the Tombs of the Maccabees," although this place bore the Arabic name *Qubūr el-Yahūd* (Tombs of the Jews), the burial style indicates that these tombs postdate the Hasmonean period and are apparently non-Jewish. The actual tombs of the Maccabees described in the sources can likely be found in close proximity to these tombs, but their precise location is difficult to pinpoint with certainty. Several sites in the area were suggested as the tombs of the Maccabees during the last 150 years, and perhaps the truth will become clearer in the future. The important conclusion here is that the city of Modi'in and its surrounding towns – many of which bear the names of the heroes of ancient Modi'in, such as Matityahu, Hashmonaim, and Maccabim – seem to have been established in the right place after all.

For further study:

Ajdler, J. J. "Talmudic Metrology: The Mile as a Unit of Length." *BDD* 19 (2008): 57–60.

Ehrlich, Z. H. *Gevurat Beit Chashmona'i*. Jerusalem, 1986, 7–10 [Hebrew].

Goldhor, Y. *Admat Kodesh*. Jerusalem, 1913, 99a [Hebrew].

Guérin, V. *Description géographique, historique et archéologique de la Palestine: Judée*, 1, Paris, 1868, 56–59; *Samarie*, 2, Paris, 1875, 55–64; *Galilée*, 1, Paris, 1880, 46–57 [French].

(Z. Radovan)

"The Tomb of the Maccabees," formerly Qubūr el-Yahūd

Klein, S. *Eretz Yehuda.* Tel Aviv, 1939, 60 [Hebrew].

Piccirillo, M. and Alliata, E. *The Madaba Map Centenary.* Jerusalem, 1997, 71–73.

Robinson, E. and Smith, E. *Biblical Researches in Palestine, Mount Sinai and Arabia Petraea.* London, 1841, 2, 328–329; 3, 30.

Schwarz, J. *Tevu'ot Ha'aretz.* Jerusalem, (1845) 1968, 115 [Hebrew].

Taylor, J. E. *The Onomasticon by Eusebius of Caesarea.* Jerusalem, 2003, 42, 73.

Weksler-Bdolah, S. "Modi'in: Hometown of the Maccabees." *Biblical Archeology Review* 40 (2014): 52–58, 70.

Weksler-Bdolah, S., A. Onn, and Y. Rapuano. "Identifying the Hasmonean Village of Modi'in." *Cathedra* 109 (2003): 69–86 [Hebrew].

Zissu, B., and L. Perry. "Hasmonaean Modi'in and Byzantine Moditha: a Topographical-Historical and Archaeological Assessment." *PEQ* 147 (2015): 316–337.

Parashat Vayigash

Beersheba

City of the Patriarchs

We turn now to Beersheba, the city of the Patriarchs. We first encounter Beersheba in *Parashat Vayera* and then in *Parashat Toledot*, where we learn of its role in the lives of Abraham and Isaac. Following *Parashat Vayigash*, Beersheba takes an extended hiatus from the biblical narrative, disappearing from view for the remainder of the *Ḥumash*. We finally return to the city in the Book of Joshua, in the description of the portions of land allotted to the tribes of Israel. Our separation from Beersheba in *Parashat Vayigash* is perhaps a reflection of Jacob and his sons' parallel separation from Beersheba and indeed from the whole country. Jacob descends to Egypt, leaving behind the Land of Israel, where he will not return in his lifetime. To be sure, Jacob's descendants will eventually return – as conquerors and settlers in the land – but only after the fulfillment of the fateful prophecy: "They shall be enslaved and oppressed" (Gen. 15:13). It seems almost fitting that the point of departure from the Land of Israel is Beersheba:

> So Israel set out with all that was his, and he came to Beersheba, where he offered sacrifices to the God of his father Isaac. God called to Israel in a vision by night: "Jacob! Jacob!" He answered, "Here I am." And He said, "I am the God, the God of your father.

> Fear not to go down to Egypt, for I will make you there into a great nation. (46:1–3)

God's revelation to Jacob in Beersheba was the third stage of the ongoing interaction between the Patriarchs and this place, beginning with Abraham – "Abraham planted a tamarisk at Beersheba, and invoked there the name of the Lord, the Everlasting God" (Gen. 21:33) – and followed by Isaac:

> From there he went up to Beersheba. That night the Lord appeared to him ... and I will bless you and increase your offspring for the sake of My servant Abraham. So he built an altar there and invoked the Lord by name. (26:23–25)

Now God reveals Himself to Jacob in Beersheba as well – three patriarchs, three visits to Beersheba, and three divine revelations. It is no coincidence that Jacob's departure from the land of Canaan, along with the promise of "I Myself will also bring you back" (46:4), takes place in Beersheba. This was the place that his father and grandfather both invoked God's name and merited divine revelation, not to mention lived their lives and dug their wells.

Following Joshua's conquest of the land, Beersheba regains its role as a central location in the national narrative of the people of Israel. From this point forward, Beersheba is depicted in Tanakh as the primary city of the Negeb, and it is consistently used to denote the southern extreme of the inhabited part of the Land of Israel. The phrase "from Dan to Beersheba" is found in Tanakh seven times, and the phrase "from Beersheba to Dan" appears twice, both times in Chronicles. While the various historical upheavals that befell the land and its people over the years rendered this usage irrelevant, this did not detract from Beersheba's importance as a city. Following the split between the kingdoms of Judah and Israel, we find the borders of the kingdom of Judah described as "from Beersheba to the hill country of Ephraim" (II Chr. 19:4). Additionally, the borders of Josiah's kingdom toward the end of the First Temple period, following the exile of the ten tribes, are listed as "from Geba to Beersheba" (II Kings 23:8).

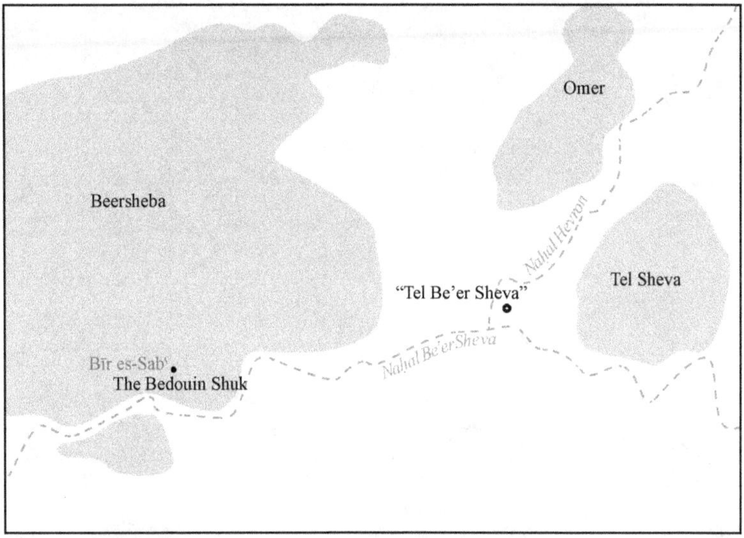

Further still, following the return to Zion, the Judean people lived "from Beersheba to the Valley of Hinnom" (Neh. 11:30). Beersheba, a place so intrinsically connected to the Patriarchs, had become the perennial capital of the South for their descendants.[1]

City of the Children

Today, Beersheba is a thriving Jewish city that ranks among the largest in Israel. It is the only city in Israel where one can find streets named for each one of the Patriarchs. Before the War of Independence, there was only a small Arab town known as Bīr es-Sabʿ, built in the late nineteenth century by the Ottomans atop a ruin that bore that name. By 1944, the city had a population of 3,700, and this number rose to about 6,500 by the start of the War of Independence. The city was conquered on Ḥol HaMoed Sukkot, October 21, 1948, its Arab residents fled, and Beersheba was once more a city belonging to the descendants of Abraham, Isaac, and Jacob. By early 1950, the Jewish population of Beersheba was 1,167, and in 2017 – 2018 it stood at around 215,000 (according to the municipality website). Today Beersheba is home to schools and yeshivas, one of Israel's major universities, several colleges, a prominent hospital, a

1. See map below.

(Tristram, 1865)

Bīr es-Sabʿ

rabbinical court and a regional court, industrial areas, a Bedouin market and modern malls, hotels, a high-tech complex, a large prison, community centers, a sinfonietta that plays for a 712-seat hall and *Glidat Be'er Sheva,* an ice cream factory that is almost as old as the state itself.

Biblical Beersheba – on Road Signs and in Scholarly Literature

Where is biblical Beersheba located? Generally, biblical Beersheba is identified with Tel Be'er Sheva, about three miles east of the Old

City of modern Beersheba, where the wadis Naḥal Hevron and Naḥal Beersheba meet. All the road signs refer to the site as Tel Be'er Sheva, as do most common encyclopedias, works of archaeological literature, and modern biblical commentaries – not to mention websites. The tell was excavated during the 1970s by Yoḥanan Aharoni, and, following his death in 1976, Ze'ev Herzog continued his work. Aharoni declared that Tel Be'er Sheva is "a location whose identification is not in doubt." An impressive array of finds was unearthed at the tell, primarily from the Israelite period, including strong fortifications, an elaborate water system, well-dressed stone blocks from a large horned altar and the deepest well in the Negev (226 ft.).

Tel Be'er Sheva is now a national park, as well as a UNESCO World Heritage Site. It is an extremely well-maintained site, with paths that are replete with clearly labeled signs explaining the archaeological finds. Partially preserved walls have been restored to their full original height, with precise indications distinguishing between what was found at the site and the restored sections. Visitors can view the deep well, as well as indentations from the rope that was used to draw water from the well in ancient times. Groups of children and teens often participate in hands-on activities, like pita baking in a traditional oven and making mudbricks using authentic materials.

Tel Be'er Sheva and Tel Sheva

A particularly perceptive driver on his way to this site might notice that alongside the brown "historical site" road sign that reads "Tel Be'er Sheva," there is another road sign that directs motorists to a Bedouin town called Tel Sheva. This town was established by Israel in 1968, was made a local council in 1984, and in the fall of 2015 had a population of 18,671 (according to Israel's Central Bureau of Statistics). But why is this Bedouin town called "Tel Sheva," while the ancient tell close by is called "Tel Be'er Sheva"? The answer is that "Tel Sheva" is the Hebrew version of the Arabic name "es-Sab‘," the Bedouins' name for the tell and its surroundings, which today include the modern Bedouin town itself.

Let us summarize what we know about the various names for these two locations. There are the Hebrew names: the city of Beersheba

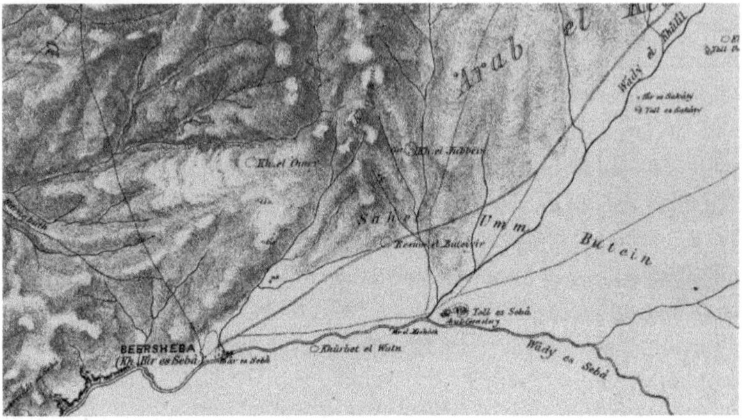

and the historical site Tel Be'er Sheva three miles east of the city. And there are the Arabic names: the city of Bīr es-Sabʿ and the tell (and town) of Tall es-Sabʿ three miles east of that city.

Turning now to Joshua 19, we encounter a surprising revelation. The first section of the chapter delineates the borders of the portion of land assigned to the Simeonites, in the Judean Negev ("The portion of the Simeonites was part of the territory of the Judahites" [19:9]). The list of the Simeonite cities begins: "The second lot fell to Simeon…Their portion comprised: Beersheba and Sheba and Moladah" (19:1–2). We see that the verse lists two distinct locations in close proximity to each other – Beersheba and Sheba. In light of the well-known fact that Arabs tend to preserve the original ancient names of many of the places in which they live, and in light of the existence of the Arabic pair Bīr es-Sabʿ and (Tall) es-Sabʿ and the biblical pair Beersheba and Sheba, it seems logical to assume that Bīr es-Sabʿ is Beersheba and (Tall) es-Sabʿ is Sheba. Sheba can also be found elsewhere in Joshua, in the list of cities in the Judean Negev (parallel, in part, to the list of Simeonite cities). There, it appears as "Shema": "Amam, Shema, Moladah" (15:26).[2]

Some commentators and scholars have posited that the phrase "Beersheba and Sheba" that appears in Joshua is actually referring to one location, and "Sheba" is either an alternate name for Beersheba or simply

2. Other examples where the letters *beit* and *mem* are interchangeable include Dibon-Dimon and Abanah-Amanah.

(Z. Radovan)

Tel Sheva ("Tel Be'er Sheva")

an unnecessary repetition of part of the name "Beersheba." This position helps provide a solution for a numerical problem in the text. At the end of the list of the first group of Simeonite cities, the verse states that there were "thirteen cities, with their villages" (19:6), but a quick count yields fourteen cities. If "Sheba" is not counted as a distinct city, this would bring the total down to thirteen, thus resolving the contradiction. In my opinion, however, nothing is gained by twisting the meaning of one verse in order to make sense of another. The simple meaning of the text is that Beersheba and Sheba are two different locations, a reading that is corroborated by both the parallel list in chapter 15 and the apparent preservation of the name as "es-Sabʿ."

The problem of the verse's reference to thirteen cities is beyond the scope of this discussion. Suffice it to say, though, that a more problematic contradiction of this type exists regarding the list of cities in the Judean Negev. Following Martin Noth and others, the solution seems to be that in desert and semi-desert regions, certain unwalled cities were mentioned in the list but not included in the final count, in which only walled cities were included.

The Archaeological View

From the archaeological point of view, Tel Sheva – the site that appears on Israeli road signs and maps as "Tel Be'er Sheva" – does not fit its depiction in Tanakh as one of the central cities in the Land of Israel. Its physical area is about 2.7 acres, which is quite small, especially in comparison to cities like Lachish, whose area is over thirty acres. In addition, Tel Sheva is not actually a tell in the archaeological sense. In archaeology, a tell is generally a fortification from the Middle Bronze (Canaanite) period, in which earth is piled up around a city, forming a trapezoidal shape. These tells preceded Joshua's conquest of the land.[3] In contrast, Tel Sheva dates from the Iron (Israelite) period, and more closely resembles an Israelite fortress than a tell, from a strictly archaeological perspective. While this Israelite fortress is certainly a thing of beauty, as well as the source of many fascinating finds, it is not Beersheba – it is Sheba.

This rejection of Tel Sheva as the identification for biblical Beersheba was proposed years ago by Professor Nadav Na'aman, a scholar with whose views I frequently disagree. This time, however, I believe that Na'aman is right. Some scholars did adopt Na'aman's position, but the predominant view among scholars – and with them, grant organizations, educational institutions, the Government Appellation Committee, the Nature and Parks Authority and mapmakers – was that Tel Sheva is indeed what remains of ancient Beersheba. Whether this was a result of Yoḥanan Aharoni's outstanding influence and authority as one of the leading

Prof. Nadav Na'aman, Tel Aviv University

3. See Josh. 11:13: "However, all those towns that are still standing on their mounds were not burned down by Israel."

speakers in the field, or because of the need to pinpoint a precise location in identifying the City of the Patriarchs, this became the accepted view.

In Beersheba, in the Bedouin *shuk* (marketplace) within the city proper, remnants of settlement from the Israelite period were found. Remnants from a walled city have yet to be discovered. There is no need to search for remnants from the Patriarchal Age, as the Torah implies that the Patriarchs lived not in a city but in tents near a well. Later in history, there was apparently a walled city here, and perhaps someday this will be found as well.

To summarize, I am certain that those who maintain that ancient Beersheba was located within the borders of modern-day Beersheba are correct. Conversely, the tell that road signs, maps, and the majority of the scholarly literature confidently label "Tel Be'er Sheva" is actually Tel Sheva, an Israelite fortress from the First Temple period.

In all likelihood, our Patriarchs – Abraham, Isaac, and Jacob – and their descendants, from the time of Joshua until the Second Temple period, lived in the vicinity of the modern city of Beersheba. This region was home to a fortified city during the Israelite period (that has yet to be found), and it was also home to Abraham's well and his tamarisk, and the altars built by Isaac and Jacob. The promise of "I will bless you and increase your offspring" (Gen. 26:24) that was made in Beersheba has come to fruition in our generation, in the tens of thousands of Jewish people living today in Beersheba and all throughout the Land of Israel.

For further study:

Aharoni, Y. "Excavations at Tel Beer-Sheba." *Biblical Archaeologist* 35 (1972): 111–127.

Aharoni, Y. "Excavations at Tel Beer-Sheba." *Tel Aviv* 1 (1974): 34–42.

Herzog, Z. "Tel Beersheba." *The New Encyclopedia of Archaeological Excavations in the Holy Land*, 1, 167–173.

Na'aman, N. "The Inheritance of the Sons of Simeon." *ZDPV* 96 (1980): 149–151.

Noth, M. *Das Buch Josua*. Tübingen, 1953, 93 [German].

Press, I. "Beersheba I." *Encyclopedia of Palestine*, I, 61–62 [Hebrew].

Parashat Vayeḥi

Goren Ha-Atad

The Problem

As we approach the end of *Parashat Vayeḥi*, we encounter a place called "Goren Ha-atad." This place raises a serious geographical difficulty.

Accompanied by a large delegation of Egyptians, Jacob's children leave Egypt in order to bury their father in Hebron:

> So Joseph went up to bury his father; and with him went up all the officials of Pharaoh, the senior members of his court, and all of Egypt's dignitaries, together with all of Joseph's household, his brothers, and his father's household; only their children, their flocks, and their herds were left in the region of Goshen. Chariots, too, and horsemen went up with him; it was a very large troop. When they came to Goren Ha-atad, which is beyond the Jordan, they held there a very great and solemn lamentation; and he observed a mourning period of seven days for his father. (Gen. 50:7–10)

When the mourning period was over, "his sons did for him as he had instructed them. His sons carried him to the land of Canaan, and buried him in the cave of the field of Machpelah … the field … near Mamre" (50:12–13).

Thus, the mourners' journey began in Egypt and ended in Hebron, stopping only in Goren Ha-atad to hold a "great lamentation" for Jacob.

It would seem logical, then, to search for Goren Ha-atad somewhere along the way between Egypt and Hebron – perhaps even in the vicinity of Hebron.

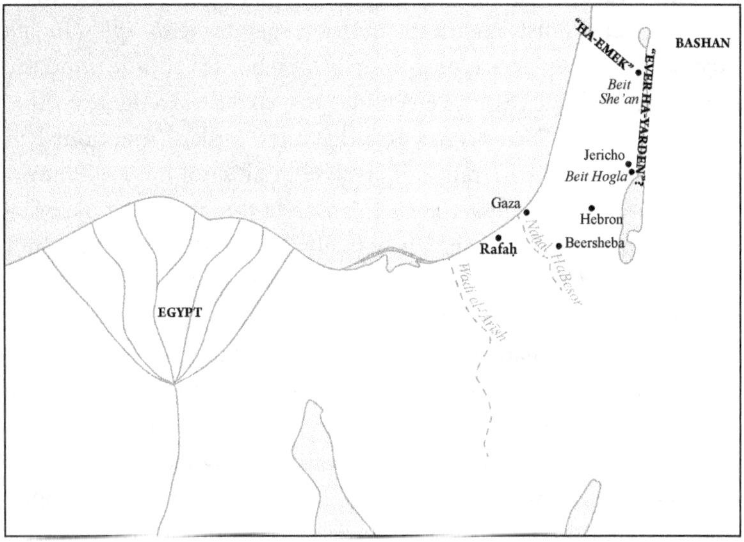

The problem is that the Torah places Goren Ha-atad elsewhere: "Goren Ha-atad, which is beyond the Jordan (*be-ever ha-Yarden*)… That is why it was named Abel-mizraim, which is beyond the Jordan" (Gen. 50:10–11). This is very strange: how did the mourners end up on the eastern side of the Jordan while traveling from Egypt to Hebron? It is somewhat surprising that most of the commentators, both classical and modern, seem unperturbed by this difficulty. In addition, the commentators who did raise this question posited solutions that are largely inadequate.

Ziv and Demsky's Solution

In 1960, Yehuda Ziv proposed an original solution to this problem, which was suggested again more comprehensively by Professor Aaron Demsky in a 1993 article. Demsky cites three chronologically disparate sources: the list of Shishak's conquests in the southern portion of Judah (no. 150), Josephus's *The Jewish War* (III, 3:5, 51) and a Christian chronicle written in Syriac recounting the Muslim conquest of the land in 634 CE. In each of these three sources there appears a place called "Jordan" (in Shishak's list: y-r-d-n; in Josephus: Iordan; in the Christian chronicle: *yrdn*) in southwest Israel. Shishak's list mentions Jordan together with *rpḥ (Rafiah, Rafaḥ)*, Josephus places it near the southern border of Judea, and the Syriac chronicle places it twelve miles east of Gaza. In light of these sources, Ziv and Demsky suggest that the "Jordan" mentioned in connection with the narrative of Jacob's burial is not the well-known Jordan River but this lesser-known Jordan in the southwest. Demsky explains that "Abel-mizraim" is actually "the wadi of Egypt,"[1] and "*be-ever ha-Yarden*" refers to a crossing (*ma'avar*) that the mourners used to traverse this wadi, which was located in the vicinity of "Jordan."

This is a brilliant and innovative theory, but unfortunately it is also unconvincing. Demsky himself admitted the unlikelihood of there existing in the Land of Israel not only two Jordans but also two separate places known as *ever ha-Yarden*. To solve this difficulty, Demsky suggested that this is a case of intentional wordplay. In my opinion, it is impossible to accept the notion that "the wadi of Egypt" referred to several different wadis over the course of history, and Demsky's interpretation of "*be-ever ha-Yarden*" seems dubious as well. It should be noted that Benjamin Mazar linked Josephus's "Iordan" to three other names: "yrḍ," which appears in the Annals of Thutmose III; "yurza," which appears in the Amarna letters; and "Orda," which appears on the Madaba Map. From a linguistic perspective, however, while the addition of the letter *nun* at the end of a word during the Second Temple period would be conceivable; dropping a *nun* from the end of a place-name during the biblical period is not. In addition, the linguistic interpretation of the word "Abel" to mean "wadi"[2] is somewhat contrived. In sum, I believe

1. This location appears several times throughout Tanakh (Num. 34:5; Josh. 15:4, 47; I Kings 8:65; II Kings 24:7; Is. 27:12; II Chr. 7:8). According to Demsky, "the wadi of Egypt" did not necessarily refer to the same wadi throughout history, and in our *parasha* it refers to Naḥal Ha-Besor.
2. Based on the word *yuval* (tributary), appearing in Daniel 8:2 in the form *uval*: "I was beside the Ulai River (*Uval Ulai*)."

that Ziv and Demsky's theory does not solve the problem, but only emphasizes its difficulty.

My Father *z"l*'s Solution

I would like to present a solution that I learned from my father, Professor Yehuda Elitzur *z"l*. He never managed to publish this idea in his lifetime, and I want to take this opportunity to do so on his behalf.

In order to understand my father's solution properly, we must first introduce two concepts, the first relating to the Tanakh's method of description, and the second relating to a certain term in the geographical terminology of Tanakh.

First, biblical descriptions. In general, when one studies Tanakh, he must be aware that the Tanakh does not describe things in the same way that historians do. Some information is described at length and in great detail in Tanakh that a historian might deem insignificant and disregard entirely. In contrast, there is material that may seem incredibly important to the objective reader that the Tanakh simply glosses over.

For example, we read that "the other events of Ahab's reign, and all his actions the ivory palace that he built and all the towns that he fortified – are all recorded in the Annals of the Kings of Israel"[3] (I Kings 22:39). The Annals of the Kings of Israel presumably dedicated many of its pages to the various wars and other exploits of Ahab, many of which the Tanakh does not deign to recount. Indeed, we only learn of the greatest war of Ahab's reign from an Assyrian account; the war seems to have been omitted entirely from Tanakh. In addition, "the ivory palace that he built" certainly sounds like an impressive building that Ahab would likely display to his visitors, but in the Book of Kings the palace is only mentioned here in passing, almost parenthetically. Instead of focusing on Ahab's military and architectural achievements, the Tanakh prefers to dwell on the story of Naboth the Jezreelite's vineyard, an incident that a historian might ignore.

In Genesis, there are several examples that fit this model. The long journey to Haran undertaken by Abraham's servant and his ten camels was certainly an arduous trek, complicated further by the problem of

3. This is considered a lost work.

finding food and water along the way. We can assume that they stopped at numerous wells in the course of their journey, but the Torah only tells us about the events surrounding one of them: the well at Haran. Clearly, this is not an objective historical account, but an account based on the narrative that the Torah intends to convey.

We are all familiar with the story of how Esau, exhausted from the hunt, sold his birthright to Jacob for a pot of lentil stew. However, this incident is surely not one to which any serious biographer or historian would devote significant attention. It may be that even the two brothers at that time saw it as a kind of joke between themselves.

But from the Torah's perspective, this is a highly important and symbolic exchange, and as such, it is presented in great detail.

Let us return now to the topic at hand. We read here that the delegation of mourners for Jacob consisted of chariots and horsemen, "a very large troop." The scope of this journey seems to more closely resemble that of a military operation than that of a mourners' procession. If we analyze the verses carefully, we will see that the delegation actually comprised two separate groups. One group consisted of Jacob's family: "Joseph's household, his brothers, and his father's household." The second group consisted of "the officials of Pharaoh, the senior members of his court, and all of Egypt's dignitaries," and with them, chariots and horsemen – a very large troop. In other words, it is a small group of Israelites traveling alongside a large Egyptian delegation. A close reading of the verses demonstrates that, following the mourning ceremony in Goren Ha-atad, Jacob's sons alone proceeded on to bury their father: "His *sons* did for him as he had instructed them. His *sons* carried him to the land of Canaan, and buried him in the cave of the field of Machpelah, the field… near Mamre, which Abraham had bought" (Gen. 50:12–13).

What perhaps seemed like a joint procession of Egyptians and Israelites was actually two separate delegations traveling alongside each other for the first leg of the journey. The Torah focuses on the actions of Jacob's sons, as well as on the large portion of the journey that was dedicated to mourning for Jacob. However, it seems very likely that the Egyptian delegation that set out to bury Jacob actually had an ulterior motive for its journey. While they certainly had great respect for

Jacob – they "bewailed him seventy days" (Gen. 50:3) and embalmed him as they would their most respected figures – the journey seems to have had a different purpose as well.

According to Egyptian sources, Egypt ruled over the land of Canaan during that period. To maintain their hold on the land, the Egyptians would set up garrisons in various locations. The most important of these garrisons were located in Beit She'an and Gaza, and each year the soldiers manning these garrisons would be replaced with fresh troops. Apparently, this annual changing of the guard would be accompanied by a large military delegation.

In light of this, the chariots, horsemen and "very large troop" from our *parasha* presumably served precisely this purpose: They set out from Egypt to take the place of the Egyptian forces who were manning the garrisons in the land of Canaan. The decision to implement this changing of the guard at that particular time was likely a result of various Egyptian military factors, but what interests the Torah is that this journey was integrated with the mourning ceremony for Jacob.

Let us turn now to the topic of biblical geographical terminology. The geographical term in question is *ever ha-Yarden*. In general, when we encounter this term in Tanakh, the verse specifies which side (*ever*) of the Jordan is being referred to. A scholar named Gemser investigated this question over sixty-five years ago and found twenty-four instances in which the expression *ever ha-Yarden* appears together with a geographical direction. Most often the reference is to the east side of the Jordan, and the word *mizracha* is appended to *ever ha-Yarden*, as in: "But we will not have a share with them in the territory beyond the Jordan, for we have received our share on the east side of the Jordan (*me-ever ha-Yarden mizracha*)" (Num. 32:19); "Those two and a half tribes have received their portions across the Jordan (*me-ever la-Yarden*), opposite Jericho, on the east, the orient side (*mizracha*)" (34:15); and "Then Moses set aside three cities on the east side of the Jordan (*be-ever ha-Yarden mizraḥa shamesh*)" (Deut. 4:41). Occasionally, the direction is west (*yama*), as in: "When all the kings of the Amorites on the western side of the Jordan (*be-ever ha-Yarden yama*)" (Josh. 5:1); and "the following are the local kings whom Joshua and the Israelites defeated on the west side of the Jordan (*be-ever ha-Yarden yama*)" (12:7).

In light of this evidence, it is worthwhile to investigate the cases in which the phrase *ever ha-Yarden* appears alone, without an east-west clarification. There are only a few examples in which this stand-alone phrase refers to Transjordan; indeed, it usually has another meaning entirely. A prime example can be found at the end of I Samuel:

> And when the men of Israel *asher be-ever ha-Emek vaasher be-ever ha-Yarden* saw that the men of Israel had fled and that Saul and his sons were dead, they abandoned the towns and fled; the Philistines then came and occupied them. (31:7)

The phrase *asher be-ever ha-Emek vaasher be-ever ha-Yarden* is usually translated as "on the other side of the valley and on the other side of the Jordan." However, from a geographical-historical perspective it is difficult to imagine that this verse is referring to the eastern side of the Jordan and the areas beyond the Jezreel Valley, since the Philistines never settled in those regions. Considering the geographical and historical context of the narrative in Samuel, the verse must be referring to the plains of the Jezreel Valley and the Jordan Rift Valley – on the western side of the Jordan River.

An example that has confounded translators and commentators can be found in the Book of Joshua: "When all the kings *asher be-ever ha-Yarden*, in the hill country, in the Shephelah, and along the entire coast of the Mediterranean Sea up to the vicinity of Lebanon heard" (9:1). Here, *be-ever ha-Yarden* – literally "beyond the Jordan" – certainly does not refer to Transjordan, but it cannot be referring to Cisjordan either. The events of this chapter and the following chapters occur on the western side of the Jordan and were written in the Land after the entire region had already been conquered; why, then, would the writer of this verse call his own location "beyond"? Based on the context, however, it seems that the verse is presenting a list of topographical regions of the land, similar to: "in the Arabah, the hill country, the Shephelah, the Negeb, the seacoast" (Deut. 1:7); "Joshua conquered the whole of this region: the hill country, the Negeb, the whole land of Goshen, the Shephelah, the Arabah" (Josh. 11:16); and "In the hill country, in the lowlands, in the Arabah, in the slopes, in the wilderness and in the Negeb" (12:8). If we view the verse in Joshua 9 in the context of these other lists, we get the impression that the phrase *be'ever ha-Yarden* does not function as a heading for the list of regions that follow, but instead refers to a distinct region in the Land of Israel. In other words, the punctuation following the phrase should be a comma ("*be-ever ha-Yarden,* in the hill country...") rather than a colon ("*be-ever ha-Yarden*: in the hill country..."), a parsing that is corroborated by the traditional cantillation marks associated with the verse. Furthermore, this new understanding can help us determine approximately to which region *ever ha-Yarden* refers. The one region found in each of the above lists, but missing from the list in Joshua 9, is the Arabah, the biblical name for the Jordan Rift Valley.[4] We can infer from this substitution of *ever ha-Yarden* for "Arabah" that *ever ha-Yarden* refers precisely to this region – the Jordan Rift Valley.

What is the linguistic background for the identification of *ever ha-Yarden* with the Jordan Rift Valley? Apparently, it can be derived from an example of *ketiv ukerei*[5] in II Samuel. The verse reads, "Look, I shall linger in the steppes of the wilderness (*be-arvot ha-midbar*) until word comes from you to inform me" (15:28). In the Masoretic text, however, the letters *resh* and *beit* in the word *be-arvot* are flipped and the word is spelled *be-avrot ha-midbar*. *Arvot-avrot* might be explained as metathesis (like *keves-kesev* and *simla-salma*). Thus, *ever ha-Yarden* can be understood to mean *arvot ha-Yarden* – the Arabah.

We read in Isaiah:

> Nevertheless this darkness shall not be the same as the affliction that came upon her when they lightly touched the land of Zebulun and the land of Naphtali, nor afterward when they more grievously afflicted her by the way of the sea, *ever ha-Yarden,* in Galilee of the Gentiles. (8:23)

The wording of the Hebrew text in this verse is somewhat vague so that one cannot be certain of its exact translation. Its historical context is also complicated and well beyond the scope of our discussion. However,

4. See the chapter on the first day of Sukkot.
5. Where the traditional pronunciation of a word conflicts with the Masoretic text

since the verse is dealing with regions in northern Israel, we can assume that *ever ha-Yarden* refers here to the Jordan Rift Valley, rather than the lands of Gilead and Bashan east of the Jordan River.

A most intriguing verse of this type is the opening verse of Deuteronomy: "These are the words that Moses addressed to all Israel *be-ever ha-Yarden*" (1:1). Ibn Ezra, in an enigmatic comment here, hints at a theological problem: Deuteronomy, along with the entire *Chumash*, was completed on the day of Moses's death in the plains of Moab, at which point the Levites were commanded to "take this book of teaching and place it beside the Ark of the Covenant of the Lord your God" (31:26). But if we understand "*be-ever ha-Yarden*" in Deuteronomy 1:1 to mean "the other side of the Jordan," then that seems to imply that this opening verse of Deuteronomy was written *after* the people of Israel had crossed the Jordan. Only once the people are situated west of the Jordan do the plains of Moab become "the other side."

According to our interpretation of *be-ever ha-Yarden*, however, there is no such contradiction. Since the phrase appears without a directional qualifier, the verse is essentially saying: "These are the words that Moses addressed to all Israel in the Jordan Rift Valley."[6] Verse 5 can be explained in the same manner: "In the plain of the Jordan (*be-ever ha-Yarden*), in the land of Moab," meaning, essentially, "in the plains of Moab."

Now let us return to Goren Ha-atad. The phrase *be-ever ha-Yarden* appears in our *parasha* as well, similarly without an accompanying direction: "When they came to Goren Ha-atad, which is *be-ever ha-Yarden*... that is why it was named Abel-mizraim, which is *be-ever ha-Yarden*" (Gen. 50:10–11). Thus, following our new understanding, we can conclude that the verse is not referring to the eastern side of the Jordan but to the Jordan Rift Valley. Goren Ha-atad, where the memorial ceremony for Jacob took place, was located somewhere in the Jordan Rift Valley, presumably on the *western* side of the Jordan River.

Support for placing Goren Ha-atad west of the Jordan can be found in verse 11: "The Canaanite inhabitants of the land saw the mourning." Throughout Tanakh, there is not one mention of Canaanites east

6. The end of the verse then highlights one particular section of the valley – "in the Arabah, near Suph."

of the Jordan. Canaanites are always portrayed as living on the western side of the Jordan, in the Jordan Rift Valley in particular, as we find in the story of the spies: "And Canaanites dwell by the Sea and along the Jordan" (Num. 13:29). In other words, the Jordan Rift Valley was the

Prof. Yehuda Elitzur z"l (1911–1997)

regional home of the Canaanites (one of the seven nations that lived in the land of Canaan).

To summarize, our *parasha* describes a large-scale Egyptian military expedition, an annual operation that involved numerous chariots and horsemen. The purpose of this expedition was to replace the troops manning the Egyptian garrisons throughout Canaan with fresh soldiers from Egypt.

Before each group of soldiers went off to its respective garrison, the delegation stopped at a central location – Goren Ha-atad – for seven days, where they also mourned the loss of Jacob, the father of the viceroy of Egypt. After this ceremony, the Egyptian troops all traveled to their designated garrisons, and Jacob's twelve sons departed for Hebron to bury their father.

Where Was Goren Ha-atad?

As we established, Goren Ha-atad was located somewhere in the Jordan Rift Valley. My father *z"l* speculated that it was in the general vicinity of Beit She'an, which was a major Egyptian military center during the time the Egyptians maintained a presence in the Land of Israel. At the time, Beit She'an also functioned as a kind of geographical midpoint in the land. From Beit She'an, roads branched out to the north, south, west, and even east, to the Bashan region where the Egyptians held important military outposts.

On the other hand, it is worth noting the existence of an ancient tradition that places Goren Ha-atad near Beit Hogla, southeast of Jericho. This tradition is mentioned by several early Christian sources: Eusebius, in the early fourth century CE in his *Onomasticon* (8:17), Epiphanius of Salamis; Jerome; and the Madaba Map. There is some substance to the claim that this tradition is rooted in Jewish sources as well, as there is a clear connection to a *midrash*. According to Eusebius, Halōn Atad (Goren Ha-atad) is now called Bethagla, meaning "place of circling," because "there (according to custom) they were circling in lamentation over Jacob." E. Z. Melamed noted the similarity between Eusebius's explanation and the following talmudic passage: "But is there a threshing floor (*goren*) for brambles (*atad*)? R. Abahu said: 'It teaches that they surrounded Jacob's coffin with crowns like a threshing floor that is surrounded by a hedge of brambles'" (Sota 13a). This connection is of special interest considering that R. Abahu and Eusebius lived during the same time period and in the same place: Caesarea in the early fourth century CE. Additionally, R. Abahu was a well-known figure, and he was held in high regard by the non-Jewish residents of Caesarea (Ketubot 17a and Sanhedrin 14a).

Goren Ha-atad on the Madaba Map (Z. Radovan). The map faces east. The main items are the Jordan River and the Dead Sea. Below the outlet of the Jordan into the Dead Sea two churches are visible. The lower church bears the caption "ΑΛΩΝ ΑΤΑΘ Η ΝΥΝ ΒΗΘΑΓΛΑ": "Halon Atath, which is now Bethagla."

Thus, it seems likely that the ancient tradition placing Goren Ha-atad in the Jordan Rift Valley, near Jericho, is actually a Jewish tradition as well. This tradition might fit with the theory we presented above regarding the main purpose of the Egyptian expedition to Goren Ha-atad.

For further study:

Demsky, A. "The Route of Jacob's Funeral Cortege and the Problem of *Eber Hayyarden* (Genesis 50:10–11)." Edited by M. Brettler and M. Fishbane. *Minḥah le-Naḥum: Biblical and Other Studies Presented to Nahum M. Sarna* (JSOT 154), Sheffield, 1993, 55–64.

Gemser, B. "*Beʿēber Hajjardēn*: In Jordan's Borderland." *VT* 2 (1952): 349–355.

Kasher, M. M. *Torah Shelema*, 7, 1870–1871 [Hebrew].
Mazar, B. *Cities and Districts in Eretz-Israel*. Jerusalem, 1976, 141–146 [Hebrew].
Melamed, E. Z. "The Onomasticon of Eusebius: An Introduction." *Tarbiz* 4 (1933): 256 [Hebrew].
Yahuda, A. S. *The Accuracy of the Bible*. New York, 1935, 39–40.
Ziv, Y. "*Yarden Levo Mitzrayim*." *Teva Va-aretz* II (1960): 412–413. Reprint: Y. Ziv, *Yalkut Gav: Iyyunim Bi-yedi'at Ha-aretz*, Jerusalem, 1991, 162–164 [Hebrew].

Exodus

Parashat Shemot

Ramesses and the Question of Dating the Exodus

Identifying Pithom and Ramesses

"And they built garrison cities for Pharaoh: Pithom and Ramesses" (Ex. 1:11).

Many have attempted to identify these two cities, and a large number of identifications have been suggested in the Nile Delta region in Egypt. It is fair to say that this question cannot be answered with certainty.

Part of the difficulty in answering this question lies in a fundamental difference between the Land of Israel and Egypt. In the Land of Israel, we encounter a phenomenon that might seem miraculous: a large percentage of the ancient place-names in the Land of Israel have been preserved by its residents until the modern era. When we returned to the Land of Israel, we found that Lod was called al-Ludd, Jaffa was called Yāfa, Bethlehem was called Bēt Laḥm, Haifa was called Ḥayfā and Acre was called ᶜAkkā. Thus, we were able to easily identify these locations, and many others as well, with a great degree of confidence.

This phenomenon did not occur in the lands of other ancient kingdoms or empires, like Egypt, Babylonia, and Turkey, where the ancient Hittite empire was located. In these lands, very few of the ancient names were preserved, and in general, the modern names are not reliable indicators for identification of ancient locations. In Egypt, place-names have been constantly changing throughout history, even into the modern era. Indeed, maps of Egypt from eighty years ago, forty years ago, and today feature significantly different sets of names.

Targum Yerushalmi identifies Ramesses as Pelusium, a famous city during the Hellenistic, Roman, and Byzantine periods. Pelusium was located on the eastern branch of the Nile, which dried up toward the end of the ancient period, and was a source of fine linen fabrics.[1] Today, Pelusium can be found east of the Suez Canal at a site known as Tell el-Farama, in a region that was called Balūza – this time actually preserving its ancient Greek name. However, this placement seems too far northeast to be an accurate identification for Ramesses. According to the Torah, Ramesses was located within the land of Goshen:

> Settle your father and your brothers in the best part of the land; let them stay in the region of Goshen… So Joseph settled his father and his brothers… in the choicest part of the land of Egypt, in the region of Ramesses, as Pharaoh had commanded. (Gen. 47:6–11)

We also learn that Ramesses was near the royal city: "Where you will be near me" (45:10); "He summoned Moses and Aaron in the night" (Ex. 12:31). Pelusium, in contrast, was situated outside the heart of Egypt. Additionally, the path between Pelusium and the land of Canaan does not pass anywhere near the Red Sea. Finally, nowhere in the vicinity of Pelusium have significant remnants been found from biblical times. Thus, it seems highly doubtful that Pelusium can be an accurate identification for Ramesses.

1. See Mishna Yoma 3:7: "In the morning he put on Pelusium linen worth twelve *minas*."

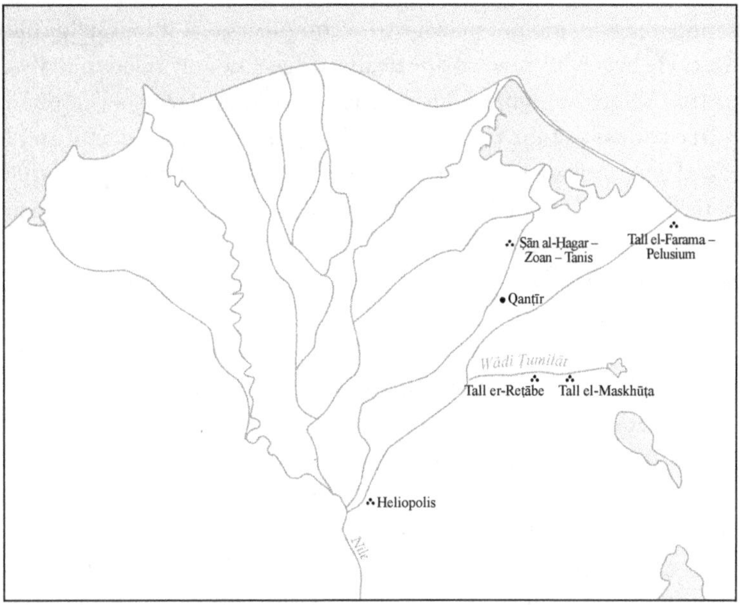

Many scholars identify Pithom and Ramesses as Tell el-Maskhūṭa and Tell er-Raṭābe, tells located west of Isma'iliya on the eastern side of the Delta. Other sites suggested as identifications for Pithom or Ramesses were further north, near Qanṭīr, and some even considered Tanis, even further north. One scholar strayed to the southwest, identifying Pithom as Heliopolis, a suburb of Cairo. Some of the sites suggested had already been identified as a different ancient location, and it would have to be assumed that the location possessed multiple names, either simultaneously or in different eras. Ultimately, it seems that the common denominator between all of these identifications is that they are all doubtful, and they all rely upon secondary considerations.

The Name "Ramesses"

The name Ramesses has critical implications for formulating the entire chronology of the biblical period. We know that there were several pharaohs called Rameses. The name first appeared at around 1300 BCE, at the start of the Nineteenth Dynasty of Egypt. No pharaohs used the name Rameses before this point, and from then on pharaohs began using the name in intermittent spurts. Rameses I was a monarch who did not manage to accomplish great things in his lifetime. He began his reign at an advanced age and only ruled for a year or two before appointing his son and heir Seti I (who was around thirty years old at the time) to rule alongside him. The reign of Seti I saw the renewal of a glorious period of conquests and Egyptian rule in the land of Canaan. This was the start of a new period of Egyptian hegemony in the Land of Israel and Syria following a period of decline. Seti I, who ruled for sixteen years, achieved great things on behalf of Egypt in western Asia.

The most interesting of all the pharaohs who took the name Rameses was Rameses II, who followed Seti I. Known as Rameses the Great, Rameses II is likely the most celebrated pharaoh in Egyptian history. First, he ruled for more than sixty-six years – longer than any other pharaoh. Such a lengthy reign may have been difficult for us to believe, if not for the existence of similarly long-reigning monarchs in modern times, such as Queen Victoria of the United Kingdom and Emperor Hirohito of Japan. Today Queen Elizabeth II, who has reigned since 1952, may yet break this record.

Rameses II began his reign at a young age, and ruled until he was elderly. He was a strong and forceful ruler, waging great wars and building extensively throughout the region. The first half of his reign was marked by great military conquests. Rameses recorded on the walls of temples and palaces more conquest lists in the land of Canaan and its surroundings than any other monarch. He also undertook numerous building projects, primarily in the second half of his reign. Among Rameses' many building achievements, one stands out in several Egyptian records: the construction of a city in his honor called Per-Rameses, or "the House of Rameses".[2]

Following Rameses II, many other pharaohs took on the name Rameses. The most important of these pharaohs was Rameses III of the Twentieth Dynasty. Rameses III was followed by many pharaohs with the same name, who were not particularly historically significant, and during whose reigns Egypt no longer ruled over foreign lands. The last of these pharaohs was Rameses XI, who ruled in the early eleventh century BCE. In all, Egypt was ruled by pharaohs named

2. *Per* is the Egyptian word for "house."

(Z. Radovan)

Rameses II – the pharaoh of the enslavement and the Exodus, according to the most common approach

Rameses for a total of 230 years. Rameses II was not only the greatest Rameses who ruled Egypt, but was also the greatest pharaoh in all of Egyptian history. He reigned for most of the thirteenth century BCE. There is some disagreement among scholars regarding the precise years of his reign, but it is clear that it began around 1300–1290 BCE and ended around 1230–1220 BCE, an extremely long period of rule for the strongest and most powerful pharaoh of all time. Furthermore, the reign of Rameses II is considered a kind of watershed moment in Egyptian history: there is the Classical period and there is the Ramesside period. His reign even is mentioned concerning the Egyptian language; there is a Ramesside dialect that has its own unique facets and nuances.

The parallel between the Rameses who appears in Egyptian sources and the Rameses who appears in Tanakh drew the attention of scholars. Many scholars assumed that if Rameses II reported that he built a city in his honor called "the House of Rameses," this certainly fits the Torah's description in the verse: "And they built garrison cities for Pharaoh; Pithom and Ramesses."[3] Thus, this notion has become very accepted, including in many historical atlases and encyclopedias, which state unequivocally that Rameses II was the pharaoh who enslaved the people of Israel and during whose reign the Exodus occurred.

The Tanakh's Chronology

A detailed historical debate on this topic is beyond the scope of this discussion. I will just explain briefly that this notion simply does not fit with the chronology that the Tanakh presents. According to the Tanakh, 480 years passed from the Exodus to the construction of the First Temple (I Kings 6:1), and other verses indicate that about four hundred years passed between the conquest of Canaan and the time of David.[4] David and Solomon reigned in the tenth century BCE, meaning that the Exodus took place around 1450 BCE and the conquest of Canaan

3. Truly, it should be noted that, according to Egyptian sources, there were several locations called "Ramesses."
4. See the list of years of the Judges, as well as the "three hundred years" (Judges 11:26) that Jephthah mentions. Also see the list of generations of high priests and Levite singers in I Chronicles 5–6.

occurred around 1400 BCE. The identification of the pharaoh of the Exodus with Rameses II would effectively cut the period between the Exodus and the conquest of Canaan in two.

(P. Lacau, 1909)

y-s-r-3-r "Israel" with the determinatives "nation" and "foreigners" in Merneptah's stele (c. 1220 BCE) – source and decipherment. In this stele, Israel is mentioned together with Gezer and Ashkelon, both with the determinative "place in foreign land."

Since we cannot accept this modified chronology in light of the Tanakh's account, we should resist the temptation to identify the pharaoh of the Exodus with Rameses II. The Torah refers to "the region of Ramesses" (Gen. 47:11) in the narrative of Joseph and his brothers, long before the enslavement. It seems that "the region of Ramesses" and the city of Ramesses preceded the rulers who took on this name[5] – and this should not surprise us. There is no linguistic evidence that suggests that the use of the name Rameses ("the god Re^{c} gives birth") only began with the pharaohs who bore this name. Apparently, the con-

5. According to the *mesora*, the name is vocalized four times as "רַעְמְסֵס" and once as "רַעַמְסֵס" (city and district; the pharaohs known by this name are not mentioned in the Tanakh). In English, it is common convention to spell the place "Ramesses" and the pharaohs "Rameses." KJV, following the masoretic punctuation renders (only in Ex 1:11) "Raamses." However, it seems that all the versions have one source.

nection between the names is coincidental; according to the Tanakh's chronology, the great accomplishments of Rameses II all took place during the period of the Judges, from the perspective of the people of Israel. The identified names in the lists of cities conquered by Seti I and his son Rameses II, as well as the later lists of Rameses III are generally either in Syria or along the coast and in the Jordan Rift Valley, in particular the towns that were situated along the "Via Maris." In other words, they conquered distinctly Canaanite regions whose inhabitants the people of Israel had never dispossessed throughout the period of the Judges. Apparently, the tribes of Israel, who lived irregularly in unwalled localities throughout the hilly and semi-arid regions of the land, were not an appropriate target for the Egyptian conquerors, who were eager to seize only valuable plunder. Because of this, the people of Israel were not mentioned in the Egyptian military records and in the lists of their conquests. Rameses II's heir Merneptah mentions Israel in his victory stele, which he had carved in the fifth year of his reign (circa 1220 BCE), along with Canaan and the Canaanite cities of Ashkelon, Gezer, and Yenoam; this is the first extra-biblical source that mentions Israel.

Responding to the Accepted Chronology

The later dating of the conquest and settlement of the Land of Israel was accepted by the majority of scholars for most of the twentieth century, and it was based primarily on three pillars: (a) The connection to Ramesses, presented above. (b) Archaeological evidence: The archaeology of the Land of Israel features an abrupt transition from the Bronze Age to the Iron Age. Fortified cities built atop tells were conquered and destroyed, often by intense fire. In their place, small villages sprouted up, meager in comparison to their predecessors and generally unwalled. Scholars dated this transition to around 1200 BCE, speculating that the people who destroyed the fortified cities and built simple towns for themselves were none other than the Israelites. According to the Tanakh's account, the people of Israel conquered the land by storm but quickly entered the period of the Judges, when there was no central leadership and the tribes of Israel were weak in relation to their neighbors. (c) Egypt's absence from the books of Joshua and Judges. According to Egyptian sources, Egypt ruled over Canaan for centuries,[6] their power in Canaan only abating after the reign of Rameses III. Thus, if Israel had entered the Land during those centuries, they would have had to deal with Egypt, rather than with the thirty-one Canaanite kings. If there had been some kind of agreement with Egypt allowing them to enter, it would mean that from a political perspective they had essentially never left Egypt.

The Tanakh's chronology, however, obviously does not fit all this. What, then, is the solution?

Let us first point out that the whole framework the scholars established in developing their chronology was somewhat phony to begin with; even the scholars' chronology is riddled with problems. With respect to the "third pillar" mentioned above, the people of Israel would have had to enter the land only after Rameses III, who reigned for thirty-two years and left a legacy of seven lists of conquests in the land of Canaan. The problem is that Merneptah, who died about twenty years before Rameses III's reign began, already mentioned the presence of Israel in the land. Furthermore, if the pharaoh who enslaved the people of Israel was Rameses II, how could they have managed to be already entrenched in the Land of Israel by the start of the reign of Merneptah, his heir? These problems forced the scholars to employ a technique that my father *z"l* called "contracting and stretching": On the one hand, they shortened the length of the enslavement, the Exodus, and the period of wandering in the wilderness so that these events could fit within the reign of Rameses II (writing off the "forty years" in the wilderness as a "typological number"); on the other hand, they stretched out the period of entry into the Land of Israel over the course of several decades, viewing it as a slow process that began before Merneptah and ended after Rameses III. They also went on to minimize the significance of Rameses III's conquests, painting a picture of a monarch who only struggled to defend his own land from the invasion of the Sea Peoples.

The solution to the archaeological question (the "second pillar") was developed by several archaeologists who refused to accept the

6. The Torah hints at this as well: "Both the land of Egypt and the land of Canaan languished because of the famine" (Gen. 47:13); "Chariots, too, and horsemen went up with him" (50:9).

conventional scholarship. I will attempt to explain this solution here in brief. Scholars of this period noticed an interesting phenomenon: Settlement in the Land of Israel in the Late Bronze Age is most prominent in the cities of the Shephelah, the coast, and the valleys, and even there settlement was, by and large, diminished compared to the Middle Bronze Age that preceded it. In contrast, in most mountainous areas, settlement in the Late Bronze Age is completely nonexistent. In light of this, members of the archaeological mainstream concluded that there was a settlement gap during that period (fifteenth–thirteenth centuries BCE) in the mountainous regions. The few scholars who stuck with the straightforward understanding of the Tanakh's chronology explained this archaeological phenomenon differently. According to these archaeologists, there was no settlement gap in the mountain cities during that period. Rather, the Iron Age – the Israelite period – began here earlier. The Canaanites continued to reside in the Shephelah, the coast, and the valleys; the people of Israel did not dispossess them "for they had iron chariots" (Judges 1:19). It was there that the "Late Bronze" culture began to develop, while the mountain regions saw the beginning of the material "Iron" culture, ushering in the Israelite period in the land.[7]

As for the "third pillar": According to the accounting of the Tanakh, the people of Israel entered Canaan and established themselves in the land over the course of the last hundred years of the Eighteenth Dynasty. This was a period of great decline for the Egyptian empire, during which Egypt lacked practical control outside its own borders. When Egypt regained its power and increased it further during the time of Seti and Rameses II – who, according to our chronology, reigned during the period of the Judges – the people of Israel consisted of a collection of meager mountainous tribes, of no interest to the marauding Egyptians. At that time, the pharaohs concentrated their efforts on international roads and the fortified Canaanite cities situated along these roads.

7. This discussion is connected to another, secondary discussion regarding the question of dating the transition from the Middle Bronze Age to the Late Bronze Age. Those interested in reading a more comprehensive analysis are encouraged to consult the bibliography.

Tuthmose III Temple gate in Upper Egypt (depiction from the nineteenth century CE). Tuthmose III (Eighteenth Dynasty, fifteenth century BCE) was one of the strongest kings of Egypt; he reigned 54 years. According to the biblical chronology, he was probably the pharaoh of the enslavement.

In terms of positive Egyptian evidence supporting our proposed chronology, I will briefly summarize the two most important historical points. First, according to our chronology, the kings of the Hyksos dynasty (who were Semitic in origin) were the ones who accepted Joseph and, later on, Jacob and his family. Their violent expulsion from Egypt may be hinted at in the verse, "A new king arose over Egypt" (Ex. 1:8). Second, the Amarna letters (written during the time of Amenhotep III and his son, Amenhotep IV, better known as Akhenaten) contain a possible eyewitness account of the Israelite conquest of the land of Canaan and the dread that gripped the Canaanites at the time.[8]

Finally, I feel the need to add that this entire discussion has become somewhat dated in recent years. Over the last two or three decades, a new fad has begun to dominate in academic settings: the complete denial of the historicity of the Tanakh as a whole. According to this approach, there was no enslavement and there was no Exodus; we did not conquer Canaan and we never set up judges and leaders; if David and Solomon did exist, they were marginal local leaders. The history of the nation of Israel began sometime in the middle of the period of the two separate kingdoms of Israel and Judah. When faced with such extreme positions, the distance between the two sides of the playing field in the age-old debate on the chronology of the Exodus and the conquest of Canaan becomes largely negligible.

Year (BCE)	Archeological period	Dynasty	Important pharaohs	Israel
~2000	Middle Bronze I			
~1700	Middle Bronze II B	*Hyksos*		
~1550	Late Bronze	*18*	Ahmose I – expulsion of the Hyksos Tuthmose III	
~1450			Amenhotep II	Exodus according to Tanakh
~1400			Amenhotep III – Amarna letters[En] Amenhotep IV = Akhenaten	Conquest of Canaan according to Tanakh

8. See the sources listed in the bibliography for more on the Amarna letters.

Year (BCE)	Archeological period	Dynasty	Important pharaohs	Israel
~1320		19	Seti I	
~1290			Rameses II	Exodus (accepted)
~1230			Merneptah – "Israel Stele"	Conquest of Canaan (accepted)
~1200	Iron I	20	Rameses III	
~1100	Iron II		Rameses XI	
~1070		21		
~1010				David
~970				Solomon – construction of First Temple

For further study:

Breasted, J. H. *A History of Egypt from the Earliest Times to the Persian Conquest.* New York, 1964.

Bimson, J. J. *Redating the Exodus and Conquest.* Sheffield, 1981.

Elitzur, Yehuda. "*Yetziat Mitzrayim Le'or Hahistoriya.*" *Israel and the Bible,* Ramat Gan, 2000, 51–53 [Hebrew].

Elitzur, Yoel. "*Al Ofnot Beḥeker Toledot Yisrael.*" *Al Atar* 7 (2000): 23–41 [Hebrew].

Garstang, J. "Chronology and Dates." *Joshua Judges,* London, 1931, 51–66.

Garstang, J. "The Hornet." *Joshua Judges,* London, 1931, 112–115.

Holladay, J. S. "Maskhuta, Tell el," *ABD* 4:588–591.

Meitlis, I. *Excavating the Bible.* Baltimore, 2012.

Wei, T. F. "Pithom," *ABD,* 5:376.

Wente, E. F. "Rameses (Place)," "Ramesses II." *ABD* 5:617–620

Parashat Va'era

People Named for Places

Places Named for People and People Named for Places

"The following are the heads of their respective clans. The sons of Reuben…The sons of Simeon…The sons of Levi…" (Ex. 6:14–19).

Among the names of the sons of Levi, we find one prominent place-name, which, in every other context, is a geographical location: "The sons of Kehath: Amram, Izhar, Hebron and Uzziel" (Ex. 6:18). Hebron, which, in every other context, is the name of a city, here is the name of a person – Levi's grandson. This phenomenon, where a person's name and a place-name are identical, is found numerous times throughout Tanakh. In these cases, either the person bears the name of the place or the place bears the name of the person. But which is it? Which came first: the person or the place?

On modern Israeli maps, we find many places named for people. In the late Second Temple period, several such place-names became established, some of which remained until today. These include Caesarea (for Augustus Caesar), Tiberias (for Tiberius) and Petza'el (for Herod's brother Phasael). Names of this type from the modern era include Herzliya (for Theodor Herzl), Netanya (for Nathan Strauss), as well as dozens of other names in memory of more or less prominent people, such as Kiryat Motzkin, Kfar Vitkin, Kfar Hess and Netzer Sereni. All these places were named for people.

Even in the opening chapters of the Torah, we find a prominent example of this phenomenon. The Torah says that Cain "founded a city, and named the city after his son Enoch" (Gen. 4:17). Other people in the Torah were named Enoch as well: "Ephah, Epher, Enoch, Abida, and Eldaah" (25:4). In our *parasha* as well, we read: "Enoch and Pallu, Hezron and Carmi" (Ex. 6:14). It is clear that in this case the personal name came first, and the place was named for it.

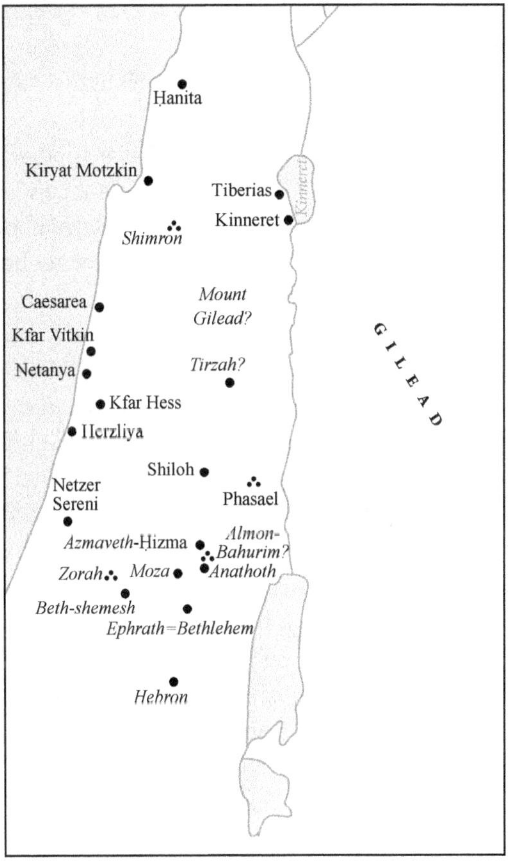

But concerning Levi's grandson Hebron, logic would dictate that the person was named for the place and not vice versa. This can be assumed from a historical perspective, since Hebron was settled by Abraham as early as *Parashat Lekh Lekha*: "And Abram moved his tent, and came to dwell at Elonei Mamre, which is in Hebron" (Gen. 13:18).

It is thus inconceivable that the city of Hebron was named for this Egyptian-born Levite who lived years after Abraham's journeys. From a linguistic perspective as well, the name Hebron bears a nominal pattern typical of many place-names across the country, such as Eglon, Heshbon and Ashkelon.[1] Thus, it is reasonable to conclude that, in this case, the person was named for the place.

Tribal Names

Before we begin to discuss this phenomenon, let us first familiarize ourselves with the phenomenon of tribal names in Tanakh. Some names pass from generation to generation within a particular tribe, while remaining exclusive to that tribe alone. Even today we are familiar with this phenomenon; in some families, a name like "Yissakhar" or "Zevulun" is common, while in other families these names have not been used for centuries.

Take, for example, the family of *nesi'im* in the tannaitic period; we find repeated alternating instances of the names Hillel, Simeon, Gamaliel, and Judah. These names recur generation after generation within this particular family; each new generation is given the name of one of his recent ancestors. This phenomenon even has a scientific name: patronym – name for one's father. The Tanakh features examples of this as well. In the list of family members in this *parasha*, we read of Korah's three sons: "The sons of Korah: Assir, Elkanah, and Abiasaph. Those are the families of the Korahites" (Ex. 6:24). Later, in the parallel list of Korahites in Chronicles, which includes the lineage of Samuel the prophet and Heman the singer, we find the name Elkanah three more times, precisely among the descendants of Abiasaph, the brother of the original Elkanah (I Chr. 6:7–22).

In the Book of Judges, we find a judge from the tribe of Issachar named Tola son of Puah (10:1). Tola is the name of one of the families of Issachar, and Puah/Puvah is the name of a different household within the

1. Wilhelm Borée, a scholar who investigated the patterns and meaning of place-names in the Land of Israel during the biblical period, enumerated eighty-four place-names with the ending -on. There are, however, people whose names use this nominal pattern as well.

tribe of Issachar (Gen. 46:13). It is clear that this judge came from the tribe of Issachar, and that both he and his father were named for two great households within the tribe.

In the tribe of Benjamin, we encounter Ehud son of Gera and Shimei son of Gera, who lived in two separate generations. Sure enough, Gera is one of the ten households of the tribe of Benjamin: "Gera, Naaman, Ehi, Rosh" (Gen. 46:21), and apparently two people in two different periods were both named for Gera, one of the forefathers of the tribe.

In all of Tanakh, there are only two people named Mephibosheth,[2] and they are related to each other: One was the son of Saul by his concubine (II Sam. 21:8) and the other was Mephibosheth son of Jonathan, "whose feet are crippled" (9:3), the nephew of the original Mephibosheth.

Jeremiah clashed with a priest named Pashhur son of Immer (Jer. 20:1). Pashhur is the name of one of the priestly divisions (an alternate name for the division of Jakim) and Immer is the name of a different priestly division.[3] This priest, who was the "chief officer in the House of the Lord," could equally have been from any other division as well.

Similarly, we read in Esther: "In the fortress Shushan lived a Jew by the name of Mordekhai, son of Jair son of Shimei son of Kish, a Benjaminite" (2:5). We are familiar with the Benjaminite names Shimei and Kish from the time of Saul; in fact, Saul and the Shimei of his time were distant relatives ("a member of Saul's clan" [II Sam. 16:5]). The Book of Esther takes place in the generations after the Exile. According to the simple understanding of the text, "Kish, a Benjaminite" was exiled from Jerusalem along with King Jeconiah of Judah. Now, four generations later, Mordekhai is born in Shushan.[4]

2. Originally Merib-baal (I Chr. 8:34, 9:40); all names that include the root *baal* are altered in the Book of Samuel.
3. See I Chr. 24:7–18; Ezra 2:36–39; 10:20, 22; Neh. 7:39–42.
4. Compare to Zerubbabel, who was probably four generations removed from his ancestor King Jeconiah of Judah; see I Chr. 3:17–19. A similar context, in which a historical note relates to the first generation on a list, is "And Ahiah, the son of Ahitub, Ichabod's brother, the son of Phinehas, the son of Eli, the LORD's priest in Shiloh, wearing an ephod" (I Sam 14:3); Eli had been the the priest in Shiloh and Ahiah was now wearing an ephod.

In all these examples, and in many other instances as well, it is clear that the name in question is a tribal name that can appear in different generations, in any family within the tribe. This straightforward understanding of the text runs parallel to the reality that we find in many cultures throughout history, and reflects a wholly understandable phenomenon. Nevertheless, we must stress the existence of this phenomenon, because alternate approaches to the question of repeated names abound. In midrashic sources there is a tendency to conflate different characters with the same name into one. For instance, the Talmud cites an *aggada* that claims that the Shimei that appears in Mordekhai's lineage is the same Shimei who cursed David as he fled from his son Absalom (Megilla 13a).

Surprisingly, many Bible scholars advocate this same aggadic approach, often formulated in critical language. For instance, Shmuel Aḥituv writes: "According to Genesis 46, Numbers 26 and I Chronicles 7, Tola was Puah's brother; but according to Judges 10, Tola was Puah's son." In a more extreme manifestation of this approach, Yairah Amit writes: "The details on Tola son of Puah, who lived at Shamir, seem to indicate that this was a fictitious personality, a personification of the families of Issachar: Tola, Puvah, Jashub, and Shimron." According to Jacob Liver in Encyclopedia Biblica, as well as according to *Daat Mikra* on Judges and Samuel, Ehud son of Gera and Shimei son of Gera were merely members of the household of Gera. It is not that their fathers' names were both Gera, but rather that the phrase "son of Gera" refers to their broader family heritage. This begs the question: Why should these people be any different from all the rest of their contemporaries, who were frequently and consistently mentioned with their fathers' names – such as "Joshua son of Nun," "Saul son of Kish" or "David son of Jesse"?

In the opening to the narrative of Jephthah, we read:

> Jephthah the Gileadite was an able warrior, who was the son of a prostitute. Jephthah's father was Gilead; but Gilead also had sons by his wife, and when the wife's sons grew up, they drove Jephthah out. They said to him, "You shall have no share in our father's property, for you are the son of an outsider." (Judges 11:1-2)

The name "Gilead" is well known: it is the name of the family's early forefather, Gilead son of Machir son of Manasseh, as well as the name of the region where Jephthah lived. The simple explanation – that in the middle of the period of the Judges, the family name Gilead was given to a certain member of the family who lived in the Gilead region – for some reason seems inconceivable to Bible scholars. German theologian Bernhard Stade took the literary-anthropological route, explaining that Gilead here refers to the tribe of Gilead, which produced Jephthah and his household. Jephthah's household was inferior in status among the other households, as manifested in the words "the son of an outsider." American scholar George Foot Moore proposed a more inventive solution. According to Moore, the original text read, "Jephthah the Gileadite was an able warrior, and Jephthah fled from his brothers…Jephthah replied to the elders of Gilead, 'You are the very people who rejected me and drove me out of your midst.'" The original intent of the text was to portray Jephthah as a man of the Gilead region, and "his brothers" as the local residents and his extended family. A later editor who did not understand what he was reading thought that "the Gileadite" meant "the son of Gilead," and "his brothers" meant his literal brothers. Therefore, he added extra verses to the original text, by way of (inaccurate) commentary.

Strikingly, just like in the other examples, here too the solutions offered by scholars and modern Bible critics fall unexpectedly in line with positions found in early *midrashim*. We, on the other hand, will dispense with speculations and homiletics and follow the words of the Tanakh themselves, which demonstrate clearly that tribal names existed among the people of Israel.

Names of People and Names of Places

I will begin with two preliminary remarks. First, there are several lists of family members throughout Tanakh, particularly in descriptions of the early periods, in which names of different nations and ethnic groups are often interwoven. For example: "And Mizraim begot the Ludim, the Anamim, the Lehabim, the Naphtuhim, the Pathrusim, the Casluhim and the Caphtorim, whence the Philistines came forth" (Gen. 10:13–14); and "The descendants of Dedan were the Asshurim, the Letushim, and the Leummim" (25:3). But there is no reason to broaden this genre as various scholars have done, applying its attributes to normal lists of family ties in Tanakh, where the name of a man and the name of his father are actually no more than what they appear to be. Second, the phrase "father of..." commonly found in the "family tree" chapters in the Book of Chronicles, is always followed by the name of a city in which the subject of the verse established settlement. For instance, we find: "father of Bethlehem" (I Chr. 2:51), "father of Kiriath-jearim" (2:50) and "the father of Birzaith" (7:31). This is a unique usage and not just a casual integration of a place-name within a list of people's names.

Let us now return to the topic of people who were named for geographical locations. If we understand that tribal names existed during the biblical period, passed down through the generations in honor of the tribal forefathers or simply because these were the popular names within a particular tribe, it should not surprise us that some tribe members were named for geographical locations within their tribe's territory. We find among the sons of Issachar the name Shimron (Gen. 46:13; Num. 26:24; I Chr. 7:1), which is also the name of a city bordering the territories of Issachar and Zebulun (Josh. 12:20; 19:15). We also find in the lists of Judah the name Ephrath (I Chr. 2:19), which is more commonly known as an early name for Bethlehem, in Judea. In the same vein, it is not outside the realm of possibility that the great warrior Samson, who was born in Zorah, was named for the neighboring city of Beth-shemesh. Scholars have noted the connection between the two names, but used this connection to advance their romantic-critical claims that Samson was a kind of mythological figure representing sun (*shemesh*) worship. I recall a panel discussion broadcast on the radio decades ago in which Yigael Yadin and my father *z"l* participated. When Yadin connected Samson with sun worship, my father challenged him in response: Does this mean that the modern last name Sonnenfeld ("field of sun" in German) is connected to sun worship as well? According to my claim, it is quite reasonable to connect Samson with Beth-shemesh, but the connection is a purely human one. It may very well be that the city of Beth-shemesh was named at the dawn of history for an ancient sun temple, but when Samson was named for the city, this was an act of pure tribal patriotism without any mythological or ritual connotations. By Samson's time, the connection to paganism had been long since forgotten.

Even today, people in Israel are still being named for places. People give their children names like Ḥanita, Kinneret, or Shiloh to express the spiritual connection that they feel to these places. The difference between this modern phenomenon and the parallel phenomenon in the biblical period is that today there is no geographic or familial element that limits the use of certain names to a particular tribe. In the biblical period, tribal attitudes dominated the people's way of life, which explains why they named their children for place-names within their tribal territory.

The tribe of Benjamin was extraordinary in this regard. If we look at the Benjaminite family listing in I Chronicles, we find among the descendants of King Saul: "And Ya'arah begot Alemet, Azmavet, and Zimri; Zimri begot Moza" (9:42). The people mentioned here were seven or eight generations removed from Saul. It was now the middle of the period of Israelite monarchy, by which time Israelite settlement in the land of Benjamin was already centuries old, and in such a case one would not expect new settlements to be established there. Yet we find that Alemeth is a place-name in the Benjamin region, known today as Khirbet Almit; Azmaveth is a place in Benjamin as well, likely located in modern-day Hizma; the name Zimri was preserved in the name of a wadi below Pisgat Ze'ev called Wadi Zimra; and Moza is Motza, a formerly agricultural colony and now a neighborhood on the western edge of Jerusalem.[5] Some scholars may still claim that geographical names got "mixed into" the Benjaminite family listing, but once again, the biblical text here speaks for itself. If we take the text as it is, this is a clear example of the phenomenon of people named for places. Two particularly interesting examples are one Benjaminite named "Anathoth" (7:8) and another with the unique name "Anthothiah" (8:24). Incidentally, many

5. The name Moza is most probably a shortening of *moza mayim* ("spring of water"), called after the nearby fountain. In the time of the Second Temple, willow branches were brought from Moza to the Temple on Sukkot. See Mishna Sukka 4:5: "There was a place below Jerusalem called Moza. They went down there and gathered from there young willow branches."

scholars believe that the place-name Anathoth, upon which the names of these Benjaminites were based, was pagan in origin. The Benjaminites were certainly not aware of this, and were not interested in such matters in any case. From their perspective, to name someone Anathoth (or Anthothiah, by adding the theophoric ending *yod-he*) was an expression of pride and admiration for an esteemed location in their territory. In the variant Anthothiah in particular, its form demonstrates that we are dealing here with a person's name that was derived from a place-name and not vice versa – and surely not that the person was "representing" the place-name.

Saul's daughter Michal was given as a wife to Palti son of Laish from Gallim (I Sam. 25:44). However, it turns out that Laish and Gallim are two adjacent locations in the Benjamin region (see Is. 10:30). What this means is that Palti's father lived in Gallim and was named for the neighboring town of Laish. And one more Benjaminite example: One of David's warriors was named Azmaveth the Bahrumite (I Chr. 11:33; II Sam. 23:31), who came from Bahurim but was named for a different place in the Benjaminite territory.

As we have mentioned, members of the tribe of Manasseh were also named for places. Gilead son of Machir son of Manasseh was obviously named for Mount Gilead on the eastern side of the Jordan. But in an entirely different generation, during the period of the Judges, one of his descendants was given this name as well – the father of Jephthah the Gileadite: "Jephthah's father was Gilead" (Judges 11:1). The original Gilead's sons and grandsons settled in both Gilead and Samaria (Num. 26:30–33; Josh. 17:5–6). A mountain named Gilead on the western side of the Jordan appears once in Tanakh (Judges 7:3; 12:4 as well according to *Daat Mikra*), and it may be speculated that this less-renowned Mount Gilead was named for one of the original Gilead's descendants who bore that name.

Among the descendants of Manasseh we find the name Tirzah, which is the name of an important city mentioned in the list of Joshua's conquests: "the king of Tirzah, one" (Josh. 12:24). Tirzah was even the capital city of Israel for a period of time. Similarly, Tirzah's grandfather was named Hepher, which is the name of another city-kingdom conquered by Joshua: "the king of Hepher, one" (12:17).

The most interesting point is that the people mentioned here, including Gilead son of Machir son of Manasseh and including Hepher and Tirzah his granddaughter, were all born in Egypt. This observation led my father *z"l* to propose a novel suggestion: Even as the descendants of Jacob were exiles in Egypt, they maintained a connection to locations in the Land of Israel, and apparently in particular to locations designated to become part of their respective territories. In other words, even before Jacob's family descended to Egypt, there was already a basic plan for dividing the land into territories, and their knowledge of this planned division motivated them to name their children for locations designated for them.

It seems that Hebron, with whom we opened this discussion, was a product of this approach as well. Here was an Egyptian-born Israelite who bore the name of the revered city of the Patriarchs – Hebron. Incidentally, Hebron the man was a Levite, and the city of Hebron was both a city of refuge and a Levite city; it functioned, essentially, as a city of Priests. Hebron, the uncle of Moses and Aaron, was apparently named in Egypt as a symbol of longing for Hebron, city of the Patriarchs, to which we, their descendants, have merited to return.

For further study:

Ahituv, S. "Tola." *Encyclopaedia Biblica* 8, 466 [Hebrew].

Amit, Y. *Judges: Introduction and Commentary* ("Bible for Israel" series). Tel-Aviv/Jerusalem, 1999, 181 [Hebrew].

Borée, W. *Die alten Ortsnamen Palästinas*. Hildesheim, 1968, 57–61.

Elitzur, Y. "*Anashim Venaḥalot BiMenashe Uveshivtei Yisrael.*" *Al Atar* 4–5 (1999): 243–249 [Hebrew].

Kahane, T. "The Priestly Courses and Their Geographical Settlements." *Tarbiz* 48 (1979): 9–29 [Hebrew].

Liver, J. "Relation." *Encyclopaedia Biblica* 3, 66 [Hebrew].

Moore, G. F. *A Criticial and Exegetical Commentary on Judges*. (ICC), Edinburgh, 1989, 284–285.

Pike, D. M. *Israelite Theophoric Personal Names in the Bible and their Implications for Religious History*. Pennsylvania, 1990, 199–201.

Parashat Bo

The Land of Goshen

Where Is the Land of Goshen?

"But on that day I will set apart the land of Goshen, where My people dwell…that you may know that I the Lord am in the midst of the land" (Ex. 8:18). The people of Israel lived in the land of Goshen from the time they descended to Egypt until the time they left it. Immediately after Joseph revealed himself to his brothers, he invited his father and the entire family to the land of Goshen: "You will dwell in the land of Goshen, where you will be near me – you and your children and your grandchildren, your flocks and herds, and all that is yours" (Gen. 45:10). Indeed, while the family was still en route to Egypt, Judah was sent ahead to prepare accommodations for the family in Goshen: "He had sent Judah ahead of him to Joseph, to point the way before him to Goshen. They came to the land of Goshen" (46:28). But where is this land of Goshen, where the people of Israel lived?

One hint to Goshen's location is in the message that Joseph sent to his father: "You will dwell in the land of Goshen, where you will be near me." We see from this that Goshen must have been close to the centers of the Egyptian government. We read in Exodus that the location among the reeds by the bank of the Nile where Jochebed placed the basket containing the infant Moses was near Pharaoh's palace, where Pharaoh's daughter went to bathe. In the context of the plagues as well, we read of the direct connection between Moses and Pharaoh, which reaches a climax during the plague of the firstborn: "He summoned Moses and Aaron in the night and said, 'Up, depart from among my people'" (Ex. 12:31). The description of this scenario demonstrates once more that the people of Israel lived in close proximity to Pharaoh.

The land of Goshen bore another name as well – Ramesses. Even as early as Genesis, the Torah recounts that Joseph settled his father and brothers "in the choicest part of the land [of Egypt], in the land of Ramesses" (47:11). When the period of enslavement began, the people of Israel built "garrison cities for Pharaoh: Pithom and Ramesses" (Ex. 1:11), and the Exodus, described in our *parasha*, begins in Ramesses: "The Israelites journeyed from Ramesses to Succoth" (12:37).

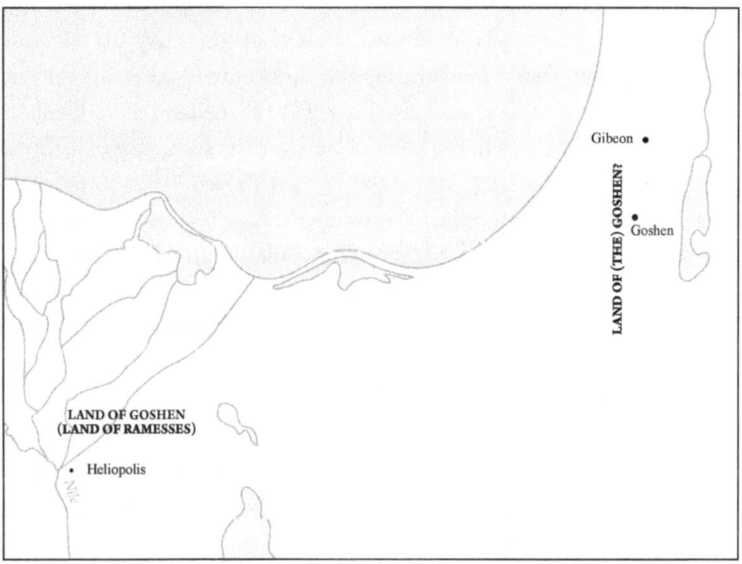

Ancient Egypt was shaped like a kind of long sausage, following the Nile from the heights of the south to the Mediterranean Sea in the north. Near Heliopolis, in the vicinity of modern Cairo, the Nile splits into tributaries, forming a triangular shape. The Greeks called the land within this triangle the "Delta," due to the region's similarity to the shape of the Greek letter delta. The Nile Delta is known as "Lower Egypt," and its Egyptian hieroglyph was a wasp or a bee. Pithom and Ramesses have not been identified with certainty, but it is reasonable to assume that they were located within the Delta, apparently on its eastern portion.[1]

Goshen in the Land of Israel

What is known, from a linguistic perspective, about the name "Goshen"? Attempts to ascribe Egyptian or Semitic etymological roots to the name have not been fruitful. It is worth noting, however, that the name "Goshen" appears in a non-Egyptian context three times in the Book of Joshua – as locations in the Land of Israel. Apparently, there were two different Goshens in the Land of Israel at the time, both located in Judea. One was a city and the other was a "land," more accurately a region, similar to the "land" of Goshen in Egypt. The city of Goshen is enumerated in the southwestern group of cities in the region of southern Mount Hebron, along with Jattir, Debir, Anab, Eshtemoh, and Anim (Josh. 15:48–51). In contrast, the land of Goshen – also referred to as the land of *the* Goshen – is the name of a region in the Land of Israel. In the summary of Joshua's conquests in the southern part of the Land, we read: "Thus Joshua conquered the whole country: the hill country, the Negeb, the Shephelah, and the slopes ... Joshua conquered them from Kadesh-barnea to Gaza, all the land of Goshen, and up to Gibeon" (10:40–41). Later, in the general summary, we read: "Joshua conquered the whole of this region: the hill country [of Judah], the Negeb, the whole land of the Goshen, the Shephelah, the Arabah, and the hill country and coastal plain of Israel" (11:16).

Rabbi Yisrael Ariel, in his atlas of the borders of the Land of Israel (following the commentary of *Daat Zekenim Mibaalei HaTosafot* on Genesis 46:29, and a *derash* cited critically by Radak in his commentary on Joshua 11:16) includes the Egyptian Goshen within the borders of the Land of Israel, stretching the territory of the tribe of Judah to the point where it reaches the Nile Delta! This detail is possibly the most extreme of his generally maximalist positions regarding the borders of the Land. I believe that this kind of view is patently impossible. The idea that Joshua could have conquered land in the eastern Nile Delta from the Canaanites is perplexing. As we will explain in the chapter on *Parashat Mishpatim*, the borders of the tribal territories fall within

1. See the chapter on *Parashat Shemot* and map there.

the smaller version of the Land's borders. These borders reach in the southwest to the "wadi of Egypt," whose identification with modern-day Wadi el-Arish is reasonable and accepted.

Most modern commentators and scholars of biblical geography maintain that the land of Goshen mentioned in Joshua 10–11 refers to the territorial area of the city of Goshen mentioned in chapter 15. Nevertheless, this view does not make sense for a number of reasons:

- The city of Goshen was a small city, mentioned only once in Tanakh, and its territorial area certainly did not exceed a few square miles. In its vicinity lay the well-known cities of Debir, Anab, and Eshtemoh. The area of southern Mount Hebron was certainly named for these cities rather than for Goshen.
- The land of Goshen in the summaries of Joshua's conquests is a vast region, mentioned alongside the hill country, the Shephelah, the Arabah, the Negeb, and the slopes. The "hill country" refers to the mountainous region of Israel, the Shephelah is what is known today as the "inner Shephelah," the Arabah is the Jordan Rift Valley and the Dead Sea, the Negeb refers to the northern Negeb region, and "the slopes" are the steep, rocky slopes of the east. The only region remaining in the land where the land of Goshen can possibly be placed is the western hillside region between the mountains and the Shephelah, which, as the verse specifies, extends to Gibeon at its northern end.
- An important linguistic consideration, discerned by John Gray in 1967, is the use of the definite article in Joshua 11:16 – "the whole land of *the* Goshen (*Eretz Ha-Goshen*)." As a rule in Biblical Hebrew, and to a great extent in Modern Hebrew as well, the regions of the land are referred to using the definite article: *the* Negeb (*Ha-Negev*); *the* Sharon plain (*Ha-Sharon*); *the* Galilee (*Ha-Galil*); *the* Lebanon (*Ha-Levanon*); *the* Carmel region (*Ha-Karmel*); *the* Bashan (*Ha-Bashan*); *the* Gilead (*Ha-Gil'ad*). What we see from this is that Goshen belongs to this same family of names, and like the other items on this list, it too is apparently an ancient Semitic name for a large geographical area. It has a three-letter root, and it is formed from a common nominal

pattern. Although we do not have the slightest idea how to understand the meaning of this root (suggestions proposed by scholars connecting Goshen to the root G-W-Š or to the name Geshuri are unlikely), we can estimate that it expresses something connected to the topographic scenery or to the agriculture of the region, or perhaps to the manner in which animals were raised. Apparently, the same geographical characterization existed in the eastern Nile Delta as well.

Hebrew Names in Egypt?

It should come as no surprise that a Hebrew-Canaanite name existed in the eastern part of Lower Egypt. In the main part of Egypt, the place-names are always Egyptian (examples mentioned in Tanakh include No-Amon, Tahpanhes, On, Moph, and Syene). However, in northeast Egypt we find a number of Hebrew or Canaanite names, including Succoth, Migdol, Baal-zephon and apparently Etham, and in the neighboring desert to the east we find the Semitic names Marah and Elim. In the same vein, the oldest known record of the Hebrew alphabet (from the Middle Bronze Age) was found in the site Serabit el-Khadim in the western Sinai Peninsula. Apparently, the Hebrews and the Canaanites left their mark – even from ancient times – on the local place-names in this region. Roads originating in this region lead directly to the land of Canaan, which the Book of Genesis (referring to at least part of the land) calls "the land of the Hebrews" (40:15).

The strip of land where the people of Israel lived in Egypt had two names, one Egyptian – Ramesses, and one Hebrew – Goshen. This was certainly a result of the region's location: between the center of Lower Egypt and the eastern border between Lower Egypt and the Semitic lands.

There is a symbolic message in the language of the verse, "The Israelites journeyed from Ramesses to Succoth" (Ex. 12:37). Ramesses is an Egyptian name, meaning "child of the god Re^{c}," the sun god. Succoth, on the other hand, is a Hebrew name. The first step of the journey from Egypt undertaken by the people of Israel symbolized the transition from the Egyptian experience to the Israelite experience: "For the Egyptians whom you see today you will never see again" (14:13). From now on – from a linguistic perspective as well – you are in a Hebrew world, the first step on the path to "when you have freed the people from Egypt, you shall worship God at this mountain" (3:12).

For further study:

Ariel, Y. *Atlas Eretz Yisrael Ligvuloteha al pi Hamekorot.* Jerusalem, 1993, 85–85 [Hebrew].

Baumgartner, W. and J. Stamm. *The Hebrew and Aramaic Lexicon of the Old Testament.* Leiden-New York-Köln, 1994, 205–206.

Brawer, A. J. "*Eretz Goshen Shemimizrach LaDelta.*" *Beit Mikra* 28 (1966): 91–92 [Hebrew].

Cooke, G. A. *The Book of Joshua.* Cambridge, 1918, 98.

Gray, J. *Joshua, Judges and Ruth* (The Century Bible). London, 1967, 116.

Kil, Y. *Joshua, Daat Mikra.* Jerusalem, 1970, 81 [Hebrew].

Loewenstamm, S. "Goshen 1"; B. Mazar, "Goshen 2." *Encyclopaedia Biblica,* 2, 569–570 [Hebrew].

Levin, Y. "The Land of Goshen, Gibeon: the Southern Frontier of the Early Monarchy." *Maarav* 10 (2003): 195–220.

Parashat Beshallaḥ

The War of Deborah and Barak: A Different Geographical Perspective

The Historical Significance of the Victory over Sisera and His Army

In the *haftara* of *Parashat Beshallaḥ*, we read the story of the remarkable victory of the people of Israel, under the leadership of Deborah and Barak, over Sisera, the army commander of King Yavin of Canaan. This was a war of liberation that carried historical significance for generations to come. In order to understand the context of this narrative, let us contemplate our own generation for a moment. The divine process in which we have participated of the return of the nation of Israel to its land began more than two hundred years ago, reaching climaxes that were unprecedented in history with the establishment of the State of Israel and the War of Independence, the miracles of the Six-Day War, and the salvation of the Yom Kippur War. Through all these years, we have defended ourselves against the same, unchanging enemy: the Arabs who live in the Land and their neighbors in the surrounding countries. Indeed, it is difficult to imagine a change in this fundamental status quo in the foreseeable future.

Returning to Tanakh, we find that our ancestors who lived in the Land had a constant enemy as well: the Canaanites, for whom the land was named "the land of Canaan." From the initial arrival of Abraham to this land, the Canaanites were here – "the Canaanites were then in the land" (Gen. 12:6). When the people of Israel returned under Joshua's leadership more than four hundred years later, they found the land in the same state. The conquest of the land left Canaanite enclaves, both large and small, and when the power of the tribes of Israel waned in the period of the Judges following the death of Joshua and the elders, the Canaanites reared their heads. From their perspective, the time had come for them to restore their former glory, and they proceeded to crown King Yavin as ruler of the northern part of the land.

But there is a twist to our story. After the victory over Sisera, we read, "The hand of the Israelites bore harder and harder on King Yavin of Canaan, until they destroyed King Yavin of Canaan" (Judges 4:24). From a historian's perspective, this verse is more important than the entire dramatic story that preceded it. It represents a historical watershed: From this point on, we no longer learn – in the rest of Tanakh or in any later source – of a Canaanite enemy daring to challenge Israel militarily. The remnants of the Canaanite people became merchants of the Mediterranean coast and servants of King Solomon (I Kings 9:20–21). It seems that the verses in Joshua and at the beginning of Judges – "When the Israelites became stronger, they imposed tribute on the Canaanites" (Josh. 17:13; cf. Judges 1:28 and *Daat Mikra* commentary there) – refer to this period, when the hand of the Israelites bore harder and harder on the Canaanites. Through this lens, we can view the Song of Deborah as a song celebrating the completion of the conquest of the Land of Israel, in the same way that the Song of the Sea was a victory hymn for the Exodus.[1]

1. Based on Dr. Yael Ziegler's lectures at Herzog College.

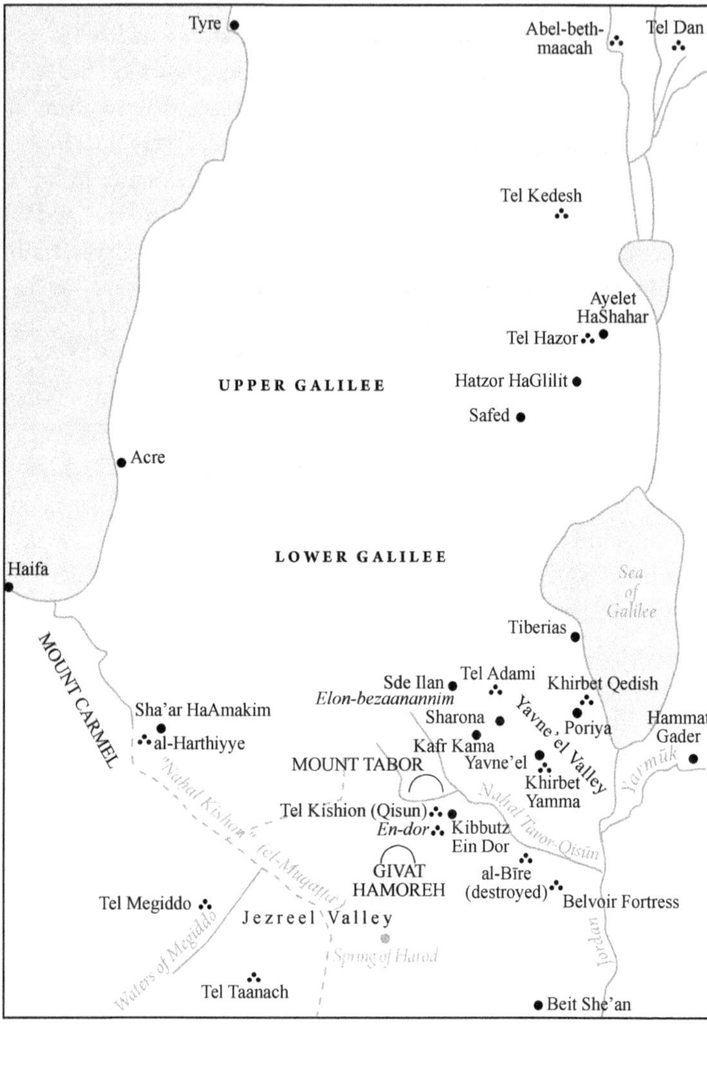

How Did the Victory Happen?

The story of the victory of the people of Israel, under the leadership of Deborah and Barak, is described in prose form in chapter 4, and in poetic form in chapter 5. The two chapters have much in common, but there are also fundamental differences between the two versions of the story. In order to understand properly the precise nature of the events, we must integrate elements from the song in chapter 5 into the prose narrative of chapter 4.

The narrative relates that Barak assembled ten thousand men in Kedesh, and then ascended with them to Mount Tabor. Sisera ordered all his chariots and troops to Naḥal Kishon. We read:

> Then Deborah said to Barak, "Up! This is the day on which the Lord will deliver Sisera into your hands: the Lord is marching before you." Barak charged down Mount Tabor, followed by the ten thousand men, and the Lord threw Sisera and all his chariots and army into a panic before the onslaught of Barak. Sisera leaped from his chariot and fled on foot. (Judges 4:14–15)

According to the reasonable and accepted interpretation of this passage (since Josephus, *Antiquities* V, 205), the deciding factor in the battle was a sudden, intense, unseasonal rainstorm: "The Lord is marching before you!" This interpretation is not written explicitly, but it is implied in the text: Compare "and the Lord threw Sisera and all his chariots and army into a panic" to a similar verse from the crossing of the Red Sea – "[The Lord] threw the Egyptian army into a panic. He removed the wheels of their chariots so that they moved forward with difficulty" (Ex. 14:24–25). The sudden inundation of water that caused the panic described in the crossing of the Red Sea seems to have played the same role in the battle against Sisera.

The song adds to the narrative: "The heavens dripped, yea, the clouds dripped water" (Judges 5:4)[2]; "the stars fought from heaven" (5:20); "Naḥal Kishon swept them away" (5:21). It is clear that heavenly intervention was at work here. Barak himself was initially surprised, but then knew enough to seize the opportunity. But what was Barak's original plan of action?

2. A bit of literary wisdom: The opening of the song speaks generally about the mighty acts of God, but prepares us for the rainstorm that will arrive and decide the outcome of the battle. Compare to Elihu's speech in Job 36–37, which describes the might of God manifested in storm, rain, and thunder, and immediately thereafter God reveals himself to Job "out of the tempest" (38:1).

Comparing the story in chapter 4 with the song in chapter 5 can help us answer this question. The song states: "Then the kings came, they fought: The kings of Canaan fought at Taanach, by Megiddo's waters" (Judges 5:19). This piece of information is not mentioned in the description of the battle in chapter 4. My father *z"l* connected this to another difference between the two chapters – the role of the tribes of the central region of the land. In the song, Deborah praises the tribes of Benjamin, Ephraim, and Machir (Manasseh) who came to join in the battle (5:14). In the prose narrative of chapter 4, however, there is no mention of them.

According to my father *z"l*, Deborah and Barak had prepared for a difficult war against vast Canaanite forces scattered throughout the whole northern part of the land. The Canaanite strongholds of Taanach and Megiddo, which, as we learn from the song, had their own kings who were subordinate to Yavin, had certainly planned to support Sisera from the south. The tribes of Benjamin, Ephraim, and Manasseh, whose territories bordered these Canaanite strongholds on the south, took it upon themselves to attack those cities in an attempt to stop them in the southern part of the valley, undoubtedly at great human cost. The sudden heavy downpour that turned the entire region into a mass of mud and raging streams neutralized Sisera's nine hundred iron chariots and turned the horsemen into an unorganized mob trying to flee and survive. This turn of events practically eliminated the need for the central tribes to intervene, and thus they were not mentioned in the narrative of chapter 4.

Similarly, the song describes the tribe of Zebulun as "a people that mocked death" (Judges 5:18): The plan was for the Zebulunites to draw out Sisera's army – inevitably causing many of them to be trampled by the Canaanite chariots – so that the soldiers of Naphtali and Issachar could attack Sisera from the rear. The downpour eliminated the need for this plan as well. The only thing left was for Deborah to thank God for his kindness and to praise the tribes for their readiness to go to war for the sake of their brothers.

Following our general approach in this series, our discussion will focus on geography, and the conclusions we draw will lead us to different perspectives as well. This story of war and victory revolves around seven geographical names: Hazor; Harosheth-goiim; Kedesh Naphtali;

Mount Tabor; Naḥal Kishon; Elon-bezaanannim, which is near Kedesh; and Taanach, by Megiddo's waters.

Hazor

Hazor is mentioned in this narrative twice: "And the Lord surrendered them to King Yavin of Canaan, who reigned in Hazor" (Judges 4:2); and "for there was friendship between King Yavin of Hazor and the family of Ḥever the Kenite" (4:17). Hazor was, at the time, the most respected conquest of Joshua. At the time of Joshua's conquest of the land, King Yavin of Hazor recovered from the initial shock of the Israelites' sudden intrusion into the land, assembled a large coalition of all the kings in the north and prepared to wage a large-scale war against Joshua. But Joshua surprised them "suddenly" (Josh. 11:7) at their initial place of assembly at the Waters of Merom, conquering in one blow the entire northern part of the land, including, most significantly, Hazor itself.

The narrative in Joshua stresses that "Hazor was formerly the head of all those kingdoms" (Josh. 11:10). In the archives from the nineteenth–eighteenth centuries BCE found in ancient Mari, on the Euphrates River, the only city in the Land of Israel mentioned is Hazor. In the Amarna letters from the fourteenth century BCE (which, according to the chronology I have adopted, dates back to the conquest of Canaan; see the chapter on *Parashat Shemot*), the ruler of Hazor is the only ruler who dared to give himself the title of "king." Hazor is enumerated in Joshua 19 among the cities of Naphtali, whose territory extends through the length of the eastern Galilee. According to I Maccabees 11:68, Hazor is located on the border between the hill country and the valley north of the Sea of Galilee, and is not far from Kedesh. According to *Antiquities* V, 199, it is located above the lake Semechonitis, known today as Lake Hula. The identification of Hazor is accepted by all as Tel Hazor, adjacent to Kibbutz Ayelet HaShahar and north of the city of Hatzor HaGlilit. This fortified tell is enormous for the standards of its time (approximately two hundred acres; compare to Tel Megiddo – approximately fifteen acres – and Tel Lachish – approximately thirty acres). Based on excavations of the tell in the 1950s and 1960s, and again in the 1990s and 2000s, it has become clear that the Canaanite city of Hazor was destroyed by a huge fire, consistent with the events recorded in Joshua. One particularly interesting find at the site was a wide variety of idolatrous statues and figurines that were intentionally destroyed and thrown into the fire throughout the city!

Many scholars have had difficulty answering two historical questions in connection with Hazor, in the context of the story of Deborah and Barak. First, if Hazor was destroyed by fire in the time of Joshua, how is it that King Yavin reappears in Hazor during the time of Deborah and Barak? Second, why was Sisera's base in Harosheth-goiim and not in Hazor, the city of Yavin his king? Furthermore, why doesn't the text apprise us of the fate of Hazor following the war of Deborah and Barak? The critical scholarship has tended to provide answers to these questions that are either critical and overly complicated (different, contradictory sources were stitched together haphazardly by an unintelligent editor) or critical and overly simplistic (the words "who reigned in Hazor" are the result of a clerical error, influenced by Joshua 11). The correct solution was provided by the Radak, and my father *z"l* followed his approach in an article dedicated to this topic. The answer is that "Yavin" is a dynastic name (as hinted at in the verse, "The hand of the Israelites bore harder and harder on King Yavin of Canaan, until they destroyed King Yavin of Canaan"). The phrase "who reigned" is conjugated in the past perfect,[3] indicating that in the past, before the conquest of Canaan at the hands of the people of Israel, this royal house was situated in Hazor. Now, since Hazor was destroyed, it is situated in Harosheth-goiim.

Harosheth-goiim

We do not possess enough information in order to identify the location of Harosheth-goiim. The general region where it can be found is a derivative of our geographical interpretation of this entire narrative. Various identifications have been suggested. Some are based on etymology,

3. In a narrative sequence characterized by the so-called waw consequtive or waw conversive, a relative clause with regular past relates to pluperfect. Thus, the phrase asher malakh rendered commonly "who reigned" is actually a syntactic conjugation by which biblical Hebrew expresses past perfect in contrast with the participle ham-molekh that is the way to express regular past. Hence, our verse should be translated "And the Lord surrenered them to Yavin king of Canaan who had reigned in Hazor" (as opposed to Esther 1:1: "Now it came to pass in the days of Ahasuerus, this is Ahasuerus who reigned, from India even unto Ethiopia."

connecting the word *ḥaroshet* to craftsmanship, as in "to cut stones (*uvaḥaroshet even*) for setting and to carve wood (*uvaḥaroshet etz*) – to work in every kind of designer's craft" (Ex. 35:33), forests and woodlands, as in "a cedar in Lebanon with beautiful branches and shady thickets (*veḥoresh*)" (Ezek. 31:3) or to plowed land, as in "You shall not plow (*lo taḥarosh*) with an ox and an ass together" (Deut. 22:10). Other identifications are based on a slightly similar Arabic name (Ḥaris or Ḥarthiyye). However, all these are mere speculations. The identification with Ḥarthiyye is especially common in the scholarly literature. In truth, however, Ḥarthiyye is a modern-era name for a place where the members of the Arab family known as "the sons of Ḥāritha" lived. Benjamin Mazar argued that Harosheth-goiim was a territorial name and not the name of a city. In addition, a new speculation has arisen in the last decade: Professor Adam Zertal wrote an entire book built on the speculative connection of Sisera to the island of Sardinia, in light of a lone place in Sardinia whose name sounds similar to "Sisera." Based on this, Zertal identified Harosheth-goiim, the city of Sisera, with an archaeological site above Wadi 'Āra that bears resemblance to parallel Sardinian sites.

Based on a parallel in the Book of Joshua, it seems to me that the second element, "goiim," was a place-name, rather than a reference to "gentiles." This conclusion can be drawn from the verse: "the king of Goiim in Gilgal (*melekh Goyim le-Gilgal*)," at the end of the list of Canaanite kings in Joshua 12:23. In this list, when we find the pattern "the king of X in Y," X is always the name of a city and Y is always the name of a large region. What might be the region described here as "Gilgal"? It is reasonable to suggest that our "Gilgal" here is a similar form to "Galil."[4] Indeed, the Septuagint translates in this vein: "Basilea Gōim tēs Galilaias" – the king Goim of the Galilee. The expression "Galilee of Goiim (*Gelil Ha-goyim*)" is mentioned in a northern context in Isaiah 8:23, and apparently in the Hebrew substrate of I Maccabees 5:15 as well. This expression should be interpreted as "the part of the Galilee that is in the vicinity of the location Goiim" (compare to "the Negeb of Arad," "the Negeb of the Jerahmeelites" and "the Negeb of the Kenites"). In my opinion, the expression *Charoshet*

4. From a linguistic perspective, the roots G-L-L and G-L-G-L are identical in meaning; compare Josh. 15:7 to 18:17.

Ha-Goyim bears the same form as *Timnat Cheres* – Timnah in the vicinity of Heres, and *Ta'anat Shilo* – Taanah in the Shilo region. According to this, our case is referring to a place called Harosheth that is adjacent to the city of Goiim. As for more precise identifications for Harosheth and Goiim, as we have stated, there is simply not enough information.

Kedesh Naphtali

The identification of Kedesh is seemingly clear: Tel Kedesh (formerly Qadas) in the eastern part of the Upper Galilee, near Yiftah, Malkiya, and Ramot Naftali. The certainty of this identification is based on six factors:

- General consideration: The three cities of refuge in the land of Canaan were Hebron, Shechem, and Kedesh in the Galilee, in the hill country of Naphtali (Josh. 20:7). The principle of "You shall… divide into three parts the territory of the country" (Deut. 19:3), which the Talmud explains to mean, "so that [the distance] from Hebron to the south is equivalent to [the distance] from Hebron to Shechem, and [the distance] from Hebron to Shechem is equivalent to [the distance] from Shechem to Kedesh" (Tosefta Makkot ch. 3; and Bavli and Yerushalmi ch. 2) leads us to place Kedesh within the limits of the Upper Galilee.
- Kedesh is enumerated in Joshua 19:37 in the list of Naphtalite cities between Hazor and Iron, which have been identified in that area.
- "In the days of King Pekaḥ of Israel, King Tiglat Pileser of Assyria came and captured Ijon, Abel-beth-maacah, Janoah, Kedesh, Hazor…" (II Kings 15:29). Janoah is not mentioned anywhere apart from this verse, and its identification is unknown.[5] Connecting Ijon (Tel Dibin, adjacent to Marj Ayyun), Abel-beth-maacah (Tel Abel, south of Metula), Tel Kedesh, and Tel Hazor yields a continuous north-south line.
- Post-biblical sources, including I Maccabees 11:63–74 (Kedes/Kades in the Galilee, near Hazor); Josephus, in *The Jewish War* II,

5. Based on the geographical context, it seems that it should not be identified with either of the two Arab villages in the western Galilee that bear the same name, one of which lies east of Tyre, and the other of which lies east of Nahariya.

459 (Kadasa/Kedasa "of Tyre"); and Eusebius, in the *Onomasticon* (Kades [Cades] – "It is now called Kydissos, twenty miles from Tyre, near Paneas") all point to this region.

- The name is preserved in the form of Qadas.
- It is the largest tell in the mountainous Upper Galilee region (approximately twenty-five acres), with a spring at its feet and walls sixteen feet thick (it is listed in Joshua 19 among the "fortified cities"). Excavations of the site have yielded rich findings from the early and middle Canaanite periods, while findings from the late Canaanite period and the Israelite period are meager in comparison. Later findings prominently include remnants from a pagan temple from the Roman period.

Mount Tabor

There is no need to elaborate on the identity, location, and prominent appearance of Mount Tabor, as these features are well known and well documented in sources throughout history.

Naḥal Kishon

Outside of the narrative of Deborah and Barak, Naḥal Kishon is mentioned one other time in Tanakh. After the fire descended from heaven at Mount Carmel, I Kings 18 relates:

> When they saw this, all the people flung themselves on their faces and cried out: "The Lord alone is God, The Lord alone is God!" Then Elijah said to them, "Seize the prophets of Baal, let not a single one of them get away." They seized them, and Elijah took them down to the Naḥal Kishon and slaughtered them there. (18:39–40)

Since Naḥal Kishon is mentioned in connection with both Mount Carmel and Mount Tabor, it must be identified with a stream connecting these two regions. The modern-day Kishon River (known in Arabic as Nahr el-Muqaṭṭaʿ) is the only stream that fits this description. However, a certain difficulty remains, as the upper tributaries of the Kishon do not reach Mount Tabor itself. Rather, Mount Tabor itself is surrounded on all sides by the tributaries of Naḥal Tavor, which flows east, toward the Jordan. The upper tributaries of the Kishon are located approximately three miles from Mount Tabor. An additional difficulty is the use of the word *naḥal*. Most of the Jezreel Valley and the Kesulot Valley is within the drainage basin of the Kishon, and while maps of these valleys generally contain dashed blue lines indicating surface flow channels, ultimately most of the area covered by the Kishon is a large plain rather than a clearly defined stream. If what transpired here was flooding and troops sinking into mud and standing water, then it was not quite that "Naḥal Kishon swept them away" (Judges 5:21), but more that "the Jezreel Valley flooded them." We will return to these questions later on.

Elon-bezaanannim, Which Is near Kedesh

The term "*Elon*" is an ancient feature of the geographical terminology of Tanakh. It is the first component of nine non-settlement geographical names in the ancient parts of Tanakh (i.e., from Genesis to Samuel). Today, it is commonly accepted that *Elon* refers to a tree or woodland. In an article published in 2003, I brought proofs supporting the early Targumic interpretation that *Elon* actually refers to a plain.

The verse states that Elon-bezaanannim is located in the vicinity of Kedesh. Elon-bezaanannim is mentioned one other time in Tanakh – in the description of the territory allotted to the tribe of Naphtali: "Their boundary ran from Heleph in Elon-bezaanannim, Adami-nekeb and Jabneel to Lakkum, and it ended at the Jordan" (Josh. 19:33). Does the information provided by this verse match the descriptor "which is near Kedesh" found here in Judges? We will attempt to answer this question later on.

Taanach, by the Waters of Megiddo

Taanach and Megiddo are paired together here and in other sources as well, both biblical and extra-biblical. They have been identified with certainty in the southwestern edge of the Jezreel Valley, in two tells five miles apart that are rich in findings. "The Waters of Megiddo" are apparently the Naḥal Qina springs (Wadi al-Lajjūn) adjacent to Megiddo Junction. From a territorial perspective, it seems that these springs were associated at the time with Taanach, while the territory associated with Megiddo included the sections of the valley that lay north and west of the city.

Two Geographical Questions

a. Kedesh Naphtali is located almost thirty miles from Mount Tabor. Why did Barak summon thousands of men from the tribes of Naphtali and Zebulun to Kedesh, only to send them shortly thereafter to Mount Tabor? Barak's actions are particularly puzzling with respect to the Zebulunite draftees, since Mount Tabor is located on the border of their territory. The Zebulunites, then, had to travel back and forth this entire distance needlessly.

b. How could Sisera have fled on foot twenty-five to thirty miles to Elon-bezaanannim, which is near Kedesh, after a long day of battle and defeat, without stopping for food or rest? My father *z"l* (in *Daat Mikra*) and others answered that the text was referring to the general nomadic area of the household of Ḥever the Kenite. Those who know that the descendants of Moses' father-in-law generally lived in the southern part of the land would be surprised to read that Yael, wife of Ḥever the Kenite, suddenly appeared in the north. Therefore, the text informs us that Ḥever the Kenite had recently separated from the other Kenites, and was wandering in the northern part of the land, as far north as Elon-bezaanannim, which is near Kedesh. During the battle at the Kishon, Ḥever's tent was near Mount Tabor, and it was there that Sisera fled. With all due respect, however, this answer seems insufficient. Furthermore, the answer does not fit well with the description of the borderline of Naphtali in Joshua. Let us examine this point.

Mt. Tabor – picture from the 1890s

Elon-bezaanannim on the Southern Borderline of Naphtali

We read in Joshua: "The sixth lot fell to the Naphtalites ... Their boundary ran from Heleph in Elon-bezaanannim, Adami-nekeb, and Jabneel to Lakkum, and it ended at the Jordan. The boundary then turned westward to Aznoth-tabor" (19:32–34). It would seem that the borderline described here is the southern border of Naphtali. The verse uses a technique found several times in Joshua: delineating a borderline by moving east from a certain midpoint, and then returning to move west from that same midpoint. In this case, the midpoint is Heleph, located within Elon-bezaanannim. The borderline then moves east, toward Adami-nekeb, Jabneel, Lakkum, and the Jordan. Returning to Heleph, the borderline then moves west toward Aznoth-tabor. Many of the locations mentioned here can be identified, at least to a certain extent. "Aznoth-tabor" is a two-word place-name that should be interpreted as "Azenoth, which is near Tabor." It is clear that the western end of the borderline described here is close to Mount Tabor. On the east, the borderline ends at the Jordan, south of the Sea of Galilee, in the general area of the modern-day moshava of Menahamiya. An excellent identification has been suggested for Adami, in the middle of this borderline: Tel Adami, a prominent, fortified, Canaanite-Israelite tell from the biblical period, above the Yavne'el Valley, two miles east of Sde Ilan.[6]

Ḥazal had a traditional identification for each of the sites listed in this verse, three of whose names were preserved until the modern era: "Adami – Damin, Nekeb – Siyadathah, and Jabneel – Caphar Jama" (Y. Megilla 1:1). "Damin" is linguistically equivalent to "Adami," in a variant typical to the period of the Talmud Yerushalmi, and it is also equivalent to the later "Dāmyeh."[7] Ṣiyadathah is Khirbet Ṣiyāda (three miles southeast of Tel Adami) and Caphar Jama is Khirbet Yamma (south of the moshava of Yavne'el). The borderline described in the verse makes topographical sense. It seems that it follows the length of the steep grade that delimits the Yavne'el Valley from the southwest. In order to complete

6. The Arabic name of the site was Khirbet et-Tell, and the later ruins nearby were known as Khirbet Dāmyeh.
7. Regarding the dropped *aleph*, compare to "Lazar" (Eleazar) and "Rabbi Ba" (Rabbi Abba). Regarding the added *nun*, compare to "Zipporin" (Zippori) and "Caesarin" (Caesarea).

the picture in a logical manner, we must estimate that Aznoth-tabor was located several miles north of Mount Tabor. Thus, our analysis of this borderline described in Joshua leads us to the conclusion that Elon-bezaanannim, which lay between Adami on the east and Aznoth-tabor on the west, was apparently the plains region of modern-day Sde Ilan, Sharona, and Kafr Kama.

How Can Elon-bezaanannim Be "near Kedesh"?

The conclusion drawn from the previous section leads to a new problem: Kedesh lies more than twenty-five miles north of the location we proposed for Elon-bezaanannim! A solution to this problem was suggested by Isaiah Press (in an important article with whose details I do not entirely agree), and consequently advanced by many others as well. Press explained that we have no choice but to conclude that there was a different place called Kedesh in the vicinity of Mount Tabor. This name duplication should not surprise us; in Judea, for example, there are two places named Ziph (Josh. 15:24, 55) and two places named Socoh (15:35, 48). Within the small territory allotted to the tribe of Benjamin, there were two places named Gibeah (Gibeah of Saul/Gibeah of the Benjaminites and Gibeah of Kiriath-jearim), not to mention Geba and Gibeon as well. The name Kedesh itself is found in other contexts in Tanakh as well (not including instances of Kadesh, which is a different name entirely). Different locations named Kedesh are found in Judah (15:23) and in Issachar (I Chr. 6:57). It may be that the Kedesh mentioned in the story of Deborah and Barak is actually the Issacharite Kedesh, whose identification is not agreed upon. However, it is more likely that Barak son of Avinoam of Kedesh, in Naphtali, assembled his soldiers to his own hometown, and therefore we can conclude that there were two places named Kedesh within Naphtali – one in the north and one in the south. There is even a plausible suggestion for this southern Kedesh's identification: Khirbet Qedish in the topographical terrace below Poriya, located above a steep incline that descends to the Sea of Galilee. This ruin contains remnants of a fairly large settlement inhabited during the Canaanite period and the Israelite I period, and later in the Roman and Byzantine periods. In light of this information, it appears that all mentions of Kedesh in the story of the war of Deborah and Barak do not refer to the northern Kedesh but to the southern Kedesh, which is not far from Mount Tabor (nine miles, if the identification with Khirbet Qedish is correct). It was to this southern Kedesh that Barak assembled ten thousand men, and it was from there that he brought them to Mount Tabor. Sisera fled by foot only a few miles before he reached Yael's tent in Elon-bezaanannim, the plains region northeast of Mount Tabor.

Naḥal Kishon – a Reassessment

We concluded our discussion of Naḥal Kishon with two questions. These questions do not constitute serious problems, but they are somewhat discomfiting. First, Mount Tabor is surrounded on all sides by the tributaries of Naḥal Tavor, while the tributaries of the Kishon are at least three miles away. Second, the upper tributaries of the Kishon are virtually unrecognizable as part of the stream; as we said, it would be more fitting to say that "the Jezreel Valley flooded them" rather than "Naḥal Kishon swept them away" (Judges 5:21).

Before I drop the coming bombshell, I would like to say a few words about Naḥal Tavor. This stream has tributaries surrounding Mount Tabor on all sides, and is blessed with an abundance of springs, ensuring a constant flow in the stream. Some four miles southeast of Mt. Tabor, the stream becomes deep with steep banks, and thus it flows, descending to the Jordan Valley at the foot of Belvoir Fortress. Because of the combination of this abundance of water and the steep inclines on either side of the stream, several ancient settlements were built on the streambed, close to the stream itself, and an ancient road passed through the streambed as well. Until the foundation of the State of Israel in 1948, the stream was known as Wadi al-Bīreh, after the village of al-Bīreh that lay at the edge of the plain above its southern bank.

And now for the twist: Rabbi Ishtori Haparḥi, a resident of Beit She'an, who completed his well-known work *Kaftor Vaferaḥ* in 1322 CE, writes:

> South of Tiberias about a half day [journey] lies Beit She'an, and in the middle of the way lies Naḥal Kishon, which is called Qīsūn" (ch. 11, p. 287 [Lunz ed.]).

The large stream that lies in the middle of the road between Tiberias and Beit She'an is Naḥal Tavor. That is to say that Rabbi Ishtori Haparḥi is informing us that in his time, seven hundred years ago, the Arabs called this stream Qīsūn, and he thus identified it as the biblical Naḥal Kishon. This Naḥal Kishon is mentioned twice more in *Kaftor Vaferaḥ*. First: "South of the where the Yarmuk meets the Jordan about a half hour [journey], Naḥal Kishon meets the Jordan, and it descends from the west, south of Mount Tabor" (ch. 7, p. 125). Actually, the distance from the mouth of the Yarmuk River, where it meets the Jordan River, to the mouth of Naḥal Tavor is about two miles. Second, and more significantly: "West of Mount Tabor is Chisloth-tabor...directly to the south about an hour [journey] is Kishon, and from there extends the stream" (ch. 11, p. 293).

Lower Galilee scholar Neḥemiah Zimbalist-Zori visited the southern springs of Naḥal Tavor in the summer of 1943, and found that the ruin above the springs was known to the Arabs as Khirbet Qīsūn. The ruin is an exceptionally large tell (35–50 acres) made up of four mounds, and containing remnants from the prehistoric, Canaanite, Israelite, Hellenistic, Roman, and early Arab periods. This city was apparently Kishion, a Levite city in Issachar (Josh. 19:20; 21:28). Kishon may be a parallel version of the same name.[8] In the list of the conquests of Tuthmose III of Egypt, the name *qswn* appears (immediately preceding Shunem) and it is reasonable to claim that this name also refers to this same city. Upon further examination, Zori found that in an early map originating in the Byzantine period and attributed to Jerome, as well as in a few other maps from the medieval period and even in a map from 1830, Naḥal Kishon is labeled as flowing southeast from Mount Tabor to the Jordan. In addition to the sources collected by Zori I can cite the English traveller John Sanderson who in 1601 mentioned the Kishon stream east of Mt. Tavor.

The apparent conclusion is that just as we have found that there were two distinct locations named Kedesh approximately on the same longitude, there were also two streams named Kishon roughly on the same latitude. The Kishon associated with Elijah was located on the slopes

8. In one version of the Septuagint, Kishion is rendered as "Kisōn."

of Mount Carmel,[9] while the Kishon associated with Barak was apparently Naḥal Tavor. The meaning of the name "Kishon" is unknown, as is its linguistic root.[10] It is likely that the early meaning of the name was relevant in both districts and thus led to its use for two different streams. Another (late) example of two streams on parallel opposite sides of a watershed bearing the same name is 'Ūja or 'Ōja ('Auja in literary Arabic; the meaning of the word is "twisted" or "convoluted"), wich is the Arabic name for both Naḥal Yitav, which descends to the Jordan Rift Valley, and the Yarkon River on the west.[11] It may also be speculated that the apparently obscure expression *naḥal kedumim naḥal kishon* (Judges 5:21)[12] might simply be interpreted as "the eastern torrent Kishon" (*kedumim* like *kedem* might mean "east"). In light of the fact that there were indeed two different streams known as Naḥal Kishon along the same line of latitude, the verse is stressing that it is the eastern Kishon that featured in the battle.[13]

We may add that there is another hint to the identification of the Naḥal Kishon of Judges with Naḥal Tavor in the writings of Josephus. He writes:

9. Consequently, we cannot be certain that this was the same river as the modern-day Kishon (Nahr el-Muqaṭṭaʿ); perhaps it was a different wadi or stream.
10. Suggestions include: *Kish* + suffix *-on*; the root K-Š-N; and the root K-Š-Y + *-on*. The connection to Kishion fits well with the last suggestion.
11. I am grateful to my friend Yaki Fried for this insight.
12. Translators and commentators have been perplexed by this verse. Some, including the Septuagint version A, the Vulgate, Douay-Rheims 1899 American Edition, and (recently) the Orthodox Jewish Bible, transliterated the Hebrew word "Kedumim" without translation. Most of the versions and commentaries (beginning with the Septuagint version B and *Targum Yonatan*, continuing with Radak and terminating with the majority of the English translations and *Daat Mikra*) translated it "that ancient river" or the like, suggesting a variety of interpretations to explain this title. Other interpretations have been suggested as well. According to the Peshitta, *nḥla dqrmin* (!) was another stream that swept away the Canaanites together with the Kishon. Additionally, some modern sources translated *kedumim* as "onrushing" or "raging," others (on the basis of an Arabic parallel) translated as "of the daring men," or "stream of encounter," i.e., the meeting point of the two armies. As can be expected in such cases, some researchers emend the difficult expression to read *naḥal kishon gerafam, kiddemam naḥal kishon* ("Naḥal Kishon advanced before them").
13. This theory was proposed by my friend Yehuda Etzion.

> And when they were come to a close fight, there came down from heaven a great storm, with a vast quantity of rain and hail, and the wind blew the rain in the face of the Canaanites, and so darkened their eyes ... while the storm did not so much incommode the Israelites, because it came in their backs. (*Antiquities* V, 205)

Josephus understood that the Canaanites advanced facing west, while the Israelites advanced facing east. This description only makes sense if the stream in question is Naḥal Tavor, and not the tributaries of the Kishon (el-Muqaṭṭaʿ) in the Jezreel Valley.

The *Daat Mikra Bible Atlas* cites a unique eyewitness account of a sudden, heavy downpour that occurred in this region. The author of the account is Yifraḥ Ḥaviv of Kibbutz Beit Keshet, who writes:

> It was ... Independence Day [April 16] of 1964. It was a typical spring-sirocco day ... Suddenly in the evening, lightning cleaved the sky from horizon to horizon ... There was deafening thunder as in the time of the Deluge and the gates of the heavens opened wide. Within two hours, 120 millimeters [almost five inches] of rain fell. The thunder and lightning never let up during those two hours ... Tens of millions of cubic meters of water flowed ... in the handful of wadis in the area, sweeping away titanic rocks and trees, destroying fences, changing the look of the land ... Naḥal Tavor ... turned into a roaring river. (p. 176)

What is curious about this anecdote is that while the authors of the *Daat Mikra Bible Atlas* surely followed the prevailing opinion that Naḥal Kishon, which swept away the army of Sisera, refers to the tributaries of the modern-day Kishon River in the Jezreel Valley, the account that it cites describing a "roaring river" refers to none other than Naḥal Tavor!

A Glimpse at the Story of Gideon

Begging the permission of the readers, I would like to jump for a moment to the geography of the story of Gideon. We read in Judges: "All Midian, Amalek, and the Kedemites joined forces; they crossed over and encamped in the Valley of Jezreel" (6:33). In response, Gideon and his men assemble as well: "Early next day, Jerubaal – that is, Gideon – and all the troops with him encamped above En-harod, while the camp of Midian was on the north side of them, by Gibeath-moreh, in the valley" (7:1). Following the test of the "lappers" (7:4–8), three hundred men remained with Gideon: "The Midianite camp was below him, in the plain" (7:8). Gideon and his attendant descended to this Midianite camp at the beginning of the night and heard a dream and its interpretation (7:9–14). Gideon then returned to the Israelite camp and attacked the Midianite camp just before midnight, "at the beginning of the middle watch" (7:19). The geographical picture here is clear: The vast Midianite camp was spread out in the Jezreel Valley between Gibeath-moreh in the north and En-harod in the south, and Gideon attacked this camp from the south, from the direction of En-harod.

This geographical description makes perfect sense, as long as you take what you read in the chapter at face value while looking at a map of the region. However, the moment you open any modern work or commentary on the conflict between Gideon and the Midianites, you are in for a shock. Modern Bible atlases and commentators move the Midianite camp more than six miles to the north, past Gibeath-moreh, forcing Gideon and his men to march a total of seven miles in the beginning of the night, including ascending and descending the ridge of Gibeath-moreh (Jabel ed-Dahi). This geographical shift is accompanied by a linguistic distortion as well. *Daat Mikra*'s commentary on verse 1 reads:

> "While the camp of Midian was in the plain to the north of him, at Gibeath-moreh.": "To the north" – this phrase refers to both the words preceding it and the words following it; it is as if it was written twice. The camp of Midian was to the north of Gideon, to the north of Gibeath-moreh, in the plain. The Midianites encamped north of Gibeath-moreh, far north of Gideon's camp.

Daat Mikra's commentary on verse 8 reads:

> "Retaining only the three hundred men" – Here end the events that transpired at En-harod at the foot of Mount Gilboa, about

> eleven kilometers [seven miles] from the Midianite camp, which was encamped in the Ksalot Valley (north of Gibeath-moreh).
>
> "The Midianite camp was below him, in the plain" – Here the verse teaches us that at nightfall, Gideon's three hundred men traveled secretly to Gibeath-moreh, preparing themselves there next to the Midianite camp, from above. The Midianites ... did not notice a handful of men moving through the plain in the darkness.

What Is Going On Here?

What is going on here? Why is it that in the story of Deborah, where, according to the simple reading of the text, the military clash took place at the foot of Mount Tabor, the scholars moved the battlefield more than three miles to the west, while in the story of Gideon, where the text seems to place the attack in the Jezreel Valley (seemingly even in its southern part), the scholars moved the story seven miles north, to the vicinity of Mount Tabor?

The key factor here can be found in Psalms: "Deal with them as You did with Midian, with Sisera, with Yavin, at Naḥal Kishon – who were destroyed at En-dor, who became dung for the field" (83:10–11). Ancient En-dor is well known; it was located in the ruined village of Indūr (some say in the adjacent site of Khirbet Ṣafṣāfeh) about two miles south of Khirbet Qisun above the tributaries of Naḥal Tavor. The simple meaning of the verse from Psalms makes sense in light of our analysis: Sisera and Yavin's army was destroyed in the fields of En-dor, and from there it was swept away by Naḥal Kishon, which is none other than Naḥal Tavor.

Despite this, virtually all the scholars and modern commentators, in their confidence that Sisera and his army were defeated between Afula and Nazareth, far west of En-dor, were forced into a farfetched interpretation of the verse in Psalms. They explained that it was not Sisera who was destroyed at En-dor, but the Midianite army at the hands of Gideon and his three hundred "lappers." This interpretation distorted the meaning of the verse in Psalms, and dragged not only the story of Deborah and Barak, but the story of Gideon as well into this convoluted mess.

In this context, here is some more food for thought: The Book of Judges teaches us that the tribe of Asher did not come to the aid of Deborah and Barak in their war against Sisera, and was admonished as a result (5:17).

However, the same tribe of Asher did participate in the war between Gideon and the Midianites (6:35). According to the prevailing view, the battle between Barak and Sisera took place in Asher, while Gideon's battle at En-dor took place in Issachar. It might have been expected, then, that the people of Asher would participate precisely in the war of Deborah and Barak, as it took place in their own territory. In contrast, according to the new geographical perspective we have presented here, Gideon's battlefield was located in the Jezreel Valley on the border of Asher, while Barak and Sisera clashed further east – in the basin of Naḥal Tavor, far from Asher.

Summing Up

It seems clear that the Kedesh in the story of Deborah and Barak is not the well-known Kedesh in the northern part of Naphtali, but a different Kedesh near Mount Tabor. Furthermore, the Naḥal Kishon of Deborah and Barak is not Elijah's Naḥal Kishon, but Naḥal Tavor at the foot of Mount Tabor. This stream preserved its ancient name at least until the end of the Middle Ages. Sisera's chariots and soldiers were defeated in the area around En-dor and Kishion-Kishon, south of Mount Tabor – and it was Naḥal Tavor that "swept them away." Sisera himself fled on foot north three to six miles to Yael's tent, where he met his demise at the hands of a woman. "So may all Your enemies perish, O Lord!" (Judges 5:31).

Addendum

On *Rosh Ḥodesh Av* 5769 (July 22, 2009), I gave a lecture at the Tanakh Study Days at Herzog College on the topic, "Who Was Destroyed at En-Dor?" Several days later, I received a fascinating letter from one of my former students, David Cohen, who today is a resident of the moshav HaZor'im in the Lower Galilee. In it, he gives his personal perspective on this entire discussion. I felt that I should share this letter with my readers, so I present it here, in his own words:

> *"Nahal Tavor Swept Them Away": Memories of a Rainy Navigation at Nahal Tavor*
>
> Winter 1993 – We set out for a series of solo navigations at night, our unit's first navigation on this particular trail. The truck bus

dropped us off at Kochav HaYarden Junction and we began the climb to Belvoir Fortress, all together in the pouring rain. From Belvoir Fortress we split up, each man going his own way. The waypoints were scattered throughout the Issachar Heights, while the endpoint of the navigation was the summit of Mount Tabor. The rain did not stop the entire night. When I arrived at Naḥal Tavor and prepared to cross, I saw that the current was strong. Based on my calculations, I had planned to cross about a kilometer east of where Naḥal Tavor intersects the paved road connecting Kfar Tavor and Afula. It was late at night, and in my laziness I decided to cross the stream by foot rather than walk to the highway – "The water will probably go up to my knees; I'll get to the end of the navigation and change clothes then," I thought to myself. Upon entering the water, I suddenly realized (too late to change course) that I was no longer standing, and I was forced to cross the stream in a panicked swim. At the other side, I became tangled in the bushes and managed to drag myself to the mud at the opposite bank. Dripping wet at this point, I attempted to turn on my two-way radio and call for help, but the wet equipment did not work. I realized that I had no choice – I had to climb Mount Tabor soaking wet. My platoon mate Eitan attempted to cross Naḥal Tavor in a similar manner, and he too ended up swimming as I did. Unfortunately for him, however, the opposite bank was too high where he crossed and he was unable to climb onto the other side. He shouted for help until one of the members of the platoon in the area heard him and managed to pull him out of the stream. The other members of the platoon were smarter than the two of us and crossed the stream via the road.[14]

On the second night we set out for another navigation, this time from the junction at the entrance to Dabūryeh through the

14. I cannot refrain from remarking that the conduct of the army and the soldiers in this case was irresponsible and life-threatening, and it is only by a miracle that this navigation ends with an experience that is told cheerfully and not in a coffin. On January 7, 2019, Eviatar Yosefi, a soldier in an elite IDF unit, lost his life in a stormy river in the Galilee in very similar circumstances. I pray that in the future the IDF, its commanders and soldiers will be more careful.

Kesulot Valley, to the Nazareth Mountains, and ending at Nahalal Junction. By that time the rain had stopped falling, but the entire valley was wet and muddy. One or two kilometers from the start of the navigation, my platoon mate Yaron became stuck in the mud, unable to move. Zohar, who was in the area, tried to reach him, but then he too became stuck in the mud up to his hips, unable to move as well. I tried to approach them, but the mud was too deep and I couldn't really get close. Meanwhile, the rest of the platoon continued on in the navigation. Shai, the platoon leader, attempted to help the two men using the Abir [a tactical military vehicle], but the Abir became stuck as well (it was only extracted close to dawn by a large excavator brought from Kibbutz Gazit). In the end, Shai was able to get close enough to the men to throw them ropes, which he used to pull them out to safety. They then boarded a truck bus and were brought to the midpoint of the navigation. I, on the other hand, was instructed by the platoon leader to continue on the navigation, so I found myself wading through the mud by myself, while the rest of the platoon had already arrived at the midpoint. I remember that at every step I took I was afraid that my boot would remain stuck in the deep mud. Later in the navigation, Amit reported that he was seeing a village on his coordinates. It became apparent later on that the mud caused his compass to malfunction; instead of heading west he had been heading generally northward, and had reached the village of Iksāl. It was only when we reached the Nazareth Mountains region that it became possible to progress more easily until the end of the navigation.

At the time, I thought of the story of Barak and Deborah and what we were taught about the chariots becoming stuck in the mud of the Jezreel Valley – I felt that we were in a similar situation.

Today, with a new understanding of the battle, I truly believe that the incident of the first night fits the phrase, Naḥal Kishon swept them away," more than the incident of the second night. There, in the valley, even elite infantry soldiers were only able to move through the mud-filled valley with difficulty.

For further study:

Arnon C., and R. Amiran. "Tel Kishion." *NEAEHL* 3, Jerusalem, 873–874.
Dabbagh, M. M. "Al-Harthiyya." *Biladna Filastin*, VII, Kefar Qara' 1991, 676 [Arabic].
Elitzur, Yehuda. *Sefer Shofetim. Daat Mikra*, Jerusalem, 1989, 47–75, 86–89 [Hebrew].
Elitzur, Yehuda, and Yehuda Kiel. *Daat Mikra Bible Atlas*. Translated by L. J. Schramm. Jerusalem, 2011, 176.
Elitzur, Yehuda. "*Lefarashat Ḥatzor*." *Israel and the Bible*, Ramat-Gan, 2000, 78–84 [Hebrew].
Elitzur, Yoel. "*Elon – Mishor – αὐλών*." *Eshel Beer-sheva* 8 (Yaakov Bentolila Jubilee Volume), Beer-sheva, 2003, 1–11 [Hebrew].
Elitzur, Yoel. "Toponyms in the Land of Israel: Two-word Place Names." *Encyclopedia of Hebrew Language and Linguistics*, Leiden and Boston, 2013, 3: 783.
Elliger, K., and W. Rudolph. *Biblia Hebraica Stuttgartensia*. Stuttgart, 1990, 408.
Ish-Shalom M. "The Travels of John Sanderson in Eretz-Israel." *Yerushalayim: Review for Eretz-Israel Research*. Edited by M. Ish-Shalom, M. Benayahu and A. Shohet. Jerusalem, 1953, 150 [Hebrew].
Kaufman, Y. *The Book of Judges*. Jerusalem, 1978, 113–147 [Hebrew].
Mazar, B. "Beth-sheᶜarim, Gaba and Haroshet of the Peoples." *The Early Biblical Period: Historical Essays*. Edited by S. Ahituv and B. A. Levine. Jerusalem, 1986, 203–212.
Moore, G. F. *A Criticial and Exegetical Commentary on Judges* (ICC). Edinburgh, 1989, 159–160.
Press, I. "Kedesh Naphtali and Elon Beṣaᶜananim." Bulletin of the Jewish Palestine Exploration Society 3, Jerusalem, 1934, 26–31 [Hebrew].
Rainey, A. F. "Toponymic Problems: Harosheth-hagoiim." *Tel Aviv* 10 (1983): 46–48.
Zertal, A. *Sisera's Secret*. Or Yehuda, 2010 [Hebrew].
Zimbalist (Zori) N. "Kishon and Kishyon." Bulletin of the Jewish Palestine Exploration Society 13, Jerusalem, 1946–47, 28–32 [Hebrew].
Zori, N. *The Land of Issachar: Archaeological Survey*. Jerusalem, 1977, 110–113 [Hebrew].

Parashat Yitro

Stone Altars and Earthen Altars in the Archaeology of the Land of Israel

"An Altar of Earth" and "An Altar of Stones" – the First Commandment After God's Revelation

After the spiritual pinnacle of the revelation at Mount Sinai and the lofty verse following it – "You yourselves saw that I spoke to you from the very heavens" (Ex. 20:19), both encapsulating and amplifying the nature of this singular event – God chooses to brief the people of Israel on the laws of altars:

> With Me, therefore, you shall not make any gods of silver or any gods of gold, nor shall you make such for yourselves. Make for Me an altar of earth and sacrifice on it your burnt offerings and your sacrifices of well-being, your sheep and your oxen; in each place where I cause My name to be mentioned I will come to you and bless you. And if you make for Me an altar of stones, do not build it of hewn stones; for by wielding your tool upon them you

have profaned them. Do not ascend My altar by steps, that your nakedness may not be exposed upon it. (20:20–23)

Why this mitzva specifically? Umberto Cassuto gave a compelling answer to this question (the main points of which were advanced years earlier by Abrabanel):

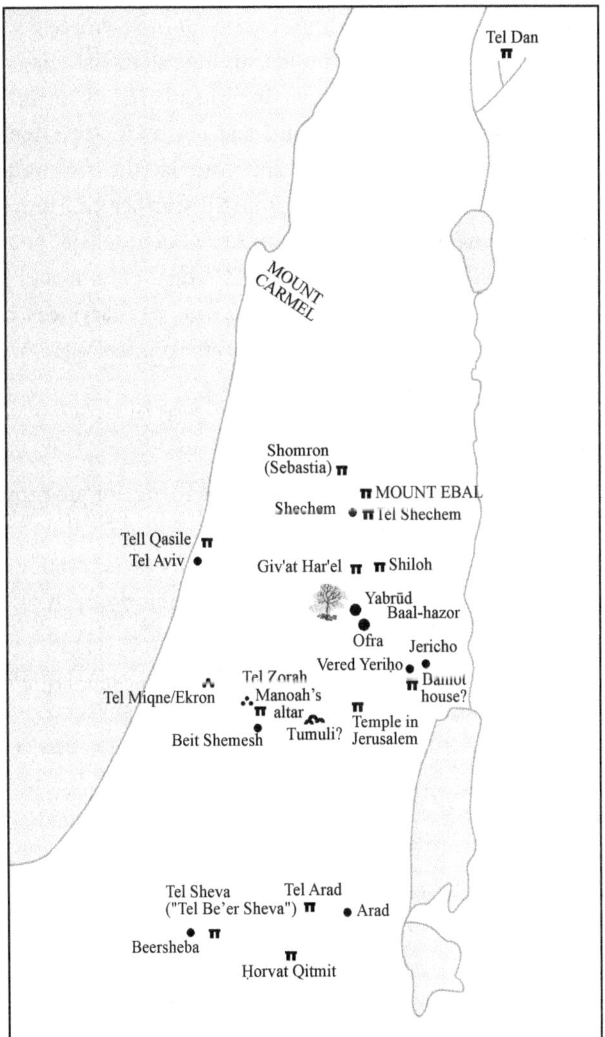

> "With Me, therefore, you shall not make any gods of silver, nor... gods of gold" – Even if the aim be to honor the God of Israel ("with Me"), and even if such precious metals as silver and gold be used, with which other nations do honor to their gods, you may not make any divine image. Even the most exquisite ornamentation cannot serve as a fitting symbol of the Invisible God.
>
> Even the worship in My honor should not resemble the ornate ritual of the gentiles, who build elaborate altars to their gods, but should be very simple: "Make for Me an altar of earth," a modest altar of clods of earth..."and sacrifice on it" – on this simple altar – "your burnt offerings and your sacrifices of well-being," that is, all the oblations that you will sacrifice to Me...namely, the oblations of "your sheep" and the oblations of "your oxen." The fourfold emphasis on the word "your" connotes as it were: Know that it is not I (God) who have need of sacrifices, but you alone require them, in order to express your feelings toward Me. The sacrifices are your sacrifices.

"In Each Place"

At this juncture, we must dedicate a few words to the unique expression: "In each place where I cause My name to be mentioned I will come to you and bless you" (20:21). The critical Bible scholarship is certain that this statement is antithetical to the statement in Deuteronomy that one may only sacrifice "in the place that the Lord will choose" (12:14). Cassuto rightfully points out that this interpretation views the text as detached from its surroundings, and that this is an incorrect approach – a verse can only be understood in light of its context. In reality, this verse is a continuation of the passage that immediately followed the revelation at Mount Sinai, and it cannot be understood without considering this background.

The nation of Israel merited experiencing God's revelation at Mount Sinai, but were scheduled to travel from Sinai shortly thereafter, to continue their journey through the wilderness. Perhaps some people feared that by distancing themselves from the Mountain of God, they would also be distancing themselves from God Himself. In order to prevent this misconception, God explained that He is not connected to Mount Sinai or to any other physical place. "In each place where I cause My name to be mentioned" – meaning that in each place where I allow My name to be mentioned and worship in My honor to take place... in each place where I will reveal Myself... "I will come to you and bless you." Another important point to note is that in this entire passage, the word "altar" is used in the singular, meaning that even in this passage the intent is for divine worship to be concentrated in one place.

In this context there is an important linguistic point to make as well: The expression "in each place" (*bekhol hamakom*) contains a kind of internal contradiction. The word *kol*, which means "each," serves to broaden and expand the scope of the term that follows it. This is the exact opposite function of the definite article prefix *ha* that is appended to the word *makom*. The purpose of the prefix *ha* is to exclude all subjects other than the one in question. Yeḥiel Bin-Nun addressed this question, explaining that we have here an internal contradiction unique to Biblical Hebrew. In this case, *ha* does not single out *makom* completely – only partially. To quote Bin-Nun:

> [The partial *ha*] does not limit the following substantive precisely, but rather designates a certain area around it. It does not point, therefore, to the object, but limits it, distinguishes it... In modern language we can thus express approximately the message of the above text like so: "*In any particular place* that is chosen at that time or in that generation." The text does not intend to suggest to us that mentioning God's name is truly possible anywhere... (as could be implied by the language of *bekhol makom asher* without *ha*), and not even that multiple places can serve that purpose simultaneously (as could be implied by the language of *bekhol hamekomot asher*, "in all the places to which..."). Rather, it suggests to us that there are a number of potential sanctified places, one of which will be chosen, or occasionally chosen to be actually sanctified.

In the chapter on *Parashat Re'eh*, we will address the deeper meaning of the word *hamakom* – the location of the Divine Presence –in contrast to *kol makom* ("Take care not to sacrifice your burnt offerings in *any place you like*" [Deut. 12:13]) and to *kol hamekomot* ("You must destroy *all the sites* at which the nations... worshipped their gods" [12:2]), which are both terms used in connection to idolatry. The unique phrase in our *parasha* – *kol hamakom* – avoids these linguistic-theological obstacles and delivers the unique message of one single, yet changing location of the Divine Presence.[1]

Altars in Archaeological Findings

Ritual sacrifice is one of the identifying characteristics of all early civilizations. According to the Torah's account, the Canaanites would frequently sacrifice to their gods "on lofty mountains and on hills or under any luxuriant tree" (Deut. 12:2). The people of Israel perpetuated this custom as well, to the great chagrin of the prophets, and would sacrifice on altars and on shrines (*bamot*) "in all their settlements" (II Kings 17:9), as well as in open fields, "like stone heaps upon a plowed field" (Hos. 12:12). With the exception of short periods during the reigns of Hezekiah and Josiah, even believers in monotheism would sacrifice to God all through the land on *bamot* and altars, throughout the Israelite period. During the Second Temple period, the *bamot* ceased to function in Jewish-inhabited areas, and apparently in Samaritan-inhabited areas as well, but the pagan population that resided in large parts of the land continued in their idolatrous folk culture until Christian rule arose in the land.

For some reason, the archaeological findings do not represent this reality properly. In temples from the Israelite period that were excavated throughout the land, and even outside ritual buildings, close to fifty small incense altars were found, usually featuring four horns. Several incense altars dating from the Late Bronze period on have been found in regions outside the Land of Israel as well.[2] One site in Israel – Tel Miqne, near

1. Regarding another two verses that feature the phrase *kol hamakom*, see Bin-Nun in his article cited below.
2. Menaḥem Haran claimed that all these altars were not meant for incense offerings but rather for meal offerings, but he did not bring convincing evidence to support his position.

Prof. Adam Zertal, Haifa University

Kibbutz Revadim, identified with great certainty with the biblical city of Ekron – is home to the largest collection of these altars. Nineteen incense altars were found there, as well as several unfinished altars, seemingly attesting to the existence of a kind of factory for the production of altars. In the post-biblical periods, several similar incense altars were unearthed in the Land of Israel and in neighboring lands as well.

"Joshua's Altar" on Mt. Ebal

However, only a very small percentage of findings were recognized as ancient altars dedicated to animal sacrifice, and of these, only a handful were recognized as such by a consensus of scholars. From the Chalcolithic period and from the Bronze periods, only between eight and fifteen such altars were unearthed in Israel in archaeological excavations, and from the Israelite period only between three and eight such altars were found, in addition to two altar horns. Two of these Israelite altars were found in fortresses from the First Temple period, one in Tel Sheva ("Tel Be'er Sheva"; see the chapter on *Parashat Vayigash*), which was found dismantled, its stones and horns embedded in a wall, and the second in Arad. The third altar is the large stone altar unearthed by Adam Zertal in the 1980s at the settlement site on Mount Ebal. Its large dimensions, ramp, and surrounding ledge located at half the altar's height fit the descriptions of the altar found in the Mishna and the Talmud with incredible accuracy. Zertal identified the altar that he found with the altar mentioned in Joshua 8. The very identification of the structure as an altar, and in particular its connection to the Book of Joshua, stirred up great debate that transcended the professional field of archaeology.

The three altars mentioned here provide an excellent illustration of the passage from our *parasha*. The altar in Arad was an earthen altar, the altar in Mount Ebal (assuming it is indeed an altar) was an altar of "unhewn stones, over which an iron tool was not wielded" (see Deut. 27:5, Middot 3:4), while the dismantled altar at Tel Sheva was made of hewn stones, against the Torah's injunction!

Another type that is not mentioned in the Torah is an altar that is hewn wholly in the rock. Several Nabatean altars of this type can be found in Petra, but these are not relevant for those who are studying Tanakh. Throughout Israel, however, three examples of this type of altar, which, in theory, date back to the biblical period, can be found. One of these is a huge altar at the foot of the tell of ancient Samaria (Sebastia). The other two are "Manoah's altar" below Tel Tzor'a (located today at the edge of the Shimshon industrial area) and the beautiful four-horned altar found by Doron Nir-Zvi in Giv'at Harel, near Shiloh, whose details I publicized in 2003.

Altar in Giv'at Har'el, sight from west

It should be noted that the dimensions of the altar in Arad, Manoah's altar, and the altar in Giv'at Harel approximately match the dimensions of the burnt-offering altar described in Exodus – five cubits long and five cubits wide and three cubits tall! The latter two altars, as well as the altar at Mount Ebal, are all located in open areas, at the

(Courtesy of L. Leipnik)

Altar in Giv'at Har'el, top and horns

middle of the mountain and not at its peak. This information allows us to speculate that these altars were designed for worshipping God and not for idolatry. It is likely that those who carved the altars out of the natural rock felt that this method of building was fundamentally similar to building an earthen altar.

More doubtful cases are the altars (or altar bases) in Shechem, in Tell Qasile in north Tel Aviv, in Dan, and in Ḥorvat Qitmit in the Negev (an Edomite site). A fortified structure from the end of the First Temple period located south of Jericho, featuring two raised platforms with steps leading up to them, might be added to this list as well. This structure, excavated in 1982 was interpreted (somewhat hesitantly) by the site's excavator Avi Eitan as a "*bamot* house."[3] An early *bama* that most probably did not serve as an altar can be found in the village of Yabrud, 1.5 miles northwest of modern Ofra. The *bama* is built from large stones and surrounds a centuries-old Mediterranean hackberry tree, which was apparently preceded by an even more ancient tree (*celtis australis*) before it. It is difficult to determine how old this *bama* is, but it should be noted that one of the stones of the *bama* is pentagonal, and contains

3. Eitan himself did not repeat his cultic suggestion in his 2008 publication; see reference list below.

small pentagonal depressions of the kind found occasionally in Byzantine churches. Aside from these examples, various hewn stone sites have been identified as altars by scholars searching eagerly for remains of ritual.

In the end, the number of incense altars found far outstrips the number of animal altars. The proportion between these two types of altars is surprising, since animal sacrifice is the more basic ritual act. In fact, the Hebrew word for altar – *mizbe'aḥ* – is fundamentally connected to the word for slaughtering an offering – *zeviḥa*. Thus, the expression *mizbaḥ haketoret* (incense altar) is a borrowed phrase by its very nature. Why, then, are there so many incense/meal-offering/libation altars and so few animal altars?

Drawing of an altar of incense, Henry Baker Tristram, 1865

(courtesy of Meir Rotter)

Incense altar *in situ* at Tel Dothan

Why So Few Animal Altars Survived: A Difficult Question

The answer to this question might be that much of the ritual animal sacrifice was performed on alternative surfaces, including natural rock surfaces, large stones, and earthen altars that were not designed to be preserved. The first of these can be found in the story of Manoah and the angel – "and [he] offered them up on the rock to the Lord" (Judges 13:19), and perhaps in archaeological findings as well in the tumuli of western Jerusalem.[4] The second type – large stones – is mentioned in the account of the Battle of Michmas in I Samuel (14:33), and the third type – earthen altars – is mentioned by Naaman, the Aramean army commander (II Kings 5:17). Despite this, it is unclear if this solution is sufficient. The Tanakh does not merely mention explicitly the existence of ritual animal sacrifice, but also describes the construction of altars, the destruction of altars, and the altar stones themselves. In the story of Gideon (Judges 6), the beginning of the revelation takes place when Gideon places an offering of meat and matzot on a rock, but in that same place an altar was later built and another altar was destroyed. Even the large stone upon which King Saul sacrificed later became an actual altar (I Sam. 14:35). When Elijah challenges the prophets of Baal on Mount Carmel, a sacrifice ostensibly takes place in an open area "large enough for two seahs of seed" (I Kings 18:32) surrounded by a hastily erected trench, but there is also a destroyed altar that is restored and an (additional?) altar made up of twelve large stones.

In the end, the hundreds of instances in Tanakh where the word "altar" is mentioned attest to the fact that there is no simple solution to this question. We might claim that altars made of unhewn fieldstones are not designed to be preserved over time, or perhaps that it is difficult to distinguish between them and generic field clearing piles. However, the earthen altar found in Arad and the altar at Mount Ebal demonstrate that even altars made of unattached bricks or of rough stones can be preserved. Perhaps we can assume that the lack of altars is a result of the massive,

4. These are about twenty mounds of earth and stones covering small pits in the areas of Givat Massuah, Ir Ganim, Ora, Aminadav, and Beit Zayit. The mounds feature burn marks and are surrounded by short fences. According to the excavator of two of them, Ruth Amiran, and my late father Yehuda Elitzur, who published two papers concerning this subject, these sites served as altars; according to archaeologist Gabriel Barkay, however, they were lamentation sites of the kings of Judah.

far-reaching campaigns to purge the land of altars undertaken by Hezekiah and especially Josiah, as recounted by the Tanakh.[5] The two kings were not as meticulous in their destruction of incense altars, possibly because their small size made it easier for worshippers to hide them. Another possibility is that offering incense outside the Temple in Jerusalem was not considered as grave an offense as animal sacrifice outside the Temple.[6]

For further study:

Barkay, G. "Mounds of Mystery: Where the Kings of Judah Were Lamented." *Biblical Archeology Review* 29 (2003): 32–39, 66.

Ben-Yosef, S. "Yabrud." In *Israel Guide: An Encyclopedia for the Study of the Land* 8 (1980), edited by A. Yitzḥaki, 316–318 [Hebrew].

Bin-Nun, Y. *Eretz HaMoriya: Pirkei Mikra Velashon*. Alon Shevut, 2006, 219–221 [Hebrew].

Cassuto, U. *A Commentary on the Book of Exodus*. Jerusalem, 1967, 255–256.

Eitan, A. "Vered Yeriḥo." *Excavations and Surveys in Israel* 2 (1983): 106–107.

Eitan, A. "Vered Yeriḥo." *NEAEHL* 5 (2008): 2067–2068.

Elitzur, Yehuda. "*Lemahut Haregamim Bema'arav Yerushalayim.*" *Israel and the Bible*, Ramat Gan, 2000, 164–171 [Hebrew].

Gitin, S. "The Four-Horned Altar and Sacred Space: An Archaeological Perspective." In *Sacred Space: Archaeology and the Religion of Israel*, edited by B. Gittlen, 95–123, Winona Lake, 2002.

Haran, M. "Altar-ed States: Incense Theory goes up in Smoke." *Bible Review* 11 (1995): 30–37, 48.

Kempinski, A. "Joshua's Altar – An Iron Age I Watchtower." *BAR* 12 (1986): 42, 44–49.

Mazar, A. *Archaeology of the Land of the Bible*. New York, 1990, 492–502.

Nir-Zvi D., and Yoel Elitzur. "A Rock-Hewn Altar Near Shiloh." *The Palestine Exploration Quarterly Volume* 135 (2003): 30–36.

Porten, B. *The Elephantine Papyri in English: Three Millennia of Cross-cultural Continuity and Change*. Atlanta, 2011, 151.

Shanks, H. "BAR Interviews Avraham Eitan: Antiquities Director Confronts Problems and Controversies." *BAR* 12 (1986): 30–38.

Zertal, A. "Has Joshua's Altar Been Found on Mt. Ebal?" *BAR* 11 (1985): 26–43.

---

5. There are, however, two archaeological contexts that seem to indicate that Josiah's agents preferred to bury ritual sites dedicated to the God of Israel rather than destroy them: the altar in Arad (according to Yoḥanan Aharoni) and the tumuli in western Jerusalem (according to my father *z"l*).
6. This last theory is supported by testimony in the Elephantine papyri, which date back to the fifth century BCE: "And sheep, ox, and goat (as) burnt-offering are [n] ot made there, but (only) incense (and) meal-offering."

Parashat Mishpatim

The Destined Borders of the Land of Israel

> I will set your borders from the Sea of Suph to the Sea of Philistia, and from the wilderness to the Euphrates; for I will give into your hands the people who live in the land, and you will drive them out before you. Do not make a covenant with them or with their gods. (Ex. 23:31–32)

Expansive Borders Described Four Times in the Torah

Four times in the Torah the borders of the Promised Land are described as extraordinarily vast, reaching all the way to the Euphrates River. The first time we find this description is in God's promise to Abraham at the Covenant of the Pieces: "On that day the Lord made a covenant with Abram, saying, 'To your offspring I assign this land, from the river of Egypt to the great river, the river Euphrates'" (Gen. 15:18).

The second time is in our *parasha,* in the closing lines of the covenant of Sinai: "I will set your borders from the Sea of Suph to the Sea of Philistia, and from the wilderness to the Euphrates" (Ex. 23:31).

The third time is in the opening of Moses' first speech at the beginning of Deuteronomy. Moses cites God's command to Israel in anticipation of their journey from Horeb:

> The Lord our God spoke to us at Horeb, saying: You have stayed long enough at this mountain. Start out and make your way to the hill country of the Amorites and to all their neighbors in the Arabah, the hill country, the Shephelah, the Negeb, the seacoast, the land of the Canaanites, and the Lebanon, as far as the Great River, the river Euphrates. See, I place the land at your disposal. Go, take possession of the land that the Lord swore to your fathers, Abraham, Isaac, and Jacob, to assign to them and to their heirs after them. (Deut. 1:6–8)

The fourth time is at the end of the series of faith chapters that open the Book of Deuteronomy:

> The Lord will dislodge before you all these nations: You will dispossess nations greater and more numerous than you. Every spot on which your foot treads shall be yours; your territory shall extend from the wilderness and the Lebanon and from the River – the Euphrates – to the Western Sea will be your border. (Deut. 11:23–24)

These four sources complete one another. The verses describe six geographical points that delineate the borders of the land:

- In the north – *the Euphrates River*. The Euphrates River is mentioned in all four parallel passages. It seems that this refers to the northwestern section of the river, north of the river's "knee." Today, this area contains an artificial lake adjacent to the Syrian town of Maskaneh, about sixty miles east of Aleppo.
- In the west – *the Mediterranean Sea,* called the Sea of Philistia or the Western Sea in these passages.
- In the south – *the Sea of Suph,* and in Genesis 15, *the river of Egypt.* The Sea of Suph divides into two gulfs: the Gulf of Eilat on the east

and the Gulf of Suez on the west. North of the Gulf of Suez lies the easternmost branch of the Nile Delta, which carried a stream in ancient times but subsequently ran dry. In the Hellenistic period and the Roman period, this branch was known as the Pelusian arm, after the city of Pelusium, located in what is now Tell el-Farama near Baluza in the northwest Sinai Peninsula. The city was situated on the riverbank and became known for producing fine linen fabrics.[1]

- In the east – the wilderness, and in Deuteronomy 11, *the wilderness and the Lebanon.* "The wilderness" is apparently the large Syrian Desert east of the inhabited region of Transjordan. This enormous desert was impassable in ancient times. Therefore, even though the Land of Israel is situated west of Babylonia (which accounts for its sobriquet in the Babylonian Talmud: "Ma'arava"), ancient travelers to the Land of Israel from Babylonia, Assyria, or Aram would have to journey along the northern Euphrates and enter the land from the north.[2]

The inclusion of the Lebanon among the borders of the Land of Israel presents some difficulty, as ostensibly the Lebanon region does not lie on the border but falls within it. A solution to this problem can be found in the Septuagint, which translates the word *Ha-Levanon* in Deuteronomy 11 as "Antilibanos," meaning the Anti-Lebanon mountains, the long mountain range that begins at Mount Hermon and trends northeast, east of the Beqaa Valley. This range is known in Arabic as "al-Lubnān esh-Sharqi" – the eastern Lebanon. It can also be demonstrated that in Biblical Hebrew as well this range is occasionally called "the Lebanon." The strongest evidence can be found in Song of Songs: "Your brow like the Lebanon tower[3] that faces toward Damascus" (7:5). From western

1. See Mishna Yoma 3:7: "In the morning he put on Pelusium linen worth twelve minas."
2. This explains Jeremiah's references to Nebuchadnezzar and the Babylonians: "From the north disaster will be poured out on all who live in the land" (Jer. 1:14), and "For I am bringing disaster from the north" (4:6).
3. "Tower" here seemingly refers to a steep mountain range.

> Lebanon it is impossible to see Damascus; from eastern Lebanon, on the other hand – the Anti-Lebanon mountains – it is certainly possible. If we review the borders of the land, the Torah seems to be referring to the northeastern slopes of the Anti-Lebanon mountains, near the town of al-Qaryatēn. The line that follows the length of the border of the Syrian Desert from south to north, toward the "knee" of the Euphrates mentioned above, passes through this very region.

To summarize, these passages speak of expansive borders, which include all the inhabitable land east of the Mediterranean Sea. Defined another way: all of Greater Syria between Egypt and Mesopotamia, the middle portion of what is known as the Fertile Crescent. This vast region was defined in a national sense, in a manner typical of the zeitgeist of Isaiah's time: "In that day, Israel shall be a third partner with Egypt and Assyria as a blessing on earth" (Is. 19:24).

An Alternate Border in the Book of Numbers

In addition to these borders, there is a destined border different from the one described above. *Parashat Masei* delineates entirely different borders for the Land of Israel: "Instruct the Israelite people and say to them: When you enter the land of Canaan, this is the land that shall fall to you as your portion, the land of Canaan with its various boundaries" (Num. 34:2). The chapter goes on to describe the borders in great detail. Many have dealt with these borders and suggested identifications for the names mentioned here. Instead of discussing these borders from a geographical perspective, however, we will first highlight what is missing from these borders: the Euphrates River, the Sea of Suph, the wilderness, and the river of Egypt.

In place of these expansive borders, we find much smaller borders. In the north, the border extends to Lebo-hamath and Mount Hor.[4] According to the identification advanced by *Ḥazal* (in halakha, Aggada, and *Targumim*) and supported by evidence from Tanakh

4. This refers to the northern Mount Hor, rather than the southern Mount Hor where Aaron died.

Mount Hor in the Nur Mountains

(II Kings 14:25–28),[5] this peak is located in the Amanus ridge, today the Nur Mountains, above the northeast corner of the Mediterranean Sea. In the south, the border extends to the wilderness of Zin and Kadesh-barnea (in the region known today as the Negev Mountains), in the southwest to the Wadi of Egypt, identified with Wadi el-Arish, and in the east to the Jordan and the Dead Sea. The same borders are mentioned in brief in the description of the land that the spies scouted: "From the wilderness of Zin to Rehob, at Lebo-hamath" (Num. 13:21). The only component in the border delineated in *Parashat Masei* that matches the borders we recognize from Genesis, Exodus, and Deuteronomy is the western border – the Mediterranean Sea.

The entire history of the nation of Israel, from the Exodus to the conquest of the land of Canaan, is based on these reduced borders. If the borders of the land had been defined then by the Sea of Suph and the river of Egypt, this would mean that the people of Israel had already entered the Land of Israel the moment they crossed the Sea of Suph. If so, they could have remained in Marah and Elim and saved themselves all those years of wandering in the wilderness! The spies were sent to scout out the land, starting from the region of Kadesh-barnea and the wilderness of Zin, which were the southern borders of the smaller land

5. In these verses, whose wording corresponds with the borders of Numbers 34, the borderline delineated through Lebo-hamath includes Hamath itself inside the Land of Israel, and thus suits the northern approach of Ḥazal.

of Canaan described in Numbers 34. The entire story of the spies and the subsequent decree that the nation would wander in the wilderness can only be understood if these were the actual borders of the Land of Israel.

In light of these considerations, it seems that the Torah presents two different sets of borders for the Land of Israel, one expansive and one more limited. If we examine the Book of Joshua, we find that it, too, presents two sets of borders. At the opening of the book, the expansive borders are presented (Josh. 1:4), using language that closely resembles the passage from Deuteronomy 11. However, Joshua 13 uses the borders of *Parashat Masei* – "to Lebo-hamath" – as a point of contrast for the achievements of the conquest. Two sets of borders for the Land of Israel are hinted at in Deuteronomy as well, in the passages on the cities of refuge: "And when the Lord your God enlarges your territory... then you shall add three more towns to those three" (19:8–9). In other words, there is the basic state in which there are three cities of refuge (in addition to those that Moses designated in Transjordan), and there is also an expanded state, when God enlarges the borders of Israel, and they will have to add another three cities.

According to the plain meaning of the text (as opposed to the wishful thinking of certain scholars), these two sets of borders are not a practical description of the territory that was conquered or that was settled by the people of Israel during any particular historical period. Rather, these are both theoretical sets of borders mentioned in the Torah prior to the entrance of the people of Israel into the land. However, we must still answer a question that arises from this conclusion: Why was the Land of Israel given two different sets of borders from the start?

Why Are There Two Sets of Borders?

Some solve this problem by defining the expansive borders as the "promised borders." According to this interpretation, it is not incumbent upon the people of Israel to realize these borders; this was simply an abstract promise that only God is required to fulfill. When God desires to bestow these expansive borders upon His nation, He will do so. This approach does not make sense conceptually and does not accord with the language of the text. Conceptually, according to the

Jewish faith, God does not make promises that are not applicable to man in a practical sense. Even regarding the manna that sustained the people of Israel in the wilderness – an unparalleled miracle – the people were still required to toil: "The people would go about and gather it, grind it between millstones or pound it in a mortar and boil it in a pot" (Num. 11:8). And from a textual perspective, consider that the commandment to take possession of the land is said in connection with the expansive borders in Deuteronomy: "Start out and make your way... as far as the Great River, the river Euphrates. See, I place the land at your disposal. Go, take possession of the land..." (1:7–8). In his addenda to *Sefer HaMitzvot*, Nahmanides cites these verses from Deuteronomy 1 as the primary basis for the positive commandment of taking possession of the land.[6] Thus, the expansive borders constitute destined borders that the people of Israel are commanded to realize, and not merely "promised borders."

What Is the Solution?

It seems[7] that the text in our *parasha* (and similarly in *Parashat Ekev* in Deuteronomy 7) answers this question. The Torah speaks of the fact that the conquest of the land will be accomplished in a slow process: "I will drive them out before you little by little, until you have increased and possess the land" (Ex. 23:30). The Torah presents two obstacles that may stand in the way of Israel's conquest of the land. The first is: "lest the land become desolate and the wild beasts multiply to your hurt" (23:29), and the second is: "You shall make no covenant with them and their gods. They shall not remain in your land, lest they cause you to sin against Me; for you will serve their gods – and it will prove a snare to you" (23:32–33). The land that was designated for the people of Israel is large and expansive. In the future, Israel will grow and become as numerous as the stars of heaven and the sands on the seashore; but at the time, their population numbered about 600,000 men, and it was thus impossible to take possession of the entire land. Even if they would be able to

6. I would like to thank Rabbi Yoel Bin-Nun for pointing this out to me.
7. Malbim suggested a similar explanation in his commentary to Numbers 34.

conquer all of it, they would be forced to choose between two evils: either to allow their enemies to remain in the land and forge a treaty with them that will inevitably "prove a snare" to Israel; or to destroy the nations of the land without being able to then settle the empty tracts of land generated as a result. This second option is a bad one as well, not to mention immoral. God is prepared to expel the land's inhabitants if they would be substituted by the people of Israel, but not at the cost of bringing utter desolation to the world. The proper, correct solution is to conquer the land by stages. In the first stage, the Torah outlines the borders of a smaller version of the land, one that the people of Israel would be able to conquer and settle within the same generation. Subsequently, when the people of Israel grow in number and in strength, it will be incumbent upon them to finish taking possession of the entire land, in its full, expansive form. Just as the commandments of appointing a king and building a permanent temple were intended to be relevant only in the future, the completion of the conquest and settlement of the entire land was only intended for the future as well – for the second stage.

This principle – that God designated a territorial nucleus for immediate conquest and established a stage-based program for the remainder of the land – was implemented by Joshua, following God's command even in the context of the limited borders described in *Parashat Masei*. In Joshua 13, after the overview of "the territory that remains" (13:2), which he did not manage to conquer, Joshua accepts a divine promise and, with it, a divine command: "I Myself will dispossess those nations for the Israelites; you have only to apportion their lands by lot among Israel, as I have commanded you" (13:6). In Joshua's final speech to the nation, he declares that he carried out this command:

> See, I have allotted to you, by your tribes, [the territory of] these nations that still remain, and that of all the nations that I have destroyed, from the Jordan...The Lord your God Himself will thrust them out on your account and drive them out to make way for you, and you shall possess their land as the Lord your God promised you. (13:4–5)

If we pay close attention to the tribal borders, it is apparent that Joshua formally added two large swaths of land to the territorial regions of two powerful tribes that were not actually conquered: the southern coast – Philistia – to the tribe of Judah (15:44–47)[8] and the northern valleys – the Beit She'an Valley, the Jezreel Valley, and the northern Sharon plain, to the tribe of Manasseh (17:11). Joshua did not allot the remaining land in the north – "to Lebo-hamath" – to the tribes even formally. Joshua estimated correctly that conquering this land was not a goal that could be achieved in the near future, so he left this task to the leaders who would follow him, even on the declarative level.

On the other hand, there was also a significant reversal from the original plans. As a result of the war and conquest of the land of Sihon and the request of the Gadites and the Reubenites, this territory was given to these tribes under a special contract. The territories of Reuben and Gad, which were located beyond the Jordan River and therefore were originally intended to be conquered and settled only during Stage B, were advanced to Stage A. Thus, while Joshua did accomplish his task, he deviated somewhat from the form in which it was given to him; assessing the reality in light of the principles of the Torah, he added land in the east and neglected land in the north.

Returning to the two sets of borders delineated in the Torah, the Torah not only designates all of "Greater Syria" for the people of Israel, but also commands them to conquer and settle this land. This region includes land stretching from Egypt to the Euphrates River, on both sides of the Great Rift Valley, including the Sinai Peninsula. But this is a destiny for the future, when the nation grows and becomes capable of fulfilling its mission properly. For the first stage, however, the plan is to conquer a much more limited region – the land east of the Mediterranean between the Great Rift Valley and the sea, and in particular, Cisjordan until the Makhtesh Ramon area in the south.

---

8. A smaller unconquered region that was given to Judah as a duty for the next generation was apparently the land of Jerusalem, including Bethlehem and the vicinity of modern Gush Etzion (Josh 15:63). The next generation indeed accomplished this task, as indicated in some passages in the books of Judges and I Chronicles. See the reference to my recent article about Bethlehem in the bibliography below.

The prophetic messages that appear frequently in the books of the Prophets in Tanakh, which foretell that in the future the desert will bloom and contain sources of water, are connected to this idea. The ability to take true possession of the entire land – not through imperial rule from above and not over a desolate land – will come in tandem with the divine blessing that allows the desert regions of the land to bloom.

The (Potential) Holy Land

There is another interesting conceptual, perhaps mystical point that we can add to this discussion. It seems that the entire land, in its expansive version, possessed a kind of "potential for holiness" even before it was conquered, which lay dormant until that time. R. Yehuda HaLevi writes in his *Kuzari* that the prophecy of Moses, Aaron, and Miriam was a result of the special quality (*segula*) of the Land of Israel, because

> Sinai and Paran are reckoned as belonging to the Land of Israel, because they are on this side of the Sea of Suph, as it is said, "I will set your borders from the Sea of Suph to the Sea of Philistia, and from the wilderness to the Euphrates" [Ex. 23:31]. (2:14)

R. Yehuda HaLevi's purpose was certainly not to contradict the Torah's assertion that Moses, Aaron, and Miriam never entered the land, and that they wandered through Sinai and Paran on the way to the Land of Israel. Rather, he was undoubtedly referring to the deeper message that we mentioned above – the land where Moses, Aaron, and Miriam prophesied was not the Land of Israel in actuality, but only in potential.

We may add that, according to this, the moment that the people of Israel crossed the Sea of Suph and entered the greater boundaries of the Promised Land, even though this was not technically considered part of the Land of Israel, the people immediately merited the virtue of song: "Then Moses and the Israelites sang this song to the Lord" (Ex. 15:1). The virtue of song is intrinsically connected to the Land of Israel, as the Talmud states: "Hallel is not said for a miracle which occurred outside of the Land of Israel" (Megilla 14a). The

Talmud challenges: "How then do we come to say it for the Exodus from Egypt, which was a miracle which occurred outside the Land of Israel?" and answers:

> As it has been taught: Until they entered the Land of Israel, all lands were counted as proper for chanting a hymn of praise [for miracles done in them] – After they had entered the land, other countries were not counted as proper for chanting a hymn of praise [for miracles done in them].

Thus, we may argue on a deeper level that in the end, the Song of the Sea was recited in a place that will one day be included in the holiness of the Land of Israel.

One day, the nation of Israel will fulfill its destiny and merit the realization of the Torah's message:

> And when the Lord your God enlarges your territory, as He swore to your fathers, and gives you all the land that He promised to give your fathers – if you faithfully observe all this Instruction that I enjoin upon you this day, to love the Lord your God and to walk in His ways at all times. (Deut. 19:8–9)

When this occurs, it will become clear, in retrospect, that both song and the Torah were given to Israel – in the Land of Israel.

For further study:

Elitzur, Yehuda. "*Gevulot HaAretz Bemasoret Yisrael.*" *Israel and the Bible,* Ramat Gan 2000, 375–383 [Hebrew].

Elitzur, Yoel. "*Hagam HaLevanon BeEretz Yisrael?*" *Nekuda* 48, (1983): 10–13 [Hebrew].

Elitzur, Yoel. "*Beit Lehem Bizman Kibbush Ha-Aretz Uvi-Yemey Ha-Shoftim.*" *Meḥqerey Ḥevron Vi-Yehuda* 5, (2016): 26–39 [Hebrew].

The Destined Borders of the Land of Israel

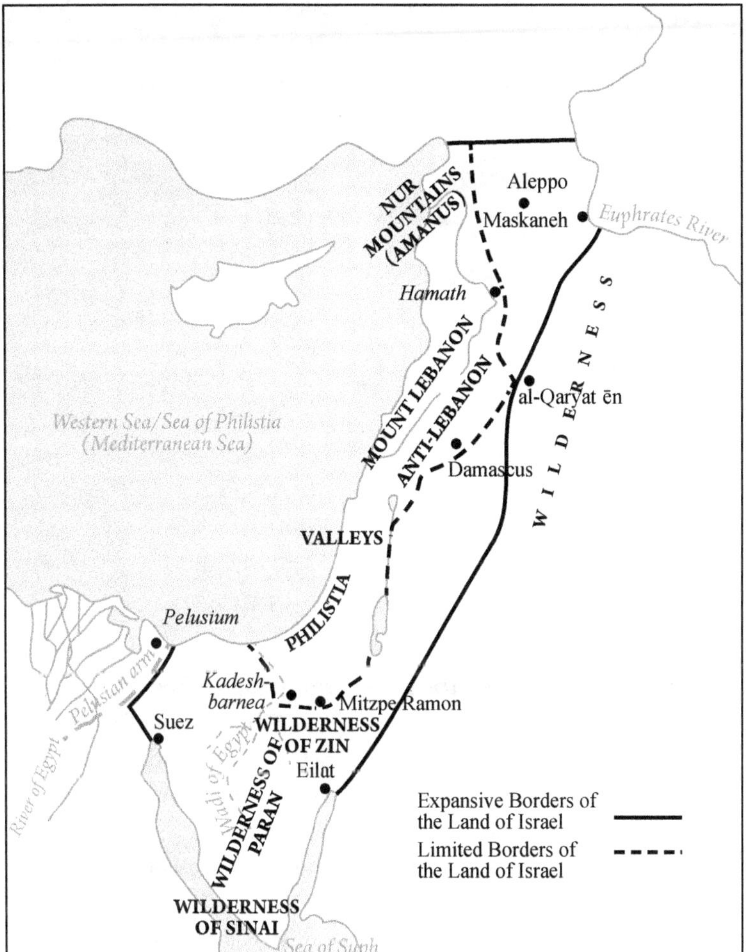

Parashat Teruma

The Givlim

Were the Givlim Named for Their Profession or Their Location?

The *haftara* for *Parashat Teruma* relates that the people of Israel were not the only ones engaged in the construction of the Temple; members of other nations participated as well, including Ḥiram's masons and the *Givlim*: "Solomon's masons, Ḥiram's masons, and the *Givlim* shaped them. Thus the timber and the stones for building the house were made ready" (I Kings 5:32). Who are the *Givlim*?

Targum Jonathan translates the word as *argovlaya,* a rare word that only appears in the *Targum* one other time, in its translation of "and the masons and the stonecutters" (II Kings 12:13). Similarly, the Syriac Peshitta translates *givlim* as *argovlei,* and uses this same word in its translation of "and the laborers" (12:12). Apparently, there is a common Targumic tradition that manifests itself in both Targum Jonathan and the Peshitta. Based on the context in II Kings 12, it is clear that this term refers to a kind of craftsman who specializes in building or stonecutting. Writers of historical dictionaries have had difficulty locating an etymological background for this strange word. According to some scholars, it is derived from the Greek word *ergolabos,* meaning "work manager," while others connected it to the ancient Sumerian word BUR.GUL, meaning stonecutter. In the end, no one has suggested a truly precise parallel for this word.

However, all our classical commentators (Rashi, Rabbi Joseph Qara, Radak, Ralbag, and also the *Metzudot*) rejected the interpretation of the *Targum*, which states that *hagivlim* refers to the name of a profession. Instead, they argue, *HaGivlim* is the name of a nation – the residents of the city of Gebal. Indeed, the Latin Vulgate also interpreted the word in this manner, and this interpretation is accepted in modern exegesis as well.

(Z. Radovan)

Ancient temple in Gebal – Byblos

Gebal is a large, ancient port city that is rich in archaeological findings, located on the northern Lebanese coast between Beirut and Tripoli. The northern section of the Mount Lebanon region is named for this city – "the land of the Gebalites" (Josh. 13:5). Besides the mention of *HaGivlim* in I Kings and "the land of the Gebalites" in Joshua, the city is mentioned one other time in Tanakh, in a context critical for understanding the narrative here in I Kings. It appears when Ezekiel is instructed by God to "intone a dirge over Tyre" (Ezek. 27:2). He laments: "Gebal's elders and craftsmen were within you, making your repairs" (27:9). We learn two things from this: First, that in the time of Ezekiel, the city of Gebal was subject to Tyre, and second, that it was home to expert builders. It seems that in Solomon's time as well, the expert builders that King Ḥiram of Tyre sent to assist in building the Temple hailed from Gebal. Furthermore, the proximity of Gebal to the cedar-rich Mount Lebanon range certainly made it an important source of cedar wood for building.

The form *givli/givlim* indicates that the name Gebal is derived from the so-called "segolate" nominal pattern. This pattern features one syllable consisting of a consonant followed by a vowel and then a cluster of two consonants, as in *malk* (king) or *qudš* (holiness).[1] The form *geval* found in Ezekiel probably constitutes the Aramaic equivalent of this same segolate pattern.[2] Arabic sources record the city's name in the form Jubayl (pronounced today Žbayl).

Comprehensive archaeological excavations conducted at Gebal during the 1920s yielded many impressive discoveries, including remnants of a fortified royal city with a magnificent castle. The antiquities found in Gebal included Canaanite inscriptions commemorating the kings of Gebal and their households. The earliest of these kings was Aḥiram (the biblical form Ḥiram was apparently a shortening of this name), who, according to scholars, predated Solomon by about a century. (A)ḥiram/Ḥirom was a common Phoenician name. In the time of Solomon, it was the name of both the king of Tyre and an Israelite master craftsman – "the son of a widow of the tribe of Naphtali, and his father had been a Tyrian" (I Kings 7:14) – who created the copper

1. A similar indication can be found in the Amarna letters of the fourteenth century BCE, where the forms *gubla* and *gubli* can be found, rendered in Greek as Βύβλος (Byblos). It is presumed that the Greek word *biblos/byblos*, meaning "book," originated from the Greek version of the name of the city of Gebal, since in ancient times the Egyptian papyrus passed through Gebal on its way to the Aegean world. It may be that the Hebrew-Canaanite alphabet reached ancient Greece via Gebal as well. (According to Herodote 5:58 both the papyrus and the script reached Greece through the Phoenicians who came with Kadmos).
2. Compare to the Aramaic *gevar*, which is parallel to the Hebrew *gever*, and the Aramaic *melakh*, which is parallel to the Hebrew *melekh*. In addition, there are several segolate words in Hebrew that are pronounced in the Aramaic manner, such as *devash* (honey), *sevakh* (thicket), and the city Benei Berak.

(Z. Radovan)

Sarcophagus of Ahiram, king of Gebal – Byblos (tenth century BCE)

vessels for the Temple. One of the more significant findings at Gebal was a statue bearing the name of King Shishaq of Egypt, depicting Shishaq sitting on his royal throne. Shishaq's name is inscribed in Egyptian, alongside the Canaanite inscription "to King Abibaal of Gebal in Egypt." From Tanakh, we learn that Shishaq invaded the Land of Israel and that King Reḥavam of Judah succeeded in dissuading him from attacking Jerusalem by presenting him with a large bribe. The inscription found in Gebal reveals that Shishaq conquered Gebal in the north as well, and that its king Abibaal was, like Reḥavam, a vassal king to Shishaq.

Gebal is not merely a location that appears in the *haftara*; it is also an integral part of the Land of Israel. In the chapter on *Parashat Mishpatim*, we addressed the fact that the Land of Israel possesses two sets of borders, one expansive and one more limited. As it turns out, Gebal falls within the borders of the Land of Israel even according to its limited borders. We learn this explicitly from Joshua 13. The text delineates the "territory that remains" (13:2) that the people of Joshua's generation were meant to conquer but did not succeed in reaching. The borders of this remaining territory which follow the limited set of borders described in *Parashat Masei*, include:

> The land of the Gebalites, with the whole [Valley of the] Lebanon, from Baal-gad at the foot of Mount Hermon to Lebo-hamath on the east, with all the inhabitants of the hill country from the [north of the] Lebanon to Misrephoth-maim, namely, all the Sidonians. I Myself will dispossess them for the children of Israel. (13:5–6)

Thus, according to the Tanakh, it is the nation of Israel's responsibility to aspire to reach all the way to Gebal.

Two Gebals

There is one final point to make. It is important to distinguish between two different vocalizations of the word Gebal: גְּבַל with a *pataḥ* and גְּבָל with a *kamatz*. All the instances of Gebal that we have mentioned in our discussion thus far are examples of the *pataḥ* vocalization. The *kamatz* vocalization can be found in Psalms: "the clans of Edom and the Ishmaelites, Moab and the Hagrites, Gebal, Ammon, and Amalek" (83:8). The geographical context here indicates that the verse is speaking of a strip of land in the southern Transjordan. This Gebal is apparently the northern part of Edom, southeast of the Dead Sea. The Jerusalem *Targum* translates Mount Seir (*Har Se'ir*) as "Gebala." This name is found in Greek-Roman sources (in the form "Gebalene") and was adopted by the Arabs in the form "al-Jibāl."

The Talmud recounts two incidents that took place in Gebal (גבלא). In the first, R. Ḥiyya b. Abba, the prominent disciple of the *Amora* R. Yoḥanan, visited Gebal and encountered a weak, half-assimilated Jewish community (Yevamot 46a, Avoda Zara 59a). The second incident is a beautiful story, one of a series of *aggadot* in praise of the Land of Israel at the end of Tractate Ketubbot:

> R. Yehoshua b. Levi once visited Gebal, where he saw vines laden with clusters of ripe grapes standing up [to all appearances] like calves. "Calves among the vines!" he remarked. "These," they told him, "are clusters of ripe grapes." "Land, O Land," he exclaimed, "withdraw your fruit; for whom are you yielding your fruit? For those Arabs who rose up against us on account of our sins?"

> Toward [the end of that] year R. Ḥiyya happened to be there and saw them standing up [to all appearances] like goats. "Goats among the vines!" he exclaimed. "Go away," they told him, "do not you treat us as your friend did." (Ketubbot 112a)

Which Gebal is the Talmud referring to in these two incidents? The proper vocalization of the Aramaic גבלא is unclear: Is it Gabla – the northern Gebal (Byblos) or is it Gebala – the southern Gebal (Gebalene/Seir)? Most scholars of talmudic geography are certain that it is Mount Seir, on account of the mention of "Arabs" in the story in Ketubbot. However, Professor Saul Lieberman correctly noted that the scholars were misled here by their use of print versions of the Talmud. The appearance of the word "Arabs" is actually the result of internal censorship implemented in European printings of the Talmud because of fear of the Christians. In the manuscripts and in the first printing (MS Venice 1521), the original text was still in place: "For those *goyim* ("gentiles") who rose up against us on account of our sins." The nature of this story and its context within Ketubbot teach us that, as *Tosafot* point out (in Avoda Zara 59a), the Talmud here refers to a location in the Land of Israel. Because of this, Lieberman maintains that this story relates to the northern Gebal, which is included in the Land of Israel even within its more limited borders delineated in Numbers 34 and mentioned again in Joshua 13. Rabbi Ishtori Haparḥi already suggested this identification in his *Kaftor Vaferaḥ* (ch. 11). Finally, the first story has parallel versions in the Yerushalmi, and the northern connection is apparent from there as well. It seems therefore that in these two talmudic stories, the place under discussion was Gabla (which is identical with the biblical Gebal – with a *pataḥ* – and the Greek Byblos) and not Gebala (the later name of Mount Seir).

For further study:

Albright, W. F. "Gebal." *Encyclopaedia Biblica*, II, 404–411 [Hebrew].

Haparḥi Ishtori. *Kaftor Vaferaḥ*. Lunz ed., 251 [Hebrew].

Lieberman, S. *Studies in Palestinian Talmudic Literature*. Jerusalem, 1991, 413, 584–585 [Hebrew].

Mazar, B. "Gebāl." *Encyclopaedia Biblica*, II, 403–404.

Reeg, G. *Die Ortsnamen Israels nach der rabbinischen Literatur*. Wiesbaden, 1989, 157 [German].

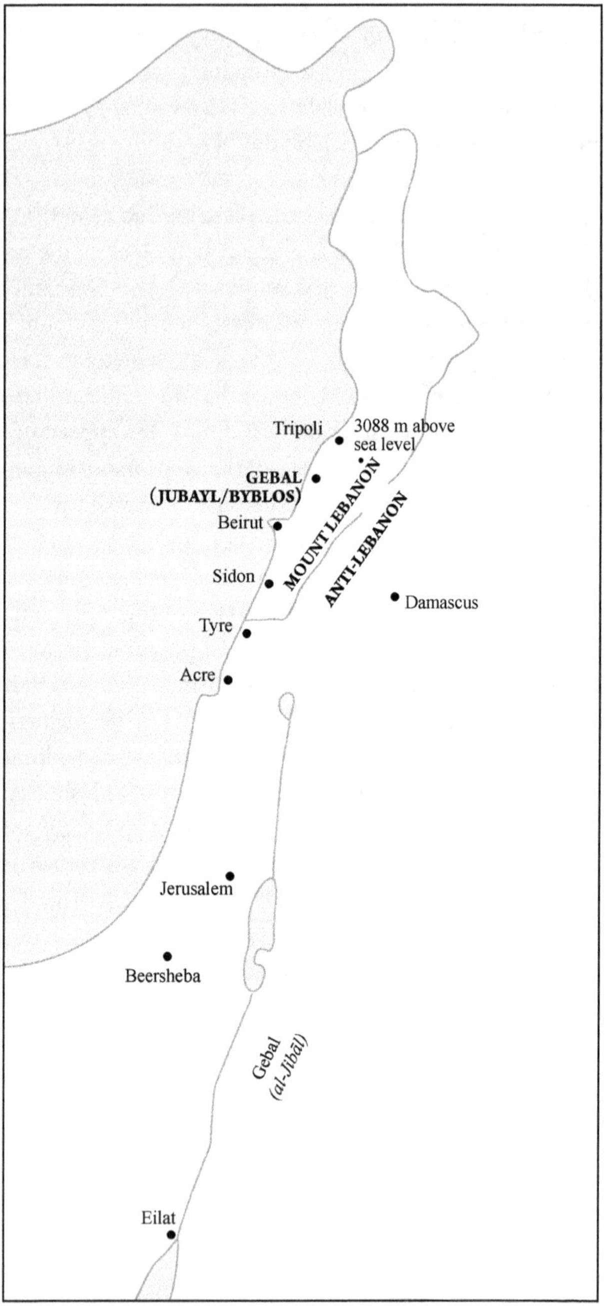
Tripoli
3088 m above sea level
GEBAL
(JUBAYL/BYBLOS)
Beirut
Sidon
MOUNT LEBANON
ANTI-LEBANON
Damascus
Tyre
Acre
Jerusalem
Beersheba
Gebal
(al-Jibāl)
Eilat

Parashat Tetzaveh – Zakhor

Remembering Amalek

"Remember what Amalek did to you" (Deut. 25:17). Before we discuss the Amalek incident and attempt to understand it fundamentally, we must first ask a more basic question: Who was Amalek, and where did this nation live?

Who Was Amalek?

Amalek was a nomadic nation, spread out across large desert expanses. The Amalekites were related to the Ishmaelites, the Midianites, and the Kedemites, known as the "tent dwellers" (Judges 8:11). Periodically they would penetrate inhabited settlements, and, according to Judges, "their camels were countless" (7:12).

What is the origin of Amalek? According to the list of the descendants of Esau at the end of *Parashat Vayishlaḥ* (Gen. 36:12), Amalek was Esau's grandson, or in other words, a second cousin of the nation of Israel. However, "the territory of the Amalekites" (14:7) is mentioned even in Abraham's time, in the story of the war of the four kings. *Ḥazal* explained: "Amalek had not yet arisen, yet you say, 'and subdued all the territory of the Amalekites'? Rather, 'declaring the end from the

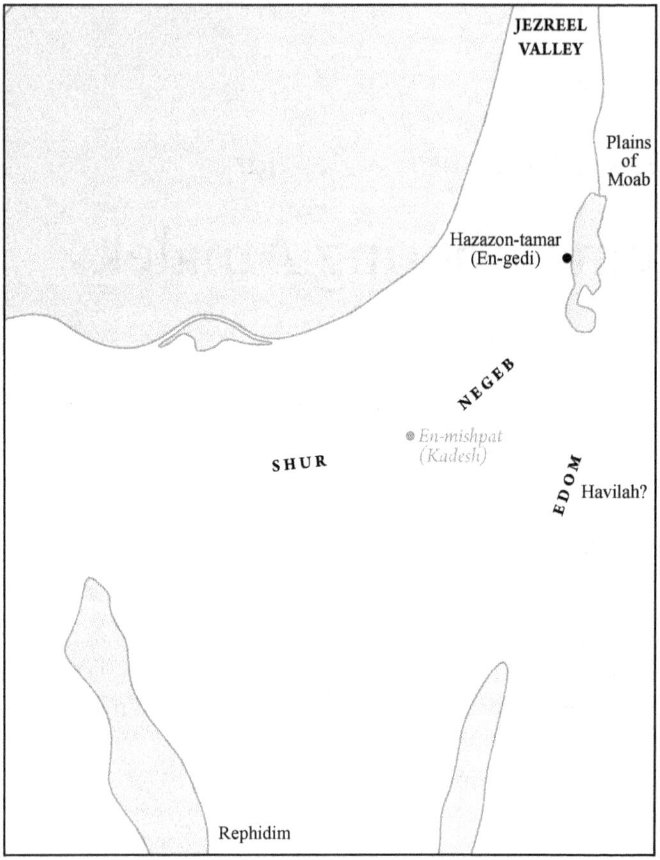

beginning'" (Genesis Rabba 41). In other words, the name written in Genesis 14 is merely a reflection of the reality at the time the Torah was written, and not an indication that the Amalekites already existed at that time. However, Balaam later prophesies, "The first of the nations was Amalek; but its fate is to perish forever" (Num. 24:20). The interpretation of the *Targumim* and the classical commentaries that Amalek was the first nation to attack Israel following the Exodus seems unlikely in light of the simple reading of the text. The interpretation advanced by Nahmanides, Samuel David Luzzatto, and others that Amalek was the premier nation at the time does not at all fit the image of Amalek as a nation of bandits and raiders who preyed on stragglers. It seems, then, that the correct interpretation is that of Grintz, who wrote that in the Tanakh's view, Amalek and its lifestyle exemplify the early state of humanity. Grintz cites I Samuel 27:8: "the Geshurites, the Gizrites, and the Amalekites – who were the inhabitants of the land from of old." According to Grintz's position, Amalek was apparently the name of an ancient nation that spread out over large expanses on the outskirts of the settled part of the land. As for Amalek son of Eliphaz son of Esau, it is reasonable to assume, following Nahmanides in his commentary to Genesis 14:7, that he was named for this nation, or alternatively, joined them, similar to the other sons of Esau assimilated with the sons of Seir the Horite.

Where Did Amalek Live?

In Numbers, the spies report that "Amalekites dwell in the Negeb region" (13:29), and we read later on in the narrative of the spies that "the Amalekites and the Canaanites occupy the valleys" (14:25); "the Amalekites and the Canaanites will be there to face you" (14:43); and "the Amalekites and the Canaanites who dwelt in that hill country came down" (14:45). This placement of the Amalekites fits "the territory of the Amalekites" found in Genesis 14:7 – between "En-mishpat, which is Kadesh" and Hazazon-tamar (En-gedi).[1] This was the basic extent of their territory. But in reality, Amalek reveals itself in many additional places, including Rephidim (Ex. 17), the plains of Moab (Num. 24), and the Jezreel Valley (Judges 6). Amalek reaches their greatest level of dispersion in I Samuel: "Saul destroyed Amalek from Havilah all the way to Shur, which is east (*al penei*[2]) of Egypt" (15:7). This area itself is defined in Genesis as the area to which the Ishmaelites spread: "They dwelt from Havilah, by Shur, which is east (*al penei*) of Egypt, all the way to Asshur; they camped alongside all their kinsmen" (25:18).[3] This regional description returns in I Samuel, in an extremely significant context:

1. II Chr. 20:2.
2. The preposition *al penei* should be interpreted here as *kedem* – east.
3. The Asshur mentioned here is not Asshur in northern Iraq, but the name of the territory of one of the descendants of Ketura (Gen. 25:3).

> David and his men went up and raided the Geshurites, the Gizrites, and the Amalekites – who were the inhabitants of the region from of old, all the way to Shur and to the land of Egypt. When David attacked the region, he would leave no man or woman alive. (27:8–9)

It seems that this emphasis on equivalent geographical areas serves to establish a contrasting parallel between the first two kings of Israel. Saul was disgraced and lost his kingdom when he did not heed the word of God, neglecting to annihilate Amalek completely as commanded. In contrast, David presents a "dowry" to God – even before his crowning – that rectifies the very issue that constituted Saul's failure. He destroys the same nation of Amalek in exactly the same region – but in contrast to Saul, "he would leave no man or woman alive."

"From Havilah all the way to Shur, which is east of Egypt": Where is this region? Shur can be found in other places. In the stories of the Patriarchs, Shur marks the edge of the western Negeb: "Then Sarai treated her harshly, and she ran away from her. An angel of the Lord found her by... the spring on the road to Shur... between Kadesh and Bered" (Gen. 16:6–7, 14); "[he] settled between Kadesh and Shur" (20:1). On the other hand, it is also mentioned immediately following the crossing of the Sea of Suph: "Then Moses caused Israel to set out from the Sea of Suph. They went on into the wilderness of Shur" (Ex. 15:22). We can infer from the combination of these sources that "Shur" refers to the region known today as northern Sinai.

Havila, on the other hand, is not easy to identify. It is mentioned in Genesis, in the Garden of Eden narrative: "the land of Havilah, where the gold is" (2:11). In addition, Havilah is the name of one of the sons of Cush (10:7), and the name of one of the sons of Yoktan as well (10:29). All of these Havilahs are located in regions far to the south of the Land of Israel and its neighboring lands, and thus it seems that our Havilah is a different place entirely. Since Havilah had never been mentioned in the context of southern Canaan, and the Torah states that Abraham's sons by concubines (among whom the Ishmaelites were certainly included) were sent eastward, to the land of the East, we can estimate that the Havilah of the Ishmaelites and Amalek was some desert region in the southern Transjordan, near Edom. This means that the Amalekites spread out over a large area that apparently included the entire northern Sinai Peninsula, Negeb Mountains, and southern Transjordan. If so, this large expanse was the home of various nomadic peoples, including the Ishmaelites – and the Amalekites as well.

The Question

Now we must ask the main question: What is the meaning of our eternal conflict with Amalek? "I will utterly blot out the memory of Amalek from under heaven" (Ex. 17:14); "You shall blot out the memory of Amalek from under heaven. Do not forget" (Deut. 25:19); "Now go, attack Amalek, and proscribe all that belongs to him. Spare no one, but kill alike men and women, infants and sucklings, oxen and sheep, camels and asses!" (I Sam. 15:3). The difference between these harsh commands and the attitude that the Torah displays toward Egypt is stark: "You shall not abhor an Egyptian, for you were a stranger in his land" (Deut. 23:8). But is the crime of having "cut down all the stragglers in your rear" (25:18) truly worse than the crime of "every boy that is born you shall throw into the Nile"? Is it not simply the way of warfare to pinpoint and exploit the enemy's weaknesses? Why is the Torah so much more stringent in its response to a one-time incident that occurred in a military context than in its response to a long period of enslavement, replete with mortar, bricks, and cruel taskmasters?

One original solution to this problem, rooted in a simple reading of the text, was suggested by Ariella Deem, a writer and Bible scholar from Jerusalem, who died at a young age in 1985. Deem examined the various incarnations of Amalek throughout Tanakh, and discovered some intriguing information: Apparently, Amalek serves, in a way, as the nation of Israel's "evil twin." When the people of Israel leave Egypt and reach Rephidim, on the verge of entering the wilderness of Sinai, Amalek suddenly appears and attacks them. (Note the language of the verse: "And Joshua overwhelmed *the nation* of Amalek with the sword" (Ex. 17:13) – the moment Israel becomes a *nation*, we hear the term "the *nation*" applied to Amalek as well.) Israel continues to wander, and in the fortieth year they encamp at the edge of the Promised Land, in the

Ariella Deem (1935–1985)

plains of Moab, at the Jordan near Jericho, atop the ruins of the kingdom of King Sihon the Amorite. Whom do they encounter at this critical moment? Once again, none other than Amalek. The Torah relates that Balaam peered out from the mountaintop at Israel in its tribal encampment, and immediately thereafter: "He saw Amalek" (Num. 24:20). In the time of the Judges, when Israel was already settled in their land, there was no king in Israel, and each tribe had to fend for itself, we find Amalek again by their side with tribes of their own: "Now Midian, Amalek, and all the Kedemites were spread over the plain, as thick as locusts; and their camels were countless" (Judges 7:12). The Amalekites spread throughout the land, raiding produce from the farmlands and filling the Jezreel Valley. When Israel starts to become an organized nation, led by their first king, Saul, Amalek acquires their first king as well – Agag. This is also the first we read of the *city of Amalek*: "Then Saul advanced as far as the city of Amalek and lay in wait in the wadi" (I Sam. 15:5).

In contrast to the rest of Esau's descendants, who chose the land of Edom and became integrated therein, dispossessed some of the Horites and assimilated into the rest, Amalek instead clings to Israel, refusing to let go. When Israel sets its eyes on the land of Canaan, Amalek does the same. Ariella Deem writes: "Before us a monstrous figure begins to appear, inching closer to us like a murky shadow, a kind of twin of ours, growing and developing with us, wrapped around our ankles, a dark specter, our menacing twin."

Amalek refuses to leave us alone. Wherever we go, Amalek is there as well. At every stage of our national development, Amalek develops along with us. Whenever we attempt to take possession of a piece of land, we find that Amalek is interested as well. Amalek is a figure that competes with us for our identity and for our place – in our land, in the world, in history. The war with Amalek is more than just revenge; it is an act of defense – it is either us or them. We are commanded to blot out the memory of Amalek, but it is no less important for us to be able to distinguish between Israel and Amalek. The harsh war with Amalek is, in essence, Israel's only means to survive and endure.

My father *z"l* added that the command to annihilate Amalek in the time of Samuel and Saul was not rooted in the events of the past. In the Book of Samuel, the Amalekites are a corrupt people that subsists on theft and pillaging. I Samuel recounts the decisive battle between Israel and the Philistines. The Amalekites wait until the moment is right and take advantage of the departure of the two armies from their respective camps, gleefully plundering both sides of the conflict: "And there they were, scattered all over the ground, eating and drinking and making merry because of all the vast spoil they had taken from the land of the Philistines and from the land of Judah" (30:16). The Amalekites stormed in, burning Ziklag (David's city at the time), taking all the women and children captive and seizing all their possessions. As they traveled from Ziklag, they abandoned an Egyptian boy who was taken captive in one of their earlier raids because he fell ill with the flu, or with indigestion.[4]

Saul is commanded to "go and proscribe the sinful Amalekites; make war on them until you have exterminated them" (I Sam. 15:18). When Samuel is about to execute Agag, he does not recite a blessing over the fulfillment of the mitzva of destroying Amalek; rather, he proclaims:

4. His ailment must not have been very serious – David and his men were able to restore him to health with merely a pressed fig cake, two raisins, and a jug of water!

"As your sword has bereaved women, so shall your mother be bereaved among women" (15:33). According to the simple understanding, Saul and Samuel's war with Amalek had little to do with Agag's family ties or with his historical provenance. Amalek was a generic name that included other nomadic raiders of their type as well; only the Kenites, who performed an act of kindness for the nation of Israel, were commanded to "withdraw from among the Amalekites, that I may not destroy you along with them" (15:6). This was a war for survival.

In one of the last sentences in Ariella Deem's short article, she writes: "It is almost difficult to avoid modern-day comparisons, and every generation has its own Amalek."

The mitzva to remember Amalek is eternal. We remember Amalek even when the historical nation of Amalek has already been mixed up throughout the nations. According to Ariella Deem, when we search for the quality of "Amalek-ness" in the world, we are not necessarily referring to evil, but rather to competition with Israel. When a religion claims that it is the true Israel – when a nation claims that it is the chosen race, while the Jews are an inferior nation that must be destroyed – when people claim that this land is not the Land of Israel, but a land with a different name, belonging to them – perhaps this is the essence of Amalek, about whom the Torah commanded: "Remember" and "Do not forget."

For further study:

Deem, A. "*Reishit Goyim Amalek.*" *Maariv* (literary supplement), 3/1/85 [Hebrew].[5]

Elitzur, Yehuda. *Israel and the Bible*. Ramat-Gan, 2000, 125 [Hebrew].

Grintz, Y. M. *Studies in Early Biblical Ethnology and History*. Tel Aviv, 1969, 95–96 [Hebrew].

Daat Mikra commentary on Numbers 24:20 and I Samuel 15:3 [Hebrew].

5. The article was published posthumously several weeks after Deem's passing.

Parashat Ki Tissa

The Nation of Canaan and the Girgashites

While this book is entitled "Places in the Parasha," this chapter's discussion will focus on a group of people glaringly absent from *Parashat Ki Tissa*. On two occasions in the *parasha*, God promises the people of Israel that He will expel the Canaanite inhabitants of the land from before them:

> I will send an angel before you, and I will drive out the Canaanites, the Amorites, the Hittites, the Perizzites, the Hivites and the Jebusites. (Ex. 33:2)

> I will drive out before you the Amorites, the Canaanites, the Hittites, the Perizzites, the Hivites and the Jebusites. (34:11)

Perceptive readers will note immediately that each of these two lists includes only six nations. One of the nations of Canaan is missing: the Girgashites! While it may be that the Torah hints at the Girgashites in the text – "I will drive out (*vegerashti*)"; "I will drive out (*hineni goresh*)" – nevertheless it is curious that only six nations are listed outright.

The Girgashites and the Lists of the Nations of Canaan

The nations of Canaan are enumerated in Tanakh twenty-three times, mostly in the Torah and in Joshua. Only three of these lists actually include all seven nations – twice in Joshua (3:10 and 24:11) and only once in the Torah:

> When the Lord your God brings you to the land that you are about to enter and possess, and He dislodges many nations before you – the Hittites, Girgashites, Amorites, Canaanites, Perizzites, Hivites and Jebusites, seven nations much larger than you. (Deut. 7:1)

It is no accident that the Torah punctuates this list of nations with the words, "seven nations much larger than you," as this is the only time in the *Chumash* that all seven nations are listed. The list of nations appears seven times in Exodus, all of which omit the Girgashites (in one list, the Perizzites are omitted as well, and in another only three nations are listed). The list appears another six times in Joshua and the beginning of Judges, and again, the Girgashites are missing from four of these lists![1]

In Genesis, it is a different story. There, the nations of Canaan are enumerated twice. The first time is in chapter 10, in the "Table of Nations," which lists the names of the seventy nations of the world descended from Shem, Ham, and Japheth. The second time is in chapter 15, in the Covenant of the Pieces, when God promises the land of Canaan to Abram. In both instances, more than seven nations are listed.

1. Some inaccurate versions of the Bible emended the text to "correct" perceived errors. Thus, the Samaritan Pentateuch added the Girgashites to each of the seven lists in Exodus, so that all of them include seven nations. In the Septuagint a similar emendation was implemented six times. In fragments of the Book of Exodus found in Qumran, four lists were found, two of which are identical with the Masoretic text, one contains all seven nations like the Samaritan Pentateuch and the Septuagint, and in one case the Girgashites replace the Amorites of our text.

In the Table of Nations, twelve names are enumerated among the "clans of the Canaanites." Six of these are northern names that do not recur in the later lists of the nations of Canaan, and the remaining six are familiar to us from the other lists of Canaanite nations – Canaan, Heth, Jebusites, Amorites, Girgashites, Hivites. Here the missing nation is the Perizzites. In the Covenant of the Pieces, ten nations are enumerated: four that are unique to that *parasha* (the Kenites, Kenizzites, Kadmonites and Rephaim) and six that are familiar to us from the other lists – the Hittites, Perizzites, Amorites, Canaanites, Girgashites, and Jebusites. This time it is the Hivites who are left out.[2]

Thus we can summarize by saying that in the earliest periods, the Girgashites existed and even wielded greater power than the Hivites and Perizzites. However, from the time of Moses and on we barely hear of the Girgashites; they only appear three times, in celebratory lists that intentionally include all seven nations.

What do we know from Tanakh about the Girgashites? The answer is: virtually nothing. The Girgashites are not mentioned in any place in connection to a city or any particular place in the land. In the two verses that detail the regions throughout the land where each Canaanite nation resided (Num. 13:29 and Josh. 11:3), the Girgashites are not mentioned. Josephus mentions the Girgashites once in his writings (*Antiquities* 1.139, on Gen. 10:15–18), noting regarding them and several other Canaanite nations that all we know about them from Scripture is their names.

What Happened to the Girgashites?

Ḥazal cite a surprising tradition that provides a historical-geographical solution to the omission of the Girgashites from most of the lists:

> This is in line with what R. Shmuel b. Naḥman said: "Joshua sent three proclamations to [the Canaanites in] the Land of Israel prior to the [Israelites'] entry into the land: 'Whoever wishes to emigrate should emigrate; [whoever wishes] to make peace

2. Here again, the Samaritan version (but not the Septuagint) insists on adding the Hivites in order to ensure that the list contains seven nations.

> should make peace; [and whoever wishes] to wage war should do so.' The Girgashites emigrated, for they believed in the Holy One, blessed be He, and they went to Afrike. [This is in line with II Kings 18:32:] 'To a land like your own' – this refers to Afrike. The Gibeonites made peace. [This is in line with Joshua 10:1:] 'The people of Gibeon had come to terms with Israel.' Thirty-one kings waged war and fell [in battle]."[3]

At the time, "Afrike" referred to what is known today as North Africa, in particular the Tunis region. *Ḥazal* claimed that Afrike was a land like our own. To be sure, it does not possess the same spiritual character as our land, but perhaps the two lands share some physical characteristics, like climate and economic opportunities. From this minimalistic approach, at least, it is a land like our own.

Over the course of many generations, North Africa was home to nations of Canaanite origin who left numerous inscriptions written in the Phoenician language and alphabet. There were Canaanite towns scattered all along the coast of the Mediterranean Sea throughout the entire first millennium BCE and apparently even earlier. From the Israelites' perspective, apparently when King Solomon forged a treaty with King Hiram of Tyre, this treaty included in practice economic control over these Canaanite coastal towns. The capital of these towns was Carthage (today a suburb of Tunis), known to the Phoenicians as *Qart-ḥadašt*, to the Greeks as *Karkhēdon* and to the Romans as Carthago. The Carthaginians were culturally connected to Tyre, which was known as *Qart*, meaning "city."[4] According to a Greek myth of Carthaginian origin, *Karkhēdon* was founded by Queen Dido of Tyre. Incidentally, it seems that the Zarephath mentioned in Obadiah – "And that exiled force of Israelites [shall possess] what belongs to the Phoenicians as far as Zarephath" (1:20) – is not the more well-known "Zarephath of

3. Y. Shevi'it 6:1 and similarly Vayikra Rabba 17:6, Devarim Rabba 5:14; compare to Tosefta Shabbat, end of chapter 7, and Mekhilta Bo 18 (p. 69), where the residents of Afrike are depicted as descendants of the Canaanites and the Emorites respectively.
4. Compare to "on the heights of the town (*al gapei meromei karet*)" (Prov. 9:3), and to the Aramaic *karta*.

Sidon" (I Kings 17:9), which, being part of the territory of the tribe of Asher, would not truly qualify as an "exile." Rather, it is a city on a distant Mediterranean coast that was named for the city in the Land of Israel.[5] In the fifth century BCE (early Second Temple period), Carthage became the most important naval superpower in the Mediterranean Sea, and in the third to second centuries BCE it fought three great wars against Rome (the "Punic Wars"). In the Second Punic War, Rome was almost defeated by the Carthaginian military commander Hannibal (a Canaanite name par excellence!) and in 146 BCE Carthage was destroyed. About two hundred years later, Carthage was rebuilt as a Roman city.

The historical connection between North Africa and the land of Canaan is also expressed in another tradition cited by *Ḥazal*. According to this tradition, in the time of Alexander the Great, the people of Afrike brought a claim against Israel, arguing that the land of Canaan belonged to them. Gebiha son of Pesisa then argued against them and defeated the people of Afrike in the debate.[6]

A remarkable incarnation of this rabbinic tradition is found in the Greek work *History of the Wars*, by Procopius of Caesarea, a Byzantine writer who was a member of the court of Justinian I in the sixth century CE. In this work, Procopius mentions the Moors, early Semitic residents of North Africa, and relates that they are descended from the Girgashites, the Jebusites, and "some others with other names by which they are called in the history of the Hebrews" (book IV, chapter 10). These nations fled from Joshua, were not able to settle in overcrowded Egypt, and so continued onward to Libya.

> And they established numerous cities and took possession of the whole of Libya as far as the Pillars of Heracles [the Strait of Gibraltar], and there they have lived even up to my time, using the Phoenician tongue. They also built a fortress in Numidia [the Atlas Mountains region], where now is the city call Tigisis.

5. The late Ḥezi Katz, a resident of Yagur, pointed this out to me, and his suggestion appears reasonable. See Radak and Ralbag on the verse in I Kings.
6. Megillat Taanit, 25 Sivan, according to Scholion P; Sanhedrin 91a; Genesis Rabba 61:7.

> In that place are two columns made of white stone near by a great spring, having Phoenician letters cut in them which say in the Phoenician tongue: "We are they who fled from before the face of Joshua, the robber, the son of Nun!"[7]

We will not discuss here the question of how much we can trust the testimony of this author, who did not know but was still able to relate the fantastical content of a unique inscription written in this language. Rather, let us return to our own sages.

Rashi accepted the core of R. Shmuel b. Naḥman's claim, citing it twice in brief: "They were six nations [listed here], and [this is because] the Girgashites rose and emigrated because of them [the Israelites] of their own accord" (commentary on Exodus 33:2). In contrast, Ibn Ezra and Nahmanides (in their commentaries on 3:8) apparently maintained that this is simply a homiletical interpretation that does not properly reflect the real history and the simple understanding of the text.[8] Therefore, they suggested alternate solutions. Ibn Ezra states: "And [the Torah] did not mention the Girgashites because it was the smallest of the seven [nations]... and the text included them in the word 'Canaanites.'" Nahmanides speculates: "Perhaps the [Girgashites'] land was not flowing with milk and honey [like the lands of the other nations]."

A nation with a name similar to *Girgashi* is found in an extra-biblical source from the biblical period. This Egyptian source recounts the war between Rameses II (thirteenth century BCE) and the Hittites, who had joined forces with a tribe or nation whose name was written in Egyptian as ḳrḳš3. Other sources mention first names that are similar to *Girgashi*. Aside from examples in Ugaritic texts[9] (*grgs* and *bn* grgš), it is noteworthy that the greatest concentration of names of this type

---

7. This same story about Canaanites who fled from Joshua appears, with minor changes, in excerpts from the work of Christian historian John of Antioch, as well as in the *Suda*, a Byzantine encyclopedia written circa 1000 CE.
8. Compare to Yoḥanan Aharoni's claim that the source of this aggadic story is the linguistic similarity between *vegerashti* and *goresh mipanekha* and *Girgashi*.
9. Ugarit was an ancient city and kingdom on the banks of the Mediterranean Sea in northern Syria. It was destroyed in the middle of the period of the Judges.

(Wikipedia)

Naḥum Slouschz (1871–1966)

is found in Phoenician-Carthaginian inscriptions from Qart-ḥadašt in Tunis – or in the language of *Ḥazal*, Afrike. Dedication inscriptions for pagan temples in the city feature the names of donors to the temple, including *bʿlytn bn grgš, grgš bn - -*, and *mtn bn grgšm*. In light of these findings, Professor Naḥum Slouschz permitted himself to speculate: "In the Talmud it is told that the Girgashites went to Africa … and perhaps the donator is of Girgashite descent."

Investigation of the Findings in Light of Scripture

The archaeological findings from Carthage serve to support the rabbinic tradition that commentators and scholars had written off as an imaginative homiletical interpretation. However, the Tanakh seems to indicate a slightly different version of this tradition; the Girgashites had already disappeared by the events of Exodus, and they were apparently not significant among the nations living in Canaan by the time the Israelites left Egypt. The departure of the Girgashites from Canaan at the behest of Joshua, then, is an aggadic formulation of the actual history. On the other hand, the three mentions of the Girgashites in Deuteronomy and Joshua seem to demonstrate that not all the Girgashites had left the land.[10] At this point in time Ibn Ezra's solution is correct. In the period of the Exodus and the conquest, the Girgashites were indeed a smaller nation than the rest of the Canaanite nations, and thus were not listed independently aside from the celebratory lists that presented all seven nations. Instead, they were included within the general term "Canaanites." Ibn Ezra's solution on its own does not fit the information that can be inferred from Genesis, where we see that the Girgashites were seemingly more important than the Hivites and the Perizzites. Nonetheless, in combination with the information that we have gleaned from analyzing the texts and connecting this with the archaeological findings, it seems that we should accept Ibn Ezra's solution, but limit it to the period following the departure of most of the Girgashites from the land.

Thus, our conclusion integrates the tradition cited by R. Shmuel b. Naḥman with the interpretation of Ibn Ezra.

For further study:

Aharoni, Y. "*Girgashi.*" *Encyclopaedia Biblica* 2, 551 [Hebrew].

Gordon, C. H. *Ugaritic Textbook.* Rome, 1998, 381.

Levy, J. *Studies in Jewish Hellenism.* Jerusalem, 1969, 60 [Hebrew].

Lieberman, S. *Tosefta Ki-Fshutah,* Part III: Seder Mo'ed. New York, 1962, 105 [Hebrew],

Procopius. Translated by H. B. Dewing, II, London and Cambridge, Massachusetts, 1953, 286–289.

Slouschz, N. *Thesaurus of Phoenician Inscriptions,* Tel-Aviv, 1942, 266, 273, 301 [Hebrew].

10. Compare to the migration of the Danites from Zorah and Eshtaol to Laish in the northern part of the Land of Israel. Six hundred armed men, with their children and wives, moved to the north, but generations later we find that the Danites Manoah and Samson seem to have remained in Zorah and Eshtaol.

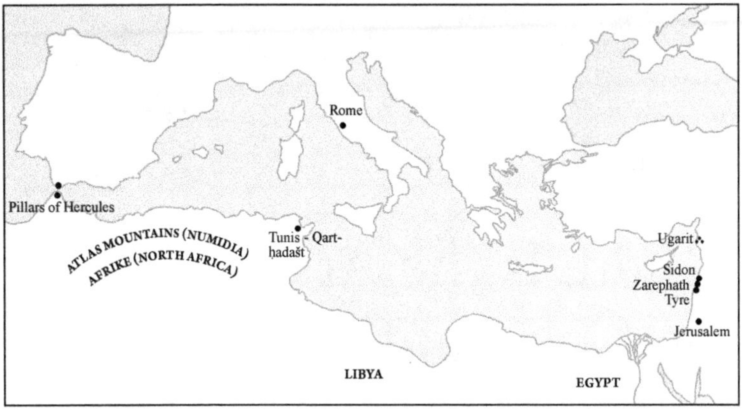
Rome
Pillars of Hercules
ATLAS MOUNTAINS (NUMIDIA)
AFRIKE (NORTH AFRICA)
Tunis - Qart-
ḥadašt
Ugarit
Sidon
Zarephath
Tyre
Jerusalem
LIBYA
EGYPT

Parashat Vayak'hel

Where Is the Ark of the Covenant?

The crowning glory of the Tabernacle and its vessels, the focal point that exemplifies more than anything else the presence of the Divine Presence within Israel, is the Ark of the Covenant, also known as the Ark of the Testimony. Located in the Holy of Holies, the Ark was plated with gold inside and out and contained both the broken and the newly made tablets upon which the Ten Commandments were inscribed. Beside it were the jar of manna (Ex. 16:33), the rod of Aaron (Num. 17:25) and a Torah scroll (Deut. 31:26).[1] The word of God emanated from atop the Ark, where the golden cover and cherubim were situated, as the Torah states: "There I will meet with you, and I will impart to you – from above the cover, from between the two cherubim" (Ex. 25:22). The high priest

1. According to the plain meaning of both this verse and I Kings 8:9 the Torah scroll was placed next to the Ark on the outside, and this is R. Yehuda's opinion in Bava Batra 14a. But R. Meir (ibid.) argued that the scroll was also placed inside the Ark.

would burn the incense between the two poles once a year (Mishna Yoma 5:1). *Ḥazal* regarded the Ark and the cherubim as the pinnacle of the intimate connection between God and Israel. The Talmud describes the poles of the Ark:

> They pressed forth and protruded as the two breasts of a woman, as it is said: "My beloved to me is a bag of myrrh lodged between my breasts" (Song. 1:13). R. Kattina said: "Whenever Israel came up for the festival, the curtain would be removed for them and the cherubim were shown to them, whose bodies were intertwisted with one another, and they would be thus addressed: 'Look! You are beloved before God as the love between a man and a woman.'" (Yoma 54a)

What happened to the Ark of the Covenant? Does it still exist?

The Ark of the Covenant Today?

The Christian residents of Ethiopia are certain that the Ark does exist there today, inside a church in the sacred city of Axum in northern Ethiopia. A guardian monk is charged with the care of the Ark, and even he only enters the chamber that houses the Ark on rare occasions. According to an Abyssinian legend, the Ark was brought to Axum by Menelik, the son of King Solomon and the queen of Sheba. Solomon prepared an exact replica of the Ark for Menelik, but at the last second the original was switched with the replica. Menelik took the original Ark with him and Solomon was left with the replica.... Replicas of the Ark are a central motif in Abyssinian Christianity; they are known as *tabot*[2] and are found in churches throughout Ethiopia. Every year, on January 19, members of the Ethiopian Orthodox Church conduct large processions surrounding *tabot* arks. The arks are concealed from view, so that those who are "unfit" do not gaze upon it. These processions open the ceremonies of the festival of Timqat, which lasts three days.

2. Compare to the Hebrew *teva*; the Aramaic *tēvōta* found in *Targum Onkelos*, the Palestinian *Targumim* and the Samaritan *Targum*; and the Arabic *tābūt*.

An Ethiopian priest with a tabot – a replica of the Ark of the Covenant (AP)

The ark in Axum is brought out as well, in a closely guarded procession; it is wrapped in cloths on all sides.

From a critical perspective, it may be speculated that this tradition surrounding the "true" Ark of the Covenant originated with the custom of creating symbolic replicas of the Ark and distributing them during the public religious celebrations. It is only natural that in the most ancient and central church in the land, greater effort was invested into creating and preserving an outstanding replica of the Ark. Over time, people likely became so convinced of this replica's authenticity that they began to attribute it to Bezalel son of Uri and King Solomon. Note that even in the Menelik legend itself, there seems to be some uncertainty as to which ark is the original and which is the replica.

One of the most famous films of the twentieth century was dedicated to the riddle of the current location of the Ark of the Covenant. The film was Steven Spielberg's *Raiders of the Lost Ark*, which became an international sensation in 1981. In this suspense-filled action film, the brave and adventurous Indiana Jones saves the beautiful daughter of his mentor from the clutches of the Nazis, who are pursuing her because she possesses the means of finding the Ark of the Covenant. By the end of a plot that takes its characters around the globe, traversing exotic locales and exciting landscapes, all the while battling the Nazis and their agents, the forces of good finally triumph over the forces of evil. The Nazis are prevented from obtaining the Ark and using it for their nefarious aims. The film ends with a brilliant comic twist: The American victors transport the Ark, covered in a military tarpaulin, to an enormous army warehouse, where a busy worker attaches a tag to the Ark and places it in a bottomless pile of similar-looking crates. There, the Ark is seemingly lost once again – forever.[3]

Second Temple Period

Legends attempting to solve the mystery of the fate of the Ark of the Covenant existed during ancient times as well. II Maccabees 2 cites an earlier book, which relates that shortly before the destruction of the Temple, Jeremiah was commanded to take the Tent of Meeting, the Ark of the Covenant, and the Incense Altar, and hide them in a cave in Mount Nebo. Jeremiah rebuked the people who wanted to mark the path

3. By the way, the historical conception behind the narrative of Spielberg was that the Ark had been spoiled from Jerusalem by Shishak (cf. I Kings 14:26; I am indebted to Elyakum Berman of Beit Shemesh for this note). To the best of my knowledge there are no commentators or scholars who support this approach, probably because it seems to contradict II Chr. 35:3.

to this cave, informing them that the location must remain hidden until the day comes when the glory of God will reveal itself in a cloud, as it did for Moses and Solomon. This story also found its way into *Josippon,* a Hebrew chronicle from the early medieval period, containing selections from Josephus' writings with various additions. In the version of the legend found in *Josippon,* the ending is slightly different:

> The priests in those days chased after Jeremiah in order to find the location [of the Ark]. Jeremiah looked to his rear and saw the priests, and he became enraged and he swore, saying: "This place will not become known until I and Elijah, the servant of God, return. Then, we will restore the Ark to its place in the Holy of Holies, under the wings of the cherubim."

In II Baruch 6, another pseudopigraphical work,[4] a different story appears. Here, the story is attributed to Baruch son of Neria, who speaks in the first person:

> And it came to pass on the morrow that the army of the Chaldeans surrounded the city... Suddenly a strong wind raised me, and bore me aloft over the wall of Jerusalem. And I beheld four angels standing at the four corners of the city, each of them holding a torch of fire in his hands. And another angel began to descend from heaven and said to them: "Hold your lamps, and do not light them until I tell you. For I am first sent to speak a word to the earth, and to place in it what the Lord the Most High has commanded me." And I saw him descend into the Holy of Holies, and take from there the curtain, and holy ephod, and the cover, and the two tables, and the holy raiment of the priests, and the altar of incense, and the forty-eight precious stones, which adorned the high priest[5] and all the holy vessels of the Tabernacle.

4. This book was most likely written originally in Hebrew; it was preserved in Greek.
5. This number apparently included the clappers within the bells on the robe of the ephod.

> And he spoke to the earth with a loud voice: "Earth, earth, earth, hear the word of the mighty God, and receive what I deposit to you, and guard them until the end times, so that, when you are ordered, you may restore them, so that strangers may not get possession of them..." And the earth opened its mouth and swallowed them up.

A Tannaitic Dispute

Three different positions regarding the fate of the Ark can be found in rabbinic sources, one of which is based on an *aggada* as well. Thus we read in Shekalim 6:

> There were in the temple...thirteen prostrations. [Members] of the household of Rabban Gamaliel and of R. Hananiah the chief of the priests used to prostrate themselves fourteen [times]. And where was the additional [prostration]? In front of the store of wood,[6] for they had a tradition from their forefathers that the Ark was hidden there.
>
> It once happened that a certain priest who was busy [there] noticed that the pavement was different [there] from the others. He went and told his fellow, but before he had time to finish his words his soul departed. Then it became known with certainty that the Ark was hidden there.[7]

Despite this tradition, the other sages – including the first opinion in the same mishna, which enumerates only *thirteen* prostrations – either did not believe the veracity of the story, or did not take it into account in their ruling. Perhaps they believed that the priest in the story simply died of a sudden heart attack, unconnected to the problem of the Ark's location. If so, according to them, what was the eventual fate of the Ark?

---

6. This was located in the northeast section of the court of the women (Middot 2:5).
7. A different version reads: "He struck it with a hammer, and a fire came out and burned him" (Y. Shekalim 6:2 and similarly Bavli Yoma 54a).

The Talmud states: "R. Eliezer said, 'The Ark went into exile to Babylonia...' R. Yehuda b. Lakish said, 'The Ark was hidden in its own place'" (Yoma 53b; Tosefta Shekalim 2; Baraita Dimelekhet HaMishkan 7). R. Yehuda b. Lakish appears rarely in the Talmud, and as a result, in some parallel versions his name was erroneously rendered as R. Yehuda b. Ilai or R. Shimon b. Lakish. According to one *baraita* in the Talmud Bavli, R. Shimon b. Yoḥai maintained that the Ark was "hidden in its own place" as well, but according to a different *baraita* in the Bavli and according to the Tosefta, R. Shimon actually supported R. Eliezer's position. It is interesting to note that the Tosefta opted to omit entirely the opinion that the Ark was hidden in the store of wood, despite the fact that the whole discussion of the fate of the Ark came about as a result of the dispute over the thirteen prostrations. The Bavli cites the tannaitic dispute in connection to the passage in the mishna, "After the Ark had been taken away..." pointing out that "the mishna does not teach 'after the Ark had been *hidden* away,' but 'after the Ark had been *taken* away' – this is in accord with him who holds that the Ark went into exile to Babylonia."

All agree that during the Second Temple period there was no Ark: "In five things the First Temple differed from the Second: in the Ark, the cover, the cherubim,[8] the fire, the Divine Presence, the Holy Spirit, and the *Urim VeTummim* (Yoma 21b and parallels). In contrast to the other vessels in the Temple, the Ark could not be constructed anew, since the most important part of the Ark is the tablets contain within. "And even though Solomon made a pattern for all the vessels, he did not make a pattern for the Ark" (*Baraita Dimelekhet HaMishkan* 7). The question is when and how the Ark disappeared. Those who maintain that the Ark was exiled to Babylonia are supported by the words of Isaiah: "nothing will remain behind" (II Kings 20:17; Is. 39:6) and by the description of the exile of Yehoyachin: "At the turn of the year, King Nebuchadnezzar sent to have him brought to Babylon with the precious vessels of the House of the Lord" (II Chr. 36:10). Those who maintain that the Ark was

8. Rashi explains that the Ark, the cover, and the cherubim were all considered one "thing."

hidden in its own place rely on the description of the Ark in Solomon's Temple in the Book of Kings: "The priests brought the Ark of the Lord's Covenant to its place ... the cherubim shielded the Ark ... the poles were long ... and there they remain to this day" (I Kings 8:6–8). According to this approach, the phrase "to this day" should be interpreted to mean until the time at which the Book of Kings was written and redacted following the destruction of the Temple.[9] Those who follow R. Eliezer's position must respond that "to this day" was written as a description of Solomon's Temple during an earlier period, and the line was simply copied verbatim into the Book of Kings. According to a different *baraita* (Tosefta Sota 13:1; Bavli Yoma 52b; Y. Shekalim 6:2; and parallels), Josiah hid the Ark. (The *baraita* does not say whether he hid the Ark in the store of wood or in some other place.) The *baraita* cites a unique verse in support of this theory – part of the description of Josiah's preparations for Passover in Jerusalem: "He said to the Levites, consecrated to the Lord, who taught all Israel, 'Put the Holy Ark in the House that Solomon son of David, king of Israel, built; as you no longer carry it on your shoulders'" (II Chr. 35:3). The *baraita* explains: "What was his reason for hiding it? He saw the passage, 'The Lord will drive you, and the king you have set over you' (Deut. 28:36) – therefore he hid it." The verse in Chronicles is difficult to understand. According to the commentary attributed to Rashi, Manasseh and Amon, in their wickedness, removed the Ark and put their idols in its place. As a result, Josiah ordered that the Ark be returned to its place.[10] However, Radak (who cited this explanation) took issue with it: Why did Josiah wait? Why did he not return the Ark to its place immediately, just as he removed the idol from the House of the Lord? The words "you no longer carry it on your shoulders" have generally not been interpreted satisfactorily by both the classical and modern commentators. The *baraita* explains that Josiah is commanding the Levites to *hide* the Ark in the place that had been designated for this purpose from the time of Solomon, interpreting the words "you

9. The Talmud (Yoma 54a) rejects Ulla's position that "'until this day' means everywhere 'forever,'" but cannot reject the words of the *baraita* that cited this verse.

10. This interpretation does not fit *Ḥazal's* opinion mentioned above that the verse refers to hiding the Ark.

no longer carry it on your shoulders" to mean: "He said to them, 'If it is exiled with you to Babylonia, you will no longer return it to its place.'"

Both *Rishonim* and *Aḥaronim* marshaled textual support for *Ḥazal*'s interpretation. Rosh, in his *Tosafot,* noted the unique emphasis in the words, "the House that Solomon son of David, king of Israel, built," explaining that this hints at a special construction commissioned by Solomon for the purpose of hiding the Ark. *Tosefot Rosh* goes on to explain that the words "the Levites, consecrated to the Lord, who taught all Israel" indicate that certain exceptionally pious priests and Levites were charged with preserving the knowledge of the Ark's secret location, transmitting this secret from generation to generation. The Maharsha inferred from Josiah's choice of the words "*put* the Holy Ark," rather than "*return* the Holy Ark," that the command was to move the Ark to a new location, a place where it had not been previously. The Chida speculated that even those who maintain that the Ark was exiled to Babylonia agree that the verse in Chronicles indicates that the Ark was hidden during the time of Josiah, only to be discovered later by Israel's enemies (as a result of the people's sins) and fall into their hands.

Modern Scholarship

Like the early exegetes, today's scholars are similarly divided over the question of the Ark of the Covenant's fate. Some maintain that the Ark was looted and exiled to Babylonia. In addition to the verses that *Ḥazal* cited in support of this position, modern scholars cited the verse: "He did not remember His footstool on His day of wrath" (Lam. 2:1). This, however, is not a particularly strong proof that the Ark was exiled, as "His footstool" could be a reference to the Temple as a whole, or even to the city of Jerusalem. Menaḥem Haran claimed, in support of the second approach, that such a valuable and symbolic object would certainly have been mentioned explicitly in the list of the spoils of Nebuzaradan (II Kings 25; Jer. 52) if it had been taken to Babylonia.[11] Yehuda Kiel

11. It should be noted, however, that the golden vessels taken to Babylonia were mentioned in the account of the exile of Yehoyachin without naming each vessel individually, whereas Nebuzaradan's list from the exile of Zedekiah primarily included copper vessels.

was another scholar who maintained that the Ark was hidden. He suggested an original explanation for the verses in Chronicles, in particular regarding "the Levites, consecrated to the Lord, who taught all Israel." According to Kiel, during the time of Manasseh the Ark was situated in the Holy of Holies alongside a statue of Asherah that Manasseh had erected (II Kings 21:7). A group of bold, God-fearing Levites entered the Holy of Holies surreptitiously in the middle of the night, smuggled away the Ark and hid it in a secret location known only to them and their close friends. The verse in Chronicles relates that Josiah instructed these Levites to move the Ark from where they had concealed it to a different secret location that had been set aside for this purpose from the time of Solomon.

My father *z"l* lectured on this topic at the Twelfth World Congress of Jewish Studies in 1997 (a few months before he passed away); the lecture was later published in the Congress's proceedings and in a collection of his articles. He focused on a prophecy that appears toward the beginning of the Book of Jeremiah that is difficult to understand:

> And when you increase and are fertile in the land, in those days – declares the Lord – men shall no longer speak of the Ark of the Covenant of the Lord, nor shall it come to mind. They shall not mention it, or miss it, or make another. (Jer. 3:16)

This is a prophecy of consolation, describing the ideal state of things that will be in the future. But why should the people forget the Ark of the Covenant of the Lord? Why does Jeremiah stress this so emphatically – "Men shall no longer speak ... nor shall it come to mind. They shall not mention it, or miss it, or make another"?

Some commentators focused on the connection between this prophecy and Jeremiah's rebuke in chapter 7:

> Don't put your trust in illusions and say, "The Temple of the Lord, the Temple of the Lord, the Temple of the Lord are these [buildings]"... therefore I will do to the House which bears My name ... just what I did to Shiloh. (7:4, 14)

In other words, Jeremiah is denouncing the approach that held that the Temple was indestructible due to its holiness – that God would not allow it to be destroyed.

According to my father *z"l*, Jeremiah's prophecy in chapter 3 contains much more at first appears. If we read between the lines of the prophecy, we can discern the deep, real-life conflict in the nation at the time regarding the Ark. Some believed that the Temple was no longer a secure place. Since the Temple would likely fall into enemy hands, as they claimed, the prudent course of action would be to preemptively conceal the nation's prized possession – the Ark of the Covenant – in a secret and secure location. In contrast, others believed that the Temple, and in particular the Ark, were so supremely holy that they could never be harmed. Jeremiah stresses that the Sanctuary itself is not protected simply because God's name is invoked in connection with it. Rather, its continued existence within the nation depends on the actions of the people, and considering the actions of the people at the time, this did not bode well for the Temple.

Josephus records a surprising tradition: When Hasmonean leader John Hyrcanus found himself in financial distress, he took out three thousand silver talents from the treasures of King David's sepulchre (*Antiquities* 13:249). It is clear that the treasures preserved in King David's sepulchre would not have survived Nebuzaradan's plundering at the time of the Temple's destruction had they not been concealed in a hiding place whose location was known to only a select few. My father points out that King Manasseh of Judah changed the official burial site of the royal house, and as a result, he, his son, and apparently his grandson Josiah were all buried in this new site: the garden of Uzza. Paradoxically, and in contrast to other kings who were more righteous than he was, Manasseh was the only king who followed the diplomatic policies advocated by the prophets. The prophets consistently preached fealty to the dominant superpower, encouraging kings to avoid misguided pacts and adventurous foreign policy. By following the advice of the prophets in this regard, Manasseh merited fifty-five years of continuous reign. My father estimates that Manasseh began a systematic operation to hide the royal treasures, among them the Ark.[12] These actions, my father claims, garnered blessing from Jeremiah, and Josiah continued in his grandfather's path in this regard as well. My father cites two important archaeological findings that, according to his interpretation, reflect a policy of hiding holy sites and artifacts during the time of Josiah: the tumuli west of Jerusalem and the Israelite temple and altars in Arad. According to this approach, the verse in Chronicles refers to a temporary removal of the Ark from its hiding place by the faithful priests and Levites who were charged with preserving the secret location of the royal treasures, and its placement in the Holy of Holies for the great Passover observance in Jerusalem. All the while, however, the intent was to return the Ark to its hiding place at the conclusion of the festival.

Maimonides' Position

I will conclude this discussion with a surprising ruling found in Maimonides' *Mishneh Torah*:

> When Solomon built the Temple, he was aware that it would ultimately be destroyed. [Therefore,] he constructed a chamber, in which the Ark could be entombed below [the Holy of Holies] in deep, maze-like vaults. King Josiah commanded that [the Ark] be entombed in the chamber built by Solomon, as it is said: "He said to the Levites, consecrated to the Lord, who taught all Israel, 'Put the Holy Ark in the House that Solomon son of David, king of Israel, built…'" (II Chr 35:3). (*Hilkhot Beit HaBeḥira* 4:1)

This is unusual, as Maimonides generally does not rule on historical questions in *Mishneh Torah*, including the interpretation of texts and even halakhic questions that were only relevant in the past (such as the permissibility of the *bamot*), unless there is some practical halakhic implication for the present or the future, or if the question touches on

12. It should not come as a surprise that Manasseh, who famously worshipped many gods, would show respect to the Ark and the God of Israel, as polytheists generally do not object to worshipping an additional god.

a fundamental foundation of faith. So why did Maimonides choose to rule with such certainty in our case, weighing in on what amounts to a tannaitic historical dispute?

It is likely that the reason behind this ruling can be found in the Talmud Yerushalmi:

> R. Yassa said in the name of R. Yoḥanan: "This is the rule – whenever the Ark is within [the Sanctuary], the *bamot* are forbidden; when it has left [the Sanctuary], the *bamot* are permitted." R. Ze'ira asked R. Yassa: "Even [when the Ark has left the Sanctuary] temporarily, as in the case of Eli?" (Y. Megilla 1:12)

In the style of the Yerushalmi, R. Ze'ira's question that was seemingly left unanswered serves as its own conclusion: indeed, even when the Ark leaves the Sanctuary temporarily, the *bamot* become permitted. Rabbi Meir Simcha of Dvinsk, in his *Meshekh Ḥokhma* commentary on *Parashat Re'eh,* expanded on this notion, using it to explain the apparent violation of the prohibition on *bamot* during the Shiloh period. According to him, during the time of the *Mishkan* in Shiloh, the Ark would be removed regularly from its place to be present at national gatherings elsewhere, and sometimes it would even remain in those other locations for extended periods of time. During those periods when the Ark was absent from the *Mishkan* in Shiloh, claims the *Meshekh Ḥokhma,* the *bamot* were permitted.

Now we can return to Maimonides' unusual ruling. In a different, well-known statement that is accepted as the normative halakha, Maimonides rules that the "first consecration" performed by Solomon in Jerusalem applied "for that time and for eternity" (*Hilkhot Beit HaBeḥira* 6:14). This ruling has several halakhic implications, both positive – we can offer sacrifices on the Temple site even without the Temple itself; we can eat the "most holy" sacrifices even without the "hangings" of the Courtyard; we can eat sacrifices of lesser sanctity and *maaser sheni* even without the wall surrounding Jerusalem (Mishna Eduyot 8:6; *Hilkhot Beit HaBeḥira* 6:15) – and negative – the impure may not enter the area of the Courtyard; and *bamot* are prohibited outside Jerusalem. In order to reconcile this ruling with

illustration from c. 1900

The Ark of the Covenant

the statement of the Yerushalmi, Maimonides was forced to rule in accordance with R. Yehuda b. Lakish – the Ark was hidden in its own place![13] If so, according to Maimonides the Ark is still in its original location, waiting for us in the depths of the Holy of Holies, beneath the Foundation Stone in Jerusalem.

For further study:

Chida. *Sha'ar Yosef* on *Horayot* 104b [Hebrew]. http://www.hebrewbooks.org/pdfpager.aspx?req=19259&st=&pgnum=223&hilite=

Elitzur, Yehuda. "*Pulmus Aron Haberit Biyemei Yoshiyahu.*" *Israel and the Bible*, Ramat-Gan, 2000, 230–234 [Hebrew].

Flusser, D. *The Josippon*, 1. Jerusalem, 1981, 45 [Hebrew].

Haran, M. "The Removal of the Ark of Covenant." *Bulletin of the Israel Exploration Society* 25, Jerusalem, 1961, 211–223 [Hebrew].

Kiel, Y. *Sefer Divrei HaYamim* II. *Daat Mikra*, 917–918 [Hebrew].

Wikipedia entries: "Ark of the Covenant," "Axum," "Indiana Jones," "*Raiders of the Lost Ark.*"

13. Incidentally, Rabbi Yoḥanan who authored the above statement in the Yerushalmi ruled explicitly in the Bavli that the prohibition on *bamot* applies even today, because the first consecration applies for eternity (Zevaḥim 107b).

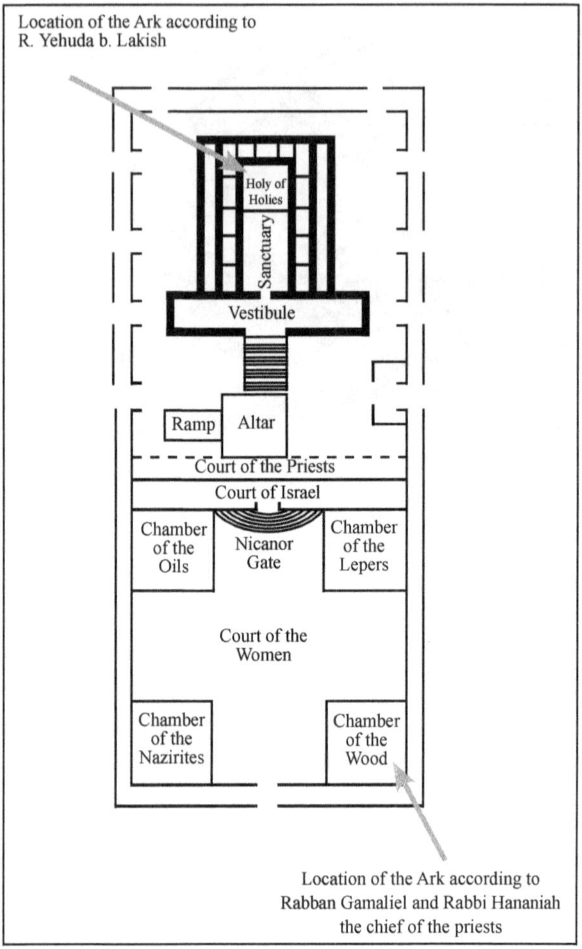
Location of the Ark according to
R. Yehuda b. Lakish
Holy of Holies
Sanctuary
Vestibule
Ramp
Altar
Court of the Priests
Court of Israel
Chamber of the Oils
Nicanor Gate
Chamber of the Lepers
Court of the Women
Chamber of the Nazirites
Chamber of the Wood
Location of the Ark according to
Rabban Gamaliel and Rabbi Hananiah
the chief of the priests

Parashat Pekudei

Tarshish

Tarshish Stone

The *tarshish* stone is one of the twelve gemstones embedded in the high priest's breastplate: "And the fourth row: *tarshish, shoham,* and *yashfe*" (Ex. 28:20, 39:13). It is also mentioned in the similar list of the gemstones that beautify the Garden of Eden, in Ezekiel's prophecy of Tyre: "*Odem, pitda,* and *yahalom; tarshish, shoham,* and *yashfe*" (Ezek. 28:13). In Ezekiel's vision of the chariot, we read: "As for the appearance and structure of the wheels, they gleamed like *tarshish*" (1:16; 10:9). In Song of Songs, the hands of the beloved are "rods of gold, studded with *tarshish*" (5:14), and in Daniel's vision, a man appears "dressed in linen" whose "body was like *tarshish*" (10:5–6).

What does this *tarshish* stone look like? *Targum Onkelos* and *Targum Yerushalmi* translate the word *tarshish* as *khrom yamma,* which seems to refer to a version of aquamarine, a blue-green variety of beryl.[1] Similarly, Jerome in the Latin Vulgate on Ezekiel 1:16 (circa

1. *Chroma* is the Greek word for "color"; *yamma* is Aramaic for "sea," parallel to the Hebrew *yam.*

400 CE, parallel to the latter part of the Amoraic period in the Land of Israel) translates it as *quasi visio maris* (like the appearance of the sea), perhaps as a result of the influence of his Jewish teachers. There is an apparent connection between the *khrom yamma* translation of the biblical *Targumim* and the practice of the *Targum* of the Prophets to translate the place-name Tarshish as *yamma* and the phrase "the ships of Tarshish" as *sefināt yamma* (see below). This tradition identifying *tarshish* as an aquamarine-colored gemstone continues to the time of Rav Saadia Gaon, who translates *tarshish* as *azraq*, Arabic for "blue." Ibn Ezra, in his commentary on Song of Songs 5:14, translates *tarshish* as *ke'ein hashamayim* (like the sky). In contrast, the Greek Septuagint on Exodus translates *tarshish* as *chrysolithos*, an adjective meaning "gold-stone," and the Syriac Peshitta in Song of Songs translates it as *kēfay dahavā* (golden stones).

There are also other possibilities. The Septuagint on Ezekiel translates *tarshish* as *anthrax* (coal), whereas Rashi on Ezekiel translates it as crystal.

Tarshish – the Place

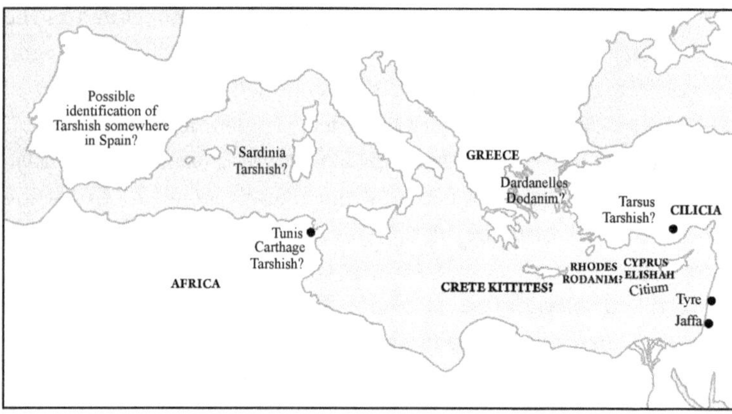

However, the name Tarshish is known primarily as an ethnic and geographic name associated with the Mediterranean Sea. In the list of nations of the world in Genesis 10 (and its parallel in I Chronicles), Tarshish is one of the nations descended from Javan: "Elishah and

Tarshish, Kittim and Dodanim [in Chronicles: Rodanim]." In this context, these nations represent islands in the Mediterranean Sea or places on its coast. According to various sources, Elishah is identified with the island of Cyprus; Kittim with Kition, a city in Cyprus, or with the island of Crete; Dodanim possibly with the Dardanelles; and Rodanim with Rhodes. Tarshish must therefore be located in that general region as well. Tarshish is mentioned in the Prophets as the most prominent city among the Mediterranean kingdoms, possessing a unique connection to Tyre. (In Isaiah's prophecy against Tyre, Tarshish is mentioned four times!). The "ships of Tarshish" are mentioned many times throughout the books of Prophets and Writings, and Jonah boarded such a ship in Joppa in order to escape to Tarshish and flee from God's service. Outside the Tanakh, Tarshish is mentioned in an inscription of the Assyrian king Esarhaddon (681–669 BCE), who boasts: "All the kings from amidst the sea from Yadanana (Cyprus), Yaman (Ionia, Hebrew *Yavan*), as far as Tarsisi (evidently biblical Tarshish) – bowed to my feet and I received heavy tribute [from them]."

Where is Tarshish? There are several opinions. In several instances, the authors of the Septuagint identified Tarshish with Karchedon (Carthage), today known as Tunis. Targum Jonathan on the Prophets, in several instances, points to approximately the same region, translating *Tarshish* as *Afrika* and *oni Tarshish* as *sefināt Afrika.*[2] However, it is worth noting that Targum Jonathan generally translates *Tarshish* as *yamma* or *medinat yamma*, and *oniyot Tarshish* as *sefinei yamma.*[3] Josephus, in his *Antiquities of the Jews* (1:127; 9:209) identifies Tarshish with Tarsos in the Cilicia region (the Mediterranean coast in southern Turkey). Various other authors, both ancient and contemporary, followed Josephus in this identification. In Tanakh, the information regarding the various metals that originate in Tarshish provides clues as to its identification. Jeremiah describes how idol worshippers would craft their idols, saying: "Silver beaten flat, that is

2. Before the modern era, "Africa" referred to what we now call North Africa; only later did the name begin to be applied to the entire continent.
3. Rashi integrates both of these interpretations in his commentary on Daniel 10:6: "A sea whose name is Tarshish, which is the sea of Africa."

brought from Tarshish, and gold from Uphaz" (10:9). Ezekiel, in his prophecy of Tyre, which is located "at the gateway of the sea" (27:3), lists Tarshish among the cities and lands that would bring their finest creations to the markets of Tyre: "Tarshish traded with you because of your wealth of all kinds of goods; they bartered silver, iron, tin, and lead for your wares" (27:12). Searching for metal mining centers in light of these verses, various scholars sought to place Tarshish in the Iberian Peninsula (Spain and Portugal), which was known in the ancient world as the international center for the mining of gold, silver, and other precious metals.[4] Many scholars thus point to a Spanish city mentioned in Greek and Roman sources called Tartessus, situated near a river of the same name that flows from the so-called "Silver Mountains," as the location of ancient Tarshish. In fact, the identification of biblical Tarshish with Tartessus was already offered by a Christian Roman presbyter named Hippolytus in the third century CE. Among modern authors, Edward Lipiński is apparently the most ardent adherent of this theory. Indeed, the Greek sources do not provide accurate information in order to identify the precise location of the city and river in question. However, Lipiński, following earlier researchers, points to some sources that lead him to conclude that the region in question must be located in southwest Spain, near the Atlantic coast. In his view, Tarshish-Tartessus was the ancient name of the vicinity of Huelva and the Rio Tinto River, some 150 miles northwest of Gibraltar. One of these sources is Herodotus (4:152), who recounts the story of a ship that was carried by the eastern wind past the Pillars of Hercules and reached Tartessus. From both the story of Jonah and the juxtaposition of Tarshish and the most southern Sheba and Seba in Psalms 72:10, along with the inscription of Esarhaddon, he infers that Tarshish was considered in antiquity "the western end of the world." This fits well with a location west of the boundaries of "the Great Sea" – the Mediterranean.

4. Compare to I Maccabees 8:1-3: "Now Judas had heard of the fame of the Romans, that they were mighty and valiant men... It was told him also of their wars and noble acts... And what they had done in the country of Spain, for the winning of the mines of the silver and gold which were there."

A very important source for the question of Tarshish's identification is a fragment of a Phoenician inscription found accidentally in 1773 in Nora, a town on the southern seashore of the island of Sardinia. The fragment mentions the name "TRŠŠ," which led a few scholars to conclude that Tarshish was located in Sardinia.

Additionally, one scholar claimed that there existed several places bearing the name Tarshish (possibly even outside the Mediterranean region; see below).

בתרשש
וגרשהא
בשרדנש
למהאשל
מצבאמ
לכתנבנX
שבמנגד
לפמי

right, courtesy of Rivka Leiman

Nora Inscription (right, courtesy of Rivka Leiman) and deciphered text (left). F. M. Cross, who identifies Tarshish with Sardinia, reads in line 7 "שבננגד" and translates: [a. He fought (?)] [b. with the Sardinians (?)] 1. at Tarshish 2. and he drove them out. 3. Among the Sardinians 4. he is [now] at peace, 5. (and) his army is at peace: 6. Milkaton son of 7. Shubna (Shebna), general 8. of (king) Pummay. According to Lipińsky, who supports the identification in Spain, the content of the inscription is not military, but rather a thanksgiving to the god Pummay, who saved sailors near Šrdn-Sardinia who were on their way to Tarshish in Spain.

What Is the Source of the Word *Tarshish*?

Some maintain that the word *tarshish* derives from the Greek *tarsos*, meaning "oar." The word *tarsos* appears in the writings of the historian Thucydides as a collective noun referring to a row of oars along one side of a ship. According to this approach, the word *tarshish* was first used as part of the expression *oniyot tarshish*, and from there it may be that the word began to be used to refer to the city or cities whose port was noted for the ability to accommodate large ships. The well-known scholar William F. Albright, following Wilhelm Gesenius, speculated that the word is Semitic in origin, with the root R-Š-Š. According to Albright, it can refer to a flame or to the color red (based on the Akkadian ruššu, meaning "red," or rašāšu, meaning "to glow with heat"). Two eminent Israeli linguists accepted this interpretation and developed it further in two opposite directions. Chaim Rabin explained, following Albright, that the word *tarshish* refers to a precious stone of either red or bright gold color. This was the *tarshish* stone found in the priestly breastplate, and "according to this hypothesis, the color of the *tarshish* [stone] would be red. Apparently the word *tarshish* bears no connection to the place-name Tarshish" (*Encyclopaedia Biblica*, 8, 946). The opposite approach was taken by Yechezkel Kutscher, who explained:

> Therefore, Albright had in his hands a simple solution: *Tarshish* is no more than the ancient Phoenician-Hebrew word for "smelting plant"! Thus it follows that, according to his view, it is unsurprising that the name surfaces in various places where the Phoenicians established "smelting plants." And of course, it is no wonder that the ships that set out from Ezion-geber were called *oniyot tarshish*, as they sailed to *tarshishim* established by King Solomon and Hiram somewhere in Ophir, in order to produce and smelt metals.[5]

Kutscher does not mention the *tarshish* stone. Apparently he believed – like Rabin but on the other side of the same coin – that there is no connection between the stone and the place.

---

5. Kutscher's interpretation here comes to reconcile a difficulty in II Chronicles 9:21 and 20:37; see Abrabanel on I Kings 10:22. It may be that this difficulty led *Targum Yonatan* on the Prophets to interpret *tarshish* as a general name for any large sea, as we noted above.

I believe that we need not overexert ourselves in our attempts to understand the etymological background of the place-name Tarshish. As Ibn Ezra and Nahmanides noted: "Do not seek out the reason for all the names if it has not been written" (Ibn Ezra's short commentary on Gen. 10:8)[6]; "There is no need to seek out the reason for names of places" (Nahmanides's commentary on Gen. 23:9). In addition, the connection between a *possibly* red or yellow stone and an Akkadian root that is unheard of in Hebrew and other northwestern Semitic languages seems somewhat tenuous. On the other hand, the connection between the name of such a unique place and the name of the precious stone seems much more likely. Precisely because *tarshish* does not have any clear meaning in Hebrew and its neighbor languages, it is hard to believe that, by chance, this word was used as a name for two wholly unconnected things. Materials, animals, foods, spices, and clothing are frequently named for the places that would export them or for the places to which they would be attributed. Today we have Angora wool, turkeys (mistakenly thought to have originated in Turkey, but actually native to the Americas)[7] and china (porcelain, which originated in China). In Arabic, oranges are called *burduqan*, for Portugal. It is reasonable to speculate that the word *barzel* (iron) was derived in an early period from the name of a place that was home to iron crucibles. On the morning of Yom Kippur, according to the Mishna (Yoma 3:7), the high priest would don his white *pilusin* garments (named for Pelusium in northeast Egypt) and in the evening he would don his *hinduin* garments (named for India). In many languages, the names of certain types of woven fabric are derived from the name of the city of Damascus, which was an international center for the production of textiles and clothing. Often, in naming these fabrics for Damascus, a language will use a version of that name that differs significantly from the normal way the name is rendered in that language. For instance, among the European

6. I am indebted to my student Yael Gvili for this reference.

7. In Hebrew, a turkey is called (also misleadingly!) *tarnegol hodu*, meaning "Indian rooster." In Yiddish it is called *indik*; but in the past, European Jews called it *english han* (Magen Avraham, who lived in the seventeenth century, uses the term in *Shulḥan Arukh Oraḥ Ḥayim* 79:14). In Arabic it is called *dīk Ḥabash* ("Ethiopean rooster") and in Egyptian Arabic *dīk Rūmi* ("Roman rooster").

languages we find *damast, damas* and *damasco;* in Greek, *metaxa;* in Arabic, *dimaqs* or *midaqs,* and in Amos 3:12: *demeshek ares* (probably referring to fabric spread on a couch).

Returning to Tarshish, it is reasonable to speculate that the precious stone of the same name originated in the land of Tarshish along with the silver and gold that were imported from there. If, in fact, *tarshish* was a golden gemstone, it may be that it referred to topaz, which was mined in abundance in Spain in ancient times.

Incidentally, there are two individuals in the Tanakh who bear the name Tarshish, one of whom was a Benjaminite (I Chr. 7:10) and the other a Persian sage "next to" Ahasuerus (Est. 1:14). It has been suggested that both were named after the precious stone Tarshish. This might be reasonable if we assume that the name of this stone was a "wandering word" that was transported from culture to culture and from language to language over the course of history. Compare, for example, the biblical Sapir, the Sanskrit *sanipriya,* the Greek *sampheiros,* the rabbinic *sampirinon* or *sanpirinon,* the Syriac *sappīlā,* the Ethiopian *sanpīr,* the English "sapphire" (which originally referred to lapis lazuli) and the modern Israeli girl's name Sapir.

For further study:

Altbauer, M. "Tarshish." *Encyclopaedia Biblica,* 8, 942–945 [Hebrew].

Baker, D. W. "Tarshish." In *The Anchor Bible Dictionary,* 6, 331–332.

Day, J. "Where was Tarshish?" In *Let us go up to Zion: Essays in Honour of H. G. M. Williamson,* edited by I. Provan and M. J. Boda, 359–369. Leiden-Boston, 2012.

Elat, M. "Tarshish in Isaiah 23 and in History." *Shnaton* 10 (1986–1989), 17–30 [Hebrew].

Elitzur, Yoel. *Ancient Place Names in the Holy Land.* Jerusalem-Winona Lake, 2004, 200.

Gmirkin, R. E. *Berossus and Genesis, Manetho and Exodus.* New York-London, 2006, 271–276.

Koehler, L., W. Baumgartner, and J. J. Stamm. *The Hebrew and Aramaic Lexicon of the Old Testament* (HALOT) 4. 1797–1798.

Kutscher, E. Y. *Words and their History,* Jerusalem, 1974, 39–41 [Hebrew].

Lipiński, E. *Itineraria Phoenicia* (Orientalia Lovaniensia Analecta 127). Louvain, 2004, 225–246.

Leviticus

Parashat Vayikra

Tzafon

"The Most Holy Sacrifices are Slaughtered in the North"

The insistence that the sacrifices possessing the highest level of sanctity be slaughtered specifically on the northern side of the altar (Mishna Zevaḥim 5:1) is a basic principle in the laws of sacrifices. At the opening to the Book of Leviticus, this law is mentioned in connection with the burnt offering: "It shall be slaughtered before the Lord *on the north side of the altar*" (1:11). Later, the Torah reemphasizes this requirement in connection with the sacrifices that are eaten in the court of the tent of meeting:

> It shall be slaughtered at the spot where the burnt offering is slaughtered before the Lord; it is a sin offering. (4:24)
>
> And the sin offering shall be slaughtered at the place of the burnt offering. (4:29)
>
> And it shall be slaughtered as a sin offering at the spot where the burnt offering is slaughtered. (4:33)

> The sin offering shall be slaughtered before the Lord, at the spot where the burnt offering is slaughtered. (6:18)

> The guilt offering shall be slaughtered at the spot where the burnt offering is slaughtered. (7:2)

Ibn Ezra and Rabbi Samson Raphael Hirsch explained that slaughtering the holy sacrifices on the northern side of the altar is parallel to the placement of the table in the northern part of the Sanctuary. Rabbi David Zvi Hoffman added to this suggestion, explaining that the showbread and the sacrifices represent material divine worship, whereas the Menora represents spiritual divine worship. The "spiritual" Menora was situated at the sunlit southern end of the Sanctuary, while the "material" meat and bread were situated on the shaded end – in the shade of the divine wisdom.

The Cardinal Directions in Biblical Hebrew

Rabbinic Hebrew and Modern Hebrew both resemble English with respect to the cardinal directions; only one word exists that corresponds to each of the directions – *tzafon* (north), *darom* (south), *mizraḥ* (east) and *maarav* (west). In contrast, Biblical Hebrew features a wealth of synonyms for the cardinal directions. For "east," not only do we find *mizraḥ* and *mizraḥ shemesh* ("sunrise"), but also *motza* ("origin"; Ps. 75:7) and the more common *kedem* ("front"). The word *penei* ("the face of") seems to refer to east in some instances as well. The word *maarav* appears only rarely in Tanakh; usually *yam* ("sea") is used, and occasionally *mevo hashemesh* ("sunset"). The word *darom* appears frequently in Ezekiel and in Ecclesiastes but almost not at all throughout the rest of Tanakh. Instead, *negev* is generally used, though occasionally we find *teiman* or *yamin* ("right"; Ps. 89:13 and others). In one instance, the word *yam* refers to the south (Ps. 107:3). The north is almost always called *tzafon* in Tanakh, as it is in today's Hebrew, but we do find a few instances where the word *semol* ("left") is used, such as "And he pursued them as far as Hobah, which is north (*misemol*) of Damascus" (Gen. 14:15).

The difference between Biblical Hebrew and Rabbinic Hebrew in this regard is not anomalous; the existence of multiple synonyms for a given word is a typical characteristic of Biblical Hebrew, while in Rabbinic Hebrew this phenomenon is rare.

By examining the various examples in Tanakh listed above from a semantic perspective, we can divide them into three basic categories: The first category comprises words that describe the state of the sun: The sun *rises* in the morning in the east, or, in other words, it leaves its place of origin – its *motza* ("as the sun rose [*yatza*] upon the earth," Gen. 19:23; "as the sun rising [*ketzeit hashemesh*] in might," Judges 5:31; "not from the east [*mimotza*] or the west," Ps. 75:7; and in ancient and royal Aramaic, *moka shemesh* or *mo'a shemesh* respectively). In the evening, the sun sets – *mevo hashemesh* – as if it were going to sleep for the night ("When the sun set [*ba'a*] and it was very dark," Gen 15:17; "thus his hands remained steady until the sun set [*ad bo hashemesh*]," Ex. 17:12). In Ugaritic, the root *ᶜrb* means "enter," and thus *ᶜrb.špšm* means "sunset"; *yᶜrb.bḥdrh.ybky* means "he entered his room crying." Similarly, the Akkadian verb *erēbu* means "to enter." We see from this that the Hebrew word *maarav* was originally a synonym for "sunset."[1]

The second category is based on one's orientation when facing east. Why would one face east? Some connect this notion to ideas found in ancient pagan sun worship. Others maintain that this is rooted in primitive man's dependence on the sun; each day one would eagerly await the sunrise, which would allow him to set out on a journey or begin his work in the fields. It seems, however, that it would be best to avoid such unprovable anthropological speculation and focus instead on facts. In Hebrew and in related languages we find that the words for the cardinal directions are based on an east-facing orientation. East is therefore called *kedem*,[2] west is called *aḥor* ("back"),[3] north is called *semol* and south is called *yamin*. All four of these terms appear together

1. In Arabic, however, the root uses the velar consonant *ghayn*, as in *gharb* and *maghreb*. Apparently this is a case in which similar phonemes are switched, like the pairs Ṣ-Ḥ-Q/Ś-Ḥ-Q, Z-ᶜ-Q/Ṣ-ᶜ-Q, and Š-M-Š/Š-P-Š.
2. And occasionally *panim*, as in "from Havilah, by Shur, which is east of [*al penei*] Egypt," Gen. 25:18, I Sam 15:7; "and he encamped east of [*al penei*] the city," Gen. 33:18. Of course, the word *penei* is used in Tanakh in other senses as well.
3. The Mediterranean Sea is called *Hayam HaAḥaron*, which the *Targumim* translate as *yama ma'arva'a*/*ma'arvaya*.

in the Book of Job, when Job searches for God in every direction but cannot find Him:

> But if I go east (*kedem*) – He is not there; west (*aḥor*) – I still do not perceive Him; north (*semol*) – since He is concealed, I do not behold Him; south (*yamin*) – He is hidden, and I cannot see Him. (23:8–9)

The third category is perhaps the most intriguing of all. The cardinal directions are named for regions in the Land of Israel, teaching us that the Hebrew language is, by its very nature, intrinsically connected to the land. This category includes *yam*, referring to the Mediterranean Sea in the west, and *negev*, referring to the arid region in the south.[4] Once the use of these words to refer to cardinal directions was initially established, they began to be used to mean west and south even without any connection to the eponymous regions. Thus, for example, the "west wind (*ruaḥ yam*)" (Ex. 10:19) that carried the locusts from Egypt was actually a land breeze originating in Libya, which is west of Egypt. In addition, the region "south of Chineroth (*negev kinerot*)" (Josh. 11:2) is located in one of the most fertile regions of the country, nowhere near the actual Negev region. As we mentioned above, there is one instance where *yam* surprisingly refers to the south: "*Mimizraḥ umimaarav, mitzafon umiyam*" (Ps. 107:3). It seems that the word *yam* here refers to the Sea of Suph in the southern part of the Land of Israel.[5]

Not all the names used in Tanakh for the cardinal directions are easy to understand and categorize. Several explanations have been suggested for *darom*, but Eliezer Ben-Yehuda said it best when he wrote in his dictionary, in the entry for *darom*: "Its origin is unclear." The explanation generally given for *teiman*, in dictionaries and in the research literature, is that it is a synonymous form of *yamin*. However, there is no evidence that *teiman* was ever used consistently to mean "right" in the normal directional sense of the word. It seems to me that a combination of factors is at work here. The word *teiman* possesses a nominal

4. The root N-G-B means "dry" in Hebrew (albeit not in Tanakh) and Aramaic.
5. Some claim instead that *yam* here is a shortened form of *yamin*.

derivation pattern that is commonly found in names of people and places (e.g., Tifsach [Thapsacus], Tirzah, Timnah and Timna^c). Teman is a well-known town and region in Edom, and based on ancient inscriptions found in Kuntillet Ajrud in the western end of the southern Negev Mountains, another Teman probably existed in that region as well.[6] Thus, it is reasonable to assume that the word *teiman* in the sense of "south" fits into the third category – cardinal directions named for places in the Land of Israel – but that the place-name Teman was originally derived from the fact that it was located on the "right" – *yamin*.[7]

Returning to Tzafon

The word *tzafon* is written as *tzefon* in its construct state, its inflected form and sometimes in its absolute state as well (as in Joshua 11:2). The classical grammarians maintained that the word *tzafon* fit into the first of the three categories detailed above – relation to the sun. According to Radak, "The path of the sun is not on [the northern] side but rather on the southern side, and it is as if that direction is hidden (*tzafun*) from the sun" (*Sefer Hashorashim*). This interpretation seems overly homiletical, though.

The explanation suggested by German theologian Otto Eissfeldt seems more likely. According to Eissfeldt's suggestion, *tzafon* would fit into the third category – directions named for places in the Land of Israel. In documents found in Ugarit – an important city, kingdom, and cultural center on the northeastern Mediterranean coast between the Patriarchal Age and the period of the Judges – the name *ṣpn* appears many times. *Ṣpn*, or *ṣrrt ṣpn*, is a tall mountain or ridge where the gods lived, according to Ugaritic myth (similar to Mount Olympus for the

6. Several biblical verses can potentially corroborate this speculation.
7. There is, of course, no connection between the nation of Yemen in the southern Arabian Peninsula, called *Teiman* in Modern Hebrew, and either of the ancient locations known as Teman. Jews began to use the word *Teiman* to refer to Yemen in the medieval period, when they would frequently (and imaginatively) use names culled from Tanakh to refer to their places of residence in the Diaspora. These included Ashkenaz, Sepharad, Togarmah, the land of Hagar and even the land of Canaan, each of which bore some similarity in linguistic form or in content to the lands in which they lived.

Greeks). The chief gods were associated with *ṣpn,* and are often mentioned in names that combine the two terms, such as *il ṣpn, bᶜl ṣpn,* and *ᶜnt ṣpn*. Thanks to the Ugaritic texts, we understand that Baal-zephon, located on the Egyptian border (Ex. 14:2; Num. 33:7), was apparently home to a temple in honor of the Baal who revealed himself on Mount Zaphon. This understanding also helps contextualize Isaiah's statement regarding the king of Babylonia:

> Once you thought in your heart, "I will climb to the sky; higher than the stars of God I will set my throne. I will sit in the mount of assembly, *be-yarketei tzafon*: I will mount the back of a cloud – I will match the Most High." (Is. 14:13–14)

The expression *yarketei tzafon* in this verse is parallel in nature to "the highest mountains…*yarketei levanon*" (II Kings 19:23; Is. 37:24).

Where is this tall mountain located? It is assumed that the peak in question is Mount Aqraʿ (Greek Casios, Turkish Kel), which is located north of the ruins of Ugarit.[8] This mountain/ridge is prominent within its surroundings, its slopes reaching the Mediterranean Sea, and its highest point is 5,670 feet above sea level. Almost seven centuries ago, Rabbi Ishtori Haparḥi visited this mountain and was impressed by it, as he writes in his book, *Kaftor Vaferaḥ*:

> A very, very tall mountain, whose name in Arabic is *Jabal al-*Aqraʿ, which means Bald Mountain. This mountain stands alone, its nose enters the sea and on it are tall cedar trees that reach to the heart of the heavens, as well as pistachio trees. There are water springs and towns there, which add to its blessing, and its circumference is about [a] one or two days' [journey].[9]

8. The southern border of modern-day Turkey runs this mountain's southern slopes.
9. Haparchi identified this mountain with the northern Mount Hor, the northwestern point in the description of the boundaries of the land of Canaan in Numbers 34. However, *Ḥazal* identified Mount Hor with *Turei Amanon/Tauros Amanos,* the next ridge to the north, which is even higher and more impressive than Mount Aqra' (see the chapter on *Parashat Mishpatim*).

(Anthiok at en.wikipedia)

Mount Aqra'

It seems, therefore, that the name of the direction *tzafon* was coined in reference to this prominent mountain. From a linguistic perspective, *tzafon* is a very appropriate name for a tall mountain. The ending *–on* is a common ending for geographical names in general (consider Hebron, Eglon, Ashkelon, and Sidon), and in particular for names of tall northern mountains (such as Lebanon and Hermon – "Sidonians called Hermon Sirion" [Deut. 3:9]; "as far as Mount Sion, that is, Hermon" [4:48]). The root of the word *tzafon*, according to this approach, is *Ṣ-P-Y*, meaning "to look out" – fitting for a tall mountain from which people can look out to great distances.[10]

Yarketei Tzafon in the *Mishkan* and in Jerusalem?

We will conclude with a subtle point. In the Book of Psalms we find a title for Jerusalem that reflects its honor and holiness: "Mount Zion, *yarketei tzafon*, city of the great king" (48:3). But what is this *yarketei tzafon* in Jerusalem? In light of what we established above, it would be difficult to accept simple topographical explanations in this case, such as that the Temple Mount is located on the northern edge of Jerusalem. It

10. Compare to *Tzefat* (Safed), a name derived from the same root, but with a feminine ending.

seems, rather, that this expression – like many other concepts and expressions found in Tanakh – was first used by Israel's neighbors in a pagan context. The expression was then given new meaning in the spirit of the monotheistic faith of Israel. While the King James Version – the classic English translation of Tanakh – translates *yarketei tzafon* as "the sides of the north," many newer translations render the phrase more accurately as "the heights of Zaphon."[11] The psalm addresses the kings who gathered together and passed through Jerusalem, informing them that Mount Zion is the true "heights of Zaphon," where the Divine Presence rests.

Perhaps we can suggest that even the mitzva to slaughter the most holy sacrifices on the northern end of the altar in the *Mishkan* represented an effort to clothe a concept from that period's world of worship in new Israelite garb, consecrating it with the holiness of the God of Israel. Amos Ḥakham noted the linguistic similarity between the phrase *yerekh hamizbe'aḥ tzafona* ("the north side of the altar") and the phrase *yarketei tzafon*. The Torah often adopts concepts from the cultural and legal world of the time, injecting within them an entirely different meaning. I will provide two examples here. The first is the law of the city of refuge. The idea that a holy place can act as a safe haven for any fugitive, whether his crime was intentional or unintentional, whether he is an escaped felon or a political dissident, was prevalent at the time of the revelation at Sinai (and to some extent today as well). The Torah vehemently rejects this kind of safe haven: "When a man schemes…you shall take him from My very altar to be put to death" (Ex. 21:14). Instead of this arrangement, the Torah suggests a haven for the unintentional murderer alone, situated not in the Temple, but in a city of Levites – those who taught Torah to the populace. In addition, a person's flight to a city of refuge was fully coordinated by the elders of the nation. The Torah's institution of this law effectively preserved the foreign concept of the city of refuge in name only, while changing its essence entirely by adapting the law to the Torah's ethical principles.

The second example I will cite emphasizes the linguistic perspective: the law of the Hebrew slave (*eved ivri*). Throughout Tanakh, the

11. Thus reads the New International Version; others translate similarly.

word *ivri* is not used in the context of the nation of Israel. Instead, terms like "the people of Israel (Benei Yisrael)," "your kinsman (*aḥikha*)," "your fellow (*amitekha*)" and "the men of Israel (*ish Yisrael*)" are generally preferred. In contrast, the term *ivri* was originally a name for the larger group of peoples that included Israel ("ancestor of all the descendants of Eber [*ever*]," Gen. 10:21; "Abram the Hebrew [*haIvri*]," Gen. 14:13). It was only later that *ivri* became a name for the people of Israel, and even then, this usage was generally limited to the conversations of non-Israelites among themselves or of Israelites with non-Israelites – including Egyptians, Philistines, and the sailors in Jonah's ship. When the Torah uncharacteristically uses the term *eved ivri*, it is clear that it is borrowing the precise language of the legal systems of the time (which apparently dealt with the Ḫabiru/'Apiru slave trade). However, the Torah emphasizes the brotherly relationship between slave and master in the people of Israel. The Torah even states explicitly, "If a fellow Hebrew is sold to you" (Deut. 15:12).

To return to our discussion, the Torah is not influenced here by the views of foreign nations.[12] While the world of sacrifices found in the Torah was clearly anchored in the world of the worship of the time, the Torah refined this institution, uprooting from within it the principles of ecstasy, licentiousness, and self-mutilation – the latter with swords and spears to the point of blood loss (cf. I Kings 18:28). Perhaps the same principle can be applied here: The Torah adopts terminology like *tzafon* – a common term in the context of the pagan worship of the time – but couches it within its own sacrificial system.

For further study:

Bendavid, A. *Biblical Hebrew and Mishnaic Hebrew* I. Tel-Aviv, 1967, 13–59 [Hebrew].

Cassuto, U. *A Commentary on the Book of Exodus*. Translated by I. Abrahams. Jerusalem, 1974, 265–266.

Dahood, M. "Psalms I 1–50." In *The Anchor Bible*. New York, 1966, 288–290; idem. "Psalms III 101–150." New York, 1970, 81.

12. Rabbi David Zvi Hoffman challenged those who believe that the law of slaughtering sacrifices in the north is based on the notion of a deity that resides in the northern part of the world, asking why, if so, the Holy of Holies was not situated in the northern part of the Sanctuary.

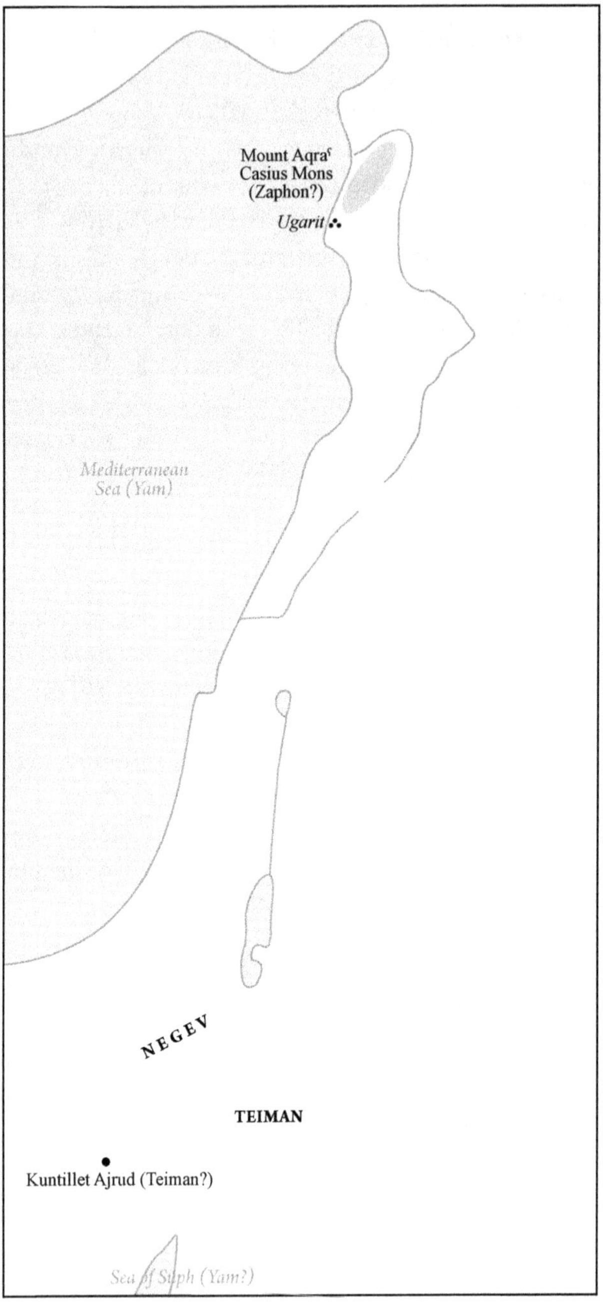
Mount Aqraʿ
Casius Mons
(Zaphon?)
Ugarit
Mediterranean
Sea (Yam)
NEGEV
TEIMAN
Kuntillet Ajrud (Teiman?)
Sea of Suph (Yam?)

Ḥakham, A. *Sefer Tehillim 1. Daat Mikra,* Jerusalem, 1990, 273 [Hebrew].
Haparḥi, Ishtori. *Sefer Kaftor Vaferaḥ.* Lunz ed., ch. 11, p. 250 [Hebrew].
Hoffman, D. Z. *Leviticus with a Commentary.* Translated by Z. Har-Shefer and A. Liebermann. Jerusalem, 1976, 98 [Hebrew].
Qimron, E. "The Names of the Cardinal Points in Ancient Hebrew Sources." *Beth Mikra* 25 (1979): 41–47 [Hebrew].
Talshir, D. "The Relativity of Geographic Terms." *Journal of Semitic Studies* 48 (2), Oxford, (2003): 259–285.

Parashat Tzav

Mul

El Mul Panav

"And he set the headdress on his head; and on the headdress, *el mul panav*, he put the gold frontlet, the holy diadem – as the Lord had commanded Moses" (Lev. 8:9).

The word *mul* is a common preposition in modern, spoken Hebrew. It means "opposite" – on the opposite side. If, for example, a Hebrew speaker tells you that the Cohen family lives *mimuli,* he is saying that he lives on one side of the street and the Cohens live on the other side.

If we only consider this contemporary usage, the above verse makes little sense. The headdress is, of course, placed on the head of the high priest, and we read in Exodus that the frontlet is placed beneath it – "on Aaron's forehead" (Ex. 28:38). How can Aaron's forehead possibly be considered the "opposite" side of Aaron's face?

Slaughtering the Bird Offering

A similar usage of *mul* is found in the Torah's instructions for slaughtering a bird as a sin offering: "He shall pinch its head *mimul* the nape without severing it" (Lev. 5:8) – a process known as *melika*. What is the meaning of *mimul* here? Once again, if we interpret *mul* the way that it is used in modern Hebrew, we would have to conclude that *melika* is performed by pinching the bird's head on the side opposite its nape, namely, on its neck. But if that were true, then why would the Torah mention this explicitly? Animal offerings are unquestionably slaughtered at the neck, so a statement indicating that birds are slaughtered at the neck as well would be superfluous. Moreover, why would the Torah use such a circumlocutory phrase as "opposite the nape" instead of saying, simply, "at the neck"?

Therefore, it is clear that *melika* is not performed at the neck but at the nape, as *Ḥazal* state:

> If one cut at the nape, the slaughtering is invalid; if one pinched off [the head] from the nape, the *melika* is valid. If one cut at the neck, the slaughtering is valid; if one pinched off [the head] from the neck, the *melika* is invalid. For the whole of the nape is the appropriate place for *melika*, and the whole of the neck is the appropriate place for slaughtering. It follows, therefore, that the place which is appropriate for slaughtering is inappropriate for *melika*, and the place which is appropriate for *melika* is inappropriate for slaughtering. (Mishna Ḥullin 1:4)

Thus, it is well documented that a bird offering is slaughtered at the nape. However, our linguistic question remains unsolved: Why did the Torah use the word *mimul* when describing the appropriate place for *melika*, instead of simply saying "He shall pinch its head at the nape"?

Origin of *Mul* and Its Appearances in Tanakh

The key to solving this problem is a close examination of the word *mul*. The results of this examination will likely have a significant impact on several areas of Tanakh, and on biblical geography in particular.

First, we learn that the preposition *mul* has no equivalent in any Semitic language besides Hebrew. Even in Hebrew, *mul* is not used in the language of *Ḥazal*, and even in Tanakh it appears only in the prose sections; it is absent from the poetry sections of Tanakh. In the prose sections of Tanakh, however, *mul* does appear relatively frequently – over thirty times.

In addition, we find instances of *mul* throughout the biblical period, from Exodus to Nehemiah and Chronicles. The word is usually vowelized with a *shuruk* (מוּל – *mul*), but it is vowelized in one instance with a *ḥolam* (מוֹל – *mol*) and once with a *ḥolam* and an additional *aleph* (מוֹאל – *mol*). The etymological background of the word is unknown, and it is difficult to find another word or root that might be connected to it. In the scholarly literature, I found ten different suggestions attempting to explain the linguistic background of the word *mul*, none of which is convincing.

I would like to propose an additional, albeit speculative, theory. Perhaps we might view the word *mul* as a kind of expansion of the prepositional prefix *le-*. The letter *mem* is commonly added to the ends of common or proper nouns in Semitic languages.[1] In biblical poetry, the word fragment *mo* is often appended to the prepositional prefixes *le-*, *be-* and *ke-*, creating the words *lemo*, *bemo* and *kemo*. It may be that in our case, *mo* was added to the beginning of the preposition instead of to the end of it. Regardless, this entire discussion is marginal. Ultimately, understanding the etymology of *mul* will not truly help us, and, as usual, we are better off trying to understand the word through the various contexts in which it appears.

Mul in Unambiguous Contexts

In many of the dozens of times that the word *mul* appears in Tanakh, the context is unclear. Let us attempt to isolate the instances where the context is clear and unambiguous, and use these examples to arrive at an accurate understanding of the word.

One example can be seen in the story of Balaam, when the messengers of Balak inform Balaam: "There is a people that came out of Egypt; it hides the earth from view, and it is settled *mimuli*" (Num. 22:5). Where were the people of Israel settled at the time? The answer is provided a few verses earlier, in the final verse of *Parashat Ḥukkat*: "The Israelites then marched on and encamped in the steppes of Moab, across the Jordan from Jericho" (22:1). Balak and his dignitaries lived in the hills of Moab, and wandered with Balaam through the hills overlooking the Israelite encampment. In other words, *mimuli* means "at my feet" in this context. If Balak were speaking in Modern Hebrew,

1. In Tanakh, compare Laish (Judges 18) and Leshem (Josh. 19:47).

he would only have been able to say "and it is settled *mimuli*" – meaning, "opposite me" – in earnest once Joshua conquered the part of the Land of Israel west of the Jordan and apportioned it to the twelve tribes!

Another example is in the Book of Joshua: "All Israel, with their elders, officials, and magistrates, stood on either side of the Ark... half of them *el mul* Mount Gerizim and half of them *el mul* Mount Ebal" (8:33). In modern Hebrew, "*el mul* Mount Gerizim" means "on Mount Ebal" and "*el mul* Mount Ebal" means "on Mount Gerizim" – as the two mountains stand opposite each other. It is almost nonsensical to imagine that the verse would use such a backward phrase to describe the place where the nation stood. Rather, the solution follows the description found in the Mishna:

> And the priests and Levites with the Ark were stationed below in the center, the priests surrounding the Ark, the Levites [surrounding] the priests, and all Israel on this side and that side, as it is said: "All Israel, with their elders, officials, and magistrates, stood on either side of the Ark." (Sota 7:3)

(David Roberts, 1849)

Nineteenth-century Nablus, where the tribes of Israel stood "half of them el mul Mount Gerizim and half of them el mul Mount Ebal"

In other words, half the nation stood *at the foot of* Mount Gerizim or *on its slopes*, and the other half stood *at the foot of* Mount Ebal or *on its slopes*.

Perhaps the most prominent example is in the story of the battle at Michmas in I Samuel 13–14. In describing the place where Jonathan and his attendant surprised the Philistines, the verses go into great detail regarding the scenery:

> At the crossing by which Jonathan sought to reach the Philistine garrison, there was a rocky crag on one side, and another rocky crag on the other, the one called Bozez and the other Seneh. One crag was located on the north, *mul* Michmas, and the other on the south, *mul* Geba. (14:4–5)

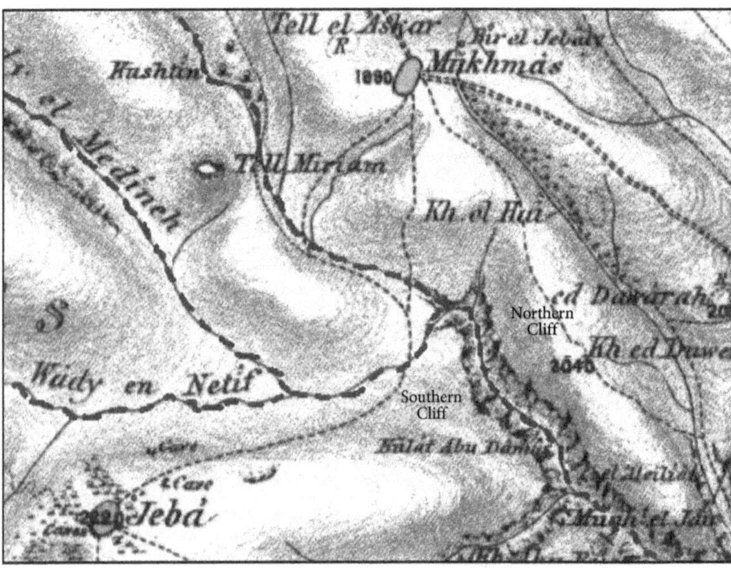

Geba and Michmas are well-known locations, both of whose names have been preserved until the modern era. They are situated on either side of Naḥal Michmas (Wadi Suweinit in Arabic), a deep and rocky wadi. The modern Arab village of Mikhmas is located north of the wadi and the village of Jabaʿ is located south of the wadi.[2] Years ago, when I was wandering around this region, I was happy to run into a group from the Society for the Protection of Nature in Israel. The members of the group were carrying Tanakhim and following the trail of the dramatic biblical story of Michmas in the very places where the events unfolded. The tour guide graced the members of his group with an original explanation of the names of the two villages on either side of the wadi, relating that this was a prime example of the phenomenon of "name wandering." Place names in the Land of Israel, said the tour guide, frequently shift to a different location up to a few kilometers away. But this place is unique, he claimed, in that the names of these two spots not only moved, but actually switched places! As we see in the Tanakh, the northern crag was *mul* – opposite – Michmas, and the southern crag was *mul* – opposite – Geba; today, however, the town of Mikhmas is in the north and Geba is in the south.

(Courtesy of Alexander Lysyi)

Bozez and Seneh, "one crag...on the north, *mul* Michmas, and the other on the south, *mul* Geba."

With all due respect to this tour guide's originality, the simple explanation is that "*mul* Michmas" does not mean "opposite Michmas"

2. See the map, taken from the 1880 map of the Palestine Exploration Fund.

but "on the same side as Michmas" or "at the foot of Michmas" – and the same is true for "*mul* Geba" as well.

Mul in Other Contexts

Apparently the word *mul* took on a new meaning in Modern Hebrew that runs counter to its original meaning. In the biblical period, *mul* meant "on the same side as" or "at the foot of," the exact opposite of the meaning of *mul* today. If a Modern Hebrew speaker were to meet Joshua, King David, Isaiah, or Ezra and tell them that the Cohen family lives *mul* his own house, they would undoubtedly conclude that the Cohen family lives adjacent to him – either next door or directly below him.

Returning now to Leviticus, it is clear that *melika* is performed on the same side as the bird's nape. The verse seemingly uses *mul* here to indicate that there is no need to insist on pinching any specific point on the bird's nape; rather, it is as the mishna cited above states: "For the whole of the nape is the appropriate place for *melika*." The same principle applies to the golden frontlet as well: it is placed adjacent to the headdress on the same side as the priest's face.

Understanding the meaning of *mul* has implications for several issues in Tanakh. For instance, when Yitro says to Moses, "You represent the people *mul* God" (Ex. 18:19), we now understand this to mean that Moses will be on the same side as God. Moses will be God's representative to the nation rather than the nation's representative to God.[3] In another example, the command, "Let the seven lamps give light *el mul* the front of the Menora (*penei hamenora*)" (Num. 8:2), is not easy to understand; the early sages disputed its precise meaning. We will suffice in noting that the basic intent of the statement is to bring the seven lamps closer to "the front of the Menora," not to distance them from the Menora or to situate them opposite it. Compare to the parallel verse: "The lamps shall be lighted as to give the light on its front side (*al ever paneha*)" (Ex. 25:37).

The Altar of the Gadites and the Reubenites

The most powerful episode in which we can arrive at a novel explanation thanks to our new understanding of the word *mul* is the episode

---

3. This interpretation follows Ibn Ezra's approach and differs from that of Nahmanides.

involving the altar of the Gadites and the Reubenites in Joshua 22. The Reubenites, the Gadites, and the half-tribe of Manasseh built an altar in the steppes of the Jordan, "*el mul* the land of Canaan" (22:11). Most commentators, especially the modern ones, maintained – in an explanation that may seem justified from a logical perspective as well – that the tribes of Transjordan built an altar in their own territory, on the side of the Jordan opposite the land of Canaan. However, according to our analysis, it seems that they actually built the altar on the same side as the land of Canaan, in Cisjordan – outside their own territory. A more thorough review of this episode is beyond the scope of our discussion. In brief, however, this chapter hints at a kind of contradiction between the intense anger directed at the Gadites and the Reubenites and the severity of their actual transgression. The atmosphere in the chapter is extremely tense. The actions of the Gadites and the Reubenites constitute a rebellion and a betrayal of God, akin to the heresy of Peor. In response, the rest of the tribes amassed their troops and prepared to go to war against the two and a half rebellious tribes. On the other hand, the only "crime" that they were charged with was building a *bama* – an altar dedicated to God, considered illicit only in that it was constructed outside the *Mishkan*. Throughout Tanakh, such a transgression is generally considered a relatively light offense. Even the most righteous kings of Israel, who always strove to do what was pleasing in the eyes of God, were unable to eradicate this phenomenon; most did not even attempt to do so.

The solution, it seems, is that it was precisely the act of building an altar west of the Jordan, outside their territory, that caused the tense conflict. If the Gadites and the Reubenites had built the altar within their own territory, perhaps the nation's leaders would have sufficed in sending two or three elders to explain to them that from the moment the *Mishkan* in Shiloh was built, it was no longer appropriate to worship God anywhere else. The conflict would have been completely resolved then and there. Instead, the Gadites and the Reubenites built the altar in the steppes of the Jordan, adjacent to their territory but pointedly outside its borders – in the western part of the Land of Israel. This was an extremely problematic gesture; it indicated that the Gadites and the Reubenites believed that only Cisjordan constituted the Holy Land, whereas they regarded their own home in Transjordan as "unclean" (Josh. 22:19). They saw themselves not as true members of the people of Israel, but as tribes that simply accompanied that nation into their land, allies of Israel who recognized the God of Israel and occasionally chose to participate in His worship, similar, for example, to the Kenites. In other words, they completely misunderstood the nature of the agreement that they had arranged with Moses, and as a result they had essentially become mere desert nomads with loose contact to the nation of Israel and its territory. The creation of such a deep schism constituted an unforgivable act of rebellion and betrayal.

For further study:

Ben Yehuda, E. *A Complete Dictionary of Ancient and Modern Hebrew*. Jerusalem, 1908–1959, 2843–2844 [Hebrew].

Elitzur, Yoel. "מול: 'Near, Below, On the Same Side As.'" *Lĕšonénu* 67 (2005): 7–20 [Hebrew].

Reider, J. "The Etymology of Hebrew MŪL or MŌL." *HUCA* 12–13 (1937–1938): 89–96.

Parashat Shemini

Kiriath-Jearim and the *Giv'a*: Not (Exactly) What You Thought

Kiriath-jearim and *Ba'alei Yehuda*

This week's *haftara* recounts the story of the Ark of Testimony's journey from Kiriath-jearim to Jerusalem. Kiriath-jearim is alternately known as "Baalah" and "Kiriath-baal," and Psalms refers to it poetically as "Ephrath" and "the region of Jaar" (132:6).[1] Our *haftara* contains a unique expression that has proved confusing for translators and commentators alike: "Then David and all the troops that were with him set out from *ba'alei Yehuda* to bring up from there the Ark of God" (II Sam. 6:2). *Ba'alei* is a term that appears several times in the Early Prophets; it always refers to the residents of a city – usually to its aristocratic ruling class. Thus we find *ba'alei Yericho, ba'alei Shekhem, ba'alei Migdal Shekhem, ba'alei*

1. For "Ephrath" compare to I Chronicles 2:50.

Ha-Giv'a, ba'alei Ke'ila and *ba'alei Yavesh Gil'ad.*[2] Once the quality of life and governance in the land changed at the onset of the period of monarchy, the use of the expression died out. Thus, it would seem that the term *ba'alei* refers to people – the noblemen and dignitaries of the tribe of Judah who accompanied David as he escorted the Ark to its destination in Jerusalem. Accordingly, the verse should be translated, "Then David and all the troops that were with him of *ba'alei Yehuda* set out to bring up the Ark of God." Indeed, the Septuagint, the Peshitta, and the Vulgate all translate *ba'alei* in this manner. However, the continuation of the verse – "to bring up *from there*" – seems to indicate otherwise, implying that *ba'alei Yehuda* is the name of a place. But if *ba'alei Yehuda* is a place-name, why is it in plural form (*ba'alei* rather than *ba'al*)? And why does the verse read "*from ba'alei Yehuda*" when "*to ba'alei Yehuda*" would make more sense, since David and his followers would have first traveled *to* the location to take the Ark "from there"?

To answer these questions, we turn to the earliest commentary on the Book of Samuel: the Book of Chronicles. As it does in many other places in its retelling of events depicted elsewhere in Tanakh, Chronicles replaces this difficult expression with a simpler one: "David and all Israel went up to Baalah, Kiriath-jearim of Judah, to bring up from there the Ark of God" (I Chr. 13:6). One manuscript from Qumran even uses this version of the verse for the passage in Samuel. Influenced by this verse from Chronicles, all the classical commentators (Rashi, Radak, Rid, Abrabanel, and the *Metzudot*) wrote that *ba'alei Yehuda* refers to Baalah, which is in Judah. The commentators sensed the syntactical difficulty of the verse's use of "from" instead of "to," and provided unconvincing solutions to the problem. Targum Jonathan was troubled by the use of the plural form *ba'alei*, and translated the phrase "from the cities of the house of Judah." This translation is difficult: Since when are cities called *be'alim*?[3] More significantly, in the end Targum Jonathan leaves unresolved the question of the verse's use of "from." Modern commentators and scholars

2. "Citizens of a city" occurs also in an ancient Aramaic treaty inscribed on basalt stelae revealed in northern Syria

3. I will point out, however, that the word *be'alot*, which appears in Joshua 15:24, is translated in the Septuagint (B) as "villages."

rushed to suggest a plethora of textual emendations to reconcile this problematic verse, none of which merits mention here. Disregarding those suggestions, is there a satisfactory solution to the problem?

I believe that I can suggest one. It involves a general approach concerning which I intend to write a comprehensive article. Here, though, I will suffice with presenting the fundamental principles of this approach in brief. Several twentieth-century scholars have already discussed the notion that a biblical verse does not need to be limited to one "correct" interpretation. Often in Tanakh, there is a dual meaning embedded in the original text. David Yellin was the first to deal with this subject in depth, in a comprehensive study published in 1934 in which he provides twenty-one detailed examples of this phenomenon. For instance: "Wolves of *erev*, they leave no bone until morning (*boker*)" (Zeph. 3:3). At first glance, the word *erev* seems to mean "evening," creating a phrase that runs parallel to the end of the verse. But are there really some wolves that are unique to the evening and others that are unique to the daytime? The answer is clear: The prophet is using the alternate meaning of the word *erev* and actually referring to "wolves of the steppe" – more commonly found in the feminine form *arava/aravot*. Thus, the verse seems to be hinting at both meanings of *erev* simultaneously – "steppe" and "evening." Our *haftara* begins with a good example of this phenomenon: "David again gathered (*vayosef od*) all the chosen men of Israel." *Vayosef* is a common verb from the root Y-S-P meaning "he added," "increased," or "he did something again," and the adverb *od* usually accompanies it. But here the context dictates "gathered," that can also suit *vayosef* since in rare cases we find forms like *osifkha* (I Sam. 15:6) and *osefa* (Mic. 4:6) from the root ʾ-S-P. Four verses before our verse (II Sam. 5:22) we find *vayosifu od* in its regular meaning. It seems therefore that the intent in our *vayosef* is both "added" and "gathered."[4]

I would like to add a new layer to this analysis. I believe that the Tanakh contains examples not only of words with dual meanings, but also of words that imply two versions of the original text. An excellent example of this phenomenon is a verse from Isaiah's prophecy against

4. See Targum Jonathan and Radak loc. cit.

Egypt, "one shall be called 'city of *heres*'" (Is. 19:18). Isaiah is very clearly speaking of the "city of the sun (*ḥeres*),[5]" a reference to On, an ancient city located in modern-day northern Cairo. Later renamed Heliopolis by the Greeks, this city was home to the center of sun worship in Egypt. By replacing *ḥeres* with *heres*, meaning "destruction," Isaiah was predicting the imminent destruction of the city's pagan temples, as is reflected in the translation of *Targum Yonatan*: "The city of the house of the sun, which will one day be destroyed." In this case, *ḥeres* and *heres* do not constitute two alternate readings of the verse, but rather two versions of the original text that are meant to be read and understood simultaneously. Ideally, the reader recites the word *heres*, but knows in his heart that *ḥeres* is implied – or vice versa; otherwise the verse is meaningless. *Ḥeres* is an uncommon word, chosen here to convey this dual content.

Returning now to *ba'alei Yehuda*, it seems that here too the intention of the verse was to include both meanings – that the tribal dignitaries were with David when he took the Ark, and that the Ark was taken from Baalah/Kiriath-jearim – simultaneously. The conflation of these two statements resulted in the unique expression *ba'alei Yehuda*, which differs from other similar expressions in that its second clause is not the name of a city but the name of a tribe or geographical region. This caused a certain degree of oddness in the syntax of the verse as well.[6]

Kiriath-jearim in Tanakh

Kiriath-jearim is mentioned in Tanakh in seven contexts:

- In the story of the pact that the disguised Gibeonites made with Joshua: "Their cities were Gibeon, Chephirah, Beeroth and Kiriath-jearim" (Josh. 9:17).
- In the description of the tribal territories, Kiriath-jearim is a border city between Judah and Benjamin (Josh. 15:9, 60; 18:14–15, 28).

5. See Job 9:7: "Who commands the sun (*laḥeres*) not to shine."
6. I would like to mention here that the question of *ba'alei Yehuda* was treated similarly, albeit with somewhat different points of emphasis, in an article by Professor Yisrael Rosenson in 1996.

- It was home to several prominent families from the tribe of Judah (I Chr. 2:50–53).
- The Danites encamped in its environs before they set out to conquer Laish (Judges 18:12).
- The Ark of the Testimony was brought there after it was captured by the Philistines and returned to Beth-shemesh. Years later, David removed the Ark from Kiriath-jearim and brought it to Jerusalem (I Sam. 6:21–7:2; I Chr. 13:5–6; II Chr. 1:4).
- It was the home city of the prophet Uriah, who was murdered by King Yehoyakim (Jer. 26:20–23).
- Kiriath-jearim was one of the destinations of the people who returned from exile – "each to his own city" – in the time of Zerubbabel (Ezra 2:25; Neh. 7:29).

A remarkable tradition concerning Kiriath-jearim was preserved in a *baraita* (Tosefta Makkot 2:2; Y. Makkot 2:7 [31d]), which states that Kiriath-jearim served as a city of refuge until Shekhem was conquered. Samuel Klein, a scholar of talmudic geography, believed that this tradition originated in the early Hasmonean period. Based on various proofs, Klein claimed that the Hasmoneans reinstated the laws of the city of refuge as a kind of Jewish counterbalance to the autonomous Hellenistic asylum cities that were established during that period.[7]

Kiriath-jearim and the *Giv'a*

We read in our *haftara*: "They loaded the Ark of God onto a new cart and conveyed it from the house of Avinadav, *which was on the giv'a…*" (II Sam. 6:3). A similar statement is found earlier in the Book of Samuel as well: "The men of Kiriath-jearim came and took up the Ark of the Lord and brought it into the house of Avinadav on the *giv'a*; and they consecrated his son Eleazar to have charge of the Ark of the Lord" (I Sam. 7:1). The meaning of the word *giv'a* is "hill," and thus this verse seems to be stating that there is a hill in Kiriath-jearim where the Ark of God was located, remaining there for all those years until David

7. See the chapter on *Parashat Masei*.

arrived to bring it to Jerusalem. Indeed, this is the interpretation found in the Septuagint's translation, followed by Edward Robinson in his reports of his 1838 exploration of the Land of Israel – that *giv'a* here is no more than a common noun meaning "hill." Despite this, other translators and commentators generally maintained that *giv'a* here is a proper noun, referring to a place-name: Gibeah. The Gibeah of Kiriath-jearim was mentioned earlier, in the Book of Joshua, and it is interesting to examine the relationship between Kiriath-jearim and the Gibeah of the Book of Joshua. The borderline between Judah and Benjamin is described in Joshua twice: first in chapter 15 (from the side of Judah) and a second time in chapter 18 (from the side of Benjamin). The Tanakh's emphasis in the latter description is unusual:

> The boundary now turned and curved onto the western rim; and the boundary ran southward from the hill on the south side of Beth-horon till it ended at Kiriath-baal – that is, Kiriath-jearim – a city of the Judahites. That was the western rim. The southern rim: From the outskirts of Kiriath-jearim ... (Josh. 18:14–15)

This passage describes the territorial border of Benjamin, and Kiriath-jearim is a key point in the description, as it constitutes the southwestern corner of the border. However, the verse emphasizes that the city of Kiriath-jearim itself belongs to the Judahites, while the territory of Benjamin only reached "the outskirts of Kiriath-jearim."

"Kiriath-baal – that is, Kiriath-jearim" is enumerated in Joshua 15:60 as one of the hill cities belonging to the tribe of Judah, while the tribe of Benjamin's list mentions "Gibeath Kiriath" (18:28; see below). Thus, it seems that Gibeah is a satellite town of Kiriath-jearim.[8] When the Tanakh states that the Ark was "*in* Kiriath-jearim," it is making a territorial statement: The Ark was in the *city* of Gibeah in the *region* of

8. We must distinguish between the current Gibeah and "Gibeah of Benjamin/Saul," an entirely different Benjaminite city that is also often called simply "Gibeah." There is also a third Gibeah, mentioned in Joshua 15:57 – "Kain, Gibeah, and Timnah" – in the southern Mount Hebron region, in addition to the Benjaminite Geba and Gibeon, which are different cities as well.

Kiriath-jearim. The boundary between the two tribes ran between the two cities: Kiriath-jearim, the more prominent Judahite city; and the nearby Benjaminite city of Gibeah.

Identification of Kiriath-jearim – Information from the Sources

The accepted identification for Kiriath-jearim is in the Abu-Ghosh/ "Telz-Stone" area just west of Jerusalem. This identification is based on several considerations:

- First, the information found in the various biblical passages seems to point to this region. Kiriath-jearim is located between Beth-shemesh and Jerusalem not only in the story of the Ark in Samuel, where it is not entirely clear if the narrative is referring to a contiguous line drawn between those two cities. It is also mentioned as part of the northern borderline of the territory of Judah, which is undoubtedly a more-or-less straight line. What is more, Kiriath-jearim is the point of intersection of two presumably straight biblical lines: the northern border of Judah (Josh. 15:5–11), whose eastern half coincides with the southern border of Benjamin (18:15–19) and which runs east-west, and the western border of Benjamin (18:14), which runs north-south. The northern border of Judah runs from Jerusalem and the Waters of Nephtoah toward Kiriath-jearim, and continues west, passing through Mount Seir and "north of the slope of Mount Jearim – that is, Chesalon" toward Beth-shemesh. Chesalon is identified strongly with the ruins found at the top of a tell in the ruined Arab village of Kasla (destroyed during the War of Independence in 1948), north of modern-day Moshav Ksalon. The site is situated atop a steep slope south of Naḥal Ksalon. Beth-shemesh is identified with a great degree of certainty with Tel Beth-shemesh (formerly Tell 'Ain Shams), west of modern-day Beit Shemesh above a perennial stream. The western border of Benjamin begins at "the hill south of Lower Beth-horon" (18:13). Lower Beth-horon is identified with the village of Beit 'Ūr at-Taḥta. There is no prominent hill, either in appearance or in height, south of this village; the verse simply wished to emphasize that the territory does not include Beth-horon itself, leaving it instead to the tribe of Ephraim.[9] In any case, the line that runs south from the Lower Beth-horon border is the line that passes along the slopes between the high mountains and the lowlands. This line intersects the Jerusalem-Ksalon-Beth-shemesh line somewhere in the area of Abu-Ghosh and Telz-Stone.

- On the entry "Baal," Eusebius writes: "This is…city of Iarim… There is a village Cariathiarim (today) on the road descending from Aelia [Jerusalem] to Diospolis [Lod] at the tenth milestone." On the entry "Cariathiarim (also known as Cariathbaal)," he asserts that the place is located on the way between Jerusalem and Diospolis, at the ninth mile. The road from Jerusalem to Lod was approximately equivalent to the modern Jerusalem-Tel Aviv highway.[10] It passed through Jerusalem along modern-day Jaffa Street and the Givat Shaul neighborhood, and continued to the Castel and Sha'ar HaGai.[11] Keeping in mind that one Roman mile is slightly less than one standard modern mile, one who travels 9.5 Roman miles from the Jaffa Gate will reach the Abu-Ghosh region.
- Kiriath-jearim is mentioned as well in two early Christian accounts of pilgrimages to the Holy Land. The first, a twelfth-century source that was apparently copied from the fourth-century original, writes: "Nine miles from Jerusalem, at the place called Cariathiarim, where there was the Ark of God, a church was built." The second, an early sixth-century source, writes:

9. See the chapter on *Parashat Vezot HaBerakha.*
10. An interesting proof for the identification of the Roman-Byzantine road from Jerusalem to Lod with the general route of the modern-day Jerusalem-Tel Aviv highway is in Lamentations Rabba, which contains material from Eusebius' lifetime. The Midrash mentions that among all the walls and towers of Jerusalem, the only thing that Titus left intact was the city's western gate, which provided access to the road to Lod (1:31). This is a reference to the Jaffa Gate and to the enormous Herodian towers adjacent to it. We can infer from this that the road to the Shephelah that originated at the Jaffa Gate was known in the time of the Amora'im as "the road that goes to Lod (*pylē ma'arvita de-nafqa le-Lod*)."
11. An ancient fortress that once guarded this road is preserved in the courtyard of Herzog Hospital, a geriatric-psychiatric hospital in Givat Shaul.

"From Jerusalem to Silona (Shiloh), where there was the Ark of the Testimony of God, nine miles. From there to Emmau, today called Nicopolis, nine miles." It is clear that the author was referring to the road to Lod, and simply confused the Ark with the *Mishkan*.

(Wood engraving, from C. W. Wilson, *Picturesque Palestine*, Sinai and Egypt, 1, London, 1881)

Qaryat al-Inab

- The preservation of the name. The modern village of Abu-Ghosh was named for a prominent family originating in Egypt, which took control of the village in the sixteenth century upon the Ottoman conquest of the land. Suleiman I (known as "the Magnificent"), who was sultan at the time, permitted the family to collect tolls from all travelers on the road between Jerusalem and Jaffa.[12] The

12. They often accomplished this by means of violent attacks. The Chida, in his travel diary entitled *Ma'agal Tov* ("The Good Journey"), describes a frightening conflict with the Abu-Ghosh family that took place in 5524 (1764 CE). He relates that Abu-

> Abu-Ghosh family retained both their control over the town and their right to collect taxes for approximately three hundred years. These rights were finally abrogated in the time of Ibrahim Pasha, following the suppressed Peasants' Revolt of 1834 CE. "Abu-Ghosh" is a shortened version of "Qaryat Abu Ghosh," but the true original name of the village was "Qaryat al-'Inab" and it is this name that is found ubiquitously in historical documentation, from the mid-eleventh-century travel records of a Persian traveler to British maps from the Mandatory period.

At first glance, one might think that the preservation of this name is not particularly valuable, since seemingly the only element from the name that was preserved is the first word – *kiryat/qaryat*; the second word, *ye'arim*, seems to have been lost. However, this is a good preservation. In most of the early place-names in the Land of Israel, including the Arabic names, comprised of two words, the first word is generally the primary one, while the second is merely an additional word that serves to distinguish that place from other places with the same primary name. Examples of Arabic place-names that follow this principle include: al-Mazra'a ash-Sharqiya ("the eastern") as against al-Mazra'a al-Qibliya ("the southern"); and al-Lubban ash-Sharqiya as against Lubban Rantīs. Examples from Tanakh include: Timnath-heres as against Timnah in Judah; and Abel-meholah, Abel-beth-maachah and Abel-cheramim. In each of these examples, the second word can easily be interchanged, since it is only an external descriptor for the name. Thus, we find that al-Mazra'a al-Qibliya is also called Mazra'at Bani Murra, named for the Arabic tribe that lived there. Similarly, Abel-beth-maacha is also called Abel-maim[13] and, in later periods, Ābil al-Qamḥ (Ābil of wheat).

In an article that I published twenty-eight years ago on two-word place-names, I demonstrated that even names of the form Kiriath-X

Ghosh, "the great snake, chief of the violent men," was accompanied by "the offspring of the wicked, a pack of evil ones – two hundred fifty." Together, they assaulted the guards escorting the Chida and his men, "and we settled the dispute [by paying] one hundred *zilotas* – blessed [is God] who redeems and saves."

13. II Chr. 16:4 as opposed to I Kings 15:20.

follow this principle. In contrast to the current norm, in early periods very few names beginning with Kiriath- existed, and the name of such a place was effectively "Kiriah" or "Kiriath." Thus, we find that the city of Debir was also known as both Kiriath-sepher and Kiriath-sanna (Josh. 15:15, 49). Returning now to Kiriath-jearim, we find that it is called both Kiryat-baal and simply "Kiriath."[14]

Identifying Kiriath-jearim and Gibeah: The Archaeological Findings

Since the time of geographer Rabbi Joseph Schwarz (mid-nineteenth century), it has generally been accepted to identify the Judahite city of Kiriath-jearim with the village of Qaryat al-'Inab/Abu-Ghosh, and the Benjaminite city of Gibeath Kiriath-jearim with the tell overlooking that village from the north.[15] Archaeological excavations are currently conducted in this site by Prof. Israel Finkelstein, but they have not yet been published. Surveys in the area have yielded pottery from the Neolithic period and the Canaanite and Israelite periods, as well as tesserae from the Byzantine period. Based on these findings, the border between Judah and Benjamin must have been the old Jerusalem-Tel Aviv highway, which passes between Abu-Ghosh and the tell and church.

Difficulties

To my mind, this accepted identification is somewhat problematic:

- First, as we established above, Chesalon is identified strongly with the ruins of Kasla, located north of the moshav of Ksalon, at the northern edge of a mountainous region that continues east. It is at the top of a steep slope that descends to Naḥal Ksalon, which flows south of the Abu-Ghosh/Telz-Stone area. Joshua 15:10 mentions that Chesalon is located on the northern border

14. See Josh. 18:28; the word *arim* following the name Kiriath is meant to hint at the name Kiriath-jearim, but the simple meaning of the word in this context is "cities."

15. In 1924, a monastery was built on this tell, atop the ruins of an ancient church, crowned by a statue that could be seen from afar. The site was labeled Deir al-'Azar in old British maps, Deir al-Azhar in some scholarly literature, and Tel Kiryat Ye'arim in today's maps.

of Judah, two border points after Kiriath-jearim, and it is given a topographical descriptor: "The boundary passed north of the slope (*katef*) of Mount Je'arim – that is, Chesalon."[16] In light of our interpretation of "Kiriath-jearim" as "Kiriat" with the appended identifying element "jearim," this would mean that the "jearim" element was coincidentally given to both the city of Kiriath north of Naḥal Ksalon and the mountainous region south of the wadi. Even though the scenery on both sides of this deep wadi was likely very similar, and was probably wooded (as *ye'arim* means "forests"), it is still somewhat strange that the proper name "jearim" was seemingly duplicated on either side of the wadi.

- The overall border of northern Judea is very logical from a topographical perspective. It apparently follows Wadi Og on its eastern end[17] and Naḥal Sorek on its western end. Its proximity to Naḥal Sorek is particularly prominent in the Shephelah between Beth-shemesh and the Mediterranean, passing through Ekron, Timnah and Jabneel/Yavne along the way. In Naḥal Sorek's mountainous portion, the borderline deviates from the stream twice. The first deviation is in the Jerusalem area – the borderline continues south, following Naḥal Kidron until En-rogel. From there it turns west, following the Valley of Ben-hinnom and "the hill that flanks the Valley of Hinnom on the west" (Josh. 15:8) – the primary mountain of modern Jerusalem. Then it descends to the spring of the Waters of Nephtoah, identified according to most scholars as Lifta, and finally returns to Naḥal Sorek. The purpose of this deviation is apparently to include Jerusalem in the territory of Benjamin.

  The second deviation is in the area of the Castel. The existence of Chesalon on the borderline proves that in this section the border follows Naḥal Ksalon, a more northern tributary of Naḥal Sorek. This deviation is essentially a correction of a natural deviation. When Naḥal Sorek reaches this area, it curves

16. See the chapter on *Parashat Bemidbar* regarding the topographical term *katef.*
17. Explaining the reasoning behind this determination is beyond the scope of this discussion.

sharply to the south, circumventing the entire Castel ridge, Tzova, Giv'at Ye'arim, and Ksalon from the south. Naḥal Ksalon, which originates at the Castel bridge and flows west in a more-or-less straight line, helps the border remain a logical east-west line until the wadi merges back into Naḥal Sorek near Beit Shemesh.

Based on this information, topographical logic dictates that the border must have run from the spring of the Waters of Nephtoah/Lifta, following Naḥal Sorek until Motza, then similarly ascended along with what is today the Jerusalem-Tel Aviv highway until the Castel bridge. Once there, it could continue along the southern slopes of Naḥal Ksalon in the direction of Beit Shemesh. The inclusion of Abu-Ghosh in the borderline utterly reverses the topographical logic of the line, adding an ascent to Abu-Ghosh, a steep descent to Naḥal Ksalon, and then another steep ascent to the ridge south of the wadi.

- The approach to defining land boundaries in the biblical period was territorial. Biblical cities were, in practice, the regional centers of larger tracts of agricultural land that might cover several thousands of acres. Every city was surrounded by such a swath of land, making it unreasonable for Kiriath-jearim and Gibeath Kiriath-jearim to be located in such close proximity to each other.
- From an archaeological perspective, no remnants of an ancient city have been found in either Abu-Ghosh or Telz-Stone. The scattered sherds of pottery found in the area of the spring in Abu-Ghosh and in the rest of the area most likely belong to the city situated on the tell overlooking the area. The approach that connects this Arab village from the medieval or modern era with an ancient biblical site is typical of many nineteenth-century scholars, who often misguidedly assumed that the existence of an Arab village automatically meant the existence of a biblical city. This assumption bears out in many cases, but the fact is that many Arab villages are not situated on an ancient site, and conversely, many ancient sites are located in tells or ruins in open areas.

Where Should We Search for Kiriath-jearim?

It seems to me that the Judahite city of Kiriath-jearim must be located south of Naḥal Ksalon. The name al-Qarya/Qaryat al-'Inab/Qaryat Abu-Ghosh, which is a continuation of the Byzantine Cariathiarim, preserved the ancient name within the territorial area of Gibeath Kiriath-jearim, located in modern-day Tel Kiryat Ye'arim (Deir al-Azhar). The name Kiriath-jearim was not preserved in the area of the chief Judahite city south of the stream. The tall ridge that runs west from the summit of the Castel, passing through Tzova and Giv'at Ye'arim in the direction of Ksalon, was known as Mount Jearim in the biblical period.[18] In the eastern or central part of this ridge, there was a central city – Kiriath-jearim. West of this city, within the Mount Jearim ridge, was Mount Seir,[19] and further west lay Chesalon/Kasla, at the top of the slope overlooking the wadi.

Mahaneh-dan and Kiriath-jearim

Before the Danites set out to conquer Laish in the northern part of the land, they encamped in Mahaneh-dan, which literally means "the camp of Dan." The Tanakh states:

> They departed from there, from the clan seat of the Danites, from Zorah and Eshtaol, six hundred strong, girt with weapons of war. They went up and encamped at Kiriath-jearim in Judah. That is why that place is called "Mahaneh-dan" to this day; it lies west of Kiriath-jearim. (Judges 18:11–12)

Kiriath-jearim is mentioned in this passage twice, the first in reference to its territorial area and the second time to the city itself. The Danites encamped in the *land* of Kiriath-jearim, in a space west of the city

18. It is today a wooded area once again, after becoming bare and rocky, and remaining so for centuries due to uncontrolled chopping and pasturing by the Arab villagers.
19. The mountain was actually named for its ample vegetation, which resembled hair (*se'arot*). The word *se'ira*, which appears in Judges 3:26, probably also refers to a vegetated area. (Rashi points to a similar phrase in the Mishna in his commentary on the verse.) This local Mount Seir is to be distinguished from the huge hilly massif Mt. Seir of Edom.

of Kiriath-jearim. Even though this was a piece of land within an open area, the passage makes a point of emphasizing that this is Kiriath-jearim in Judah, which – in light of what we have seen above – is certainly meant to stress that this location belonged to the Judahite city of Kiriath-jearim rather than the Benjaminite city of Gibeath Kiriath-jearim. This passage supports our assumption that the distinction between the Judahite Kiriath-jearim and the Benjaminite Gibeath Kiriath-jearim was most significant for its territorial implications, and was not merely a distinction between two points on the same plot of land.

(Z. Radovan)

Abu-Ghosh and Tel Kiryat Ye'arim

In addition, it stands to reason that the Danites, who set out from Zorah and Eshtaol, would encamp in a location close to Zorah and Eshtaol. This logic is also supported by a second mention of Mahaneh-dan in a different generation and a different context[20]: "The spirit of the Lord first moved him in Mahaneh-dan, between Zorah and Eshtaol" (Judges 13:25). Zorah and Eshtaol are a constant pair; they are always mentioned together. Zorah has a strong identification with the ruins of

20. This incident occurred later in history than the previous one, despite the story's earlier placement in Tanakh.

the village of Ṣar'a (captured in 1948) at the top of a hill between Tarum and the Naham-Hartuv industrial zone northeast of the contemporary Kibbutz Tzora. Eshtaol does not have a clear identification,[21] but it must be somewhere near Zorah. Tell Zorah is located 7.5 miles southwest of Abu-Ghosh and about four miles west of Kasla/Chesalon. It may be that "between Zorah and Eshtaol" can be interpreted as the area located off to the east of both Zorah and Eshtaol themselves.[22] Either way, since the area is named for Zorah and Eshtaol, it cannot be too far away from the two towns. In terms of the territorial division of the land in this region, the Zorah ridge can be considered a continuation of the mountainous area south of Naḥal Ksalon. Thus, Mahaneh-dan and its surroundings are so distant and disconnected from Abu-Ghosh and Tel Kiryat Ye'arim (i.e., the Benjaminite Gibeah) that linking the two would be incongruous.

One Final Thought

On the northern border of Judah, between the Waters of Nephtoah and Kiriath-jearim, we find "the cities of Mount Ephron" (Josh. 15:9). Based on the implied logic of the borderline, it is reasonable that "Mount Ephron" refers to the Castel ridge. But we must ask: What is the meaning of the plural "*cities* of Mount Ephron"? After all, a borderline must follow a specific path – one that cannot be defined by such a general term referring to multiple cities. As a result of this difficulty, most versions of the Septuagint omitted the word "cities (*arei*)," and the Peshitta replaced it with the word "tip (*keren*)." Some modern commentators dealt with the problematic word by explaining that it was the result of a scribal error, but the wide variety of interpretations only reinforces the authenticity – and the problematic nature – of the Masoretic text.

In a similar case – "he was buried in the cities of Gilead" – the aggadists questioned the vague description of Jephthah's burial site, and explained that "Jephthah died through the loss of his limbs. Wherever he went, a limb would fall off, and they would bury it there" (Genesis Rabba 60 and parallels). Radak and other peshatists interpreted "in one of the

21. See the chapter on *Parashat Naso*.

22. Compare to the usage of the word *bein* ("between") here to its usage in the verse, "you shall not… shave the front of your heads (*bein eineikhem*)" (Deut. 14:1).

cities of Gilead" to mean that at the time the Book of Judges was written, Jephthah's precise burial site was unknown (*Daat Mikra*, Judges 12:7). This kind of solution is impossible in our case. But it is worth noting a different example of the same variety: one of David's warriors, known as "Hiddai of *Naḥalei Ga'ash*" (II Sam. 23:30). The meaning of Hiddai's hometown is unclear. If *naḥalei ga'ash* is translated as "the brooks of Gaash," then, as above, this is too broad a location. The best solution here (suggested by Karl Elliger) is that *naḥalei ga'ash* refers to one town whose name consists of two words: the name of the town – Nehalim or Nehalin – and the name of the mountainous region where the town was located – Mount Gaash, named for the city of Gaash. Perhaps we can suggest a similar approach in our case as well. It may be that the name of the town was "Arim," and it was located in the Mount Ephron region. "Arim" may be a shortened form of "Jearim" (as in Hezekiah/Jehezekiah and Balaam/Ibleam), and the name appears in Tanakh both explicitly (Ezra 2:25) and implicitly (Josh. 18:28). According to this speculation, (Je)arim was the name of a city in Mount Ephron, a name that very aptly described the regional landscape as well. This city and its surroundings were thus the basis for the name of the whole nearby ridge – Mount Je'arim – and the city of Kiriath within that ridge was thus called Kiriath-(je)arim.

Open Questions

Let us summarize what we have established until this point. The identification of Chesalon with Kasla at the top of the southern slope of Naḥal Ksalon is certain. The border passes through here, apparently running all along the ridge south of Naḥal Ksalon. The Tanakh calls this ridge Mount Jearim. Thus, the Judahite city of Kiriath-jearim must be located on this ridge, at a point further to the east, and it is likely that even further to the east there was a site called (Je)arim. According to the Tanakh, an uninhabited wooded mountain called Mount Seir, actually a part of the ridge of Jearim, was situated between Kiriath-jearim and Chesalon.

We assume that the borderline ran all along the ridge and did not rise or fall sharply at any point. However, it is difficult to ascertain with certainty precisely where, within this region, it ran. The borderline might have passed through Tzova, Eitanim, and Ramat Raziel. In order to suggest a precise identification for Kiriath-jearim, we must see what information we can glean from the regional sites themselves. The most prominent site in the region is the conical hill of Ṣūba – which the crusaders called Belmont ("the nice hill") – atop Kibbutz Tzova, but the fact that this site has its own ancient Hebrew name[23] is an argument against its identification with a different name.

From the perspective of preservation of ancient names, we assumed that the name "Qaryat al-'Inab" (Abu-Ghosh) constituted a preservation of the ancient name "Kiriath," but this is problematic, as it is located adjacent to the Benjaminite city of Gibeath Kiriath. Let us add a piece of information that will confuse matters further: The moshav of Giv'at Ye'arim, located south of Naḥal Ksalon, is situated atop a ruin known as Khirbet Jab'a, and according to our analysis, is located in the territorial area of the Judahite city of Kiriath-jearim. It turns out that a strange transposition occurred here. In the biblical Kiriath (Jearim) area, the name Gibeah (Jaba') was preserved, while in the Gibeah (Gibeath Kiriath-jearim) area, the name Kiriath (Qaryat al-'Inab) was preserved. At this point in our discussion, though, we must leave these questions for another time.

For further study:

Abegg, M., P. Flint, and E. Ulrich. *The Dead Sea Scroll Bible*. New York, 1999, 241.

Bernard, J. H. *Theodosius* (Palestine Pilgrims' Text Society). London, 1893, 9.

Elitzur, Yoel. "Toponyms in the Land of Israel: Two-word Place Names." In *Encyclopedia of Hebrew Language and Linguistics*. Leiden and Boston, 2013, 3, 783.

Elitzur, Yoel. "The Concept of Territory in the Arab Village and in Biblical Geography." *Israel – Land and Nature* 7 (1982): 146–150.

Fitzmyer, J. A. "The Aramaic Inscriptipns of Sefire I and II," JAOS 81 (1961): 188.

Freeman-Grenville, G. S. P., R. L. Chapman, and J. E. Tailor. *The Onomasticon of Eusebius of Caesarea*. Jerusalem, 2003, 34, 65.

Freimann A., ed. *Sefer Ma'agal Tov, Vehu Sipur Mas'ot Harav R. Ḥayim Yosef David Azulai*. Jerusalem, (1921) 1967, 47 [Hebrew].

Klein, S. "The Cities of the Priests and the Levites, and the Cities of Refuge." *Journal of the Jewish Palestine Exploration Society* (1934–35): 81–107 [Hebrew].

23. This name may have been mentioned in the addition of the Septuagint in its translation of Joshua 15:59, and perhaps in a document from the time of Bar Kokhba.

Levin, Y. "Baal Worship in Early Israel: An Onomastic View." *Maarav* 21 (2014): 214–216 (203–222).
Robinson E., and E. Smith. *Biblical Researches in Palestine and in the Adjacent Regions: A Journal of Travels in the Year 1838* 2. Boston, 1856, 12.
Rosenson, Y. "Kiriath-jearim – Baalah." *Al Atar* 1 (1995): 83–88 [Hebrew].
Schwarz, J. *A Descriptive Geography and Brief Historical Sketch of Palestine.* Michigan, 1899 (Jerusalem, 1850), accessible at [http://www.tevuot.org/aretz/eng/cities_of_benjamin.html].
Wilkinson, J. *Egeria's Travels to the Holy Land.* Revised Edition, Jerusalem, 1981, 186–188.
Yellin, D. "*Mishneh Hahora'a BaTanakh.*" *Tarbiz* 5 (1933): 1–17 [Hebrew].

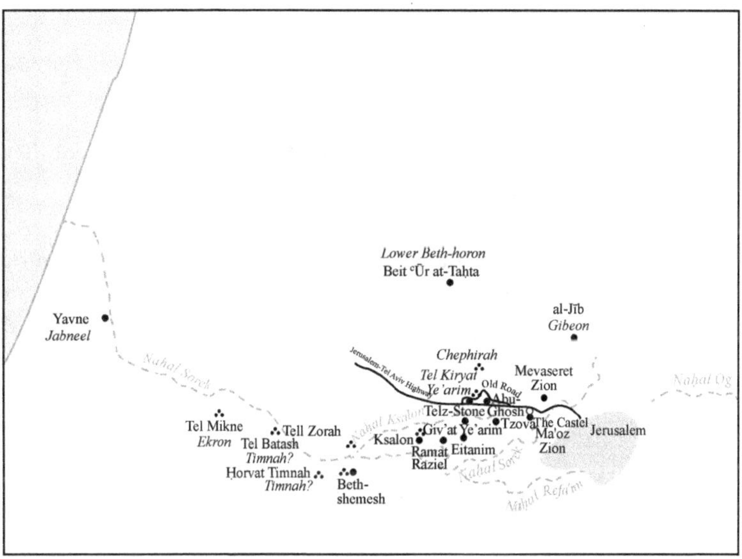

Tazria

Baal-Shalishah

Shalishah: Two Appearances in the Tanakh

The *haftara* of *Parashat Tazria* opens with the wondrous incident that occurred while Elisha the prophet stayed at Gilgal:

> A man came from Baal-shalishah and he brought the man of God some bread of the first reaping – twenty loaves of barley bread, and some fresh grain in his sack. And [Elisha] said, "Give it to the people and let them eat." (II Kings 4:42)

Shalishah is mentioned in the Tanakh only one other time, in the story of Saul's search for the asses that belonged to his father Kish: "He crossed the district of Shalishah, but they did not find them" (I Sam. 9:4). In both instances, the name is written in *ketiv ḥaser*, without a *yod* (שָׁלִ֫שָׁה), and in both cases the masoretic vocalization features a *ḥirik*, as well as *mile'eil* stress (stress on the penultimate syllable: *sha-LI-sha*).[1] The prefix "Baal" does not tell us much about the nature of the place. In the

---

1. This pattern is generally common when the text is expressing a direction of movement. For example, we find: *chev-RON-a* (to Hebron); *mitz-RAY-ma* (to Egypt); and *ha-BAY-ta* (to the house). But sometimes we find this kind of ending in place-names that do not express a direction of movement, such as: *b-almon div-la-TAY-ma* (in Almon-diblathaim); *mechevel akh-ZI-va* (by the region of Achzib); and *el ketef LU-za NEG-ba* (to the shoulder of Luz to the south).

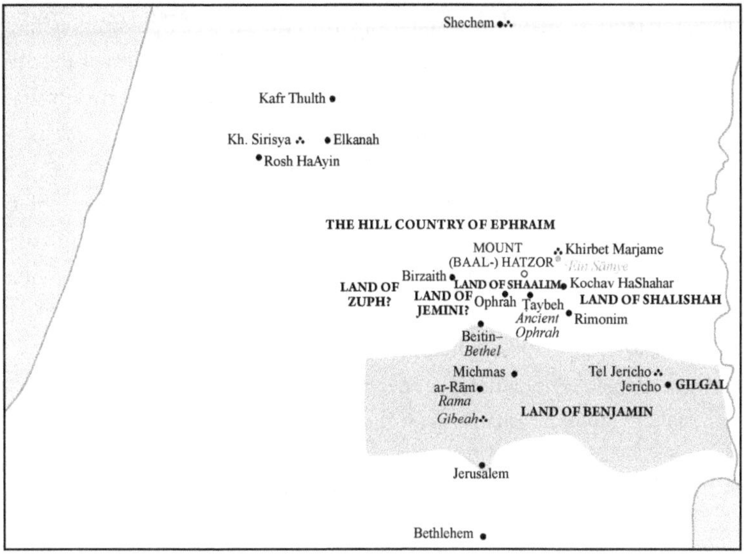

Tanakh, we find "Baal-meon," which is a city, "Baal-hermon" and Baal-hazor" which are tall mountains and "Baal-gad," which is a valley. Two early translations rendered the word *shalisha* somewhat strangely. *Targum Yonatan* translates it twice as "south," while the Peshitta translates it as "in the land of glowing coals" and as "from the province/city of the giants." It is difficult to find an etymological background for these interpretations, and from a geographical perspective, "south" fits neither the story of the asses nor the story of Elisha. The Septuagint in Samuel leaves the name in its original form – "Salissa" (or in another manuscript: Selkha, a corrupted version of the same name) – and in Kings presents the name as "Baithsarisa." Eusebius, who was only familiar with the Tanakh in Greek, identified Baithsarisa in the vicinity of Thamnitikē (Timnath-heres), fifteen miles north of Diospolis (Lod) (*Onomasticon* 56:21). Eusebius was referring to Khirbet Sirisia, located on a prominent hill between Kafr Qāsem and Elkanah adjacent to the Trans-Samaria Highway, near the army checkpoint. Several modern writers accepted this identification for Baal-shalishah, connecting Shalishah to Kafr Thulth, located about 3.5 miles to the north. But Eusebius, who was familiar only with the Septuagint and not with the original Hebrew Bible did not intend to find the name Shalishah here – only the Septuagint's "Baithsarisa." In addition, there is no reason to place the land of Shalishah so far away from the land of Benjamin, where Kish's asses were lost. From the point of view of the preservation of ancient names, ascribing Kafr Thulth to Shalisha is farfetched, since it means that the local Arab peasants understood etymologically the Hebrew Shalisha and were witty enough to exchange it with Thulth.

Aside from these two biblical sources that we mentioned, there is apparently only one source that perhaps attests to a real familiarity with Baal-shalisha. This source is the words of Rabbi Meir in the Tosefta (Sanhedrin 2:9) and Talmud Bavli (Sanhedrin 12a): "There is no other place in the Land of Israel where the fruit ripens earlier than in Baal-shalishah."[2] But it is possible that this was merely a logical inference from the text, rather than actual familiarity with the place.

What Can the Story from Kings Tell Us About the Location of Baal-shalishah?

Some have clung to the story in the Book of Kings and inferred from it that Baal-shalishah must be located near Gilgal. This is possible, but not necessarily true. A person who admires a prophet or who requires his assistance and wants to honor him with bread of the first reaping will likely be willing to travel a great distance to reach him. Naaman, commander of the army of Aram, for example, came to Elisha from far away in Damascus. Those who advance this approach have also relied on the early ripening of fruit that is characteristic to Baal-shalishah, which fits with the Valley of Jericho ("'Benjamin is a ravenous wolf; In the morning he consumes the prey' [Gen. 49:27] – this is Jericho, in that it produces its fruit early" [Genesis Rabba 99:1276 and parallels]). However, as we will see shortly, the land of Shalishah and Baal-shalishah must be places in the hill country, and not in the Jordan Rift Valley.

The "Lands" in the Story of the Search for the Asses

The most significant source for the identification of the land of Shalishah is the story of the search for the asses in I Samuel 9. In this context, I

2. In the printed version of the Bavli (Sanhedrin 12a) the text reads "Rabbi" instead of "Rabbi Meir," but the manuscripts and the citations of the *Rishonim* corroborate the version reading "Rabbi Meir."

will generally follow the approach of the late Professor Zecharia Kallai, one of the most venerable scholars of biblical historical geography of our generation. Kallai presented an excellent analysis of this topic, connecting the biblical information to the geographical reality. I accept most of his approach – but not his conclusion.

Saul and his father Kish lived in the land of Benjamin.[3] The story begins: "Once the asses of Saul's father Kish went astray, and Kish said to his son Saul, 'Take along one of the servants and go out and look for the asses'" (I Sam. 9:3). The ensuing journey in search of the asses is described as follows:

> He traversed the hill country of Ephraim. He crossed the land of Shalishah, but they did not find them. They crossed the land of Shaalim, but they were not there. They crossed Eretz Yemini, and still they did not find them. When they reached the land of Zuph, Saul said to the servant who was with him, "Let us turn back." (9:4–5)

The structure of the verse demonstrates that "He traversed the hill country of Ephraim" is a heading for what comes afterward; in other words, that all these "lands" are situated within "the hill country of Ephraim." Some believe that "the hill country of Ephraim" in the Tanakh included the land of Benjamin, especially based on the verse here in which Eretz Yemini is part of the hill country of Ephraim, and in light of the fact that Sheba son of Bichri was known as both "a Benjaminite (*ish yemini*)" and "a man from the hill country of Ephraim" (II Sam. 20:1, 21). But in other places, it is implied that the land of Benjamin is not part of the hill country of Ephraim (see Judges 19:16–18: "This man hailed from the hill country of Ephraim and resided at Gibeah, where the townspeople were Benjaminites"; "We are traveling from Bethlehem in Judah to the other end of the

3. Saul, his uncle and "all who knew him previously" (I Sam. 10:11) lived in Gibeah (of Benjamin), later named Gibeah of Saul after him. Gibeah's accepted identification is in Tell el-Ful above Pisgat Ze'ev or in its vicinity. Kish himself was perhaps in Zela' in the land of Benjmin (II Sam. 21:14), whose identification is unknown.

hill country of Ephraim"). In our case, we must pay attention to the fact that the verse does not refer to the land of Benjamin as *Eretz Binyamin*, but as *Eretz Yemini*. Throughout the Tanakh, *yemini* serves distinctly as an ethnic name, used to describe people from the tribe of Benjamin, unlike *binyamin*, which can be used as a geographic name describing the territory of Benjamin. Therefore, we must interpret here that *Eretz Yemini* refers to an area of land within the hill country of Ephraim that was populated by people from the tribe of Benjamin. In the territorial apportionment chapters in Joshua, there is a phenomenon of extending to the north in a sort of "domino effect." The text enumerates among the Benjaminite cities even Ophrah, which is located a few miles north of the line of latitude of Bethel (Josh. 18:13, 23). The northern border of Ephraim passes through Wadi Kanah, but the text notes twice that Ephraim had cities north of Wadi Kanah, within Menashe's territory (16:9; 17:9), and Menashe had cities and areas of land north of its own territory, within the territories of Issachar and Asher (17:11). Thus, it seems that Eretz Yemini was an area of land occupied by Benjaminites, but located within the hill country of Ephraim.

We will now dedicate a few words to "the land of Zuph." The Tanakh states that the land of Zuph was where Samuel – the seer – lived, and it was there that Saul and his servant arrived. The verse emphasizes that they had come "from the land of Benjamin" (I Sam. 9:16), and we can infer from here once again that "the land of Zuph" itself is in the hill country of Ephraim and not in Benjamin. From the words of Saul's servant – "there is a man of God in that town" – it seems that this was Samuel's permanent residence (thus interpreted already Josephus in *Antiquities* 6:47). We know from other places that Samuel's city of residence was Ramah ("Then he would return to Ramah, for his home was there" [I Sam. 7:17]). Ramah was also the city of his father Elkanah ("and they went back home to Ramah" [1:19]), and its full name was "Ramathaim-zophim,[4] in the hill country of Ephraim" (1:1). Rabbi Isaiah di Trani and Ralbag, in their commentaries on the Book of Samuel, addressed the connection between the name "Ramathaim-zophim" and "the land of Zuph," as well as the connection

4. The pseudo-dual suffix in "Ramathaim" is often found in place-names. There is seemingly no essential difference between "Ramah" and "Ramathaim."

between these two names and Elkanah's great-great-grandfather Zuph. Elkanah's genealogy presented in the first verse of the Book of Samuel includes five generations: "Elkanah son of Jeroham son of Elihu son of Tohu son of Zuph." In the parallel passage in I Chronicles 6:19–22, twenty generations are listed from Jacob the Patriarch until Elkanah. There must be a reason for the fact that precisely five generations are enumerated here, rather than the usual practice of either listing merely two generations or providing the entire genealogy such as in Chronicles. It seems that Elkanah's lineage was traced back to Zuph because Zuph was the founder of the family's regional settlement. The region was called "the land of Zuph" after him, as was the city of "Ramathaim-zophim" – Ramathaim in the land of Zuph.

The land of Shaalim is apparently "the land of Shual," mentioned in the story of the war of Michmas in I Samuel 13:17: "The raiders came out of the Philistine camp in three columns: One column headed for the Ophrah road that leads to the land of Shual."[5] Ophrah is identified with certainty in Taybeh, in the southeast part of the hill country of Ephraim, about two miles east of the modern town of Ofra. The region surrounding Ophrah was probably the land of Shual/Shaalim.

As we already clarified above, we do not have any information about the land of Shalishah beyond the two places where its name is mentioned, in Samuel and in Kings. Nevertheless, an accurate analysis of the story in Samuel will help us approximate its location. Let us summarize what we already know. It seems that the four "lands" that are enumerated here were territorial regions in the hill country of Ephraim, apparently not large in area. We know the names of cities that existed in two of these regions Ophrah in the land of Shual/Shaalim; and Ramah in the land of Zuph – but the "lands" were not named after the cities. Eretz Yemini was apparently named for its inhabitants, who were of Benjaminite descent, and the land of Zuph was named for the man who first established the settlement in the region. There is therefore room to propose that the land of Shual and the land of Shalishah were also named after people. The journey in search of the asses took three days, while the return trip took only one

5. For other examples of two such versions of the same place, compare to Nimrah/Nimrim and Moserah/Moseroth.

day. We see from here that Saul and his servant did not travel far into the heart of the hill country of Ephraim. In light of the reason for the journey in the first place – finding the lost asses – we must assume that this could not have been a journey of more than fifteen to twenty miles. Thus, it seems that the "lands" where Saul and his servant traveled are situated along the hill country of Ephraim, in the region where the hill country of Ephraim and the land of Benjamin meet. The description of their journey, which was written in the verses using terse, concrete language, allows us to assume that the names are listed in geographical order. The land of Shalishah, where the barley ripens early, seems to be in the east, east of the area of Ophrah, in the warmer areas,[6] but nonetheless must be in the hill country of Ephraim and not in the Jordan Rift Valley. To its west is the land of Shual/Shaalim surrounding Ophrah, followed by Eretz Yemini and the land of Zuph.

Why Did Saul Search for the Asses Specifically in the Hill Country of Ephraim?

The asses were lost in the land of Benjamin, but the search took place in the hill country of Ephraim. What is the explanation for this?

The undersized land of Benjamin was the Israelite area with the highest concentration of settlements. Along the watershed (about ten miles from Bethel in the north to Jerusalem in the south) and on the line parallel to it in the east, the following settlements were enumerated in Isaiah 10:28–32: Aiath, Migron, Michmas, Geba, Ramah, Gibeah of Saul, Bath-gallim, Laish(ah), Anathoth, Madmenah, Gebim, Nob, and Jerusalem. To this list we can add Bethel and Mizpah on the mountain ridge, as well as Azmaveth, Alemeth, Zimri, and Parah/Perath in the east. To the east of these locations is a semi-desert area where one could find shepherds and their flocks. To the west was the land of the Gibeonites, which during Saul's time was already inhabited mostly by Israelites, some of whom were Saul's family members (I Chr. 8:29–33; 9:35–39; compare to II Sam. 21:1). To the south of Benjamin, in northern

6. Compare to Michmas in eastern Benjamin, which, in the Second Temple period, was considered *alfa la-solet* – a place that ranked first for the quality of its fine flour for use in the Temple meal offerings.

Judah, was Bethlehem, which was apparently a bustling urban center at the time.[7] Aside from Jerusalem, a city that was a Jebusite enclave, no matter where the asses might have wandered throughout the rest of the region, Saul's father Kish might have hoped that they had ended up in the hands of a person who would be willing to fulfill the mitzva of "And it shall remain with you until your fellow claims it…You shall do the same with his ass" (Deut. 22:2–3).

(Courtesy of Prof. Amihay Mazar)

Khirbet Marjame and Ein Samia – Baal-shalishah according to Kallai

In contrast, the hill country of Ephraim was seemingly heavily forested at the time, with few settlements. Even during the Patriarchal Age, we find that one could ask a random person about a few brothers who were herding sheep in Shechem – "Could you tell me where they are pasturing?" – a reality fitting for a region that is sparsely populated.

7. In the Book of Ruth, Bethlehem was a crowded place where those without ancestral lands would gather sheaves in the field; in the episode of Micah's idol, the young Levite had left Bethlehem "to take up residence wherever he could find a place" (Judges 17:8); and in the episode of the concubine in Gibeah, Bethlehem was where the concubine's father tried to stall her husband day after day, to prevent him from living with his wife in the hill country of Ephraim as he insisted.

The Book of Joshua describes the conquest of the south, then the conquest of the north, followed by the summary "Joshua conquered the whole of this land" (Josh. 11:16). The conquest of the center of the land is not mentioned. Even in the list of the thirty-one kings of Canaan, the center of the land is barely featured; the tribes of Ephraim and Manasseh do not have lists of cities; and Joshua suggests that they clear out the forests (end of chapter 17). Between Bethel and Ai, Joshua spends a full day hiding thousands of soldiers in preparation for an ambush, presumably in the same forest from which the lion that killed the man of God in I Kings 13 and the bears in the time of Elisha (II Kings 2:24) would one day emerge. In the episode of Micah's idol, the young Levite from Bethlehem sets out to "find himself" in the hill country of Ephraim, and Micah's house in the hill country of Ephraim is a place that is reminiscent of a saloon from the American Wild West of the nineteenth century. The hill country of Ephraim was the dangerous place that worried the father of the young woman from the episode of the concubine in Gibeah. It is the area where Zuph – who was of Levite descent – decides to establish an ancestral land for his family without being concerned that someone would interfere by claiming ownership of the territory. Tola son of Puah of the tribe of Issachar served as Judge of Israel not within the boundaries of his tribal territory but in the hill country of Ephraim (Judges 10:1). In light of this reality of life and in light of the sparse nature of settlement in this region, it is no surprise that Kish sends his son to search for the asses in the heavily wooded hill country of Ephraim, where they would likely disappear in the forest.

The Asherite Theory

In I Chronicles 7–8, there are genealogical lists that contain, interwoven within them, geographical names associated with the tribes of Issachar, Benjamin, Ephraim, Asher, and, once again, Benjamin, at great length. The position of Asher here between Ephraim and Benjamin is somewhat surprising, since Asher's territory is located in the western Galilee. Furthermore, some scholars noted that the Asherite list contains names that are typical of the southern Ephraim/northern Benjamin area, while, on the other hand, none of the names gives any indication of a northern association. Among the names that fit with the southern Ephraim area, two prominent names are Beriah (mentioned in the list of Ephraimites in the same chapter) and Japhlet (which appears in Joshua 16:3 as the name of a family in whose territory the southern boundary of Ephraim runs). A particularly interesting phrase from this list is "who was the father of Birzaith." The expression "the father of" in the genealogical lists in Chronicles always relates to the names of cities. In general, the phrase is used for well-known cities, such as "the father of Bethlehem," "the father of Kiriath-jearim," or "the father of Mareshah," and it seemingly refers to the founders of the settlement in these places. Birzaith, in contrast, is a unique name in the Tanakh, reappearing in Josephus (Bērzēthō, Birzitho, Barzēthō, Birzēthō, or in other versions, Bēthzēthō, zēthō; *Antiquities* 12:397, 422). Moreover, even today there is only one settlement in the world bearing this name: Birzeit, located north of Ramallah.

It is well known that the genealogical lists in Chronicles are not systematic, and that they sometimes contain duplicate entries and contradictions. There are some tribes and families about whom there is copious information, while others are not mentioned at all. Even a Torah sage like Rabbi Arye Leib Ginzburg, the author of *Sha'agat Arye* (1695–1785), allowed himself to say that these eccentricities are all a matter of coincidence, and that whatever lists were found at the time the book was written were included. Scholars therefore speculated that the list of Asherite families that found its way into the Book of Chronicles included only those families that, like many others at the start of the Israelite period, seized territories in the southern hill country of Ephraim. In contrast, the genealogical lists of the northern Asherite families were never included in Chronicles, just as the genealogical lists of Zebulun, Naphtali, and Dan were likewise omitted.

From here we return to the matter at hand. In the Asherite list in Chronicles, we find people named Shelesh, Shilshah, and Shual (I Chr. 7:35–37). We may speculate that these individuals were the eponyms of the land of Shalishah and the land of Shual/Shaalim.

Kallai's Identification

After all these analyses, we can summarize by saying that the land of Shalishah was apparently located east of the area of Ophrah/Taybeh and north of the northern border of Benjamin. The northern border of

Benjamin in this area apparently ran along Wadi Makūk/Nuwei'meh, indicating that the land of Shalishah was in the area of modern-day Kokhav HaShahar or Rimonim.

This is where Kallai's suggested identification enters the equation. North of Kokhav HaShahar there is a large spring called 'Ein Sāmyeh and a nearby site called Khirbet Marjame, a prominent ruin of an ancient Israelite city. The scholars found it difficult to suggest a biblical identification for this city. Kallai suggested identifying Baal-shalishah with this city. In my opinion, although Kallai's overall way of approaching the biblical data is certainly convincing, this identification is incorrect. As we have seen, all the "lands" in the story of the search for the asses bear names of people – not of cities; even in the case where the territory contained a well-known city, the territory was not named for the city. In addition, the expression "Baal-X" does not necessarily allude to a populated city. Therefore, there is no reason to look for a city in searching for Baal-shalishah's identification. Regarding Khirbet Marjama, I have a different suggestion for identification that is beyond the scope of this discussion. Despite this, Kallai was correct in stating that the land of Shalishah was located in this region. It seems that the man who came from Baal-shalishah to Gilgal to bring "bread of the first reaping" to Elisha was a rural settler who came from his family's ancestral territory. From his home, he traveled about twelve miles until reaching the man of God and the disciples of the prophets sitting before him.

For further study:

Breuer, M. "*Torat Hate'udot shel Baal HaSha'agat Arye.*" *Megadim* 2 (1987): 9–22 [Hebrew].

Edelman, D. "Asher." In *The Anchor Bible Dictionary* 1, 482.

Edelman, D. " The Asherite genealogy in I Chronicles 7:30–40." *Biblical Research* 33 (1988): 13–33.

Edelman, D. "Saul's Journey through Mt. Ephraim and Samuel's Ramah." *ZDPV* 104 (1988): 44–58.

Elitzur, Yoel. "*Zihuyan shel 'Eretz Tzuf' Ve'Harama,' Ir Shmuel.*" In *Lifnei Efrayim UBinyamin UMenashe*, edited by Z. Ehrlich, 101–115. Jerusalem, 1985, [Hebrew].

Elitzur, Yoel. "A New Proposal for the Identification of an Israelite City at Ein Samia." *Judea and Samaria Research Studies* 3 (1994): 17–28 [Hebrew].

Elitzur, Yoel. "*Hapasuk Harishon Besefer Shmuel: Historiya, Geografiya Umashma'ut.*" In *Minhat Sapir*, edited by I. Rozenson and Y. Spanier, 51–63. Elkana-Rehovot, 2013, [Hebrew].

Kallai, Z. "Baal-shalishah and Ephraim." In *The Bible and Jewish History: Essays in Memory of Jacob Liver*, edited by B. Oppenheimer, 191–206. Tel Aviv, 1972, [Hebrew].

Kallai, Z. "*Ba'al-shalisha.*" *Encyclopaedia Biblica* 2, 292; "*Shalisha, Eretz Shalisha.*" *Encyclopaedia Biblica* 7, 716 [Hebrew].

Parashat Metzora

The *Tzara'at*-Affected House

Tzara'at as a Real-life Phenomenon in the Second Temple Period and Thereafter

The *tzara'at* that the Torah describes is not a recognized disease today, and its prominent symptoms – hair turning white (or yellow, in the case of an affliction on the head or beard) and a patch of healthy flesh within the swelling – are unknown to us. Traditional translations, following the Septuagint, refer to the biblical *tzara'at* as "leprosy" and the *metzora* as "leper," as *lepra* was a generic name for any skin disease in ancient and classical Greek. In modern English and other contemporary European languages, the word "leprosy" or its cognates – as well as *tzara'at* in Modern Hebrew – commonly refers to elephantiasis or Hansen's disease, a serious illness that has affected people throughout history, particularly before the last century. Left untreated, Hansen's disease can cause disfiguring skin lesions and can even lead to loss of limbs, as well as paralysis, hearing loss, and vision loss, and finally death. However, modern leprosy bears little actual connection to the biblical *metzora* and *tzara'at* and to the *lepros* and *lepra* of the Septuagint. As mentioned above, the biblical *tzara'at* has different symptoms, and in the time of the Septuagint, the Greek word *lepra* was used for any kind of skin illness.

Moreover, Hansen's disease apparently did not even exist during the biblical period. Clear descriptions of this disease first appear in Greek writings from the first and second century CE. Among numerous skeletons from Egypt and the Land of Israel dated to the first millennium BCE that were examined by scholars, not one case of Hansen's disease was found. The most ancient skeleton with signs of Hansen's disease was revealed in Jerusalem in 2009 inside an ossuary dated to the first century CE. Echoes of Hansen's disease exist in rabbinic sources,[1] but *Ḥazal* never connected leprosy with *tzara'at*. In the Cairo Geniza, fifteen touching letters from the eleventh century were found, written in Hebrew by a group of lepers who stayed near the hot springs of Tiberias in an attempt to heal their affliction. In the letters, the lepers request financial assistance from the Jewish communities. The lepers describe their suffering, using biblical terminology like *sheḥin* ("inflammation") and *garav* ("scurvy") for the disease itself, and words like "pained" and "afflicted" to describe themselves, but even they never used the word *tzara'at* in connection with their condition.[2] In addition, leprosy can be contagious (though not highly contagious, as it was thought to be in previous generations), unlike biblical *tzara'at*, which is not contagious at all.[3] Finally, a person can recover from *tzara'at* in the span of one week, while leprosy is a chronic illness.

Tzara'at existed during the Second Temple period; a forty-cubit by forty-cubit unroofed chamber was designated specifically for *metzora'im* in the Women's Court of the Temple (Mishna Middot 2:5). Two generations following the destruction of the Temple, R. Yehuda

1. See Genesis Rabba 60 and parallels: "Jephthah died through the loss of his limbs. Wherever he went, a limb would fall off."
2. The first to identify Hansen's disease with the *tzara'at* of the Bible was apparently R. Ya'akov ben Moshe Badarshi, who translated in the thirteenth century Maimonides' commentary on the order of *Nhasim* into Hebrew. In Tractate Ketubot (3: 5) Maimonides interpreted *mukkat sheḥin* as *mujadhdhama* and he passed it on to *metzora'at*. R. Yosef Qāfeḥ commented on this in his comments on Maimonides' interpretation of this Mishna.
3. The *metzora* separates himself from the camp because he is ritually impure, not for medical reasons. This can be seen from the fact that the *metzora* does not always have to separate himself, such as: if "he has turned all white" (Lev. 13:13); or according to *Ḥazal*, during the seven days of celebration following his marriage or during the three festivals (Sifra Tazria 5); and if he is in an unwalled city (Mishna Kelim 1:7).

provided a detailed description of the precise way in which R. Tarfon purified three *metzora'im* (*Torat Kohanim, Metzora Parasha* 1).

Tzara'at of the House

In contrast to the *tzara'at* that would afflict a person's body, the *Tanna'im* viewed the laws of *tza'arat* afflicting clothing and the walls of a house as entirely theoretical. *Ḥazal* interpreted *tzara'at* of the house in alternately positive and negative lights. The positive:

> R. Shimon b. Yoḥai taught: When the Canaanites heard that Israel were coming to their country, they arose and hid their wealth inside their walls and in their fields. The Holy One said: I did not promise their forefathers that I would bring their descendants into a land laid waste, but rather to a land full of all kinds of goodness, as it is written: "And houses full of all kinds of goodness" (Deut. 6:11). What, then, did the Holy One do? He caused sores to appear on a person's house, and when he took it apart he would find the treasure. (Leviticus Rabba 17)

And the negative:

> "The owner of the house (*asher lo habayit*; literally, 'he that the house is for him') shall come" (Lev. 14:35). Why then, "for him"? [That means to say that] if one devotes his house to himself exclusively, refusing to lend his belongings by pretending he did not own them, the Holy One, Blessed Be He, exposes him as he removes his belongings. (Yoma 11b)

And:

> So it is with *tzara'at* affections. First they come on his house. If he repents – good; if not – then the [affected stones of the house] must be pulled out, as it says, "The priest shall order the stones to be pulled out" (Lev. 14:40). If he repents – good; if not – then [the house] must be torn down. If he repents – good; if not – [the *tzara'at* affections] come on his clothes and they must be washed.

> If he repents – good; if not, [the affection] must be torn out, as it says, "He shall tear it out from the cloth" (13:56). If he repents – good; if not, [the clothes] must be burned, as it says, "The cloth shall be burned" (13:52). Then [the affections] come on his body. If he repents – good; if not – [the priest] goes and returns. If he repents – good; if not – "he shall dwell apart; his dwelling shall be outside the camp" (13:46). (Ruth Rabba 2)

The common denominator between all of these homilies is that none of them portrays this form of *tzara'at* as a real-life phenomenon.

Did Tzara'at of the House Exist?

The *Tosefta* states:

> There was never an affected house, and there never will be one. Then why was this law written? That you may study it and receive reward. R. Elazar b. R. Shimon said: There was a place in the vicinity of Gaza that was called *Churveta Segirta* ("ruins of affected houses"). R. Shimon b. Yehuda of Kefar Akkum said: There was a place in the Galilee that they would mark off, saying: "Affected stones were there." (Nega'im 6:1)

The Talmud (Sanhedrin 71a) cites this dispute along with two other similar disputes regarding the wayward and defiant son and the idolatrous city, but there is a distinction between these two examples and that of the *tzara'at*-affected house. In the other two cases, the dispute is formulated differently:

> There was never a wayward and defiant son, and there never will be one. Then why was this law written? That you may study it and receive reward. R. Yonatan said: I saw him and sat on his grave…

> There was never an idolatrous city, and there never will be one. Then why was this law written? That you may study it and receive reward. R. Yonatan said: I saw it and sat upon its ruins.

From a statistical perspective it seems surprising that among all the sages, R. Yonatan was the one who sat on both the grave of the wayward and defiant son and the ruins of the idolatrous city. I once heard a solution – that in each of these two instances, R. Yonatan is using a poetic metaphor, and both times he is referring to Jerusalem. To explain, Jerusalem is called an "idolatrous city" because of the widespread idolatry practiced there in the years leading up to the destruction of the Temple. Likewise, the people of Jerusalem are represented metaphorically by the wayward and defiant son, who disobeyed his father and met his demise as a result.

The dispute over the *tzara'at*-affected house diverges from the uniform schematic structure of these two disputes cited in the Talmud. In the case of the *tzara'at*-affected house, the first opinion that rejects its existence is followed by the names of not one, but two sages – the son of R. Shimon b. Yoḥai and a prominent disciple of his. Both of them cite traditions that include specific information concerning the remnants of a *tzara'at*-affected house.

The Gazan Tradition

R. Elazar b. R. Shimon provides a piece of information that cannot be interpreted as a literary homily, neither does it resemble a traditional folk identification. R. Elazar was at least a second-generation resident of the Upper Galilee; his father lived in the Galilean city of Tekoa and they were both buried in Meron. Gaza is more than ninety miles from the region where R. Shimon, his children, and his disciples spent their days. What is more, during that period there were no Jews at all living in Gaza, which was entirely Hellenistic since the Roman conquest of the land in 63 CE. There was a Jewish presence in the agricultural areas surrounding Gaza until the Bar Kokhba rebellion, but these communities were eliminated following the rebellion's suppression.[4]

On the other hand, it should be noted that R. Elazar b. R. Shimon does not attest explicitly to the existence of *tzara'at*-affected houses – only that there was a place called "Churveta Segirta," which he believed

4. A small number of Jews found their way back to this region during the Amoraic period; see the chapter on *Parashat Toledot.*

referred to this phenomenon. The sages heard this information from R. Elazar but did not alter their position regarding *tzara'at* of the house. If they had done so, the *baraita* would have been formulated differently; it might have stated: "In the beginning, it was said that there was never an affected house, and there never will be one, until R. Elazar b. R. Shimon came and said: There was a place in the vicinity of Gaza that was called Churveta Segirta." What, then, is the position of the sages? Do they accuse R. Elazar of lying? Certainly not. It seems, then, that the sages do accept R. Elazar's testimony, but maintain that the existence of such a name does not necessarily prove the existence of *tzara'at* of the house. As Nahmanides states: "There is no need to seek out the reason for names of places" (commentary on Gen. 23:9). There are many place-names whose meanings are completely unclear to us, and there are sometimes place-names with multiple possible interpretations. If one insists on attempting to understand the meaning of this name, he might take into consideration that the root S-G-R is found in various Aramaic dialects referring to closing or locking. Thus, it may be that the ruin that R. Elazar spoke of was described as *segirta* not due to *tzara'at,* but because the site was considered "shut tight" or fortified, closed off from public access.

Is it possible to identify this place that R. Elazar describes? Today, there is no known site in the country, neither near Gaza nor in any other region, called "Churveta Segirta" or any name of that nature.[5] Isaiah Press suggested identifying Churveta Segirta with the nondescript ruin of "al-Kharba" or "er-Rasm"[6] between Deir al-Balaḥ and the ruins of Kfar Darom. This kind of identification is a product

5. Names similar to either *churveta* or *segirta* individually do exist: In the southwestern Mount Ephraim region there are two Arab villages whose names were preserved in the Aramaic form – Kharbata – and in Lebanon there is a similarly named village – Ḥarbata. As for *segirta,* the Lower-Galilean moshav of Ilaniya was originally called Sejera, after the nearby Arab village al-Shajara. In addition, there exists in the Upper Galilee a Druze village called Sajur. However, Sejera/al-Shajara was apparently an Arabic name in origin (meaning "the tree"), and it is accepted that Sajur is an Arabic version of the talmudic name Shezor.
6. The Arabic word *rasm* means "remnant of ruins." Almost all ruins in the Land of Israel bearing this name are found in the Gaza/Ashkelon region; apparently the term was used particularly frequently in the Arabic dialect of this region.

ספר כפתור ופרח

אשר נמצא בבית גנזי החכם סיני ועוקר הרים הלא הוא
הגאון נגיד מקצרי' עשיר עניו בו נמצא תורה וגדולה
במקום אחד כמהרר יצחק כהן שולל וכו
נמצא רוב התועלת שמדבר בדיני
ארץ ישראל הנהמרת הוים
הארץ ובשאר דינים יפים
כאשר תראה בסימני
פרקים שלו:

אותו העיר: הבחור מאיר: במשפחתו הצעיר:

פה ויניציא

(hebrewbooks.org)

Title page of Rabbi Ishtori Haparḥi's *Kaftor Vaferaḥ*, Venice, 1549

of the "identify at all costs" school of thought, and should not be given credence.

The *tzara'at*-affected house in the Gaza region interested Rabbi Ishtori Haparḥi from a halakhic perspective, concerning the holiness of the land and its borders. The *tzara'at*-affected house is a mitzva that is bound by the land, as the Torah states: "Upon a house in the land you possess" (Lev. 14:34). The mention of the *tzara'at*-affected house in the Gaza region indicates that Gaza is imbued with the holiness of the Land of Israel. Some *Aḥaronim* dealt with the question of whether Gaza was included within the territory consecrated by the returnees from Babylonia. It is well known that places that were not recaptured by the returnees from Babylonia were generally exempt from tithes and the laws of *Shemitta*. These places were also viewed as bearing "impurity of the land of the nations" like all land outside the Land of Israel (Gittin 8a and others) unless they were interpolated within the Land of Israel proper. Impurity of the land of the nations is similar in severity to the impurity of a corpse, and thus the *tzara'at*-affected house – which bears a lesser degree of impurity – would not be an important consideration in such an area. Maharit maintained that the Gaza region was not consecrated, and the tradition cited by R. Elazar may have been from the First Temple period, while Rabbi Jacob Emden maintained that the Gaza region was indeed consecrated by "the returnees from Babylonia." In the chapter on *Parashat Toledot*, we cited evidence supporting the latter position.

The Galilean Tradition

In contrast to the Gazan tradition, which, on the one hand, was an authentic testimony concerning a place-name, and on the other hand, did not possess the characteristics of a traditional folk legend, the second tradition is precisely the opposite case. R. Shimon b. Yehuda, who cites the tradition, was a prominent disciple of R. Shimon b. Yoḥai. In most places where his name appears in rabbinic literature, he cites views and statements in the name of R. Shimon. The name of his place of residence appears in numerous variations: Kefar Akko; Akkom; Akkos; Eikom; Eikos; Kefar Abbom; Eibom; Abbos; Eibos; and Kefar Eitam. The sources do not provide any indication of the identification of this place. Most scholars of talmudic geography preferred the version *Kefar Akko* and tied this name to Caphareccho, which Josephus mentions in *The Wars of the Jews* (II:573). These scholars identified this site near Acre.[7] In such a case, I prefer to leave this identification as an open question; in any case, it stands to reason that a prominent disciple of R. Shimon would live in the Galilee near his mentor.

R. Shimon b. Yehuda makes a general statement, without pointing to any specific location, and relates that there was a certain place in the Galilee that contained stones labeled as *tzara'at*-affected. The tradition he cites is written in the past tense: "There *was* a place in the Galilee that they marked off." Even though he was speaking of the

7. Compare to the similar case of Kefar Ludim, which was adjacent to Lod (Gittin 2a).

same Galilee where he and his mentors spent their lives, R. Shimon b. Yehuda is unable to point to any specific location. In light of this, it seems that he was merely citing a vague tradition, a story passed from one person to another outside the halls of the beit midrash. It is no wonder that the sages are not convinced by this anecdote, and stand firm in their position: "There was never an affected house, and there never will be one."

For further study:

Browne, S. G. "How Old is Leprosy?" *British Medical Journal* (1970): 3:640–641 (http://www.ncbi.nlm.nih.gov/pmc/articles/PMC1701736/pdf/brmedj02305-0068.pdf).

Cohen, C. "Literary and Philological Aspects of BH צרעת." *Korot* 21 (2011–2012): 255–291.

Gil, M. *Palestine During the First Muslim Period.* Tel Aviv, 1983, 2, 457–475 [Hebrew].

Gil, M. *A History of Palestine.* 634–1099 (trans. E. Broido), New York, 1992, 183–185.

Haparḥi, Ishtori. *Kaftor Vaferaḥ*, Lunz ed., Jerusalem, 1897, 129 and citations in notes [Hebrew].

Hyman, A. "R. Shimon ben Yehuda." *Toldot Tanna'im VaAmora'im*, 1177 [Hebrew].

Press, I. "*Churveta Segirta.*" *A Topographical-Historical Encyclopaedia of Palestine*, 2, Jerusalem, 1948, 252; "*a-Rasm*," 4, 882 [Hebrew].

Reeg, G. "Meron." "Tekoa." *Die Ortsnamen Israels nach der rabbinischen Literatur*, Wiesbaden, 1989, 423–424, 621–622 [German].

Wright D. P. and R. N. Jones. "Leprosy." In *The Anchor Bible Dictionary*, 4, 277–281.

Parashat Aḥarei Mot

Slaughtering Outside the Tabernacle Courtyard: The Temple of Onias

The Prohibition of Slaughtering Outside the Tabernacle Courtyard

> If anyone of the house of Israel slaughters an ox or sheep or goat in the camp, or does so outside the camp, and does not bring it to the entrance of the Tent of Meeting to present it as an offering to the Lord, before the Lord's *Mishkan*, bloodguilt shall be imputed to that man: he has shed blood; that man shall be cut off from among his people....Say to them further: If anyone of the house of Israel or of the strangers who reside among them offers a burnt offering or a sacrifice, and does not bring it to the entrance of the Tent of Meeting to offer it to the Lord, that person shall be cut off from his people. (Lev. 17:3–9)

We learn from here that one who slaughters and offers a sacrifice to God outside the Sanctuary during a period when the use of *bamot* (altars outside the Temple, literally "high places") was prohibited, would be liable to be punished by *karet* (spiritual excision) – once for slaughtering and once for offering the sacrifice (Mishna Zevaḥim 13:1). Nonetheless, the prohibition against the use of *bamot* was generally viewed in the Tanakh as a minor prohibition. Even with regard to upright kings from the Davidic line, such as Asa, Jehoshaphat, and Jehoash, the Tanakh relates that they did what is right in the sight of the Lord – "however, the *bamot* were not removed." In addition, Elijah the prophet was permitted to sacrifice on Mount Carmel due to exceptional circumstances. When Josiah destroyed the *bamot,* he distinguished between the priests who had served at *bamot* designated for idolatry – whom he slaughtered upon their own altars – and those of the *bamot* that were used in God's name – whom he brought to Jerusalem. These priests were invalidated from service in the Temple in Jerusalem, but they were permitted to eat *kodashim* (sacrificial donations) along with their kinsmen (II Kings 23:8–9; compare to 23:19–20).

During the Second Temple period, there were three temples used to serve God outside Jerusalem, all of which were in violation of the prohibition against the *bamot.* One was the Samaritan altar on Mount Gerizim, which was destroyed by John Hyrcanus (*Antiquities* 13:256), while the two others were Jewish altars in Egypt. The first of the Jewish altars existed in the Persian period in Elephantine, in southern Egypt. The second, the subject of this discussion, is the Temple of Onias on the Nile Delta, which existed during the latter half of the Second Temple period. The existence of a temple for divine service in Egypt is anchored in Isaiah's prophecy, and the sources that speak of the Temple of Onias – Josephus, the Talmud Bavli and the Talmud Yerushalmi – indeed quote this prophecy:

> In that day, there shall be an altar to the Lord inside the land of Egypt and a pillar to the Lord at its border. They shall serve as a symbol and reminder of the Lord of Hosts in the land of Egypt. (Is. 19:19)

During the Second Temple period as well, there was a relatively forgiving attitude toward these prohibited temples. When the Jews of Elephantine were attacked and their temple defiled and ruined by rioters who were antagonistic to the Jews, they requested assistance from the priests and leaders in Jerusalem to help them rebuild their temple. It is not known if there was a response from Jerusalem to this request, but the very fact that such a request was made demonstrates that the temple in Egypt possessed a certain degree of legitimacy, at least in the context of expressing solidarity against a common enemy – an enemy of Israel. In a different letter, the people of Elephantine accepted upon themselves (apparently as a condition for being permitted to restore their temple following its destruction) to sacrifice only frankincense and meal offerings, and not animals. This was apparently an acceptable compromise for the priests of Jerusalem, and it led them to use their influence to benefit their fellow Jews in Egypt. *Ḥazal,* following this approach, were not overly harsh in relating to the Temple of Onias. In the Mishna at the end of Tractate Menaḥot, the sages applied the same principles to the priests of the Temple of Onias as Josiah did in his time:

> The priests who ministered in the Temple of Onias may not minister in the Temple in Jerusalem; and needless to say [this is so of priests who ministered to] another matter; for it is written, "'The priests of the *bamot,* however, did not ascend the altar of the Lord in Jerusalem, but they ate matzot along with their kinsmen" (II Kings 23:9). Thus they are like those that had a blemish: They are entitled to share and eat [of the *kodashim*], but they are not permitted to offer sacrifices. (Menaḥot 13:10)

We find a surprising statement in the Talmud Bavli:

> R. Yitzḥak said: I have heard that sacrifices may be offered in the Temple of Onias at the present day. He was of the opinion that… the first holiness [of Jerusalem] was conferred on it for the time being but not for all time. (Megilla 10a)

Later on in the passage, the Talmud relates that after some time, R. Yitzḥak retracted his opinion on the matter of the Temple of Onias. When he was asked, "Did you really say so?" he replied, "I did not say so." Nevertheless, we learn from here that the Temple of Onias is a legitimate term in the discourse of the beit midrash.

The Name *Ḥonyo*

In the Bavli and in the Tosefta, the name Onias appears as Ḥonyo. In the Land-of-Israel traditions of the Mishna, the version is Neḥunyon or Neḥonyo.[1] It is interesting to note that Maimonides' autograph of the Mishna reads Neḥonyo, while he himself, in his commentary on the same mishna, follows the Bavli, reading Ḥonyo (each form seven times, so that it is clear it is not accidental). The Bavli's version is supported by Josephus' Greek version, which reads "Onias."[2] Onias is also Josephus' version (*Antiquities* 14:22) for the name of Honi the Circle-drawer (Ḥoni HaMe'agel). In the eleventh century CE, Rabbi Nathan, the author of the *Arukh*, related in his entry entitled "Ḥonyo": "And the Gaon [Hai Gaon] vowelized it Ḥonyei." From a linguistic perspective, it seems that Ḥonyo is a shortened version of Neḥunyo.[3] It is somewhat surprising that the Yerushalmi presents a more original form of the name than Josephus, who predates it. A proof for the assumption that Ḥonyo is a shortened or spoken version of Neḥunyo can seemingly be found in the *Sifra*: "He called for his son Neḥunya. He said to him, 'My son Ḥunya'" (*Sifra Emor* 1:14). However, this version only appears in the printed editions, and is not corroborated by the manuscripts.

---

1. Neḥunyon in MSS Kaufmann, Parma and Lowe, in *Melekhet Shlomo* on the Mishna and in Talmud Yerushalmi; Neḥunyo in Maimonides' autograph, MS Cambridge I (according to the *variae lectiones* in the Vilna edition of the Mishna) and the Naples printed edition, 1492.
2. This version is a reflection of Ḥonya, with a Greek suffix appended to it. Names whose origins end with the divine suffix *-yahu* were sometimes contracted, as early as in the First Temple period (in particular in the kingdom of Samaria) to end in *-yo*. Another development that such names have experienced, especially from the beginning of the Second Temple period on, was omission of the final vowel, causing the suffix to become *-ya*. Among *Ḥazal*, most names of this type that we find end in *-ya*, though we also find some instances of *-yo*. Noteworthy are Bavli Makkot 21a and parallel passages, which enumerate some laws stated by R. Malkia as against others stated by R. Malkio.
3. The final *nun* of Neḥunyon is connected to the common pronunciation in the Land of Israel at the time, in which the ends of words ending in a vowel were nasalized. Some examples of this phenomenon include Tzipporin (Sepphoris); Keisarin (Caesarea); *lema'alan* (above); and *lematan* (below).

Who Is Onias and When and Where Was the Temple in Egypt Built? *Ḥazal's* Version

There is a significant discrepancy on this matter between the rabbinic tradition and Josephus. According to *Ḥazal* (Bavli Menaḥot 109b–110a; Y. Yoma 6:3, 43d), Onias (Ḥonyo) and Shim'i[4] were the sons of Simeon the Just. Because of the jealousy between the two, when each son wanted to inherit the priesthood from his father, one thing led to another and Onias traveled to Alexandria in Egypt and built an altar. According to the Aggada, one of the two brothers convinced the other to perform the temple service in the sanctuary while wearing women's clothing. The story is given in two versions, that of R. Meir and that of R. Yehuda. The two versions differ with respect to the details of the story, but also primarily with the question of whether the Temple of Onias was designated for idolatry or for divine service. The following is the account in the Bavli:

> Before his departure [from life, Simeon the Just] said to them, "My son Onias will succeed me [in high priesthood] after me." His brother Shim'i, who was two years and a half older than he, was jealous of him and said to him, "Come and I will teach you the order of the Temple service." He thereupon put upon him a housecoat,[5] girded him with a girdle,[6] placed him near the altar, and said to his brethren the priests, "See what this man promised his beloved and has now fulfilled: 'On the day in which I will assume the office of high priest I will put on your housecoat and gird myself with your girdle.'" At this his brethren the priests sought to kill him. He ran from them but they pursued him. He then went to Alexandria in Egypt, built an altar, and offered thereon sacrifices in honor of idols.... This is the view of the events according to R. Meir. R. Yehuda said to him: That was not what happened, but the fact

4. The Yerushalmi reads "Shimon," in which case the names of the father and the son would be the same.
5. In the Hebrew source *onkelei*, probably corrupted from the Greek *anakōlē* "above the thigh."
6. In the Hebrew source *tziltzul* – some type of womanly ornamented belt.

> was that Onias did not accept the office of high priest because his brother Shim'i was two years and a half older than he. Despite this, Onias was jealous of his brother Shim'i and he said to him, "Come and I will teach you the order of the Temple service." He thereupon put on him a housecoat, girded him with a girdle, placed him near the altar, and said to his brethren the priests, "See what this man promised his beloved and has now fulfilled: 'On the day that I will assume the office of high priest I will put on your housecoat and gird myself with your girdle.'" At this his brethren the priests sought to kill him, but he explained to them all that occurred. They thereupon sought to kill Onias; he fled from them but they pursued him. He ran to the king's house, but they pursued him there; and whoever saw him cried out, "This is he! This is he!" He thereupon went to Alexandria in Egypt, built an altar, and offered thereon sacrifices in honor of God; for so it is written, "In that day, there shall be an altar to the Lord inside the land of Egypt and a pillar to the Lord at its border" (Is. 19:19).

In the Yerushalmi, instead of "he ran to the king's house" (in R. Yehuda's version), the text reads, "he fled to the king's mountain." It may be that the two Talmuds were referring to the same thing: the mountainous region north of the area of Jerusalem known in rabbinic sources as "the King's Mount" and in some sources "the King's House." However, it is not clear from the story why he fled to this region specifically.[7]

The entire *aggada* is puzzling in several respects. What is the meaning of the "practical joke" of convincing a person to wear a womanly garment with a decorated girdle? Could it be that someone who had been raised by Simeon the Just – who served as high priest for forty years and said that the world is based upon three things: the Torah, divine service and the practice of kindliness – would not know what even small children know: "These are

7. Maimonides, in his commentary on the Mishna at the end of Menaḥot, explained that he fled to the king, but the king could not protect him, since all of Israel sought to kill him. The problem is that the nearest kings to Jerusalem at the time were in Antioch, far to the north, and in Alexandria, far to the southwest. Moreover, the king in question could not have been in Alexandria, since the story relates that he fled to Alexandria immediately thereafter.

the vestments they are to make: a breastpiece, an ephod, a robe, a fringed tunic, a headdress, and a sash" (Ex. 28:4)? And if these were indeed the sons of Simeon the Just, and the apple fell far from the tree – they had assimilated or were ignoramuses to such an extent – how could Simeon the Just have even considered appointing one of them to succeed him as high priest?

We can summarize that according to rabbinic sources, the passage was referring to an altar that was erected during a period long before the Hasmonean Revolt, and the entire background to its initial construction was no more than a dispute between two brothers over inheritance, jealousy, and lust for honor. The location of the altar was apparently Alexandria (especially according to the Yerushalmi: "From there he fled to Alexandria and stood and built an altar *there*"), but it may be that one could claim – with difficulty – that he fled to Alexandria simply to seek refuge, and afterward he built the altar somewhere else in Egypt. We can also comment that R. Meir in our *baraita* maintains that the Temple of Onias was a place of idol worship, while R. Yehuda maintains – like the rest of the sources – that the temple was dedicated in God's name. According to the Yerushalmi's version, the positions are switched: According to R. Meir the altar was for God, while according to R.Yehuda the altar was for idolatry.

The family background of Onias according to the Talmuds is simple:

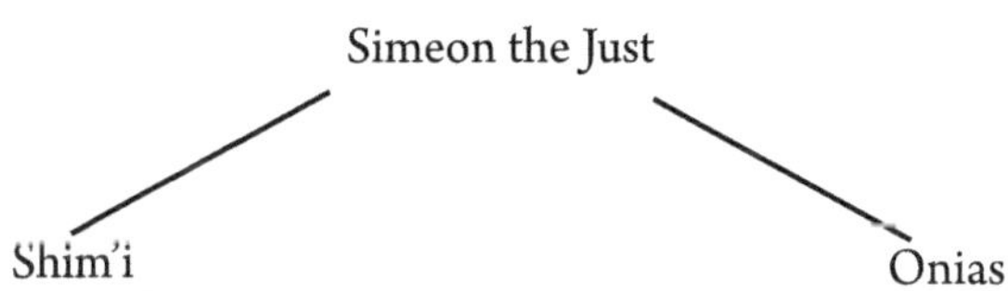

Who Is Onias and When and Where Was the Temple in Egypt Built? Josephus' Version

According to Josephus in *Antiquities of the Jews* (11:347; 12:43–44, 157–158, 224–225, 235–238, 383–387) Onias who built the temple in Egypt was the last of a fairly long line of high priests who served for generation after generation from the beginning of the return to the Land of Israel from Babylonia during the time of Zerubbabel until the Hasmonean Revolt. Onias is twelve generations removed from Joshua son of Jehozadak, the first high priest who immigrated from Babylonia to Jerusalem during the time of King Cyrus of Persia. Over the course of these generations there were sixteen high priests. Eleven of these comprised a direct father-to-son line from Joshua until the father of our own Onias. In four cases, the brother of the preceding high priest was appointed because the son was still too young to serve. Finally there was Jakim/Alcimus, the wicked Hellenized high priest who was the only high priest during this period who was not a descendant of Joshua son of Jehozadak. Alcimus was appointed by Antiochus Epiphanes during the time of the Hasmonean Revolt. The first six high priests on Josephus' list overlap with the list that appears twice in Nehemiah 12 (in verses 9–11 and in verse 22). Onias is the most common name in this family, appearing five times in the list. In the final generation, even first-degree relatives bear this name – Onias III, his Hellenized brother Onias IV (who adopted the Greek name Menelaus) and his son Onias V, who built the temple in Egypt. (Josephus emphasizes the identity of each of these three individuals in *Antiquities* 20:236). In *Wars of the Jews*, in two brief outlines that mention the matter incidentally (1:33, 7:423), there is one less generation and one less Onias. According to *Wars*, Onias III, who was high priest during the time when Antiochus Epiphanes defiled the Temple, was the one who fled to Egypt and built a temple there. In contrast, according to *Antiquities*, Jason and Menelaus (the Hellenized brothers of Onias III) and after them Alcimus, continued to serve as high priests even during the Hasmonean Revolt, and even after the purification of the Temple by Judah Maccabee. It was only after the sudden death of Alcimus that the nation gave the high priesthood to Judah Maccabee (12:414), who served as high priest for three years until he fell in battle (12:434). Onias V was the one who fled to Egypt when he saw that his uncle Menelaus was executed and the high priesthood passed from his family to Alcimus. The version in *Antiquities* is generally preferred over the version in *Wars*. *Wars* was written first, and its focus was the Great Revolt. Earlier matters described in *Wars* were presented as preludes to the events surrounding the destruction of the Temple and were written with less attention to detail and without thoroughly examining the pertinent sources. In our case, the version in *Antiquities* is supported by the book of II Maccabees (4:30–38), according to which

Onias III was murdered in Syria at Menelaus' command. A certain difficulty arises from the fact that, according to *Antiquities*, both Onias III and his brother Menelaus were called Onias in Hebrew. It may be, then, that their Hebrew names differed slightly; perhaps one was called Ḥoni while the other was called Ḥonyo or Ḥonya.[8]

The following is Onias' priestly lineage according to Josephus:

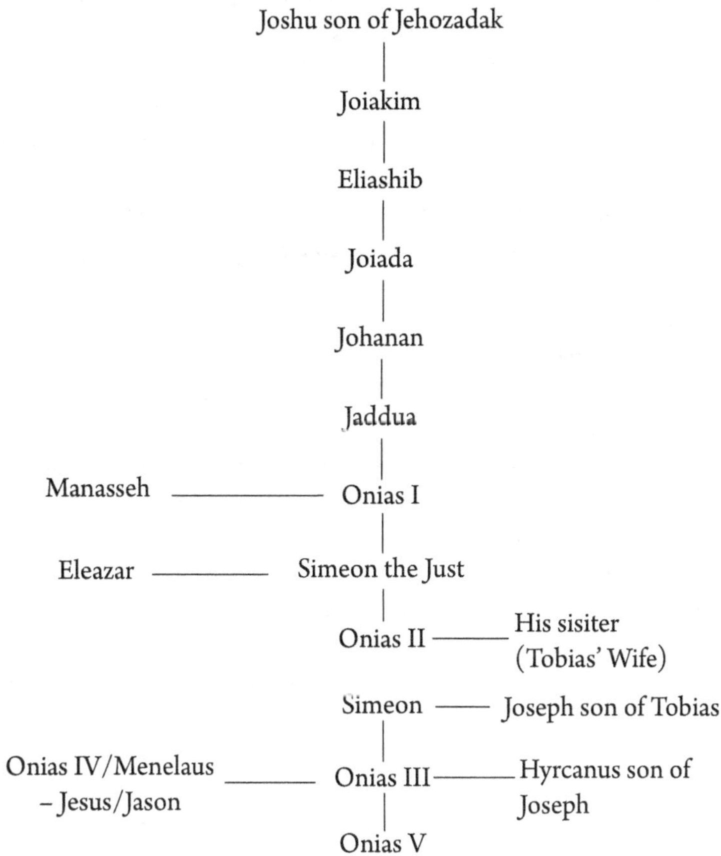

8. According to the common version of II Maccabees 3:4 and 4:23, Menelaus was not Onias' brother but a complete outsider; he was not even of priestly descent! However, many prefer a different version of chapter 3, which states that Menelaus was indeed a priest. In addition, it may be that the order of the words in the version of the verse in chapter 4 that Josephus possessed was slightly different. The matter requires further examination.

The Temple of Onias and its History

According to Greek and Roman sources, especially Josephus' *Antiquities of the Jews* (13:62–73), the Temple of Onias was built in a place called Leontopolis (lit. "city of the lions") on the ruins of an ancient pagan temple in the prefecture of Heliopolis. This entire area, which was rife with wild animals and natural vegetation, was eventually called "the land of Onias." Heliopolis, the Biblical On, was situated in the northern suburbs of modern-day Cairo. Leontopolis is identified according to most scholars with Tell el-Yahudiyya, which preserves the memory of the Jewish religious center that existed there in the past, about fifteen miles north of Cairo. Onias became deeply entrenched in Egypt, and, according to Josephus, he and another Jew named Dositheus were army generals for Ptolemy VI Philometor (ruled in the years 180–145 BCE; *Against Apion* 2:49–50). Onias' two sons, Hananiah and Hilkiah, were army generals for Cleopatra III (ruled in the years 116–101 BCE; *Antiquities* 13:284–287).

The Temple of Onias was forced to close and cease its operations about three years following the destruction of the Temple in Jerusalem by Lupus, the Roman governor in Egypt. After some Sicarii zealots who survived the destruction of Jerusalem arrived in Egypt and began to stir up the Jews of Egypt, the zealots were tortured and executed, the Temple of Onias was shut down and all its vessels were taken at the command of the Roman Emperor Vespasian. Josephus, who records this episode immediately following the story of Masada, adds that Lupus died a short time after he closed the Temple of Onias, concluding: "Now the duration of the time from the building of this temple till it was shut up again was three hundred and forty-three years" (*Wars* 7:420–436). The number of years listed here is one hundred years longer than the true number according to Josephus' chronology, and it is thus speculated that the longer number constitutes an arithmetic or copyist error.

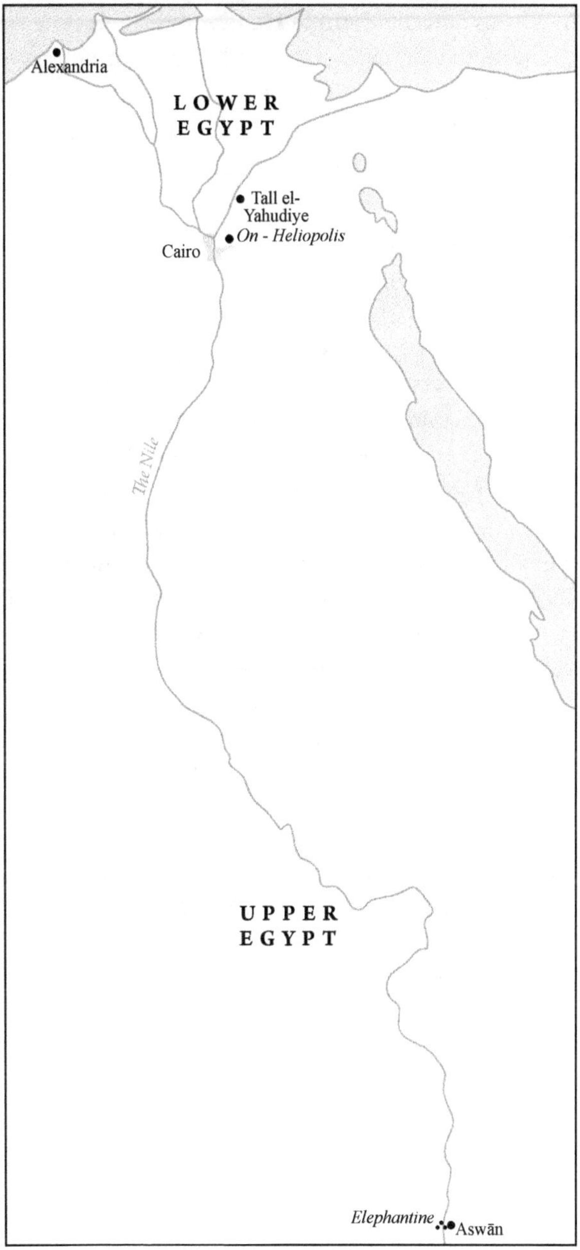
Alexandria
LOWER
EGYPT
Tall el-
Yahudiye
On - Heliopolis
Cairo
The Nile
UPPER
EGYPT
Elephantine
Aswān

Assessing Onias and the Temple He Erected

As we have said, the Talmuds and Josephus present entirely different stories about the founding of the Temple of Onias.[9] The chronological and genealogical differences between the Talmudic account and the traditions cited by Josephus have fundamental ramifications. According to the Talmuds, the entire episode is merely the result of a conflict over honor and lust for money between two jealous brothers who did not take after their righteous father, with a romantic element and possibly idolatry mixed into the equation. According to Josephus, however, there is a different background entirely. In one instance, Josephus concurs with the Talmud's negative assessment of Onias, blaming him for building the temple in "a place so unclean and so full of sacred animals" (*Antiquities* 13:70). However, in another instance Josephus praises Onias for saving the Hellenist country of Egypt from becoming embroiled in a civil war (*Against Apion* 2:49–50). He points out that Onias' sons sought the good of their people and were exceedingly respected in Egypt (*Antiquities* 13:284–287). In any case, the important part is that according to Josephus, Onias is a legitimate high priest who fled from Jerusalem, either from Antiochus Epiphanes and his decrees or from Alcimus the Hellenized high priest. He was a positive person who sought to find a place for serving God at a time of crisis when the original Temple of Jerusalem was defiled.

For further study:

Baines, J., and J. Malek. *Atlas of Ancient Egypt*. Oxford, 1986, 171–174.

Ilan, T. and Noam, V. *Josephus and the Rabbis*, 1. Jerusalem, 2017, 197–236 [Hebrew].

Porten, B. "Elephantine Papyri." In *The Anchor Bible Dictionary* 2, 445–455.

Rappaport, U. "Onias." In *The Anchor Bible Dictionary* 5, 23–24.

Stern, M. *Greek and Latin Authors on Jews and Judaism*, 1. Jerusalem, 1976, 268–270.

Tchernowitz, C. "*Hazugot Umikdash Ḥonyo*." In *Louis Ginzburg Jubilee Volume*, New York, 1946, 223–247 [Hebrew].

Thackeray, H. S. J. *Josephus: Against Apion* (LCL 186). London, n.d., 312–313.

Yavetz, Z. "*Beit Ḥonyo*." In *Sefer Toldot Yisrael, Metukan al pi Hamekorot Harishonim*, 4. Jerusalem-Tel Aviv, 1929, 4, 15–17 [Hebrew].

---

9. The historian Ze'ev Yavetz attempted to reconcile the two stories by adding details to the Talmud's account, as well as a forced interpretation of the phrase "his brother" to mean "one of the priests." His suggestion is not very convincing.

Parashat Kedoshim

Kir

Kir in Tanakh

This week's *haftara* is the closing section of the Book of Amos. The *haftara* begins: "To Me, O Israelites, you are just like the Ethiopians – declares the Lord. True, I brought Israel up from the land of Egypt, but also the Philistines from Caphtor and the Arameans from Kir" (Amos 9:7). Kir is mentioned one other time in Amos, at the opening of the book:

> Thus said the Lord: For three transgressions of Damascus, for four, I will not revoke it: Because they threshed Gilead with threshing boards of iron. I will send down fire upon the palace of Hazael, and it shall devour the fortresses of Ben-hadad ... and the people of Aram shall be exiled to Kir – said the Lord. (1:3–5)

This prophecy of Amos was indeed fulfilled relatively soon thereafter: "The king of Assyria responded to his request; the king of Assyria marched against Damascus and captured it. He deported its inhabitants to Kir and put Rezin to death" (II Kings 16:9). Aside from the two verses in Amos and the verse in Kings, Kir is seemingly mentioned in one other place in Tanakh: "While Elam bore the quiver in troops of mounted men, and Kir bared the shield" (Is. 22:6). The meaning of this last verse is disputed (some interpret *kir* as a substantive: "wall"), but the prevailing opinion is that it refers to warriors in the Assyrian army who were native to Kir. Another approach maintains that the preceding verse – *mekarkar kir vesho'a el hahar* – refers to the people of Kir as well, translating the verse "Kir raged…and Shoa on the hill." It seems more likely, however, that the word *kir* here simply means "wall," and the verse should be translated, "a battering down of walls and a shouting to the mountains." The repetition of the word *kir* in the following verse can be ascribed either to coincidence or the use of wordplay.

Thus, Kir is mentioned four times in Tanakh, all during the same period – the period of Amos and Isaiah. Three of these instances are connected to the Aramean nation, which originated in Kir and was eventually exiled back to Kir.

The Location of Kir According to Scholars

Most of the early translators identified Kir with the ancient city of Cyrene (*Kyrēnē* in Greek), due to the linguistic similarity between the two names. But from a geographical-historical perspective, Cyrene – located in modern-day Libya in North Africa – could not have been the homeland of the Arameans, nor could it have been the place where the Assyrian king Tiglat Pileser III exiled them.

Modern scholarship has not fared any better in identifying Kir. The name does not appear in any extrabiblical sources (one suggestion to identify it using an Akkadian source was rejected in the scholarly literature), and we do not possess any Assyrian sources describing the conquest of Damascus and the exile of the Arameans. Most of the suggested identifications are based on the method of searching for geographical names that bear some slight resemblance to Kir. Some scholars attempted to search for names that translate to "wall" or "city" (based on the word *kir* in Moabite) in various ancient languages. This method led some scholars to place Kir in northern Syria, Babylonia, or Assyria, while others strayed as far as eastern Media and Ararat, northern Armenia, and even as far north as Georgia.

The First Clue: A Talmudic Source

I believe that I have discovered a clue that may aid in identifying Kir. I lectured on this topic at the Fifteenth World Congress of Jewish Studies, and published the content in a scholarly forum.

The clue is an aggadic anecdote found in the Talmud Bavli:

> [As to] the Garden of Eden, Resh Lakish said: If it is in the Land of Israel, its gate is Beth-shean; if it is in Arabia, its gate is Beth Gerem; and if it is between the rivers, its gate is Dumaskanin. In Babylon, Abaye praised the fruit of Eber Yamina and Rava praised the fruit of Harpania. (Eiruvin 19a)

The manuscripts contain several textual changes, none of which is particularly interesting for us here except for one: the name Dumaskanin is rendered as Durmaskanin.

The phrase "between the rivers" appears several other times in the Talmud referring to the region between the Tigris and the Euphrates north of Babylon. Following the Arabian conquest, the region became known as "al-Jazira," a name whose literal meaning in Arabic is "the island." This name was fitting because the region is surrounded by two great rivers like an island in the middle of the sea.

What is the source of the name Du(r)maskanin? Clearly, this is a reference to the city of Damascus, whose name has taken on several variant forms in different sources – apart from the common "Dammesek" – including: Dummesek, Darmesek (found consistently in Chronicles and in the Great Isaiah Scroll from Qumran), and Durmesek. It is worth quoting from *Sifrei*: "R. Yose b. Durmaskith said to him … I call upon heaven and earth to witness that I am from Damascus ("Dammesek" in the Hebrew text) …" (*Sifrei* Deuteronomy 1).

It seems, then, that Du(r)maskanin was a place that was home to people who originated in Damascus. It stands to reason that these people from Damascus arrived at "between the rivers" in the time of King Tiglat Pileser III of Assyria, who destroyed Damascus in 733 BCE and exiled its inhabitants.

At this juncture, it is worth mentioning an interesting source from the Persian period: the archives of the Murashu family of the Babylonian city Nippur, unearthed in the nineteenth century CE. The Murashu family consisted of wealthy landowners who acquired numerous plots of land, employed a large number of sharecroppers, and conducted many financial transactions during the time of Artaxerxes I and Darius II (464–404 BCE).

In the documents found in the archive (written mostly in Akkadian cuneiform) several place-names are mentioned that – scholars speculate – were the new Babylonian homes of groups of exiles from various locations: Ishqalluna, named for Ashkelon in the land of Philistia; Khazati, for Gaza; Khammanai, for Amman; Khashbaya, for Heshbon; and Khattai, for Khattu, the coast of Syria and Lebanon in Akkadian terminology. Other similar examples from the archive include: Bît Ṣurrai – "the house of the people of Tyre"; sha Nêrebaya – "of the people of Nayrab" in northern Syria; Qidish, for Kedesh in the Galilee or Kadesh in Syria; Khatalua, for Hethlon (Ezek. 48:1); and Qidari, for Kedar. In the last two decades, Babylonian documents were published that mention exiles from Judea! The earliest of these documents (from 572 BCE, fourteen years after the destruction of the First Temple) mentions a city called URU sha LÚ Iakhudaia – "city of the people of Judea" – and the later documents shorten this name to URU Iakhudu – "city of Judea" – and other variations.

Against the background of this reality, it is no wonder that there existed a place for exiles from Damascus that was named for their native city. Fortunately for Du(r)maskanin, its name was preserved until the talmudic period. According to the Talmud, this was a warm, well-watered place, similar to Beth-shean in the Land of Israel, and it was thus worthy of being considered "the gate to the Garden of Eden." This brings up an interesting point: The original Damascus possessed similar physical characteristics to those that the Talmud ascribes to Du(r)maskanin. It is a warm region, receiving ample water from the Amanah and Pharpar (modern-day Barada and A'waj) Rivers, which flow from the Anti-Lebanon Mountains and transform a large expanse of land into a green, fertile desert oasis. It may be that here too the Assyrians implemented their policy of "I will take you away to a land like your own" (II Kings 18:32; Is. 36:17).

"Between the Rivers" – Where?

We have thus established that Durmaskanin is located in "between the rivers," and it seems to have been the most fertile place in that strip of land.

What else do we know about "between the rivers" from the Talmud? Kiddushin 72a mentions two places in "between the rivers," one in the south called Ihi Dekira and one in the north called Shot-Mishot. Briefly, the background to the talmudic discussion there is as follows: It is well known that the Jews who lived in Babylonia during the amoraic period enjoyed two privileges that were not shared by those who were exiled to other lands. The first was the ability to produce a valid *get* without having to declare that "it was written in my presence and it was signed in my presence." The second was genealogical purity likened to "pure fine flour," which was unparalleled even compared with that of residents of the Land of Israel. These Babylonian Jews took immense pride in their lineage, saying: "All countries are as dough in comparison with the Land of Israel, and the Land of Israel is as dough relative to Babylonia" (71a). The most genealogically inferior places were the mountainous lands of Media and Elam east of Babylonia: "Media is sick, and Elam is dying." Regarding "between the rivers," the law was unclear. On the one hand, the Talmud took great care to point out the borders between Babylonia and "between the rivers," and there were even differences of opinion regarding the precise location of the border. On the other hand, the Talmud relates an anecdote stating that Rabbi Isaac Nappaha permitted a man from Shot-Mishot to enter into the congregation, using as his rationale the fact that Shot-Mishot is located between the rivers. His verdict was based on the statement: "Said Abaye in the name of R. Ḥama b. Ukba in the name of R. Yose b. R. Ḥanina: Between the rivers is as Babylonia with respect to genealogy." The Talmud certainly chose Shot-Mishot as an example that would allow them to establish a general rule about the broader region of "between the rivers," so Shot-Mishot was probably located in the far reaches of the region, a great distance from Babylonia. In the vicinity of the northern Euphrates, there are, in fact, two Arabic place-names that resemble Shot-Mishot: Sumaysāṭ (Samosata in Roman sources) and Shimshāṭ. It may be speculated that one of these names constitutes a preservation of the talmudic Shot-Mishot.

In the southern part of "between the rivers," the Talmud mentions Ihi Dekira (in another version: Hai Dekira): "And where is ['between the rivers'] situated? R. Yoḥanan said: From Ihi Dekira and upward." The Gemara challenges this report about R. Yoḥanan's claim in a parallel discussion:

> How far does Babylonia extend?...How far [does it extend] on the upper reaches of the Euphrates? Rav said: To Fort Tulbakene (MS: Tulbaneke). Samuel said: To the bridge of the Euphrates. R. Yoḥanan said: As far as the ford of Gizama.

Thus, R. Yoḥanan's two statements contradict each other. The solution is: "Abaye said: A strip issues [beyond that limit]."

Ihi Dekira is found in two other places in the Talmud, both of which can help us learn more about its location and its population. The first is the following passage:

> Rami b. Abba said in the name of R. Yitzḥak: If one sees the River Euphrates by the Bridge of Babylon, he says, "Blessed is He who has wrought the work of creation." Now, however, that the Persians have changed it, only if he sees it from Be Shavor and upward. R. Yosef says: From Ihi Dekira and upward. (Berakhot 59a)

The blessing of "who has wrought the work of creation" is recited only upon witnessing forces of nature that have not been altered by human hands. The Euphrates from Ihi Dekira and upward originally flowed on a completely straight course, without veering away at all, and without any canals connecting it to the Tigris or redirecting its waters for irrigation purposes.

For our geographical discussion, the second mention in the Talmud of Ihi Dekira is more critical:

> It has been stated: If a barrel of wine is found floating on the River [Euphrates]. Rav says, if it is opposite a town where the majority of the inhabitants are Jews, the wine is permitted, and if opposite a town where the majority of the inhabitants are non-Jews, the wine is prohibited. Samuel, however, says that even if it is found opposite a town where the majority of the inhabitants are Jews, it is prohibited, because it may be supposed to have come from Ihi Dekira. (Bava Batra 24a)

In the continuation of the passage, the Talmud explains that Rav is not concerned with the possibility that the barrel originated in Ihi Dekira, because according to him, if the barrel came from there it would not have survived the "bays and the shallows" of the Euphrates. The barrel would have either become stuck or sunk before reaching Rav's city of Sura or Samuel's city of Nehardea, both of which were situated along the Euphrates. Based on this passage, Ihi Dekira was a non-Jewish city situated on the banks of the Euphrates north of the Jewish region in the northern part of Babylonia. It was also a city where wine barrels were commonly found.

In Greek and Roman Sources

Ihi Dekira is mentioned by name in non-Jewish sources as well. The earliest of these is the famous geographer Ptolemy, who lived in Alexandria during the tannaitic period (second century CE). In his Greek work *Geography*, Ptolemy includes a city named Idikara in a list of Mesopotamian cities, but does not write anything about it. For our discussion, it is important that we quote two historians who lived during the talmudic period and mentioned Ihi Dekira in their writings, adding essential information in their descriptions of the city. The first is Ammianus, the last of the great Roman historians (330–400 CE), who served in the Roman army in the east and describes the army's attack on the Persians: "We then crossed the river, and ... we entered the city of Diacira ... which we found empty of inhabitants but full of corn and excellent salt ... and [we] passed a bituminous spring..."

The second historian is Zosimus, a Byzantine historian who, in the years following 425 CE, wrote a six-volume work in Greek entitled *New History*, which outlined the events that transpired in the Roman Empire and in the rest of the world (with an emphasis on the East) from the time of Augustus until the year 410 CE. He writes:

> He arrived at Dakira, a town on the right hand, sailing down the Euphrates. The soldiers, finding this place forsaken by its inhabitants, took away a large quantity of corn that was laid there, and many other things ... on the opposite shore was a fountain of asphalt ...

We learn from these sources that the place was rich in corn and that it contained mines of fine salt, as well as a unique attraction – a bituminous spring.

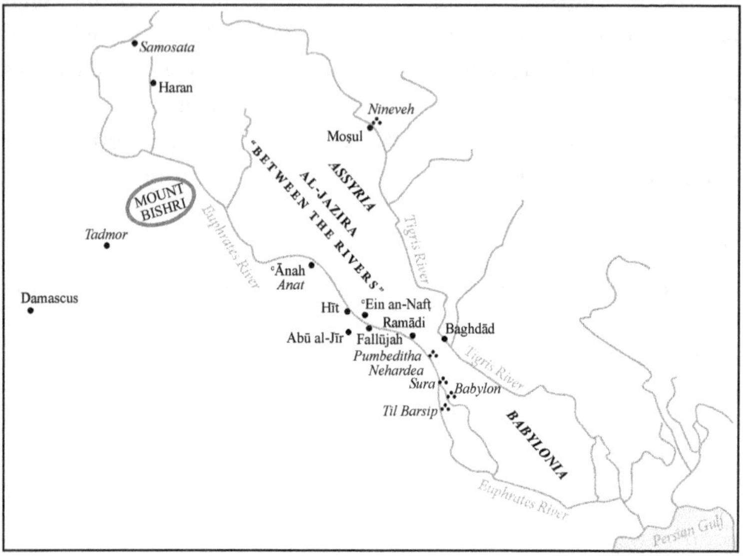

Bitumen (in Latin), or asphalt (in Greek), is mentioned in both of the above historical accounts, and its presence is a vital piece of information. Using this information, we can identify the place in other sources, and in today's reality as well. We should first explain here that asphalt – the material that the Tanakh calls *ḥemar*[1] – was very important in Babylonian culture. It was used as mortar in the large buildings and fortifications that abounded in Babylonia, echoing the verse, "and asphalt (*ḥemar*) served them as mortar (*ḥomer*)" (Gen. 11:3). This fact is reflected in the archaeology of Babylonia as well. In ancient times, materials like asphalt, pitch, tar, and petroleum were only produced in places where natural layers of the earth containing these resources were discovered. In the Iraq-Iran region there are three areas rich in asphalt:

1. The word *ḥemar*, in its "asphalt" sense, also exists in a similar form in Arabic, ancient South Arabian languages, the Christian Aramaic of the Land of Israel, Egyptian, and Coptic.

one area east of the Tigris, between the river and the mountains; a second area on the opposite side of the Karun River, near the city of Susa (Shushan); and a third area – the richest of the three – between Ramadi and Hīt on the Euphrates (see map). This center of asphalt production is the closest to ancient Babylon and was the source of the asphalt used in its ancient buildings. The asphalt was shipped to Babylon on boats, which sailed all along the river. Ihi Dekira must have been located in this region.

The famous historian Herodotus (c. 440 BCE) described a city in this region that bore a different name:

> Now there is another city distant from Babylon a space of eight days' journey of which the name is Is; and there is a river there of no great size, and the name of the river is also Is, and it sends its stream into the river Euphrates. This river Is throws up together with its water lumps of asphalt in great abundance, and thence was brought the asphalt for the wall of Babylon. (Herodotus I, 179)

In light of Greek linguistic patterns, the name Is may have been a Greek version of the word *id* or *idu*. Indeed, a city named ID or Idu, on the Euphrates, north of Babylon, is found in Akkadian sources as early as the Mari Letters (from the Patriarchal Age) and one Assyrian source mentions explicitly that bituminous springs existed on the eastern bank of the Euphrates, opposite Idu. It is generally assumed that the Arabic name Hīt (recognized from the birth of Islam until today) is a later version of that very name.[2] Hīt is situated on the western bank of the Euphrates, about 120 miles from Baghdad. In the medieval period, Hīt was a commercial center, due to the nearby presence of a bridge crossing the Euphrates, on which convoys traveled from Baghdad to Aleppo in Syria, and onward toward the Land of Israel and Egypt. The Islamic geographers praised Hīt's grains and dates, and poets sang of its excellent wine. Even today Hīt is home to ample fruit orchards, as well as date

2. However, linguistically speaking, since Sumerian, Akkadian, and Greek do not have the phoneme *h*, Hīt might be the original name, while ID/Idu and Is might be its Sumerian/Akkadian and Greek attestations respectively.

and grain plantations. Hīt's fertile nature, its wine, and its neighboring bridge across the Euphrates seem to clearly evoke the traits of Ihi/Hai Dekira of the talmudic period.

A third name of a city in this area is mentioned in a source from the Roman period: Isidore of Charax, a Greek writer who lived in southern Mesopotamia during the first century BCE and the first century CE. In about 25 CE, Isidore wrote *The Parthian Stations*, an itinerary listing all the caravan stations on the trade route from Babylon to Alexandria in Egypt. There, he mentions the city of Aipolis, "where there are springs of asphalt." It may be that the "Ai" component in this city's name is equivalent to "Ihi" or "Hai" in the name Ihi/Hai Dekira.

And now for a linguistic revelation: In Akkadian, the ancient language spoken by the nations of the Tigris and the Euphrates, there are actually two words for asphalt/bitumen. Crude asphalt is called *ittû* or *iddû*, whereas refined asphalt is called *qīru*.[3] Most probably, the placename Id(u)/Hīt is derived from the former, and the name Ihi Dekira is derived from the latter!

Here we reach the crux of the matter. It is reasonable to speculate that Du(r)maskanin, "the gate to the Garden of Eden," was situated in this region in the vicinity of Hīt – the most fertile part of "between the rivers," making the connection between the biblical city of *Kir* and the Akkadian *qīru* and Ihi Dekira of the *Amora'im* and the Greek and Roman sources seem self-evident. Apparently, it was to this region that the Assyrians exiled the Arameans from Damascus, and it was there that the name Damascus was preserved for centuries in the form of Du(r)maskanin.

"And the Arameans from Kir"

All that is left for us to do now is to clarify what might be the historical background of the emigration of the Arameans from Kir of which Amos speaks: "True, I brought Israel up from the land of Egypt, but also the Philistines from Caphtor and the Arameans from Kir."

3. This last word appears in the Aramaic of the Talmud Bavli in the form *qira*. This should not be confused with the Talmud's word for wax, which is spelled the same way in Aramaic but derives from a different, Greek source.

The Arameans are a nation whose history is characterized by extreme change. We may speak of three major periods:

- *The Ancient Period: From the Patriarchal Age to the time of Saul*

  In the stories of the Patriarchs, we encounter the family of Abraham's brother Nahor. Nahor, his son Bethuel, and his grandson Laban are Arameans living in Aram-naharaim. They and the other inhabitants of Aram-naharaim live as shepherds, and everyone seems to know one another: "'My friends, where are you from?...Do you know Laban the son of Nahor?'...'Yes, we do'...'Is he well?'...'Yes, he is; and there is his daughter Rachel, coming with the flock'" (Gen. 29:4–6). Their lives seem to operate at a leisurely pace: "Until all the flocks are rounded up; then the stone is rolled off the mouth of the well and we water the sheep" (29:8). When someone's daughter is married, the entire town is invited to the wedding: "And Laban gathered all the people of the place and made a feast" (29:22). For these early Arameans, kings and wars are nowhere on the horizon. There is a three-day journey connected with the streaked, speckled, and spotted flocks, and there is a sheep-shearing in a distant location, but there is no hint of ornate temples, priests, and worship – with the sole exception of Laban's household idols.

  Not far from there was Pethor, "which is by the Euphrates" (Num. 22:5) – the city of Balaam, also described as "Pethor of Aram-naharaim" (Deut. 23:5). We might theorize that the group of Arameans living in Aram-naharaim was part of a larger Aramean region that was not mentioned in the Torah. Even the term "Aramean" was sometimes used as a symbol for a penniless nomad, or for a homeless refugee, as in: "My father was a fugitive Aramean" (26:5).[4]

4. As Rabbi Ovadia Seforno interprets: "My father Jacob was, for a time, a fugitive Aramean, without a home of residence, and thus he was not prepared to establish a nation worthy of inheriting the land."

- *The Period of the Aramean Kingdoms*: The Tanakh gives no indication that the status of the Aramean nation had changed until Saul's time.[5]

  During the time of Saul, there is, for the first time, a laconic mention of "the kings of Zobah" (I Sam. 14:47) in the list of enemies surrounding Israel whom Saul fought successfully. David had already fought wars against the kings of Aram, wars that were, in practice, the greatest military accomplishments of David and his talented commanders Yoav and Avishai, the sons of Tzeruya. II Samuel 8 and 10 mentions several aggressive Aramean kingdoms, possessing extensive armies. The Tanakh records that David defeated Aram of Zobah and Aram of Damascus, Maacah, and the men of Tob, and even "the Arameans from across the Euphrates." He forged a treaty with King Toi of Hamath, who was the enemy of King Hadadezer of Zobah. Thousands of Aramean charioteers were killed, along with tens of thousands of foot soldiers, and a vast amount of copper was taken as plunder. David knew full well why he was investing such a tremendous effort in subduing the Arameans; this was a preventative strike that delayed the rise of Aramean power by more than a hundred years.

  In the Book of Kings, as early as Solomon's time, the Arameans began to show signs of recovery. Rezon son of Eliada established a kingdom in Damascus and was an "adversary" to Solomon and to Israel (I Kings 11:23). From the time of Asa until the time of Ahaz, Aram was Israel's bitter enemy. The Tanakh states that during certain periods, the king of Aram "trampled [Israel] like the dust under his feet" (II Kings 13:7). At the end of this difficult period, Aram's power began to decline, to the point that Isaiah called its king Rezin "a smoking stub of a firebrand" (cf. Is. 7:4). The conquest of Damascus at the hands of Tiglat Pileser, the

5. The one exception is the episode involving Cushan-rishathaim, king of Aram-naharaim, who was seemingly not a typical Aramean.

execution of Rezin, and the exile of the inhabitants of Damascus to Kir signified – all at once – the endpoint of the history of Aram.

- *The Rise of the Aramaic Language*

Paradoxically, and for reasons that are beyond the scope of this discussion to trace, it was only after the destruction of the Aramean nation that the Aramaic language rose to prominence. The Assyrian kings made Aramaic the international diplomatic language, and it continued to serve in this role during the rise of the Babylonian Empire and thereafter during the rise of the Persian Empire, until the conquests of Alexander the Great. At first, only members of the ruling classes were able to speak Aramaic, and not the masses (II Kings 18:26; Is. 36:11), but the language eventually became a vernacular language as well. For more than 1,300 years until the Arab conquest, Aramaic even became the most commonly spoken language in vast areas of the world.

From the perspective of the nation of Israel, the first half of this lengthy period yielded two books of the Tanakh, half of which was written in Aramaic: Ezra and Daniel. In the second half of this period, some of our greatest spiritual works were created, written in Aramaic or in a fusion of Aramaic and Hebrew: the Talmud Bavli, the Talmud Yerushalmi, the midrashim and the *Targumim*.

Let us return now to the Arameans. The transition from the pastoral first stage to the second stage, the period of the militarily powerful Aramean kingdoms, is correlated with a change in location. The Aramean kingdoms described in Samuel and Kings were generally in the West, north of the Land of Israel. Geshur and Maacah, Tob, Helam, and Rehob were located in the Golan region and by the headwaters of the Jordan; Zobah and Hamath were located in western Syria; and between them lay Damascus, the strongest and most important of all the Aramean cities.

The archaeological findings corroborate this notion. In various places, usually along the length of western Syria, more than thirty royal inscriptions written in Aramaic have been found, dating from the tenth, ninth, and eighth centuries CE. The inscription among them found farthest south was discovered about twenty-five years ago in Tel Dan. In contrast, the Arameans from the ancient periods lived in Haran (as well as Nahor and Serug, geographic names not far from Haran), which was situated far to the east, across the Euphrates, over 150 miles from the Mediterranean coast. Some critical scholars, basing themselves on the wealth of Aramean findings from the period of Aramean kingdoms compared to the complete lack of Aramean findings from earlier periods, rejected the authenticity of the Torah's description of the Aramean origin of the patriarchs. These scholars view the mention of Arameans and the Aramaic name Yegar-sahadutha (Laban's name for the mound of stones that marked his pact with Jacob) in the Torah as a "historical anachronism." However, the reason for the lack of inscriptions from the early period is the nature of the Aramean nation, which, during the early periods, was a nation of tribal shepherds with no walled cities and no kings or the wars that accompany them.

The first extrabiblical sources that mention the Arameans are the inscriptions of King Tiglat Pileser I of Assyria, who reigned during the years 1114–1076 BCE. This was actually toward the end of the period of the Judges, one generation before Saul and two generations before David. The information contained in these inscriptions is interesting, and helps to complete the picture of the Arameans that arises from the Tanakh. In the inscriptions, the Arameans are categorized into groups called "houses," meaning households.[6] In two inscriptions he describes how he attacked and defeated the Arameans, but in a third inscription – written toward the end of his lifetime – he is forced to admit that the Arameans defeated him in battle (an unusual display of frankness for an Assyrian inscription!) and conquered the great city of Nineveh for a certain period of time.

The Location of the Arameans According to Tiglat Pileser I

Now we arrive at the geographical angle of the discussion. Where did the Arameans live during the time of Tiglat Pileser I? The inscriptions mention explicitly that they lived in the Sūḫu region (i.e., the middle Euphrates), the northern part of the Syrian Desert and Mount Bishri. In

6. Compare to the Midianites, another nomadic nation: "He [Zur] was the tribal head of an ancestral house in Midian" (Num. 25:15).

the summarizing inscription of his wars, he describes the areas where he defeated the Arameans: "From the foothills of Mount Lebanon, Tadmor of Amurru, Anat of Sukhu, until Rapiku of Babylonia." The last location is not identified, but it is certainly located in northern Babylonia. Anat is known today as 'Ānah on the Euphrates, about eighty miles north of Hīt. Hīt and its surrounding area, where, according to our conclusion above, the Talmud's Ihi Dekira and the Tanakh's Kir were located, is situated at the midpoint between Anat and Babylon. This is where the tribes of Aram were most heavily concentrated at the end of the period of the Judges, and from there they began to invade westward, establishing aggressive kingdoms during the early stages of the monarchy in Israel.

It seems that it is to this transitional phase – the movement of the Aramean nation's center of gravity, accompanied by its rise to political and military power – that Amos refers when he states, "I brought Israel up from the land of Egypt, but also…the Arameans from Kir."

(Wikimedia Commons)

Hīt, Iraq, in 2004, as seen from a bridge over the Euphrates. The Arameans probably originated here, and were later exiled back here as well

From a prophetic perspective, the return of the Aramean exiles from Damascus to Kir and their subsequent decline into oblivion perhaps signify that they have come full circle in a moral experiment. God may transport nations from one place to another, giving them roles that are appropriate for them at a given time. He may even use them, unbeknownst to them, as the proverbial rod that will punish His chosen people who have gone astray. But the Arameans abused their position, losing their sense of humanity and engaging in excessive hatred and wickedness far beyond their divine dispensation. "Because they threshed Gilead with threshing boards of iron," they were sentenced to return to their meager beginnings and forfeit all their power.

For further study:

Abramski S. and A. Parnas. "*Ḥemar.*" *Encyclopaedia Biblica* 3, 187–190 [Hebrew].

Elitzur, Yoel. "Qīr of the Aramaean: A New Approach." *Shnaton: An Annual For Biblical and Ancient Near Eastern Studies*, 21 (2012): 141–152 [Hebrew].

Grintz, Y. M. *Studies in Early Biblical Ethnology and History*. Tel Aviv, 1969, 58–59 and notes [Hebrew].

Lipiński, E. *The Aramaeans: Their Ancient History, Culture, Religion*. Leuven, 2000, 39–45.

Mattingly G. L. and H. O. Thompson. "Kir." in *The Anchor Bible Dictionary* 4, 83.

Mazar, B. "The Aramaean Empire and its Relations with Israel." In *The Early Biblical Period: Historical Studies*, edited by S. Ahituv & B. A. Levine, Jerusalem, 1986, 151–172.

Millard, A. R. "A Wandering Aramean." *JNES* 39 (1980): 153–155.

Oppenheimer, A. *Babylonia Judaica in the Talmudic Period*. Wiesbaden, 1983, 164–168, 436–442.

Postgate, J. N. "Idu." *Reallexikon der Assyrologie*, 5, 33.

Streck, M. "Hīt." *The Encyclopaedia of Islam: New Edition*, 3, 510.

Parashat Emor

Sunset and *Teruma*: The Haifa Connection

Sunset and the Permission to Eat *Teruma*

> The person who touches such shall be unclean until evening and shall not eat of the sacred donations (*ha-kodashim*) unless he has washed his body in water. As soon as the sun sets, he shall be clean; and afterward he may eat of the sacred donations, for they are his food. (Lev. 22:6–7)

In this passage, the Torah relates to two different types of *kodashim*: one that may be eaten immediately after one washes his body in water; and one that may only be eaten after the sun sets. An even higher level than these two is described in *Parashat Tazria*:

> On the completion of her period of purification, for either son or daughter, she shall bring to the priest, at the entrance of the Tent of Meeting, a lamb in its first year for a burnt offering, and a pigeon or a turtledove for a sin offering…The priest shall make expiation on her behalf, and she shall be clean. (Lev. 12:6–8)

The sages explained that there are three types of *kodashim* in total, each of which demands a process of purification to permit eating it that corresponds to its level of sanctity: "If he immersed himself and came up, he may eat of the [second] tithe; after sunset he may eat *teruma*; and after he has brought his atonement he may eat the *kodashim*" (Yevamot 74b, based on Nega'im 14:3). This explanation, that the second *kodashim* the Torah mentions in the first passage above refers to *teruma*, is indeed the simple meaning of the text. The Torah's addition of the phrase "for they are his food" is an explicit reference to *teruma*, as both the second tithe on one side and the sacrifices of the Temple on the other side may be eaten by Israelites as well – and not only by priests.

The consumption of *teruma* was once an everyday occurrence; the *halakhot* of *teruma* were thus important and highly relevant. The priests were systematically supported by the gifts of *teruma* that they received from the rest of the nation, and they were required to eat the *teruma* in a state of *tahara* (ritual purity). In contrast to the second tithe and the *kodashim*, which could only be eaten in Jerusalem, *teruma* could be eaten anywhere in the Land of Israel. The consumption of *teruma* is not connected to the existence of the Temple, but only to the reality of *tahara*. Hundreds of years after the destruction of the Second Temple, priests in the Land of Israel had preserved ashes from the red heifer and were thus still able to purify themselves and eat *teruma*. In the time of the *Amora'im*, there was a group of people in the Galilee who took great care to keep their wine and oil in the highest state of *tahara*, so that if the Temple were rebuilt in their lifetimes they would be able to produce pure wine and oil for meal offerings and libations (Ḥagiga 25a, Nidda 6b). Finally, *Sefer Hamaasim Livenei Eretz Yisrael*, a halakhic work found in the Cairo Geniza, implies that some residents of the Land of Israel still maintained a state of *tahara* until the end of the Geonic period.

The first mishna in the six orders of the Mishna opens: "From what time may one recite the *Shema* in the evening? From the time that the priests enter [their houses] in order to eat their *teruma*" (Berakhot 1:1). The formulation of the mishna teaches us that during the tannaitic period, eating *teruma* was a basic and practical reality.

When Does the Evening Begin?

In this chapter, I will attempt to present in the simplest way possible a considerably complicated talmudic subject. The main locus for the treatment of this subject in the Talmud Bavli is Shabbat 34b–35b and in the Talmud Yerushalmi at the beginning of Tractate Berakhot.

According to the sages, there is a received tradition that each day following sunset there is a period of time called *bein hashemashot* (literally, "between the suns") when it is uncertain whether it is day or night. This period is followed by certain night. When exactly does *bein hashemashot* occur? The answer to this question is subject to a tannaitic dispute:

- R. Yehuda: "From sunset as long as the face of the east has a reddish glow, and if the lower [horizon] is gray but not the upper, that is *bein hashemashot*. But when the upper horizon is gray and the same as the lower, it is night."[1] The *Amora'im* were divided over the interpretation of this statement. According to Rabba, *bein hashemashot* begins immediately following sunset and ends when the upper horizon becomes gray, whereas according to R. Yosef and the anonymous opinion of the Yerushalmi, *bein hashemashot* begins only when the lower horizon becomes pale. A different version of the dispute between Rabba and R. Yosef is cited in the Bavli as well: According to Rabba, *bein hashemashot* lasts for the time it takes a person to walk three-quarters of a mil (13.5 minutes[2]), and according to R. Yosef it lasts for the time it takes a person to walk two-thirds of a mil (12 minutes).
- R. Neḥemia: For the time it takes a person to walk half a mil from sunset (9 minutes).

1. The Yerushalmi cites this position as an anonymous *baraita*.
2. This calculation is based on the most accepted opinion, according to which one walks one *mil* in eighteen minutes (Maimonides' commentary on Mishna Berakhot 1:1, based on interpretation of Bavli Pesaḥim 94a, adopted by *Shulḥan-Arukh Oraḥ Ḥayim* 459:2; this was also the last opinion of the Vilna Gaon as stated in *Shenot Eliyahu* Berakhot 1:1 and in a note attached to Tractate Sanhedrin in *Shas Vilna* after *Haggahot Yaabetz*, 46a).

- R. Yose: "*Bein hashemashot* is as the twinkling of an eye, one entering and the other departing, and it is impossible to determine it." As R. Tanḥuma in the Yerushalmi formulates it: "It is like a drop of blood placed on the edge of a sword; in the time it takes for the drop to divide to this side and the other – that is *bein hashemashot*." When does *bein hashemashot* occur according to R. Yose? The Yerushalmi cites two opinions: the first is that it occurs following the half-mil time interval advocated by R. Neḥemia; and the second is that every "twinkling of an eye" within R. Neḥemia's half-mil time interval possesses the uncertain status of *bein hashemashot*. The Bavli (Nidda 53a) cites two other opinions: that R. Yose's *bein hashemashot* occurs at a particular point within R. Yehuda's *bein hashemashot*, and that it occurs after R. Yehuda's *bein hashemashot* ends. This last opinion suits the conclusion of the Talmud's discussion in Tractate Shabbat (which, as we stated above, is the main locus for the Talmud's treatment of this subject), so it may be considered the primary opinion. The *Rishonim* proved from the discussion that R. Yose's *bein hashemashot* does not occur immediately following the conclusion of R. Yehuda's *bein hashemashot*, but only after a certain unspecified period of time has passed.

Both Talmuds cite another definition for *bein hashemashot* and the beginning of the night: *tzeit hakokhavim* (literally, "the emergence of the stars"). The term *tzeit hakokhavim* is mentioned in Tanakh (Neh. 4:15) and the Talmud is precise in interpreting it: "When one star [is visible], it is day; when two [appear], it is *bein hashemashot*; three, it is night." This definition is cited in both Talmuds by *Amora'im*,[3] and both Talmuds ignore the question of the relation between the use of *tzeit hakokhavim* to determine nightfall and the opinions of the *Tanna'im* R. Yehuda, R. Neḥemia, and R. Yose. In practice, the emergence of three medium-sized stars occurs about 20–30 minutes after sunset.[4]

3. Later, the Bavli does quote a *baraita* that supports this definition.
4. In *Mishneh Torah Terumot* 7:2 (according to the manuscript version), Maimonides estimates this interval as "about a third of an hour." In Israel today, most calendars

The reasonable solution to this problem is that *tzeit hakokhavim* is equivalent to R. Yose's "twinkling of an eye," which occurs, according to this, about ten minutes (or slightly less) after the conclusion of R. Yehuda's *bein hashemashot*. Another possibility is that *tzeit hakokhavim* is equivalent to R. Yehuda's *bein hashemashot* itself. Both measurements cited as calculations of R. Yehuda's *bein hashemashot* (three-quarters of a mil and two-thirds of a mil) were reached based on the simple understanding of the *baraita* – that one must observe the color of the sky after sunset while facing east. However, according to Rava's interpretation in Shabbat 35a, R. Yehuda's *bein hashemashot* is calculated while facing west, where the darkening of both the upper and lower horizons occurs much later. This can easily be corroborated by anyone who wishes to verify Rava's observation in reality.[5]

I want to dedicate another few words to the position known as "*tzeit hakokhavim* of Rabbeinu Tam." Rabbeinu Tam's position is that night begins after the time it takes a person to walk four mils after sunset (72 minutes). The source for his position is a passage in Tractate Pesaḥim that states that travelers continue walking five mils after sunset until night falls (this is eventually revised to four mils in the conclusion). In order to resolve the contradiction between the positions of three-quarters of a mil found in Shabbat and four mils found in Pesaḥim, Rabbeinu Tam explained that there are actually two "sunsets," the second occurring three and one-quarter hours after the first. Several great *posekim* adopted Rabbeinu Tam's position, but it is difficult to square his approach with the empirical reality. The Vilna *Gaon* rejected Rabbeinu Tam's position, explaining the contradiction between the talmudic passages simply: The "four mils" position derived from Pesaḥim was not referring to halakhic times, but only to the habits of travelers who would try to take advantage of the twilight period in order to continue walking until the last light had truly faded.

---

listing Shabbat times follow the observations of Rabbi Yechiel Michel Tukachinsky, who found that the emergence of three small stars (taking the stringent approach) occurs in practice 35 minutes after sunset.

5. I heard this idea from Rabbi Yoel Bin-Nun.

A Geographical Tradition for Calculating Bein Hashemashot

Alongside the tannaitic dispute over the exact definition and nature of *bein hashemashot*, both Talmuds cite a tradition for calculating the times of *bein hashemashot* that is connected to Mount Carmel, immersion in the sea and eating *teruma*. Both Talmuds attribute the tradition to R. Ḥanina, but they differ regarding the details of the tradition.

The Talmud Bavli states: "R. Ḥanina said: One who wishes to know R. Neḥemia's period should leave the sun on the top of the Carmel, descend, dip in the sea, and ascend, and this is R. Neḥemia's period."

In contrast, the Talmud Yerushalmi states:

> R. Shmuel b. Ḥiyya b. Yehuda said in the name of R. Ḥanina: If the sun's orb has begun to set, one standing atop Mount Carmel descends and dips in the Great Sea, ascends, and eats his *teruma* – it is presumed that he dipped in the day. Under what circumstances is this true? When one travels on the shortcut. But one who travels on the promenade is not included in this.

Historical and Geographical Background

Before we explain this passage – in both its versions – let us present some background information on the personalities involved in the discussion and on the region in question.

R. Ḥanina (son of Ḥama) was a prominent disciple of R. Yehuda the Prince. One of the first *Amora'im*, R. Ḥanina was apparently born in Babylonia and immigrated at a young age to the Land of Israel. Citations of his *halakhot* and customs can be found scattered throughout rabbinic literature. When R. Yehuda the Prince was on his deathbed, he commanded: "Ḥanina son of Ḥama shall preside [at the college]" (Ketubbot 103b). R. Ḥanina lived a long life, notably retaining his vigor even in old age:

> It was said of R. Ḥanina that at the age of eighty years he was able to stand on one foot and put on and take off his shoe. R. Ḥanina said: The warm baths and the oil with which my mother anointed me in my youth have stood me in good stead in my old age. (Ḥullin 24b)

In contrast, R. Shmuel b. Ḥiyya b. Yehuda was an obscure sage, about whom nothing is known. He is mentioned in six contexts in the Talmud Yerushalmi and in three additional contexts in the midrashim of the Land of Israel. In each of these nine instances he cites statements in the name of R. Ḥanina!

Haifa was a Jewish city during the time of the *Tanna'im* and *Amora'im*. Sources from the biblical period do not indicate the existence at the time of settlements in the Haifa region. In sources from the Hellenistic-Roman-Byzantine period, four place-names are mentioned in this area: Shikmona (Sycamina in Greek and Roman sources), Haifa (Hēpha), Castra or Gastra, and Porphyreon.

Etymology

The name Shikmona apparently derives from the word *shikma*, meaning "sycamore" – "as plentiful as sycamores (*kashikmim*) in the Shephelah" (I Kings 10:27). In Greek, *sykaminon*/*sykaminos* means "mulberry." Since this was not one of the central cities in the land, and it is mentioned in its Hebrew version in rabbinic sources, it seems that the Hebrew version is the original one and the name was adapted to the Greek.

The name Haifa seems to be connected to the word *ḥof*, meaning "seacoast," as Rabbi Ishtori Haparḥi speculated almost seven hundred years ago. This speculation was proposed again in the nineteenth century. Among the names of the coastal cities in the Land of Israel, we find another two examples in which a *ḥolam* vowel (as in the "o" sound in *ḥof*) becomes a *tzerei* (as in the "ai" sound in Haifa): The Hebrew *Akko* (Acre) and *Yaffo* (Jaffa) became *ᶜky* and *ypy* in Phoenician inscriptions, and Akē and Ioppē in Greek sources.[6]

Castra means "fortress" in Latin. The site was also known as Castra Samaritanorum, or "fortress of the Samaritans."[7]

6. A shift from *ḥolam* to *tzerei* is found in some Hebrew pronunciation traditions. Manuscripts with Babylonian punctuation attest to this phenomenon, and it can be seen in modern times in the Hebrew pronunciation of many Yemenite and Lithuanian Jews.
7. This was not necessarily a reference to the Samaritan ethnoreligious group, but likely to a Roman military unit that transferred to the site from the Samaria region.

Porphyreon was named for the *porphyra* (in Latin *purpura*, related to the English word "purple"), a genus of sea snails of the variety used to produce the blue and red-purple dyes used in the *Mishkan*. As the Talmud states: "These are those that catch snails from the promontory of Tyre as far as Haifa" (Shabbat 26a). An additional place bearing this name is known to exist between Beirut and Sidon.

(Drawing from the nineteenth century)

The Carmel Ridge, bare of any vegetation. Visible are ancient Haifa, the German Colony, and the Carmelite Monastery.

Identification

Ancient Haifa is situated near the western side of the port of Haifa, east of the Central Bus Station of modern-day Haifa, north of Kiryat Eliyahu and south of the Rambam Hospital. Ancient Haifa was destroyed in the mid-eighteenth century by Daher el-Omar, who then established a new city approximately where today's downtown Haifa lies. Archaeological surveys (excavations have not yet been conducted) in the ancient Haifa region have yielded various antiquities, including a pool designed for salt production and a rock-hewn burial complex from the Roman period. On a PEF map from 1880, the region is labeled "Haifa el ʾAtîkah."

Tel Shikmona is the Hebrew name given to Tel es-Samak ("tell of the fish") near the sea, at the western foot of Mount Carmel, about two miles from ancient Haifa. The two sites are divided by the steep slope of "Carmel by the sea," atop which lies the Stella Maris Monastery and beside it the "Cave of Elijah." Ancient Haifa is found at the northeast foot of the mountain and Tel Shikmona is found at its western foot, on the seacoast. Israeli researchers conducted extensive archaeological excavations at Shikmona during the 1960s and 1970s, and again in 2010. The tell is small (only two acres in area), but it and the surrounding area have yielded many findings. The flat areas adjacent to the tell were inhabited during various periods throughout history. Numerous rock-hewn tombs were found on the slopes of Mount Carmel east of the tell, the earliest of which contained an Egyptian scarab seal of y'ḳbhr, a Hyksos ruler during the Middle Canaanite IIB period – the Patriarchal Age. Tel Shikmona was inhabited from the Late Canaanite period (fifteenth century BCE) until after the Arab conquest (seventh century CE). From the Israelite period, several Hebrew inscriptions were found. One prominent discovery at the tell was a burnt layer that excavators date to the time of Shishaq's conquests in the late tenth century BCE. In this burnt layer, a jug was found with the inscription "of Malkiel."

Haifa and Shikmona are not mentioned together in Hebrew or foreign sources. Shikmona is found frequently in Greek and Roman sources,[8] but is mentioned in a few instances in rabbinic sources as well. *Ḥazal* laud the *rimin*[9] of Shikmonah, which boasted higher quality than other *rimin* and are thus subject to the laws of *demai* (doubtfully tithed produce). *Ḥazal* also noted that the carobs of Shikmona were of lesser quality than other carobs, and are thus exempt from tithing. One of R. Akiva's disciples was named Shimon the Shikmonite. In the itinerary attributed to Antoninus of Piacenza from the late Byzantine period, the author describes his journey along the coastline from Ptolemais (Acre) to "the city of the Jews, Sucamina."

Haifa is mentioned frequently in rabbinic sources. In both Talmuds, R. Abdimi of Haifa is mentioned numerous times, as well as R. Abba of Haifa and R. Dimi of Haifa.[10] Yerushalmi Eiruvin 2:1 recounts a teaching given in Haifa by R. Abdimi of Haifa. There is even a site near ancient Haifa where, according to tradition, R. Abdimi is buried.

8. First, in a Greek cruise guidebook from the fourth century BCE, prior to the conquests of Alexander the Great.
9. The *rimin* are apparently the small apple-like fruit of the Christ's Thorn Jujube – thus named because some believe that Jesus' Crown of Thorns was made from it (however this plant needs hot climate and is not found in the vicinity of Jerusalem).
10. It may be that all these names refer to one person.

We read in *Sifrei* Deuteronomy:

> "For they draw from the riches of the sea" (Deut. 33:19) – this is the sea of Haifa, which is hidden for the righteous [to enjoy] in the future... for there is no boat that is lost in the Great Sea, or bundle of silver or gold or precious stones or gems or crystals or any treasure that the Great Sea does not deposit into the sea of Haifa. (354)

Pesikta DeRav Kahana relates:

> It happened that a certain pious man was walking along the sea wall of the sea of Haifa and thought to himself, and said: "How can it be that the Holy One, Blessed be He will make the eastern gate of the Temple and its two wickets out of one single gemstone?"... Immediately, a miracle occurred and the sea split before him, and he saw the ministering angels chiseling and carving and kneading [a stone]. He said to them: "What is this?" They said to him: "This is the eastern gate of the Temple – it and its two wickets – [made of] one single gemstone. (18:5)

Lastly, we learn that the residents of Haifa could not pronounce Hebrew words properly: "We do not allow to pass before the Ark men from Haifa or men from Beth-shean or men from Tib'on, because they pronounce *he* as *ḥet* and *ayin* as *aleph*" (Y. Berakhot 2:3 and similarly in Megilla 24b).

Only one non-Jewish source mentions the name Haifa: Eusebius' *Onomasticon* (108:30). His identification is surprising: "And the maritime village Sykaminos on the way from Caesarea to Ptolemais [Acre] near the Carmel is called Hēpha.[11]" The prevailing opinion among scholars is that Eusebius was not entirely precise here, and that this was actually two adjacent Jewish settlements on opposite sides of the slope of Mount Carmel that expanded and merged. The Jews generally

11. Jerome, in his edition of the *Onomasticon*, renders this name "Efa."

referred to the entire complex as "Haifa," while the non-Jews preferred the name Sycamina.[12]

The precise location of Castra is not clear from the sources. *Ḥazal* stressed the contrast between the Jewish Haifa and Castra, its hostile non-Jewish neighbor: "'The Lord has summoned against Jacob His enemies all about him' (Lam. 1:17). For example, Hallamish to Naveh, Castra to Haifa, Susitha to Tiberias, Jericho to Noaran, Lydda to Ono" (Lamentations Rabba 1:52 and parallels). The itinerary attributed to Antoninus of Piacenza from the sixth century states that Castra is one mil from Shikmona, and half a mil above it is "the monastery of Elisha the prophet" at the site where Elisha met the woman whose son he revived. The monastery described in the itinerary is estimated to have been situated at the site of the current Carmelite monastery known as "Stella Maris." It is difficult to ascertain the exact intent of the pilgrim, but the distances recorded in the itinerary – in its various versions, and in particular in the example in question – are problematic. The name "Chorvat Castra" was given in modern times to the ruins at Kfar Samir, near the bank of Naḥal Ezov beneath the Haifa neighborhood of Karmeliya and above the cemetery. In the course of excavations performed there in the 1990s, a Christian town of approximately 8.5 acres was discovered from the Roman-Byzantine period. The site yielded many findings, including fourteen winepresses, eleven olive presses, and remnants of two churches, each floored with a colorful mosaic. It seems that this is the Castra found in the sources. The shopping and cultural center built later about half a mile southwest of the ruins was named Castra as a result. On display at the Castra Center is a selection of findings from the adjacent ruin.

Porphyreon does not have a convincing identification. It is likely that this is simply another name for Haifa and/or Shikmona. On the Shikmona seacoast, piles of seashells were found, which were used to produce blue and red-purple dyes, the *tekhelet* and *argaman* of the Torah.

12. Michael Ehrlich, following Clemens Kopp, tends to accept Eusebius' testimony as an original identity between Haifa and Sycamina, suggesting that the town had two names, Jewish and non-Jewish. To my mind this approach is not plausible, since the rabbinic sources mention Shimeon the Sikmonite as well as two species of fruit related to Sikmona. According to Kopp and Ehrlich one must assume that there existed another Shikmona elsewhere in the country.

R. Ḥanina in the Talmud Bavli and Yerushalmi

It is clear that there is a dispute between the two Talmuds over the true nature of R. Ḥanina's opinion. The Bavli stresses that Rabbi Hanina's opinion follows the tannaitic position of R. Neḥemia. The Yerushalmi, in contrast, cites R. Ḥanina before mentioning R. Neḥemia at all. According to the Yerushalmi, the walk toward the sea only begins at sunset, which is certainly impossible according to R. Neḥemia's position. It seems that the two versions of the passage are not describing a hypothetical experiment, but rather are giving practical advice to a priest who wants to make the most out of his schedule within the constraints of *halakha*; he wants to immerse himself at the last possible time, and to eat an evening meal of *teruma* in a state of ritual purity at the earliest possible time. According to Torah law, immersion must take place during the day, while *teruma* may only be eaten at night. Neither of the two activities may take place during *bein hashemashot*.

R. Ḥanina's statement in the Bavli was seemingly directed at a priest living in "Haifa el-'Atikah." This priest lives in the shadow of the slope of Mount Carmel and of Stella Maris situated to his west. The sun disappears from his field of vision about ten minutes before it can be seen setting over the sea west of Mount Carmel (for one whose vision is not obstructed by the mountain). It seems that it should only take about five minutes to reach the sea from the priest's house. Until he removes his clothes and examines his body for items or substances that might invalidate his immersion, two or three minutes have passed. The immersion itself takes all of one minute, and by the time he ascends and dries off it is already sunset. It takes another two or three minutes to dress and comb his beard, and five more to return home. By the time he enters his house, greets his family members, and washes his hands, the nine minutes of a half-mil journey – the time interval of *bein hashemashot* according to R. Neḥemia – have passed and he is permitted to eat his *teruma*.

In contrast to R. Ḥanina in the Bavli, who speaks of the sun vanishing behind the peak of Mount Carmel, R. Ḥanina in the Yerushalmi speaks of a man who is himself standing atop the mountain. He is certainly referring here to the Stella Maris area above the steep slope that descends to the sea. R. Ḥanina is teaching this man that when he sees the orb of the sun beginning to set (a process that takes about three minutes), he should descend to the sea, immerse himself, ascend and eat his *teruma*. However, this is on condition that he takes the "shortcut"; he must walk in a straight path and may not stroll along the promenade at a leisurely pace. I do not know why the priest addressed by the Yerushalmi would have been at the top of the mountain in the late afternoon before the advent of taxis, buses, cable cars, or the Carmelit railway, but the language of the Yerushalmi implies categorically that the subject of the discussion is indeed standing atop the mountain. Perhaps he is equipped with a small backpack containing his dinner. The route that our priest must take is perhaps equivalent to that of the cable car that currently operates at the mountain. The route of the Haifa cable car is 1,165 feet long, and the difference in altitude between its two stations is 427 feet. Its upper station is at the top of the mountain and its lower station is by

Steps hewn in the rock near Elijah's Cave

the sea. In the lower part of the slope, above the lower station, lies the "Cave of Elijah." While this site is not mentioned in rabbinic sources, it seems to preserve an ancient tradition recorded in the dozens of Greek inscriptions and the menora engraving on its walls.

The priest of the Yerushalmi must have been in good physical shape, since the descent from the mountain is exceedingly steep, and some of the descent even consists of smooth diagonal rock. But we should note that at least near the Cave of Elijah and above it there are clearly delineated steps that were hewn from the rock in ancient periods (see the image above).

(Image courtesy of Zvi Roger, Haifa Municipality)

Mount Carmel in 2010

Which halakhic position do R. Ḥanina's instructions in the Yerushalmi follow? I believe that his statement fits with the "three stars" position, which, as we noted above, is mentioned in both the Bavli and the Yerushalmi in the name of *Amora'im*. In the Yerushalmi, not long before we encounter R. Ḥanina's passage, we read: "R. Pinḥas said in the name of R. Abba b. Papa: 'One star is certainly day; two is uncertain; three is certainly night." The steep descent toward the sea apparently takes just over twenty minutes, which, according to observations, is the amount of time that passes from the time the sun begins to set until one medium-sized star appears. At that point, the priest may still immerse in the sea, and by the time he manages to dry off and dress, three stars are already visible and he can eat his *teruma* immediately.

For further study:

Ehrlich, M. "Studies in the History of Medieval Haifa: a Reassessment." *Horizons in Geography* 71 (2008): 22–47 [Hebrew].

Elgavish, J. "Shiqmona." *The New Encyclopedia of Archaeological Excavations in the Holy Land* (1993): 1373–1378.

Elgavish, J. *The Excavations of Shikmona.* Haifa, 1973.

Elgavish, J. *Shikmona on the Seacoast of Mount Carmel.* Tel Aviv, 1994 [Hebrew].

Elitzur, Yoel. "ō-ē Interchanges in Toponyms in Moab and on the Coast." In *Studies in Hebrew and Jewish Languages: Presented to Shlomo Morag,* edited by M. Bar-Asher, 63–71. Jerusalem, 1996 [Hebrew].

Haddad, E. "Roman Byzantine Amphorae from a Terrestrial Site and its Underwater Environs: Horbat Castra and Kfar Samir (Southern Levant) as a Case Study." *Levant* 41 (2009): 79–91 (http://www.maneyonline.com/doi/pdfplus/10.1179/175638009X427602).

Newman, H. *The Ma'asim of the People of the Land of Israel.* Jerusalem, 2011, 52–57 [Hebrew].

Reeg, G. "Haifa," "Qastra," "Shiqmah." *Die Ortsnamen Israels nach der rabbinischen Literatur,* Wiesbaden, (1989): 251–253, 573–574, 612–613 [German].

Tsafrir, Y., L. Di Segni and J. Green. "Carmel Mons," "Castra Samaritanorum," "Hefa," "Porphyreon," "Sycamina." *Tabula Imperii Romani Iudaea-Palestina: Eretz Israel in the Hellenistic, Roman and Byzantine Periods,* Jerusalem (1994): 100–102, 141–142, 204, 237.

Vilnai, Z. "Haifa." *Ariel: Entziklopedia Liyediat Eretz Yisrael,* Tel Aviv (1977), 2290–2365 [Hebrew].

Yankelewitz, S. "HaArkheologiya shel Merchav Cheifa." *Ishim Uma'asim BeḤeifa Vehaseviva,* edited by S. and M. Aharoni, 10–15. Kfar Saba, 1993, [Hebrew].

Yeivin Z. and G. Finkelstein. *Castra, at the Foot of Mount Carmel: The City and its Secrets* Haifa, 1999 [Hebrew].

Zigelman, A. "Castra or Porphyrion?" *Michmanim* 15 (2001): 32–36 [Hebrew].

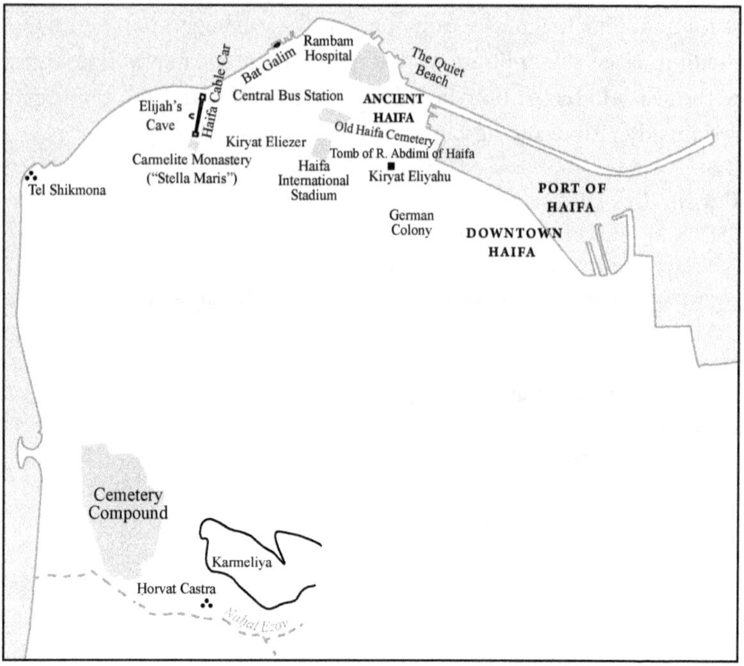
Rambam
Hospital
Bat Galim
Haifa Cable Car
The Quiet
Beach
Central Bus Station
ANCIENT
HAIFA
Elijah's
Cave
Old Haifa Cemetery
Kiryat Eliezer
Tomb of R. Abdimi of Haifa
Carmelite Monastery
("Stella Maris")
Haifa
International
Stadium
Kiryat Eliyahu
Tel Shikmona
PORT OF
HAIFA
German
Colony
DOWNTOWN
HAIFA
Cemetery
Compound
Karmeliya
Horvat Castra

Parashat Behar

Walled Cities

The Walled City: An Exception to the Laws of the Jubilee Year

Parashat Behar deals with the laws of the Land of Israel and the Jubilee year, and it is in this context that the unique phrase "a dwelling house in a walled city" appears. The Torah states:

> If a man sells a dwelling house in a walled city, it may be redeemed until a year has elapsed since its sale; the redemption period shall be a year. If it is not redeemed before a full year has elapsed, the house in the walled city shall pass to the purchaser beyond reclaim throughout the ages; it shall not be released in the Jubilee. (Lev. 25:29–30)

This law essentially constitutes an exception to the laws of the Jubilee year. According to Torah law, every field returns to its original owners during the Jubilee year. In contrast, the Torah states in the above passage that a house in a walled city does not return to its original owners (although the seller has the right to annul the transaction within a year of the sale).

What is the reason for this law? A logical assumption might be that in the reality of urban life, the concept of ancestral territory becomes irrelevant. It would be ludicrous for a person to claim, for instance, that the second floor of a luxury apartment building in Tel

Aviv is part of his ancestral territory. These buildings change over the years; they are destroyed and rebuilt, they change ownership according to the city's needs and its development. In such a reality, the notion of ancestral territory cannot exist. In contrast, "houses in *ḥatzerim* (villages) that have no encircling walls shall be classed as open country; they may be redeemed, and they shall be released through the Jubilee" (Lev. 25:31). This is an exception to the exception: a house in an unwalled town is part of the framework of rural life, and thus it is equivalent to fields for the purposes of *the Jubilee year* – it returns to its original owner.

The Walled City in Three Halakhot

The first *halakha* is the one we discussed above: the explicit Torah law that a house in a walled city is not released through the Jubilee year. The second *halakha* is presented in the Mishna:

> Walled cities are holier [than the rest of the Land of Israel], for *metzora'im* must be sent out of them; and a corpse, though it may be carried about within them as long as it is desired, may not be brought back once it has been taken out. (Kelim 1:7)

There is one other *halakha* that is stated almost explicitly in the Tanakh: the date for celebrating and reading the *Megillat Ester* on Purim. We read:

> That is why unwalled Jews, who live in unwalled cities, observe the fourteenth day of the month of Adar and make it a day of merrymaking and feasting, and as a holiday and an occasion for sending gifts to one another. (Est. 9:19)

The *Megilla* continues, immediately thereafter, "Charging them to observe the fourteenth and fifteenth days of Adar, every year" (9:21). We can infer from these two verses that residents of walled cities observe Purim on the fifteenth day of Adar and not on the fourteenth, as stated in the Talmud: "Since the "unwalled" [are to read] on the fourteenth, the "walled" [must read] on the fifteenth" (Megilla 2b).

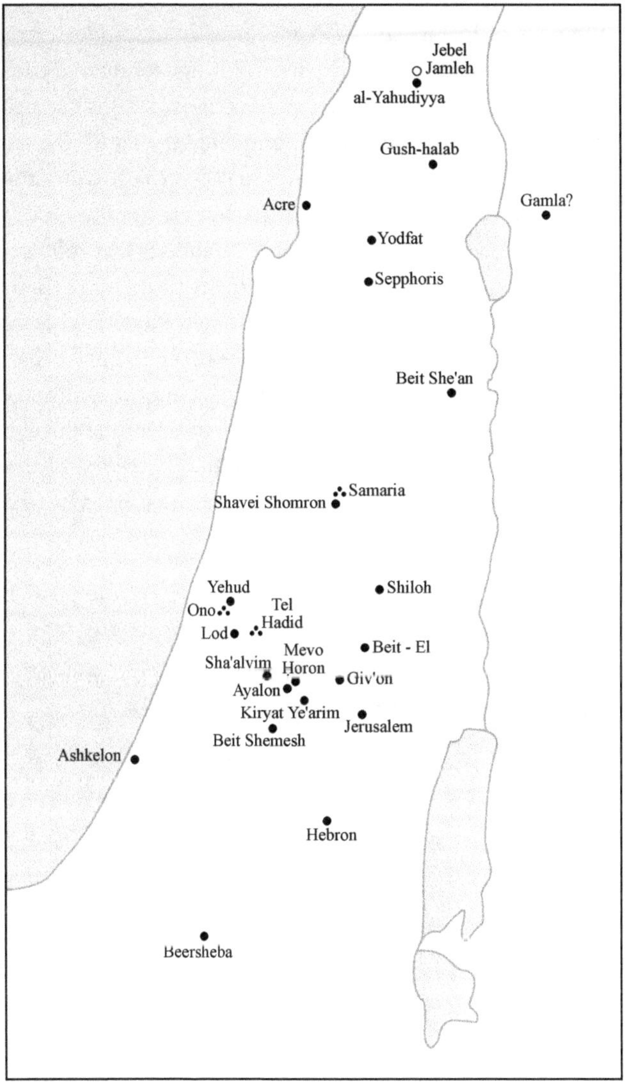

How Many Walled Cities Were There in the Land of Israel at the Time of Joshua's Conquest?

According to the Mishna (Megilla 1:1, Arakhin 9:6), the factor that determines if a city is "walled" or "unwalled" is whether it was walled during "the days of Joshua son of Nun," or as Maimonides expresses it, "surrounded by a wall at the time when Joshua conquered the land" (*Shemitta Veyovel* 12:15). How many walled cities did Joshua and the people of Israel encounter when they conquered the land? The answer is apparently hundreds. The Torah notes that in a single district in the Land of Israel – the district of Argob – there were sixty cities that "were fortified with high walls, gates and bars" (Deut. 3:5). It follows that throughout the rest of the land there were many times more than that.

Furthermore, the distinction that our *parasha* makes between a walled city and "houses in *ḥatzerim* that have no encircling walls" aids us greatly in understanding the chapters in Joshua that discuss the apportionment of the land. The formula used consistently throughout these geographical lists is "[number] *arim* (cities), with their *ḥatzerim*." Based on *Parashat Behar*, this means that all the cities listed by name in Joshua were walled cities.[1]

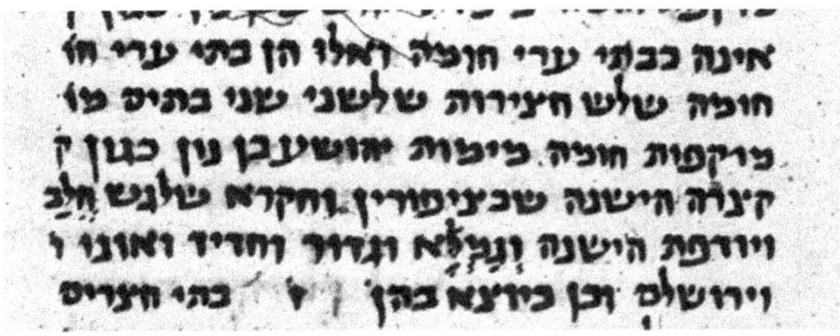
אינה כבתי ערי חומה ואלו הן בתי ערי חו
חומה שלש חצירות שלשני שני בתים מו
מוקפות חומה מימות יהושע בן נון כגון ק
קצרה הישנה שבציפורין וחקרא שלגוש חלב
ויודפת הישנה וגמלא וגדוד וחדיד ואונו ו
וירושלם וכן כיוצא בהן בתי חצרים

(Courtesy of the Bibliotheca Palatina, Parma

Mishna Arakhin 9:6 MS Parma 1

The Talmud Yerushalmi records a dispute among *Amora'im* regarding the nature of the cities listed in Joshua: "R. Shimon b. Lakish said: He counted walled cities. R. Yose b. Ḥanina said: He counted cities near the boundary" (Y. Megilla 1:1 [70a]). In the continuation of the discussion, the Yerushalmi supports the second opinion, and the Talmud Bavli echoes this approach: "R. Yehuda also said in the name of Rav: Joshua enumerated only the cities on the borders" (Bava Batra 56a). But it seems that even the

1. Some exceptions to this rule likely exist, specifically in places where the number of cities enumerated does not match the number recorded in the summarizing statement.

second opinion does not conflict with the simple meaning of the phrase "cities, with their villages." Rather, it merely adds detail to the first opinion, stating that Joshua did not enumerate all the walled cities, but only those that were situated on the borders. See also Nahmanides' commentary at the beginning of Tractate Megilla: "Also, in Hutzal of Benjamin a few of them had a tradition that it was enumerated in Joshua in the portion of Benjamin." Thus Nahmanides indicated his clear belief that every city that Joshua enumerated fell into the category of walled cities.

"And These Are the Walled Cities"

The Mishna at the end of Arakhin presents a list of walled cities in the Land of Israel. Before doing so, the Mishna defines the term "walled city":

> [A house within] a city whose roofs form its wall, or that was not encompassed by a wall in the days of Joshua son of Nun, is not considered a dwelling house in a walled city. [A house in any of] the following is accounted a house in a walled city: [Those in a city] of no less than three courtyards, having two houses each, which have been encompassed by a wall in the days of Joshua son of Nun, such as the old castle of Sepphoris, the fort of Gush-halab, old Yodfat, Gamla, Gedor, Hadid, Ono, Jerusalem, and the like. (9:6)

First of all, the Mishna clarifies that a walled city can actually be quite small. Even a plot of land containing three courtyards, each of which contains two houses, is considered a walled city if it has been encompassed by a wall since the days of Joshua. In other words, the Mishna hints here that many of the cities from the time of Joshua were small cities.[2]

In addition, the list in the continuation of the mishna implies that cities during the biblical period were relatively small. The Mishna stresses: "the old castle of Sepphoris, the fort of Gush-halab." In other

2. Compare as well to Eiruvin 26a, where the *Tanna'im* dispute whether a "medium-sized city" is as large as a *beth kor* (about 4.5 acres) or as large as forty *beth se'ah* (about six acres).

words, the fortified area overlooking each of these two cities constituted the "walled city" from Joshua's time. The implication is that Sepphoris and Gush-halab at the time of the Mishna were large cities, and according to rabbinic tradition, only their old fortresses had been walled since the time of Joshua.

We can also infer from this mishna that in the cases of Sepphoris and Gush-halab, the biblical city was situated atop a summit, while the later city extended over the surrounding slopes. This phenomenon can be found in countless sites in the archaeology of the Land of Israel; usually the Canaanite-Israelite cities were situated atop a summit and were fortified well, while the towns built during the Hellenistic-Roman-Byzantine period were larger and tended to spread out on the slopes and spurs. The reason for this, seemingly, is that in earlier periods, each city was responsible for its own defense and fortification, whereas in later periods these concerns were generally the responsibility of the central government.

The list of eight walled cities from the time of Joshua is interesting, and even at the time of the later *Tanna'im* was the focus of a dispute between R. Yishmael b. R. Yose and his brother, R. Elazar.[3] One argued that this was an exclusive list, while the other argued that it simply listed several examples, while other such walled cities did exist (a position shared by our mishna as well, as one might conclude from the language of the end of the mishna: "and the like").

According to R. Yishmael b. R. Yose, the eight cities listed were the only ones that were re-sanctified by the returning exiles, while all the others "lost their privilege when the land lost its sanctity" (Megilla 10a) following the destruction of the First Temple. According to R. Elazar, the eight cities were merely representative examples:

> And not only in these alone, but in every one in regard to which you shall find a tradition from your ancestors that it was walled from the days of Joshua son of Nun, all these precepts are to be observed.

3. Another opinion cited in the Talmud is that the disputants were two students of R. Yishmael b. R. Yose.

This dispute hinges on a critical, fundamental question in *halakha*: Was the first holiness conferred for the time being and for all future time, or was it not conferred for all future time?

In any case, both positions agree that the list refers to the cities that the returning exiles found when they entered the Land of Israel, and that at least these cities had been walled during Joshua's time and were still walled when they returned from Babylonia – which is why they were listed in the mishna.

Identification of the Cities and Archeological Findings

Almost all the places mentioned in this mishna are identified with certainty. Gamla is the only city whose identification is somewhat debatable. The *Baraita* in *Torat Kohanim, Behar* 4 and in Arakhin 32a states that Gamla is "in the Galilee," while Gamala, one of the main strongholds of the Great Jewish revolt preceding the destruction of the Second Temple which is identified today with certainty, was in the Golan. Many today believe that the western Golan, due to its close connection with the Galilee and its wealth of Jewish settlement, should be considered part of the Galilee. This suggestion is supported by the name of the Jewish rebel Judas son of Hezekiah "the Galilean," who, according to Josephus, was originally from the city of Gamala. While Josephus usually refers to Judas as "the Galilean," on one occasion he calls him "the Golanite." Regardless, Samuel Klein and Gustaf Dalman – classical scholars of rabbinic geography and sources from that period – maintained that it is impossible to call the Golan "Galilee." Moreover, in their opinion Josephus' use of the term "Golanite" is simply the error of an overly clever copyist; he must have known of the Golanite city of Gamala and "corrected" Josephus' text accordingly. Klein and Dalman identified the Galilean city of Gamala with Jebel Jamleh, north of Tibnin in the Lebanese portion of the Upper Galilee, south of the Litani River.[4] At the southern feet of Jebel Jamleh lies a small village called al-Yahudiyye,[5]

4. Dalman and Klein were preceded by the Palestine Exploration Fund's list of place names in which Kh. Jumleh was interpreted "The ruin of Gamala" and Jebel Jumleh "The mountain of Gamala (mentioned in the Talmud as a Galilean Site)."
5. The name occurs in maps until the 1970s. Since then it was substituted, probably because of nationalistic reasons, by al-Sulṭāniyye. Similar exchanges took place in the 1920s in the Shefelah where biblical Jehud (Josh 19:45), preserved as al-Yahudiyye,

(Courtesy of Dr. Zev Rothkoff)

Gamla in the Golan

which preserves a tradition of Jewish presence in the region. One consideration in support of this position and against the identification of Gamla in the Golan is that there was a time – probably during the Second Temple period – when Gamla served as a city of refuge in place of the Galilean city of Kedesh. The city of Golan in the Bashan

was changed by the Arabs to ʿAbasiyye, and in the 1950s in the Golan where the Syrian authorities changed al-Yahudiyye into Yaʿrabiyye.

(Courtesy of Dr. Zev Rothkoff)

Yodfat

served as a city of refuge at the same time, and it is unlikely that there were two functioning cities of refuge in the same region.[6]

It is interesting to note that none of the cities in the Mishna's list (with the exception of Jerusalem) is mentioned in the Book of Joshua. What is the reason for these omissions? It may be that two factors played a role here: (a) in the Galilee, most place-names were changed between the biblical period and the rabbinic period, and thus the newer names could not have appeared in the Tanakh; and (b) the cities belonging to the tribes of Ephraim and Manasseh were not enumerated in the Book of Joshua.

Archaeological examinations have been undertaken in most of the cities on the list. Some of these yielded findings that match the Mishna's account well, while others did not. In Yodfat, Gamla (in the Golan) and Sepphoris, remnants that fit with the simple understanding of the Mishna have not yet been found, but such remnants were indeed found in the other cities. In light of a survey that he conducted in the Upper Galilee, Yoḥanan Aharoni noted that Gush-halab was a fortified city from the Late Bronze or Late Canaanite Age, e.g., the period of Joshua's conquest of the land that we are discussing

6. See the chapter on *Parashat Masei*.

Hadid

here. In al-Ḥadīthe (formerly al-Haditha, a village that was destroyed in 1948, about half a mile east of the modern-day Moshav Hadid near the Jerusalem-Tel Aviv highway), remnants were found indicating the presence of a fortified city from the Late Canaanite period through all the Israelite periods. This matches the tradition cited in the Mishna excellently, despite the fact that the city is not mentioned in the Book of Joshua.

A tradition recorded by R. Yehoshua b. Levi, a resident of the city of Lod and the leader of its sages at the beginning of the amoraic period, should be added to the Mishna's list: "Lod and Ono and Ge Haharashim were walled in the days of Joshua son of Nun" (Megilla 4a).[7]

Lod contains archaeological findings that match the rabbinic tradition as well. Lod's ancient tell is almost unnoticeable within the city's flat topography. Nevertheless, remnants from the Middle and Late Canaanite periods, as well as from all the biblical periods and later,

7. Also see Yerushalmi Megilla 1:1 (70a): "Lod and Ge Haharashim." The Talmud explains that it was not necessary to mention Ono, which is enumerated in Nehemiah 11 alongside Lod and Ge Haharashim, because it is already listed in the Mishna in Arakhin.

were found at the center of the tell. The Mishna does not enumerate Lod, perhaps because it was not walled at the time of the return from Babylon.

Walled Cities in Israel Today

Today, the issue of walled cities in Israel only has practical relevance for the question of when to observe Purim and to read the *Megilla*; is it on the fourteenth day of Adar or on the fifteenth? The laws of the Jubilee year do not apply today, and *tzara'at* of the type described in the Torah does not exist today either. Since observance of the mitzva to read the *Megilla* and celebrate Purim in both walled and unwalled cities is not limited to the Land of Israel – the Talmud invokes the *Megilla*'s expression, "from India to Nubia" – it is accepted that the question of when to observe Purim is determined based exclusively on the historical question of whether a city was walled at the time of Joshua's conquest, unconnected to questions of the holiness of the Land. The walls of the city in the days of Joshua are the only determining factor, even if the city is currently unwalled.[8] As we saw above, there were hundreds of walled sites at the time of Joshua, and since according to the Talmud the adjacent suburbs of each walled city must celebrate Purim together with the city (Megilla 2b), there must be hundreds of places throughout the land today whose residents should observe Purim on the fifteenth.

However, in today's reality, only Jerusalem (including its outlying neighborhoods) has retained its identity as a walled city in this regard, its residents observing Purim on the fifteenth of Adar alone. There are other places where residents observe Purim on both days due to "uncertainty," and in most of these places the main celebrations generally take place on the first day in practice. On the second day – the fifteenth of Adar – they suffice with reading the *Megilla* without reciting a blessing, in order to discharge their obligation.[9] We are fortunate that many famous ancient

8. See Maimonides *Hilkhot Megilla* 1:4, *Tur* and *Shulḥan Arukh, Oraḥ Ḥayim* 688.
9. But in Hebron and Shiloh, and in some congregations in Lod and other ancient places, residents conduct festive Purim meals and take care to fulfill the mitzvot of sending gifts to one another and giving presents to the poor on both days (see below). A

cities in the Land of Israel have experienced a great revival in our generation, and are now settled by members of the nation of Israel in and around their ancient sites. (These include, for instance, Beit Shemesh, Beit She'an, Beersheba, Ashkelon, Acre, and Yehud.) Quite surprisingly, for various reasons, these places observe Purim as unwalled cities – on the fourteenth of Adar alone. To be sure, we can cling to halakhic technicalities such as uncertainty of a city's precise location or the question of "the city was destroyed, or became [possessed by] non-Jews," but ultimately the result cannot be right; it cannot be that the law of walled cities has practically disappeared from the face of the earth. It cannot be that out of the hundreds of walled cities that existed in the land, only Jerusalem has survived – as though the law of walled cities is just another byproduct of the sanctity of Jerusalem.

Years ago, I wrote several articles addressing this question, which piqued the interest of the Torah luminaries at the time. In 1980, I proposed suggestions with respect to the new settlements that had been established during that period of time (Beit El, Shiloh, Mevo Horon, Shavei Shomron, Giv'on, and Kiryat Ye'arim "Telz Stone"), and in 1988 I wrote an extensive article proposing that residents of the city of Lod observe Purim on the fifteenth of Adar, like in Jerusalem. The chief rabbi of Lod, Rabbi Natan Ortner, supported my line of reasoning, albeit with certain reservations regarding the complete elimination of observance on the fourteenth. Rabbi Ortner indeed went on to implement the observance of Purim in Lod on both days. I was personally invited several times to lecture on the topic in Lod before audiences of rabbis and Torah students in several of the city's batei midrash. In Beit Shemesh and in Ramat Beit Shemesh (which is adjacent to Tel Yarmuth – among the central cities in the time of Joshua) there has been a movement in recent years to observe Purim (with all its attendant *halakhot*) on both days, and the same practice has begun to take root in Beersheba and other places

unique testimony concerning Purim in Hebron 275 years ago is found in the journal of Moshe Ḥayim Capsuto's journey in the year 1734. In this year the fifteenth of Adar fell on Shabbat. Kapsuto recounts that in Hebron he experienced a "carnival" of three days: Friday, Shabbat, and Sunday. Since in such a year the reading of the Megilla is made everywhere exclusively on Friday, we can conclude definitively that the Jewish residents of Hebron celebrated Purim on both days in the same manner.

as well. Recently, most of the contemporary halakhic discussions on this topic were collected and recorded in a book by Rabbi Yehuda Zoldan.

In conclusion, despite the fact that observance of Purim on the fifteenth day alone continues to prevail only in Jerusalem, there has nonetheless been a resurgence throughout Israel of awareness of this issue, and of the desire to return the walled cities of Israel to their former glory.

For further study:

Adan-Bayewitz, D. "The Tannaitic List of 'Walled Cities' and the Archaeological-Historical Evidence from Iotapata and Gamla." *Tarbiz* 66 (1996–1997): 449–470 [Hebrew].

Aharoni, Y. *The Settlement of the Israelite Tribes in the Upper Galilee.* Jerusalem, 1957 [Hebrew].

Aharoni, Y. *The Land of the Bible.* Translated and edited by A. F. Rainey. Philadelphia, 1979, 220.

Ben-David, E. *Purim DeMukafin BiBe'er Sheva.* Beersheba, 2011 [Hebrew].

Capsuto, M. H. *Diario di un Viaggio in Terra Santa.* Translated into Hebrew by J. Rofé. Edited by M. Saltzman and D. Cassuto. Jerusalem, 1983, 25–26.

Dalman, G. *Sacred Sites and Ways.* Translated by P. P. Levertoff. London, 1935, 9.

Elitzur, Yoel. "Time of Purim in the New Settlements." *Shana Beshana* (1980): 268–279 [Hebrew].

Elitzur, Yoel. "When Purim Should Be Celebrated in Beit El and the Army Camps Around It." *Tehumin* 1 (1980): 109–136 [Hebrew].

Elitzur, Yoel. *Ancient Place Names in the Holy Land.* Jerusalem-Winona Lake, 2004, 139 and references there.

Klein, S. *The Land of the Galilee* (2nd ed.). Jerusalem, 1967, 27–28 [Hebrew].

Ortner, N. "Purim in the City of Lod," and Elitzur, Yoel. "The Time of Purim in the City of Lod." *Tehumin* 9 (1988): 341–380 [Hebrew].

Palmer, E. H. *The Survey of Western Palestine: Arabic and English Name Lists.* London, 1881, 22, 27.

Rosenson, Y. "*Arim Mukafot Choma – Reshima Akra'it O Text Megamati?*" *Sidra* 17 (2001–2002): 205–215 [Hebrew].

Zoldan, Y. *Megilla Bemukafot Choma.* Ramat Gan, 2013 [Hebrew].

Parashat Beḥukkotai – Yom Yerushalayim

Names of Jerusalem in the Tanakh

Yom Yerushalayim always falls out on the calendar not long after we read *Parashat Beḥukkotai*. This is fitting, as there is nothing like *Parashat Beḥukkotai* to remind us of the miraculous victory of the Six-Day War:

> You shall give chase to your enemies, and they shall fall before you by the sword. Five of you shall give chase to a hundred, and a hundred of you shall give chase to ten thousand; your enemies shall fall before you by the sword. (Lev. 26:7–8)

When we read about "normal" wars throughout history, a very different pattern emerges. We see, for example, how the British and Ottoman armies sat entrenched on either side of the line of the "two Aujas" for several long months during World War I. The two sides would each advance one kilometer only to be driven back two kilometers, shelling each other seemingly without end. Similarly, in the Tanakh, a war in which twenty cities were conquered – certainly an exceedingly protracted affair – was considered a great victory: "He utterly routed them – from Aroer as far as Minnith, twenty cities – all the way to Abel-cheramim. So the Ammonites submitted to the Israelites" (Judges 11:33).

(Courtesy of the Government Press Office of Israel)

"The Temple Mount is in our hands!" Rav Goren on the Temple Mount with a shofar and a Torah scroll, June 7, 1967

But in the Six-Day War, a modern-day conflict, we witnessed wonders that may have been unprecedented in history. It was the stuff of fantasy, but it all happened in real life. The villains, who had all the strength on their side, banded together to destroy Israel, declaring their intent explicitly in blustering, blood-curdling pronouncements. But in the early morning on June 5, 1967, the tables were turned, and within six days Israel had captured vast swaths of land in the north, east, and south. The once-arrogant enemy had fled into the desert sands with such haste that many even left their boots behind them to hasten their retreat. The Israeli army actually saved the lives of many of these fleeing soldiers, who were dying of thirst in the desert. But the crowning moment of this remarkable war of salvation was the recapture of the Old City of Jerusalem and the Temple Mount. All of Israel leaped to their feet, and not a single eye was dry, when the voice rang out: "The Temple Mount is in our hands! I repeat: The Temple Mount is in our hands!"

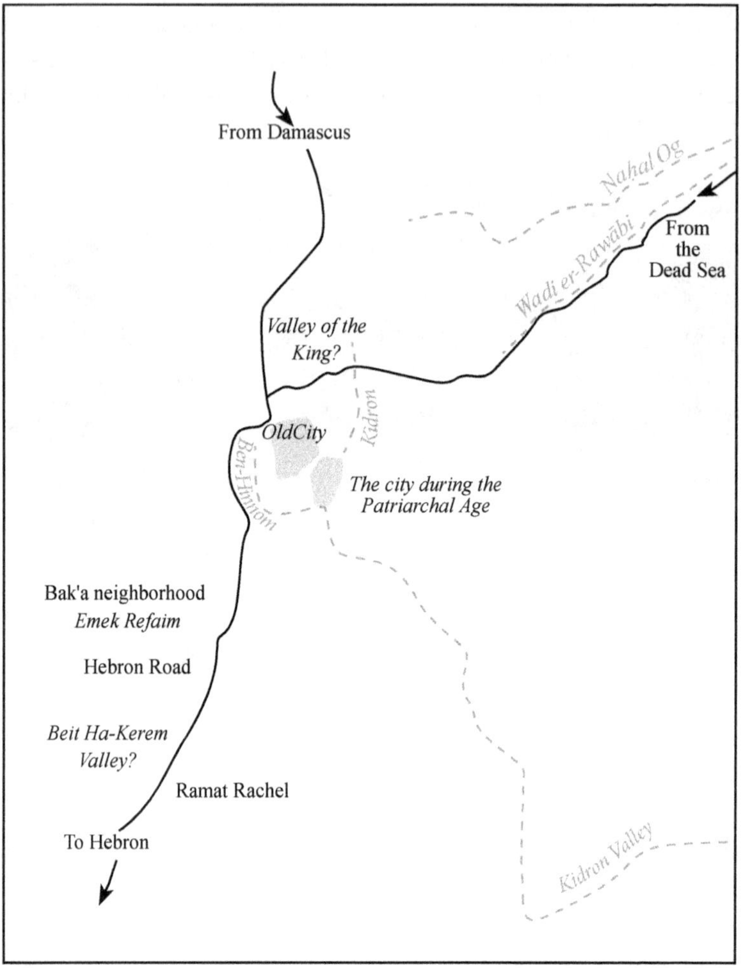

In honor of Yom Yerushalayim, I will deal here with the names of Jerusalem in the Tanakh. I will not use this forum to list all of the many epithets given to Jerusalem in the Tanakh – "perfect in beauty," "joy of all the earth," "city of God," "the faithful city," and others. My purpose in this discussion is to examine and analyze the true names of the eternal city of Jerusalem. As we will see, the city has several names, whose meanings and origins are not particularly clear.

Salem (Shalem)

The first time the city is mentioned in the Tanakh is in Genesis 14:17–18:

> The king of Sodom came out to meet him...in the Valley of Shaveh, which is the Valley of the King. And King Melchizedek of Salem brought out bread and wine; he was a priest of God Most High.

Salem is identified with Jerusalem in the simple understanding of the verse. This is derived primarily from the name of Salem's king – Melchizedek. "King Melchizedek of Salem" is parallel to "King Adoni-zedek of Jerusalem" who features in Joshua 10 (we will discuss the background for this name in greater depth below).

(Courtesy of Dr. Zev Rothkoff)

The Temple Mount and the Old City, seen from Mount of Olives, 2010

An additional piece of information is the Valley of the King mentioned in the previous verse, where Melchizedek brought out bread and wine. Melchizedek suddenly bursts onto the scene during the story of the war between the four kings and the five kings. His appearance is certainly a result of the meeting between Abraham and the king of Sodom, along with their men, on his territory. Melchizedek acts as host, bringing out bread and wine for his guests. For reasons unspecified in the verses, the king of Sodom came out to meet Abraham in "the Valley of Shaveh, which is the Valley of the King." The name "Valley of the King" recurs in the Tanakh in a much later period. The Tanakh states in II Samuel 18:18 that David's son Absalom set up a pillar in the Valley of the King, calling it "Absalom's Monument." It is reasonable to assume that Absalom set up this pillar near Jerusalem, where he aspired to rule. We thus learn that the name "Valley of the King" was an early name that referred to this place even at the time the Torah was written. We do not know the identity of the valley's royal namesake. In the time of Abraham, it was called "the Valley of Shaveh." Why did Abraham and the king of Sodom meet in the vicinity of Jerusalem? It seems that Abraham, who was returning from his victorious war north of Damascus, was traveling toward Elonei Mamre on his way home. Naturally, he traveled along the Hill Road – known as the Way of the Patriarchs – which runs from Nablus to Hebron by way of Jerusalem and Bethlehem. The king of Sodom, who was indebted to Abraham for saving the residents of his city and their possessions, set out from the Dead Sea Valley to meet him at the intersection of road leading from the northern Dead Sea region and the road that traverses the length of the Land of Israel. According to the map of the Palestine Exploration Fund from 1880, the most convenient ancient road from the northern Dead Sea region to Jerusalem ascended along a spur south of Wadi er-Rawabi from the tributaries of Naḥal Og, and reached the vicinity of Augusta Victoria Hospital in the northern part of Mount of Olives. From there, the road turned west, crossing Naḥal Kidron (Wadi al-Joz) at its northern, relatively placid section and eventually reaching the area north of the Old City of Jerusalem. During the Patriarchal Age, this area was an open plain about half a mile north of the city.

We should comment here on the identification of the Valley of the King and the location of Absalom's Monument. In an article that I published not long ago, based on the teachings of my father *z"l* I demonstrated that while the English word "valley" (following the Latin *vallis*) can refer to either wide plains or narrow ravines, the word *emek* in Biblical Hebrew (as in *emek ha-melekh* – "the Valley of the King") never refers to a wadi or a gorge. In fact, the word *emek*, meaning "plain," sometimes refers even to an elevated plateau in a mountainous region. Abraham's journey certainly took place on the main north-south road, and the Valley of the King was a plain located near Jerusalem. The plain that borders Jerusalem on the southwest is called "Emek Refaim" (according to Joshua 15:8, 18:16). Thus, perhaps we may speculate that the Valley of the King was the plain to the north of Jerusalem, through which Highway 1 currently passes. This is also a more appropriate location for a meeting between someone traveling from the north and someone traveling from the Dead Sea Valley.

Absalom's Monument was not located where the folk tradition places it. The folk tradition is based on a misunderstanding of the word *emek*, and perhaps also on the notion that there must be some connection between "the Valley of the King" and "the Garden of the King." The magnificent "nefesh" (monument placed near a grave) associated with Absalom in the Kidron Valley is actually from the late Second Temple period, with parallel structures from that same period in Petra and Herodium. Josephus (*Antiquities* 7:243) recorded that Absalom's Monument in his time was located at a distance of two stadia (1,150–1,300 feet) from Jerusalem, but he did not write to which side of Jerusalem he was referring. A different tradition from the late Second Temple period, reflected in the Qumran scrolls, connected Absalom's Monument to the Beit Ha-Kerem Valley, apparently located in the Bak'a neighborhood of Jerusalem and the Hebron Road, at the foot of Ramat Rachel (Genesis Apocryphon XXII, 14 and the Copper Scroll X 5, 12). According to what we presented above, it is reasonable to speculate that the original Absalom's Monument was located in the plains to the north of the Old City of Jerusalem.

The tradition of identifying Salem with Jerusalem is very ancient and is found even in the Book of Psalms: "Salem became His abode; Zion, His den" (76:3). Psalm 110 makes a literary-homiletical connection between Genesis 14 and David: "The Lord has sworn and will not repent, 'You are a priest forever, a rightful king (*malki-tzedek*) by My decree'" (110:4). David, a righteous king ruling in Jerusalem, is given epithets that allude to an ancient king – Melchizedek, who was a "priest of God Most High."[1] This literary connection is undoubtedly based on the firm knowledge that the Salem that appears in Genesis is the same city as David's Jerusalem.

The existence of the royal city in Jerusalem during the time of Abraham is corroborated by a famous extrabiblical source: the execration texts from the nineteenth–eighteenth centuries BCE, probably Abraham's period. The execration texts are names of enemy cities and rulers written alongside curses on pottery sherds or figurines. The sherds or figurines were then smashed and buried in Egyptian temples as a magical means of subduing those enemies. Among the cities listed on these execration texts was "ȝwšȝmm," which, according to the Egyptian transliteration rules of that period, can be read *rushalimum*. This is essentially Jerusalem, with a letter *mem* added to the end, a typical feature in Semitic languages.[2] The archaeological findings at the City of David demonstrate as well that there was a heavily fortified city there even during that period, the Middle Bronze Age IIA.

Is it possible to speculate on the origin of the name Shalem? First, as a general rule one should always remember Nahmanides' cautionary words: "There is no need to seek out the reason for names of places" (commentary on Genesis 23:9). The geographical names in the Land of Israel are so ancient; the languages spoken there at the time these places were named are not well known to us and the cultural lives and agricultural-economic reality at the time are very foreign to us. Because of all of these factors, other than instances where the meaning of a name is exceedingly clear, we are relegated to baseless speculation in these matters. Several scholars attempted to connect the name Shalem to the Assyrian deity Šulmānu (mentioned in the form *šlmn* in a Phoenician dedicatory inscription from the Tyre area), which may be equivalent to *shalem*, a theophoric component of *Ṣṭqšlm*,[3] a man's name in Ugaritic texts. According to them, this was originally the location of a

1. Similarly, in Psalms 34:1 King Achish of Gath is given the literary name "Abimelech," alluding to the Philistine king during the time of Abraham of the same name.
2. In the Tanakh, compare to "Leshem" (Josh. 19:47), which is equivalent to "Laish" (Judges 18).
3. This is the equivalent of **Ṣdqšlm*; the letter *dalet* became a *tet* to match the two emphatic consonants surrounding it.

city built around a temple dedicated to that forgotten deity, before King Melchizedek adopted the belief in the God Most High.

The prevailing scholarly view is that Shalem is simply a literary abbreviation of Yerushalem. In another direction, one scholar proposed emending the verse to read "Melchizedek, king of his peace (*melekh shelomo*)," meaning that Melchizedek was allied with the king of Sodom.[4] On a homiletical level, one can easily wax poetic on the virtues of peace (*shalom*) and wholeness (*shelemut*) that Jerusalem symbolizes. However, I believe that even the simple understanding of the name – if it is decipherable at all – is not far from this. From a grammatical perspective, the word *shalem* – like the words *kaved, zaken, ḥametz,* and even *amen* – is derived from a nominal pattern that reflects an ongoing state.[5] In these forms, as a result of their ongoing nature, the Hebrew past tense form and present tense form appear the same. A description of an ongoing state is fitting for a place-name, and thus a considerable number of biblical place-names are derived from this nominal pattern. Examples of this include *Avel, Gader, Yavesh,* and *Aner*. Other names take the feminine ending *-a,* such as *Gedera, Azeka,* and *Kehelata*. The root Š-L-M is ubiquitous in Hebrew and in other Semitic languages, and thus we can cautiously speculate that the original name of the city expressed that this was a place of peace and tranquility. Compare to place-names like Naamah (from the root N-ᶜ-M, meaning "pleasure"), Janoah, and Manahath (both from the root N-W-Ḥ, meaning "rest"), which seem to express similar ideas.

Yerushalem

Yerushalem has been the city's most distinctive name throughout history until today. The form "Yerushalayim," with its quasi-dual ending *-ayim,* is certainly secondary to Yerushalem. In the Tanakh, there is in this name a consistent *ketiv ukerei* (discrepancy between the traditional pronunciation and the Masoretic text). In 660 instances, the *ketiv* (Masoretic

4. In my view, a phrase like *melekh shelomo,* meaning "a king allied to him" or the like seems awkward in the Hebrew language.
5. This form is related to the Arabic derived stem *fa'ila* and the Aramaic stem *pe'il*; it is parallel to the Akkadian stative form *qatil*.

text) reads Yerushalem, but the *kerei* (traditional pronunciation) is Yerushalayim. There are only five instances[6] where both the *ketiv* and the *kerei* are in the form "Yerushalayim." The shorter form "Yerushalem" appears frequently in the later books of the Tanakh as well (147 times in Chronicles, 9 times in Daniel and 85 times in Ezra and Nehemiah), and even in the verified manuscripts of rabbinic sources. Furthermore, the English "Jerusalem" (apparently based on the Septuagint's "Hierusalēm") and the Aramaic Yerushlem match the *ketiv* form, not to mention the obvious connection with the early name Shalem.

What is the linguistic background for the dual form "Yerushalayim"? Doug Tushingham, who conducted excavations in Jerusalem with Kathleen Kenyon, believed that the background is historical-geographic. Tushingham and Kenyon held the "minimalist" view on the question of the size of biblical Jerusalem, maintaining that it was originally fully contained within the small confines of the City of David, and it was only during the Second Temple period that it expanded into the upper city (the Jewish and Armenian quarters and Mount Zion). Based on this approach, Tushingham suggested that the linguistic transition to the dual form "Yerushalayim" reflects the city's doubling in size, becoming two cities on either side of the Tyropoeon Valley following the biblical period. Aside from the historical problems that this theory creates, which are beyond the scope of this discussion, we must point out that Yerushalayim is not the dual form of Yerushalem but of **yerushal*. According to Aaron Demsky, the reason for "Yerushalayim" is phonetic: The proximity between the *lamed* and the *mem* at the end of the name necessitated the addition of a *yod*. Personally, I have a hard time accepting this linguistic claim, and I do not believe that the examples that Demsky cites to support his claim do so effectively.

In my opinion, the preferable explanation is that of Bauer and Leander in their work on Hebrew grammar. In their view, two linguistic phenomena have coincided here, thereby creating this suffix. On the one hand, there is a common phenomenon among geographic names involving the addition of a seemingly dual ending to the name. This ending is not an integral part of the name, like other additions, and it

6. Jer. 26:18; Est. 2:6; I Chr. 3:5; II Chr. 25:1, 32:9.

can be removed or added on easily. Thus, the demonym of Mitzrayim is *Mitzri* and the demonym of Efrayim is *Efrati*. The Book of Samuel opens: "There was a man from Ramathaim (*Haramatayim*)" and continues: "And they went back home to Ramah (*Haramata*)" (1:19). This practice continues in later periods as well, as in the name of Dalton in the Galilee, alternately written as Deltayim and Dalata, the latter preserved in the Arabic name "Dalata." On the other hand, there was a phonetic tendency in various Hebrew dialects to contract the diphthong *ay* into the vowel *ē*.[7] It seems therefore that this is an example of overcorrection. Hebrew speakers, who were used to the ending *-ayim* affixed to place-names but at the same time were also used to the contraction of *ay* to *ē*, intuitively "corrected" Yerushalem to Yerushalayim.

The name "Yerushalem" appears in very early sources. As we noted above, it is mentioned in the earliest source we know of that contains names of cities in the Land of Israel – the execration texts – in which the name occurs three times in the form 3wš3mm (*rushalimum*, with its added *mem* at the end). The Akkadian sources first mention this name in the Amarna Letters (early fourteenth century BCE), in the form *urusalim*, and in Assyrian sources in the form *ursalimmu*. The name appears in a version similar to the Akkadian one in Nabatean, Syriac, and Mandaic (three Aramean dialects) until it evolved to *Ûrshalîm al-Quds* in modern Arabic. However, it must be stressed that this last name is only used in Israeli publications written in Arabic. In actual Arab sources this is considered an artificial name, appearing only on rare occasions alongside the name *Bayt al-Maqdis*, the official name of Jerusalem.[8]

In Sumerian, which had a major influence on Akkadian, the word URU means "city." It is tempting to think, as did some scholars, in light of the persistence of the version *ur(u)salim* throughout history

7. In the Masoretic text, compare for example *ḥek* ("bosom") rather than the expected **ḥayik*, *ḥoma vaḥel* ("wall and rampart") rather than **ḥayil* and *amudei shesh* ("marble pillars") rather than *shayish*.

8. Yāqūt al-Ḥamāwi, the great thirteenth-century Muslim geographer, cites this name in three possible versions – *'ūrīšalim*, *'ūrīšalam* and *'ūrīšalm* – stating: "This is the name of *Bayt al-Maqdis* in Hebrew." Later, he adds a version in which the name is pronounced with a *sin* and not a *šin*, while others have the versions: *'ūrīšalūm*, *'ūrīšallam*, *'ūrāsalam*, or *'ūrā salim*. The multitude of versions attests to the non-currency of the name.

and through various languages, that this is the original form of the city's name, and that its original meaning was "the City of Shalem." However, we must reject this suggestion for three reasons: First, it would be unexpected for a place-name in the Land of Israel to be in Sumerian. Second, the notion that *uru*, a word with actual meaning, would transform into the meaningless *yeru* is illogical. The opposite would make much more sense – Akkadian speakers might very well have taken *yeru*, a foreign component, and adapted it to a form that was more recognizable for them – especially considering that there is no "y" sound in Akkadian. Third, the form of the name that appears in the execration texts is similar to the Hebrew version.[9] It seems, then, that *Yerushalem* is the original form. The component *yeru* can be found in the geographical name "Yeruel" (II Chr. 20:16) and in the person's name "Yerubaal,"[10] and the same root can be found as well in the geographical names "Giv'at Ha-moreh," "Elon Moreh" and "Eretz Ha-moriya." Most likely, this root expressed a certain topographical, scenic, or agricultural essence that existed in the Jerusalem area, which is why that broader region was known as "Eretz Ha-moriya." The component *yeru* as its own entity is hinted at in the verse: "And Abraham named that site Hashem-yireh ('the Lord will see'), whence the present saying, 'On the mount of the Lord there is vision (*yera'eh*)'" (Gen. 22:14). In the chapter on *Parashat Vayetzeh*, we learned that in such situations we must search for a name (a place-name or a person's name) that sounds similar to the keyword of the verse, and assume that the purpose of the verse is to connect the incident in question to the place or person's name using the homiletical approach to name interpretation. The difficulty inherent in the content and syntax of this verse, along with the doubling of the keyword *yir'eh-yera'eh* fits very well with the Torah's typical methodology for name interpretation.

9. For examples in which the *yod* at the beginning of a word is dropped, see *Yeḥizkiyahu/Ḥizkiyahu* and *Yivle'am/Bil'am*.
10. The explanation given for the name in Judges 6:32 – "Let Baal contend with him (*yarev bo habaal*)" is a homiletical interpretation; see the chapter on *Parashat Vayetzeh*.

Dr. Mordechai Mishor of the Hebrew Language Academy presented to me a solution to the discrepancy between the different versions: It is likely that the first component in the name was originally *wuru*, and each language adapted this component to its own pronunciation system. Hebrew and Aramaic, in a manner typical of northwestern Semitic languages, changed the initial "w" to a *yod* and reduced the vowel that followed to a shva due to its distance from the word's emphasis. Akkadian eliminated the weak consonant "w" entirely, beginning the word with the vowel following it.

It seems that in the beginning, the two versions "Shalem" and "Yerushalem" coexisted (as we see, for instance, in the coexistence of Beth-meon/Baal-meon/Beth-baal-meon and Kiriath-jearim/Baalah which is Kiriath-jearim/Kiriath-baal/the region of Jaar). Since the time of Joshua, however, the exclusive use of the name "Yerushalem" became established.

Jebus (Yevus)

Yevus, Ha-Yevusi, or Ir Ha-Yevusi was the primary name of the city during the period between the apportionment of the land until David's conquest of the city, named for the nationality of its residents. There were certainly Jebusites living in Jerusalem even before this time, and some may even have remained thereafter, but what is unique about the generations between the apportionment and David's time is that Jerusalem (the city, and apparently the large region south of the city as well) was at the time a large Jebusite enclave in the heart of the land. During this period, all the surrounding area, from the mountainous region north of Samaria to the region south of Mount Hebron, was already in Israelite hands. In the chapters in Joshua describing the tribal territories and in the parallel chapter in Judges 1, Jerusalem is mentioned five times, each time using the epithet "Ha-Yevusi." Of particular note is the list of Benjaminite cities at the end of Joshua 18. The chapter lists twenty-six cities in the territory of Benjamin, and "Jebus (Ha-Yevusi) – that is, Jerusalem" is twenty-fourth on the list. This placement on the list is certainly a result of the fact that Jerusalem was not a territory that was settled in practice.[11]

---

11. In Joshua 13:6, Joshua was commanded to apportion even places that had not yet been conquered. In Joshua 23:4, Joshua declared that he had fulfilled this command.

As a side comment, I will mention the following: Most critical scholars are convinced that the apportionment chapters of Joshua were written during the monarchy period, only disagreeing about which part of the period it was. Yeḥezkel Kaufmann rejected this approach, demonstrating that the lists clearly reflect that they were compiled during the tribal period that followed the apportionment. Among his other claims, Kaufmann correctly argued against scholars who dated the lists to the time of Josiah(!):

> Is it really possible that, in an official district list of the seventh century, Jerusalem – the capital of a great king, the glorious city of God – would have been mentioned in the terms used here? In the city line, as in the boundary list, Jerusalem is still *Jebus*! This name is followed by the explanation: "that is Jerusalem" (Josh. 18:28). It is listed at the end of Benjamin's second district – a remote place, one of the twenty-six cities of Benjamin. To the list of Judah's cities is attached the note, that Jerusalem was still occupied by the Jebusite (15:63).

As we have seen, this claim holds true against those who would date the lists to the time of David and later as well.

Zion (Tziyyon)

This name, more than any of Jerusalem's other names, is brimming with yearning and longing, expressing the essence of the connection between the nation and its land, between the nation and its city, from the prophets of Israel to Rabbi Yehuda HaLevi and later Hebrew poets, to Ḥovevei Zion and the Zionist movement. What is the background of this name?

Pay attention here to the historical and statistical aspects of the name's appearance in the Tanakh. The name Zion is mentioned 154 times in the Tanakh, first in II Samuel 5, in the story of the conquest of Jerusalem in the time of David. Aside from this context and one other time – the story of Solomon transporting the Ark to the newly built Temple (I Kings 8:1) – the name does not appear again in a concrete, prosaic context. It is unsurprising, then, that the name does not appear in Ezra-Nehemiah, a historical, prosaic work. It is used frequently as a literary device by the poetic authors of Psalms and the Later Prophets, but not by all of them. In contrast to the books of Isaiah, Jeremiah, and Lamentations, which mention the name frequently, it is entirely absent from all the prophecies of Ezekiel. In the books of the Twelve Prophets, the use of the name Zion varies by book: Joel, Amos, Obadiah, Micah, Zephaniah, and Zechariah mention the name; Hosea, Jonah, Nahum, Habbakuk, Haggai, and Malachi do not.

This information teaches us that the name "Zion" used by the poets and the prophets is essentially the literary adoption of a name that was only used in a narrow context during a short period, after which point it ceased to be used practically. It should come as no surprise that not every writer in the history of the people of Israel used this name, as such is the nature of literary expressions. There are additional examples of similar literary revivals of once-defunct names. We have already cited above the use of the epithet *malki-tzedek* for David and *avi-melekh* for Achish. In the chapter on *Parashat Lekh Lekha,* we noted, following Y. M. Grintz, that the name "Beth-aven" originally served as a concrete geographical name for a short time during the biblical period. Once the site was destroyed and forgotten, Hosea and Amos (and only these two prophets) used the name as a derogatory epithet for the neighboring city of Bethel.

The conclusion is that if we wish to understand the etymological background of the name "Zion," we must focus on the small number of instances in which the name bears actual geographical meaning, rather than literary meaning. Unfortunately, all we possess is the story of the conquest of Jerusalem (II Sam. 5:4–10 and the repetition in I Chr. 11:4–9) and one word in the story of the transportation of the Ark (I Kings 8:1, and again in II Chr. 5:2).

II Samuel reads, "But David captured the stronghold of Zion; that is, the City of David… David occupied the stronghold and renamed it the City of David."

I Kings reads, "To bring up the Ark of the Covenant of the Lord from the City of David, that is, Zion."

The "City of David" is the southeast hill of ancient Jerusalem, above the Gihon Spring, located today outside the city walls. A full examination of the identification of the City of David and the size of ancient Jerusalem is beyond the scope of this discussion. It must be stressed, however, that scholars erred when they interpreted the phrase "the City of David" to mean "the city belonging to David" – in other words, that the territorial extent of Jerusalem was limited to the City of David during David's time or when this passage was written. A more reasonable interpretation of the intent of the verse is that the stronghold itself was named "the City of David."[12] This stronghold was previously named – apparently by the Jebusites – "the stronghold of Zion," and after conquering it David changed its name to "the City of David."

Before we attempt to uncover the meaning of the name Zion, let us once again remind ourselves of Nahmanides' forthright assertion that in most cases it is difficult and unnecessary to track down the origins of geographical names.

What is the meaning of Zion and what is the connection between this meaning and the stronghold in Jerusalem? What do the scholars have to say about the name "Zion"? First of all, there is no consensus regarding the name's etymology. Most believe that Tziyyon is derived from the root Ṣ-Y-Y, with the addition of the ending *-on* (a common ending in the nominal patterns of names, and geographical names in particular). However, some believe that the root is Ṣ-Y-N, and the name shares a nominal pattern with words like *gibbor* and *kinnor*. The problem here is the imbalance between the etymology and the morphology. Supporters of the root Ṣ-Y-N note the Arabic root Ṣ-W-N, meaning "protection" or "defense," as well as the Arabic word *Ṣawwān*, meaning "flint." This root is the perfect match for a fortified stronghold in a rocky area. However, the downside of this position is that the nominal pattern *qittōl* is rarely found in geographical names (the only examples are *Millo, Rimmon, Meronoth* and, with a minor adjustment, *Ḥuqqōq*), while the ending *-on* is very common.[13] On the other hand, if we follow the more common nominal pattern, the name's root would be Ṣ-Y-Y, a

12. In the parallel passage in Chronicles, the phrase "the rest of the city" is mentioned explicitly.

13. Wilhelm Borée, who researched biblical place-names and sources of that period enumerated eighty-four names with this suffix.

root that produced the word *tziyya,* meaning "wilderness" or "desolation," a very poor descriptor for Jerusalem with its bountiful spring. In 1930, one particularly sharp biblical scholar, Albert Shanda, made a suggestion that miraculously seems to match modern-day Jerusalem perfectly. According to his theory, place-names with the ending *-on* are often built on the basis of animal names. One clear-cut example of this is the name "Eglon," which is related to the word *egel,* or "calf." Based on various etymological explanations, Shanda succeeded in applying his theory to the interpretation of the names "Hebron" and "Heshbon" as well. Shanda went on to connect the name "Tziyyon" with the word *tziyyim,* as in "but desert creatures (*tziyyim*) will lie there" (Is. 13:21) and "desert creatures (*tziyyim*) will meet with hyenas (*iyyim*)" (34:14). The word *tziyyim* here refers to animals that inhabit ruins, perhaps a kind of cat.[14] According to Shanda, then, Zion is "the city of cats..."

It seems to me that there is another way to integrate the more likely nominal pattern for geographical names on the one hand, and the more common dictionary definition of the root Ṣ-Y-Y, without resorting to farfetched theories. The answer is connected to two topics that we encountered in the chapter on *Parashat Shemini*: the meaning of two-word place-names and the territorial approach of the Tanakh. The territorial region that borders the City of David from the south and the east is a desert area (see Mishna Yoma 6:8), and it may be that it was called *Tziyyon,* meaning "land of wilderness and desolation."[15] It is likely that "the stronghold of Zion" meant "the stronghold of the Zion area," although the stronghold itself was not located within the desert. The biblical expressions "the mountain of the house [*kerei*: daughter] of Zion" (Is. 10:32) and the standalone phrase "the daughter of Zion" fit this approach.[16]

14. *Targum Yonatan* translates *iyyim* as *ḥatulin* – "cats."

15. Compare to *yeshimon,* which is a general term for a desolate wilderness, as well as a proper noun that the Tanakh and rabbinic sources use to refer to specific regions in the Land of Israel.

16. Some have written that "the daughter of Zion" refers to the residents of Jerusalem, but the phrases "the mountain of the daughter of Zion" and "the wall of the daughter of Zion" (Lam. 2:18) indicate that the phrase refers to the city itself.

The semantic connection between the name "Tziyyon" and the word *tziyya* can also help us to understand the Syriac and, later, the Arabic version of the name: *Ṣahyūn* (*Ṣahē* means "thirsty" in Aramaic).

I would like to comment on the erroneous name "Mount Zion" given today to the southern part of the western hill of Jerusalem (located today outside the city walls). This name apparently originated in a Christian approach from the early Byzantine period. In the Tanakh, "Mount Zion" refers to Jerusalem or to the Temple Mount.

Zedek (Tzedek)

I believe that Jerusalem had another early name: "Zedek." The names "King Melchizedek of Salem" and "King Adoni-zedek of Jerusalem" are similar in form to "Adoni-bezek": "They found Adoni-bezek in Bezek" (Judges 1:5). Using this verse as a model, the natural meaning of the first two names is that Adoni-zedek and Melchizedek were kings of a place called Zedek. Thus the meaning of the verse, "The king of Babylon made Mattania, Yehoyachin's uncle, king in his place, and changed his name to Zedekiah" (II Kings 24:17), becomes clear: Once Mattaniah was made king of Jerusalem, his name was changed to match the name of the city itself.

The literary expressions "righteousness (*tzedek*) once dwelt in her" and "afterward you will be called 'the City of Righteousness (*Ir HaTzedek*)'" (Is. 1) take on a new dimension of depth once we understand that these expressions fundamentally constitute a prophetic name interpretation. The prophet declares: You, Jerusalem – your name "Zedek" was very fitting for you, but now you are the city of oppression. When you repent and mend your ways, only then will you rightfully be called *Ir HaTzedek*, "the City of Righteousness." We find similar examples of this idea in Jeremiah, in his admonition: "Woe to him who builds his house without righteousness (*belo tzedek*)" (Jer. 22:13); in his prophecy of comfort: "I will raise up for David a righteous branch (*tzemaḥ tzaddik*)… [who] will do what is just and right (*mishpat utzedaka*) in the land…This is the name by which he will be called: The Lord Our Righteousness (*tzidkeinu*)" (23:5–6); and later: "May the Lord bless you, O abode of righteousness (*neveh tzedek*), O holy mountain" (31:22). Each of these verses hints at the name of the city that was known to the prophet, to his audience, and even to the foreign king Nebuchadnezzar.

In the documents found in URUyaḥudu, the city of the Jewish exiles in Babylon (see our discussion in *Parashat Kedoshim*), a man named Yashuv-zedek was mentioned. It seems that his parents gave him this name to express their desire to return to Jerusalem.

Kodesh?

The expression "the holy city (*ir hakodesh*)" appears twice in the Book of Isaiah as a flowery literary epithet: "For they call themselves after the holy city, and lean on the God of Israel" (48:2); "Put on your beautiful garments, O Jerusalem, the holy city" (52:1). In Nehemiah, the name is already used in a prose context: "To live in Jerusalem, the holy city" (11:1); "All the Levites in the holy city" (11:18).

In Arabic, there is a short, one-word name for Jerusalem: *al-Quds*. This name, which is used on its own today, is not the term that medieval Arab writers used to refer to Jerusalem. The earliest of these Arabic authors called Jerusalem *Iliya*, reflecting the Roman-Byzantine name *Aelia Capitolina* (despite the fact that they themselves were not aware of the origin of the name and sought to find a different etymology for it). Generally, the name of the city in medieval Arabic sources is *Bayt al-Maqdis*, while in a few instances the two names were integrated: *Iliya hia Madinat Bayt al-Maqdis*, meaning "Iliya, which is the city of the Temple." Starting from the tenth century CE, the name *al-Quds* began to be used sporadically, and as stated above, it has since become the prevailing Arabic name for Jerusalem in the modern era. Does this name have an origin that predates Islam?

My good friend Ḥanoch Alon opened my eyes here to a connection in the Tanakh. We read in Psalms: "May He send you help from the sanctuary (*mikodesh*) and support you from Zion (*mitziyyon*)" (20:3). It is well known that parallel couplets provide the most authentic commentary on the poetic chapters of the Tanakh. In this case, the parallelism in the verse seemingly teaches us that *kodesh* was synonymous with *tziyyon*. Perhaps Kodesh was an ancient name for Jerusalem that lay dormant for many generations, until finally surfacing and reappearing in the form of the Arabic *al-Quds*.

(Courtesy of Dr. Zev Rothkoff)

The Temple Mount and "Mount Zion" – Yom Yerushalayim, 2014

For further study:

Albright, W. F. "Abram the Hebrew: A New Archaeological Interpretation." *BASOR* 163 (1961): 52.

Bauer H. and P. Leander, *Historische Grammatik der Hebräischen Sprache des Alten Testamentes.* Hildesheim, 1965, 518–519 [German].

Borée, W. *Die Alte Ortsnamen Palästinas.* Hildesheim, 1968, 57–61 [German].

Demsky, A. "Hebrew Names in the Dual Form and the Toponym Yerushalaim." In *These are the Names* 3, edited by A. Demsky, 11–20. Ramat Gan, 2002,.

Elitzur, Yehuda. "*Rishumei Gevuloteha shel Mamlekhet Yerushalayim hatrom-Yisraelit bamikra uvimekorot Makbilim.*" *Israel and the Bible*, Ramat Gan (2000): 71–72 [Hebrew].

Elitzur, Yoel. *Ancient Place Names in the Holy Land.* Jerusalem-Winona Lake, 2004, 141 n. 4, 283–290.

Elitzur, Yoel. "'So He Sent Him Out of the Vale of Hebron': On the Hilly ᶜEmeq in the Hebrew Bible." *Beit Mikra* 54:2 (2009): 5–20 [Hebrew].

Elitzur, Yoel. "The Biblical Names of Jerusalem." *Maarav* 21:1–2 (A. Demsky Festschrift) (2014): 189–201.

Kaufmann, Y. *The Biblical Account of the Conquest of Canaan.* Translated by M. Dagut. Jerusalem, 1985, 24.

Klein, J. "Pray for the Peace of Jerusalem – the Origin and Meaning of the Name Jerusalem." Edited by Y. Boussidan. *Jerusalem – Names in Praise.* Jerusalem, 2005, 22–31.

Koehler L. and W. Baumgartner. "ציון" and "II שָׁלֵם." In *The Hebrew and Aramaic Lexicon of the Old Testament*. Translated and edited by M. E. J. Richardson. 3–4, 1996–1999, 1022, 1539.

Mazar, B. "*Yerushalayim: Shemot Hair Vekhinuyeha.*" *Encyclopaedia Biblica* 7, 791–793 [Hebrew].

Reich, R. "The Recent Discovery of a Middle Bronze II Fortification in the City of David, Jerusalem." *City of David: Studies of Ancient Jerusalem* 4 (2009): 13–33.

Šanda, A. Review of: P. Heimisch, *Das Buch Genesis*. Bonn, 1930, *AfO* 7 (1931–1932): 288 [German].

Simons, J. *Jerusalem in the Old Testament*, 247 n. 1.

Tsafrir, Y. *The Southwestern Hill of Jerusalem and its Place in the Urban Development of the City in the Byzantine Period*. Doctoral dissertation, Jerusalem, 1975 [Hebrew].

Tushingham, A. D. "Yerushalayim." In *Archaeology in the Levant: Essays for Kathleen Kenyon*, edited by R. Moorey and P. Parr). Warminster, 1976, 183–193.

Numbers

Parashat Bemidbar

The Golan in the Torah

Each year, *Parashat Bemidbar* is read during or shortly before the beginning of the month of Sivan. Aside from their role in heralding the upcoming festival of Shavuot, the first two days of the month of Sivan have taken on a special significance in the last several decades, as these days in 1967 were the fifth and sixth days of the Six-Day War, when we merited receiving a unique divine gift: the Golan Heights. In 1967, these two days fell out on Friday and Shabbat, June 9–10. As a final operation ending those six days of salvation, seven brigades of Israeli soldiers advanced to the Golan Heights and the slopes of Mount Hermon. For years leading up to the Six-Day War, the Syrians had been firing artillery shells at the settlements in the Hula Valley and the Jordan Valley from their position in the Golan, and these attacks increased dramatically during the first few days of the war. In addition, the Syrians built a diversion canal in the Golan with the purpose of robbing Israel of its share of the Jordan's waters.

The advance on the Golan, the subject of which had been mired in internal debates among the military and state leadership, began on Friday, 1 Sivan with difficult battles that continued through Friday night, killing many soldiers and wounding many as well. A dramatic, perhaps even miraculous

(Courtesy of Dr. Zev Rothkoff)

Ancient synagogue at Katzrin, a Jewish settlement from the talmudic period that became a flourishing modern Israeli city

turning point occurred the next morning. The Syrian command received the erroneous impression that the battle for the Golan was lost, and was suddenly seized by tremendous fear. The Syrian chief of staff instructed all Syrian forces to destroy their posts and to retreat past Quneitra for the purpose of defending Damascus, the Syrian capital. Damascus Radio broadcast the erroneous report that Quneitra had fallen to the Zionists, causing a mass exodus of Syrian soldiers and civilians eastward, accompanied by clouds of smoke from the bombing of their own outposts and stations. Israel immediately took advantage of this opportunity and stormed ahead to Quneitra and the Ruqad River, which flows north-south along the eastern side of the Golan Heights in the direction of the Yarmouk River. When the Golan region, with its prominent open plains, abundant water, and beautiful streams, fell into Israeli hands, it was entirely devoid of inhabitants. Afterward, ancient synagogues and batei midrash – including that of the *Tanna* R. Eliezer HaKappar[1] – were discovered, many settlements

1. Incidentally, my father *z"l* was the first to decipher the inscription reading "This is the beit midrash of R. Eliezer HaKappar in the summer of 1968."

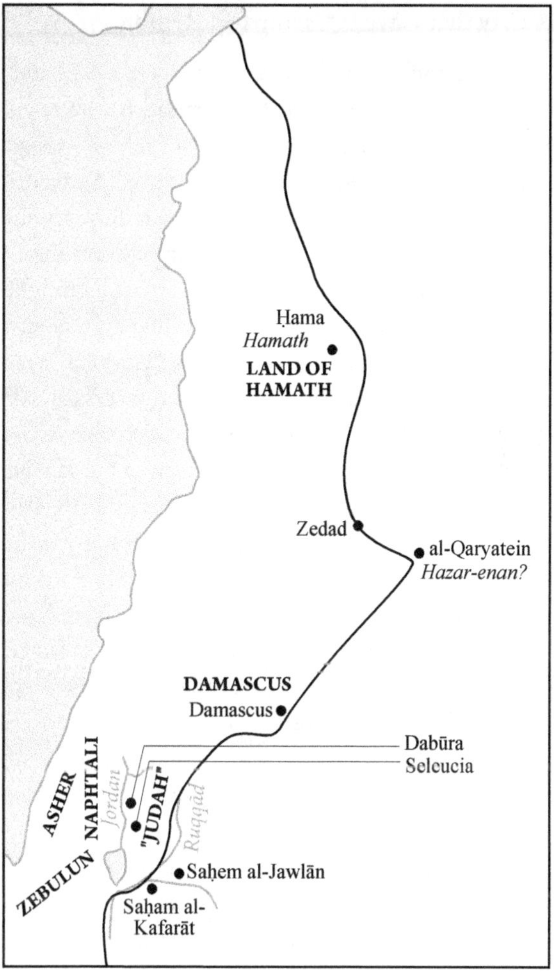

and one city were founded, agriculture and cattle-raising infrastructure was established, and the nation of Israel arrived (and continues to arrive) en masse to tour the beautiful Golan. On December 14, 1981, the Knesset passed the Golan Heights Law, which applied Israel's laws and government to the Golan Heights. On March 25, 2019, US President Donald Trump proclaimed that "the United States recognizes that the Golan Heights are part of the State of Israel." On June 16, 2019, the government of Israel declared the establishment of a new settlement in the Golan Heights named "Ramat Trump," in gratitude to the President.

Golan: A City that Gave Its Name to a Region

In the Tanakh, the name "Golan"[2] refers to a city of refuge and Levite city located in the Bashan region. Josephus referred to the city as Gaulana, mentioning it in its biblical context as a city of refuge (*Antiquities* 4:173) and in a later context, among the conquests of Alexander Jannaeus (*Antiquities* 13:393). However, the Golan *region* features more prominently and more frequently in Josephus' writings, under the Greek name Gaulanitis or Gaulanitikē, and his writings even distinguish between the Upper Golan and the Lower Golan. Rabbinic literature mentions a place called "HaGavlan," or in Aramaic, "Gavlana" or "Gavlona," a region that is equivalent to the Galilee: "In the footsteps of the Messiah…Galilee will be destroyed, Gablan (HaGavlan) desolated" (Mishna Sota 9:15). There is no settlement in rabbinic literature called Golan or Gavlan, but Eusebius, who lived during the time of the *Amora'im*, recognized in the Bashan region (which he calls "Batanaea") "a large village called Gaulōn in a district of the same name" (*Onomasticon* 64:8). Eusebius did not provide further information, and it is unclear to which site he is referring. In any case, Eusebius is the latest source that mentions a specific settlement called Golan. Since then, until today, the name "Golan" has only been used in the regional sense.

The identification of the biblical city of Golan is not truly known. The "large village" that Eusebius describes is not mentioned in other sources. In the *Targum Yerushalmi* (MS *Neofiti*) and *Targum Pseudo-Jonathan*, the city of Golan is translated as "Dabra." It is thought that the *Targum* is referring to Dabura, where the inscription from the beit midrash of R. Eliezer HaKappar was found, along with additional Jewish inscriptions, but one of the Geniza Fragments of the halakhic Midrashim identifies the city of Golan with Seleucia, which is mentioned in Josephus' writings (*Antiquities* 13:393, *Wars* 4:3) and whose name was preserved until 1967. In the scholarly literature, a different identification is very common, but this is only an error stemming from a lack of understanding. What is this mistaken identification? East of the eastern border of Israel in the Golan, about nine miles east of the moshav of Nov in the southern part of the Golan Heights,

2. In a case of *ketiv ukerei*, the Masoretic text of the Book of Joshua twice renders the name "Galon," with the traditional pronunciation "Golan." The Septuagint generally refers to the city as Gaulōn.

there is a village called Saḥem al-Jawlan. Gottlieb Schumacher, a scholar of the region during the 1880s, believed that the name of this village represented a preservation of the biblical name "Golan," and many other scholars followed in his footsteps from then until today. However, these scholars did not completely understand the nature of place-names of this variety. The second component of two-word place-names (with the exception of names of the form *ain-X, bayt-X, deir-X,* etc.) is almost never part of the actual place-name. Rather, it serves as an epithet meant to distinguish the place from a different place that bears the same name. For example, Dura al-Qarʿ ("Dura of the gourds") near Beit El bears this name to distinguish it from the town of Dura in the Mount Hebron region. Similarly, al-Lubban ash-Sharqiyya ("eastern") bears this name to distinguish it from al-Lubban Rantis near Rantis and Beit Aryeh. The same is true of Sahem in this case. The ending "al-Jawlan" is meant to distinguish it from Saḥam al-Kafarat not far from there, in the northern Gilead region, south of the Yarmouk.

The Golan and the Borders of the Land of Canaan

In Numbers 34, the borders of "the land of Canaan with its various boundaries" are outlined (34:2). These are the more limited borders compared with the vast, predestined borders of the land that we encountered in other places in the Torah, which reach until the Euphrates River.[3]

The eastern border of "the land of Canaan with its various boundaries" begins in the northeast in a place called Hazar-enan. Its identification is unknown, but general borderline logic dictates that it must be located around the town of al-Qaryatēn, about seventy-five miles northeast of Damascus. From Hazar-enan, the border continues to Shepham and "Riblah on the east side of Ain," which also lack clear identifications. The passage continues: "From there the boundary shall continue downward and abut on the shoulder (*katef*) of the Sea of Chinnereth to the east. The boundary shall then descend along the Jordan and terminate at the Dead Sea" (Num. 34:11–12). We all know the Jordan and the Dead Sea. We even recognize the Sea of Chinnereth (the Sea of Galilee). But what is the meaning of the phrase "and abut on the *katef* of the Sea of Chinnereth to the east"?

3. See the chapter on *Parashat Mishpatim*.

Upon examination, I found that the word *katef* in the topographical sense appears in the Tanakh nine times, eight of which are in Joshua 15 and 18, in the descriptions of the borders of Judah and Benjamin. The ninth time is here in Numbers 34, in the description of the eastern border of the land of Canaan.

When tracing the frequency of *katef*'s appearance in its topographical sense, it becomes clear that there is a certain defining element that accompanies the word every time it is used: direction. The word *katef* never appears alone; it is always juxtaposed with a direction. The instances of *katef* in Joshua come in the context of descriptions of east-west borderlines, and each time *katef* appears there, it is accompanied by the word *negba* ("south") or *tzafona* ("north"). In our case, where the borderline runs north-south, *katef* is accompanied by the word *kedma* ("east"). Apparently, this reflects a systematic usage.

What is the mechanism of this usage? To begin, we must first explain that the use of the word *katef* in the topographical sense at all, whose primary meaning is "shoulder," is part of a semantic system that borrows topographical terminology from the human body. Unlike European languages and Modern Hebrew, which also contain topographical terms derived from animal terminology (such as "back of the mountain" and "saddle"), Biblical Hebrew favors topographical terms derived specifically from parts of the human body. Examples include parts of the face, including "lip"; "tooth of the rock"; "tongue"; "eye"; and parts of the whole body such as "head of the mountain"; "rib of the mountain"; "navel of the land"; and finally, "shoulder."

It would be reasonable to assume that the biblical *katef* must be a topographical feature similar in appearance to a person's shoulder. In other words, it should be a flat area of ground with a steep vertical slope on one side. (Modern Hebrew uses this term in the same way.)

Let us return to our findings. We saw that the topographical *katef* is always accompanied by a direction, and that the direction is always perpendicular to the borderline described in the verse. This seems to indicate that the direction marks the point at which the *katef* begins to break downward, allowing the *katef* to serve as a kind of waypoint. When the borderline runs east-west, the point at which the table-like mountain begins to break to the north or south is a significant piece of information for mapping out the line. When the line runs north-south, the break to the east is similarly significant.

We can trace the *katef*-containing borderlines described in the apportionment chapters in the Book of Joshua. Let us cite two examples here.

(Courtesy of Dr. Zev Rothkoff)

Naḥal Ksalon with the tell of Kasla – ancient Chesalon (the bright area on the top of the central hill). The wooded slope below the tell is "the katef of Mount Jearim to the north."

On the northern border of the territory of Judah, between Kiriath-jearim and Beth-shemesh, the borderline reaches "to the *katef* of Mount Jearim on its northern side – that is, Chesalon" (Josh. 15:10). The modern-day moshav of Ksalon is located several hundred feet south of ancient Chesalon, which was situated atop a tall hill. The ancient name was preserved until the War of Independence through the name of the village of Kasla, which was situated on the ruins of the ancient city atop that same hill. This hill is located in the northern part of a large mountainous ridge, and contains an extremely steep slope down into the stream we now call Naḥal Ksalon. This large mountainous ridge is the "Mount Jearim" described in Joshua, which was certainly given this name due to its wooded scenery (then as now).[4] The site of ancient Chesalon is the

4. The literal meaning of *ye'arim* is "forests."

point where the mountain begins its steep slope into Naḥal Ksalon, or as the Tanakh describes it: "the *katef* of Mount Jearim on its northern side – that is, Chesalon."

A second example can be found in Joshua 18. On the eastern part of the southern border of the territory of Benjamin, we find the description, "to the *katef* adjacent to the Arabah northward" (18:18). The Arabah here is the Jordan Valley and the Dead Sea and "the *katef* adjacent to the Arabah" is what is known today as the "Fault Cliff," an intense, craggy slope that descends in the direction of the Dead Sea. The northernmost point of this slope is Naḥal Og in the northern Dead Sea region, near Kibbutz Almog; it serves as the southern border of the territory of Benjamin and the northern border of neighboring Judah.

Now we can return to the phrase "the *katef* of the Sea of Chinnereth to the east." In light of the other instances of *katef* in the Tanakh, we must immediately reject any interpretation that maintains that this is simply a neutral expression describing the eastern shore of the Sea of Galilee or a certain protrusion in the waterline (if indeed such a protrusion exists). "The *katef* of the Sea of Chinnereth" must be an elevated plain or a wide, horizontal ridge adjacent to the Sea of Galilee, and defined by it. In theory, this *katef* could be situated on either side of the sea, but in practice the ridges west of the sea do not come into the equation, for two reasons: First, the borderline described in the Torah originates in the northeast. Second, if we move the eastern borderline of the land of Canaan to the western side of the Sea of Galilee, this would mean that the western shore of the sea would not be included within the borders of the land of Canaan. This notion would conflict with the account in Joshua 19:35, which states that Hammath, Rakkath and Chinnereth – cities on the western shore of the Sea of Galilee – are included in the territory of the tribe of Naphtali. Thus, it seems that "the *katef* of the Sea of Chinnereth" is the Golan Heights, the large, elevated plain that runs along the length of the Sea of Galilee (similar to "the *katef* adjacent to the Arabah," which runs along the Arabah Sea, meaning the Dead Sea).

What, then, is "the *katef* of the Sea of Chinnereth to the east"? Various scholars interpreted this to mean "the *katef* that is east of the Sea of Chinnereth" – a general term for the Golan Heights – and moved the borderline to the western slope of the Golan Heights. But the parallel instances of *katef* in the Tanakh and the consistent role of the direction in each instance

(Courtesy of Samuel Klein)

Naḥal Rukad. The white slope on the left is "the *katef* of the Sea of Chinnereth to the east."

teach us that the opposite is true. In order to find the location described in the verse, we must search for the eastern slope of the Golan Heights. The eastern slope of the Golan Heights comprises the cliffs that descend from the Golan Heights into Naḥal Rukad, which is "coincidentally" the contemporary northern part of the eastern border of the State of Israel.

Did the Golan Belong to the Tribes of Transjordan or the Tribes of Cisjordan?

There is one more question that we must answer. Based on the ideas that we have developed here, it would seem that the Golan Heights were part of Cisjordan – the western side of the Jordan River. This seems difficult to accept, as the Golan lies east of the Jordan and the Sea of Galilee. It is part of the Bashan, the land of Og, a region that was given to the half-tribe of Manasseh. This region contained Havvoth-jair, named for Jair son of Manasseh (Deut. 3:13–14 and others), and "Golan, in Bashan, belonging to the Manassites" (4:43) – the northern city of refuge in Transjordan! Can it truly be that this region was included in the "land of the nine and a half tribes"?

The genealogical list of the tribe of Judah in I Chronicles 2 provides the answer to this question. According to this list (2:21–23), the famous Jair son of Manasseh was actually from the tribe of Judah, and his affiliation with the tribe of Manasseh stemmed from the fact that he was a grandson of the daughter of Machir son of Manasseh.[5] In any case, the list in Chronicles teaches us that from a certain perspective, the Golan was a kind of territorial addition for the tribe of Judah.

There are two other verses in the Tanakh that only recognition of the association of the Golan Heights with the tribe of Judah can satisfactorily explain. The first is Joshua 19:34. The chapter describes in a general sense the territory of Naphtali in the eastern Galilee: "It touched Zebulun on the south, and it touched Asher on the west, and Judah at the Jordan on the east." At first glance, this statement is completely incomprehensible: The geographical distance between the outlet of the Jordan from the Sea of Galilee (the southeasternmost point of Naphtali) and the Jordan estuary at the Dead Sea (the northeasternmost point of Judah) is almost seventy miles! How can the border of Naphtali touch the border of Judah? The classical commentators did not have a clear understanding of the geography involved, and thus were not overly troubled by this question. The *Metzudot* and the Vilna *Gaon* explained that the entire Jordan River belonged, for some reason, to Naphtali, thus enabling its territory to stretch until Judah. On the other end of the spectrum, some modern commentators excised the tribe of Judah from the verse entirely. They either suggested fanciful interpretations for the word *yehuda* or searched for a site called "Yehuda" near the Jordan. Others edited and emended the biblical text. Despite this, the verse as it stands states that the Golan Heights are part of Judah.

The second verse is II Kings 14:28. This verse describes the extensive conquests of King Jeroboam son of Joash of Israel, who restored the border of the Kingdom of Israel to Lebo-hamath. The verse ends, "The other events of Jeroboam's reign, and all his actions and exploits, how he fought and recovered Damascus and Hamath *for Judah in Israel*, are recorded in the annals of the Kings of Israel." Commentators both old and new suggested farfetched interpretations here. The simple

5. We will deal with the question of when Jair lived and, more importantly, what brought him to conquer the cities of the Bashan and settle that region along with Manassite families, in the chapter on *Parashat Matot*.

understanding is that the northeast region of the Kingdom of Israel – the Golan and the Hermon – were known as "Judah in Israel." Jeroboam added to this territory by annexing the regions of Damascus and Hamath to the north.

It should be added that in rabbinic sources as well, the northern section of the Jordan River, which lies north of the Sea of Galilee, is viewed as "not really the Jordan" compared to the section that lies south of the Sea of Galilee. *Ḥazal* stated, "The real Jordan is only from Beth-jericho[6] and below" (Tosefta Bekhorot 7:4; Bavli Bekhorot 55a). According to many scholars, *Ḥazal* also regarded Gamla in the Golan heights as part of the Galilee, and there is good reason to assume that Josephus did so as well.[7]

In the end, "the land of Canaan with its various boundaries" – the land of the nine and a half tribes – included within it the Golan Heights until Naḥal Rukad. Based on this, it turns out that the new eastern border that Israel reached by the end of the Six-Day War, upon which Israeli law was conferred in 1982, lies precisely on the eastern borderline of "the land of Canaan with its various boundaries" according to the Torah.

For further study:

"Professor Yehuda Elitzur Ubeit Midrasho shel R. Eliezer Hakappar," from "Yehuda Elitzur" website: http://www.daat.ac.il/elitzur/sipur.asp [Hebrew].

Elitzur, Yoel. "Toponyms in the Land of Israel: Two-word Place-names." In *Encyclopedia of Hebrew Language and Linguistics*, 3:783. Leiden and Boston, 2013.

Elitzur, Yoel. "*Ma hu Katef Veheikhan Ketef Yam Kinneret Kedma.*" *Al Atar* 4–5 (1999): 41–50 [Hebrew].

Elitzur, Yoel. "'*Katef*': A Topographical Term in the Benjaminite Dialect." *HUCA* 70–71 (1999–2000): 27–38.

Kallai, Z. "Kateph – כתף." *Israel Exploration Journal* 15 (1965): 177–179.

Maoz, Z. "Golan Heights." In *The Anchor Bible Dictionary*, 2, 1058–1065.

Syon, D. "The Identification of Gamla – Through the Sources and by the Results of the Excavations." *Cathedra* 78, 3–24 [Hebrew].

Yeivin, S. "To Judah in Israel (2 Kings 14:28)," *Eretz-Israel* 10 (1971): 150–151 [Hebrew].

6. "Beth-jericho" is Bet Yerah at the outlet of the Jordan from the Sea of Galilee.
7. See the chapter on *Parashat Behar*.

www.zerothkoff.com (Courtesy of Dr. Zev Rothkoff)

Naḥal Yahudiyya in the Golan. The Arabic name "*Yahudiyya*" preserved the existence of Jews in this region in the past.

Parashat Naso

Zorah and Eshtaol and the Territory of Dan

This week's *haftara* begins, "There was a certain man from Zorah, of the family of the Danites" (Judges 13:2) and concludes, "The spirit of the Lord first moved him in the encampment of Dan, between Zorah and Eshtaol" (13:25).

Zorah

Zorah and Eshtaol are two cites that are usually mentioned together. Zorah was the more important of the two, and is sometimes mentioned alone. For precision's sake, Eshtaol is mentioned eight times in the Tanakh, always together with Zorah. Zorah is mentioned an additional five times alone, as well as in one extrabiblical source from the biblical period – in the Amarna Letters from the early fourteenth century BCE: "May the king, my lord, know that the Ḫabiru wrote (or sent) to Aijalon (^{URU}a-ya-lu-na) and to Zorah (^{URU}Ṣa-ar-ḫa), and the two sons of Milkilu [the ruler of Gezer] barely escaped being killed" (EA 273). Based on the chronology that I consider correct, it may be that this letter constitutes a testimony of the Israelite conquest of the Land of Canaan.[1]

The name Zorah was preserved in the name Ṣarʿa,[2] an Arab village destroyed during the War of Independence. The village is located adjacent to a summit just over a mile northeast of Kibbutz Tzora, between the moshav of Tarum and the Shimshon industrial area. The peak overlooking the village contains two grave markers.[3] A recent Jewish tradition identifies these graves as those of Samson and his father, an identification that runs counter to the verse, "they buried him between Zorah and Eshtaol" (Judges 16:31), as these graves are adjacent to Zorah itself. The area surrounding the summit is full of ancient cuttings (including an oil press cave from the Roman-Byzantine period), which teaches us that this region was located outside the limits of the ancient city itself. In the area of the destroyed village, ancient building stones and pottery can be seen. Excavations have not been undertaken there.

At the foot of the hill, at the edge of the industrial area, there is an unusual finding – an ancient rock-hewn altar, referred to as "Manoah's altar." It is about five feet high, its surface about 8x10 feet, dimensions that are similar to those of the burnt-offering altar described in Exodus 27:1–2.[4] A positive note about this village, which was destroyed in 1948: While visiting the site, I saw a discarded concrete lintel with an Arabic inscription reading, "In the name of Allah the All-Merciful, the victory is to God and the liberation is near, year 1355 of the Hijra, 1936 of the birth [CE]." This lintel is a testimony of what is known as the Great Arab Revolt of 1936. As a God-fearing Jew, I take this inscription at face value and thank God for our victory in the War of Independence at this site and at other sites, twelve years after this inscription was engraved.

1. See the chapter on *Parashat Shemot.*
2. The pronunciation of Ṣarʿa matches the name's pronunciation as recorded in the Amarna letter, as well as that of the Septuagint: *Saraa.*
3. The site is known as Sheikh es-Samet.
4. See the chapter on *Parashat Yitro.*

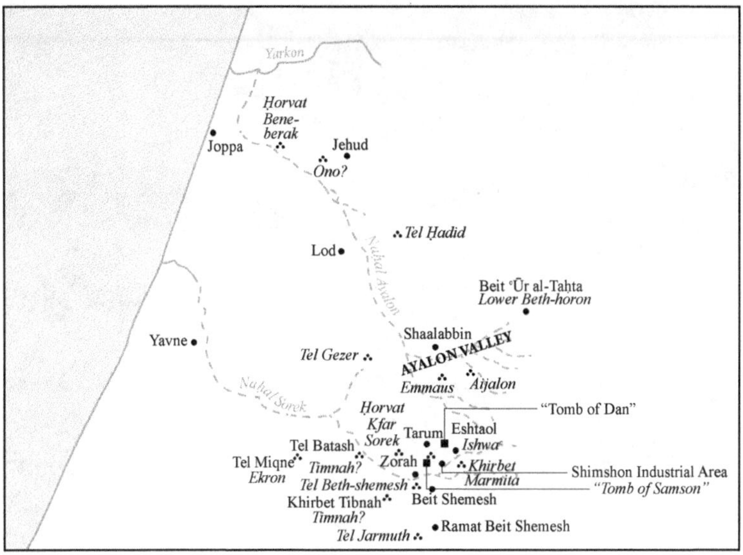

Eshtaol

The identification of Eshtaol is not known, but it is clear from the Tanakh that its distance from Zorah cannot be more than a few miles. The modern-day moshav of Eshtaol is situated atop the ruins of the village of Ishwaʿ, about one mile east of the ruins of Zorah. Scholars drew a comparison between the names "Ishwaʿ" and "Eshtaol." The French explorer Victor Guérin writes that on June 21, 1863, he heard from elderly Arabs in Bēt 'Iṭāb that the village of "Ashuaʿ" was previously known as "Ashua'l" or "Ashtua'l." The elders also told him that the wali consecrated to Sheikh Gherib between Ishwaʿ and Ṣarʿa (in recent years labeled "the Tomb of Dan, son of Jacob") was previously known as "Kabr Shamshun" – the Tomb of Samson. In truth, the connection between Eshtaol and Ishwaʿ is completely fictive. Regarding Guérin's testimony, it is highly doubtful if this information can be trusted. First, no other sources attest to such names. Second, the connection to the biblical names is so fantastic that one suspects the source of the information was actually conversations between the Arab villagers and European travelers who passed through the area prior to Guérin.

Eusebius, in his Onomasticon (approx. 320 CE), recognized Zorah and Eshtaol as existing villages during his time. He described

www.zerothkoff.com (Courtesy of Dr. Zev Rothkoff)

The Tomb of Samson, formerly Sheikh es-Samet, on the peak of ancient Zorah

the two villages, along with Beth-shemesh, with the following words: "Ten miles from Eleutheropolis [Beit Guvrin] on the road to Nicopolis [Emmaus]." This description, used for all three locations, demonstrates that there was apparently a crossroads with a path leading to each of the three settlements. In any case, the distance is too short; it is actually about twelve miles. For Jarmuth, Eusebius dedicated two entries. In one of them ("Iermus"), the description is very similar to that of Zorah, Eshtaol, and Beth-shemesh: "There is now a village Hiermokhōs[5] ten miles from Eleutheropolis on the way to Jerusalem." Eusebius is undoubtedly referring to Tel Yarmuth, known until the modern era as "Khirbet al-Yarmouk," today located near Ramat Beit Shemesh.[6] The distance between Beit Guvrin and Tel Yarmuth is indeed ten Roman miles. In the second entry dedicated to Jarmuth, the text of the Greek manuscript is defective, but fortunately this entry

5. In Jerome's edition: "Iermucha."

6. It is a shame that this new city was not named Yarmut, as this was the original historic name for the site.

Modern-day Beit Shemesh, viewed from the northwest

was cited by Procopius of Gaza about one hundred years after the Onomasticon was written. In this entry, Eusebius writes that "Ierimuth" is situated fourteen miles from Eleutheropolis, near Eshtaol, a village [in the region of] Adullam. Scholars speculated that Eusebius was not referring here to Tel Yarmuth but to a location farther north, perhaps Khirbet Marmita, about half a mile east of Naham. In any case, the distance of fourteen miles fits with the Naham area, the Shimshon Junction, and the moshav of Eshtaol.

Rabbi Ishtori Haparḥi wrote in 1322: "South of Lod about three hours east is Zorah and Eshtaol; their names have not been altered." Rabbi Joseph Schwarz wrote in 1845: "The village of Ṣara is Zorah. West of Ṣara about one hour, slightly to the south is the village of Shtual, which is Eshtaol." Rabbi Schwarz, a German-born Jew, was not sensitive to the guttural sound of the letter *ayin*, so he spelled "Ṣara" with a Hebrew *aleph* rather than an *ayin*. But it is clear that he is referring to the village of Ṣarʿa. Regarding the testimony on "Shtual" west of Zorah, I do not know of any support for this in other sources, but a certain degree of support can likely be found in Eusebius' *Onomasticon*. The

Onomasticon mentions the village of Sorek on two occasions,[7] and both times Eusebius highlights the connection to Naḥal Sorek, the brook where Samson came to meet Delilah for the first time. In one of those observations he writes that the site is near Zorah, and in the other he writes that it is near Eshtaol. The village described by Eusebius is definitely identical with Khirbet Surīk (two miles west of Ṣarʿa). Eusebius' biblical identification of Sorek is questionable, but his testimony on the ground is presumably trustworthy. Based on this, we must ostensibly seek out the Eshtaol that Eusebius recognized west of Zorah rather than east of it; this issue requires further study.

In summary, it seems that in the past Eshtaol continued to be recognized by its ancient name, but in the last few centuries its identity has been forgotten. It is likely that in the future, additional sources will be found that will shed more light on this question. The distance that Eusebius records in his "Ierimuth" entry seems to fit with the region of modern-day Eshtaol, but the other details that he recorded fit this region less; it is difficult to ascertain the truth of the matter.

To Which Tribe Did Zorah and Eshtaol Belong?

Zorah and Eshtaol are places that are typically associated with the tribe of Dan. The pair appears at the beginning and end of the series of narratives involving the Danite judge Samson: "The spirit of the Lord first moved him… between Zorah and Eshtaol" (Judges 13:25); "They buried him between Zorah and Eshtaol" (16:31). The Book of Judges contains another set of stories involving the tribe of Dan, a multi-strand narrative surrounding the conquest of Laish and Micah's idol. In this narrative as well, Zorah and Eshtaol are the centers of life for the tribe of Dan. "Valiant men" set out from there to spy out the land on behalf of their kinsmen; the spies would return there to report their findings; and "six hundred strong, girt with weapons of war" departed from there on their way to conquer Laish in the north, traveling via the home of Micah in Mount Ephraim (18:2, 8, 11). It is well known that the narrative in chapter 18 occurred chronologically

7. Once it is written as "Sōrēk" (Jerome: "Sorec"); a second time in the Greek manuscript it is written incorrectly as "Barēch" (Jerome: "Cafarsorech").

www.zerothkoff.com (Courtesy of Dr. Zev Rothkoff, 2015)

Moshav Eshtaol on the ruins of the village of 'Ishwa, surrounded by forests

at the start of the period of the Judges – the story was already recounted in brief in Joshua 19:47 and the end of the story seems to feature a grandson of Moses[8] – whereas the story of Samson that appears in prior chapters actually occurred at the end of the period of the Judges.[9] We learn from this that only a portion of the tribe of Dan traveled north, while the rest of the tribe remained in the original Danite territory. The Song of Deborah ("And Dan – why did he linger by the ships?" [5:17]) teaches us that there were some Danite sailors, who perhaps settled in Jaffa.

However, in the Book of Joshua we find that Zorah and Eshtaol are enumerated twice: in 15:33 the cities appear first in the list of the cities of the Shephelah belonging to the tribe of Judah; and in 19:41 they appear first in the list of cities belonging to the tribe of Dan. To whom do the cities belong? Rashi explained that they were border cities: "They

8. See *Seder Olam* 12 and Bava Batra 109b and parallels.
9. The reason for this reversed order is that in the Book of Judges, two long narratives were added to the end of the book – after the normal chronology of the period of the Judges was completed – to illustrate the low spiritual and national state of the nation in those days.

belonged to Judah and the border of the Danites fell near them." This explanation is difficult to accept: To whom did the cities actually belong? To Judah or to Dan? On several occasions in the allotment chapters, we find that the Tanakh stresses the status of the border cities. Regarding Kiriath-jearim on the border of Judah and Benjamin, the verse states that it was "a city of the Judahites" (Josh. 18:14). The Benjaminite border runs through the region of Beth-horon "to the hill south of Lower Beth-horon" (18:13). There is no prominent hill in the Lower Beth-horon region; the intent of the verse was to declare that Beth-horon itself belonged to Ephraim. If so, why didn't the verse explicate similarly in the case of Zorah and Eshtaol? It may be that Rashi intended to distinguish between the city and the territorial region, in the same vein as "The region of Tappuah belonged to Manasseh; but Tappuah, on the border of Manasseh, belonged to the Ephraimites" (17:8) and regarding Hebron – where the city itself was a priestly city while its territory was given to the clan of Caleb – "They gave the fields and the villages of the city to Caleb son of Jephunneh as his holding" (21:12). But why was this point not stated explicitly by the Tanakh itself? In addition, we will see below that the problem of Zorah and Eshtaol is only a small part of a wider question, one that requires an overarching solution.

The author of the *Metzudot* suggested a radical solution: "Zorah and Eshtaol: It may be that these [cities] were not those that were on the border of Judah." It is very difficult to accept this kind of solution. While there are indeed examples of multiple cities in the Land of Israel that bear the same name, most of the time these duplicate names have readily understandable meanings, most often describing the topographical or agricultural landscape. Examples include Ramah ("rise"); Mizpah ("lookout"); Gibeah ("hill"); En-gannim ("garden spring"); and Tappuah ("apple"). In contrast, unique names like Zorah and Eshtaol do not lend themselves to duplication. But more significantly, from a statistical perspective it is hard to imagine that the pair of Zorah and Eshtaol would be duplicated in two regions not far away from each other.

One ostensible solution could be that the cities were given to Judah only for the initial, temporary allotment. Joshua 18 describes two stages in the apportionment of the land. In the first stage, five tribes settled their territory semi-spontaneously: Reuben, Gad, and the half tribe of Manasseh in Transjordan; and Judah, Ephraim, and the other half tribe of Manasseh in Cisjordan. The Tanakh relates that Joshua brought the nation to Shiloh, berating the remaining tribes: "How long will you be slack about going and taking possession of the land which the Lord assigned to you?" (Josh. 18:3). He then sent delegations to determine the proper borders for the land and to divide the remaining territory among the seven remaining tribes. If so, we might suggest that Zorah and Eshtaol were given to Judah in the first allotment, only to be transferred to Dan in the second allotment. Nevertheless, this solution is also impossible. In I Chronicles at the end of chapter 2, the Tanakh lists the families of Judahite ancestry along with their places of residence. There we read the following:

> And the families of Kiriath-jearim: the Ithrites, the Puthites, the Shumathites, and the Mishraites; from these came the Zorathites and the Eshtaolites. The sons of Salma: Bethlehem, the Netophathites, Atroth-beth-joab, and half of the Manahathites, the Zorites. (2:53–54)

www.zerothkoff.com (Courtesy of Dr. Zev Rothkoff)

Yalu, the site of Aijalon. The raised area on the top of the hill was a fortress overlooking the ancient city.

In other words, the Judahite families, in practice, settled throughout the generations in Zorah and Eshtaol.

The Many Owners of Aijalon

Joshua 19:42 states that Aijalon was given to the tribe of Dan. Joshua 21:24 (and its parallel verse in I Chronicles 6:54) states that it was given to the Levites. Judges 1:35 states that the Amorites seized Aijalon and settled it, until the House of Joseph got involved: "But the hand of the House of Joseph bore heavily on them and they had to perform forced labor." To complicate matters further, I Chronicles 8:13 speaks of the Benjaminites Beriah and Shema – "chiefs of clans of the inhabitants of Aijalon, who put to flight the inhabitants of Gath."[10] That the city was given to Dan and then devoted to the Levites is a normal phenomenon. (The explanation for this is apparently that generally the fields and farmlands – the prime sections of the territory – remained in the possession of the tribe, while the Levites only received residences for themselves and their families, as well as space for their cattle and other property.) However, the fact that the city changed hands so many times indicates that Aijalon was located in a kind of "Wild West" in which the most powerful group at a given time would take control.

It seems that this collection of information illustrates well the weakness of the tribe of Dan, of whom the Tanakh states: "But the territory of the Danites slipped from their grasp" (Josh. 19:47); and "The Amorites pressed the Danites into the hill country; they would not let them come down to the plain" (Judges 1:34).

However, Judges 18:1 presents a picture that hints at the fact that the problem had already begun from the time of the apportionment: "In those days the tribe of Dan was seeking a territory in which to settle; for to that day no territory had fallen to their lot among the tribes of Israel." Let us examine the biblical description of the allotment of the tribe of Dan.

10. The exact interpretation of this verse is debated among the commentators, but it may be that the verse actually adds a sixth owner of Aijalon – the inhabitants of Gath (either Canaanites or Philistines).

We must preface this discussion by stating that we will be taking a simple step, one that begs to be taken: to read the allotment chapters in Joshua exactly as they are written; to attempt to identify the places mentioned in the verses based on biblical and extrabiblical parallels and on the facts on the ground; and to try to understand the background and historical circumstances behind the descriptions in the Tanakh. This is a lonely task, as the classical commentators were not familiar with the land or with the extrabiblical sources, and many God-fearing students today who take interest in these matters believe that they should not pursue information or sources that were beyond the purview of the classical commentators. On the other hand, most scholars of biblical geography and history do not pay attention to what the Tanakh says about itself. They date the biblical text centuries later and raise dozens of different historical theories regarding when each list was written and the "agendas" behind each one. We will take the minority approach here: We will read the Tanakh as it is written and attempt to understand what exactly it is saying, with the help of all the historical, geographical, archaeological, and linguistic tools available to us.

The Territory of Dan

The territory of Dan is described last among the tribal territories in Joshua 19:40–48:

> The seventh lot fell to the tribe of the Danites, by their clans. Their allotted territory comprised: Zorah, Eshtaol, Ir-shemesh, Shaalabbin, Aijalon, Ithlah, Elon, Timnah, Ekron, Eltekeh, Gibbethon, Baalath, Jehud, Bene-berak, Gath-rimmon, Me-jarkon and Rakkon, at the border near Joppa. But the territory of the Danites slipped from their grasp. So the Danites migrated and made war on Leshem. They captured it and put it to the sword; they took possession of it and settled in it. And they changed the name of Leshem to Dan, after their ancestor Dan. That was the portion of the tribe of the Danites, by their clans – those cities, with their villages.

Among the descriptions of the tribal territories there are several models. The territories of Judah and Benjamin are the most orderly;

the Tanakh describes the borderlines systematically at the four cardinal directions and then goes on to list the cities within the territories. In the description of the territories of Ephraim and Manasseh, the Tanakh describes only partial segments of the outer borderlines, and there is no list of cities inside the borders. For the other tribes, as a rule, the descriptions feature some combination of borderline and territorial cities.[11] The description of the territory of Dan does not include any borderline, but only a list of cities. Modern commentators and historical atlas writers have tried to map out the borders of the territory based on the enumerated cities, but they generally do not address the question of why the Tanakh itself did not provide a description of the tribe's borderline – or at least partially, as it does in the case of several other tribes.

A second question is why several important cities – situated between the southern line connecting Zorah, Eshtaol, Beth-shemesh, Timnah, and Ekron – and the northern line connecting Jehud and Bene-berak – are apparently missing from the list. According to various sources and findings, these missing cities – which include Lod, Ono, Hadid, Gezer, and Jabneh – were central cities in the region at the time. Why, then, were they omitted?

One scholar who tried to answer these two questions was Aaron Demsky. His solution is that here too, the Tanakh listed only the border cities of Dan, along Naḥal Sorek in the south, the mountain slope line in the east, and Naḥal Ayalon and the Yarkon in the north. According to Demsky, the list of cities is essentially a description of the borderline, though the text does not say so explicitly (see map). This suggestion does not solve our problem completely, however. Some of the cities on the list have not been identified, and their integration in the outer borderline is perhaps wishful thinking. The cities of Lod, Hadid, and Ono are basically situated on that line – yet they were omitted.

11. In Yerushalmi Megilla 1:1, *Ḥazal* addressed this matter, using it as a support for the position of R. Yose b. Ḥanina that the Book of Joshua only enumerated cities that were near the borders; see the chapter on *Parashat Behar*.

Prof. Aaron Demsky

However, the most important question here is a different one: the comparison of the territory of Dan to the territories of Judah and Ephraim. There is no overlap between the northern border of Judah (Josh. 15:5–11) and the southern border of Ephraim (16:1–3). On the eastern portion of the borderlines, from the Jordan to Kiriath-jearim on the border of Judah and to Lower Beth-horon on the border of Ephraim, there is a space between the two territories that is occupied by the tribe of Benjamin (18:11–20). Additionally, there is another narrow area in which there is a small amount of space – the Aijalon area. However, from there on, for over fifteen miles of Shephelah and coast, the borders basically overlap. Gezer, which is listed as part of the southern border of Ephraim, and Jabneel (Yavne), which is listed as part of the northern border of Judah, are situated along the same line of latitude. What this means is that there was no room left for the tribe of Dan. In other words: Beth-shemesh, Zorah, Eshtaol, Timnah, and Ekron were part of the territory of Judah. Shaalabbin, Jehud, Bene-berak, Gath-rimmon, and Joppa belonged to Ephraim. What land does this leave for the territory of Dan?

My Solution

It seems that the territory of Dan (19:40–46) is similar in character to the territory of Simeon (19:1–9). The descriptions of these two territories include lists of cities but no surrounding borderline. In the territory of Simeon there is an abundance of cities with no identification, whereas in the territory of Dan scholars have identified most of the cities, but both lists are similar in type. We can determine that the territory of Dan contains neither surrounding borderline nor territorial contiguity. What is the background of this character of the territory? As for Simeon, the Tanakh states: "Since the share of the Judahites was larger than they needed, the Simeonites received a portion inside their portion" (19:9). The verse reveals in Judges 1:3 that the Judahites and the Simeonites formed a pact in which they agreed to fight together in the wars of conquest and to share their territory as well. It appears that Simeon was a weak tribe without organizational abilities. We may even speculate that the tribe of Simeon was then in a state of shock following the loss of tens of thousands of their number. Simeon was the only tribe whose numbers decreased drastically; they effectively lost most of their population between the census taken in the second year since the Exodus and the census taken in the fortieth year (from 59,300 to 22,200). *Ḥazal* explained that all the 24,000 people who died in the plague following the incident of Baal-peor were from the tribe of Simeon, the tribe of Zimri son of Salu. It is well known that Moses did not impart a unique blessing to Simeon, merely hinting at the tribe in Judah's blessing: "Hear (*shema*), O Lord the voice of Judah" (Deut. 33:7).

Most of the cities that Simeon received from Judah are enumerated twice in the Book of Joshua as well, once in the list of Judah's cities in the Negeb (15:20–33) and again in the list of Simeonite cities (19:1–9). It is reasonable to assume that the Judahites did not abandon these cities, but rather that they and the Simeonites lived in the cities side by side. It is difficult to imagine that a central city like Beersheba could have been purely Simeonite. More likely, it remained in Judahite hands while the Simeonites were given the right to settle there.

From here, we can return to the Danites. The tribe of Dan was the second-largest tribe of Israel (after Judah), and it preserved its high population until the fortieth-year census. However, despite its strength in numbers, the tribe did not seem to possess actual power. In the wilderness, Judah was the vanguard while Dan was "the rear guard of all the divisions." When the people of Israel reached the land, Judah was foremost in both conquering and settling the land, whereas the Tanakh does not record any incidents surrounding the tribe of Dan during that period. The process of settling the land hinged primarily on the tribes' motivation and their ability to act. The Judahites and the Josephite tribes – the Manassites in particular – were the ones who were strong enough and ambitious enough to take possession of the land. Joshua 14 relates that upon their request, Caleb son of Jephunneh and the Judahites were granted permission to go to war against the giants in Mount Hebron and to settle Hebron and the fortified cities surrounding it. Caleb promised his daughter's hand in marriage to the man who would attack and capture Kiriath-sepher. The Manassites settled the Gilead and the Bashan, while the daughters of Tzlofhad demanded portions among their brothers. Joshua gave the land of the valleys – which had been designated for Issachar and Asher – to the Manassites, in the hope that they would be able to dispossess the Canaanites there who possessed iron chariots (17:11, 18). The indolent tribes remained in Gilgal while the five zealous tribes fought and engaged in conquering the wasteland. It is likely no coincidence that the tribe of Dan was left until the end; the Danites were the "rear guard" of the tribes in the settlement process as well.

In Joshua 18, the nation assembles and Joshua urges the seven remaining tribes to follow in the footsteps of the five industrious tribes and discharge their responsibility with respect to conquering and settling the land. Joshua establishes a just principle: "Judah shall remain by its territory in the south, and the house of Joseph shall remain by its territory in the north" (18:5). In other words, the entire nation of Israel shows its thanks to the industrious tribes for their initiative in conquering and dispossessing the land. The thought that these five tribes would be required to clear out the places they conquered for the benefit of other tribes was never even entertained. They would stay where they were, while the rest of the tribes would divide the remaining land. We may even speculate that this secondary allotment of the remainder of the land was dependent to some extent on the eagerness and demand of the tribes to receive their portion. By the time Dan's turn was reached, there was no portion left for the tribe. I can picture the scene: The elderly Joshua turns to his close friend and partner in loyalty to God and to the cause of settling the Land of Israel Caleb son of Jephunneh, saying: Look, we need to solve the problem of the tribe of Dan, the most laggardly of the laggardly tribes. Let us give them the right to settle in the cities of our Shephelah, where the Canaanites still need to be dealt with – half from your territory and half from mine.

"Of the Family of the Danites"

This understanding explains another unique feature of the Danites of Zorah and Eshtaol. All the stories involving the Danites in the Book of Judges include the word *mishpaḥa,* meaning "family." Regarding the Danites who travel north, the verse reads: "The Danites sent out five of their number, from their family seat (*mimishpeḥotam*) at Zorah and Eshtaol – valiant men – to spy out the land and explore it" (Judges 18:2). Then again later: "They departed from there, from the family seat of the Danites (*mimishpaḥat HaDani*), from Zorah and Eshtaol, six hundred strong, girt with weapons of war" (18:11). And our *haftara* opens similarly as well: "There was a certain man from Zorah, of the family of the Danites, whose name was Manoah" (13:2). What is the nature of this emphasis? My father *z"l* explained in the *Daat Mikra* commentary on Judges 13:2:

> Every tribe is divided into families (extended divisions, each consisting of numerous households) and in the tribe of Dan there was only one family (Num. 26:42). Therefore Dan may be called a tribe and it may be called a family.

Begging my father's forgiveness, I would like to offer a different interpretation. In my humble opinion, the explanation is tied to the reality of the settlements in question. The reality was that Zorah and Eshtaol were Judahite cities, in which one Danite family was given permission to settle alongside the Judahites, dividing the cities' lands between them. When the Tanakh refers to the Danite residents of Zorah and Eshtaol, it feels the need to emphasize that the group in question is the Danite family in Zorah.

The Omission of Dan (and Simeon) from the List of Levite Cities in Chronicles

I Chronicles 6 enumerates the Levite cities. This list is parallel to the list of Levite cities in Joshua 21, but the lists differ from each other in several details. While the list in Joshua contains forty-eight cities (forty-four cities plus four more that appear in a minority of versions of the text, but are omitted from the primary versions), in line with the Torah's account (Num. 35:7), the list in Chronicles enumerates only forty-two cities, and some of the names of the cities have changed. In contrast to the prevailing view in the scholarly literature that the two lists are two versions of the same text, and that the differences between them are merely minor textual variations, the Tanakh itself provides a different answer: In Joshua, the Tanakh states that it is listing an apportionment plan that was devised during the time the land was being settled, whereas in Chronicles it states that it is providing a snapshot of the current state of the Levite cities from generations later.[12]

The list of Levite cities is also a list of the tribes of Israel, as the verses point out which cities were given over to the Levites by each tribe. This leads us to an interesting discovery. In the list in Joshua, which, as we said, reflects the original plan for the territorial allotment, all twelve tribes of Israel are mentioned. However, in the list in Chronicles, the tribe of Dan is missing and Simeon is only mentioned in a summarizing note appended to the section on Judah (I Chr. 6:50). This effectively reflects the settlement status of these two tribes. Both Simeon and Dan are essentially subtenants of Judah and Ephraim. Presumably, there was

12. In the chapter on *Parashat Masei*, I will expand on this matter.

not one city that was given over for the exclusive use of Simeon or Dan. From the official, schematic perspective of Joshua 21, both Simeon and Dan are mentioned. But from the practical perspective of Chronicles, Simeon and Dan are not landowners, and so are unable to give cities to the Levites from their territory. As they themselves are "guests" in the home of another tribe, they certainly cannot invite new "guests" of their own.[13]

After this chapter has been completed and published in Hebrew, I found the main idea proposed here in *Divrey Yoseph* of R. Joseph Schwartz, published in 1861.

For further study:

Demsky, A. "The Boundary of the Tribe of Dan (Joshua 19:41–46)." *Sefer Moshe: The Moshe Weinfeld Jubilee Volume*, edited by C. Cohen, A. Hurvitz, and S. M. Paul), 261–284. Winona Lake, 2004.

Elitzur, Yoel. *Ancient Place Names in the Holy Land*. Jerusalem-Winona Lake, 2004, 111, 361.

Freeman-Grenville, G. S. P., R. L. Chapman, and J. Tailor, *The Onomasticon of Eusebius of Caesarea*. Jerusalem, 2003, 36, 52, 61, 62, 86, 87, 88.

Guérin, V. *Description Géographique, Historique et Archéologique de la Palestine*, II. Paris, 1869, 382 [French].

Haparḥi, Ishtori. *Kaftor Vaferaḥ*. Edited by Lunz. Jerusalem, 1897, 302 [Hebrew].

Moran, W. L. *The Amarna Letters*. Baltimore-London, 1992, Letter 273.

Schwarz, Joseph. *Tevu'ot HaAaretz*. Edited by Lunz, Jerusalem, (1845) 1968, 121 [Hebrew].

Schwarz, Joseph. *Divrey Yoseph*, 3-4, Jerusalem 5621 (1861), 17-18 [Hebrew].

13. It may be supposed that the unique description of the Tribe of Dan – "Dan shall judge his people *as one of the tribes of Israel*" (Gen 49:16) – hints at its inferiority to the other tribes; cf. Josh 10:2: "because Gibeon was a great city, *like one of the royal cities*" (I am indebted to Itamar Haddad for this note). It is noteworthy that the closing words of the blessing to the tribe of Dan in the Book of Genesis, "I wait for thy salvation, O Lord" (Gen. 38:18), a desperate plea of pleading to God unlike any other phrasing in the blessings of the tribes, perhaps anticipate the difficulties of this tribe in relation to the other tribes (this has already been observed by some commentators).

Parashat Behaalotekha

The Wilderness of Paran

Just Under a Year in the Wilderness of Sinai

Parashat Behaalotekha marks the endpoint of the nation of Israel's encampment in the wilderness of Sinai. The nation of Israel arrived at Sinai on 1 Sivan of their first year in the wilderness: "On the third new moon after the Israelites had gone forth from the land of Egypt, on that very day, they entered the wilderness of Sinai" (Ex. 19:1); they settled there for almost a year. During this year, the nation of Israel underwent several powerful experiences that shaped their identity, for better and for worse. Sinai was where the people experienced both the divine revelation and committed the sin of the Golden Calf. Sinai was where the *Mishkan* was constructed and dedicated, and where Aaron's sons died a fiery death. Sinai was where the tribal chieftains were appointed and where the nation's judicial and administrative infrastructure – including magistrates and officials, as well as chiefs of thousands, hundreds, fifties, and tens – was established. Sinai was where the firstborn initially performed the divine service, until the priests and Levites took their place in that role. The wilderness of Sinai is the setting for all the events of the Book of Exodus starting from *Parashat Yitro*, the entire Book of Leviticus, and the Book of Numbers until the middle of *Parashat Behaalotekha*. The nation of Israel's stay in Sinai begins with the formation of a covenant, reading from the "record of the covenant" and the proclamation that "all that the Lord has spoken we will do!" (19:8); and "all that the Lord has spoken we will faithfully do!" (24:7). It ends with blessings, curses, and the promise of "I will remember in their favor the covenant with the ancients" (Lev. 26:45). It is in this dualistic light that the *Sifrei* on Deuteronomy[1] 1:6 stresses:

> "You have stayed long enough at this mountain": You *profit* from lingering at this mountain! You made for yourselves the Dwelling; you made for yourselves the Table; you made for yourselves the Lamp. Another word: You *benefit* from lingering at this mountain! You accepted upon yourselves the Torah; you appointed over yourselves seventy elders; you appointed over yourselves chieftains of thousands, of hundreds, of fifties, and chieftains of tens. See how beneficial it is for you to linger at this mountain! Another word: You *are harmed* from lingering at this mountain!

From Sinai to Paran, to Zin and Kadesh

In *Parashat Behaalotekha* we depart Sinai:

> In the second year, on the twentieth day of the second month, the cloud lifted from the Tabernacle of the Pact and the Israelites set out on their journeys from the wilderness of Sinai. The cloud came to rest in the wilderness of Paran. (Num. 10:11–12)

Their first stop came after a three-day journey (10:33), and they stayed there for at least a month (11:20); this was where the incidents of Taberah and Kibroth-hattaavah took place.[2] "Then the people set out

1. In the Venice edition 1546 and other versions, as well as Rashi's citation of the *Sifrei* in his commentary on this verse, the last sentence is missing.
2. Taberah and Kibroth-hattaavah are two names for the same place; for more on this phenomenon, see the chapter on *Parashat Vayetzeh*.

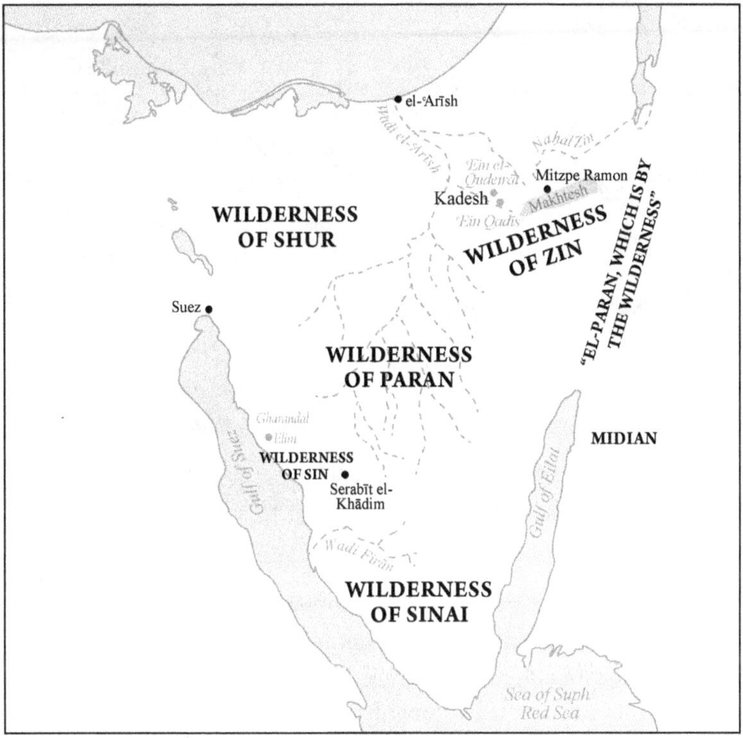

from Kibroth-hattaavah for Hazeroth" (11:35), where Miriam was shut out of the camp for seven days. "After that the people set out from Hazeroth and encamped in the wilderness of Paran" (12:16), which was the point of departure for the spies. This place was also called Kadesh ("at Kadesh in the wilderness of Paran" [13:26]), and its full name was Kadesh-barnea ("when I sent them from Kadesh-barnea to survey the land" [32:8 and similarly in Deuteronomy 1:19]). Kadesh-barnea, which is also located in the wilderness of Zin ("They went up and scouted the land, from the wilderness of Zin" [Num. 13:21]), is the midpoint of the southern border of "the land of Canaan with its boundaries" (34:2). The entire southern border is entitled "the wilderness of Zin alongside Edom" (34:3) and the point nearest to Kadesh-barnea on this border is Zin (34:4).

We see from the above descriptions that the entire area between the wilderness of Sinai and Kadesh-barnea (an eleven-day journey according to Deuteronomy 1:2) is known as the wilderness of Paran.

Typical view of the wilderness of Paran

Since the wilderness of Paran is mentioned both before Hazeroth and after it, it is clear that Hazeroth is a point within the wilderness of Paran. Most probably Hazeroth was an oasis, and was mentioned by name simply because it had one. In contrast, the other places within the wilderness of Paran did not have any known names, and thus the Torah sufficed with giving these places the general name "the wilderness of Paran." The region in the northern part of the wilderness of Paran, on the border of the land of Canaan, was called the wilderness of Zin, where Kadesh-barnea was located. The area where the people of Israel encamped at the time the spies were sent on their mission was originally given the general, neutral name "the wilderness of Paran" and afterward was labeled more specifically as "Kadesh" or "Kadesh-barnea." The spies' point of departure was called "the wilderness of Zin" as well. In the list of the marches of the people of Israel, this particular place was called Rithmah (Num. 33:18). In other words, even "Kadesh/Kadesh-barnea" is a territorial name in our context, referring to the "wilderness of Kadesh" (Psalms 29:8). The specific point or small region of Kadesh-barnea is located farther north, within the boundaries of the land of Canaan, as the borderline delineated in *Parashat Masei* indicates ("south of Kadesh-barnea" [34:4]).

www.zerothkoff.com (Courtesy of Dr. Zev Rothkoff)

Naḥal Masor – a typical view in the wilderness of Zin

Identifying Kadesh

About twenty miles west of Mitzpe Ramon and about two miles west of the western border of modern-day Israel, there is a spring called 'Ain Qadīs that represents a precise preservation of the name Kadesh. There is a larger spring called 'Ain el-Qudeirāt (pronounced Gdērāt) about five miles northwest of 'Ain Qadīs, surrounded by a large oasis containing remnants from prehistoric times, as well as a fortified Israelite castle that was in use from Solomon's time until the destruction of the First Temple. Following the return to Zion, the site was home to an unwalled Jewish settlement that was abandoned before the Hellenistic period and has not been settled since. Israeli archaeologists have excavated the site, starting in 1956 – immediately after the Sinai War – and again during the years 1976–1982, when the Sinai Peninsula was in Israeli hands. The findings at the site include several Hebrew inscriptions written on pottery from the First Temple period and from the Persian period. (To our great sorrow, all these Israelite findings were handed over to the Egyptians as a condition of the "Egypt-Israel peace treaty" of 1979.) The name "Qudeirat" is the name of a Bedouin tribe and its meaning is unimportant for our purposes. Upon traveling in the region in 1838, Robinson and Smith pointed out that the Bedouins generally refer to the spring as simply "el-'Ain," without any addition. Modern maps reflect this observation as well, labeling the wadi that originates at the spring and flows in the direction of Wadi el-'Arish "Wadi el-'Ain." The region containing these two springs is generally identified with the biblical Kadesh, which, as we said, was a territorial name for an entire desert expanse and not for one specific point alone. "En-mishpat, which is Kadesh" (Gen. 14:7) likely refers to one of the two springs mentioned here. Placing Kadesh-barnea in this region fits with the descriptions of the southern border of the land of Canaan in Numbers 34 and that of the territory of Judah in Joshua 15. In the description of the Land of Canaan the borderline runs "south of Kadesh-barnea." However, as we have said, even the region where the people of Israel were situated during their second year in the wilderness – when the spies were sent out – and again in the fortieth year when they returned from their wanderings (Num. 20:1) – which was presumably slightly south or west of this border – was given the territorial names Kadesh and Kadesh-barnea.

The expression "Kadesh-barnea" is mentioned in Tanakh in connection with the sin of the spies that took place during the second year in the wilderness, and it is usually found alongside either the Amalekites and the Canaanites or the Amorites. In contrast, "Kadesh, in the wilderness of Zin" and "the wilderness of Zin, which is Kadesh" are mentioned in connection with the fortieth year in the wilderness, and they are usually mentioned alongside the Edomites. Some classical commentators and modern scholars believe that the names represent two places located at a great distance from each other. Using this theory, it is possible to solve several biblical questions and even to corroborate the tradition that Aaron's tomb is located next to Petra. In practice, however, this theory is impossible; as we demonstrated above, even Kadesh-barnea is located within the wilderness of Zin. Despite this, it is quite logical to assume that Kadesh-barnea and Kadesh in the wilderness of Zin were two subregions in relatively close proximity to each other within the wilderness of Kadesh. Compare to the expressions "the Negeb of Arad," "the Negeb of the Kenites," "the Negeb of the Jerahmeelites" and similar expressions in the Negeb cities on Shishaq's list. Here too, these are two subregions within one large semidesert region.

The name Rithmah is certainly derived from the word *rotem*, referring to the broom bush, because of the high concentration of these plants at that location. Whether it is possible for us to identify Rithmah, however, is uncertain. As we said, it must be a relatively anonymous place in a region that was defined in Tanakh alternately as Kadesh-barnea, the wilderness of Zin, and the wilderness of Paran. However, it cannot be located at the site of one of the Kadesh springs themselves, as the springs were located within the land of Canaan. With due caution, I will permit myself to direct the attention of the reader to the information recorded by Robinson and Smith in the description of their travels in 1838. Robinson and Smith mention one of the tributaries of Wadi el-'Arish called Wadi Abu Retemât. This wadi, located about three miles west of 'Ain el-Qudeirāt on the opposite side of a mountain that separates between them, contains a high concentration of broom bushes and desert scrub. Nevertheless, this is not considered a clear name preservation, as the Hebrew word *rotem* exists in Arabic as well (in Arabic *ritm*), with the same meaning, and a place-name derived from this word should have arisen naturally at a late date. (There are several known Arabic names derived from the name of this plant, in several locations in the desert.) In any case, the location seems to be well in line with the information found in the biblical text, and thus this identification may indeed be reasonable.

Sections of the Sinai Peninsula

The application of the name "Sinai" to the entire vast area between the Mediterranean Sea and the two arms of the Red Sea is a phenomenon of modern terminology. In the Tanakh, as we have already seen, Sinai is only a small part of this area. The Sinai Peninsula, including what is known today as the central and southern Negev, can be divided into three main sections. The northern section bordering on the Mediterranean Sea contains dune fields, but its climate is not extreme; indeed, its high groundwater levels have allowed for the existence of settlements throughout history. The southern section is primarily known for its lofty granite mountains, which reach an altitude of 8,500 feet above sea level and contain flowing streams. The central section, which constitutes most of the area of the Peninsula and includes within it the Negev from Makhtesh Ramon southward, is known in Arabic as *at-Tīh* or *Tīh bani 'Isra'īl* (after the people of Israel's wanderings). It is an absolute desert, mostly flat and large in area – almost 7.5 million acres with virtually no signs of life.

The southern section is Sinai or Horeb. The region northwest of the Sinai Massif is called the wilderness of Sin "which is between Elim and Sinai" (Ex. 16:1). Elim is identified with Wadi Gharandal, near Rās Malʿab, south of Rās Sudr, which was an Israeli military center during the time when Israel controlled Sinai. The region between Elim and the Sinai Massif includes mountains that are not as high. One famous historical site in this region is the ancient turquoise mines and the Egyptian-Canaanite temple in Sarabīṭ el-Khādim, where the earliest-known alphabet was discovered. Between the wilderness of Sin and the wilderness of Sinai is Rephidim. It makes sense to identify Rephidim in the area of Wadi Firān (no connection to the biblical Paran).[3]

The northern section of the Sinai Peninsula is known in the Torah as Shur. It is mentioned in Genesis in connection with the Patriarchs and their settlement in the western Negeb (Gen. 16:7, 20:1); in the description of the settlement patterns of the Ishmaelites (25:18; compare to I Sam. 15:7, 27:8); and in Exodus as the wilderness that the people of Israel entered after they crossed the Sea of Suph (Ex. 15:22).

The large, desolate central section is the wilderness of Paran, which features in our *parasha*, stretching from the wilderness of Sinai to the border of the land of Canaan. It is interesting to note the language that Moses uses in Deuteronomy to describe the wilderness of Paran as he summarizes the marches of *Parashat Behaalotekha*: "We set out from Horeb and traveled the great and terrible wilderness that you saw, along the road to the hill country of the Amorites, as the Lord our God had commanded us, and we reached Kadesh-barnea" (Deut. 1:19). *Parashat Ekev* adds to the description of this "great and terrible wilderness": "Who led you through the great and terrible wilderness with its seraph serpents and scorpions, a parched land with no water in it" (8:15). It seems that within a certain oasis in this territory there was

3. The name "Rephidim" was given after the Six-Day War to the IDF encampments in the Bir Gafgafa area, far from the original Rephidim.

also a settlement called Paran. I Kings 11:17–18 relates the story of the Edomite Hadad, who traveled from Midian (east of the Gulf of Eilat) toward Egypt via Paran, where additional men joined him.

In the northern part of the wilderness of Paran, in that part's eastern section, around Kadesh-barnea, was the wilderness of Zin. Based on Numbers 34:3 and its parallel in Joshua 15:1, the entire desert region between the southern edge of the Dead Sea (which apparently reached past the modern-day moshav of Neot HaKikar at the time the Torah and the Book of Joshua were written) and the "wadi of Egypt," i.e., Wadi el-Arish – in other words, lower Naḥal Zin and the areas to its south and the Makhtesh Ramon area and the territory to its west, "south of Kadesh-barnea" – was called the wilderness of Zin. The southern borderline of "the land of Canaan with its boundaries" and of the territory of Judah in the southern part of the land is the same line that separates between the wilderness of Zin and the inhabited area. The view of Ze'ev Meshel placing the borderline atop the cliff of Makhtesh Ramon seems quite reasonable.

"El-Paran, Which Is by the Wilderness"

This unique expression appears in Genesis 14:6. Amraphel, Chedarlaomer, and their allies attacked the Horites of Mount Seir "as far as El-paran, which is by the wilderness." It is accepted in the scholarly literature to identify "El-paran, which is by the wilderness" with Eilat on the banks of the Red Sea. In my opinion, this identification is not likely at all, for three reasons: First, Eilat is always written with a feminine ending (such as Elath, Eloth, Aela Elana in Greek-Roman sources and 'Ayla in Arabic sources); second, Eilat is always connected to the Red Sea and to Edom – and not to Paran; and third, based on the context, it is likely that El-paran represents a line demarcating the edge of the land of the Horites, and not a point within it.

The descriptor "which is by the wilderness" is also surprising. Since Mount Seir is surrounded by deserts on all sides, to what can this expression possibly refer? In my article on the biblical concept of *elon*, I cited evidence supporting the interpretation of the Aramaic *Targumim* and the Midrash, which translate *elon* as *meshar*, meaning "plain." This is in contrast to the translation of the Septuagint, the Peshitta, and the accepted view today, which maintains that *elon* refers to a kind of tree

"El-paran, which is by the wilderness"; a view in the southern Arabah

or clump of trees.[4] In my article, I also lent support to these targumic interpretations in their application to El-paran, translating the name as *meshar Paran*. The verse should thus be understood as saying, "as far as El-paran, which is by the wilderness of Paran." The most fitting candidate for "the plain of Paran, which is by the wilderness of Paran" is the Arabah between the Dead Sea and the Red Sea, which truly marks the edge of Mount Seir for its entire length.

For further study:

Elitzur, Yoel. "*Elon – Meshar – αὐλών*." *Eshel Beer-sheva* 8 (Yaakov Bentolila Jubilee Volume), Beer-sheva 2003, 1–11 [Hebrew].

Elitzur, Yoel. "Geographical Terminology in the Bible: *nhr, nḥl,* and *nḥl 'ytn*." *Iggud: Selected Essays in Jewish Studies* 1 (2008): 6–7 [Hebrew].

Frumkin A. and Yoel Elitzur. "The Rise and Fall of the Dead Sea." *Biblical Archaeology Review* 27:6 (2001): 42–50.

Gilead I. and R. Cohen. "Kadesh-barnea." In *The New Encyclopedia of Archaeological Excavations in the Holy Land* 3, 841–847. Jerusalem, 1993.

Hamilton, J. M. "Paran." In *The Anchor Bible Dictionary*, 5, 162.

Jaffee M. *Sifre Devarim* Translated to English, ḥttp://jewisḥstudies.wasḥington.edu/book/sifrc-dcvarim/.

Meshel, Z. "The Southern Border of Canaan and Judah—The Geographical Aspect." *Judea and Samaria Research Studies* 9, Ariel (2000): 27–37 [Hebrew].

Robinson E. and E. Smith. *Biblical Researches in Palestine, and in the Adjacent Regions, A Journal of Travels in the Year 1838*^{2}, I, Boston, 1858, 189–190.

4. Jerome, in his Vulgate – the most common Latin translation of the Tanakh – and in his commentaries, as well as Nahmanides in his commentary on the Torah, integrated these two interpretations in an unconvincing manner.

Parashat Shelaḥ

Emek or *Har*? The Dwelling Place of the Amalekites and Canaanites

The Valley or the Hill Country?

After the decree that our ancestors would not enter the land of Canaan, God adds an implicit warning: "Now the Amalekites and the Canaanites dwell in the valley (*emek*). Start out, then, tomorrow and march into the wilderness by way of the Sea of Suph" (Num. 14:25; see Rashi there). The following day, the people of Israel prepare to violate God's instructions: "We are prepared to go up to the place that the Lord has spoken of, for we were wrong" (14:40). Moses repeats God's warning, this time making it explicit:

> Do not go up, for the Lord is not in your midst... For the Amalekites and the Canaanites will be there to face you, and you will fall by the sword, inasmuch as you have turned from following the Lord and the Lord will not be with you. (14:42–43)

The nation does not heed the warning: "Yet defiantly they marched toward the crest of the hill country (*har*)... And the Amalekites and the Canaanites who dwelt in that hill country came down and dealt them a shattering blow at Hormah" (14:44–45).

The contradictory information in this passage is plain to see. Verses 40–45 stress that the Amalekites and the Canaanites dwell in the crest of the hill country. According to the verses, one must go up to reach this place and one must come down to return. But verse 25 states that they lived in the valley. How can this be?

An excellent "correction" to the verse is found in the Peshitta, the Syriac translation of the Bible used by many churches of Eastern Christianity (the prevailing view is that the Peshitta was the work of Jews). The Peshitta's translation of verse 25 states that the Amalekites and the Canaanites dwelt in the *tura* – meaning the hill country. However, the fact that no other known source features this word substitution found in the Peshitta indicates that this change was entirely arbitrary, an emendation to the word that the translator felt should really have appeared in the verse.

Ibn Ezra writes: "'Dwell in the valley' – to ambush you. And some say: Even though the Amalekites and the Canaanites dwell in the valley, start out by way of the Sea of Suph and do not be afraid." Here, Ibn Ezra presents two improbable solutions to the hill country/valley contradiction: First, while it is true that the Amalekites and the Canaanites dwell in the hill country of the land of Canaan above you, they are lying in ambush in the valley at the moment; and second, most of the Amalekites and the Canaanites indeed dwell in the hill country of the land of Canaan, but some of them dwell in the opposite direction as well, in the valley that awaits you when you make your way back. Do not fear them; since you are fulfilling God's decree they will not harm you.[1]

I found an unusual suggestion in Elliger and Rudolph's *Biblica Hebraica Stuttgartensia*, a critical edition of the Bible (fourth edition, Stuttgart 1990). They suggest, without citing support for their proposal, attaching the first half of verse 25 to verse 24 and changing the text and vocalization accordingly, to read:

> But My servant Caleb, because he was imbued with a different spirit and remained loyal to Me – him I will bring into the land that he entered, and his offspring shall hold it as a possession, and the Amalekites and the Canaanites will dwell in the valley.

1. Ḥizkuni presented similar suggestions.

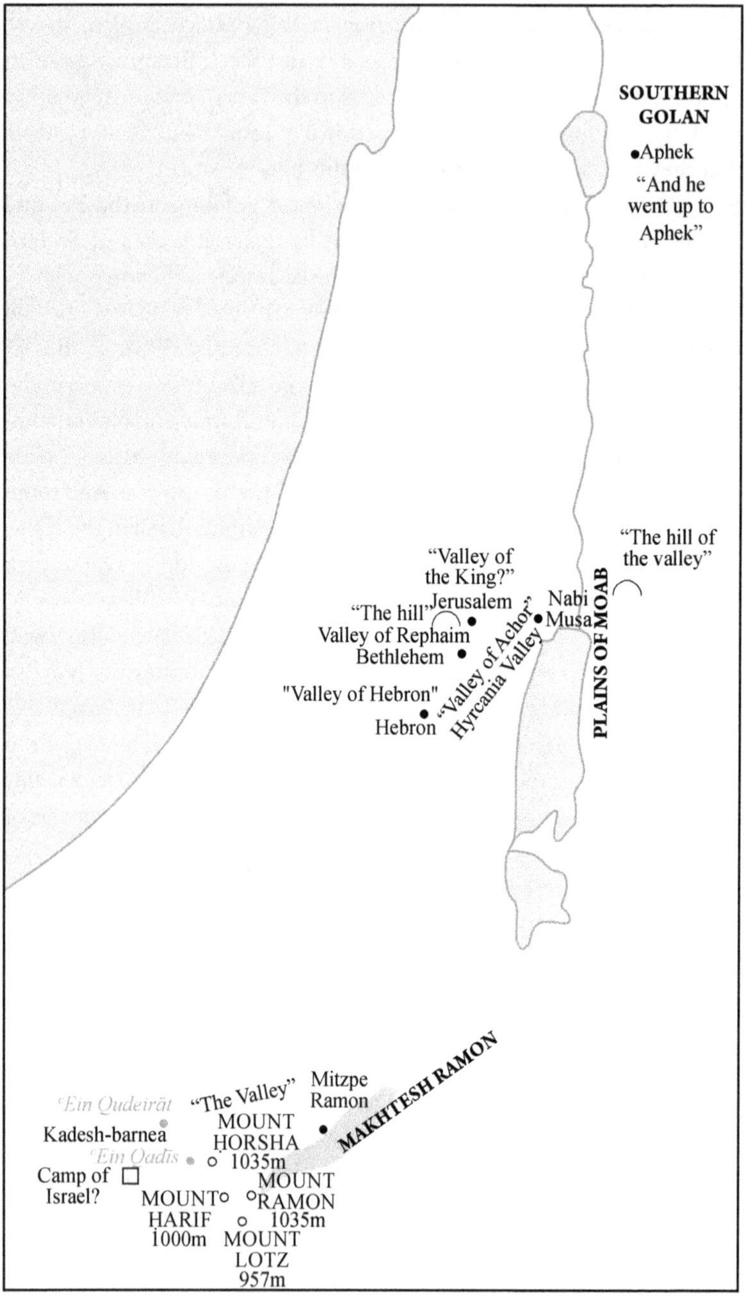
SOUTHERN GOLAN
Aphek
"And he went up to Aphek"
"The hill of the valley"
"Valley of the King?"
Jerusalem
"The hill"
Nabi Musa
Valley of Rephaim
Bethlehem
"Valley of Achor"
Hyrcania Valley
PLAINS OF MOAB
"Valley of Hebron"
Hebron
MAKHTESH RAMON
Mitzpe Ramon
"The Valley"
ʿEin Qudeirāt
Kadesh-barnea
MOUNT HORSHA 1035m
ʿEin Qadīs
Camp of Israel?
MOUNT RAMON 1035m
MOUNT HARIF 1000m
MOUNT LOTZ 957m

It seems that they based themselves on a few biblical passages that teach us that the Canaanites dwelt in the valley and the people of Israel were not able to dispossess them because they had iron chariots. But it is very strange that when God praises Caleb son of Jephunneh and promises him the inheritance of the land, He finds it necessary to mention in advance what the people will not succeed in doing in conquering the land. Thus, this "emendation" seems to be merely another testimony to the difficulty of our question here: Why does the verse say "valley" and not "hill country"?

Other Examples of "Going Up" to a Valley

Upon examination, it appears that our case is not the only one in the Tanakh involving "going up" to a valley. The Valley of Achor is mentioned twice in the Book of Joshua. The first time is in the incident of Achan: "And they brought them up to the Valley of Achor" (7:24). The second time is in the description of the northern border of the tribe of Judah:

> On the northern side, the boundary began at the tongue of the [Dead] Sea at the edge (mouth) of the Jordan. The boundary ascends to Beth-hoglah ... then the boundary ascends to the Stone

www.zerothkoff.com (Courtesy of Dr. Zev Rothkoff)

Hyrcania Plain between Jerusalem and the Dead Sea. It is most probably identical with Emek Achor, mentioned in Joshua 15 and 18.

> of Bohan son of Reuben. The boundary ascends from the Valley of Achor to Debir and turns north. (15:5–7)

It seems from the passage that the borderline ascends twice from the point where the Jordan meets the Dead Sea until the Valley of Achor, and it ascends an additional time after that point. It is accepted and reasonable to identify the Valley of Achor with the Nabi Musa region and the Hyrcania Valley – a plain much higher than the Jordan Valley but lower than the mountains to its west.

Another somewhat more complex example of this phenomenon is Aphek, mentioned twice in I Kings 20. After the Arameans lost to Israel in battle in the Samaria region, they interpreted their defeat in theological terms: "Their God is a God of the mountains; that is why they got the better of us. But if we fight them in the plain (*mishor*), we will surely get the better of them" (20:23). Thus, King Ben-hadad of Aram prepared for the next battle in Aphek: "And he went up to Aphek to fight" (20:26). A man of God approached the king of Israel and quoted the Arameans' declaration, with a minor change that is nonetheless extremely significant for our purposes:

> Then the man of God approached and spoke to the king of Israel, "Thus said the Lord: Because the Arameans have said, 'The Lord is a God of mountains, but He is not a God of valleys (*amakim*),' I will deliver that great host into your hands; and you shall know that I am the Lord." (20:28)

The king of Aram *goes up* to Aphek, yet the region surrounding Aphek is called a "plain" and a "valley."

As for the identification of Aphek, the site that features in I Kings 20 cannot be the same Aphek that is located at the headwaters of the Yarkon, and neither can it be the Aphek that the Asherites neglected to dispossess (Judges 1:31). It must be between Israel and Aram of Damascus, on a plain that one must ascend to reach. Thus, we may identify this Aphek with Afik/Fiq in the Golan Heights; the battle must have taken place in the southern part of the Golan Heights. Once again, we see that *emek* can refer to a high place.

Additional Examples of the Hilly *Emek* in the Tanakh

We know where the Valley of Rephaim is located from the description of the border between Judah and Benjamin. This border is described in detail twice in the Book of Joshua, once in the description of the northern borderline of Judah in chapter 15 and another time in the description of the southern border of Benjamin in chapter 18. Both of these parallel

www.zerothkoff.com (Courtesy of Dr. Zev Rothkoff)

The Wadi of Ben-hinnom with "the hill that flanks the Wadi of Ben-hinnom"

www.zerothkoff.com (Courtesy of Dr. Zev Rothkoff)

Hebron Road in modern-day Jerusalem, in the middle of the biblical Valley of Rephaim

passages use similar language to describe a certain point west of the Valley of Ben-hinnom: "The hill that flanks the Wadi of Hinnom on the west, at the northern end of the Valley of Rephaim" (15:8); "The hill that flanks the Wadi of Ben-hinnom at the northern end of the Valley of Rephaim" (18:16).

In light of the topography of Jerusalem, this area undoubtedly refers to the hill that is today an important part of the New City of Jerusalem, which includes the King David Hotel area, Heichal Shlomo, and the Yeshurun Central Synagogue. At the peak of this hill sits the Ratisbonne Monastery on Shmuel HaNagid Street. Based on the description in Joshua 15 and 18, scholars as early as the nineteenth century came to the convincing conclusion that the "Valley of Rephaim" is located in the area that today includes the Old Train Station, the Liberty Bell Park, and Emek Refaim Street. However, while this identification is true, it is not the whole truth. The verses do not say, "the hill north of the Valley of Rephaim," but "the hill… at the northern end of the Valley of Rephaim." In other words, the hill itself is part of the Valley of Rephaim, situated in the northern part of the valley.

Another biblical story – the story of the three warriors who brought water to David (II Sam. 23:13–17; I Chr. 11:15–19) – teaches us where the southern end of the Valley of Rephaim was located. There, we read that the Philistines were then encamped along the Valley of Rephaim, with their headquarters at Bethlehem. When David voiced his craving for the waters of Bethlehem, his birth city now captured by the enemy – "If only I could get a drink of water from the cistern which is by the gate of Bethlehem!" – three warriors took him seriously. They "got through" the Philistine camps, drew water from under the noses of the Philistine generals, crossed through the enemy camps once more in darkness and brought the water to David. From the story, it is clear (as Josephus indicates in *Antiquities* as well) that the Philistine camps were scattered throughout the Bethlehem area, while the commanders were situated within the city itself.

By integrating the information that we gleaned from Joshua and Samuel, we can infer that the entire area from Jaffa Street in Jerusalem to beyond Bethlehem is called "the Valley of Rephaim." This area is quite flat, but it contains several hills that are not particularly prominent compared to the area surrounding them, including the hill of Ramat Rachel, that of Tantur (by the entrance to the Tunnels Road leading out of the city to the south) and, of course, "the hill that flanks the Wadi of Hinnom on the west" in the northern part of this area. This "valley" does not fit the classic appearance of a valley that we have in our minds. It is not a low area between tall mountains, like the Jezreel Valley, the Beit She'an Valley, the Elah Valley, or the Ayalon Valley, which we recognize from other places in the Tanakh. The Valley of Rephaim is an elevated plateau, with an average height of about 2,500 feet above sea level, close to the watershed of the country in most of its area.

www.zerothkoff.com (Courtesy of Dr. Zev Rothkoff)

Modern-day Naḥal Refaim, located far west of the original Valley of Rephaim, which designated a hilly plain and not a deep gorge.

As a marginal point to this discussion, it must be said loudly and clearly that the modern-day Naḥal Refaim was conceived and born in error. First, there is no equivalence in Biblical Hebrew between "valley (*emek*)" and "stream (*naḥal*)." *Emek* always refers to a wide area and not to a narrow ravine. Geographically as well, "Naḥal Refaim" also skews far to the west of the biblical Valley of Rephaim.

Jeremiah refers to Jerusalem as "inhabitant of the valley": "I will deal with you, O inhabitant of the valley, O rock of the plain – declares the Lord – You who say, 'Who can come down against us? Who can get into our lairs?'" (Jer. 21:13). Several farfetched interpretations have been suggested in attempts to resolve this verse. Bearing in mind our conclusion that *emek* can refer to a relatively flat area within a hilly area, we can understand this verse as well. It seems that the valley in this verse does not refer to the Valley of Rephaim but to the plains north of the Old City of Jerusalem. Jerusalem borders on deep wadis on the east, south, and west. To the north, a plain stretches out, where Highway 1 and the northern neighborhoods of the city now lie. This area north of the ancient city was, on the one hand, "the weak part of Jerusalem – it could easily be captured from there" (Tosefta Sanhedrin 3:4), but on the other hand, it represented the potential for the expansion of the city. In Jeremiah's prophecy of comfort regarding the future expansion of the city, he says, "See, a time is coming – declares the Lord – when the city shall be rebuilt for the Lord from the Tower of Hananel to the Corner Gate… and the entire Valley of the Corpses and Ashes" (Jer. 31:37–39). These two passages from Jeremiah are apparently referring to the same hilly plain.

Two places in the Tanakh speak of the Valley of the King near Jerusalem. The first is Genesis 14:

> The king of Sodom came out to meet him in the Valley of Shaveh, which is the Valley of the King. And King Melchizedek of Salem brought out bread and wine; he was a priest of God Most High. (14:17–18)

The second is II Samuel 18:18: "Now Absalom, in his lifetime, had taken and reared up for himself a pillar which is in the Valley of the King… and it has been called Absalom's Monument to this day." In contrast to the folk tradition identifying Absalom's Monument in the Kidron channel (based on the incorrect assumption that *emek* refers to a wadi), it seems that it was actually located in one of the elevated plains surrounding Jerusalem – possibly to the north of the city.[2]

Now that we have established that *emek* can refer to an elevated plain, we can grapple with a famous problem. Everyone knows Rashi's comment, citing the Midrash:

2. For a more detailed explanation, see the chapter on *Parashat Beḥukkotai*.

> "So he sent him from the valley of Hebron": But is not Hebron on a mountain? As it is said, "They went up into the Negeb and came to Hebron" (Num. 13:22). Rather, [he sent him] from the deep counsel of the righteous man who is buried in Hebron (Abraham), to fulfill what was said to Abraham [at the Covenant] between the Pieces, "Your offspring shall be strangers" (Gen. 15:13). (Commentary on Gen. 37:14)

Nineteenth-century illustration of the so-called "Absalom's Monument" in the Kidron Valley. The mistaken identification of Absalom's Monument here is based, among other things, on the incorrect interpretation of the Hebrew word *emek*.

The problem here is rooted in *peshat* – we cannot understand the simple reading of the text – but the answer given here is super-*derash*. There must be a simple, *peshat* solution as well. In light of all we have seen, we can understand the plain meaning of the verse perfectly, and it is as follows: The Hebron area, which is generally quite flat – including Elonei Mamre, the dwelling place of the Patriarchs from the time of Abraham – is called by the Torah "the Valley of Hebron." This "Valley of Hebron," somewhat paradoxically, is one of the highest regions in the Land of Israel, 3,100–3,300 feet above sea level – but it is still called an *emek*.

www.zerothkoff.com (Courtesy of Dr. Zev Rothkoff)

The hilly *emek* of the Amalekites and the Canaanites north and northwest of Mitzpe Ramon

Returning to Our Parasha

The region that was the setting for both the incident of the spies and that of the *maapilim* (those who marched defiantly to the land before being defeated at Hormah) was apparently located at the foot of the massif west of Makhtesh Ramon, namely, the area of Mount Horsha, Mount Harif, and Mount Lotz. In this region, whose altitude is about 1,300–1,600 feet above sea level, the huge, dry wilderness of Paran meets the mountains, whose altitude is about 3,300 feet above sea level. The area of these high mountains, albeit quite arid, has a climate that can support life, and therefore it is included in the borders of the land of Canaan. The camp of the people of Israel was located below the mountains, south of Kadesh-barnea, outside the borders of the land;

on the other hand, its region bore the same name – the wilderness of Kadesh.[3] Above these mountains, north and northwest of the cliff of the *makhtesh*, in the environs of Mishor HaRuhot near the Bahad 1 IDF Officers' School and the road that runs from there to the peak of Mount Harif, there are areas that are quite flat – at an altitude of about 3,000 feet above sea level. In the terminology of Biblical Hebrew, it can justifiably be called an *emek*, similar to "the Valley of Hebron" discussed above. In order to reach this *emek*, one must ascend a steep rise of about 1,600 feet.

A Hill Within the Valley

We have seen that there is a hill at the edge of "the Valley of Rephaim." The high *emek* in the southern part of the land of Canaan contained a hill as well, one that dominates the landscape of the edge of the wilderness of Paran – where the people of Israel were encamped – from above: "Yet defiantly they marched toward the crest of the hill... And the Amalekites and the Canaanites who dwelt in that hill came down" (Num. 14:44–45). The best candidate for identification with this peak may be the tall Mount Harif overlooking the desert plains south of Kadesh. There are apparently two additional examples in the Tanakh of a hill within a valley:

- "The hill of the valley (*har ha-emek*)" (Josh. 13:19) in the territory of Reuben. This expression, which seems self-contradictory, is now easily understandable: it refers to a certain prominent hill recognizable within a valley. The valley in the territory of Reuben appears to be the southern part of the eastern Jordan Rift Valley (in 13:27 an *emek* is mentioned in the territory of Gad, which refers to the remainder of the eastern Jordan Rift Valley – until the Sea of Galilee). Thus, *har ha-emek* represents the parallel opposite of *hor ha-har* – a prominent hill within a hill country.
- "The hill of Perazim" in the Book of Isaiah – "For the Lord will arise as on the hill of Perazim, He will rouse Himself as in the valley of Gibeon" (28:21). This verse in Isaiah alludes to David's first

3. See the chapter on *Parashat Behaalotekha.*

two victories over the Philistines (II Sam. 5:17–25; I Chr. 14:8–16). The war took place in Baal-perazim in the Valley of Rephaim. Isaiah calls that place "the hill of Perazim," indicating that this is another example of a hill within the Valley of Rephaim.[4]

The Takeaway Lesson

We must learn from this discussion to be cautious when dealing with etymology. From a linguistic perspective, it is clear that the word *emek* is derived from the Semitic root ᶜ-M-Q, meaning "deep" or "deepening." Despite this, a deep wadi is never called an *emek* in the Tanakh, whereas an elevated plain is called an *emek* on multiple occasions. We may speculate that the term was originally used solely to describe low valleys, and only afterward its usage expanded to include elevated plains. In any case, the meaning of the word and its linguistic connections should not get in the way of the task that should always come first: scouring the biblical contexts

www.zerothkoff.com (Courtesy of Dr. Zev Rothkoff)

The hilly *emek* north and northwest of Mitzpe Ramon. Note the modest vegetation in the bed of the wadi, attesting to the region's ability to sustain life and agriculture.

4. This is alluded to in the passage in I Chronicles: "They *ascended* to Baal-perazim" (14:11).

in which the word appears in order to learn how to interpret it properly. A similar example can be seen in the case of the word *arava,* whose literal meaning does not seem to fit well with the strip of land known in the Tanakh as the Arabah.[5] Likewise, the Mizpah (literally, "lookout") does not need to be located in the highest site with the greatest view of the land, and the Sea of Suph (literally, "reeds") is, in all likelihood, not located in a place where reeds grow.[6] There is no substitute for simply studying each verse and each term used in the Tanakh within its context.

The basic principle of this discussion and the analysis of some of the sources cited here were based on the unwritten teachings of my father *z"l.*

For further study:

Elitzur, Yoel. *Ancient Place Names in the Holy Land.* Jerusalem-Winona Lake, 2004, 124–125.

Elitzur, Yoel. "'So He Sent Him Out to the Vale of Hebron.' On the Hilly *'Emeq* in the Hebrew Bible." *Beit Mikra* 54 (2009): 5–20 [Hebrew].

5. See the chapter on the First Day of Sukkot.
6. See the chapter on the Seventh Day of Pesaḥ.

Parashat Koraḥ

Guarding the Sanctuary and the Gates of the Courtyard

The Commandment to Guard the Temple

After the ground opened up and swallowed Koraḥ and his company, and the two hundred fifty incense-offerers died fiery deaths, after the complaints, the plague, and the flowering of Aaron's staff came the additional complaint of "Lo, we perish! We are lost, all of us lost! Everyone who so much as ventures near the Lord's Tabernacle must die. Alas, we are doomed to perish!" (Num. 17:27–28). Immediately thereafter, Aaron and his sons, and with them the tribe of Levi, are commanded to guard the Tent of Meeting and the altar, to prevent the encroachment of "outsiders":

> The Lord said to Aaron: You and your sons and the ancestral house under your charge shall bear any guilt connected with the sanctuary; you and your sons alone shall bear any guilt connected with your priesthood. You shall also associate with yourself your kinsmen the tribe of Levi, your ancestral tribe, to be attached to you and to minister to you, while you and your sons under your charge are before the Tent of the Pact. They shall discharge their

> duties to you and to the Tent as a whole, but they must not have any contact with the furnishings of the Shrine or with the altar, lest both they and you die. They shall be attached to you and discharge the duties of the Tent of Meeting, all the service of the Tent; but no outsider shall intrude upon you as you discharge the duties connected with the Shrine and the altar, that wrath may not again strike the Israelites. I hereby take your fellow Levites from among the Israelites; they are assigned to you in dedication to the Lord, to do the work of the Tent of Meeting; while you and your sons shall be careful to perform your priestly duties in everything pertaining to the altar and to what is behind the curtain. I make your priesthood a service of dedication; any outsider who encroaches shall be put to death. (18:1–7)

The commandment to guard the sanctuary applies in future generations as well, as we read in *Sifrei*:

> "To be attached to you and to minister to you," in their service, and appoint from among them treasurers and supervisors…"while you and your sons under your charge are before the Tent of the Pact," the priests on the inside and the Levites on the outside. (*Parashat Koraḥ* 116)

We read further in the Mishna (Middot 1:5) and in the parallel *baraita* (Tamid 26b): "The priests guard above and the Levites below." Regarding the number of watches and the places where they were stationed, the Mishna states:

> In three places priests guard in the Temple – in the Chamber of Abtinas, in the Flash Chamber, and in the Fire Chamber. The Levites guard in twenty-one places – five at the five gates of the Temple Mount, four at its four corners on the inside, five at the five gates of the Courtyard. Four at its four corners on the outside, one at the Offering Chamber, one at the Chamber of the Veil and one behind the place of the mercy seat. (Middot 1:1; and in brief in Tamid 1:1)

The source for the three guarding places for the priests is revealed in the Talmud's interpretation of the verse, "Those who were to camp before the Tabernacle, in front… were Moses and Aaron and his sons, attending to the duties of the sanctuary, as a duty on behalf of the Israelites" (Num. 3:38). The verse is used as a source for the three guards in two ways: First, just as Moses was in one place by himself, so Aaron and his sons were each in one place by themselves; and second, *Shomerim* (attending to) – one, *mishmeret* (duties) – two and *lemishmeret* (as a duty) – three (Tamid 26a). The twenty-one watches of the Levites were derived from I Chronicles 26:17–18 (27a).

Maimonides recorded two surprising and innovative halakhot regarding this matter. In both cases he based himself on what he called *Mekhilta,* which was apparently his name for the Midrash Halakha that we call *Sifrei Zuta.* These two halakhic innovations were generally accepted by the authorities who came after Maimonides, but both halakhot are somewhat questionable.

- Maimonides enumerated "guarding the sanctuary" as a positive commandment (*Sefer HaMitzvot,* PC 22), but he added a negative commandment (NC 67) as well – the prohibition of neglecting to guard the sanctuary. For the source of this negative commandment, Maimonides based himself on the *Mekhilta* (our *Sifrei Zuta*). However, in the text of *Sifrei Zuta* that we possess, the formulation is different from the version cited by Maimonides. Our version reads: "'But no outsider shall intrude upon you' – this refers to a negative commandment. From where [do we learn that it includes] a positive commandment? Say, [from the verse,] 'As you discharge the duties connected with the Shrine.'" According to this version, the negative commandment is a prohibition imposed upon outsiders from entering to serve in the sanctuary (Negative Commandment 74 in Maimonides' enumeration), and the Midrash adds the novel element of a positive commandment imposed on the priests to guard the sanctuary, blocking outsiders from entering. In this version, there would be no prohibition involved for neglecting to guard the sanctuary. The Midrash Halakha as presented by Maimonides is quite problematic. Maimonides cites:

"Discharge (*veshameru*) the duties of the Tent of Meeting" – this refers to a positive commandment. From where [do we learn that it includes] a negative commandment? We learn this [from the verse], "As you discharge (*ushmartem*) the duties connected with the Shrine...."

The notion that *ushmartem* designates a negative command is certainly based on the principle that "Every instance of *hishamer* ('take care'), *pen* ('so that you do not') and *al* ('do not') refers to a negative commandment." However, although our verse does contain language related to *hishamer*, it is in the context of a positive command. Thus, it should be considered a positive command. Indeed, the Talmud states on three occasions that even *hishamer* refers to a positive commandment if the word is used in a context that suggests this (Eiruvin 96a and parallels; see *Minḥat Ḥinukh* 391). In any case, one wonders why *ushmartem* is at all different from *veshameru*, such that one refers to a negative commandment and the other refers to a positive commandment. (It may be that the teaching is based on the very repetition of this verb).

- Regarding the reason for the commandment, Maimonides cites the *Mekhilta* (our *Sifrei Zuta*): "A palace without guards cannot compare to a palace with guards," and emphasizes several times:

> There is a positive commandment to guard the sanctuary. [This commandment] applies even though there is no fear of enemies or thieves, for guarding [the sanctuary] is an expression of respect for it. A palace without guards cannot compare to a palace with guards. (*Beit Habechira* 8:1 and similarly in *Sefer HaMitzvot* and the Commentary on the Mishna)

There is a fundamental problem here. The reason for the commandment, as presented by Maimonides, explicitly contradicts what is written in the Torah. Quite surprisingly, no one commented on this point before the Vilna *Gaon*. The Vilna *Gaon*, in his commentary on Mishna Tamid, disagrees with Maimonides' opinion without mentioning his name, writing simply: "It is written explicitly in *Seder [Parashat] Koraḥ* that this guarding is so that no outsider will enter it." According to this approach, the statement of the Midrash Halakha that "a palace without guards cannot compare to a palace with guards" can simply be a saying that complements the law and not the primary reason for it.

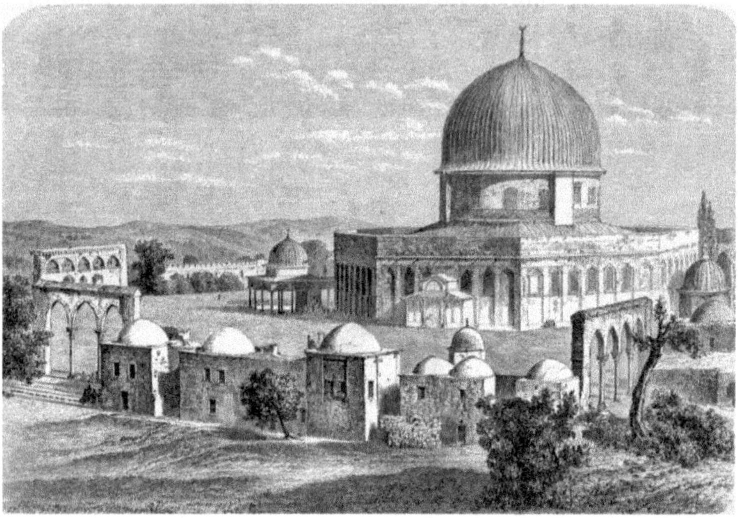

(L. C. Lortet, 1884)

The higher platform of the Dome of the Rock in the middle of the Temple Mount, as seen from the northwest. The platform includes the whole space of the Courtyard of the Temple. The lower dome to the left of the Dome of the Rock is probably situated where the altar once stood.

It may be that the dispute over the reason for guarding the sanctuary hinges on a different dispute – whether the commandment to guard the sanctuary applies during both day and night.[1] If the reason for guarding the sanctuary is to prevent outsiders from entering, then the optimal time for fulfilling the commandment is during the day, when the gates

1. According to Maimonides and Rabbeinu Shemaya (a prominent disciple of Rashi), it applies only at night. According to the anonymous commentator on Tamid, the commentary attributed to Ra'avad and Rosh, it applies during both day and night. Later authors continued this dispute more forcefully. Rabbi Yissachar Ber of Eilenburg, in his work *Be'er Sheva*, and Rabbi Yehuda Rosanes, author of *Mishneh Lamelekh*, maintained that the opinion that guarding the sanctuary applies during both day and night is impossible. On the other hand, Rabbi Yosef Babad, author of *Minḥat Ḥinukh*, claimed just the opposite – that the other opinion "requires examination."

are open and people are entering the courtyard. However, if the whole reason for guarding the sanctuary is to show respect and highlight the site's importance, then it may be that the guarding is only required at night. As Rabbi Yisrael Lipschitz writes in *Tiferet Yisrael* at the beginning of Tamid, "During the day there is no need to guard as a sign of respect, as even without this, by virtue of the priests walking back and forth as they perform their service, all say 'Glory!' [see Psalms 29:9]."

The Gates of the Courtyard

The Mishna teaches that the Levites guard in twenty-one places, five of which are in the five gates of the Temple Mount and five of which are in the five gates of the Courtyard. The five gates of the Temple Mount mentioned here fit with the five gates of the Temple Mount enumerated in the continuation of the chapter in Middot:

> There were five gates to the Temple Mount: the two Gates of Huldah on the south, which were used both for entrance and exit; the Gate of Kiponus on the west, which was used both for entrance and exit; the Gate of Taddi on the north, which was not used [by the public] at all; and the eastern gate, over which was a drawing of the palace of Susa, and through which the high priest who burned the red heifer and all who assisted with it used to go forth to the Mount of Olives. (1:3)

In contrast, the number of gates of the Courtyard mentioned in our mishna does not fit with the number mentioned in the continuation of the chapter:

> There were seven gates in the Courtyard: three in the north and three in the south and one in the east. In the south there was first the Gate of Kindling, then the Gate of Offering [alternately: the Gate of the Firstborn[2]], then the Water Gate. In the east there

2. "The Gate of Offering" appears in the most reliable manuscripts of the Mishna, while "the Gate of the Firstborn" appears in the printed editions. The former is quite difficult since the Gate of Offering appears in the northern wall as well. The latter also

> was the Gate of Nikanor, which had two rooms attached, one on its right and one on its left – one the room of Phineas the dresser and one the room of the griddle-cake makers.
>
> On the north was the Gate of the Flash, which was shaped like a veranda. It had an upper chamber built on it, and the priests used to guard above and the Levites below, and it had a door opening into the *ḥeil*. Next to it was the Gate of Offering and next to that the Fire Chamber.

The Talmud notes this seeming contradiction and cites two solutions. According to Abaye, there were actually seven gates, but watches only took place at five of these. (Perhaps the two middle gates on the south and the north did not require guarding, since there were already guards posted to the right and to the left of them.) But Rava maintains that the contradiction between the mishnas reflects a dispute over the historical reality:

> Rava said: There is a difference of *Tanna'im* on this point, as it has been taught: There must not be less than thirteen treasurers [attached to the Courtyard] and seven supervisors. R. Natan said: "There must be not less than thirteen treasurers corresponding to the thirteen gates." Subtract five for the Temple Mount, and eight are left for the Courtyard. We see therefore that there is a *Tanna* who says there were eight, and one who says there were seven, and one who says there were five.[3] (Tamid 27a)

---

seems more reasonable because it fits with the four gates of Abba Yose b. Ḥanan (see below). However, as the credible manuscripts agree on "Offering," it would seem that in this case *lectio difficilior potior* – the more difficult reading is the stronger. It may be that there were two gates devoted to offerings; after all, this was the main activity performed in the Temple.

3. According to Rabbi Betzalel Ashkenazi's version in his *Shita Mekubetzet* here (his editions are generally based on manuscripts), as well as MS Firenze and MS Vatican 120–121, the words "and one who says there were seven" should be deleted.

Indeed, the number of gates of the Courtyard is disputed explicitly in the Mishna. Aside from the seven gates mentioned in the above mishna, there is another attestation of Abba Yose b. Ḥanan at the end of Middot 2, as well as that of an unnamed *Tanna* in Shekalim 6, enumerating thirteen gates in the Courtyard:

> And thirteen prostrations were made there. Abba Yose b. Ḥanan says: They were made facing thirteen gates. On the south adjoining the west there were the Upper Gate, the Gate of Kindling, the Gate of the Firstborn, and the Water Gate. Why was it called the Water Gate? Because they brought in through it the pitcher of water for libation on the festival. R. Eliezer b. Yaakov says: In it the water welled up, and in the time to come they will issue from under the threshold of the Temple. Corresponding to them in the north adjoining the west were the Gate of Jeconiah, the Gate of the Offering, the Women's Gate, the Gate of Song. Why was it called the Gate of Jeconiah? Because Jeconiah went forth into captivity through it. On the east was the Gate of Nikanor; it had two wickets, one on its right and one on its left. There were further two gates in the west that had no special name.

Rava in our discussion does not cite this position, and according to the manuscripts, neither does he cite the position in chapter 1 that there were seven gates; it may be that he simply wanted to focus on novel ideas. However, Maimonides, in his commentary on Middot 1:1, cites Rava somewhat differently:

> And his statement here is that "five gates of the Courtyard" is according to the position of one particular *Tanna*, as among the *Tanna'im* there is one who said that there were five gates to the Courtyard, and it is he who is speaking here. Among them there is also one who said [there were] seven [gates] – this is the view of the sages – and among them there is one who said [there were] thirteen [gates], as we explained in the sixth [chapter] of Shekalim and as will be explained in the second [chapter] of this tractate.

Apparently, Maimonides' version of the Gemara was different from ours – and simpler. According to him, there is no position maintaining that there were eight gates.

Another different testimony regarding this matter can be found in the writings of Josephus. Josephus' description of the Courtyard and, east of the Courtyard, the Women's Court, is similar to the description in Middot 2. However, according to him, there were nine gates to the Courtyard and another three gates to the Women's Court, totaling twelve gates:

> Of these there were eight on the north and south, four on either side, and two on the east, necessarily; since in this quarter a special place of worship was walled off for the women rendering a second gate requisite; this approach opened opposite to the first. On the other sides there was one gate on the south and one on the north giving access to the women's court... The west end of the building had no gate, the wall there being unbroken... Of the gates, nine were completely overlaid with gold and silver, as were also their door-posts and lintels; but one, that outside the sanctuary, was of Corinthian bronze,[4] and far exceeded in value those plated with silver and set in gold. (*War of the Jews* V 5:2–3)

Contradictory Firsthand Accounts

Let us make some sense of the various accounts, which total between three and five different traditions:

- Unnamed *Tanna* (Mishna Middot 1:4–5): Seven gates total – three in the north (Gate of the Flash, Gate of Offering, Fire Chamber), three in the south (Gate of Kindling, Gate of Offering [or Gate of the Firstborn], Water Gate), and one in the east (Gate of Nikanor)

4. The magnificent gate made from "Corinthian bronze" was certainly the Gate of Nikanor in the eastern part of the Courtyard "because the copper of them gleamed [like gold]" (Middot 2:3).

- Abba Yose b. Ḥanan (Mishna Middot 2) and unnamed *Tanna* (Shekalim 6): Thirteen gates total – four in the north (Gate of Jeconiah, Gate of Offering, Women's Gate, Gate of Song), four in the south (Upper Gate, Gate of Kindling, Gate of the Firstborn, Water Gate), three in the east (Gate of Nikanor and two wickets attached on its right and left), and two unnamed gates in the west
- Josephus (*War of the Jews*): Nine gates total – four in the north, four in the south, and one in the east (Gate of Nikanor)
- First mishna in Tamid and first mishna in Middot (according to Rava and against Abaye): Five gates total
- R. Natan (according to the Talmud's deduction within Rava's opinion, and according to our edition but not that of Maimonides): Eight gates total

The two latter positions are not agreed upon, and they are possibly even problematic. In order to insist that among the *Tanna'im,* there is a position maintaining that there were only five gates altogether, one must understand that the unattributed mishna in Middot 1 is presenting two contradictory positions in two near-consecutive mishnas in the same chapter – without indicating the existence of any dispute and while leaving both positions unattributed.

The final position attributes an independent tradition specifically to R. Natan, one of the later *Tanna'im.* Not only does this position go against every position on the issue that preceded it, but R. Natan expresses the position not as a tradition in its own right, but incidentally, as an explanation of an entirely different matter. The very essence of this position is based on a sophisticated exegesis that R. Natan never actually stated explicitly. If we take R. Natan's position at face value, as Maimonides does, it turns out that R. Natan is simply presenting a tangential statement based on the second position in our above list – which is found twice in the Mishna.

Thus, in the following discussion I will limit my focus to the first three positions listed above. What is the common thread among the three?

- All three positions are stated explicitly. None of these positions is a sophisticated deduction from a different statement.

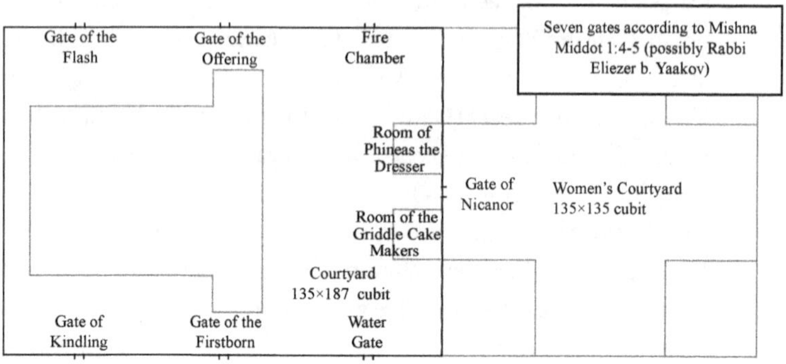
Seven gates according to Mishna Middot 1:4-5 (possibly Rabbi Eliezer b. Yaakov)
Gate of the Flash
Gate of the Offering
Fire Chamber
Room of Phineas the Dresser
Room of the Griddle Cake Makers
Courtyard 135×187 cubit
Gate of Nicanor
Women's Courtyard 135×135 cubit
Gate of Kindling
Gate of the Firstborn
Water Gate

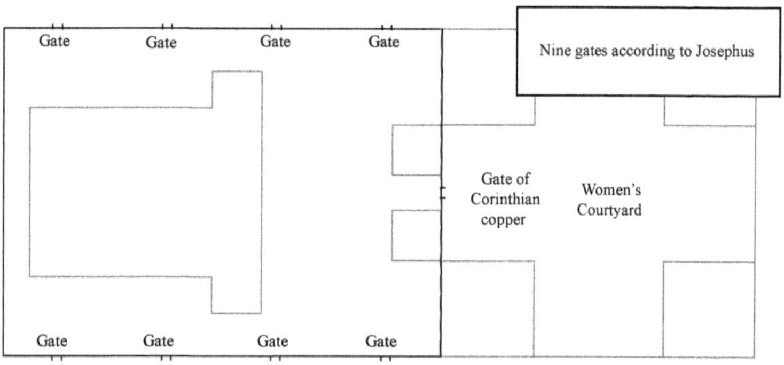
Nine gates according to Josephus
Gate
Gate
Gate
Gate
Gate of Corinthian copper
Women's Courtyard
Gate
Gate
Gate
Gate

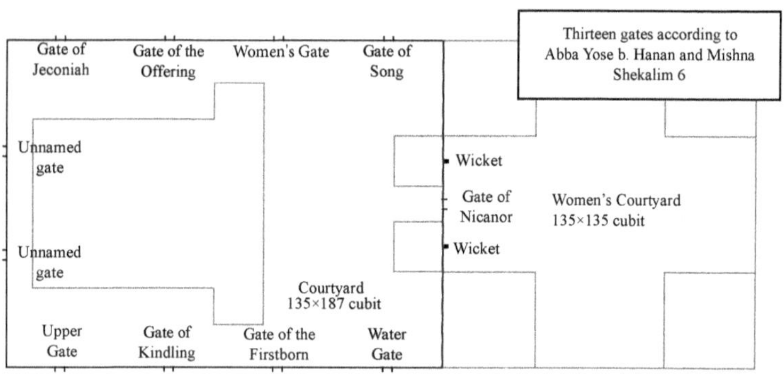
Thirteen gates according to Abba Yose b. Hanan and Mishna Shekalim 6
Gate of Jeconiah
Gate of the Offering
Women's Gate
Gate of Song
Unnamed gate
Wicket
Gate of Nicanor
Women's Courtyard 135×135 cubit
Unnamed gate
Wicket
Courtyard 135×187 cubit
Upper Gate
Gate of Kindling
Gate of the Firstborn
Water Gate

- All three represent firsthand accounts from people who saw the intact Temple with their own eyes. The first position, an unattributed mishna in Middot, can be ascribed to R. Eliezer b. Yaakov (I), who lived during the Second Temple period. The Gemara (Yoma 16a) makes this deduction from the recurring line, "Eliezer b. Yaakov said: I forget what it was used for" (Middot 2:5; 5:4). In addition, R. Eliezer b. Yaakov said, "Once they found my mother's brother asleep, and they burned his clothes" (1:2). Scholars of the language of the Mishna even claimed that the language in Tamid and Middot is not entirely identical to the standard language of the Mishna; there are signs that the language used in these two tractates is early in comparison.

  The second position is attributed to Abba Yose b. Ḥanan, a sage whose name is mentioned several times in rabbinic literature. On one of these occasions, a popular song was quoted in his name: "Woe is me because of the house of Boethus… Woe is me because of the house of Kathros… Woe is me because of the house of Ishmael son of Phabi" (Pesaḥim 57a) – a charming personal testimony from a time when the Temple still stood.

  The third position is that of Josephus Flavius, a native Jerusalemite. According to his own testimony about himself, he was a Pharisee priest from the family of Yehoyariv (*The Life of Flavius Josephus* 1:12). Josephus describes numerous incidents that occurred in Jerusalem and in the Temple during the years prior to its destruction; his is undoubtedly an eyewitness account.

- All three positions include details that could only have been provided by someone who knew the place personally. The divisions of the gates, their dimensions, and their names, as well as Josephus' detailed description of the copper gate – all of these are the typical elements of a primary source.

How can it be that three eyewitnesses who lived during the same time period – who saw the same Temple with their own eyes – gave

The Temple Mount from the east. In front of the golden Dome of the Rock, four arches can be seen above a staircase. This is the assumed location of the Gate of Nicanor and the fifteen stairs between the Courtyard and the Women's Court.

such different detailed testimonies? Here we must emphasize that none of the three testimonies includes any kind of conceptual statement or attempt to connect these details to a particular biblical verse; nor is any of the testimonies describing a miraculous occurrence. Each testimony is a technical account with no discernible agenda.

Before we try to answer this question, I would like to present a prefatory comment. As of today, there is no archaeological evidence in our possession supporting any side in this discussion. By contrast, the topic of the gates to the Temple Mount can be studied with an eye to the well-known gates at the walls of the Temple Mount compound,[5] but there are no clear remnants of the walls of the Temple courtyards and their gates. Perhaps when the legal status of the Temple Mount changes

5. There are two ancient gates at the southern wall of the Mount that are parallel to the Huldah Gates mentioned in the Mishna; in the west and in the north there is no fitting parallel, and in the east there is a questionable parallel. There is a general problem that the entire compound – according to the Mishna and Josephus – should be square, whereas today it is rectangular. All these topics are beyond the scope of the current discussion.

for the better, allowing for excavations beyond those authorized by the Jerusalem Islamic Waqf, we will be able to determine the answer to this question as well, along with several other important questions surrounding the Temple and the Temple Mount. In the present state of things, we are limited to the sources to which we have access.

Is There a Solution?

I will now examine each of the three major traditions regarding the number of gates in the Courtyard, and attempt, to the best of my ability, to suggest a few partial solutions to the problem before us.

We will begin with the tradition of Abba Yose b. Ḥanan – thirteen gates. The number thirteen was first presented as one of a list of three series consisting of thirteen elements. Thus we read in Shekalim 6 of thirteen chests, thirteen tables, and thirteen prostrations in the Temple. It is interesting to note that this mishna, which is clearly highlighting groups of thirteen, does not explicitly enumerate thirteen gates, but only explains that the thirteen prostrations were "made facing thirteen gates." In Middot 2, the thirteen prostrations are mentioned twice, each time with a different explanation. First we read:

> Within it was the *soreg* [a kind of lattice work], ten handbreadths high. There were thirteen breaches in it; these had been originally made by the kings of Greece, and when they repaired them they enacted that thirteen prostrations should be made facing them. (2:3)

Then, at the end of the chapter, in a section that appears to be a kind of appendix, we read: "The whole of the Courtyard was a hundred eighty-seven cubits in length by a hundred thirty-five in breadth, and thirteen prostrations were made there. Abba Yose b. Ḥanan says: They were made facing thirteen gates…" (2:6). The prostrations seem to have taken place on the Temple Mount, outside the *soreg* encompassing the *ḥeil*, which surrounded the Courtyard and the Women's Court, indicating that the source of the number thirteen in this context was the prostrations, while the two historical explanations served to explain the source. Thus, it may be that some of the thirteen gates were not exactly attested to firsthand. The main contingent of the group of thirteen gates certainly did exist: They were the

(L. C. Lortet, 1884)

A closer view of the staircase and the four arches.

Gate of Nikanor in the east, the four in the north, and the four in the south. These nine gates were enumerated by name and in order, and it is clear that the Mishna's description of these gates constitutes real testimony and not merely exegetical speculation. These nine also fit perfectly with the testimony of Josephus.

What about the remaining four gates? These were the two wickets to the right and to the left of the Gate of Nikanor and two in the west that "had no special name." Regarding the wickets attached to the Gate of Nikanor, it should be noted that the *Tanna* in Middot 1 who enumerated seven gates felt the need to add a seemingly unnecessary detail unconnected to the number of gates in the Courtyard: "In the east there was the Gate of Nikanor, which had two rooms attached, one on its right and one on its left – one the room of Phineas the dresser and one the room of the griddle-cake makers." What was the purpose of this comment? Perhaps this is an allusion – embedded by the redactor of the tractate – to the dispute with Abba Yose b. Ḥanan. This *Tanna* (apparently R. Eliezer b. Yaakov) maintains that there were only two rooms here, recalling the precise name and function of each of them. It is difficult to imagine that Abba Yose b. Ḥanan would dispute this testimony, nor have we heard anything to that effect.

On the other hand, it is unsurprising that a dispute would arise in such a case regarding the existence of open doorways from these rooms to the rest of the Courtyard. Wickets are small openings that are not meant for the general public; it would have been difficult for the average person to know if such doorways – only used by a select few professionals – existed at all. It may even be that all agree that there were small wickets here, but the proponent of the "seven gates" position and Josephus felt that these were not significant enough to enumerate. The Mishna stresses: "All the doorways (and the gates) in the Temple were twenty cubits high and ten cubits broad"[6] (Middot 2:3). Only Abba Yose b. Ḥanan, in his position explaining the connection between the thirteen prostrations and the thirteen gates, must either mention the existence of the two wickets here, or else enumerate the small wickets as gates. The two unnamed gates on the west must be explained in a similar manner.

What is left for us now is to address the question of the north and the south. In the south, there is only a small difference between the positions. Both the "seven gates" *Tanna* and the "thirteen gates" *Tanna* agree, more or less, on three consecutive gates in the south (apparently listed from west to east) – the Gate of Kindling, the Gate of the Firstborn (or the Gate of the Offering; the firstborn is one of the most common offerings brought by individuals), and the Water Gate – but the full list adds another gate on the western end – the Upper Gate. The name "Upper Gate" alludes to where it is situated topographically (it is clear from Middot 2–3 that the terrain rises gradually from east to west). This, along with this gate's lack of a defined function, may allude to the possibility that this gate was less important than the others (despite its appearance in Josephus' account). In addition, the Upper Gate was located in the area of the Chamber of Hewn Stones (Middot 5:4, according to the Mishna's version, which is primary), which had one opening on holy ground and one opening on non-holy ground (Yoma 25a). It may be, then, that the gate was situated inside the chamber, and thus the "seven gates" *Tanna* did not enumerate it.

The differences are starker in the north. Only one name appears on both lists: the Gate of Offering. The short list includes: the Gate of the Flash, the Gate of Offering, and the Fire Chamber. The long list includes: the Gate of Jeconiah, the Gate of Offering, the Women's Gate, and the Gate of Song. The necessary conclusion is that many of the gates had multiple names. It

6. Josephus' measurements are larger than those of the Mishna.

is not easy to interpret these names; the commentators struggled to do so. The Mishna itself interprets the Gate of Jeconiah: "Because Jeconiah went forth into captivity through it." In other words, it is a historical name for an early one-time incident from an ancient reality that has since been destroyed and rebuilt. It is only logical, then, that this gate would have a new name that is more appropriate for the reality of the Second Temple period.

The name "Gate of the Flash" is not easy to understand, and it is unclear what the Women's Gate was, considering that women would not usually enter the Courtyard.[7] Regarding the question of the coexistence of two authentic traditions, one of three gates and another of four gates, it may be that here too the answer lies in the existence of a wicket. Middot 1:7 reads:

> The Fire Chamber had two gates, one opening onto the *ḥeil* and one onto the Courtyard. R. Yehuda says: The one that opened onto the Courtyard had a small wicket through which they went in to search the Courtyard.

The commentators generally explained that this wicket was a small opening in the door of the large gate. However, if we explain that it refers to a small wicket *near* the large gate, it may be that the longer list chose to enumerate it while the shorter list chose to exclude it.

For further study:

Babad, Y. *Minḥat Ḥinukh* (commentary on *Sefer HaḤinukh*). Mitzva 388.

Epstein, J. N. *Introduction to Tannaitic Literature*. Jerusalem and Tel-Aviv, 1957, 15–58 [Hebrew].

Geva, H. "Jerusalem: The Temple Mount and its Environs." In *The New Encyclopedia of Archaeological Excavations in the Holy Land* 2, 736–744,1993.

Hyman, A. "R. Eliezer ben Ya'akov I" and "Abba Yose ben Ḥanan." *Toledot Tanna'im VaAmora'im*, 181, 726 [Hebrew].

7. *Tosefot Yom Tov* explained, in the name of Ra'avya, that women would stand there during the *semicha* and slaughtering of their offering.

Parashat Ḥukkat

Wadi Zered

Wadi Zered on Maps and in Encyclopedias

On modern maps, Wadi Zered can be found southeast of the Dead Sea. This wadi, known in Arabic as Wadi al-Ḥasa or al-Aḥsa,[1] is over fifty miles long, thirty miles of which maintain a constant flow of water west-northwest. The wadi discharges near eṣ-Ṣafi (which most accept as the identification for the biblical Zoar) into the salt marshes south of the Dead Sea.[2] This wadi is one of the four major east-west streams in Transjordan: Yarmouk, Jabbok, Arnon, and Zered. Wadi Zered is the border between the mountains of Edom to its south and the mountains of Moab to its north. The mountainous region south of the wadi contains the notable towns of Ṭafileh and Buṣeira (identified with Bozrah, a famous Edomite city). The mountainous region north of the wadi contains the notable city of al-Karak (identified with the biblical Kir of Moab) and the town of Rabba (Rabbath Moab).

This identification of Wadi Zered with Wadi al-Ḥasa is also accepted in all encyclopedias, in modern biblical exegesis, and in scholarly literature

1. The Arabic word used to mean "irrigated places in a sandy area."
2. In the early twentieth century and in other periods throughout history, the water level of the Dead Sea was higher than it has been over the last seventy years, and extended farther south. In those times, this stream would discharge directly into the sea.

in general. Other positions regarding its identification are mentioned occasionally in passing, but the prevailing opinion in both exegesis and scholarship confidently identifies Wadi Zered with Wadi al-Ḥasa.

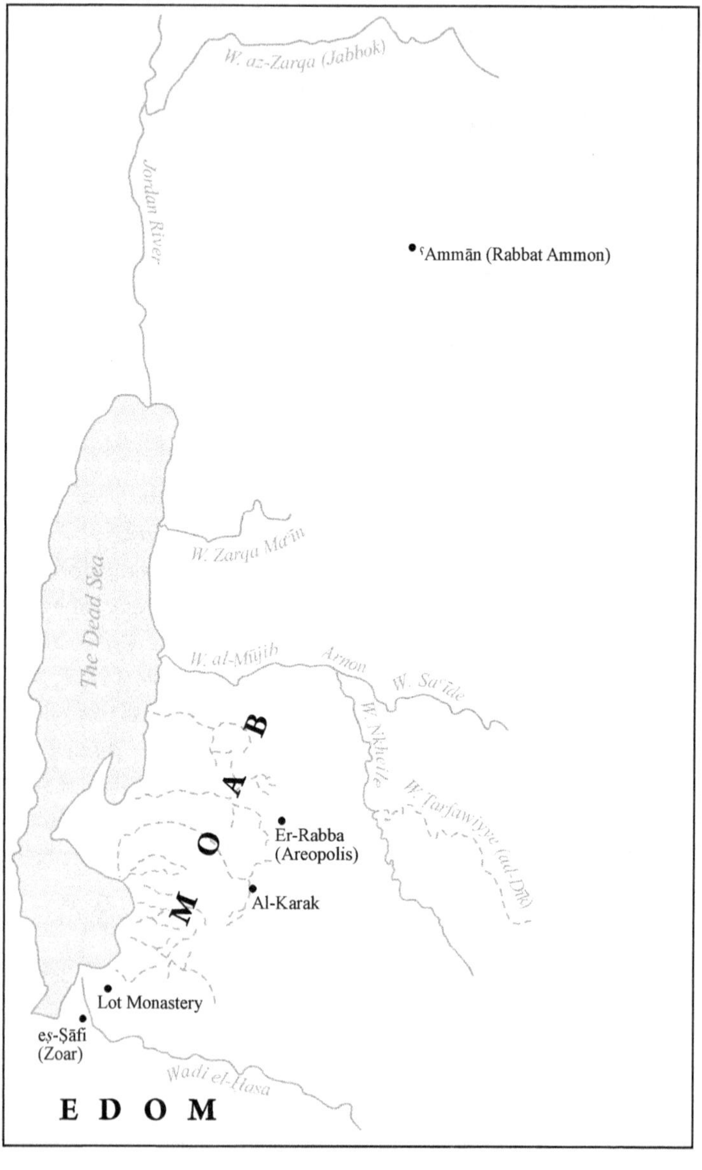

What Does the Torah Say?

Our *parasha* describes the people of Israel's journey around the land of Edom and the southern part of Transjordan. The people of Israel did not receive permission to pass through Edom, and after Aaron died at Mount Hor on the border of Edom, they set out to circumnavigate the land of Edom. Let us examine the Torah's account of the continuation of the people of Israel's journey:

> The Israelites marched on and encamped at Oboth. They set out from Oboth and encamped at Iye-abarim, in the wilderness bordering on Moab to the east. From there they set out and encamped at Wadi Zered. From there they set out and encamped beyond the Arnon, that is, in the wilderness that extends from the territory of the Amorites. (Num. 21:10–13)

The identification of Oboth is unknown. The direction that the people take here is south to north. This passage teaches us that the people of Israel first passed through "the wilderness bordering on Moab to the east" and then crossed Wadi Zered. Immediately afterward, they apparently crossed the Arnon River as well, which was then the northern border of the land of Moab (after Sihon king of the Amorites conquered the entire region north of the Arnon from Moab; see 21:26). They then found themselves east of the land of the Amorites – "in the wilderness that extends from the territory of the Amorites." This indicates that Wadi Zered flows basically east-west in the northeastern part of the land of Moab.

A similar picture is painted in *Parashat Devarim*, with an additional point of emphasis. There, Moses stands before the nation and reviews the details of the journey through the wilderness that they have undergone:

> We then moved on, away from our kinsmen, the descendants of Esau, who live in Seir… And we marched on through the wilderness of Moab (*derekh midbar Moav*). And the Lord said to me: Do not harass the Moabites or provoke them to war...Up now! Cross the wadi Zered! So we crossed the wadi Zered. The time that we spent in travel from Kadesh-barnea until we crossed the

> wadi Zered was thirty-eight years, until that whole generation of warriors had perished from the camp, as the Lord had sworn concerning them. Indeed, the hand of the Lord struck them, to root them out from the camp to the last man. When all the warriors among the people had died off, the Lord spoke to me, saying: You are now passing through the territory of Moab, which is Ar. You will then be close to the Ammonites; do not harass them or start a fight with them... Up! Set out across the wadi Arnon! See, I give into your power Sihon the Amorite, king of Heshbon, and his land. (Deut. 2:8–25)

The order of events that Moses recounts fits well with the order in our *parasha*. After they go around the land of the Seirites, they pass through the wilderness east of Moab, then cross Wadi Zered and immediately afterward cross the Arnon River. This passage in Deuteronomy contains an important emphasis absent from our *parasha*. The crossing of Wadi Zered is portrayed here as a festive event possessing historical significance. Wadi Zered represents the end of the period of Israel's wanderings, the termination of thirty-eight years of wandering that were decreed following the sin of the spies. What is so special about Wadi Zered that it was chosen to mark the momentous conclusion of this period of exile? The answer is that it is the final point before entering the land of the Amorites, which is part of the Land of Israel, as it was bequeathed to the tribes of Israel.[3]

It is very easy to see that in both passages, which are the only two places in the Tanakh that mention Wadi Zered, the location of the wadi does not match its location on modern maps! According to the verses, Wadi Zered is located in the northern part of Moab, whereas modern maps place it on Moab's southern border.

How Do Scholars Resolve This Discrepancy?

Several solutions have been suggested in order to resolve the discrepancy between the Torah's account and the accepted identification, each

3. See the Midrash Tanḥuma's description (cited in Rashi) of the miracles that occurred at the Arnon: "The mountain of the Land of Israel trembled, like a maidservant going out to greet her mistress."

solution in line with the views of its author. Some explained that since Biblical Hebrew does not recognize diagonal directions (such as northeast or southeast), the term *mizraḥ hashemesh*, generally translated simply as "east," can actually mean "southeast." Thus, the people of Israel passed south of the eastern section of Wadi al-Ḥasa, which the Torah called *mimizraḥ hashemesh*. This solution is farfetched; why would the Torah call the wilderness of Edom "the wilderness of Moab"? II Kings 3 relates that the king of Judah, the king of Israel, and the king of Edom traveled on "the road through the wilderness of Edom" and eventually reached Kir of Moab and attacked it. If so, why wouldn't the Torah use the proper name for this region here as well?

Some writers, using linguistic sophistries, succeeded in matching the accepted identification of Wadi Zered with the Torah's account – at least in Deuteronomy 2. They explain that *derekh midbar moav* should not necessarily be interpreted as "through the wilderness of Moab," but "in the direction of the wilderness of Moab" meaning, "on the road that will eventually lead to the wilderness of Moab." Furthermore, "You are now passing through the territory of Moab" means "You are now *entering* the territory of Moab." Moderate Bible critics suggested a slight emendation of the words of the verse, or alternatively, a change in the order of the verses, so that the verses match the "correct" wadi. One radical Bible critic named J. Maxwell Miller (and others following him) decided that, in light of this difficulty and others in this chapter, it is clear that not only is the history described here completely fictional, but the same is true of the geography – it is based entirely on rumors. Thus, claims Miller, the author of Numbers 21 may have lived in the Babylonian exile and was not familiar with the geography of the land of Moab. The author or redactor of Deuteronomy 2 was influenced by the author of Numbers 21 and copied his errors.[4]

Why Did Most Scholars Identify Wadi Zered with al-Ḥasa?

First, it seems to me that this identification was influenced by the schematic structure of the eastern bank of the Jordan River. The mountainous center of the western bank of the Jordan splits into numerous tributaries

4. Incidentally, upon reading Miller's article, I was unsurprised to find basic errors in his biblical citations and in his understanding of the Hebrew language.

that reunite into a sizeable number of streams, some of which flow into the sea and others into the Jordan Rift Valley. In contrast, vast sections of the eastern bank of the Jordan consist of high plateaus, all the drainage of which flows west. In addition, the main part of the drainage is through large, deep wadis – from north to south: Yarmouk, Jabbok (Zarqa in Arabic), Arnon (al-Mūjib), and Zered (al-Ḥasa). The centrality of these wadis, which divide the bank of the Jordan into five large plateaus, causes many – perhaps unwittingly – to identify them with the large wadis mentioned in the sources.[5] Other questions of identification are beyond the scope of this discussion, but it seems that we can establish with certainty, based on various pieces of information, that the identifications of the Jabbok with the Zarqa River and the Arnon with Wadi Mūjib are entirely accurate. As a result, completing the picture by identifying Wadi Zered with Wadi al-Ḥasa may seem to be the next logical step.

The Madaba Map

However, the main source that served as the basis for the identification of Wadi Zered with Wadi al-Ḥasa is the Madaba Map, the famous Greek mosaic map from the sixth century CE (some say the seventh century CE). The Madaba Map is the oldest map of the Land of Israel known to us in the original, and not from a copy. All the scholarly literature points out that the Madaba Map features an illustration of a wadi descending westward, south of "[XAP]AXMWBA" (Charach Moba, identified with the biblical Kir of Moab, today al-Karak) and discharging into the southern part of the Dead Sea near "ZOOPA" (Zoora/Zoar, today eṣ-Ṣāfi) and the "Sanctuary of Saint Lot." This wadi, which, according to its geographical features, must be Wadi al-Ḥasa, is adorned on the map with the caption "[Z]APEΔ" (Zared).

This information demonstrates that at least at the end of the Byzantine period it was already accepted to identify Wadi Zered with Wadi al-Ḥasa. While there is no guarantee that this Christian identification tradition is necessarily accurate, it certainly represents a point of departure for the discussion, and anyone arguing against this tradition must bear the burden of proof.

5. Yarmouk is not mentioned in the Tanakh, but it appears in other sources.

Is It True?

(Courtesy of the *Studium Biblicum Franciscanum*)

ΔAN (Dan) and IOYΔA (Judah) in the Madaba Map. Note the shapes of the delta (Δ) and the alpha (A).

After examining the Madaba Map carefully, the answer to this question became clear to me: absolutely not. The first thing I noticed was that the last letter in the caption accompanying the name of the wadi is not, in fact, delta (Δ), as we had previously stated. In all the captions on the Madaba Map, the letter delta and the letter alpha (A) appear quite similar. Both look much like an isosceles triangle. In the case of the delta, its base is a horizontal line forming a complete triangle. In contrast, the crossing stroke of the alpha is slightly diagonal; on the left side it touches the bottom of the left stroke of the letter, while on the right side it touches the right stroke at a slightly higher point. This distinction between the two letters is consistent throughout the map, and can be illustrated clearly by comparing names such as "Dan" and "Judah," both of which contain the two letters side by side.

Having established the distinction between the appearance of the letters alpha and delta on the Madaba Map, we can see that in the last letter of the word generally read as "Zared," the base of the letter is clearly diagonal. In other words, the last letter is clearly not delta, but alpha. Once I began to suspect that this was the case, I took measurements and found that the presumed addition of the letter zeta ([Z]) at the beginning of the name is not actually possible. The wadi is accompanied on the map by cliffs on both sides as well as at its head. The section of the cliffs at the head of the wadi was damaged over the course of time and was not preserved. The wadi's caption was integrated within these cliffs, and through careful and precise measurements, it is possible to

(Courtesy of the *Studium Biblicum Franciscanum*)

APEA (Area) and not [Z]APEΔ (Zared)

continue the line of cliffs that have been preserved and determine that there is no room for the letter zeta in the damaged section. We must then conclude that the caption of this wadi on the Madaba Map does not read ZAPEΔ (Zared) but APEA (Area).

What does "Area" mean in Greek? It is not particularly important. What is important is that this is not Wadi Zered. By way of speculation, I thought that perhaps this is a Greek version of the biblical name Ar, which is sometimes used as an alternate name for Moab in general (or for its southern part), and on one occasion it refers to a Moabite city. In Byzantine-era sources, a city is mentioned south of the Arnon River called Areopolis, which preserves the biblical name Ar. Eusebius, in his *Onomasticon*, writes that this is the Greek name for Rabbath Moab.

Rabbath Moab is known today as Rabba, about six miles north of al-Karak, and thus it may be that Area was the name of the entire region surrounding this city. However, if we follow this interpretation, we must assume that the artisan who created the Madaba Map erred by placing the caption close to the wadi instead of spreading out its letters across the region to its north.

Here is another minor discovery in the Madaba Map. We have already seen that the wadi illustrated in the Madaba Map is not Wadi Zered. It seems that this wadi does not represent Wadi al-Ḥasa either. According to the illustration on the map, the wadi discharges into the Dead Sea at a significant distance from the southern edge of the sea, between Charach Moba on one side and Zoora and the Sanctuary of St. Lot on the other – closer to Charach. This information does not fit with Wadi al-Ḥasa, which flows more than twelve miles south of al-Karak and discharges into the salt marshes south of the Dead Sea, very close to eṣ-Ṣāfi. In the past, this discrepancy could perhaps have been resolved by assuming that the map was not precise in its geographical proportions, and further assuming that the water level of the Dead Sea was higher during the Byzantine period (though according to recent geological research, modern geologists believe that the water level was actually low during that time). But then an archaeological discovery came to light that may very well close the discussion once and for all. The discovery was the Sanctuary of Lot, situated atop the cave where tradition has it that the incident involving Lot and his daughters transpired – and containing an inscription reading "Hagios Lot" (St. Lot). The monastery was found in 1983 at a site called Deir 'Ain 'Abāṭa, *north* of Wadi al-Ḥasa, and was excavated during the years 1988–1996. This monastery is undoubtedly the sanctuary illustrated on the Madaba Map, while its location on the Madaba Map is south of the wadi that appears on the map. It seems that the wadi illustrated on the map is one of the two wadis between al-Karak and Wadi al-Ḥasa, likely the southern of the two. It is somewhat surprising that the map chose to depict this wadi and not the larger Wadi al-Ḥasa. In the area northwest of the Dead Sea as well, the map depicts Naḥal Og rather than the larger Naḥal Prat (Wadi Qelt).

In short, the common identification of Wadi Zered was completely erroneous. The Madaba Map is entirely irrelevant to our discussion, as it depicts neither Wadi Zered nor Wadi al-Ḥasa. The accepted identification of Wadi Zered with Wadi al-Ḥasa is not rooted in any ancient source, and it clearly contradicts the two places in the Tanakh that mention Zered.

So What Is Wadi Zered?

Wadi Zered must be a significant wadi, one worthy of the festive remarks surrounding its appearance in Deuteronomy: "Up now! Cross the wadi Zered! So we crossed the wadi Zered. The time that we spent in travel from Kadesh-barnea until we crossed the wadi Zered was thirty-eight years…" (2:13–14). The people of Israel crossed the wadi in northeast Moab, just before they crossed the Arnon River.

One prominent candidate, which fits with these pieces of information, is Wadi Nukheile, a wadi in the eastern part of the land of Moab that flows south-north, with a slight tilt to the west. It discharges in the Arnon, below Aroer, near the place where the main road crossed the Arnon from ancient times until today. Not long ago, an ancient road was discovered that crossed Wadi Nukheile and immediately thereafter Wadi Saʿīde – the eastern section of the Arnon. This road may fit with the path taken by the people of Israel described in our *parasha* and in *Parashat Devarim*.

One other possible suggestion is Wadi Tarfawiyye (called Wadi ad-Dīk on some maps), a long, intermittent stream that discharges into Wadi Nukheile about six miles south of where Wadi Nukheile discharges into the Arnon. This suggestion was proposed by Yisrael Zev Horowitz in the early twentieth century. The benefit of this suggestion is that it fits with an ancient identification tradition mentioned in the Aramaic *Targumim* of the Land of Israel (as *tarvaya* and similar variations), but it might be assumed that this name referred in the past to Wadi Nukheile, the stream into which Wadi Tarfawiyye discharges.[6]

6. Alternatively, *tarvaya* may have referred to both wadis. *Atlas Daat Mikra* determines justly that the identification of Zered with Wadi el-Ḥasa is erroneous. However, there is a contradiction between the text of the atlas that identifies it with Wadi Tarfawiyye and the map in which the caption "Nahal Zered" relates to Nukheile.

Did the People of Israel Pass Through the Land of Moab?

The verses seem to contradict one another on this matter. Based on the two passages that we examined in *Parashat Ḥukkat* and *Parashat Devarim*, the people of Israel passed through "the wilderness bordering on Moab to the east" but did not actually enter the land of Moab. The passage in Deuteronomy emphasizes that Israel was warned not to harass the Moabites, "for I will not give you any of their land as a possession; I have assigned Ar as a possession to the descendants of Lot" (2:9). In our *parasha*, the Torah states that the people of Israel requested permission from the king of Edom to pass through his territory; when the king refused, they went around his land. In Jephthah's retelling of this story to the king of the Ammonites, who demanded the return of all the land from the Arnon to the Jabbok, he adds that "they also sent a mission to the king of Moab, and he refused," and emphasized that "they kept to the east of the land of Moab until they encamped on the other side of the Arnon; and they never entered Moabite territory" (Judges 11:17–18).

On the other hand, in that same chapter in Deuteronomy, which tells of the nation's passage through the wilderness east of Moab, the Torah seems to tell a different story in its description of Moses' entreaty to Sihon: "Let me pass through your country…What food I eat you will supply for money…as the descendants of Esau who live in Seir did for me, and the Moabites who dwell in Ar" (2:28–30). Rashi's solution – that the Moabites did not allow the people of Israel to pass through their land, and that Moses' statement to Sihon was in reference to their sale of food and water to the Israelites – seems farfetched in terms of *peshat*. The most important part of Moses' request was permission to pass through, while "what food I eat you will supply for money" is an additional statement meant to put Sihon at ease so he would not reconsider allowing Israel's passage. Why, then, would it make sense to cite as a reference a nation that did not allow Israel to pass through its land?

Ibn Ezra challenged this notion further, invoking a verse from later in Deuteronomy: "Because [the Ammonites and the Moabites] did not meet you with food and water on your journey after you left Egypt, and because they hired Balaam son of Beor…to curse you" (23:5). Commentators old and new resolved this contradiction in various ways. (These solutions include: they did not *meet* Israel with food and water, but they did *sell* them these provisions; the Ammonites were the ones who did not provide food and water, whereas the Moabites were the ones who hired Balaam; some of the Edomites and Moabites gave Israel permission to pass through, while others did not; the descendants of Esau who live in Seir were different from the rest of the Edomites, and the Moabites who live in Ar were different from the rest of the Moabites. I will note that, in the context of our discussion here, critical writers had difficulty resolving this problem as well. Since the contradiction in Deuteronomy 2 is within the same sequence of events, this precludes the possibility of splitting the passage into two or more assumed contradictory sources.

If we accept the identification of Wadi Zered with Wadi Nukheile, this means that the people of Israel passed through the semidesert region in the eastern part of Moab, but west of Nukheile – in other words, inside the land of Moab, but not in the settlement centers or the agricultural areas. After they requested permission to pass through the inhabited areas and the Moabites denied them permission to do so, they chose to travel through the semiarid eastern region. By doing this, the people of Israel made it clear to the Moabites that they were not planning to attack them or to harm them in any way. As a result, the Moabites allowed them to pass through this eastern region of their land and purchase food and water from them. This permission was not given at first, nor was it given wholeheartedly or even amicably; it was a kind of compromise. This understanding may provide a harmonious explanation for all the texts dealing with the passage of the people of Israel through the land of Moab. (The contradiction regarding the descendants of Esau may perhaps be resolved with a similar explanation.)

Summary

According to our conclusion, the Wadi Zered mentioned in Numbers 21 and in Deuteronomy 2 does not appear on the Madaba Map. Based on the information in the Tanakh, it is located in the northeast part of Moab. It should be identified with Wadi Nukheile or perhaps with Wadi Tarfawiyye, which discharges into Nukheile, but certain considerations suggest that Wadi Nukheile may be a better match. Wadi al-Ḥasa, which serves as the border between Moab and Edom, is not Wadi Zered.

Final Note

Wadi Zered is mentioned in one other source that we did not mention here: the *baraita* that discusses the regions of the Land of Israel (preserved in *Sifrei* on *Parashat Ekev,* in the Yerushalmi and the Tosefta of Tractate Shevi'it and in the Rehov Inscription in the Beit She'an Valley). Our identification of Zered with Nukheile might suit the geographical logic of the *baraita* as well. However, this topic is beyond the scope of this discussion.

For further study:

Ben-Gad, D. "'Waheb be Suphah' and the Settled Country of Ar." *Cathedra* 95 (2000): 7–24 [Hebrew].

Donner, H. "The Sanctuary of St. Lot." *The Near East in Antiquity* 4 (1994): 87–92.

Elitzur , Yehuda and Yehuda Kiel, *Atlas Daat Mikra,* Jerusalem 1993, 34-35 [Hebrew].

Elitzur, Yoel. "Zared or 'Αρεα'? One Significant Detail in the Madaba Map." *Scripta Classica Israelica* 19 (2000): 155–162.

Elitzur, Yoel. "Naḥal Zered in the Bible and the *Baraita de-Teḥumim.*" *PEQ* 145 (2013).

Politis, K. "The Sanctuary of Agios Lot, the City of Zoara and the Zared River." In *The Madaba Map Centenary*, edited by M. Piccirillo and E. Alliata, 225–227. Jerusalem, 1999.

Parashat Balak

The Land of Moab

Parashat Balak: Entirely in the Land of Moab

The final verse in the previous *parasha* is the opening verse for the Balak narrative, according to the accepted division of chapters: "The Israelites then marched on and encamped in the plains of Moab, across the Jordan from Jericho" (Num. 22:1). From this point on, through the end of the Torah until Joshua 3, the people of Israel remain in the same location – the plains of Moab across the Jordan from Jericho. Our *parasha* emphasizes that this place is adjacent to the land of Moab: "And Moab said to the elders of Midian, 'Now this horde will lick clean all that is about us as an ox licks up the grass of the field'" (22:4); "There is a people that came out of Egypt; it hides the earth from view, and it is settled next to me" (22:5).

King Balak of Moab and his dignitaries set out to meet Balaam in "Ir-moab, which is in the vicinity of the Arnon, at the edge of the border" (Num. 22:36) and then the entire party accompanies Balaam to Kiriath-huzoth, where they eat and spend the night. The next morning, they ascend to Bamoth-baal, where they "could see a portion of the people" (22:41). Balaam advances from there on his own until he sees the entire encampment of Israel, at which point he returns to Balak, bearing a blessing instead of a curse for the people of Israel. The second attempt to curse Israel occurs at Sedeh-zophim, on the summit of Pisgah, where only a small portion of the nation's encampment was visible (23:13–14).

This attempt was unsuccessful as well, leading Balak to bring Balaam to the peak of Peor, which overlooks the wasteland (23:28).

> As Balaam looked up and saw Israel encamped tribe by tribe, the spirit of God came upon him. Taking up his theme, he said: Word of Balaam... How fair are your tents, O Jacob, your dwellings, O Israel! (24:2–5)

Balak's furious response to this blessing inspires Balaam to take up his theme once more in the same place, going on to guarantee to Moab that "in days to come" they are destined to succumb to Israel, along with "all children of Seth" and the nation of Edom (24:14-19). From this vantage point, Balaam was also able to look out at Amalek and at the Kenites, who were encamped next to Israel, and to speak briefly about them as well. Before Balaam returns home, he ends with a mysterious prophecy concerning events far in the future: "Alas, who can survive except God has willed it!" (24:23). In total, Balaam delivers seven prophecies.

As usual, in this discussion too, we will focus less on the story itself and on Balaam's lofty speeches and more on the geography involved. Most of the places we mentioned above are difficult to identify precisely, but the general framework of the region is clear. The plains of Moab are a vast, flat area of land in the southeast Jordan River Valley, northeast of the Dead Sea "across the Jordan from Jericho." This region is also known in the Torah as "the valley near Beth-peor" (Deut. 3:29 and others), and at the end of the list of the marches of the people of Israel it is described in detail: "they encamped by the Jordan from Beth-jeshimoth as far as Abel-shittim, in the plains of Moab" (Num. 33:49). Beth-jeshimoth is the southern border of this region, generally identified with Suweimeh in the northeast Dead Sea region, and Abel-shittim is the northern border of the region. *Ḥazal* estimated that the area of this region is twelve mil by twelve mil (Eiruvin 55b, Y. Shevi'it 6:1 and parallels). This estimate fits well with the actual geography of the region (despite its source in the Bavli – Rabba bar bar Ḥana, who was known for his exaggerations; in the Yerushalmi, the estimate is unattributed, indicating that it was a fact known to all). In fact, this estimate is the source of the statement that

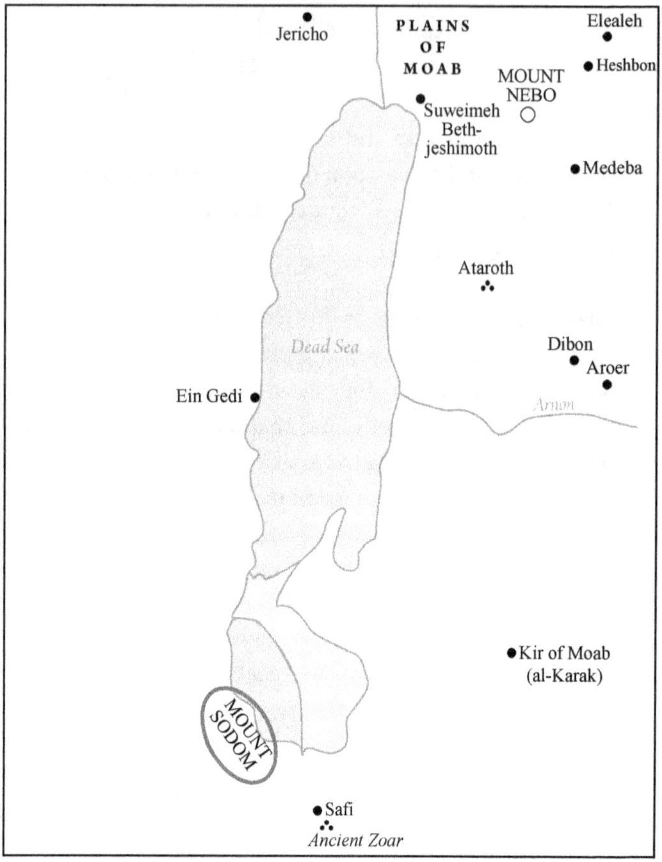

appears throughout rabbinic literature that the size of the Israelite camp was twelve mil by twelve mil (*Sifrei Devarim* 343 and parallels), a figure that has halakhic ramifications. All the points where Balak and Balaam stood and looked out upon Israel are located atop hills that overlook this large plain, and thus cannot have been very far from the plain itself. The one point that was located at a significant distance from the plain was the first point mentioned in the narrative – "Ir-moab, which is in the vicinity of the Arnon, at the edge of the border." The Arnon River is one of the central streams in Transjordan, flowing east-west and discharging into the Dead Sea about twenty-two miles south of Beth-jeshimoth and the plains of Moab. The Torah refers to this point as "the edge of the border," and we will soon clarify the meaning of this name.

"Ammon and Moab Became Purified Through Sihon"

The primary question here is if the people of Israel were permitted to enter the land of Moab. In *Parashat Ḥukkat* (chapter 21), we learned that the people of Israel requested permission from the king of Edom to pass through his territory. When he refused, they circumnavigated his land. In the case of Moab as well, they did not pass through the land, but only through "the wilderness bordering on Moab to the east" (21:11). In the Book of Judges, Jephthah recounts the story from Numbers 21, adding the clarification: "They also sent a mission to the king of Moab, and he refused...they kept to the east of the land of Moab...and they never entered Moabite territory" (11:17–18). In his overview of the nation's journey in Deuteronomy 2, Moses relates that God was the one who prohibited the people of Israel from entering Mount Seir, the land of Moab and the land of the Ammonites. The reason for this prohibition was that the land of Seir was given as an inheritance to the descendants of Esau and that the lands of Moab and the Ammonites were given as an inheritance to the descendants of Lot.[1]

If so, Israel did not battle Moab, nor did they enter the land of Moab (though they did receive permission to pass through the semidesert at the eastern edge of this territory, as we explained in the chapter on *Parashat Ḥukkat*). How, then, can we explain the fact that the people of Israel dwelled in the plains of Moab? The answer to this question, which the Torah deals with in great detail, is well known. The verse toward the end of *Parashat Ḥukkat* reads: "Now Heshbon was the city of Sihon king of the Amorites, who had fought against a former king of Moab and taken all his land from him as far as the Arnon" (21:26); immediately thereafter comes the "Song of the Bards" accompanying this conquest: "For fire went forth from Heshbon, flame from Sihon's city, consuming Ar of Moab, the lords of Bamoth by the Arnon. Woe to you, O Moab! You are abandoned, O people of Chemosh!" (21:28–29). In other words, at first the land of Moab included the entire territory north of the Arnon, until Heshbon. But Sihon set out from Heshbon and conquered half the land of Moab until the Arnon, leaving only the territory south of the Arnon to the Moabites. Following this conquest, the northern border of Moab became the Arnon

1. See the chapter on *Parashat Devarim*.

River: "For the Arnon is the boundary of Moab, between Moab and the Amorites" (21:13); "since Moab ends at the Arnon" (Judges 11:18). Thus, the moment that Israel crossed the eastern section of the Arnon River, they immediately entered "the wilderness that extends from the territory of the Amorites." And when Sihon denied them permission to pass through his land peacefully, they went to war against him and took possession of his land, "from the Arnon to the Jabbok, as far as [the land] of the Ammonites" (21:24). In light of this, the plains of Moab where the people of Israel were then sojourning are actually "Moab" in name only; at the time the territory was captured by the people of Israel it was part of the kingdom of Sihon. In essence, Sihon's conquest of this territory allowed Israel to conquer it in turn, as they were not prohibited from conquering Amorite territory as they were that of the Moabites and the Ammonites. *Ḥazal* summarized this phenomenon, pronouncing that "Ammon and Moab became purified through Sihon" (Gittin 38a).[2]

Moab De Facto, Sihon De Jure

Our conclusion at this stage of the discussion is that the region north of the Arnon was formerly a Moabite territory, which was then conquered by Sihon king of the Amorites, after which the Israelites took it from him. In our *parasha* as well, there is one piece of information that fits into the picture we have illustrated thus far – the first meeting between Balak and Balaam: "He went out to meet him at Ir-moab, which is in the vicinity of Arnon, at the edge of the border." Indeed, Arnon is the border of Moab and the city situated near the Arnon is located at the extreme end of this border.

However, the continuation of the *parasha* teaches us that things are not so simple. If the area north of the Arnon was captured from the Moabites years prior to this point, by the Amorites who then lost the territory to the Israelites, how can Balak and all his dignitaries stroll through the region in broad daylight, traveling from summit to summit overlooking the Israelite camp, more than twenty miles north of the edge

2. The Torah only mentions this "purification" in the case of Moab, but a similar process in the case of the Ammonites can be inferred from the verse in Joshua: "Half of the country of the Ammonites" (13:25).

of their kingdom, building seven altars at each point to sacrifice oxen and sheep? Even the expressions that Balak uses at the beginning of the *parasha* – "all that is about us"; "and it is settled next to me" – alludes to a much closer proximity between Moab and Israel. In other places in Numbers and Deuteronomy as well, it is apparent that the residence of the people of Israel is consistently referred to as "the plains of Moab." There are even a few instances where the location is actually called "the land of Moab": "On the other side of the Jordan, in the land of Moab, Moses undertook to expound this Teaching" (Deut. 1:5); "These are the terms of the covenant which the Lord commanded Moses to conclude with the Israelites in the land of Moab" (28:69); "Mount Nebo, which is in the land of Moab" (32:49); "So Moses died there… in the land of Moab… He buried him in the valley in the land of Moab" (34:5–6). Can it truly be that all of these are no more than historical names – bearing no significance to the geographical reality at the time?

During later periods, we find that the entire area that Moses conquered north of the Arnon, including cities like Dibon, Medeba, Heshbon, Elealeh, Nebo, and Baal-meon, were considered part of the land of Moab for all intents and purposes. This area contained Israelite cities belonging to the Reubenites and the Gadites, but it never completely shed its Moabite identity. At the beginning of the period of the Judges, Ehud son of Gera killed King Eglon of Moab. According to the description in Judges, Eglon lived somewhere in the plains of Moab opposite Jericho and Gilgal, while his soldiers occupied the City of Palms in the Jericho area. Several centuries later, the royal city of King Mesha of Moab was Dibon, north of the Arnon, where his famous stele was discovered, which enumerated numerous Moabite cities by name – especially in the northern part of Moab. Mesha captured the Israelite cities Ataroth and Nebo, decimated and enslaved their inhabitants, and reinhabited the cities with his own people. In Isaiah and Jeremiah's Moab prophecies (Is. 16 and Jer. 48), numerous Moabite cities are enumerated once more, again with an emphasis on the north.[3] In the end, the general picture

3. According to my father *z"l*, there is a connection between the lists of cities in the Moab prophecies and Mesha's list.

from the Tanakh is that the land of Moab included the entire territory east of the Dead Sea, from its northern end to its southern end, extending until the wilderness in the east (parallel to the territory of Judah to its west) – for most of its history. Our *parasha* teaches us that even during and following the time of Moses' conquests, when the people of Israel dwelled in the plains of Moab, the region north of the Arnon was still considered a de facto integral part of the land of Moab. From Balak's perspective, the conquests of Sihon merely represented a temporary episode. The land was his land, and the people of Israel were no more than desert raiders who had seized control of a portion of his territory. It would seem that even some members of the nation of Israel were convinced by his version of the reality: Zimri son of Salu, chieftain of a Simeonite ancestral house, who saw fit to cohabit with the daughter of one of the five chieftains of the nomadic nation of Midian, certainly saw himself as one of the chieftains of the nomadic nation of Israel.

Despite this, the Torah regards the people of Israel as a nation conquering what is rightfully his. From the Torah's perspective, Sihon's conquest from Moab was a critical historical – one might even say halakhic – event. It determined that this strip of land between Heshbon and the Arnon River was no longer in Moabite hands; it now belonged to the Amorites, which meant that it became permissible for Israel to conquer it. Toward the end of the period of the Judges, the historical debate over what exactly occurred in this region during Moses' time flared up again. The king of the Ammonites, who decided that he represented Moab as well, claimed: "They seized the land which is mine, from the Arnon to the Jabbok as far as the Jordan. Now, then, restore it peaceably!" (Judges 11:13). Jephthah, though he was not one of the better leaders of Israel, was able to respond courageously, in a manner befitting the solid concept of the nation of Israel: "Israel did not seize the land of Moab or the land of the Ammonites… Now, then, the Lord, the God of Israel, dispossessed the Amorites before His people Israel; and should you possess their land?" (11:15–23).

The moral of the story for us today is that from a national-historical perspective, it is the *definition* of historical events and situations that is important, and that should matter for the future. Even before we begin to discuss questions of physical control of the land, it is important to maintain a stable way of looking at past events, in order to see events clearly in the face of "alternative narratives" and give those past events their proper names.

For further study:

Elitzur, Yehuda. "*Yiftaḥ* Bedoro KiShmuel Bedoro." *Israel and the Bible,* Ramat-Gan (2000): 85–88 [Hebrew].

Elitzur, Yehuda. "*Massa Mo'av Uketovet Meisha.*" *Israel and the Bible,* Ramat-Gan (2000): 175–182 [Hebrew].

MacDonald, B. *East of the Jordan*. Boston, 2000, 171–174.

Parashat Pinḥas

Tzlofhad's Daughters and Their Portion

The Tribe of Manasseh Is Counted for the First Time

Parashat Pinḥas relates that in the fortieth year of the people of Israel's sojourn in the wilderness, a census was implemented. The total population of the people of Israel comes out to 601,730, a number that is similar to the result obtained in the previous census, conducted in the second year following the Exodus: 603,550. During the time between the two censuses, the population was completely replaced:

> Among these there was not one of those enrolled by Moses and Aaron the priest when they recorded the Israelites in the wilderness of Sinai. For the Lord had said of them, "They shall die in the wilderness." Not one of them survived, save Caleb son of Jephunneh and Joshua son of Nun. (Num. 26:64–65)

The obvious difference between the two censuses is that in the census of the fortieth year, each family is mentioned by name. A parallel can thus be drawn between the census of *Parashat Pinḥas* and the list in *Parashat Vayigash* of the seventy people who descended to Egypt (Gen. 46). While the list of families in *Parashat Pinḥas* and the list of families in *Parashat Vayigash* are largely parallel, there is one glaring difference: the inclusion in the later census of the tribes of Ephraim and Manasseh. Ephraim and Manasseh were born in Egypt, and their families are not listed among the seventy immigrants to Egypt listed in Genesis. In *Parashat Pinḥas*, however, they are enumerated in detail.

Tzlofhad's Daughters in the Torah and in the Book of Joshua

I would like to focus here on the families of the tribe of Manasseh that are particularly interesting. The Torah lists six sons born to Gilead, Manasseh's grandson, forming six families:

> These were the descendants of Gilead: [Of] Iezer, the clan of the Iezerites; of Helek, the clan of the Helekites; [of] Asriel, the clan of the Asrielites; [of] Shechem, the clan of the Shechemites; [of] Shemida, the clan of the Shemidaites; [of] Hepher, the clan of the Hepherites. (Num. 26:31–33)

The account continues, focusing on one particular individual: "Now Tzlofhad son of Hepher had no sons, only daughters. The names of Tzlofhad's daughters were Mahlah, Noah, Hoglah, Milcah, and Tirzah" (26:33). The five daughters of Tzlofhad are central characters from our *parasha* and onward. Immediately following the account of the census, we read that the five daughters stand before Moses, the tribal chieftains, and the entire congregation, presenting their claim: "Let not our father's name be lost to his family just because he had no son! Give us a holding among our father's kinsmen!" (Num. 27:4). Their argument is accepted, and God commands Moses: "The plea of Tzlofhad's daughters is just. You should give them a hereditary holding among their father's kinsmen; transfer their father's share to them" (27:7).

Later on, in Numbers 36, the "Tzlofhad's daughters incident" returns to the headlines. The leaders of the Gileadite families listed above voice their concern that Tzlofhad's daughters will marry men from a different tribe, causing each daughter's territory to be transferred to the tribe of her husband, and thereby diminishing the overall territory belonging to the tribe of Manasseh. The ruling was handed down, instructing the daughters to marry their cousins, thus ensuring that their portions remain in the hands of Manasseh. The Book of Numbers closes with the acknowledgment that the daughters did just this: "Mahlah, Tirzah, Hoglah, Milcah, and Noah, Tzlofhad's daughters, were married to sons of their uncles" (36:11).

An additional detailing of these events, with special emphasis on the practical apportionment of territory to the families of Manasseh and on the integration of Tzlofhad's daughters into the territorial map, can be found in Joshua 17. The list of families here should be familiar to us from our *parasha*:

> And this is the portion that fell by lot to the tribe of Manasseh – for he was Joseph's firstborn ... And now assignments were made to the remaining Manassites, by their clans: the descendants of Abiezer, Helek, Asriel, Shechem, Hepher, and Shemida. Those were the male descendants of Manasseh son of Joseph, by their clans. Now Tzlofhad son of Hepher son of Gilead son of Machir son of Manasseh had no sons, but only daughters. The names of his daughters were Mahlah, Noah, Hoglah, Milcah, and Tirzah. They appeared before the priest Eleazar, Joshua son of Nun, and the chieftains, saying: "The Lord commanded Moses to grant us a portion among our male kinsmen." So, in accordance with the Lord's instructions, they were granted a portion among their father's kinsmen. *Ten districts* fell to Manasseh ... as Manasseh's daughters inherited a portion together with his sons, while the land of Gilead was assigned to the rest of Manasseh's descendants. (Joshua 17:1–6)

What Are the "Ten Districts" of Manasseh?

According to a simple reading of the account in Joshua, the calculation is as follows: Gilead son of Machir son of Manasseh had six sons. One of these sons – Hepher – had one son – Tzlofhad – who, in turn, had five daughters. This adds up to ten portions: one portion for each of the five Gileadite families – Abiezer, Helek, Asriel, Shechem and Shemida – and one portion for each of Tzlofhad's five daughters, the heirs of Hepher.

While this interpretation may reflect the most straightforward reading of the text, from a logical perspective this is very difficult to understand. As R. Papa points out in the Talmud: "Whom does [the verse 'ten districts fell to Manasseh'] enumerate? If [all] children are enumerated, there were [surely] more [than ten]; if fathers' houses are enumerated, [these] were [only] six!" (Bava Batra 118b). Seemingly, the five portions designated for Tzlofhad's daughters are merely five subdivisions of one of the six portions allotted to Gilead's six sons. Just as the portion allotted to Hepher was divided between his five granddaughters, surely Hepher's five brothers produced numerous male progeny between whom to divide their respective portions. But the verse seems to bestow equal standing in this regard upon Tzlofhad's daughters and Abiezer and his brothers. But how can this be? Let us recall what Tzlofhad's daughters requested in the first place: to be regarded as the equals of their male peers. How can it be that they are suddenly given the same hereditary status as their five great-uncles?

For this reason, the sages explained that the "ten districts" of Manasseh do not include the personal portions of Mahlah, Noah, Hoglah, Milcah, and Tirzah. Rather, the sum of ten was reached by factoring in additional portions – not mentioned in the Scripture – that the five daughters inherited as a group. First, Tzlofhad was among those who participated personally in the Exodus from Egypt, each of whom received his own portion in the initial distribution of the land. Furthermore, the sages continue, Tzlofhad managed to amass additional portions by inheriting those of an unnamed brother (or two brothers, as some claim) who died childless in the wilderness. Finally, Tzlofhad merited an extra portion by virtue of being the firstborn in his family. While the calculations are somewhat murky,[1] the sages conclude that Tzlofhad himself held five portions of land, which his five daughters inherited collectively.

Malbim, in his characteristic pursuit of the simplest understanding of the text, suggests that the ten districts of Manasseh are actually

1. The exact breakdown is quite complex, and the details are debated in the Mishna, Tosefta and both the Talmud Bavli and Talmud Yerushalmi. In the end, even *Ḥazal*'s combination does not provide perfect uniformity, since Tzlofhad's original inheritance and his "firstborn portion" are two subdivided portions within Hepher's primary portion.

ten distinct geographic portions, entirely unconnected to the intricacies of the Manasseh family tree.

Yet both of these interpretations seem strained in light of the actual text in Joshua. The subject of that passage is the list of the families of Manasseh and of Tzlofhad's daughters. The verse states, "Ten districts fell to Manasseh" (17:5), and immediately clarifies: "as Manasseh's daughters inherited a portion together with his sons" (17:6), implying that these ten portions were tied to the families of Manasseh and to Tzlofhad's daughters.

Do we truly have no alternative but to favor the logical explanation here, despite the contextual indications to the contrary?

An Archaeological Finding that Supports the Simple Reading

An important and famous archaeological finding seems to support the simple reading of the text unambiguously. This is the Samaria Ostraca, dozens of inscriptions written in ink on sherds that were found in 1910 in the treasury of the palace of the kings of Israel in ancient Samaria. The Samaria Ostraca are receipts, tax records, or shipment records, which mention the year, names of officials, names of places, and occasionally names of families as well. Some of these sherds also list the name of the product being transported, such as *nbl yn* ("a jar of wine") or *nbl šmn rḥṣ* ("a jar of fine oil" or "a jar of anointment oil").

Here are a few examples:

> Ostracon 6: ***bšt.*** (in the year) ***htšʿt.*** (the ninth) ***mqṣh.*** (from the place *qṣh*) ***lgdyw.*** (to the official *gdyw*, i.e., Gaddiyau) *nbl. yn. yšn.*

> Ostracon 28: *bšt.* ˥Λ (digits, perhaps 15) *m'bʿzr.* (from the family of Abiezer) *l'š'. 'ḥmlk. bʿl'.* (to Asha, Ahimelekh, Baala, apparently names of officials or the like) *m'lmtn.* (from the place Elmatan)

> Ostracon 42: *[b]št.* ˥Λ *mšr'[l]* (from *šr'l*, apparently a shortened version of the family name Asriel) *lydʿyw. mrnyw. gdy[w]* (from the officials *rnyw* and *gdyw*) *mʿšrt* (from the place ʿAseret)

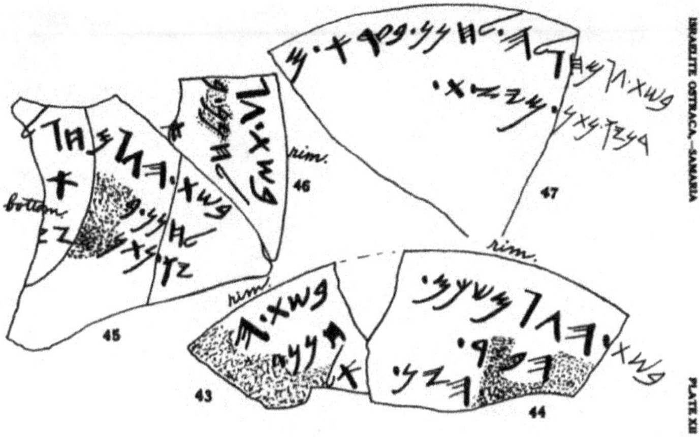

Samaria Ostraca nos. 43–47 (G. A. Reisner, *Israelite Ostraca from Samaria* [no date])
43: In the year…[to] Hanan…El...
44: [In the year] ¬Λ from Shekhem…*hp.r*…*hyn*
45: In the year ¬Λ from Holg[ah] to Hanan (son of) *b*…'…yw (son of) Nathan from Yaz[ith].
46: In the year ¬Λ to Hanan (son of) *b*…'
47: :…from Hoglah to Hanan (son of) Ba'ara *m*…from Yazith.

> Ostracon 50: *bšt.* ¬Λ *lgmr. mn'h.* (from the family Noah) *'bdyw.* (Obadiau) *l'byw.* (to Abiau; apparently names of officials)

Scholars have disputed almost every detail that can be disputed. During which king's reign were the ostraca written? How to decipher the digits of the year numbers? What is the commercial or administrative function of each ostracon? We will leave all these questions to the historians and linguists. The details that interest us most for this discussion are the family/territory names mentioned in the ostraca. Seven such names appear in the ostraca: Shemida, Abiezer, Helek, [A]sriel, Shechem, Hoglah, and Noah.

This finding proves that the simple reading in Joshua 17 is the correct one; the districts were indeed given permanent names for the major households of Manasseh, as well as for Tzlofhad's five daughters! We see in the ostraca that there are districts called Hoglah and Noah just as there are districts called Abiezer and Shemida.

(Courtesy of the Israel Antiquities Authority).

The last passage in the Rehov Inscription: The permitted towns in the district of Sebaste Iqbin and Kefar Kasdaya and Zir and Azilin and Shappirin and 'Ananin and Higher Bil'am and Mazharu and Dothan and Kefar Mayya and Shilta and Pentakumwata, Labaya and Pardislaya and Yazith and Arbanurin and Monarith and half of Shalaf.

The Territory of Hoglah

There is one clue in the Samaria Ostraca that can even point to the location of the territory of Hoglah. The two ostraca that mention Hoglah also mention the city of Yazith (Ostracon 45: *bšt h* ˥Λ *mḥgl[h] lḥnn. b'r' ywntn. myṣ[t]*. Ostracon 47: *...mḥ]glh. lḥnn b'r' m[...]. myṣt)*. Yazith is mentioned in three other ostraca, along with the official aḥn'm (or adn'm). This official is mentioned in an ostracon labeled *nbl. yn. yšn* ("a jug of aged wine") that arrived from the city of Geba. This leads us to conclude that the two cities of Yazith and Geba were located in the same district – the district of Hoglah. The two cities appear in much later Hebrew sources as well. Geba is mentioned in the Mishna, the Tosefta[2] and the Yerushalmi alongside a place called Bedan (in other editions: Badan). Geba and Bedan/Badan became famous for their high-quality agricultural produce: the pomegranates of Bedan and the vegetables of Geba, which the sages declared must

2. Known here as "Geba of the house of the Cutheans."

www.zerothkoff.com (Courtesy of Dr. Zev Rothkoff)

Bedan, whose pomegranates must always be tithed

www.zerothkoff.com (Courtesy of Dr. Zev Rothkoff)

Yazith – modern-day Yāṣīd

always be tithed, no matter where they are acquired.[3] Yazith is mentioned in the mosaic inscription from the ancient Rehov synagogue in the Beit She'an Valley, the longest ancient Hebrew inscription ever found in the Land of Israel. This inscription, a halakhic-geographic inscription dealing with the land-bound commandments and the commandments that relate to the sanctity of the land, lists Yazith among the "permitted towns in the territory of Sebaste." In other words, these were towns in the district of Sebaste (Samaria) that were inhabited by non-Jews during the tannaitic period, and thus they were exempt from the laws of tithes and the Sabbatical year.

Yazith is identified with the village of Yāṣīd[4] in northern Samaria, north of Mount Ebal. Four miles southeast of Yāṣīd are the Bāḏān springs, and four miles northwest of Yāṣīd is the village of Jabaᶜ – Geba of the house of the Cutheans. The two villages west of Jabaᶜ – Fandaqumiya and Sīlat ad-Dhahr – are apparently mentioned in the same list in the

www.zerothkoff.com (Courtesy of Dr. Zev Rothkoff)

Shilta – modern-day Sīlat ad-Dhahr

3. This rule was enacted because the Cutheans would not tithe the produce they would sell to others.

4. The *t-d* substitution at the end of the name is similar to that of *Tzefat-Ṣafad*.

Pentakumwata – modern-day Fandaqumiya

www.zerothkoff.com (Courtesy of Dr. Zev Rothkoff)

Ruins of the settlement of Homesh

Rehov Inscription, as Shilta and Pentakumwata. At the top of the hill above Fandaqumiya and Sīlat ad-Dhahr, are the ruins of the settlement of Homesh, destroyed in 2005 by the Sharon administration.[5] The name Homesh is the Hebrew version of the Greek name Pentakomia ("[center of] five villages"), which evolved into "Pentakumwata" (featuring an Aramaic ending) and Fandaqumiya (Arabic version). Atop a small hill at the foot of Fandaqumiya and Sīlat ad-Dhahr stand the remnants of the settlement of Sa-Nur. A British police station and a synagogue[6] were left intact, thus serving as memorials. Apparently, all these places – both the Arab villages that took the place of the ancient Israelite cities and the Israeli settlements that the Israeli government decided to depopulate and destroy – are located within the district of Hoglah, the daughter of Tzlofhad.

Returning to Our Original Question

How can it be that the granddaughters of the tribal elders were given equal status to that of their forebears? The exact turn of events is difficult for us – thousands of years removed from that era – to grasp. The Book of Joshua teaches us that the procedure for territorial inheritance was not simple; it was not merely the administrative matter of casting lots. Much effort and practical ability was needed, as well as courage and valor in order to dispossess the Canaanites, deforest the land, and rejuvenate desolate areas. We read in Joshua 18 that Joshua rebuked the tribes who dawdled in inheriting the land. The Manassites were among the strongest and swiftest tribes in inheriting the land – on both sides of the Jordan – so Joshua also instructed them to dispossess the Canaanites who dwelled in the valley, an area that had originally been designated for the less enthusiastic tribes (Josh. 17:11–13, 18). We may speculate that there was something special about the personalities of the five daughters that helped launch them upward in hereditary status. The text of the Tanakh

5. Owing to a stubborn group of young people, Jewish presence continues to exist here. In recent years, Homesh has been home to a permanent semi-underground yeshiva.
6. This was the only synagogue in all the settlements that were destroyed in 2005 that was not razed and burned. Instead, it was completely covered in earth, and the site now appears like a small mound.

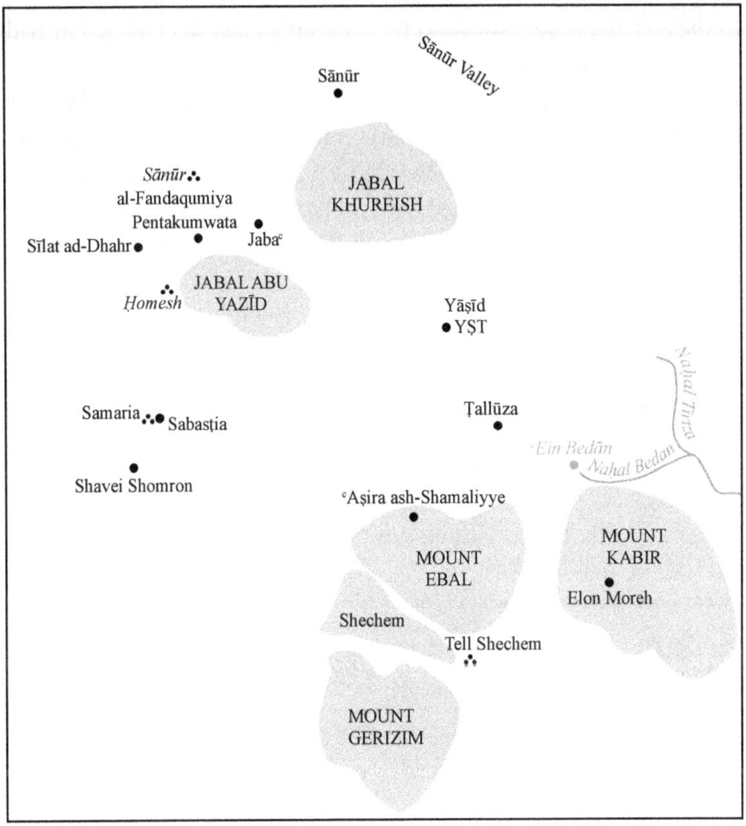

gives the impression that these were unique women, unusually eloquent and assertive.[7] It seems that these women were tribal leaders in their own right and wielded such a great degree of influence that the districts they inherited were named for them. That is to say, this was not simply a matter of equal rights. Tzlofhad's daughters' request – "Give us a holding!" (Num. 27:4) – can perhaps be compared to the Judahites' request, voiced by their chieftain Caleb son of Jephunneh: "So assign to me this hill country... if only the Lord is with me, I will dispossess them, as the Lord promised" (Josh. 14:12). Like the Judahites, Tzlofhad's daughters were volunteering for a mission beyond that of requesting equal rights.

7. The Talmud states: "The daughters of Tzlofhad were wise women; they were exegetes; they were virtuous" (Bava Batra 119b).

In the end, the reward they received was far greater than what they had requested, which was to be considered equal to their Manassite cousins. It is no coincidence that the cousins who eventually married Tzlofhad's daughters remain anonymous. These cousins may have been lesser than their wives in terms of both power and communal influence. As a result, the districts that they inherited were named for the daughters rather than the men, teaching us that feminism predated the modern era.

For further study:

Aharoni, Y. *The Land of the Bible: A Historical Geography*. Translated and edited by A. F. Rainey. Philadelphia, 1979, 356–368.

Aḥituv, S. *Echoes from the Past: Hebrew and Cognate Inscriptions from the Biblical Period.* Translated and edited by A. F. Rainey. Jerusalem, 2008, 258–310.

Demsky, A. "The Permitted Villages of Sebaste in the Reḥov Mosaic." *IEJ* 29 (1979): 182–193.

Ehrlich, Z. M. "The Inheritance of Hoglah, Daughter of Tzlofhad." *Beit Mikra* 28:3 (1983): 232–235 [Hebrew].

Elitzur, Yoel. *Ancient Place Names in the Holy Land.* Jerusalem-Winona Lake, 2004, 299.

Press, I. "Bedan." In *A Topographical-Historical Encyclopaedia of Palestine*, 1. Jerusalem, 1951, 63; "*Geva*[3]," 139 [Hebrew].

Sussmann, J. "The Inscription in the Synagogue at Reḥob." In *Ancient Synagogues Revealed*, edited by L. I. Levine, 146-151. Jerusalem, 1981. "The Reḥob Inscription: A Translation." Ibid. 152–153.

Parashat Matot

The Conquests of Machir, Jair, and Nobah

The Absence and Sudden Reappearance of the Manassites

The central section of *Parashat Matot* is dedicated to the long and difficult negotiations between Moses and the Gadites and Reubenites over their colonization in the recently captured Transjordan (chapter 32). The Torah repeatedly emphasizes the identity of the petitioners:

> The Reubenites and the Gadites owned cattle in very great numbers... the Gadites and the Reubenites came and spoke to Moses and Eleazar the priest... Moses replied to the Gadites and the Reubenites... Then they stepped up to him and said... Moses said to them... The Gadites and the Reubenites answered Moses... Then Moses gave instructions concerning them to Eleazar the priest, Joshua son of Nun, and the family heads of the Israelite tribes. Moses said to them, "If every armed fighter among the Gadites and the Reubenites crosses the Jordan with you to do battle, at the instance of the Lord..." The Gadites and the Reubenites

> said in reply, "Whatever the Lord has spoken concerning your servants, that we will do." (Num. 32:1–31)

Once each side was satisfied with the terms of the agreement, the Torah states:

> So Moses assigned to them – to the Gadites, the Reubenites, and the half-tribe of Manasseh son of Joseph – the kingdom of Sihon king of the Amorites and the kingdom of King Og of Bashan, the land with its various cities and the territories of the surrounding towns. (32:33)

The Torah refers to the Gadites and the Reubenites by name six times. When the back-and-forth deliberations finally conclude and the time comes for the territorial allotment, suddenly the half-tribe of Manasseh enters the scene!

At the end of the chapter, in the description of the conquests of the two and a half tribes, the Manassites figure prominently in the narrative:

> The Gadites rebuilt... The Reubenites rebuilt... The descendants of Machir son of Manasseh went to Gilead and captured it... so Moses gave Gilead to Machir son of Manasseh... Jair son of Manasseh went... And Nobah went and captured Kenath and its dependencies, renaming it Nobah after himself. (Num. 32:34–42)

Why were the Manassites absent from the entire discussion and why were they suddenly and surprisingly included in the practical territorial allotment? These questions become much sharper when viewed in the context of the serious accusations that Moses levied toward the Reubenites and the Gadites:

> Are your brothers to go to war while you stay here? Why will you turn the minds of the Israelites from crossing into the land that the Lord has given them? That is what your fathers did when I sent them from Kadesh-barnea to survey the land...

> they turned the minds of the Israelites from invading the land that the Lord had given them... And now you, a breed of sinful men, have replaced your fathers, to add still further to the Lord's wrath against Israel...you will bring calamity upon all this people. (32:6–15)

This whole lecture does not include the Manassites. Why?

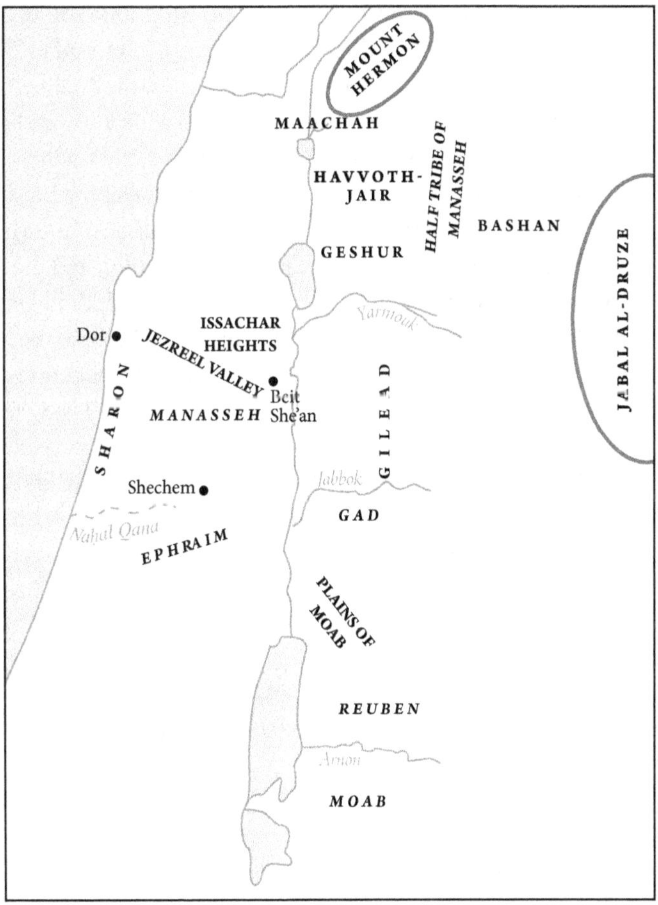

The Samaritan "Solution"

The Samaritan version of the Torah contains a miracle solution to our problem. The version reads:

> The Gadites, the Reubenites, and the half tribe of Manasseh owned cattle in very great numbers ... the Gadites, the Reubenites, and the half tribe of Manasseh came to Moses and Eleazar the priest ... Moses replied to the Reubenites, the Gadites, and the half tribe of Manasseh ... Then they stepped up to him and said ... Moses said to them ... The Reubenites, the Gadites, and the half tribe of Manasseh answered Moses ... Then Moses gave instructions concerning them to Eleazar the priest, Joshua son of Nun, and the family heads of the Israelite tribes. Moses said to them, "If every armed fighter among the Reubenites, the Gadites, and the half tribe of Manasseh crosses the Jordan with you to do battle, at the instance of the Lord ..." The Reubenites, the Gadites, and the half tribe of Manasseh said in reply, "Whatever the Lord has spoken concerning your servants, that we will do ..." So Moses assigned to them – to the Reubenites, the Gadites, and the half tribe of Manasseh son of Joseph – the kingdom of Sihon king of the Amorites and the kingdom of King Og of Bashan, the land with its various cities and the territories of the surrounding towns.[1]

The Samaritans have a well-known predilection for solving difficulties in the Torah by means of textual emendations. There are many cases throughout the Samaritan Torah that can serve as a didactic tool: Almost every time we find a difficulty in the Torah or a contradiction between parallel verses, the Samaritan Torah records what "should" be written. In each of these cases, a teacher would do well to ask his students: Why indeed wasn't the original text of the Torah written like the Samaritan version?

"They Marched On and Went Up the Road to Bashan"

In the course of the people of Israel's passage through Transjordan, which the Torah describes in detail in Numbers 21 and again in Moses'

1. The Samaritan text features the expression "and the half tribe of Manasseh (*velaḥatzi shevet HaMenashe*)" six times. The Hebrew text of the seventh occurrence, *velaḥatzi shevet HaMenashe ben Yosef*, is syntactically curious; it literally means "and the half tribe of *the* Manasseh son of Joseph." This point, along with the very use of "son of Joseph" in the final case rather than in the first occurrence in the passage here, is evidence of the clumsiness of this renovated text.

speech at the beginning of Deuteronomy, we read that after the people of Israel avoided entering the lands of Edom and Moab, they approached Sihon and requested permission to enter his land. When their request was denied, they attacked him and conquered his land. Then the Torah makes the surprising statement, "They marched on and went up the road to Bashan, and King Og of Bashan, with all his people, came out to Edrei to engage them in battle" (Num. 21:33). Why did they go to Bashan? The path to the Jordan and the land of Canaan had become clear for passage with their conquest of the kingdom of Sihon, so what is the explanation for their deviation northward to Bashan?

It seems therefore that the land of Bashan, the territory of the half tribe of Manasseh, is part of the land that had already been designated for conquest. As *Ḥazal* commented: "The Manassites did not take [the land] of their own accord" (Y. Bikkurim 1:8 [64b]). The Reubenites and the Gadites requested to remain in territory that had not been designated for allotment to the tribes, and because of this Moses compared them to the spies, who wanted to remain in the wilderness of Paran and not enter the land. In contrast, the Manassites received a territory in the northern part of Transjordan that was designated for them in the first place. The question is merely how and when this connection between the Manassites and Gilead and Bashan was established.

Territorial Apportionment in the Patriarchal Age

In the chapter on *Parashat Va'era*, I cited my father *z"l* who demonstrated that many of Jacob's grandsons who were born in Egypt were named for places in the Land of Israel. This phenomenon was particularly common among the Manassites, who used names like Gilead, Hepher, Shechem, and Tirzah – all of which refer to places in Manassite territory on both sides of the Jordan – while they were still in Egypt.[2] My father *z"l* explained that Jacob's children, men of action, related seriously and practically to the national destiny that they received from their ancestors: "To your offspring I assign this land." With this in mind, they began apportioning the regions of the land between themselves before their

2. As we discussed there, it is more likely that the geographical names preceded the personal names.

www.zerothkoff.com (Courtesy of Dr. Zev Rothkoff)

Naḥal Yahudiya

immigration to Egypt. Of course, this kind of apportionment was necessarily general, as, in the end, the size of each tribe and its abilities were the deciding factors in the final apportionment. The brothers also wandered through the Land of Israel setting up residence in places that were designated for them. (Thus, Judah set up residence in Timnah, Adullam, and Chezib in the Judean foothills.) The immigration to Egypt disrupted this natural process, but even in Egypt Jacob's sons continued to pine for their territories in the Promised Land and thus gave their children names that fuelled their love for the land. As a result, when the people of Israel finally returned to the land in the time of Moses and Joshua, they were able to relate to and connect with the places whose memory had been preserved for all those years.

According to my father, the geographical allusions to tribal territories in the verse, "He went in pursuit as far as Dan" (Gen. 14:14), and in the blessings of Jacob and Moses to the tribes, referred to that first, theoretical territorial map. Not all the territorial boundaries established in that map became reality later on. The factors that led to changes in the map were the transplantation of the Reubenites and the Gadites to Transjordan against the original plan, Joshua's inability to dispossess the far north of the land, the differences in ability and motivation between the various tribes, and perhaps other reasons as well. Bible critics generally take the opposite approach in their explanation, claiming that the later reality influenced the narrative of the earlier generations after the fact. However, those who explain in this manner become stuck over the details of the earlier texts that never became reality in the future. For instance, in the end Zebulun never dwelled "by the seashore…until Sidon" – this territory was inherited by the tribe of Asher. Similarly, the Reubenites never played a prominent role in the leadership of the nation of Israel.

Returning to our subject, we learned that the Manassites had an early connection to Gilead and Bashan on one side of the Jordan and to northern Samaria on the other side, a connection that had been recognized by the sons of Jacob themselves. Thus, when the road leading up to Gilead and Bashan became clear, the entire nation joined in going up and engaging in battle against King Og of Bashan, and the northern part of Transjordan was rightfully given to the Manassites.

The Novel Solution of "The Student of Rabbi Saadia Gaon"

Two questions arise at this point. First, considering that Manasseh was born in Egypt, how and when did he develop connections to his territory? Second – a larger question about the apportionment map in general – if Manasseh, as one of Joseph's two children, was only a half tribe in the first place, why was his territory so enormous? Indeed, Manasseh's territory is the largest of the tribes of Israel. In Transjordan, Manasseh inherited the entire land of King Og of Bashan, from half of Gilead in the south up to and including Mount Hermon in the north, and from the Sea of Galilee and the northern Jordan in the west until Jabal al-Druze in the east. In Cisjordan, Manasseh's territory includes

View of the Bashan and Hermon – the land of the half tribe of Manasseh

northern Samaria from Shechem and Naḥal Qana in the south until the Jezreel Valley in the north, including most of the Sharon plain in the west and the Jordan Rift Valley in the east, as well as additional territory in the valleys and in the northern Sharon (see Josh. 17:11). How did such a thing come about?

The answer to these questions was supplied by an early and original commentator on the Book of Chronicles, known as "the student of Rabbi Saadia Gaon."[3] The genealogical lists in Chronicles (I Chr. 2:21) mention the conquests of Jair son of Manasseh (who was related to Manasseh through his paternal grandmother and to Judah through his paternal grandfather[4]) in Gilead and Bashan in connection with the early generations of the tribe of Judah, without mentioning at all the Egyptian enslavement, the Exodus, or the conquests of Joshua. "The student of Rabbi Saadia Gaon," in his commentary there, maintains that

3. This name was given to him by the Tosafists. He apparently lived during the tenth century CE. He quotes extensively from the writings of Rabbi Saadia, but also from the first grammarian R. Yehuda ibn Quraysh and from the teachings of the sages of Kairouan, in modern-day Tunisia.

4. See the chapter on *Parashat Bemidbar*.

View of Mount Hermon – the land of the half tribe of Manasseh

Machir and his sons took possession of territory in the Land of Israel "during the rulership of Joseph, who was king of the land." After Joseph died, the land changed hands:

> The gentiles attacked them, took [the territories] from their hands and settled in them until [Israel] came to the Land of Israel [during the time of Moses]. Because of this, the descendants of Machir desired to settle the land of Gilead, so Moses gave them land from the holdings of their ancestor.

The presumption of "the student of Rabbi Saadia Gaon" that there were Egyptian provinces in the Land of Israel on both sides of the Jordan was apparently based on various verses in Genesis (e.g., "So all the world came to Joseph in Egypt to procure rations" [41:57]; "And the money gave out in the land of Egypt and in the land of Canaan" [47:15]; "Chariots, too, and horsemen went up with him ... they came to Goren Ha-Atad" [50:9–10]). Today this approach might be supported by the Egyptian sources and by the Amarna Letters.[5]

5. See the chapter on *Parashat Vayeḥi*.

"The student of Rabbi Saadia Gaon" points out another significant verse in this context: "Since Machir, the first-born of Manasseh, was a valiant warrior, Gilead and Bashan were assigned to him" (Josh. 17:1). *Ḥazal* interpreted this verse to mean that Machir lived to be almost two hundred fifty years old. He was born during Jacob's lifetime and died after Moses' death, and at the age of about two hundred thirty-five he fought in battles and conquered territory (*Seder Olam* 9 and parallels). It is clear that this is a homiletic explanation, but what is the simple truth? From a linguistic perspective it is difficult to interpret this verse to mean that the family of Machir consisted of valiant warriors. The phrase "a valiant warrior" is rendered in the singular and not in the plural. According to "the student of Rabbi Saadia Gaon," however, this verse is not referring to the time of Joshua but to the time of Joseph. Machir – the man, Joseph's grandson, whose children were "born upon Joseph's knees" (Gen. 50:23) – was a valiant warrior and Gilead and Bashan were assigned to him. Since Machir and his sons held possession of the territories of Gilead and Bashan years earlier, their descendants were given these territories during the time of Moses and Joshua.

Having established this interpretation of the verse, "the student of Rabbi Saadia Gaon" suggests an innovative explanation for the final verses in *Parashat Matot*: "Know, now, an excellent explanation – that those details in the *Ḥumash* regarding Machir, Jair, and Nobah are related retroactively, for Machir, Jair, and Nobah did not take any [land] in the wilderness" (i.e., in the time of Moses after the period of wandering in the wilderness). Yehuda Kiel, in his introduction to his *Daat Mikra* on Chronicles, cites another original author who developed similar ideas: Rabbi Yehuda the Pious, the leader of Ḥasidei Ashkenaz during the time of the Tosafists, in his commentary on the Torah in the name of his father Rabbi Samuel the Pious. Rabbi Samuel draws our attention to the Tanakh's description of Ephraim son of Joseph in I Chronicles:

> The sons of Ephraim: Shutelaḥ, his son Bered, his son Taḥat, his son Elada, his son Taḥat, his son Zavad, his son Shutelaḥ, also Ezer and Elad. The men of Gath, born in the land, killed them because they had gone down to take their cattle. And Ephraim their father mourned many days, and his brothers came to comfort him. He

> cohabited with his wife, who conceived and bore a son; and she named him Beria, because it occurred when there was misfortune in his house. His daughter was She'era, who built both Lower and Upper Beth-horon, and Uzzen-sheerah. His son Refaḥ, his son Reshef, his son Telaḥ, his son Taḥan, his son Laadan, his son Ammihud, his son Elishama, his son Non, his son Joshua. (7:20–27)

She'era daughter of Ephraim lived six generations before Joshua son of Nun and built cities in the land (in the territory of Ephraim!). Rabbi Yehuda the Pious writes (in his commentary on Exodus 1:7):

> My father would prove from Chronicles that throughout the time that Israel was in Egypt, they would occasionally travel to the soil of Jacob our father and would build cities there. And I believe that the descendants of Joseph specifically would do this, and they had permission [to do so] from Pharaoh; in respect to Joseph, Pharaoh would treat them with respect, [allowing them] to improve and strengthen their inheritance. And they would settle the land with tenants and charge them a tax…

A similar opinion, slightly different in tone, is found in the commentary of Rabbi Isaac Abrabanel on our *parasha*:

> Some say that Joseph, *a"h*, bought these cities during the time of famine in Egypt, and after his death Ammon and others seized them. And now that Israel had gained the upper hand over them and the cities have been restored to Israel's possession, the descendants of Machir requested the inheritance of their matriarch.[6]

To summarize: The picture that arises from the innovative approach advocated earliest by "the student of Rabbi Saadia Gaon," later by Rabbi Samuel the Pious and his son Rabbi Yehuda, then by Abrabanel, and in the previous generation by my father and Yehuda Kiel, is that the

6. I am indebted to my friend Professor Ḥaim Ben David for bringing this source to my attention.

sons of Jacob had already drawn up a general, basic plan for apportioning the land between themselves in the future – even before they immigrated to Egypt. In addition, the sons of Joseph were active in settling whole regions of the land during the time that their father served as second-in-command to Pharaoh, perhaps even at his behest. After Joseph, his

(Courtesy of the Kiel family)

Yehuda Kiel *z"l*

brothers, and that entire generation died out, when "a new king arose over Egypt who did not know Joseph," the people's grip on these holdings in the Land of Israel collapsed. However, their yearning for the land and the territories that were designated for each of the tribes continued to resonate within the people. This yearning influenced the names they gave their children, the blessings that Moses bestowed upon the people and, in the end, the very conquest of the land and its apportionment.

Adding Another Level to the Theory of "The Student of Rabbi Saadia Gaon"

My own generation, which already grew up on *Daat Mikra* and was familiar with my father's teachings, has paved a new path within this discourse, one that continues in the same direction as that of the older generation, but with a more radical bent. These new ideas have percolated among us for a long time as a kind of oral tradition. In 2010, Rabbi Yaakov Medan formulated these ideas elegantly and convincingly in print. I will follow in his footsteps, with slightly different points of emphasis.

Let us begin with the strongest point: the comparison between the two censuses in the Book of Numbers. The first census took place at Sinai, not long after the Exodus. The second census took place in the plains of Moab, in the fortieth year following the Exodus. Between the two censuses, an entirely new generation took the place of the old one. By the second census, the members of the people of Israel who left Egypt had died and their children, who were about to enter and settle the land of Canaan, were the ones who were counted. It is interesting to note that the total population of the nation had not changed by much. At the first census, the total count was 603,550, while at the second census the count was 601,730. The counts for each individual tribe had grown or shrunk – though not excessively. (Reuben: 46,500–43,730; Gad: 45,650–40,500; Judah: 74,600–76,500; Issachar: 54,400–64,300; Zebulun: 57,400–60,500; Ephraim: 40,500–32,500; Benjamin: 35,400–45,600; Dan 62,700–64,400; Asher: 41,500–53,400; Naphtali: 53,400–45,400.) The counts for two tribes, however, did change dramatically: Simeon, which shrank from 59,300 to 22,200 and Manasseh, which grew from 32,200 to 52,700.

Ḥazal addressed the question of why Simeon shrank to such an extent, explaining that all of the 24,000 people who died at the incident of Baal-peor were from the tribe of Simeon. This supposition has ramifications for our understanding of the sin of Baal-peor in general and in particular of Simeon's role in the conquest of the land and its apportionment. But the tribe under discussion here is Manasseh: What is the background for the unexpected surge – over twenty thousand additional men – in Manasseh's population?

Perhaps we may make a bold speculation, going one step beyond the suggestion of the previous generation's scholars. It may be that the twenty thousand men added to the tribe of Manasseh in the plains of Moab were descendants of Machir, Jair, and Nobah, who never returned to Egypt after establishing cities in Transjordan, but rather remained in the land of Bashan. Because these representatives of the nation of Israel stayed in the Land of Israel for all those years, they were able to avoid the bitter experience of the harsh Egyptian enslavement, never toiling with "mortar and bricks" and never encountering the edict of "Every boy that is born you shall throw into the Nile." On the other hand, these people also missed out on the high points of Israel's period of early nationhood, such as the Exodus, the Song at the Sea, and the pronouncement of *naaseh venishma* – "we will faithfully do." Imagine our ancestors arriving in the plains of Moab after all the hardships of the wilderness, after thirty-eight years of wandering during which the entire previous generation died, when suddenly a group of tanned "sabras" – who have never felt the sting of exile – come riding out from the hills. Imagine how emotional this meeting with their Hebrew-speaking cousins – partners in the heritage of Abraham, Isaac, and Jacob, keeping the flame alive in the Land of Israel – must have been. Their lives here were certainly not easy once they lost the protective support of the sympathetic Egyptian government. It must not have been easy to weather the rise to power of Geshur and Maacah (see I Chronicles 2:23), heralding the reign of King Og of Bashan to whom they were certainly subject. But they survived and continued to settle the northern Gilead and Bashan, and perhaps some of their counterparts existed here and there in Cisjordan as well, Ephraimites or descendants of Aner, Eshkol, and Mamre, members of Abraham's household or servants in Jacob's household who never immigrated to Egypt.

The primary task at hand was to liberate the land of these new/old brothers from the hegemony of King Og of Bashan. Moses and the people of Israel happily and hastily accomplished this task. After the victory over King Og and his people, it was understood that the vast territory throughout which the Manassites were scattered would be immediately authorized as the tribal territory of the people who had preserved it throughout those difficult years.

Rabbi Yaakov Medan explains that from a spiritual and religious perspective it was very important at this juncture to incorporate these brothers – who had retained the ethos and belief system of the Patriarchs – into the divine covenant as it was formulated at the Exodus and at Sinai. Because of this, the covenant was forged anew at the plains of Moab.[7]

---

7. It may be that the covenant at Mount Ebal during the time of Joshua was similarly forged for the purpose of assimilating the parallel Hebrew population in the land of Canaan into the nation of Israel.

"Just as Israel Did"

This theory may also explain a seemingly problematic expression found in *Parashat Devarim,* when Moses outlines the changes that occurred in Transjordan: The Moabites dispossessed the early Emim, the descendants of Esau wiped out the Horites and settled the land in their place, and the Ammonites dispossessed the Zamzummim. Moses then presents an analogy: "Just as Israel did in the land of their inheritance, which the Lord had given to them" (Deut. 2:12). The difficulty is clear: The people of Israel had not yet conquered any part of the land at this point! Several farfetched answers have been proposed: that Moses' comment here is one of several statements that deviate chronologically from the order of the Book of Deuteronomy and actually refer to the conquest of Sihon and Og that occurred later (Chizkuni, Seforno); that these statements refer to Joshua's future conquest of the land of Canaan (Nahmanides, Abrabanel); or that this is a later editorial comment regarding the conquest of Canaan (most modern scholars). Based on its structure, the chapter seems to be referring generally to the nations living in various parts of Transjordan (with an addition concerning the Caphtorim who dispossess the Avvim in Cisjordan) and the time frame of the chapter precedes the Israelite conquest in both sides of the Jordan. The assumption that the descendants of Manasseh were consistent residents of the northern Transjordan during the generations of slavery and wandering through the wilderness may shed new light on this verse as well. Upon reaching Transjordan, the people of Israel meet the nations of Edom, Moab, and Ammon, as well as the two Amorite kings. They also meet tens of thousands of Israelites with an ancient territory in the northern region of Transjordan. In this framework, it is certainly appro priate to include these Israelites among the nations who carved out a territory in Transjordan – "just as Israel did in the land of their inheritance."

The First Aliya

The entry into the land of the people of Israel during the era of Moses and Joshua can be compared to Israel's revival in our own time. The State of Israel was born in the years following the Holocaust, when Holocaust survivors banded together with Jews from Arab countries in the Land of Israel, fought against the Arab nations, and triumphed. In addition to these immigrants, there were already many Jews in the land, some of whose families had been living there for over two hundred years or more. This group included Sephardim, Hasidim, students of the Vilna *Gaon* and immigrants from the First Aliya in the late nineteenth century. Struggling with Arab terror attacks, disease, and lack of resources, these people nevertheless built colonies and, afterward, moshavim and kibbutzim. These were the "sabras" who never felt the sting of exile. If one were to write a history of Israel in the modern era, from a national-historical perspective, one might very well ignore the presence of these early settlers, since the critical contours of the nation-building process never passed their way. One might highlight Herzlian Zionism, the later Aliyot, the Holocaust, and the mass immigration that took place after the birth of the state. Despite this, a different author might recount the development of the Land of Israel specifically from the perspective of these early "Land-of-Israel" Jews.

Both approaches are correct – each in its own framework and context. We must view the events of the Tanakh and the way they are described in the same way. The "mainstream" faction of the people of Israel experience the enslavement in Egypt, the Exodus under Moses' leadership, the journey through the wilderness, and the conquest of the land; indeed, the Torah and the Book of Joshua follow the narrative of this primary faction. In contrast, the genealogical chapters in Chronicles focus on the other members of the people of Israel, who preserved the reality of Israel's continuous settlement in the land.

For further study:

Elitzur, Yehuda. "*Anashim Venaḥalot BiMenashe Uveshivtei Yisrael.*" *Al Atar* 4–5 (1999): 243–249 [Hebrew].

Kiel, Y. *Daat Mikra: Divrei Hayamim* I (Introduction), 64–66; II, 87–89 [Hebrew].

Kirchheim R. (compiler), *Peirush al Divrei Hayamim: Meyuchas Le'eḥad Mitalmidei Sa'adia Ga'on, Mutza Le'or al pi Shelosha Kitvei Yad.* Jerusalem, 1966 (Frankfurt am Main 1874) [Hebrew].

Medan, Y. "*Ḥavira el HaEretzyisraelim.*" *Makor Rishon: Shabbat, Erev Shabbat Parashat Matot-Masei, 27 Tammuz 5770* (July 9, 2010): 2–3 [Hebrew].

Viezel, E. "Context, Harmonization, and the Uniqueness of the Commentaries to the Book of Chronicles." *Jewish Studies Quarterly* 22 (2015): 10–15.

Parashat Masei

Were the Levite Cities Also Cities of Refuge?

The Lord spoke to Moses in the steppes of Moab at the Jordan near Jericho, saying: Instruct the Israelite people to assign, out of the holdings apportioned to them, cities for the Levites to dwell in; you shall also assign to the Levites space around their cities. The cities shall be theirs to dwell in, and the space shall be for the cattle they own and their possession and all their sustenance. The city space that you are to assign to the Levites shall extend a thousand cubits outside the city wall all around. You shall measure off two thousand cubits outside the city on the east side, two thousand on the south side, two thousand on the west side, and two thousand on the north side, with the city in the center. That shall be the space for their cities.

The cities that you assign to the Levites shall comprise the six cities of refuge that you are to designate for a manslayer to flee to, to which you shall add forty-two cities. Thus, the total of the cities that you assign to the Levites shall be forty-eight cities, with their spaces. In assigning cities from the holdings of

> the Israelites, take more from the larger tribes and less from the smaller, so that each assigns cities to the Levites in proportion to the share it receives. (Num. 35:1–8)

Were the Levite Cities Also Cities of Refuge?

Certainly not. The verse says this explicitly:

> The cities that you assign to the Levites shall comprise the six cities of refuge...to which you shall add forty-two cities. Thus, the total of the cities that you assign to the Levites shall be forty-eight cities, with their spaces.

According to the simple meaning of the text here, the parallel between the two types of cities goes in one direction only: the six cities of refuge are also Levite cities, but the remaining forty-two cities are Levite cities only – and not cities of refuge. In Joshua 20, six cities of refuge are enumerated: Kedesh, Shechem, and Hebron; and Bezer, Ramoth, and Golan – and their unique role is explained. The list of Levite cities is given in chapter 21 (including these six cities of refuge).

Why were the cities of refuge also Levite cities? It seems that this question contains a characteristic found in other mitzvot in the Torah. The Torah generally takes into consideration the prevalent customs and laws of the world, while giving these mitzvot an ethical framework that fits with the belief system of the people of Israel. This is the case regarding the laws of *yibbum* (levirate marriage) and of the redemption of lands, which were prevalent laws at the time when the Torah was given. The Torah limited the scope of these laws, presenting them as a mitzva only in cases where the deceased had no children. The case of marrying the widow of one's deceased brother when the brother did have children and the case of marrying the widow of one's deceased uncle were considered forbidden sexual relations. Indeed, the Torah says of those who engage in such a relationship: "They shall die childless" and "They shall remain childless" (Lev. 20:20–21), meaning that in these cases, the attempt to preserve the name of the deceased will not succeed. In cases of more distant family connections, redemption and *yibbum* remained optional. Slavery was permitted but limited, and different laws were established

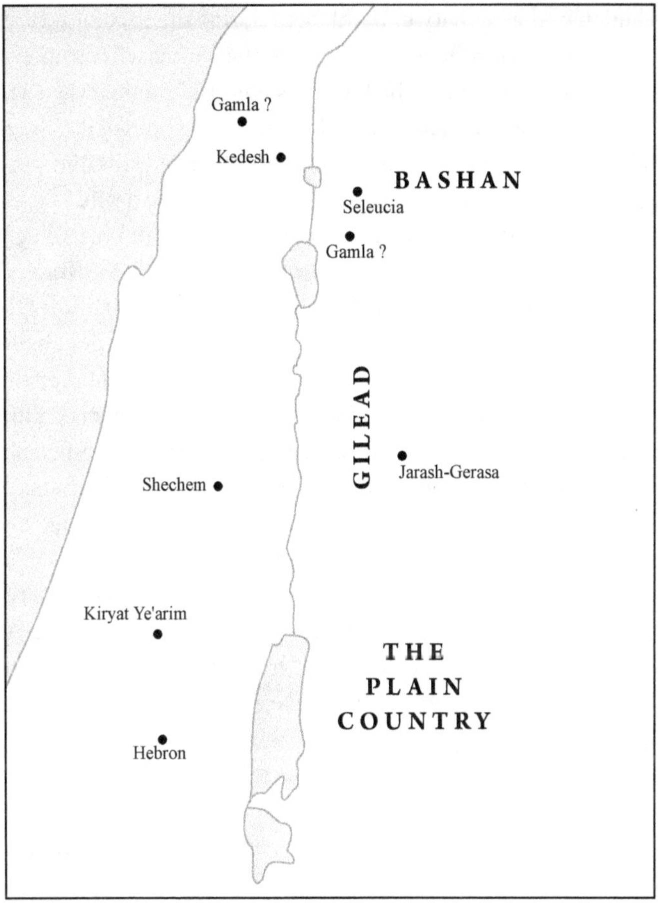

for a gentile slave and a Hebrew slave.[1] Taking a beautiful woman as a captive of war was permitted but modified, as was avenging the blood of a person who was killed, as well as several other mitzvot.

The mitzva of the cities of refuge falls into this category. In the cultures of the ancient world, and even today, there are places that are designated as "extraterritorial" locations and can provide asylum for individuals who are being pursued for political reasons or for various kinds of criminals. Many will recall the case of the terrorists who fled to

1. Even the gentile slave was protected from excessive cruelty: "He must be avenged" (Ex. 21:20); "He shall let him go free on account of his eye" (21:26).

the Church of the Nativity in Bethlehem during the Second Intifada in 2002, when Israeli forces refused to storm the church, choosing instead to lay siege to the site until the terrorists emerged on their own accord. The Torah establishes categorically that protecting oneself in this way is unethical: "When a man schemes against another and kills him treacherously, you shall take him from My very altar to be put to death" (Ex. 21:14). In fact, Solomon, the king of Israel, followed this dictum regarding Joab son of Zeruiah (I Kings 2:29–34).[2] On the other hand, the Torah does not reject the notion of asylum altogether. The Torah establishes that it is possible for an unintentional manslayer to seek refuge, though not for an intentional murderer. According to the Torah, an unintentional manslayer is also considered a murderer, and the blood avenger is permitted to pursue him and kill him. However, it is the community's responsibility to offer the manslayer protection. The Torah intentionally refrains from establishing the *Mishkan* or the Temple as places to seek refuge to convey the idea that the Divine Presence does not negate the laws of basic morality. Because of this, Bethel, Shiloh, and Jerusalem are not cities of refuge (despite the greatest efforts of various scholars to foist a "tradition of sanctity" onto the Levite cities). Instead of holy cities, the Torah sets aside some of the Levite cities as places where a murderer can seek refuge. We can provide a monetary-legalistic explanation or an ethical-educational explanation for this decision; the two possible directions do not necessarily contradict each other. The monetary-legalistic explanation is that each city of Levites was removed from the jurisdiction of the tribe in whose territory it was situated and set aside for national purposes. Therefore, it was possible to add a national purpose tied to communal responsibility. The ethical-educational explanation is that the Levites were the nation's educators and Torah teachers, and it was fitting that one who killed another person inadvertently through negligence should learn a proper way of life from these role models. *Sefer Ha-Ḥinukh* (Mitzva 408) proposes that such holy men, entrusted with the task of teaching Torah to

2. Contrary to some approaches in rabbinic sources, the plain meaning of the Torah agrees with R. Yoḥanan's saying: "And I say that the altar does not afford protection, nor does its roof afford protection, nor even does that of Shiloh afford protection, nor does the Eternal House afford protection" (Y. Makkot 2:6).

the nation, could also be trusted to provide support to the person being pursued and to prevent the blood avenger from harming him.

A Surprising Talmudic Passage: All Levite Cities Were Also Cities of Refuge!

The Talmud raises the following question about the Mishna's statement, "To where are they banished? To the cities of asylum, to the three [cities] in Transjordan and to the three [cities] in the land of Canaan" (Makkot 9b):

> Were three cities [necessary] in Transjordan (a land of two and a half tribes), [the same as] three cities for the [whole] Land of Israel (a land of nine and a half tribes)? Abaye said: Murderers were common in Gilead, as it is written, "Gilead is a city of evil-doers, tracked up with blood" (Hos. 6:8). (Makkot 9b–10a)

The Talmud adds to this a new question:

> But were there no more [than six cities of refuge]? Is it not written, "To which you shall add forty-two cities"?... Abaye said: [The main six cities] afforded asylum with or without cognizance,[3] while [the additional cities] only afforded asylum knowingly, but not without cognizance. (*Makkot* 10a)

In other words, it was clear to the authors of both the question and the solution in this passage that all forty-eight Levite cities were also cities of refuge, and that the only difference between these cities and the six additional special cities of refuge was that the six cities would accept a manslayer even "without cognizance."

3. According to Rashi, Rambam, and Ritva, one might enter a city of refuge "without cognizance" by entering without knowing that the place is a city of refuge, or by entering while sleeping on the back of an animal. Another interpretation is that "cognizance" refers to that of the *beit din* or the city's elders. In other words, the main six cities are considered designated places for accepting a manslayer; no one may bar his entrance, and the city's elders are obligated to accept him into the city. However, in the forty-two cities, the elders have the liberty to decide if they want to accept the manslayer or not (compare to Josh. 20).

The same approach returns at the end of the chapter (Makkot 13a). The Mishna states: "They used to pay rent to the Levites; these are the words of R. Meir. R. Yehuda says that they did not pay them any rent." Following this statement, the Talmud cites a dispute between Rav Kahana and Rava. Rav Kahana says that "the difference of opinion is only with regard to the [main] six cities [of refuge]...but, with regard to the other forty-two cities, they are agreed that they did pay them rent." Rava argues on this, stating that "the difference of opinion is rather about the other forty-two cities... but with regard to the [main] six they are fully in agreement that no rent was paid to them." Again, the point of departure is that all Levite cities would accept manslayers, and the *Amora'im* only disputed the issue of paying rent to the Levite landlords. In the main six cities of refuge, there is reason to claim that the unintentional manslayer is considered the owner of the land, as these cities were largely established on his behalf, and therefore he does not need to pay rent to the landlord. But in the forty-two other Levite cities, the manslayer is considered a guest, and therefore there is more reason to require him to pay rent.

Maimonides accepted the principle that the above two Talmudic passages presumed, and, in his characteristically terse and clear manner, extracted the bottom line that arose from them:

> All Levite cities offer refuge; each one of them is a city of refuge. As it says, "To which you shall add forty-two cities. Thus the total of the cities that you assign to the Levites shall be forty-eight cities." The verse thus established an association between them; all of them offer refuge.
>
> What, then, is the difference between cities of refuge that are set aside for refuge and the other Levite cities? The cities of refuge offer refuge with or without cognizance; once one enters their confines, he attains refuge. The other Levite cities only offer refuge with cognizance. Also, a murderer who lives in a city of refuge does not pay rent. If, by contrast, he lives in one of the other Levite cities, he must pay his landlord rent. (*Hilkhot Rotze'aḥ* 8:9–10)

Nahmanides: Only Six Cities of Refuge

In the face of the position outlined above and its supporters, Nahmanides, in his commentary on *Parashat Masei* (in the section added after he moved to the Land of Israel), rejected this approach. He writes:

> "And even though in the land of Canaan there were nine tribes [and a half], and here [on the east side of the Jordan] there were only two [and a half], Scripture gave them an equal number of cities of refuge, because in Gilead [on the east side of the Jordan] murderers were numerous, as it is written, 'Gilead is a city of evildoers, tracked up with blood' (Hos. 6:8)." This is Rashi's language, based on the words of our Rabbis. Now even though the [cities of] refuge were only for those who killed in error [and these murderers of Gilead killed deliberately], they would kill in treachery and make themselves appear as if they had done it in error, and therefore it was necessary to increase [proportionately] the number of their cities of refuge, in order to be able to take in all of them, since one could not tell who had killed deliberately. If so, [we must say that] The Holy One, Blessed Be He, commanded this on account of the future [since He knew that murderers in Gilead would be numerous], similar to that which it says [of the future generations], "This people will thereupon go astray" (Deut. 31:16). Or perhaps the Rabbis will say that the climate of the land of Gilead was conducive to producing murderers since it was populated.
>
> But I wonder! For in the opinion of our Rabbis, of blessed memory, the [cities mentioned in the] verse that says, "to which you shall add forty-two cities" were all commanded as cities of refuge, and thus there were thirty-six of them in the land of Canaan, and six beyond the Jordan, and they all offered protection, in the opinion of our Rabbis! Thus the cities of refuge throughout the Land of Israel were [distributed] justly and equally, for each of the [twelve] tribes received four cities of refuge. He also counted the tribe of Manasseh in the land of Canaan, because the majority of it was there. Perhaps in [the proportion of] the [six] appointed cities God increased [the number of these cities] beyond the Jordan, in honor of Moses, so that he would set

> aside half of that number [since he could not enter the land of Canaan], but in their totality [of forty-eight cities] they were all divided up by measure and according to proportion [each tribe receiving four cities].
>
> According to the simple meaning of Scripture, it appears to me that the land of the [east] side of the Jordan was very large, for it contained [the kingdoms of] the two great Amorite kings [Sihon and Og], about whose might the verses speak in superlative terms, and [this kingdom became] even greater when Ammon and Moab became a legitimate [conquest of Israel] through them [who had captured large districts of the lands of Ammon and Moab, and from whom Israel subsequently took them by the right of conquest], whereas the kings of the land of Canaan were merely kings of cities, and every ruler of a city was called a "king," as you see [from the verse]: "the king of Jerusalem, one; the king of Hebron, one" (Josh. 12:10), although between them [these two cities] there is a distance of [only] half a day's walk. Similarly, the sages mention that between Bethel and Ai is a distance of [only] four miles, and yet each of these cities had its own king. It is possible that it was the custom in those generations to call every ruler of a city "king," or perhaps [this was only in the Land of Israel] in honor of the Land of Israel, as our Rabbis, of blessed memory, explained. In any case, they were not kings of countries, but only kings of particular cities. And thus it is written, "Seventy kings, with thumbs and big toes cut off, used to pick up scraps under my table" (Judges 1:7). Thus the land on the [east] side of the Jordan was a very large land, and required three cities of refuge just as the whole of the Land of Israel on the [west] side of the Jordan did, and the forty-two cities [set aside] were for the [cities and] pasturelands of the Levites and not for refuge.

Nahmanides opens his commentary by pointing out two apparent problems with the Talmud's explanation that "murderers were common in Gilead." First, the cities of refuge were designated for unintentional manslayers, not murderers. And second, how could it be that the Torah established cities of refuge based on the social reality at the time of the

Latter Prophets? Nahmanides resolves both problems with tenuous explanations.[4]

In the main section of Nahmanides' commentary, he refers both explicitly and implicitly to two strong objections to the Talmud's question "Were three cities [necessary] in Transjordan, [the same as] three cities for the Land of Israel (Cisjordan)?" and to the given answer that "murderers were common in Gilead":

- If all the Levite cities would offer refuge, as the Talmud says, this means that there was an appropriate number of cities of refuge designated for each tribe. As we read in Joshua 21, the Levite cities were divided between the tribes of Israel justly and evenly. In Transjordan, there were only ten cities, compared to thirty-eight in Cisjordan, which fits perfectly with the number of tribes on each side. There were four cities for each tribe (with a slight deviation that Nahmanides did not mention: Judah and Simeon gave nine cities in total, while Naphtali gave only three). Therefore, there is no question of disproportionate distribution of cities of refuge.[5]

---

4. To resolve the first problem, the Tosafists proposed a clever midrashic solution. There is a well-known midrash explaining the verse "But it came about by an act of God" (Ex. 21:13). Two people killed others without witnesses, one unintentionally and one intentionally. God causes both of the killers to visit the same inn, and then causes the unintentional killer to fall upon the intentional killer, killing him. As a result, the intentional killer has died and the unintentional killer must now flee to a city of refuge. Thus, because of the meeting between the intentional killer and the unintentional killer afforded by this kind of inn, there was a need for additional cities of refuge.
   Rabbi Jonathan of Lunel suggested a different, original solution for both problems that is no less homiletic than that of the Tosafists. He wrote in his commentary on Masekhet Makkot: "Thick forests are common in Gilead, as described in II Sam. 18, and many would go there with their fellows to chop wood. Therefore, there were many unintentional murderers there."
   My good friend Rabbi Dudi Leibovich suggests a simpler solution. We learned in the Mishna: "To begin with, every manslayer, whether unintentional or intentional, was first sent forward to [one of] the cities of refuge." Therefore there was a need for cities of refuge in places where intentional murderers were common. Later, I found this approach in the commentary of Ḥizkuni.
5. It may be noted that Nahmanides related to the four Manassite cities as if they were located in Cisjordan, contrary to the explicit statement of the verses (Josh. 21:25–27).

- The distance between the cities of refuge was a function of the size of the territory and not of the size of the population. Thus, whether there were numerous unintentional manslayers in the region or only a few, there only needed to be a city of refuge close enough to protect a manslayer from the blood-avenger. And since the size of the territory in Transjordan was similar to that of Cisjordan, the equal apportionment of three cities for each region was justified.

In light of this, Nahmanides reaches the firm conclusion that, based on the simple understanding of the matter, only six cities would offer refuge, while the remaining forty-two were merely Levite cities and not cities of refuge!

How Did Nahmanides Have Permission to Disagree with the Talmud?

Almost three hundred years after Nahmanides' death, Radbaz (Rabbi David ben Zimra)[6] was asked how Nahmanides permitted himself "to interpret in Scripture the opposite of the law that was agreed upon in the Talmud."

Radbaz responds that Nahmanides relied on the Talmud Yerushalmi, in which the possibility that all the Levite cities were cities of refuge was not mentioned at all. Moreover, a *baraita* is cited in the Yerushalmi in which the *Tanna'im* use midrashic methodology to increase significantly the number of cities of refuge:

> Moses set aside three cities in Transjordan. When they entered the land they set aside three more. In the future they will set aside three more…making nine. Abba Shaul says: "'Three' (Deut. 19:2)…['Three' (19:7) – three sections that each contain three, making nine, and 'more' (19:9) – making twelve." R. Nehorai

In addition, Nahmanides' final sum of the Levite cities in Transjordan and Cisjordan requires some adjustments (35+7 instead of 36+6).

6. Radbaz was born in Spain in 1479 and died in Safed in 1573. He was famous primarily for the thousands of responsa that he wrote on all areas of Torah throughout his long and productive life.

8. says: "'Three...' (19:2); 'three...' (19:7); 'three...' (19:9) – making nine, and 'more' – making twelve. 'To those three' – making fifteen."

Radbaz argues that if these *Tanna'im* had been aware of the inference drawn by the Talmud Bavli, they certainly would have added all the Levite cities to this list.

In truth, I believe that Nahmanides himself makes stronger points in the passage cited above than Radbaz makes on his behalf. Nahmanides demonstrates that the first part of the passage in the Talmud Bavli can only be explained if one assumes that there were only six cities of refuge. In other words, the Yerushalmi is not the only source that contradicts the Bavli; even the Bavli itself – in the first part of the passage – contradicts its own points from the end of the passage.

Interim Summary

It seems, then, that most rabbinic sources, meaning all tannaitic sources, the Talmud Yerushalmi and, partly, even the Bavli, agree that there were only six active cities of refuge, whereas the remaining forty-two Levite cities were not cities of refuge. This is essentially the simple meaning of the biblical text in *Parashat Masei*. Additionally, the cities of refuge are mentioned again in *Parashat Va'etḥanan* (Deut. 4:41–43) and in *Parashat Shoftim* (19:1–10), and again in Joshua 20. In none of these places does the text mention anything about the other Levite cities serving as cities of refuge. The *Amora'im* who mention the possibility that all forty-eight Levite cities offered refuge are Abaye, Rava, and Rav Kahana,[7] and the redactor of the two talmudic *sugyot* as well. These three sages – R. Kahana, Rava, and Abaye – belong to the fourth generation of *Amora'im*.[8] This means that it can be deter-

7. The name R. Kahana appears repeatedly through the generations of *Amora'im*. In our case, the fact that Rava is the one who argues with R. Kahana and is mentioned after him indicates that this was apparently the third R. Kahana, who was the disciple of R. Yehuda and Rabba.
8. The fact that Abaye was the same person who said that "Murderers were common in Gilead" is puzzling, since, as Nahmanides explained, this view is not compatible with the view that all forty-eight cities would offer refuge. In other words, Abaye seems to contradict himself here.

mined that until the fourth generation of Babylonian *Amora'im*, the notion never occurred to anyone that all the Levite cities offered refuge to unintentional manslayers. With this background in mind, the degree of assertiveness of the two passages that indeed maintain that all the Levite cities offered refuge is somewhat baffling. In both passages, the idea that all forty-eight Levite cities offered refuge is presented as a conclusive fact, without any uncertainty or dispute.

How can we untangle ourselves from this quandary?

A Few Words on the Two Lists of Levite Cities

The Levite cities are enumerated in two places in the Tanakh. The first time is in Joshua 21 and the second time is in I Chronicles 6. The two lists are similar but not identical. The list in Joshua 21 is very schematic: Every one of the twelve tribes of Israel provides the Levites with four cities,[9] for a total of forty-eight cities.[10] The list opens with a short story:

> The heads of the ancestral house of the Levites approached the priest Eleazar, Joshua son of Nun, and the heads of the ancestral houses of the Israelite tribes, and spoke to them at Shiloh in the land of Canaan, as follows: "The Lord commanded through

9. There is one divergence from this rule. Judah and Simeon provided one additional city, yielding a total of nine cities between the two tribes. Naphtali provided only three cities, one fewer than the other tribes. It may be that the purpose of this was to fulfill – at least minimally – the injunction of "take more from the larger tribes and less from the smaller" (Num. 35:8). In some chapters of this volume (*Parashot Naso, Balak, Pinḥas, Matot*) we have learned that the process of conquest and inheritance of the country in the time of Moses and Joshua was not a technical activity of delivery or lottery of estates. It largely depended on the power, motivation, and historical memories of each tribe. Thus, the most powerful tribes of Judah and Manasseh volunteered for the challenge of fighting bitter enemies and overcoming difficult terrain, such as desert or forest. In contrast, for other tribes, especially the tribe of Dan, which was large in population but minimally active, it was adequate to receive their allotment from the public. In such a situation, it was not justified to fulfill the commandment "take more from the larger tribes and less from the smaller" in its simple meaning.
10. For some reason, the list of the four cities provided by the tribe of Reuben is missing from the primary version of the Masoretic text, though the list appears in secondary versions.

> Moses that we be given cities to live in, along with their spaces for our livestock." So the Israelites, in accordance with the Lord's command, assigned to the Levites, out of their own portions, the following cities with their spaces. (Josh. 21:1–3)

In contrast, the list in Chronicles is problematic in several respects. First, the numbers of the cities written in the verses do not fit well with the actual number. According to the numbers recorded in the verses, there are forty-eight cities. However, there are actually only forty-two cities listed: the tribe of Dan is not mentioned and the tribe of Simeon is mentioned only in the interim summary in the middle of the chapter; Judah provides eight cities, Ephraim provides six, and each of the rest of the tribes provides between two and four. Most of the names of the cities match those listed in Joshua, but a few are different, among which some are completely different cities while others are different versions of the names listed in Joshua. The list of Levite cities appears in Chronicles after several genealogical lists of Levite families, and the section is preceded by the heading: "These are their dwelling-places according to their settlements" (I Chr. 6:39). What lies behind the differences between the two lists? It is clear that part of the answer relates to the existence of two alternative forms for the same name (such as Almon/Alemeth or Holon/Hilen), or what seems to be two textual versions (like Dimnah/Rimmomo, a completely different city). In the critical and semi-critical scholarship, this approach was expanded to the point where the vast majority of differences were viewed simply as textual variations. Since the various versions of the Septuagint feature a greater similarity between the two lists, the scholars categorically followed the Septuagint in viewing them as two parallel versions of the same list. What certainly contributed to this conclusion was the underlying conception that the two lists are not ancient, and that the narrative framework in Joshua was merely a decorative element. However, I believe that anyone who reads precisely what is written in the texts will easily reach a different conclusion to the question of the major differences between the two lists (as Yehezkel Kaufmann already addressed with respect to the list in Joshua). Aside from the certain textual problems regarding discrepancies between the two lists and the problems with the numbers recorded in Chronicles, the main difference is that the Book of Joshua presents *the plan,* while the Book of Chronicles presents *the reality after several generations*. Naturally, the plan is symmetrical and orderly, but as the Israeli saying goes, every plan is a basis for change. It is perfectly reasonable that most, but not all, of the plan was realized, and that some of the cities provided were different from those originally intended.[11]

The Discovery

Now the time has come to return to our topic.

One day, I was examining the two lists of Levite cities simultaneously, when suddenly a small, but seemingly very significant difference drew my attention. The list in Joshua states: "To the sons of Aaron the priest they gave *the city* of refuge for manslayers: Hebron with its spaces, Libnah with its spaces, Jattir with its spaces, Eshtemoa with its spaces..." (Josh. 21:13–14). Its parallel in Chronicles reads, almost identically: "To the sons of Aaron they gave *the cities* of refuge: Hebron and Libnah with its spaces, Jattir and Eshtemoa with its spaces..." (I Chr. 6:42). And again, in Joshua: "They gave them (the sons of Kehath) *the city* of refuge for manslayers: Shechem with its spaces in the hill country of Ephraim, Gezer with its spaces..." (Josh. 21:21). And in Chronicles: "They gave them *the cities* of refuge: Shechem with its spaces in the hill country of Ephraim, Gezer with its spaces..." (I Chr. 6:52).

It turns out that the very dispute between Maimonides and Nahmanides – which was disputed before them between the Bavli and the Yerushalmi – was already a dispute between Joshua and Chronicles! In Joshua, Hebron is a city of refuge, while Libnah, Jattir, Eshtemoa, and all the rest are merely Levite cities. Likewise, Shechem alone is a city of refuge, while Gezer, Kibzaim, and Beth-horon are merely Levite cities. In Chronicles, in contrast, all the listed cities are cities of refuge!

11. Regarding the version conveyed by the Septuagint, it should be noted that it was typical of the less punctilious versions of Scripture (such as the Septuagint, the Dead Sea Scrolls, and the Samaritan Pentateuch) to minimize differences between parallel chapters.

In light of the differences between the character of the list in Joshua and that of the list in Chronicles, we can start out by saying that Nahmanides was certainly correct that the simple understanding of the mitzva as written in the Torah is that only the main six cities offered refuge, unlike the remaining forty-two cities. Therefore, the orderly plan for the cities of refuge following the conquest and apportionment of the land was referring only to the main six cities of refuge. On the other hand, the notion that all the Levite cities would offer refuge is also anchored in the texts. It may be speculated that the view conveyed by Chronicles was a custom or an enactment that developed over time. In the initial part of our discussion we attempted to explain the reasons that the cities of refuge were also Levite cities. It is only logical for this reasoning to have developed further and to have expanded to include the other Levite cities, similar to how, for example, the mitzva of tithes expanded at a later period from merely grain, wine, and oil to legumes and vegetables.

Thus, it seems that the "innovation" of the later *Amora'im* was not a notion created between the Tigris and the Euphrates in the year 350 CE, but an ancient concept that originated in the Tanakh. The fact that the Bavli does not mention Chronicles is very instructive. In other words, this is not a case of biblical exegesis but of an ancient tradition.

If this is so, we must ask how the tradition made its way, seemingly through underground channels, all the way to amoraic Babylonia. In addition, we must ask why the *Tanna'im* – who preceded the *Amora'im* chronologically – and the *Amora'im* of the Land of Israel – who were closer to the land and its traditions – somehow lost this tradition.

The Mitzva of Cities of Refuge During the Second Temple Period

The Tanakh contains a few testimonies as to the existence of the mitzva of Levite cities,[12] but we do not possess testimonies from the biblical period

12. Anathoth, which was designated as a city of priests in the list of forty-eight Levite cities, indeed served in practice as a city of priests throughout its history. It was

as to the practical existence of the mitzva of cities of refuge. However, absence of evidence is not evidence of absence, and therefore there is no reason to doubt the existence of the mitzva.

However, Samuel Klein drew our attention to the fact that specifically from the Second Temple period there are numerous testimonies as to the existence of the mitzva of cities of refuge. The Mishna relates that the mothers of high priests would provide unintentional manslayers with food and clothing so that the manslayers would not pray for the death of their sons. This testimony is neither a halakha, nor a homiletic interpretation of the biblical text, nor a miraculous aggadic anecdote. The statement, in its entirety, bears all the hallmarks of a historical testimony about familiar things that the Sages witnessed with their own eyes. Similarly, we read in a *baraita*: "'Asylum Asylum' was inscribed at the parting of the ways" (Makkot 10b). In addition, there are various halakhot concerning the nature of the cities of refuge: "They are to be made neither into small forts nor large walled cities"; "They should not be made into gardens or orchards; they should not be made into shops or inns; they should not be made into a potter's workshop"; "they have neither stones nor a manured field." All these laws do not appear to be theoretical, in order to "magnify and glorify the Torah," but rather practical instructions regarding an existing mitzva.

As for the question of when during the Second Temple period the cities of refuge were designated, a unique tradition recorded in the Tosefta and the Yerushalmi is of particular interest:

> And even though Shechem in the hill country of Ephraim had been designated, it did not offer refuge; they set aside Kiriath-jearim in its stead until they should take Shechem. And even

---

home to Abiathar in the time of David, as well as Jeremiah, his father Hilkiah and his cousin Hanamel son of Shallum at the end of the First Temple period. Additionally, it may be that the public altar in Hebron, where Absalom went to offer sacrifices (II Sam. 15:7), was built there specifically because Hebron was the largest of the cities of priests. II Chronicles 11:13–14 relates that in the time of Jeroboam son of Nebat, the Levites left their cities and spaces in the Kingdom of Israel and relocated to Judah and Jerusalem.

> though Kedesh in the Galilee had been designated, it did not offer refuge; they set aside Gamla instead until they should take Kedesh. (Tosefta Makkot 3:2)

First of all, this is undoubtedly an authentic tradition and not merely an *aggada*; the names Kiriath-jearim and Gamla demonstrate this conclusively. These are not names that an aggadist might choose arbitrarily.[13] During which period was the description of this tradition set? It was certainly not during the time of Joshua, when Shechem fell into his hands without a battle, and where Joshua gathered together all the tribes of Israel (Josh. 24:1). The period that fits best is the period of the Hasmonean conquests. This was the period of John Hyrcanus and his son Alexander Jannaeus (134–76 BCE), the first of whom conquered Shechem and Samaria, as well as the Samaritan city on Mount Gerizim, and the second of whom conquered the Galilee and Transjordan. Klein points to another remarkable halakha that appears in the halakhic Midrash: "They shall be cities of refuge; fight over them; give of your possessions for them" (*Sifrei Zuta*, ed. Horowitz 331). Klein writes:

> These statements could not be simply said without any special intent, or stated by people who lived at a later period who did not have any interest in wars and conquests. But the statements take on practical significance if we limit our focus to the Hasmonean period, when the Great *Beit Din* – the *beit din* of the Hasmoneans – had within its power to initiate a war for the sake of a mitzva.

Klein also found a statement in a *baraita* in the *Sifrei* giving practical encouragement toward the preparation and construction of cities of refuge during the Hasmonean period: "'And when the Lord your God enlarges your territory' (Deut. 19:8) – Carry out the mitzva that is stated in this context, in reward for which the Lord your God will enlarge your

13. Regarding the identification of Kiriath-jearim, see the chapter on *Parashat Shemini*; regarding the identification of Gamla, see the chapter on *Parashat Behar*.

territory" (*Sifrei Devarim* 184). In a halakhic midrash fragment from the Cairo Geniza (*Ginze Schechter* 2:111–112), the city of refuge Ramoth, in Gilead, is identified with Geres,[14] and Golan, in Bashan, with Seleucia. Unfortunately, the identification of Bezer, the third city of refuge in Transjordan, was not preserved in this fragment.

Here, too, Klein sees a testimony about the practical application of the injunction to designate cities of refuge in Transjordan within the lexicon of terms and names of the Hasmonean period. To this, Klein adds an ingenious comparison to Josephus' account about Alexander Jannaeus. Jannaeus was a harsh and cruel ruler. Josephus tells of fractious internal conflicts between the Jews and Jannaeus their king, over the course of which Jannaeus killed

borsaat.com

Ancient Gerasa, according to Ḥazal identical to Ramoth-gilead

14. The identification with Geres was accompanied by a comment that is difficult to understand but attests to the authenticity of the source and its direct connection to the reality of the terrain: "Why was it named Ramoth-gilead? Because it has before it two pools of water."

thousands of his rivals. Then Josephus recounts Jannaeus' wars in Transjordan and enumerates the places that he conquered: Dion, Gerasa,[15] Golan, Seleucia, and Gamla. Josephus emphasizes that when Jannaeus returned from the war, this time the Jews welcomed his reign (*Antiquities* 13:393–394; *Wars* 1:104–105). Klein provides the reason for the joy exhibited by the Jews: by conquering the cities of refuge of Transjordan in the course of his war, Jannaeus had waged a "war for the sake of a mitzva" and had fulfilled the dictum to "fight over them"!

The Historical Background for Renewing the Mitzva of Cities of Refuge During the Hasmonean Period

During the Hellenistic period, a new phenomenon developed: independent cities that boasted civil rights for their citizens and minted their own currency. One of the prominent characteristics of these cities was the right to asylum. As in other cities throughout the world, the coins minted in the most important non-Jewish cities in the Land of Israel bore the formula: "ἱερὰ καί ἄσυλος" (*hiera kai asylos*; usually rendered in shorthand: "IEP K ACYΛ"). The meaning of the phrase is "sanctuary and asylum." The source of the sanctuary's sanctity was the pagan temple or temples in the city, while "asylum" indicates that the city is not obligated to surrender an asylum-seeker to the hands of any ruler. Klein speculates that aside from the internal desire of the Hasmoneans to renew this biblical mitzva in the new independent Jewish kingdom that they had founded, they also felt a need in the reality of their time to establish an alternative Jewish model for the Hellenistic asyla.

The Number of Cities of Refuge During the Second Temple Period, and Conclusions

The sages taught: "When the First Temple was destroyed, the cities with spaces were abolished, the Urim and Thummim ceased and there was no more a king from the House of David" (Sota 48b). "Cities with spaces (*arei*

15. This is how the city's name is rendered in *Wars*; *Antiquities* features a corrupted version.

A Roman coin of the city of Dor, featuring a portrait of Dorus, the mythological founder of the city. The inscription reads: POE ΔWP(ιτwv) IEP(α) AΣYΛ (ος) AYTON(ομος) NAYAP(χις) – "Year 175 of the Holy Dora (111 CE), Asylum, Autonomic, Governs the Sea"

migrash)" refers to Levite cities, as the word "*migrash*" ("space") appears in the Tanakh dozens of times, almost only in connection with the Levite cities. During the Second Temple period, society was no longer tribal and the practice of setting aside cities of priests and Levites was discontinued. According to a *baraita* in Masekhet Taanit (Taanit 27a; Y. Ta'anit 4:2 [67d]), twelve out of the twenty-four priestly divisions were in Jericho. Rabbi Meir Simcha HaKohen wrote:

> It says in Sota that when the First Temple was destroyed, the Levite cities with spaces were abolished. Therefore, during the Second Temple period the Levite cities did not belong to them. Thus, in my opinion, only the six cities offered refuge.

Thus, we must conclude that, at the end of the day, everyone was correct. Nahmanides was correct in his statement that according to the simple reading of the verses, only the main six cities offered refuge, while the remaining forty-two were merely cities with spaces for the Levites. But the Talmud Bavli – and Maimonides, following its approach – are also correct, since the list of Levite cities in Chronicles demonstrates that all the Levite cities were indeed considered cities of refuge as well, probably as a result of a special enactment or custom. The Bavli, which omits any mention of the list in Chronicles, but nevertheless rules categorically – against the simple reading of the Torah – that all forty-eight cities offered refuge, must have been preserving an ancient tradition from the First Temple period. The tannaitic sources, as well as the first *Amora'im* until the fourth generation, were also correct, as were the sages of the Yerushalmi; they were faithfully transmitting the Torah law and the manner in which it was fulfilled during the Second Temple period.[16]

For further study:

HaKohen, Meir Simcha. *Meshekh Ḥokhma* on Numbers 35:13 [Hebrew].

Kaufmann, Y. *Sefer Yehoshua*. Jerusalem, 1976, 259–282 (appendix) [Hebrew].

Kaufmann, Y. *The Biblical Account of the Conquest of Palestine*. Jerusalem 1953, 40–46.

Klein, S. "The Cities of Priests and Levites and the Cities of Refuge." *Bulletin of the Jewish Palestine Exploration Society* 3 (Jerusalem-Tel Aviv, 1934–1935) [Hebrew].

Mazar, B. "The Cities of the Priests and the Levites." *Biblical Israel: State and People*. Edited by S. Ahituv and J. Amitai. Jerusalem, 1992, 134–145.

Neusner J., trans. *The Talmud of the Land of Israel: A Preliminary Translation and Explanation*, 31: *Sanhedrin and Makkot*, Chicago and London, 1984, 432.

Ofer, Y. and J. Jacobs. *Nahmanides' Torah Commentary Addenda Written in the Land of Israel*. Jerusalem, 2013, 489–492 [Hebrew].

Radbaz, *Responsa Radbaz* 2138 [Hebrew].

Urbach, E.E. "Abbaye," 1:235–236; S.G. Wald, "Kahana (4)," 11:709; M. Beer, "Rava," 17:118–119. *Encyclopaedia Judaica*, 2nd Edition, Detroit, 2007.

16. Some of the ideas presented in this chapter were refined and enriched during a *shiur* that I presented on this topic before my teacher Rabbi David Fuchs and the staff of *Lifneihem*, a beit midrash for Talmud instructors, in 2007.

(from R. Palmer, The Bible Atlas, London 1831, plate XIX).

Deuteronomy

Parashat Devarim

The Rephaim, Emim, and Zamzummim

A Word on the Unique Character of *Parashat Devarim*

Parashat Devarim is always read on the Shabbat immediately preceding Tisha B'Av. Tisha B'Av, the ninth day of the Hebrew month of Av, is our national day of mourning, but in the future, according to the prophecy of Zechariah, it will become a holiday, a day of joy and celebration. We may say that there is no less joy embedded in Tisha B'Av than there is mourning. The fundamental reason for Tisha B'Av's identity as a day of mourning is the sin of the spies and the malcontents within the nation. The nation rejected the Land of Israel – "a delightful land" (Ps. 106:24) – and it was decreed as a result that they would not merit seeing it. However, this is not the fundamental essence of the day. Rather, it is a complete perversion of what the essence of the day was meant to be. The ninth day of Av was designated to be a day of great celebration – the day when the spies would return from scouting out the land and sing its praises to the nation. The nation would bow to God and then, led by Moses and the Ark of the Covenant, would set out immediately to the top of the hill to storm the land. The reality of this expectation made the sin that followed all the more egregious, in the vein of the Talmud's analogy of a shameless bride who is unfaithful to her husband under the very bridal canopy (Gittin 36b). Throughout the history of the nation of Israel, this sin has never been rectified completely. When this does occur, though, the day will revert to its original, fundamental identity as a day of joy and transcendence, re-establishing our intimate connection to the holiness of the land.

Parashat Devarim is made up of two parts that express very effectively the two opposing identities of Tisha B'Av. The first part relates once more, emphatically, the story of the sin of the spies and the punishment that resulted. The second part describes, with a joyful tone and with poetic language, the journey toward the Land of Israel and the conquest of the land of Sihon and Og. There is some similarity between the second part of *Parashat Devarim* and the second part of *Parashat Ḥukkat* (many people who read the Torah using the traditional cantillation consider both these sections favorites). Like the second part of *Parashat Ḥukkat*, the second part of *Parashat Devarim* contains a combination of movement and song. The Torah uses lofty, poetic language in both places, including unique expressions, and recounts condensed versions of movement and battle, victories and dispossession.

Another similarity between the two *parashot* is quite surprising. Both *parashot* contain poetic sections that opt specifically to recount a kind of general history that is at first glance unconnected to the nation of Israel. In *Parashat Ḥukkat* it is the Song of the Bards, who sang words of encouragement to King Sihon of the Amorites during his war against Moab. In *Parashat Devarim* it is mostly information about early, mysterious nations, whose people were giants, and who were destroyed long before the people of Israel arrived in the land. In addition, there is a rather peculiar piece of information about King Og of Bashan's iron bedstead. We will now attempt to review these details and understand what it all means.

A Side Note about Giants and Anakites

The *parasha* makes reference to the notably tall *anakim* three times, twice in its description of the Emim (Deut. 2:11–12) and once in its description of the Zamzummim (2:20). There are conflicting versions of the vowelization of the word *ka-anakim*: Most printed

Ḥumashim render the word with a *pataḥ* at the beginning (כַּעֲנָקִים), but the exemplary manuscripts from the Masoretes and the newer editions based on these manuscripts, as well as the Yemenite tradition, render the word with a *kamatz* at the beginning (כָּעֲנָקִים). The difference between the two versions is manifested in the question if the word is a common noun or a proper noun. If it is a common noun (with a *pataḥ*) then the meaning of *ka'anakim* is "as giants." However, if the word is a proper noun (with a *kamatz*) then the meaning is "as the Anakites." Most translations, both old and new, follow this latter position. In any case, in terms of content it is clear that the Anakites were chosen because they were archetypical giants, so from the perspective of the spirit of the text the difference between the two versions is negligible.

The Early Nations in Our *Parasha* and Elsewhere in the Tanakh

Five early nations are mentioned in our *parasha*. Four of these lived in Transjordan, ordered from south to north: the Horites, the Emim, the Zamzummim, and the Rephaim. Another nation, the Avvim, lived in Cisjordan. The Horites lived in Seir until the descendants of Esau wiped them out and settled in their place (Deut. 2:12, 22). The Emim were the early residents of the land of Moab (2:10); the Zamzummim were the early residents of the land of the Ammonites, until the Ammonites wiped them out and settled in their place (2:20–21); and the last surviving member of the Rephaim, who had settled in Bashan, was King Og of Bashan (3:11, 13). The Avvim settled in "villages[1] in the vicinity of Gaza" until the Caphtorim, who came from Crete, wiped them out and settled in their place (2:23).

The clear biblical parallel to the text in our *parasha* is Genesis 14, which relates that when Chedorlaomer and the kings allied with him entered the land from the north, they "defeated the Rephaim at Ashteroth-karnaim, the Zuzim at Ham, the Emim at Shaveh-kiriathaim

1. The word the Torah uses here, *ḥatzerim*, refers to unwalled, nomadic villages (see Gen. 25:16 and others). The *Targum Yerushalmi* and the various versions of the Samaritan *Targum* translate in this way (*bekufranayya* or the like), while other *Targumim* maintain that *ḥatzerim* is a place-name (Onkelos identifies it with Rafaḥ).

(Courtesy of Dr. Ada Yardeni and the Hebrew University Magnes Press)

Ancient undeciphered pictographic inscriptions from Transjordan

and the Horites in their hill country of Seir as far as El-paran, which is by the wilderness" (14:5–6). This list provides us, first of all, with an exceedingly early dating for the presence of these nations in Transjordan – more than 450 years before Moses' conquest of this land. It seems that the Zuzim of Genesis are identical to the Zamzummim of Deuteronomy. The order of these nations from north to south in Genesis fits precisely with the account in Deuteronomy. We know nothing about the language or culture of these nations, but it should be noted that several ancient inscriptions were found in Transjordan, written in pictographs that have not yet been deciphered. It may be that the place-name Ham, the meaning of which is unknown, is a word in the language of the Zuzim.

Among the three cities mentioned here, two have certain identifications. Ashtaroth has been identified with Tell ʿAshtara, about eleven miles southeast of Ramat Magshimim in the southern Golan Heights. Ham has been identified with Tell Hām, about four miles southwest of Irbid in the northern Gilead.[2] Kiriathaim appears several times in the Tanakh and in the Mesha Stele among the Reubenite cities in northern Moab, and it has several suggested identifications. The meaning of the name Shaveh-kiriathaim is uncertain.[3]

The Horites also appear in *Parashat Vayishlaḥ* (Gen. 36), where it says that Esau settled peacefully in Mount Seir, and that Timna daughter of Seir the Horite was the concubine of Esau's son Eliphaz and the mother of Amalek through that union (36:12, 22). This does not contradict our *parasha*'s statement that "the descendants of Esau dispossessed them, wiping them out and settling in their place." Throughout history, it is not uncommon that during a process of population overhaul there may be incidents of both integration and intermarriage on one side and battle and dispossession on the other (similar to Israel in the land of Canaan during the time of the Judges, as well as to the Spanish in South America in the sixteenth century CE).

The Avvim appear in Joshua 13 among the "territory that remains," of which the people of Israel did not take possession: "All the districts of the Philistines … and those of the Avvim on the south" (13:3–4)[4]; in other words, there were Avvim in southern Philistia. In

2. In my visit to the tell in July 1998, we found, in addition to a wealth of pottery and residents attempting to sell sherds and ancient (possibly forged) scarabs to visitors, the tomb of a sheikh known as Nebi Hām Opposite this tomb was a Jewish burial cave from the Second Temple era containing six ossuaries and two sarcophagi, with their original covers in place. There was also an ancient pool south of the modern-day village of Hām.
3. It may be interpreted as a construct state, i.e., the town of Shaveh in the vicinity of Kiriathaim. Another possible suggestion invokes the meaning of the word *shaveh* ("even" or "flat"), which would mean that the name refers to the plain of Kiriathaim.
4. The inclusion of the word *miteiman* ("on the south") in the previous verse follows the position of Rav in Ḥullin 60b, as well as the Peshitta, contrary to the masoretic division of the verses. The Septuagint version B, although dividing the verses in accordance with the Masoretic Text, nevertheless interpreted the verse similar to Rav and the Peshitta, since they read *mᶜzh* instead of the masoretic *mᶜrh,* thus yielding "from Thaeman even to all the land of Chanaan before Gaza, and the Sidonians as far as Aphec, as far as the borders of the Amorites."

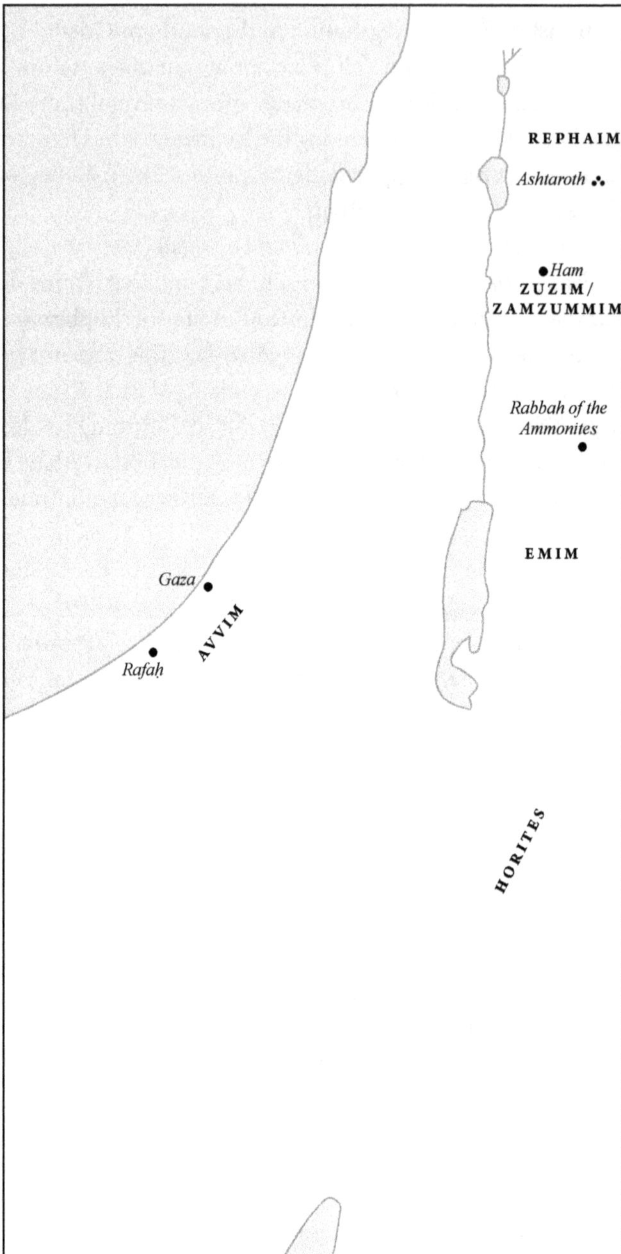
REPHAIM
Ashtaroth
Ham
ZUZIM/
ZAMZUMMIM
Rabbah of the
Ammonites
EMIM
Gaza
AVVIM
Rafaḥ
HORITES

the chapter on *Parashat Toledot*, we addressed the observation that the early Philistines described in the Torah were practically different from the later Philistines from the periods of the Judges and of Samuel (their residence was farther south, among other things). We also noted that several groups of nations that arrived from the west and settled in the southwestern part of the land over the course of several centuries became known as "Philistines." Thus, it seems that the term "Avvim" is an epithet that was used to refer specifically to the Philistines who existed during the time of the Patriarchs, while the new population that came from Crete, dispossessed the early Philistines, and settled in their place are the "Philistines" from the time of the Exodus and the conquest of the land of Canaan. We must therefore conclude that the Avvim were not dispossessed completely, and that some of them remained in the southern part of the region during the time of Joshua.

Yeiḥashevu and *Teiḥashev*

The words *yeiḥashevu* and *teiḥashev* are key words in the Torah's description of the lands of the Emim and the Zamzummim:

> And the Lord said to me: Do not harass the Moabites or provoke them to war. For I will not give you any of their land as a possession; I have assigned Ar as a possession to the descendants of Lot. It was formerly inhabited by the Emim, a people great and numerous, as tall as the Anakites. Like the Anakites, they, too, are counted (*yeiḥashevu*) as Rephaim; but the Moabites call them Emim…You are now passing through the territory of Moab, through Ar. You will then be close to the Ammonites; do not harass them or start a fight with them. For I will not give you any part of the land of the Ammonites to you as a possession; I have assigned it as a possession to the descendants of Lot. It, too, is counted (*teiḥashev*) as Rephaim country. It was formerly inhabited by Rephaim, whom the Ammonites call Zamzummim, a people great and numerous and as tall as the Anakites. (Deut. 2:9–21)

In the Hebrew text of the Torah we encounter here a case of a slightly irregular syntactic structure, where the object of the sentence (Rephaim or Rephaim country) precedes the subject (*hem*, i.e., the Emim or *hi*, i.e., the land of the Ammonites). The verses most likely use this syntax because "Rephaim" and "Rephaim country" are terms that are important to emphasize. Thus, we see that the *parasha* is especially interested in the Rephaim and their territory, stressing that the Emim and the Zamzummim are counted (*yeiḥashevu*) as Rephaim and that their lands are counted as Rephaim country.

Why does the Torah use this unusual verb that appears here in the forms *yeiḥashevu* and *teiḥashev*? This verb has legal-halakhic significance, which can be seen in the following examples. First, *Parashat Behar* teaches that, in contrast to a dwelling house in a walled city, which "shall not be released in the jubilee," "houses in villages that have no encircling walls shall be classed as open country (*al sedeh haaretz yeiḥashev*): They may be redeemed and they shall be released through the jubilee" (Lev. 25:30–31). These are houses that are legally classed as open country. *Parashat Koraḥ*, in discussing tithes, describes the tithe that the Levites are required to give to the priests:

> When you receive from the Israelites their tithes, which I have assigned to you as your share, you shall set aside from them one-tenth of the tithe as an offering to the Lord. Your offering will be accounted (*veneḥshav*) to you as the new grain from the threshing floor or juice from the winepress. (Num. 18:26–27)

A few verses later, the chapter discusses what should be done with the quantity of the tithe that is left over after separating the one-tenth: "When you have removed the best part from it, you Levites may consider it (*veneḥshav laleviyim*) the same as the yield of threshing floor or winepress. You and your households may eat it anywhere[5]" (18:30–31). In contrast to the permissible deer, gazelle, and roebuck, which are distinctly different from the forbidden camel, hare, and hyrax – or Shabbat and festivals, which are distinctly different from the days of the

5. Rashi (following Sifrei and Yevamot 86b) comments here: "Even in the cemetery."

week – tithed produce appears exactly the same as it did before it was tithed. The Torah stresses that the "tithe of the tithe" that the Levite must separate from the tithe that he receives has great sanctity and is legally equivalent to the *teruma* that Israelites must separate from their produce and deliver to the priests. The Torah then stresses that the nine tenths remaining in the hands of the Levite are completely *ḥullin* (non-sacred) and they are legally equivalent to regular produce belonging to an Israelite. A similar usage of this verb is found in Leviticus 7:18: "If any of the flesh of his sacrifice of well-being is eaten on the third day, it shall not be acceptable; *it shall not count for him* (*lo yeiḥashev lo*) who offered it. It is an offensive thing (*piggul*)." In other words, this sacrifice is not legally considered an offering; rather, it is *piggul.*

What Is the Significance of Rephaim Country?

In light of this, it is important for us to search for the meaning of "Rephaim country" as a concept in halakhic or legal terminology. It is not necessarily a concept easily recognizable on the ground, but the Torah found it important to point out the geographical regions that, from a legal perspective, are considered part of this land.

The verse here that refers to Rephaim country clearly bases itself on God's promise of the Land of Israel to Abraham:

> On that day the Lord made a covenant with Abram, saying, "To your offspring I assign this land, from the river of Egypt to the great river, the river Euphrates: the Kenites, the Kenizzites, and the Kadmonites, the Hittites, the Perizzites, the Rephaim, the Amorites, the Canaanites, the Girgashites, and the Jebusites." (Gen. 15:18–21)

Ten nations are listed here: six of the seven Canaanite nations (only the Hivvites are missing) and an additional four: the Kenites, the Kenizzites, and the Kadmonites, and the Rephaim.

In *Parashat Devarim,* as well as in the story of the war between the four kings and the five kings in Genesis 14, there is one region that is considered Rephaim country par excellence: the northern region, consisting of Ashtaroth and Bashan, the land of King Og (who was himself one of the last surviving Rephaim, despite the fact that his subjects

(L. C. Lortet, *La Syrie*, Paris 1884)

Rephaim country *de facto*: view of northern Bashan and Mount Hermon

were Amorites). In describing this region, the Torah tells us that it "is called (*yikarei*) Rephaim country" (Deut. 3:13). This teaches us another thing about the Torah's legal terminology: If the word *yeiḥashev* means *de jure* – a technical legal consideration – then the word *yikarei* means *de facto* – a consideration in practice, not necessarily by law. Gilead, the area south of Bashan, was already the land of the Zuzim (apparently the Zamzummim of our *parasha*) in Genesis 14, its eastern part later became Ammonite land, and its central and western part became Amorite land under the rule of King Sihon of Heshbon. The next area to the south, east of the Dead Sea, is – according to Genesis 14 and the "prehistoric" account in our *parasha* – the land of the Emim. The Emim were dispossessed by the Moabites, but shortly before the arrival of the people of Israel Sihon gained control over the northern half of this land, the area north of the Arnon River. The Torah stresses here that despite the fact that these two lands had been known since ancient times as the land of the Zuzim/Zamzummim and the land of the Emim (including in Genesis 14!), this is only what they are called (*yikarei*) – *de facto*. In other words, these are merely the names that the Ammonites and Moabites used to refer to the lands. From a legal perspective, however, the lands are counted (*yeiḥashevu*) as part of Rephaim country, which God had promised to Abraham. It is important for the Torah to emphasize the giant stature of the members of these nations, since this was a characteristic trait of the Rephaim, and pointing this out lends support to the idea that all these nations shared a common ethnic background. The Torah is saying that, formally, all the giants of Transjordan are members of the same nation: the Rephaim. "Emim" and "Zamzummim" are simply names for Rephaite tribes. The story of King Og of Bashan's giant bedstead serves to strengthen the *de facto* usage of "Rephaim country" to refer to Bashan. The nation living in Bashan at the time, after all, consisted mostly of Amorites. The fact that the king of this nation was not Amorite but Rephaite is reinforced by reminding the reader of the king's enormous dimensions. The reader can get a sense of these dimensions even after Og himself was already dead and buried, thanks to Og's iron bedstead, which was preserved.

The Horites

After discussing Rephaim country, the Torah goes on to describe another area in Transjordan that completes the picture: the land of the Horites southeast of the Dead Sea, which became the land of the descendants of Esau. This region is also included in the land promised to Abraham, as it is situated between the Sea of Suph and the Euphrates River, west of the large Syrian Desert.[6] It is likely that the Kenites, the Kenizzites, and the Kadmonites – or part of these nations – dwelled within this region.

"Do Not Harass Them or Start a Fight with Them"

God warns Moses and the people of Israel not to harm the descendants of Esau, Moab, and the Ammonites, "for… I have given the hill country of Seir as a possession to Esau" and "I have assigned Ar as a possession to the descendants of Lot" (Deut. 2:5, 9). These territories are part of the land that God promised to Abraham, but others aside from the people of Israel have a claim to this inheritance. Ishmael son of Hagar and the descendants of Keturah are also Abraham's heirs, but they have no claim in the inheritance of the land. This is because

6. See the chapter on *Parashat Mishpatim*.

Abraham gave them their portion in moveable property during his own lifetime, distancing them from the Promised Land, as the Torah states: "But to Abraham's sons by concubines Abraham gave gifts while he was still living, and he sent them away from his son Isaac eastward, to the land of the East" (Gen. 25:6). This was certainly not Abraham's way of shortchanging these heirs; Abraham was notably "very rich in cattle, silver, and gold" (13:2), and undoubtedly left them a considerable inheritance. The only remaining heir aside from Jacob and his descendants was Esau. On the other hand, Abraham consciously included an additional person among his heirs, giving him a gift of land during his lifetime:

> Abram said to Lot, "Let there be no strife between you and me, between my herdsmen and yours, for we are kinsmen. Is not the whole land before you? Let us separate: If you go north, I will go south; and if you go south, I will go north." (13:8–9)

Since Esau and the descendants of Lot already controlled parts of the Promised Land, in the land of the Horites and in the greater Rephaim country, and it was forbidden for Israel to dispossess them, Israel would only be able to inherit these territories on one of three conditions:

- A foreign nation could capture the land or part of the land from them, and then the people of Israel could, in turn, capture the land from that conquering force. This occurred in the northern half of Moab, in the area north of the Arnon River and in the western part of the land of the Ammonites (Josh. 13:25). These regions were conquered by Sihon, leading the sages to state, "Ammon and Moab were purified through Sihon" (Gittin 38a, Chullin 60b). This also led Jephthah to say to the king of the Ammonites, "Now, then, the Lord, the God of Israel, dispossessed the Amorites before His people Israel; and should you possess their land?" (Judges 11:23).
- Ammon, Moab, or Edom could attack Israel without provocation. This occurred in the cases of King Eglon of Moab who enslaved Israel (Judges 3:13–14) and King Hanun son of Nahash

of the Ammonites who humiliated the messengers that David had sent to him as a gesture of friendship and good will (II Sam. 10:4).

- The nations themselves could no longer exist. Every nation in the world is subject to the same basic historical laws that apply to individuals: they are born, they mature, they grow old and, in the end, they pass on. With the power of the divine covenant and promise, the eternal nation of Israel outlasts them all, regrouping and returning to the land after having been exiled and scattered. Once the descendants of Lot and the descendants of Esau had served their purposes in the world, their inheritance returned to the people of Israel. *Ḥazal* expressed this idea in a midrashic statement:

> "For I will not give you of their land so much as a foot can tread on" (*ad midrakh kaf ragel*) (Deut. 2:5). Rabbi Meir says: "Until his feet (*raglav*) stand on that day." Rabbi Samuel [Simeon?] says: "Until the one of whom it is written, 'A star rises (*darakh*) from Jacob' (Num. 24:17) comes – that is, the King Messiah. The Holy One, blessed be He, said to them: 'In this world, you do not have permission to inherit this hill country, but in the World to Come you will be redeemed and you will inherit it.' As it is said, 'For liberators shall march up on Mount Zion to wreak judgment on Mount Esau; and dominion shall be the Lord's' (Ob. 1:21)." (*Tanḥuma* Deuteronomy [Buber], addition 6[7]). In a slightly different expression of this idea, another midrash explains: "Hide yourselves from him until he passes from this world" (Deuteronomy Rabba 1:19).

The Avvim

Joshua 13 stresses that the land of the Philistines that Joshua was supposed to conquer "are accounted Canaanite (*lakena'ani teiḥashev*)" (13:3). Despite the fact that it was in Philistine hands, from a legal perspective it was part of the land of the Canaanites (who "dwell by the Sea and along the Jordan" [Num. 13:29]) and it was designated for Israel even

7. Rashi cites this midrash in brief in his commentary on Deuteronomy 2:5.

in the framework of the "limited" borders of the land.[8] In our *parasha*, the Torah stresses that the Avvim – the early Philistines who lived in the land during the Patriarchal Age – were no longer there; in their place dwelled the Caphtorim, who came from Crete. The reason for this emphasis is seemingly the covenant that Abraham and Isaac forged with King Abimelech of the Philistines and Phicol, chief of his troops: "That you will not deal falsely with me or with my kith and kin" (Gen. 21:23). The verse informs us that the land of the Avvim was already conquered by the Caphtorim, and thus the people of Israel were permitted to go to war against the current Philistines – as they are actually the Caphtorim, who were unrelated to Abimelech.[9]

For further study:

Albright, W. F. *The Archaeology of Palestine and the Bible*. New York-London-Edinburgh, 1932, 142, 211.

Astour, M. A. "Ham." In *The Anchor Bible Dictionary*, 3, 32.

Elitzur, Yoel. *Ancient Place Names in the Holy Land*. Jerusalem-Winona Lake, 2004, 109.

MacDonald, b. "Kiriathaim." *East of the Jordan: Territories and Sites of the Hebrew Scriptures*. Boston (2000): 122–123.

Naveh, J. "Undeciphered Scripts in Syria-Palestine." In *Early History of the Alphabet*. Jerusalem, 1997, 21–22.

Oded, B. "*Kiryatayim*." In *Encyclopaedia Biblica* 7, 272–273 [Hebrew].

8. See the chapter on *Parashat Mishpatim*.
9. This discussion is based primarily on Nahmanides' interpretation and, at the end, on that of Rashi.

Parashat Va'etḥanan

The Lebanon

That Good Hill Country and the Lebanon

"I pleaded with the Lord at that time, saying... Let me, I pray, cross over and see the good land on the other side of the Jordan, that good hill country and the Lebanon" (Deut. 3:23–25). What is "that good hill country and the Lebanon"? *Targum Onkelos*,[1] the midrashim of *Ḥazal*, and Rashi explain that this phrase refers to the Temple. In other words, "the Lebanon" is another name for the Temple. Indeed, this is an ancient epithet found as early as the prophecy of Zechariah: "Throw open your gates, O Lebanon" (Zech. 11:1). In any case, this name certainly began to be used only after Solomon built the Temple using the cedars of Lebanon. In our *parasha*, there is no need to look beyond the simple reading of the verse in order to understand it. Moses makes a pleading request to be permitted to see a very specific location: Mount Lebanon in the far north of the land. Moses longs to see Mount Lebanon, a site that, in his eyes, represents the very epicenter of the beauty of the Land of Israel.

1. Onkelos translates: "*Tura tava hadein uveit makdesha.*"

(Lortet, 1884)

"A land with streams and springs and fountains issuing from plain and hill" – an abundance of water under the Afqa Bridge in Lebanon

I was in Lebanon over thirty-five years ago, during the First Lebanon War in 1982. It truly took my breath away to see the arresting Lebanese landscapes, the abundant rivers and streams in particular. It seems that when the Torah states, "For the Lord your God is bringing you into a good land, a land with streams and springs and fountains issuing from plain and hill" (Deut. 8:7), it was referring primarily to the region of the Lebanon. Moses' expression of yearning for the remote Lebanon, as he stood in the plains of Moab, across the Jordan from Jericho, five miles from Jericho and twenty miles from Jerusalem, teaches us that the Torah views the Lebanon as possessing a greater degree of sanctity than Transjordan. This notion runs counter to the modern Zionist approach, and even to the approach of the Greater Israel maximalists who speak of "two banks of the Jordan – both of them ours" but never considered the Jewish connection to Lebanon.

The Lebanon's Role in the Land's Borders

We encounter the Lebanon in the Torah's description of the borders of the Land of Israel. Similarly, in the Torah's presentation of the mitzva to inherit the land within its expansive borders, we read:

> Start out and make your way to the hill country of the Amorites and to all their neighbors in the Arabah, the hill country, the Shephelah, the Negeb, the seacoast, the land of the Canaanites, and the Lebanon, as far as the Great River, the river Euphrates. (Deut. 1:7)

We see this description again in the list of the borders of the Promised Land at the end of *Parashat Ekev*: "Your territory shall extend from the wilderness to the Lebanon and from the river – the Euphrates – to the Western Sea" (11:24). As we discussed earlier (in *Parashat Mishpatim*), the Torah contains two sets of borders for the Holy Land, one limited and one expansive. The expansive set of borders (mentioned in *Parashot Lekh Lekha, Mishpatim, Devarim,* and *Ekev*) reaches north until the Euphrates, while the limited set of borders (described in detail in *Parashat Masei*) reaches only to the northern Mount Hor and Lebo-hamath. We explained that the expansive border is the ideal permanent border for the Land of Israel, intended for later generations to realize after the nation's population was to expand, allowing the people to settle the full extent of these vast regions. In contrast, the limited border is the nucleus of the Land of Israel, designated for the first stage of the conquest. For our discussion here, it is important to stress that the Lebanon was included even within the initial, limited set of borders. We can see this, first of all, from our *parasha*, where Moses is located in the very heart of the spacious Promised Land – and requests to see the Lebanon.

We see Lebanon's inclusion in the borders of the Land of Israel again in Joshua 13. The first few verses in the chapter list the "territory that remains" in Canaan, which Joshua did not manage to capture. It is easy to see that this list is based on the limited border of the Land of Israel and not on the expansive border, and it showcases the gaps between the land that was actually conquered and the borders described in *Parashat Masei.* The Euphrates River is not mentioned in Joshua 13; in its place appears Lebo-hamath, the location that best typifies the limited border of *Parashat Masei.* Sure enough, the list of "territory that remains" in Joshua 13 includes "the whole Lebanon… to Lebo-hamath on the east" (13:5) as well as "all the inhabitants of the hill country from the Lebanon (i.e., from the northern end of the Lebanon) to Misrephoth-maim" (13:6).[2] With this in mind, what does God promise Joshua? "I Myself will dispossess those nations for the Israelites."

To summarize, the Lebanon is part of the land that God promised to the nation of Israel, which He commanded them to conquer even during the early stages of that process, and which is mentioned as part of the "territory that remains" after Joshua and the members of his generation were unable to realize entirely the intended plan of conquest.

(Lortet, 1884)

The cedars of Lebanon

2. According to Yehuda Kiel's accurate analysis in *Daat Mikra,* we can see from the context in this verse as well as from Joshua 11:8 that Misrephoth-maim refers to a certain point at the top of the southern or central Mount Lebanon region.

In the language of the Tanakh, the Lebanon refers chiefly to the tall Mount Lebanon range,[3] which bears this name until today. However, it occasionally refers to the Beqaa Valley (Valley of the Lebanon) east of the range (as in Joshua 13:5, cited above), and in certain cases it even refers to the mountain range known today as the Anti-Lebanon mountains on the east, opposite Mount Lebanon.[4]

"The" Lebanon

From a linguistic perspective, it is appropriate to refer to the region as *the* Lebanon – using the definite article – as the name appears in this form (*HaLevanon*) in almost every instance in the Tanakh. Moreover, this name form has significance in the Hebrew language, especially in the Tanakh, but in the language of *Ḥazal* and in Modern Hebrew as well, in that the names of the various regions of the Land of Israel are written and said using the definite article (such as *HaGalil, HaKarmel, HaSharon, HaBashan*). In contrast, the names of other biblical lands, such as *Ammon, Moav, Bavel* (Babylon) or *Mitzrayim* (Egypt), as well as the Modern Hebrew names of most modern countries, such as *Sefarad* (Spain), *Tzarefat* (France) or *Anglia* (England), do not use the definite article. The use of the definite article in the case of the Lebanon highlights the fact that this is the name of a territory within our land, rather than the name of a foreign country.

In historical terminology, the southern part of the modern-day state of Lebanon, south of the Litani River, is essentially part of the Upper Galilee. The Tanakh refers to this region, along with the region north of this region until Sidon, using the territorial name "Sidon" or "Sidonians."[5] The First Lebanon War of the summer of 1982 (which Prime Minister Menachem Begin named "Operation Peace for Galilee") took place, for the most part, in the Lebanon, in the biblical sense of the name as well, while the Second Lebanon War of the summer of 2006 took place mostly in the Upper Galilee. The frustrat-

3. The name Levanon, from the word *lavan*, meaning "white," certainly refers to the white snow that adorns its peaks.
4. See the chapter on *Parashat Mishpatim*.
5. See the chapter on *Parashat Noaḥ*.

ing aftermath of the First Lebanon War from the perspective of the nation of Israel and the State of Israel (despite Israel's military success in that war) and the failures of the Second Lebanon War are tied, in my opinion, to the fact that the nation and its leaders – even those on "the right" – believed that they were fighting in a foreign country. Had they been familiar with the Tanakh and understood where they were located during those wars, perhaps things would have turned out differently. Even minor details connected to our perception of the land take on a grotesque appearance when a location is viewed through a lens of foreignness.

(Roberts, 1855)

Sidon

As an example, consider the village of Qana, mentioned frequently in the news during the 2006 war, as well as ten years earlier during Operation Grapes of Wrath. In both incidents, Israel launched airstrikes targeting terrorists in the village, and as a result dozens of civilians were killed alongside them. These incidents led to worldwide condemnation of Israel, and Israel apologized for the civilian loss of life in both cases. The events themselves are not the concern of this book. In the framework of this discussion, however, it is important that I address the name of the village. Due to a tendency to eagerly overcorrect in such cases, certainly owing in part to a feeling of foreignness toward the location, the name Qana was commonly spelled in Israeli sources with the initial word *kafr* and with a *kaf* as the first letter. This form is incorrect and most likely influenced by the existence of a village bearing that name (spelled with a *kaf*) in the Lower Galilee. The name of the Lebanese village is more correctly spelled with a *qof*, yielding a name that appears in Joshua 19 in the tribal territory of Asher: "The fifth lot fell to the tribe of the Asherites, by their clans. Their boundary ran along… Ebron, Rehob, Hammon and Kanah, up to Great Sidon" (19:24–28). Thus, Kanah is one of the locations given to the tribe of Asher, along with Great Sidon. It would be perfectly reasonable for the Israeli government to decide that the time is not yet right to realize the inheritance of the land in that particular location. However, the distortion of its name, relating to it as if it were some strange, foreign entity lurking beyond the edge of the known universe, is a step too far; it takes the basic concept of our immanent connection to the Land of Israel and turns it on its head.

A Personal Story

During the First Lebanon War, I was one of the infantry soldiers who advanced north through the length of the Beqaa Valley. When we passed through the area of Lake Qaraoun, the rations we had taken with us ran out. We reached a kind of dried fruit factory, where we found packs of dried figs that were grown locally. We ate them, and they were both delicious and filling. When I finished eating these figs to my heart's content and stood to recite the *berakha aḥarona,* I had to make a quick decision on the spot regarding a seemingly picayune matter – but one that at the same time bore colossal significance. According to halakha, the blessing that one recites after consuming fruit from outside the Land of Israel concludes with the formula "for the land and for the fruit (*al haaretz ve'al hapeirot*)"; after consuming the fruit of the Land of Israel, however, one recites, "for the land and for *its fruit* (*al haaretz ve'al peiroteha*)." That moment of realization filled me with exhilaration, as I recited – with utmost focus and intent – "for the land and for *its fruit*"!

(Summer 1982)

The author (right) with a friend in Kamed el-Lawz in the Beqaa Valley in Lebanon

For further study:

Elitzur, Yoel. "*Hagam HaLevanon BeEretz Yisrael?*" *Nekuda* 48 (1983): 10–13 [Hebrew].
Thompson, H. O. "Kanah." In *The Anchor Bible Dictionary* 4, 5.

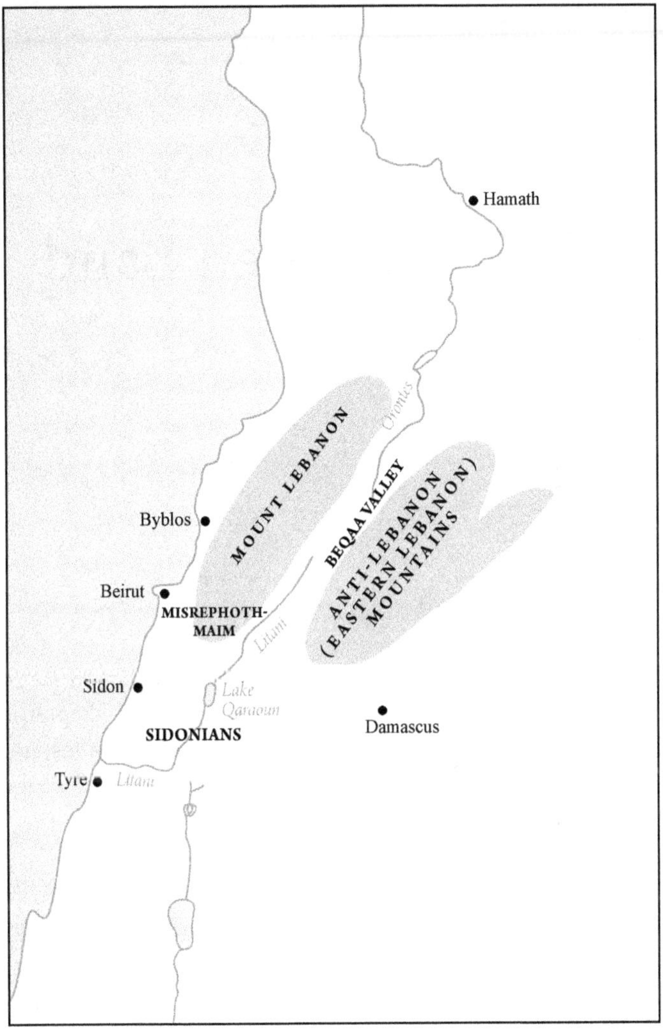
Hamath
Orontes
MOUNT LEBANON
BEQAA VALLEY
ANTI-LEBANON
(EASTERN LEBANON
MOUNTAINS)
Byblos
Beirut
MISREPHOTH-
MAIM
Litani
Sidon
Lake
Qaraoun
Damascus
SIDONIANS
Tyre
Litani

Parashat Ekev

Israel: The Chosen Land

Parashat Ekev: The _Parasha_ of the Land of Israel

The geographical location we will be discussing in this chapter is, of course, the Land of Israel. *Parashat Ekev* is full of words of inspiration and encouragement for the people of Israel in anticipation of their arrival in the Land of Israel and forthcoming possession of the land. The *parasha* opens with a promise of blessing in the land:

> And if you do obey these rules and observe them carefully, the Lord your God will maintain faithfully for you the covenant that He made on oath with your fathers: He will favor you and bless you and multiply you … in the land that He swore to your fathers to assign to you. (Deut. 7:12–13)

The *parasha* continues, addressing the possession of the land:

> You shall faithfully observe all the Instruction that I enjoin upon you today, that you may thrive and increase and be able to possess the land that the Lord promised on oath to your fathers. (8:1)

The *parasha* then praises the virtues of the land:

> For the Lord your God is bringing you into a good land, a land with streams and springs and fountains issuing from plain and hill; a land of wheat and barley, of vines, figs, and pomegranates, a land of olive trees and honey; a land where you may eat food without stint, where you will lack nothing; a land whose rocks are iron and from whose hills you can mine copper. When you have eaten your fill, give thanks to the Lord your God for the good land that He has given you. (8:7–10)

Toward the end of the *parasha* we read: "That you may long endure upon the soil that the Lord swore to your fathers to assign to them and to their heirs, a land flowing with milk and honey" (11:9), and finally:

> The Lord will dislodge before you all these nations … Every spot on which your foot treads will be yours; your territory shall extend from the wilderness to the Lebanon and from the River – the Euphrates – to the Western Sea. No man shall stand up to you. (11:23–25)

Parashat Ekev is the climax of the Torah's emphasis of the connection between the nation of Israel and its land. This connection manifests itself throughout the Torah, from the very first divine command to Abraham – "Go forth from your native land and from your father's house to that land that I will show you" (Gen. 12:1) – to Moses' message to his nation moments before his ascent to Mount Nebo: "Through it you shall long endure on the land that you are to possess upon crossing the Jordan" (Deut. 32:47).

Why Was This Land Chosen?

Are there truly no other "good lands" in the world? *Parashat Ekev* addresses this question:

> For the land that you are about to enter and possess is not like the land of Egypt from which you have come. There the grain you sowed

had to be watered by your own labors, like a vegetable garden. But the land you are about to cross into and possess, a land of hills and valleys, soaks up its water from the rains of heaven. It is a land which the Lord your God looks after, on which the Lord your God always keeps His eyes, from year's beginning to year's end. (Deut. 11:10–12)

The Midrash explains this passage:

"Not like the land of Egypt" – but better than it. In Egypt, if you work [the land] with chisel and ax, and labor assiduously on it, it will be good; if not, you will gain nothing from it. But the Land of Israel is not so; rather, there they sleep in their beds and the Omnipresent brings rain for them. R. Shimon b. Yoḥai says: In the valley, [a piece of land] produces a *beit kor*[1]; in the hill country the same piece of land produces a *beit kor* from the north, a *beit kor* from the south, a *beit kor* from the east, a *beit kor* from the west and a *beit kor* from above – in total five times as much [as in the valley]. (*Sifrei* 38–39)

"Hebron was founded seven years before Zoan of Egypt" (Num. 13:22) – What was Zoan? It was the royal city, as it says, "His officers are present in Zoan" (Is. 30:4). What was Hebron? It was the detritus of the Land of Israel. This leads to an *a fortiori* argument: If Hebron – the detritus of the Land of Israel – is finer than the finest part of the land of Egypt – which is itself the finest of all the lands – how much more so must the Land of Israel be praised. (*Sifrei* 37)

These are only a few examples of the kind of praise that the spirit of the nation heaps upon the Land of Israel. But the truth is that these words of praise do not represent the simple reading of the text. Rashi cites several of these aggadic passages, but the rest of the commentators – Rashbam, Ibn Ezra, Ḥizkuni, and especially Nahmanides – clarify that the simple reading of the text indicates the precise opposite of the message of the Midrash. If one were to ask a farmer what he would prefer: an even land that has an abundant source of natural irrigation all year long;

1. A unit of area for measuring land

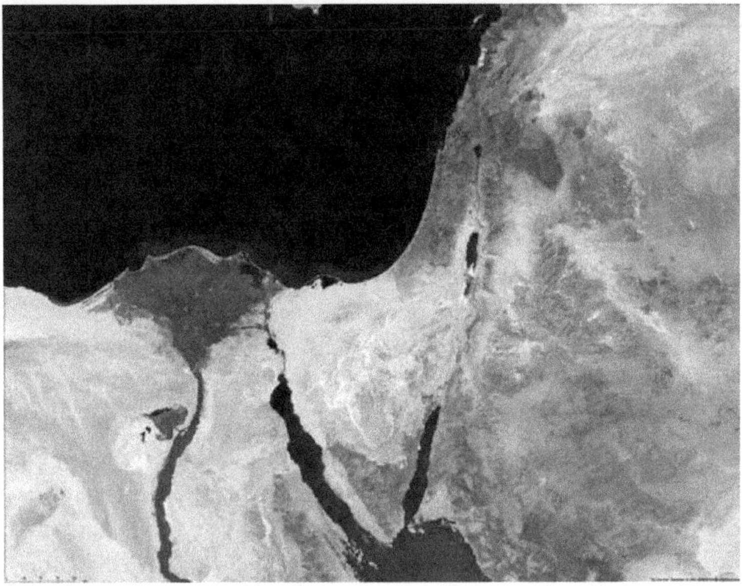

Satellite image of Israel and Egypt: Note the clear distinction in color between the lush Nile Delta and the comparatively bare Promised Land.

or a hilly land that relies on rain alone for water – he would certainly answer that the first option is preferable from a standpoint of both efficiency and economy. Even Rashi himself was aware of this, as he states in his commentary on Deuteronomy 1:27 (citing Numbers Rabba and *Tanḥuma* Buber, *Parashat Shelaḥ*):

> "It is because the Lord hates us that He brought us out of the land of Egypt" – He brought us out because He hated us. It can be compared to a king of flesh and blood who had two sons and two fields, one of which was irrigated and one of which was watered by rain. He gives the irrigated field to the more beloved son, while he gives the field watered by rain to the more hated son. The land of Egypt is irrigated, as the Nile rises up and irrigates it, and the land of Canaan is watered by rain. God took us out of Egypt to give us the land of Canaan.

Already in the Book of Genesis, Lot was confronted with the same choice between these two types of land, and did not hesitate in making his decision: "Lot looked about him and saw how well watered was the whole plain of the Jordan … like the garden of the Lord, like the land of Egypt![2] So Lot chose for himself the whole plain of the Jordan" (Gen. 13:10–11).

Thus, the Torah's purpose here is to emphasize the opposite: It is true that the land of Egypt contains excellent farmland. But the Land of Israel, in contrast, is a land "on which the Lord your God always keeps His eyes, from year's beginning to year's end" – it is a land of divine providence. It is true that God is omnipotent, and it would not be overly difficult for Him to destroy an exceptionally fertile land in an instant, or to irrigate an arid land in an instant. But the laws of nature dictate that an irrigated land is always fertile and productive, while an arid land is dry and desolate. The Land of Israel is unique in that nothing is ever certain in this regard: It can receive a large quantity of rainfall in a particular year, and will then be blessed with fertility and abundance; but in a very dry year, with little rainfall, it can become a veritable desert. God always keeps His eye on the Land of Israel, from year's beginning to year's end, to determine its fate in this respect. If God desires it, the land and its inhabitants will enjoy the highest degree of plenty, but at the same time, if God desires it, they will experience the lowest degree of destitution.

In the context of this characterization of the nature of the land, the Torah follows that passage with a warning:

> If, then, you obey the commandments that I enjoin upon you this day, loving the Lord your God and serving Him with all your heart and soul, I will grant the rain for your land … Take care not to be lured away to serve other gods and bow to them. For the Lord's anger will flare up against you, and He will shut up the skies so that there will be no rain and the ground will not yield its produce; and you will soon perish from the good land that the Lord is assigning to you. (Deut. 11:13–17)

2. The interpretation of Benno Jacob here, that "like the garden of the Lord, like the land of Egypt" is a quote from Lot is especially convincing, as this phrase seems to belie the Torah's statement in *Parashat Ekev*.

The characterization of the land leads to a reiteration of a theme that we encounter many times in the Torah and in the words of the prophets: the complete destruction and desolation of the land during the period of the exile; and the promise that the desert will bloom – "It shall blossom abundantly; it shall also exult and shout" (Is. 35:2) – during the time of the redemption.

www.zerothkoff.com (Courtesy of Dr. Zev Rothkoff)

"A land of olive trees": a view in northern Samaria

Thus, the inhabitants of the Land of Israel, by the very nature of the land, live in a constant state of miracles.

The Land of Diligence and Humility

The Land of Israel is a place where, even when God bestows upon it the full extent of His blessing, it is still necessary to work the land and invest considerable effort in it. Anyone who is familiar with traditional dryland farming,[3] still practiced today by the Arab peasants living in the Land of Israel, knows that it entails an extraordinary amount of labor and practical wisdom. In order for the rain to have its proper effect, the rainfall must be

3. Much information about this agricultural practice in earlier periods can be found in various chapters in Tanakh and in particular in rabbinic literature.

preceded by a comprehensive array of activities, including repeated plowing, stone clearing and weed removal, evoking the verse, "He broke the ground, cleared it of stones and planted it with choice vines. He built a watchtower inside it; he even hewed a wine press in it" (Is. 5:2), and the Mishna's statement, "Any field to which there are at least three trees to every *beit se'ah*... the entire area may be plowed for their sake" (Shevi'it 1:2). The farm work necessitated by dealing with seeds and trees continues throughout the year.

The diligence that this kind of farming demands is an ethical value stressed in the Book of Proverbs (see, in particular, 6:6–14, 12:11 and 24:30–34). *Ḥazal* relate in Menaḥot 85b the story of an industrious farmer in Gush Halab who was breaking up the earth around his olive trees like a menial laborer. It was only after he finished this chore that it became clear that this was a very wealthy man, who would wash his feet in a golden bowl and who owned enough oil to support an entire city in Syria and more.

Similarly, we read in Genesis Rabba 39:

> R. Levi said: At the time that Abraham was walking about Aram-Naharaim and Aram Nahor, he saw [people] eating and drinking and lazing about. He said: "I hope I have no portion of this land." Once he arrived at the promontory of Tyre, he saw [people] engaged in hoeing at hoeing time and weeding at weeding time. He said: "I hope I have a portion in this land." The Holy One, blessed be He, said to him: "To your offspring I will give this land."

From a historical and geographical perspective, this *aggada* does not fit with the simple reading of the biblical text, which states that Abraham first arrived in Elon-moreh, apparently via Succoth and Penuel like his grandson Jacob. However, it expresses very clearly the essence of the land and the lifestyle of its inhabitants. Indeed, the Land of Israel is conducive to a humble lifestyle, practiced by hardworking men of action, both in their service of God and in their work on the land. It is a land that is meant for those who work with humility and dedication, knowing that God bestows His abundance upon those who participate with Him in encouraging the land to bear fruit, rather than those who simply wait for gifts to fall from the heavens.

Zephaniah's prophetic vision of the redemption stresses this point. The prophet rages about the members of the Jerusalem aristocracy who were living a lifestyle of sin and debauchery: "I will punish the officials and the king's sons and all who don a foreign vestment" (Zeph. 1:8); "The officials within her are roaring lions; her judges are wolves of the steppe, they leave no bone until morning. Her prophets are reckless, faithless fellows; her priests profane what is holy, they give perverse rulings" (3:3–4). But when the redemption comes, Israel will come into possession of the magnificent "houses of Ashkelon" – yet they will live simple lives within those houses:

> The seacoast shall become an abode for shepherds and folds for flocks, and shall be a portion for the remnant of the House of Judah; on these [pastures] they shall graze [their flocks], they shall lie down at eventide in the houses of Ashkelon. For the Lord their God will take note of them and restore their fortunes. (2:6–7)

(Courtesy of Ma'ayan Farbstein)

"A land flowing with milk and honey"

> But I will leave within you a poor, humble folk, and they shall find refuge in the name of the Lord. The remnant of Israel shall do no wrong and speak no falsehood; a deceitful tongue shall not be in their mouths. Only such as these shall graze and lie down, with none to trouble them. (3:12–13)

"A Land Flowing with Milk and Honey"

It is worth paying some attention to the "calling card" of the Land of Israel – the famous epithet that is repeated numerous times in Tanakh: "A land flowing with milk and honey." These words describe a primordial quality of earth that is a pleasure to walk on, to sense, to breathe in, to extol in poetry. But from an economic perspective, matters are quite different; it is far preferable from an economic standpoint to possess even plains, upon which one can cultivate fields and vineyards in an orderly manner, rather than scenic hills and mountains. Furthermore, we see from Isaiah 7:21–22 that having to subsist on butter and honey is actually a sign of devastation and ruin, a state in which agricultural growth has disappeared in favor of thorns and thistles, where only a small number of cattle, sheep, and honey bees remain. In a discussion

www.zerothkoff.com (Courtesy of Dr. Zev Rothkoff)

Earth that is a pleasure to walk on, to sense, to breathe in, to extol in poetry: a view in the Judean hills described in an *aggada* in Megilla 6a, the tribe of Zebulun expresses its indignation, complaining to God for giving their fellow tribes fields and vineyards, while leaving them with hills and mountains. The Talmud is puzzled by this complaint, as the region surrounding Sepphoris – located within the territory of Zebulun – was termed by Resh Lakish "a land flowing with milk and honey." The Talmud answers: "Even so, [Zebulun] preferred fields and vineyards."

It seems that the most illustrious praise of the Land of Israel is not its production of the greatest agricultural yield, but its beautiful, spiritually uplifting landscapes, and the ability of its inhabitants to work the land, serve God faithfully and live a life of humility, diligence, and joy.

The Geopolitical Perspective

My father and mentor, Professor Yehuda Elitzur *z"l*, on whose teachings this entire discussion is based, extended the scope of this idea even further, demonstrating that this essence of the Land of Israel is not limited to economics and agriculture. The contrast between artificial irrigation and a dependence on rainwater is only one side of the story.

This idea applies to the Land of Israel from a geopolitical perspective as well. The Land of Israel is situated at the nexus of three continents. It is a land that every ruler and conqueror – indeed, anyone with any kind of political agenda in the region – immediately covets. In this sense, every political threat to the Land of Israel is an existential one. This land is called "the Promised Land," but in practice it seems that this "promise" is not at all guaranteed, whether in terms of the economic reality or the political reality. From the perspective of natural law, the Land of Israel is one of the most vulnerable places in the world. The only guarantee we have that the "promise" will be realized is the word of God, and the land is constantly and completely dependent on this word. It can be said that the Land of Israel, in its absolute essence, is the perfect match for the nation of Israel, and runs fundamentally counter to modern-day aspirations toward "peace" – merely to exist in quiet, without responsibility or obligations.

The only time in history when the nation of Israel succeeded in becoming a world empire, in the period of David and Solomon, was an era when history itself, as it were, held its breath. It was a one-time opportunity when, for the briefest moment, the strength of the northern kingdoms waned and Egypt was weakened in the south. Thousands of years have passed since then, and the balance of power in the world has shifted dramatically, but once again the State of Israel remains the only country in the world surrounded by enemies bent on its destruction – and the God of Israel alone gives us the strength to stand up to them.

Ultimately, this is a land whose very existence constantly defies the laws of nature. The reality in the Land of Israel is such that one is always subject to the divine will. As a result, one must maintain a direct connection with God, emulate Him, live a life of hard work and humility, be faithful to oneself, to the heritage of one's ancestors, to morality, and to the mitzvot. These are the means by which one can be worthy of the goodness of this good land.

For further study:

Elitzur, Yehuda. "*Eretz Pelishtim Binevuat Tzefaniya*"; "*Lama Nivchera Eretz Yisrael Mikol Haaratzot.*" *Israel and the Bible*, Ramat-Gan (2000): 247–250, 271–279 [Hebrew].

Parashat Re'eh

Hamakom

The Keyword of *Parashat Re'eh*

Upon reviewing *Parashat Re'eh*, it is virtually impossible not to notice that a certain word appears disproportionately throughout the *parasha*:

> You must destroy all the sites (*hamekomot*) at which the nations you are to dispossess worshipped their gods... Do not worship the Lord your God in like manner, but look only to the site (*hamakom*) that the Lord your God will choose... You shall not act at all as we now act here, every man as he pleases... When you cross the Jordan and settle in the land... then you must bring everything that I command you to the site (*hamakom*) where the Lord your God will choose to establish His name... Take care not to sacrifice your burnt offerings in any place (*bekhol makom*) you like, but only in the place (*bamakom*) that the Lord will choose in one of your tribal territories. There you shall sacrifice your burnt offerings... You may not eat in your settlements the tithes of your new grain or wine or oil, or of the firstlings of your herds and flocks... These you must consume before the Lord your God in the place (*bamakom*) that the Lord your God will choose.... If the place (*hamakom*) where the Lord has chosen to establish His name is too far from you.... (Deut. 12:2–21)

The same term continues to appear in other contexts in *Parashat Re'eh,* such as the passage on the mitzva of tithes:

> You shall set aside every year a tenth part of all the yield of your sowing… You shall consume the tithes… in the presence of the Lord your God, in the place (*bamakom*) where He will choose to establish His name… Should the place (*hamakom*)… be far from you… take it with you to the place (*hamakom*) that the Lord your God has chosen. (14:22–25)

Similarly, in the passage on the mitzva of consecrating the firstlings, we read: "All male firstlings that are born in your herd and in your flock… You and your household shall eat it annually before the Lord your God in the place (*bamakom*) that the Lord will choose" (15:19–20).

The passage on the mitzva of the Paschal sacrifice reads:

> You are not permitted to slaughter the Passover sacrifice in any of the settlements… but at the place (*hamakom*) where the Lord your God will choose to establish His name… You shall cook and eat it at the place (*bamakom*) that the Lord your God will choose. (16:5–7)

Regarding the festival of Shavuot we read: "You shall rejoice before the Lord your God… at the place (*bamakom*) where the Lord your God will choose to establish His name" (16:11). Regarding the festival of Sukkot we read: "You shall hold a festival for the Lord your God seven days, in the place (*bamakom*) that the Lord will choose" (16:15). And by way of summarizing all three festivals, the Torah states:

> Three times a year – on the Feast of Unleavened Bread, on the Feast of Weeks, and on the Feast of Booths – all your males shall appear before the Lord your God in the place (*bamakom*) that He will choose. (16:16)

In the following *parasha* as well, *Parashat Shofetim,* we will again encounter the recurring expression "the place that the Lord will choose" in connection to the source of judicial authority whose voice all of

Israel must obey, and in connection to the right given to the Levites (the priests) to sacrifice and serve God to their hearts' desire. Finally, regarding the mitzva of first fruits (*bikkurim*), found at the final mitzvot section in the Torah at the beginning of *Parashat Ki Tavo*, we read: "You shall put it in a basket and go to the place (*hamakom*) where the Lord your God will choose to establish His name" (Deut. 26:2).

All these examples of divine service can only be performed in the place that the Lord will choose. The opposite of *hamakom*, "the place," is *kol makom* or *kol hamekomot*:

- "You must destroy all the sites (*kol hamekomot*) at which the nations worshipped their gods"
- "Take care not to sacrifice your burnt offerings in any place (*bekhol makom*) you like"

The difference between these two examples and "the place that the Lord will choose" is a reflection of the difference between the polytheism of the Canaanite nations and the monotheism of "Hear, O Israel! The Lord is our God, the Lord alone." The Canaanites, who worshipped numerous gods, considered "all the sites" consecrated and suitable for use as places of worship. In contrast, Israel – the one chosen nation – worships the one true God, in the one chosen place, in the one chosen land that was given as its heritage: "in the place that the Lord will choose."

Does *Makom* Mean "Temple"?

There are several places throughout the Tanakh where the word *makom* is used in the sense of "Temple." The clearest example of this is in I Chronicles 16:27: "Glory and majesty are before Him; strength and joy are **in** His place (*bimekomo*)." There is a parallel verse to this one in Psalms 96:6: "Glory and majesty are before Him; strength and splendor are in His Temple (*bemikdasho*)."

From a linguistic perspective, various scholars from as early as the nineteenth century pointed out the parallel between the Hebrew word ***makom*** and the Arabic word *maqām*, which means "monument," "place

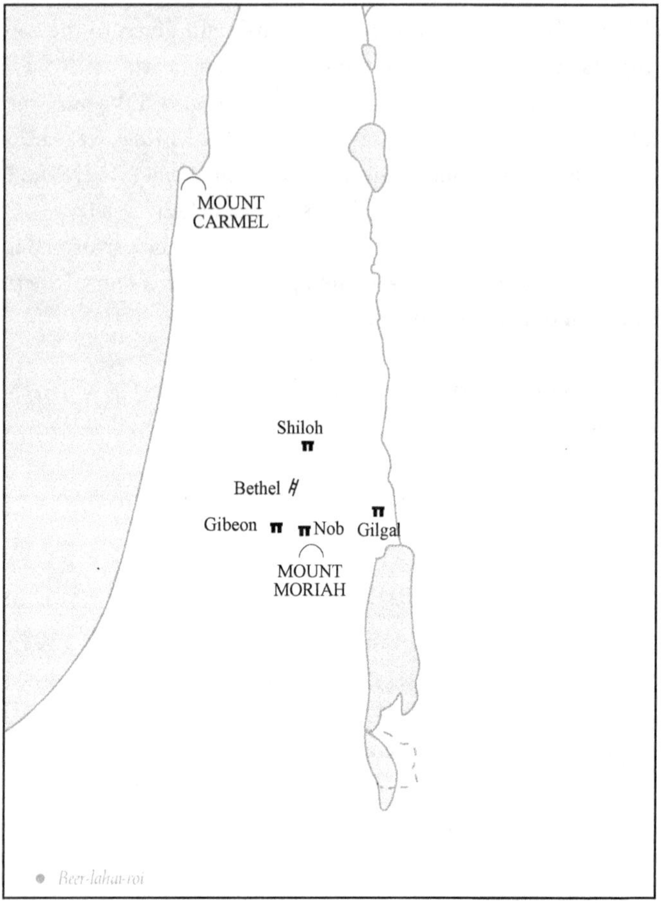

of prayer," or "sacred site."[1] The word *mqm* in the sense of "temple" also appears in Phoenician and Punic inscriptions from Carthage, as well as in a dedicatory inscription discovered in Tel Miqne, identified with the biblical city of Ekron.

1. It should be noted that in this case there is generally an opposite parallel between the Hebrew and Arabic words. The Hebrew *makom* usually appears in the Tanakh in a prosaic, mundane context, meaning simply "place," while the word *makhon* is more literary and poetic, referring to the sacred, as in the dwelling place of the *Divine Presence*. In Arabic, however, the usual word for "place" is *makān*, while *maqām* is a relatively rare term that is reserved for sacred sites.

What Is *Hamakom*?

Let us now return to our *parasha*. What is "the place that the Lord will choose"? It is commonly said to be Jerusalem, but *Parashat Re'eh* does not state this, because the Torah was not referring specifically to Jerusalem, but to a place that God will choose in the future. *Avot DeRabbi Natan* (chapter 26) reads: "The whole Land of Israel is eligible for being the place of the altar." Similarly, there is a *baraita* in *Sifrei Zuta* that is parallel to the "ten grades of holiness" mishna in Tractate Kelim (1:6–9). The *Sifrei Zuta* adds another distinction, between the two banks of the Jordan River: "The land of Canaan is more sacred than Transjordan, since the land of Canaan is suitable as a home for the Divine Presence, while Transjordan is not suitable as a home for the Divine Presence" (*Sifrei Zuta, Naso*, 228). In other words, while Transjordan possesses the same sanctity of the Land of Israel as Cisjordan for the purposes of mitzvot, *teruma*, tithes, *Shemitta* and the Jubilee year, and the mitzva of settling the land, its level of sanctity is different in one respect: "The place that the Lord will choose" can only be located in the land of Canaan, in Cisjordan. It cannot be located in Transjordan because that region has a lesser degree of sanctity than Cisjordan. The primary sanctity of the Land of Israel is in Cisjordan, in the land of Canaan, and the source of that sanctity is "the place that the Lord will choose." From this "place," the sanctity spreads throughout the Land of Israel west of the Jordan, and from there to Transjordan. The epicenter of this sanctity, the nexus "where heaven and earth touch one another" (Bava Batra 74a), must be located in the land of Canaan – but it can be anywhere within the land of Canaan. During the period when the *Mishkan* was located in Shiloh, Shiloh was "the place that the Lord will choose" and not Jerusalem. Jerusalem became "the place that the Lord will choose" when David brought the Ark to Jerusalem, and the identity of "the place" has not changed since then. As the Mishna in Megilla 1:11 states: "After the sanctification of Shiloh, there is again a time of permission (for high places [*bamot*]), but after the sanctification of Jerusalem there can be no such permission."

The same language used in the Tanakh to refer to God's choice of a location for "the place" is also used in connection with His choice of "the man" – His chosen king over the nation of Israel. The Torah states: "You shall be free to set a king over yourself, *one chosen by the Lord your God*" (Deut. 17:15), meaning that the nation's choice of a king will receive God's official approval – that this man is the king who is "chosen by the Lord your God." In his time, Saul was *the man* "whom the Lord has chosen" (I Sam. 10:24). After Saul was set aside and David was chosen, the prophet Nathan revealed a divine message to David: that from now on God had chosen David and his descendants to be kings of Israel – "your throne shall be established forever" (II Sam. 7:16). And so it was with the process of choosing "the place." "*The place that the Lord will choose*," according to its fundamental definition, could be located anywhere in the land of Canaan. But from the moment that David and Jerusalem were chosen, God announced to David through His prophet that from then on He chooses Jerusalem alone – "This is My resting place for all time; here I will dwell, for I desire it" (Ps. 132:14). Nevertheless, the eternal choice of Jerusalem applies only on the prophetic level, while on the Pentateuchal level "*the place*" can be anywhere throughout the land.

Hamakom in Genesis

Once we understand the significance of "the place," we can see that this keyword – *hamakom* – is a keyword that is emphasized in the stories of the Patriarchs in the Book of Genesis as well. It appears in the story of the Binding of Isaac and in Jacob's Bethel narrative. The proof that the prominent role of the word *hamakom* in these passages is no coincidence lies in the fact that often, the word is stressed in the biblical text much more than would be linguistically reasonable. That is to say, there are several instances in Genesis where the word *hamakom* makes it difficult to understand the simple meaning of the verse. The Torah says:

> Jacob left Beer-sheba, and set out for Haran. He came upon that place (*bamakom*) and stopped there for the night, for the sun had set. Taking one of the stones of that place (*hamakom*), he put it under (or near) his head and lay down in that place (*bamakom*). (Gen. 28:10–11)

The word appears again shortly thereafter: "Surely the Lord is present in this place (*bamakom*)...How awesome is this place (*hamakom*)! This is none other than the abode of God, and that is the gateway to heaven" (28:16–17).

The first appearance of the word *bamakom* is puzzling from a grammatical-syntactical perspective. After all, the prefix *ba-* in *bamakom* includes the definite article, implying that this is a place already known to us. What can this possibly mean? We have not yet encountered this place, or any information about it, in the Torah! As a peshatist commentator, Rashbam explains here: "In a certain place outside the city of Luz." But has Rashbam actually solved the problem? It would seem more accurate to say that rather than solving the problem, he has only highlighted its difficulty: If what the Torah means is "in a certain place," then the verse could easily have said exactly that. Ibn Ezra, in his characteristically cryptic manner, answers: "The reason for the *pataḥ* [vocalization on the letter] *beit* [in the word] *bamakom* is that these are Moses' words. The interpretation is: "in the place that is known today." In other words, the Torah here calls Bethel "the place" because it is already well known to the recipients of the Torah. By Moses' time, everyone already knew that this was an important place, so it would have been appropriate to use the definite article – *bamakom*. This solution is also difficult to accept, since the Torah speaks in "human language" – in natural, common usage – and it would thus be unusual for the text to rely on information that only comes to light later in history. Moreover, there are many similar examples in the Tanakh where the text retained its common usage and refrained from using the definite article: "They came upon a valley in the land of Shinar...That is why it was called Babel" (Gen. 11:2, 9); "A certain man of the house of Levi went and married a Levite woman. The woman conceived and bore a son... She named him Moses" (Ex. 2:1, 10); "There was a man from Ramathaim of the Zuphites, in the hill country of Ephraim, whose name was Elkanah son of Jeroham" (I Sam. 1:1); "There was a man in the land of Uz named Job" (Job 1:1). In our case as well, the text should have employed the common usage instead of relying on later information.

(1848–1910)

Claude R. Conder

Claude Reignier Conder, the well-known English scholar and explorer of the late nineteenth century, was also troubled by this question. Conder inferred from here that the place where Jacob rested in this passage was the same place where his grandfather Abraham had built an altar – between Bethel and Ai. This place was indeed already known to the readers of the Book of Genesis, hence the word *hamakom* with the definite article.

In the end, the question is better than all the answers. The repetition of the word is curious as well. Instead of saying, "He came upon that place…Taking one of the stones of that place…lay down in that place," the Torah could easily have said, "He came upon a certain place…and lay down there." It is obvious that the Torah is specifically emphasizing the word *hamakom*.

An interesting case can be found in *Parashat Vayishlaḥ*: "God parted from him at the spot (*bamakom*) where He had spoken to him" (Gen. 35:13). Rashi comments, with his typical and well-known humility: "I do not know what this teaches us." Indeed, if *hamakom* means simply "place" in the indefinite sense, then the word is entirely superfluous; how could God have parted from him at any place other than where He had spoken to him? However, if we explain, begging Rashi's forgiveness, that the Torah was emphasizing the particular location of God's revelation to Jacob, perhaps we can understand what this teaches us after all.

Are *Ḥazal* and Rashi Forcing Jerusalem into the Verses?

Upon examining several statements throughout rabbinic literature, it seems that *Ḥazal* are forcing Jerusalem into verses concerning Bethel. Those who have studied *Parashat Vayetzeh* with Rashi's commentary (on Gen. 28:17 in the common editions) will recognize three increasingly explicit ways in which *Ḥazal* do this.[2] The first way is incidental linkage: The ladder that Jacob saw in his dream was slanted such that its base was in Beersheba and its top was above Bethel – and as a result, its center was situated directly above Jerusalem. The second way is *kefitzat haaretz,* the midrashic process of shortening long distances, in which one piece of land "jumps" to another location. In this case, Jacob indeed slept in Bethel, but Mount Moriah "jumped" to his location. The third way is explicit identification, completely ignoring the simple understanding of the text. Bethel, which appears in the verse here, is actually Jerusalem.[3] This interpretation may elicit outrage from the peshatist, since the Torah says explicitly in *Parashat Vayetzeh* and again in *Parashat Vayishlaḥ* that Bethel is identified with Luz – with no connection whatsoever to Jerusalem!

Another similarly surprising rabbinic statement is quoted by Rashi here as well: "Not like Abraham, who called it a mountain, and not like Isaac, who called it a field, but like Jacob, who called it a house (*bayit,* i.e., *Beit-El*)." Again, the peshatist grows infuriated: Abraham's "mountain" is Mount Moriah; Isaac's "field" is near Beer-lahai-roi in the Negeb and Jacob's "house" is Bethel! How can all three of these places be considered one and the same?

2. The third part is missing from the reliable manuscripts, but it is confidently an original text of Rashi, since it occurs in his commentary to the Talmud in Ḥullin 91b.
3. My good friend Nissim Erez pointed out to me that this same increasing degree of connectedness can be found in each successive appearance of the word *hamakom* in the verse in question. First Jacob "came upon" that place; then he "took" one of the stones; and finally he "lay down" in that place.

The *Peshat*

Attempting to read the story of God's revelation to Jacob in Bethel from an approach of strict *peshat* is a frustrating and seemingly fruitless undertaking. As a case in point, the passage ends with the verse: "And this stone, which I have set up as a pillar, shall be God's abode" (Gen. 28:22). But one can only view this divine foretelling as having come true if one takes into consideration the temple built in Bethel by Jeroboam son of Nebat, and it seems quite unlikely that the Torah would express this kind of support for such a negative character. The Septuagint, Onkelos, and Rabbi Saadia Gaon suggested a solution. Onkelos provided a non-literal translation here: "And this stone, which I have set up as a pillar, shall be such that I will worship upon it before God." The Septuagint and Rabbi Saadia Gaon add only one short word to the literal translation of the verse: "And this stone, which I have set up as a pillar, shall be *for me* God's abode." What they mean to say is that Jacob's designation of Bethel as "God's abode" was not a permanent one, but for himself alone. And indeed, when Jacob returned from Paddan-aram, following the incident with Dinah in Shechem, he went up to Bethel and built an altar there (see Rashi here).

The problem with this simplistic interpretation is that it is extremely disappointing. All the power and intense emotion brought out by the revelation, the ladder, God's angels, "Shaken, he said, 'How awesome is this place!'" – how can all their relevance boil down to the life of one solitary person in one fleeting generation? How can this crucial moment in the life our forefather, in the formation of his intimate relationship with God, have no bearing on his descendants in future generations?

Hamakom – Where the Earth is Suspended from the Heavens

The key to understanding this whole question is that there are two basic aspects of *hamakom*. The superficial, "revealed" aspect is the simple meaning of the word: the place. But in a deeper sense, *hamakom* refers to something that transcends the simple geographical level; it is the point of contact between the chosen land and the Divine Presence, the point from which the land draws all of its sanctity and virtue. *Hamakom* is perhaps what *Ḥazal* called "the heavenly Jerusalem" (Taanit 5a; *Midrash*

Tehillim 122). When Abraham, Isaac, and Jacob wandered through the land, they were constantly searching for this place, this "heavenly Jerusalem." It was there that they wanted to worship God – to call in God's name.

Thus, in the superficial sense, "He saw the place from afar" (Gen. 22:4) refers to Mount Moriah and "He came upon that place" refers to Bethel. But in the deeper sense, *hamakom* is always "Jerusalem"; each of those places is identical in its sanctity, in its role as the nexus of heaven and earth, as the "cloud tied to the mountain" from which all the sanctity of the Land of Israel emanates. The awesome transcendence of "Jacob awoke from his sleep and said, 'Surely the Lord is present in this place… Shaken, he said, 'How awesome is this place!'… and this stone… shall be God's abode" has not been lost. Rather, it truly does exist, and continued to exist not only for Jacob, but for all the generations that followed – in Mount Moriah in Jerusalem.

I will conclude with a very original idea in this connection that I heard from Rabbi Yoel Bin-Nun. In I Kings 18, in the story of Elijah at Mount Carmel, we learn that Elijah brought a sacrifice on Mount Carmel during a period when the use of *bamot* (altars outside the Temple, literally "high places") was prohibited. *Ḥazal* defended Elijah's action, saying that this was a case of *hora'at sha'a* – an exceptional divine command, citing Elijah's statement that "I have done all these things at Your bidding" (I Kings 18:36; see Y. Megilla 1:13 [72c and parallels]). It is interesting to note the Tanakh's description of Elijah's decisive moment on Mount Carmel:

> When it was time to present the meal offering, the prophet Elijah came forward and said, "O Lord, God of Abraham, Isaac, and Israel! Let it be known today that You are God in Israel and that I am Your servant… Answer me, O Lord, answer me… Then fire from the Lord descended and consumed the burnt offering and the wood. (18:36–38)

What is the meaning of "When it was time to present the meal offering"? To which meal offering does the verse refer, and what does this offering have to do with the story? The answer is that "the meal

(Herzog College)

Rabbi Dr. Yoel Bin-Nun

offering" in question is the meal offering brought in the afternoon as one of the two daily *tamid* offerings brought in the Temple in Jerusalem. The Tanakh reveals here that the very moment Elijah requested that the fire descend upon Mount Carmel was the same moment that the *tamid* meal offering was brought in Jerusalem. In other words, Elijah's request, made under the extenuating circumstances of *hora'at sha'a,* was not to lift the prohibition on the *bamot* but to suspend the prophetic choice of Jerusalem for a moment. Elijah requested that for just one moment, "the place that the Lord will choose" would be located not in Jerusalem but on Mount Carmel. That is why he waited until the whole daily service of bringing offerings – including the final activity, bringing the afternoon *tamid* together with its meal offering in the Holy Temple in Jerusalem – had concluded. The moment that the meal offering of the afternoon *tamid* – the final activity in the daily order of sacrifices – was brought in Jerusalem, Elijah was able to request that the Divine Presence rest temporarily on Mount Carmel, only to return to its home in Jerusalem immediately thereafter.

For further study:

Conder, C. R. "The Mountains of Judah and Ephraim." In C. W. Wilson, *The Land of Judea* (Picturesque Palestine, Sinai and Egypt; reprint), edited by Z. Vilnay, 99–101. Jerusalem, n.d.

Gitin, S. "Israelite and Philistine Cult and the Archaeological Record in Iron Age II: The 'Smoking Gun' Phenomenon." In *Symbiosis, Symbolism, and the Power of the Past*, edited by W. G. Dever and S. Gitin, 279–295. Winona Lake, 2003.

Vanderhooft, D. "Dwelling Beneath the Sacred Place: A Proposal for Reading II Samuel 7:10." *JBL* 118 (1999): 625–633.

Parashat Shofetim

Naḥal Eitan

Naḥal Eitan – Earlier vs. Later Commentary

In describing the *egla arufa* ritual, the Torah states, "And the elders of that town shall bring the heifer down to a *naḥal eitan,* which is not tilled or sown. There, in the wadi, they shall break the heifer's neck" (Deut. 21:4). What is a *naḥal eitan*? For Modern Hebrew speakers familiar with the basic types of streams, the answer should be simple. A *naḥal eitan* is a perennial stream, one that contains flowing water all year long. The other major stream type is a *naḥal akhzav,* an intermittent stream, which only contains flowing water when it rains or immediately thereafter.

If we look at the interpretation of our early sources, however, we see that they did not interpret *naḥal eitan* in this manner. All the ancient translations, first among them the Greek-language Septuagint, followed by the *Targum Onkelos,* the *Targum Yerushalmi* in its different versions, the Samaritan Pentateuch translation, and the Latin Vulgate, and even Rabbi Saadia Gaon's Arabic translation, interpret *naḥal eitan* as a hard place, a rocky ravine, or something of that nature. Josephus interpreted it this way as well – "To a valley, and to a place therein where there is no land ploughed or trees planted" (*Antiquities* IV, 8:16) – as did the Mishna, according to the simple reading of Sota 9:5: "*Eitan* is to be understood in its literal sense: hard."

When I examined this question, I found that modern commentators, almost without exception, interpret *naḥal eitan* in line with its meaning in Modern Hebrew: a flowing stream, or one that flows forcefully. This interpretation is the most common among both modern commentators and contemporary English translations. These modern commentators explain that the idea behind the inclusion of the *naḥal eitan* in the *egla arufa* ritual is atonement. The murderer was not found, so the elders declare their innocence and the priests beseech God: "Absolve, O Lord, Your people Israel whom You redeemed" (Deut. 21:8). Similar, in a way, to the modern *Tashlikh* ritual customarily performed on Rosh HaShana, here too the city elders stand before a body of flowing water and wash their hands in the water, which in turn washes away their sin, as it were: "And they will be absolved of bloodguilt" (21:8). If so, we are dealing with a mitzva characterized by reconciliation.

(Courtesy of Amit Mendelsohn)

Wadi Dilb in southern Samaria: a perennial stream and an example of a *naḥal eitan* according to the later commentators and dictionaries

Thus, we find that there is a dispute between the earlier and later commentators. The early commentators maintained that *naḥal eitan* refers to a rocky, craggy ravine, while the later commentators maintained that it refers to a flowing stream. The historical inflection point when the interpretation changed occurred at a surprising time: in the heart of the Middle Ages. The early medieval commentators Rashi and Ibn Ezra continued along the lines of their predecessors. Rashi states, "*Naḥal eitan*:

hard, never tilled." Ibn Ezra explains, "*Eitan*: firm." However, beginning with Maimonides, who lived shortly after Rashi and Ibn Ezra, the "flowing water" meaning entered the scene. Maimonides writes in *Hilkhot Rotze'aḥ* 9:2: "They bring the heifer down to a stream *that flows forcefully*. This is the meaning of the term *eitan* found in the Torah." This became the predominant interpretation from that point on, both among Jewish commentators (such as Ḥizkuni and Abrabanel) and among modern-era Christian commentators, as well as in all Hebrew dictionaries, both ancient and modern. Only a small minority of commentators from the modern period deviated from the "flowing water" interpretation, while some attempted to formulate a position that would reconcile those of the earlier and later commentators (see Malbim). One prominent exception among the modern commentators is Shmuel David Luzzatto, who outlined the two conflicting approaches and sided explicitly with the earlier commentators. Among the dictionaries, the Even-Shoshan Dictionary can be singled out for siding with the earlier commentators on the *naḥal eitan* question.

Who Is Right?

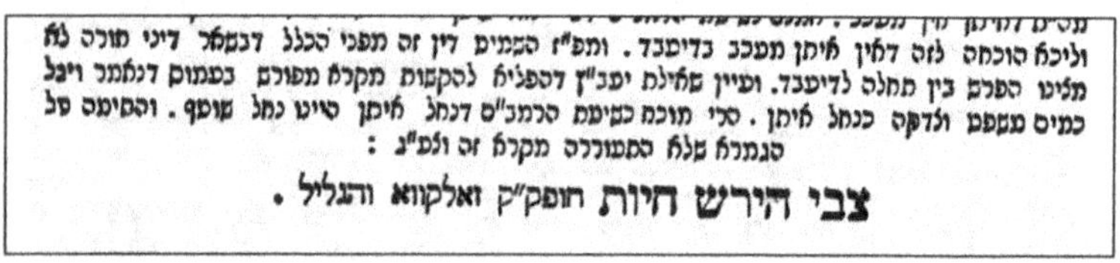
וליכא הוכחה לזה דאין איתן מעכב בדיעבד. ותפ"ז השמים דין זה מפני הכלל דבעלמא דיני תורה לא
מצינו הפרש בין תחלה לדיעבד. ועיין שאילת יעב"ץ דהפליג להקשות מקרא מפורש בעמוס דנאמר ויגל
כמים משפט וצדקה כנחל איתן. הרי מוכח כשיטת הרמב"ם דנחל איתן טיט נחל שוטף. והשיטה של
הגמרא שלא התעוררה מקרא זה וצע"ג :
צבי הירש חיות חופק"ק זאלקווא והגליל.

(Rabbi Z. H. Chajes)

See the [Responsa] *She'eilat Ya'avetz*, who argued vigorously from an explicit verse in Amos: "But let justice well up like water, righteousness like an unfailing stream (*kenaḥal eitan*)"

On the surface, it seems that the later commentators were right. Indeed, there are multiple arguments in support of their approach. First, the expression *naḥal eitan* appears one other time in the Tanakh, in a context that makes its meaning indisputable: "But let justice well up like water, righteousness like an unfailing stream (*kenaḥal eitan*)" (Amos 5:24). The parallel structure in this verse makes clear the connection between *naḥal eitan* and flowing water. Perhaps additional support can be drawn from the verse, "It was You who made mighty rivers (*naharot eitan*) run dry" (Ps. 74:15) and even, "And at daybreak the sea returned to its strength (*le'eitano*)" (Ex. 14:27). In all these cases, the word *eitan* indicates abundant water. The proof from the verse in Amos was cited by Rabbi Zvi Hirsch Chajes in his glosses on Tractate Sota, in the name of Rabbi Jacob Emden. He writes at the end of the gloss, "This requires much further study," referring to anyone who interprets *naḥal eitan* as anything other than a stream with flowing water.

In addition, the *egla arufa* passage itself contains a strong support for the later commentators. The Torah states there: "Then all the elders of the town nearest to the corpse shall wash their hands over the heifer whose neck was broken in the wadi" (Deut. 21:6). In order for the elders to "wash their hands" in the wadi, it must have contained flowing water!

Thus, it seems clear that the approach of the later commentators is indeed correct.

What Is a *Naḥal*?

However, before we discuss the question of *naḥal eitan*, we must ask what the meaning of the word *naḥal* is in general. If a person were to open a Bible concordance and examine the ways in which the Tanakh refers to streams, he would find, first of all, that there is a distinct difference between a *nahar* and a *naḥal*. Not one stream in the Land of Israel is called a *nahar* – not even the mighty Jordan. Only the largest and widest bodies of water are called *neharot* in the Tanakh, and these include only the greatest rivers by international standards: the Tigris, the Euphrates, and the Nile and its Ethiopian sources (*naharei kush*, Is. 18:1). In contrast, the Land of Israel contains *neḥalim* – smaller streams. Some of these streams contain water, such as the Kishon, the Yabbok, and the Arnon. Others are dry, like the wadi between Socoh and Azekah, where David found smooth stones to use as shots for his sling, and like Naḥal Besor, in whose vicinity David and his men found an Egyptian youth who had "drunk no water for three days and three nights." An interesting verse that effectively illustrates the meaning of a dry stream can be found in Genesis 26:19: "Isaac's servants, digging in the wadi, found there a well of spring water."

Nevertheless, my father *z"l* instilled in me the awareness that two identical phrases in the Tanakh can mean two different things depending on whether the context is one of poetry or prose. Concerning *nahar* and *naḥal* one may discern that when a verse is speaking metaphorically or using a figure of speech, *nahar* and *naḥal* generally appear in tandem, as synonyms expressing abundance. Examples of this usage include "The rivers (*naharei*) of honey, the brooks (*naḥalei*) of cream" (Job 20:17) and "Prosperity like a stream (*kenahar*), like a wadi (*ukhenaḥal*) in flood" (Is. 66:12). In contrast, when a verse is describing a physical, geographical area using concrete terms, there is a very clear distinction: all the *neharot* are mighty bodies of water located outside the Land of Israel, whereas almost all the *neḥalim* are wadis (with or without flowing water) that can be found within the Land of Israel.

Why is the same word – *naḥal* – used for both dry streams and flowing streams? The landscape of the Land of Israel itself can help explain this state of affairs. The Land of Israel is a land of hills and valleys. When one assesses the landscape from a geomorphological perspective, the only thing that is important is the valley between the hills. The question whether such a valley contains flowing water or not is immaterial to the essential definition of the visible feature; it is merely an additional detail. In other words, when the word *naḥal* is used in biblical prose, it serves to define the essence of the land formation rather than the water flowing within it. Pay close attention to the wording in Psalms 104:10: "You make springs gush forth *in* torrents (*baneḥalim*)" – the *naḥal* is the geological essence, and God causes water to flow *within it.*

Returning to *Naḥal Eitan*

If *naḥal* is the geological essence, it must be that the word *eitan* acts as a modifier for the land rather than the water – in other words, following the interpretation of the earlier commentators!

It is worth considering here the landscape of the Land of Israel. Our *parasha* discusses the case of a corpse found in a field, where the identity of the murderer is unknown. What would be done if such a corpse was found somewhere between Arad and Beersheba or between Lachish and Azekah – areas teeming with settlements during the biblical period (see Joshua 15:20–47) but nowhere near any forcefully flowing stream? Where would the elders bring the heifer in such a case? Taking logic and the geographical reality of the Land of Israel into consideration, it would be much more reasonable to think of the *naḥal eitan* as a rocky ravine rather than a flowing channel. Thus, the descriptive phrase "which is not tilled or sown" is part of the definition of *naḥal eitan* and not merely an additional piece of information.

www.zerothkoff.com (Courtesy of Dr. Zev Rothkoff)

Naḥal Darga in the Judean Desert: a rocky ravine and an example of a *naḥal eitan*, according to the earlier translations, sages, and authors

Thus, both the definition of the term *naḥal* and a consideration of the landscape of the Land of Israel seem to support the interpretation of the earlier commentators in the question of the meaning of *naḥal eitan*.

In light of this, how do we counter the strong proofs that we cited above in support of the later commentators? Regarding Rabbi Chajes' pronouncement that "this requires much further study," the solution is simple: Amos was using poetic, metaphorical language, while the *egla arufa* passage in Deuteronomy is pure prose. As we demonstrated above, *naḥal* refers to a wadi in prose, while in poetry it is a symbol of abundance and plentiful water. Professor Samuel Klein has shown that the Prophets occasionally use a literary device in which they quote an expression from the Torah or from earlier books in the Tanakh in order to extract new meaning from the expression.[1] Our case is a particularly

1. One example of this phenomenon is Migdal Eder, a place-name in Genesis and later a literary epithet for Jerusalem in Micah 4:8. Another example is Er and Onan

effective example of this device from a literary perspective. The prophet takes an expression originally used in prose, and transplants it into a context of poetic imagery. By doing so, he transforms the meaning of the expression into the polar opposite of its original sense.

"They Shall Wash Their Hands"

As for the point we made above that the elders could not possibly have washed their hands in a stream that lacked flowing water, it is worth paying attention to the division of the verse indicated by the Masoretic cantillation marks and by the diacritical marks. Specifically, in the phrase "they shall wash their hands over the heifer," the cantillation marks indicate a pause at the word *ha'egla* ("the heifer"), while the final section of the verse – *ha'arufa vanaḥal* ("whose neck was broken in the wadi") – stands as an independent segment.[2] The word *vanaḥal* is therefore clearly not an object or an adverbial adjunct of the word *yirḥatzu* ("they shall wash"), but of the word *ha'arufa* ("whose neck was broken"). The elders do not wash their hands in the water of the stream; rather, they bring a flask of water with them and use that water to wash their hands over the heifer whose neck was broken in the wadi. An internal analysis of the passage supports this interpretation as well; the words *ha'arufa vanaḥal* allude to the earlier verse: *ve'arefu sham et ha'egla banaḥal* ("there, in the wadi, they shall break the heifer's neck").

According to this interpretation, the whole essence of the mitzva takes on a new meaning. This is not an act of reconciliation, but quite the opposite: It is an act that expresses the intent to see justice done. It is an act in the vein of "She set her blood upon the bare rock, so that it was not covered" (Ezek. 24:8) and "the land can have no expiation for blood that is shed on it, except by the blood of him who shed it" (Num. 35:33). It is a stern message to the populace that they must continue to search for the murderer and bring him to justice (see Luzzatto).

(Gen. 38), two of Judah's sons who were displeasing to God and whose lives were taken by God; in Malachi, *er* and *oneh* are literary descriptions for the Judaites, who were unfaithful to God and are thus intended to be subsequently cut off by Him.

2. This division of the verse also explains why the first letter of the word *vanaḥal* ("in the wadi") loses its *dagesh*, changing from the plosive *beit* to the fricative *veit*: It is connected to the preceding word *haarufa*, which ends with a vowel.

Another point to consider: Considering all that we have seen here, it seems that we can compare the atonement of the heifer to the atonement of the "scapegoat" of Yom Kippur. Regarding the goat, which is sent off "to Azazel," the ritual's designated location is the wilderness, and *eretz gezeira* – an inaccessible region. In other words, it is a harsh, rocky land.[3]

Why the Commentators Suddenly Changed Their Minds

One more piece of the puzzle remains to be explained. How could such an extreme reversal in the approach of the commentators have occurred? How could it be that all the translators and early commentators interpreted *naḥal eitan* to mean "rocky ravine," while almost all the later commentators – both Jewish and non-Jewish – understood the phrase to mean "flowing stream"?

Perhaps the key to answering this question lies in the fact that the early authors and sages were more familiar with the Land of Israel and its landscapes. Many of them actually lived in the land itself, and others – especially Rashi, whom Luzzatto describes as having a "palate for tasting the taste of the Holy Tongue" – seemed to have had a unique sense for preserving the spirit of the Land of Israel. These earlier authors interpreted *naḥal eitan* in accordance with the landscape and atmosphere of the Land of Israel. By contrast, the later writers generally lived in completely different landscapes. Many lived near the rivers of Europe, or on the banks of the Nile in Egypt, in the case of Maimonides, and it may be that their interpretation was subconsciously influenced by the landscape in their own vicinity.

For further study:

Driver, S. R. *A Critical and Exegetical Commentary on Deuteronomy* (ICC). Edinburgh, 1901, 241–242.

Elitzur, Yoel. "Geographical Terminology in the Bible: *nhr, nḥl,* and *nḥl 'ytn.*" *Iggud: Selected Essays in Jewish Studies* 1 (2008): 319 [Hebrew].

Klein, S. *li-Sh'elat Divrey ha-Torah be-Fi ha-Nevi'im, hasoqer* 4 (Budapest 1936), 3–18 [Hebrew].

Luzzatto, S. D. *Torah Commentary*. Translated by E. Munk. Jerusalem, 2012.

3. See Rashi's commentary on Leviticus 16:8; compare to *Torat Kohanim, Parashat Aḥarei Mot* 2: "From where do we know that it must be on a cliff? We learn this from the verse 'to an inaccessible region.'"

Parashat Ki Tetzeh

"Alternate Weights, Larger or Smaller"

The Weighing of Gold and Silver

Until the advent of the coinage system, all commerce in ancient times was based on the weighing of gold and silver. In a normal transaction, the buyer would bring a gold or silver bar or jewelry and weigh it on balance scales. Every instance of buying and selling in the Tanakh involved this weighing procedure: "Abraham weighed out for Ephron the silver that he had named in the hearing of the Hittites" (Gen. 23:16); "He must weigh out silver in accordance with the bride-price for virgins" (Ex. 22:16); "Even if a thousand shekels were weighed out into my hands" (II Sam. 18:12); "Why do you spend money [lit. weigh out silver] for what is not bread" (Is. 55:2); and finally, in Jeremiah's description of his purchase of Hanamel's field, he says, "And I weighed out the silver on a balance" (Jer. 32:10).

In earlier periods, the more primitive barter method was used to carry out commercial transactions. In this system, a person would offer his cow in exchange for a donkey or one hundred sheep in exchange for a plot of land. From a linguistic perspective, it is worth noting that in the language of the Tanakh, the word *mikneh* is the general term for sheep and cattle, undoubtedly because these livestock were used in order to acquire (*liknot*) other items. The use of precious and semiprecious metals in place of livestock or grains was an early development that allowed people to purchase goods without having to carry heavy or cumbersome items long distances. The transition from cattle-based transactions to the first metal-based transactions can be seen in archaeological findings. A decorated bronze vessel from the mid-second millenium BCE found in Cyprus integrated two figures, one carrying a goat over his shoulder and a second figure a large copper bar. In the Aegean world, copper bars with the figure of an ox imprinted upon them have been found. However, in every place where people had access to gold and silver, they understandably preferred to carry a few ounces of these precious metals in their pockets rather than numerous pounds of copper. One ancient and obscure means of payment was the kesita. The kesita, whose etymological background is unknown, is mentioned in the story of Jacob's purchase of the "parcel of land" in Shechem (Gen. 33:19, Josh. 24:32) and in the description of Job's restoration in Job 42:11. The prevailing view among the ancient translations (i.e., the Septuagint, Onkelos, Jonathan, the Peshitta, the Vulgate, the Job *Targum*) is that the word *kesita* refers to a ewe, and there is room to speculate that this interpretation is based on an exegetical tradition rather than a mere guess. It is very likely that the word relates to the quantity of silver that is equal in value to a ewe.

The weights of items of jewelry were made intentionally in round numbers so that they could be used as weights for commercial transactions. This is implied in the story of Rebecca and Abraham's servant: "The man took a gold nose-ring *weighing a half-shekel* (*beka mishkalo*), and two gold bands for her hands, *ten shekels in weight*" (Gen. 24:22).

The use of the word *beka* (literally, "rift") to refer to a half-shekel alludes to the fact that originally, a half-shekel consisted of a piece of silver weighing one shekel that was actually split into two halves. Similarly, it seems that the term *betza kesef*, which appears in the Song of Deborah (Judges 5:19), and its shortened version *betza* (literally, "piece" or "slice"), which appears twenty-two times in the Tanakh, originated in the practice of slicing pieces from gold and silver bars to be used as payment.[1] Gold and silver bars that had been cut in two have been found at various

1. The verb *livtzo'a* appears in the Tanakh ten times, in the sense of robbery and theft.

archaeological sites, as well as bars with a groove in the middle indicating where to cut in order to produce two equal halves.

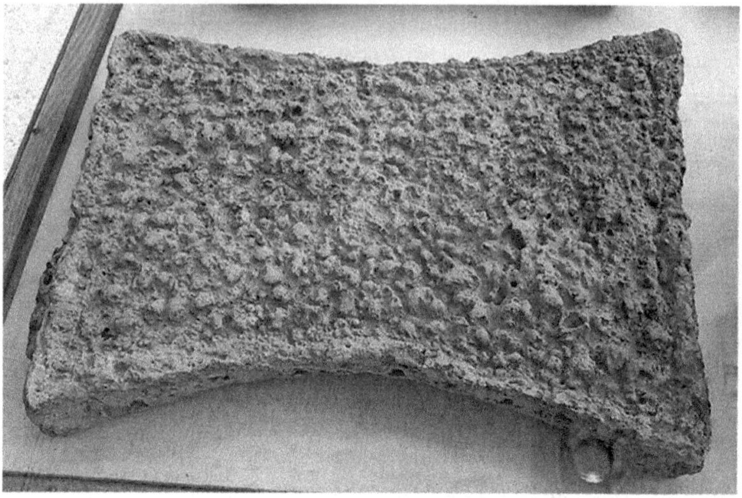

(Wikimedia Commons – User "Chris 73")

Bronze Age copper ingot found in Zakros, Crete

The Invention of Coinage

Today's coins are a form of fiat currency, possessing only symbolic value rather than actual intrinsic value. This was a very late development, which began in Europe in the seventeenth century, while the Middle East only completely converted to the system in the twentieth century. Perhaps over the course of the twenty-first century, this system will fall by the wayside as well, as electronic payment or some other more sophisticated system will supplant coins and paper bills entirely.

For more than two thousand years, the world was full of gold or silver coins whose value was assessed based on their weight. It must be stated, though, that as early as the time of *Ḥazal*, the coin had symbolic value to a certain extent; a coin maintained a fixed value even if it wore out and the quantity of metal it contained decreased. Conversely, if a government declared a coin obsolete, it would lose all its value. The Talmud distinguished between a money transaction and a barter transaction, and between *tiv'a* – the use of coinage (*matbe'a*) as a method of acquisition – and *peira* – the use of objects or merchandise for acquisition (Bava Metzia 44a–47b).

A YHD coin minted in Judea during the Persian period

The invention of coinage became possible the moment that people developed the technical ability to imprint silver tokens with intricate designs, which a simple person without sophisticated tools would find difficult to forge. The earliest coins in the world were minted in western Asia Minor during the end of the First Temple period. The technique first spread through Greece and the surrounding areas, then throughout the civilized world. The first coins mentioned in the Tanakh are *darkemonim* (Ezra 2:69; Neh. 7:69–71) and *adarkhonim* (Ezra 8:27; I Chr. 29:7). Another version of *adarkhonim* found in the Mishna is *drakhonot*[2]: "When the Israelites came up out of the captivity they used to pay the *Maḥatzit Hashekel* in *drakhonot*" (Mishna Shekalim 2:4). Despite the similarity between the names of the two coins mentioned in Ezra, most scholars believe that these are two distinct coins. These scholars identify *darkemonim* with the drachma (literally, "handful"), a common Greek coin, and the *(a)darkhonim* with the Persian daric.[3] It should be noted that a Sidonian/Greek bilingual inscription found in the vicinity of Athens (dated to the late third century BCE) mentions *drknm* and *drkmnm* as synonyms. The earliest coin discovered in the Land of Israel was found accidentally by the great coin expert, my

2. The vowelization of the word as *derakhon,* rather than *darkon,* follows credible manuscripts of the Mishna.
3. The daric was named for the Persian king Darius. According to some scholars it was originally derived from an Old Persian term meaning "gold."

teacher, Professor Yaakov Meshorer *z"l*. Meshorer was a sort of coin hunter: He had a special knack for finding coins, and would succeed in doing so almost every time he visited an ancient site. In 1960, when he was a twenty-five-year-old student, he was walking one morning in Jerusalem to the Givat Ram campus of the Hebrew University. When he passed through the site of the Binyanei HaUma convention center (then under construction), he suddenly noticed an ancient coin. Upon inspection, it became clear that this coin was an authentic tetradrachm from the sixth century BCE, apparently imported to the Land of Israel around the time of the Edict of Cyrus![4] Coins native to the Land of Israel from their conception began to be minted about one hundred years after the return to Zion, starting in Gaza (imitating the Athenian coins) and then in Ashkelon, Judah (in Jerusalem, apparently), and in Samaria. The Judahite coins are imprinted with the word *yhd* (pronounced *yehud*)[5] and sometimes (either in place of *yehud* or in addition to it) with a person's name and title, such as "Johanan the Priest"; "Jaddua"; "Judah"; and "Hezekiah the Governor." The Samaritan coins contain the word *šmryn* (pronounced *shāmrayin*)[6] and occasionally names of people: Abdael (a name that appears in the Samaritan chronicles); San(ballat); Jeroboam (!) and others. One particularly interesting finding is a Samaritan coin apparently dated to shortly after the Macedonian conquest, whose obverse depicts a bearded deity sitting on a throne and holding a scepter in his hand. Next to this figure, the word ΖΕΥΣ (Zeus) is written. The same coin's reverse depicts a rider on horseback raising a sword, beneath him the word *yhwcnh* (Jeho'anah), certainly the name of a Samaritan official. This integration of a distinctly Israelite name, characteristic of those who believed in the God of Israel, with the Greek god Zeus, fits the description of the Samaritans in the Tanakh[7] and in Josephus' writings.[8] In the Tanakh, even in the books

4. The Greek drachma is equivalent to the dinar used by the Romans (as well as by *Ḥazal*); the tetradrachm is equivalent to four dinars, a *sela* (representing the biblical shekel) in the language of *Ḥazal*.
5. Compare to Ezra 5:8: *yehud medinta* – "the province of Judah."
6. Compare to Ezra 4:10 and others.
7. See II Kings 17:33: "They worshipped the Lord, while serving their own gods."
8. See *Antiquities* XII 257–264, where he relates that the Samaritans approached Antiochus Epiphanes and requested permission to call their temple on Mount Gerizzim "the Temple of Zeus Hellenius."

set during the return to Zion, the verb "weigh out" (the root Š-Q-L) still appears frequently, in every context of monetary payment: "So they weighed out my wages, thirty shekels of silver" (Zech. 11:12); "I will weigh out ten thousand talents of silver to the stewards for deposit in the royal treasury" (Est. 3:9). Meshorer maintains that the values of coins during that period were still not uniform or completely set. As a result, people would not rely on this coinage and continued to weigh out their silver.

Stone Weights during the Biblical Period

From the Tanakh we are familiar with the shekel, the *beka* (or half-shekel), the "one-third of a shekel" (Neh. 10:33) and the quarter-shekel (I Sam. 9:8). An example of a smaller unit is the gera or agora ("twenty geras to the shekel" [Ex. 30:13]), while larger units include the talent (*kikar*, equal to three thousand shekels according to Exodus 38:25-26) and the mina (*maneh*, appearing in the later parts of the Tanakh and in rabbinic literature, equal to one hundred dinar or twenty-five *sela'im*.

The archaeological findings in the Land of Israel contain numerous weight stones from the First Temple period, each engraved with a notation indicating the weight of the stone. There were some rare weights, such as one featuring the image of a turtle labeled *peleg reva* ("a part or half of one quarter"), along with another turtle labeled *ḥamesh* ("five"). The most common symbol used to denote the shekel was **ɤ**,[9] sometimes depicted alongside digits (of the sort used at the time) indicating the number of shekels.[10] Smaller stones were also found, engraved with the words *bq*ʿ, *pym* and *nṣp*. The shekel weighed, on average, about 0.4 oz., the beka about 0.2 oz., the *pym* about 0.28 oz., and the *nṣp* about 0.35 oz. It seems that the *pym* was equal to about two-thirds of the value of the shekel, while the *nṣp* was about five-sixths of its value. When the first *pym* was discovered in the City of David in the early twentieth century, a connection to the following passage from I Samuel was immediately suggested:

9. This symbol may have been a schematic illustration of a tied bundle in which one might keep his money.
10. According to Yoḥanan Aharoni, this practice was influenced by the Egyptian writing system.

> No smith was to be found in all the Land of Israel, for the Philistines were afraid that the Hebrews would make swords or spears. So all the Israelites had to go down to the Philistines to have their plowshares, their mattocks, axes, and colters sharpened. And the sharpening was a pim for plowshares, mattocks, three-pronged forks, and axes, and for setting the goads. (I Sam. 13:19–21)

The commentators and the grammarians struggled to interpret the word *pim* here. In light of the finding, it was suggested that the Philistines would charge the Israelites a pim for every sharpening. Some understood *pym* of the weight stones as a shortened version of the expression *pi shnayim*. This expression is commonly thought to mean "double," based on a casual reading of the instances where it appears in the Tanakh. But the truth is that *pi shnayim* means two parts out of three or more. For example, in our *parasha* the firstborn son inherits *pi shnayim* of his father's estate, meaning two parts out of all the parts into which the estate was divided. Similarly, Elisha asked of Elijah that he be considered a "firstborn son" with respect to his spiritual inheritance, in relation to the other disciples of the prophets: "Let two parts (*pi shnayim*) of your spirit pass on to me" (II Kings 2:9). Finally, see also Zechariah 13:8: "Two-thirds (*pi shnayim*) shall perish, shall die, and one-third of it shall survive."[11]

Nṣp is a word that is not found in the Hebrew vocabulary. However, *niṣf* is known in Arabic meaning "half." The finding demonstrates that in the Hebrew of the First Temple period, the word was used in the sense of five-sixths.[12]

The *sela* that appears in rabbinic literature is the Tyrian tetradrachm, whose weight was about half an ounce. It is interesting to note that all the Jewish coins from the Hasmonean period, and even from the time of Herod, were cheap copper coins. On the other hand,

11. A similar expression existed in ancient Egyptian: The consonant r is represented by the mouth hieroglyph, and thus *rwy* means "two mouths," meaning two-thirds. This is the linguistic equivalent of *pi shnayim*, as the Hebrew expression literally means "two mouths" as well.
12. Compare to Isaiah 44:16–19, where the word "half" refers to any fraction, and not necessarily 50 percent.

Weight stones from the First Temple period. Clockwise from top-left: beka, pim, two shekels, and nezeph.

numerous Tyrian tetradrachms have been found in Jerusalem and in Judea, many more, in fact, than the number of such coins found in Tyre itself. Meshorer speculated that because of the quality of the Tyrian *sela'* and its importance for use in the Temple and for other halakhic purposes, the Jews in Jerusalem would mint these Tyrian coins. The first Hebrew silver coins since the ancient *yhd* coins were the beautiful and poignant coins that the Jewish rebels minted during the Great Revolt against Rome. These coins were equal in value to the Tyrian *sela'*; they bore the inscription *Shekel Yisrael* on one side and *Yerushalayim Hakedosha* ("holy Jerusalem") on the other. Nahmanides, in a letter from the Land of Israel (printed verbatim at the end of his commentary on the Torah in the Chavel edition), describes this coin, using it as a basis for establishing the halakha regarding the precise weight of the biblical shekel.[13]

13. Nahmanides confirmed Rashi's opinion on this matter, against the opinion of the *Geonim*: "And we weighed it at the money changer's tables and its weight was ten units of silver which are half an ounce, which Rashi has mentioned (see Rashi to Exodus 21:32)...This greatly supports Rashi's opinion."

It seems that the increase in the weight of the shekel from the 0.4 oz. indicated by the weights from the First Temple period to the half-ounce of the Tyrian shekel is about the same as the increase of a sixth that the sages defined as the upper limit of how much the measure of a coin may be increased.[14] It is likely that in ancient times each weight had various values, and it may be that biblical phrases like "at the going merchants' rate," "by the sanctuary weight," and "by the royal weight" referred to measures that were larger than the standard shekel.

"You Shall Not Have in Your Pouch Alternate Weights"

We can now return to our *parasha*. It is well known that a small, imperceptible increase in an object's length, width, or depth can have a significant impact on its volume. As a result, the degree of precision in the dimensions of the weights in a person's pouch could be an effective gauge of that person's moral compass: "Honest scales and balances are the Lord's; all the weights in the bag[15] are His work" (Prov. 16:11). The books in the Tanakh from the monarchy period include several references to "false balances" and "false weights" (see Hos. 12:8; Amos 8:5; Mic. 6:11; and Prov. 11:1, 20:23). The Torah states:

> You shall not have in your pouch alternate weights, larger and smaller. You shall not have in your house alternate measures, a larger and a smaller. You must have completely honest weights and completely honest measures, if you are to endure long on the soil that the Lord your God is giving to you. For everyone who does those things, everyone who deals dishonestly, is abhorred to the Lord your God. (Deut. 25:13–16)

The measures here, like the weights, are identified by their set volume, and as a result they too are easy to manipulate without causing

14. See Bava Batra 90a and *Tosafot* there; Menaḥot 77a; Bekhorot 5b. In the Torah, Onkelos translates the verse "twenty geras to the shekel" as "twenty ma'ahs to the sela"; the sela of the Second Temple period was equal to twenty-four ma'ahs, perhaps due to the influence of Mesopotamian measures.
15. The phrase *even kis* ("weight in the bag") exists in Akkadian as well: *aban kīsi*.

a noticeable change. A dishonest person might prepare a "smaller weight" that he would use when weighing out the amount of money he would need to pay when buying, as well as a "larger weight" that he would use when determining the amount of money he would receive when selling. The Torah teaches that even a small act of dishonesty, of which other people are not even aware, is an abhorrent injustice. The Book of Proverbs presents an abridged version of the passage in our *parasha*, converting the verses into a succinct adage: "False scales are an abomination to the Lord; an honest weight pleases Him" (11:1); and "False weights and false measures, both are an abomination to the Lord" (20:23).

For further study:

Aharoni, Y. "The Use of Hieratic Numerals in Hebrew Ostraca and in the Shekel Weights." BASOR 184 (1966): 13–19.

Kletter, R. *Economic Keystones: The Weight System of the Kingdom of Judah.* JSOT Supplement 276, Sheffield, 1998.

Meshorer, Y. *Ancient Means of Exchange, Weights and Coins.* Edited by R. Reich. Haifa, 1998, 15–18.

Meshorer, Y. "The Coins of Samaria in the Persian Period." *Michmanim* 6 (1992): 7–13.

Meshorer, Y. *A Treasury of Jewish Coins.* Jerusalem, 2001, 1–17, 72–78.

Meshorer, Y. *The Third Side of the Coin.* Jerusalem, 2006, 19–22 [Hebrew].

Meshorer Y. and S. Qedar. *The Coinage of Samaria in the Fourth Century BCE.* Jerusalem, 1991, esp. 13–18.

Powell, M. A. "Weights and Measures." In *The Anchor Bible Dictionary* 6, 905–908.

Slouschz, N. *Thesaurus of Phoenician Inscriptions.* Tel-Aviv, 1942, 116–118 [Hebrew].

Stern, E. "*Middot Umishkalot.*" *Encyclopaedia Biblica* 4, 846–878 [Hebrew].

Yadin, Y. "Ancient Judaean Weights and the Date of the Samaria Ostraca." *Scripta Hierosolymitana* 8 (1961): 9–25.

Parashat Ki Tavo

Mount Gerizim and Mount Ebal

The Importance of the Covenant at Mount Gerizim and Mount Ebal

The location at the heart of *Parashat Ki Tavo* is undoubtedly Mount Gerizim and Mount Ebal. The covenant of Mount Gerizim and Mount Ebal seems to be an important mitzva in the context of Deuteronomy. It is mentioned twice in Deuteronomy, in extremely significant places. The Book of Deuteronomy is divided into three parts, and since *Parashat Ki Tavo* is always read at the end of the month of Elul, it is only fitting to compare this three-part division to the three parts of each shofar blast on Rosh HaShana. It is well known that each blast (*teru'a*) is accompanied by a "plain blast" (*teki'a*) before it and after it, totaling three distinct sounds. The Book of Deuteronomy is constructed using a similar format: In the beginning, Moses presents the basic tenets of faith (*Parashot Devarim, Va'etḥanan,* and *Ekev*); then comes the complex and diverse list of mitzvot (*Re'eh, Shofetim, Ki Tetzeh,* and the beginning of *Ki Tavo*); and finally the "plain blast" returns – the covenant is forged, accompanied by song and blessing. It is noteworthy that precisely at the two points of transition between the three sections, the mitzva to bless and curse at Mount Gerizim and Mount Ebal is given. The first time, this mitzva appears only briefly, at the end of the faith chapters of Deuteronomy and before the start of the list of mitzvot in the opening to *Parashat Re'eh.*

The second time, it is described at length in *Parashat Ki Tavo,* after the mitzvot section and before the covenant section. This demonstrates that the Book of Deuteronomy assigns unique significance to the blessing and curse ritual that took place between Mount Gerizim and Mount Ebal. Its textual placement between the principles of faith and the mitzva details seemingly teaches us that within the essence of this transition lies the connection between lofty principles and practical actions.

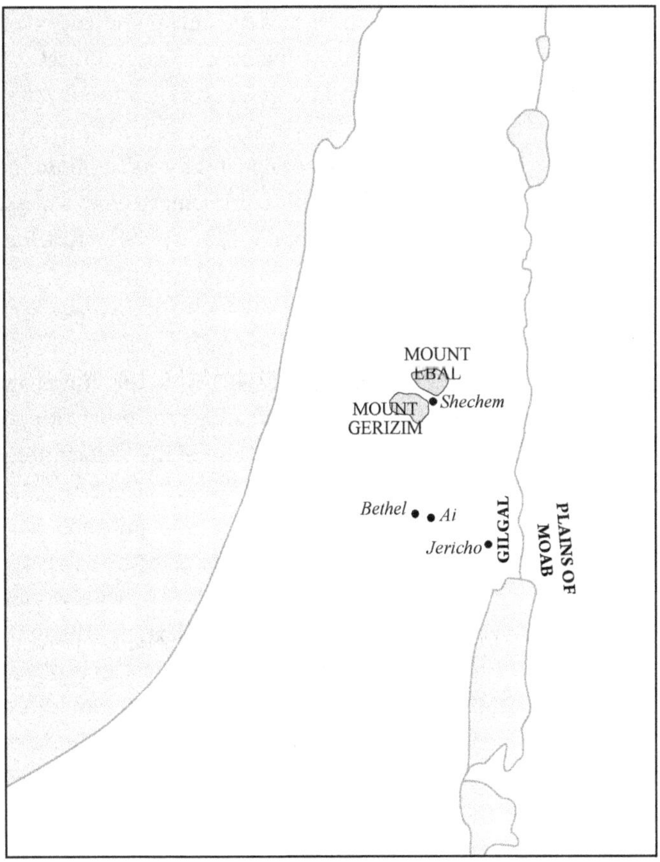

The outsize importance of the mitzva to read the blessing and the curse between Mount Gerizim and Mount Ebal is especially striking, bearing in mind that the mitzva is not applicable for future generations.

It was a one-time event that captivated the hearts of the entire nation at the time of its entry into the land of Canaan. It may be that the final two commandments in the Torah – the mitzva of *hak'hel*, which renews the covenant every seven years, and the mitzva to write down the song of *Haazinu* for future generations, "in order that this poem may be My witness against the Children of Israel" (Deut. 31:19) – represent an intergenerational vehicle for the message of this one-time event. Be that as it may, this is a unique mitzva, one intended from the start to be fulfilled only once. In addition, the Torah dedicates considerable attention to the details of the mitzva and to the precise location where it was set to take place. In order for us to understand the essence of this event, we must first try to understand the details of this mitzva, as well as the framework for the time and place that the Torah designates for its fulfillment. It is easy to become lost in the sea of rabbinic commentary on this question, so we will not attempt to review all the opinions and possibilities. Instead we will attempt to forge directly to the crux of the matter.

The Place

The place where the event took place is important to the Torah, and as such the Torah describes it in detail: "Both are on the other side of the Jordan, beyond the west road that is in the land of the Canaanites who dwell in the Arabah – near Gilgal, by Elonei Moreh" (Deut. 11:30). This is a highly detailed description, but at the same time quite enigmatic. It is worth considering that while the Torah goes on at length in describing this location, it refrains from mentioning the place that we would certainly have expected to see in this geographical context: Shechem! In the remainder of our discussion, we will attempt to suggest an explanation for this exclusion.[1] Most of the components in this geographic description cannot be deciphered easily, but the parts that can be understood present a kind of internal contradiction. "The Canaanites who dwell in

1. The Samaritans solved this problem in a characteristic manner: In their version of the Torah, they add the phrase "near Shechem." *Ḥazal* were familiar with this version, as we read in Sota 33b and parallels: "You have falsified your Torah but you gained nothing thereby."

the Arabah" and "Gilgal" seem to direct us to the Jordan Rift Valley,[2] but "by Elonei Moreh" clearly leads us to Shechem (see Gen. 12:6: "Abram passed through the land as far as the site of Shechem, at Elonei Moreh.")

The Time

www.zerothkoff.com (Courtesy of Dr. Zev Rothkoff)

"[Jotham] went and stood on top of Mount Gerizim…'Citizens of Shechem, listen to me!'" A view of ancient Shechem from the top of Mount Gerizim. Note the city wall and the temple with the large stone to its right.

A similar contradiction exists with respect to the time at which the event was set to take place. On the one hand, the Torah states that the matter of Mount Gerizim and Mount Ebal must be done "as soon as you have crossed the Jordan" (Deut. 27:2), "after you have crossed the Jordan" (27:12), meaning that it must happen immediately after entering the land. On the other hand, the Torah also states that the ritual must take place specifically on Mount Gerizim and on Mount Ebal, which, as far as we know, are located in the heart of the land, near Shechem – or as *Ḥazal* put it, sixty mil from the Jordan. Thus, the ritual could not

2. Compare to "Canaanites dwell by the Sea and along the Jordan" (Num. 13:29) and "They encamped at Gilgal on the eastern border of Jericho" (Josh. 4:19).

possibly take place immediately upon entering the land. This contradiction requires one either to assume that a miracle took place that was not mentioned in the verses – that the people were able to travel a distance of 120 mil in one day (as the *baraita* in Sota suggests) – or to follow R. Elazar's suggestion that Mount Gerizim and Mount Ebal were actually located near the Jordan: "They put up two mounds and called one Gerizim and one Ebal" (Y. Sota 21c).[3] But the simple geographical fact is that Mount Gerizim and Mount Ebal are located in Samaria, near Shechem. This is written explicitly in Judges 9:7: "When Jotham was informed, he went and stood on top of Mount Gerizim and called out to them in a loud voice. 'Citizens of Shechem!' he cried, 'Listen to me, that God may listen to you.'" In other words, Mount Gerizim is within earshot of Shechem. It seems that the Torah is expressing that, on the one hand, this is a mitzva that applies immediately the people of Israel enter the land, but on the other hand it is a mitzva intimately linked to the epicenter of the land – the environs of Shechem. As in other similar examples, the Torah is not a book of halakhic guidelines in the vein of the *Shulḥan Arukh*. Rather, it presents both possible directions and then places the responsibility to find the proper solution on the nation of Israel – in this case, on Joshua and his generation. One who reads the Book of Joshua on a simple level will find that Joshua indeed found a practical solution to the Gerizim-Ebal contradiction that did not match any of those proposed by *Ḥazal*. This solution took into consideration the two principles stated in the Torah and weighed them against the reality of Joshua's own practical considerations. Joshua believed that once the nation of Israel entered the land, it was their responsibility to put in the utmost effort to conduct the ritual as soon as possible. The moment that Jericho and Ai were in his hands, Joshua could have relied on the paucity of Canaanite settlement in the Mount Ephraim area and

3. R. Elazar was preceded by a biblical scroll from Qumran, in which the passage of the blessing and curse was inserted into Joshua 4, after the crossing of the Jordan River, and followed by Eusebius of Caesarea (see below). A third and no less farfetched approach is that of Josephus (Ant. 5: 68–70) and Yerushalmi accordibg to R. Yishmael, who distinguish between the erecting and coating of the stones that took place immediately after crossing the river and the ceremony of the blessing and curse that followed the conclusion of the conquest and the division of the allotments.

taken the whole nation of Israel to Mount Ebal to forge the covenant of the blessing and the curse.

The Details

What happened at Mount Gerizim and Mount Ebal? Once again, the limited scope of this discussion forces us to skip over many long and rich disputes on this question. We will suffice by saying, in brief, that the nation apparently stood between Mount Gerizim and Mount Ebal in the valley where the modern-day city of Nablus can be found. Joshua 8:33 states: "All Israel – stranger and citizen alike – with their elders, officials, and magistrates, stood on either side of the Ark... half of them *el mul* Mount Gerizim and half of them *el mul* Mount Ebal." Based on what we explained in the chapter on *Parashat Tzav*, this means that six tribes stood at the foot of Mount Gerizim or on its slopes and six tribes stood at the foot of Mount Ebal. The area in which the event took place was an enclosed space between the two mountains; the Ark and all of Israel stood on either side. The explanation for the division of the tribes into two groups that are not familiar from other contexts – Simeon, Levi, Judah, Issachar, Joseph, and Benjamin opposing Reuben, Gad, Asher, Zebulun, Dan, and Naphtali – was discovered by Michael Broyde and Steven Weiner. It turns out that from a mathematical perspective, this was the division that would split the nation most effectively (based on the census of *Parashat Pinḥas*) into two equal halves.

What is the nature of the "large stones" that we were commanded to "coat them with plaster and inscribe upon them all the words of this Torah" (Deut. 27:4, 8)? First, according to the simple reading of the verse, there is no connection between these stones and the altar stones, nor between these stones and the twelve stones that were taken from the Jordan and set up at Gilgal. My father *z"l* taught me to follow Rabbi Saadia Gaon's interpretation on this matter, cited in Ibn Ezra's commentary here, that these stones served as posters or placards, such as those used today at important ceremonies. In other words, the stones were coated with plaster in order to emphasize the text written upon them, in this case, select verses from the Torah that would have the capacity to inspire the hearts of the event's participants and draw their attention to the magnitude of the event and the significance of the covenant. These included verses such as "Hear, O Israel! The Lord is our God, the Lord alone" (Deut. 6:4); "Today you have become the people of the Lord your God" (27:9); "You have affirmed this day that the Lord is your God… and the Lord has affirmed this day that you are His treasured people" (26:17–18); "There is none beside Him" (4:35); and "For thereby you shall have life and shall long endure upon the soil that the Lord swore to your ancestors, Abraham, Isaac, and Jacob, to give to them" (30:20).

What Did the Levites Proclaim?

Again, there is a contradiction between the *peshat* and the midrashic tradition. According to the Mishna, the twelve "Cursed be" verses in the passage were also accompanied by twelve parallel blessings:

> They turned their faces toward Mount Gerizim and opened with the blessing: Blessed be anyone who does not make a sculptured or molten image, abhorred by the Lord, a craftsman's handiwork, and does not set it up in secret. And both parties respond, Amen. They then turned their faces toward Mount Ebal and opened with the curse: Cursed be anyone who makes a sculptured or molten image, abhorred by the Lord, etc. And both parties respond, Amen. (Sota 7:5)

This interpretation is difficult to accept: If the Torah decided to present an abridged version of the Levites' proclamation, why would it choose to present only the curses? Would it not make more sense to present the blessings and allow the reader to "fill in" the implied curses? Another difficulty was raised by one of my students after we studied this passage together. She asked: I can understand why a person who does not make idols or who "upholds the terms of this Torah and observes them" deserves to be blessed. But can it truly be that thousands of Levites were instructed to stand up and proclaim out loud, for the whole nation of Israel to hear: "Blessed be anyone who does not lie with his father's wife" or "Blessed be he who does not lie with any beast"? People who engage in these depravities are certainly worthy of being cursed, but that does not mean that anyone who does not do so automatically earns a blessing or a *yasher ko'aḥ*!

Rabbi David Zvi Hoffman found that the blessing passage following the twelve "Cursed be" verses contains six short "Blessed be" clauses; similarly, the passage of the curse begins with six parallel "Cursed be" clauses. These six blessing/curse pairs form a kind of basic skeleton for the blessings and the curses in general:

> Blessed/Cursed shall you be in the city;
> Blessed/Cursed shall you be in the country;
> Blessed/Cursed shall be the issue of your womb, the produce of your soil, and the offspring of your cattle, the calving of your herd and the lambing of your flock;
> Blessed/Cursed shall be your basket and your kneading bowl;
> Blessed/Cursed shall you be in your comings;
> Blessed/Cursed shall you be in your goings.

According to Rabbi Hoffman, these twelve blessings and curses were directed at the twelve tribes, six "Blessed be" clauses for Mount Gerizim and six "Cursed be" clauses for Mount Ebal.

It seems that a preferable position is that of Ibn Ezra, who explains that the twelve unpaired "Cursed be" verses are merely an introduction. The actual blessings and curses are: "Now, if you obey... all these blessings shall come upon you and take effect... But if you do not obey... all these curses shall come upon you and take effect..." (Deut. 28:1–2, 15). These passages detail at length the blessings that will come upon the people if they faithfully observe God's commandments, and at much greater length the curses, the exiles, and the torments that will befall the people if they betray their God. Admittedly, there is still one difficulty with this interpretation, namely, the final verse: "These are the terms of the covenant which the Lord commanded Moses to conclude with the Israelites in the land of Moab" (28:69). This means that the lengthy blessing and curse sections were meant to be read in the plains of Moab and not at Mount Ebal. Ibn Ezra resolves this difficulty by proposing an original syntactical understanding. He explains, in brief, that "the land of Moab" is an adverbial adjunct of the phrase "which the Lord commanded" and not of "to conclude." Thus, it is as if the Torah is saying,

"These are the terms of the covenant which the Lord commanded Moses in the land of Moab to conclude with the Israelites."[4]

The very fact that Moses, on the eve of his departure, stood up and transmitted the entire lengthy blessing and curse before the nation of Israel created a "covenant at the plains of Moab" here. Moses himself preceded the commandment regarding the blessing and curse of Gerizim and Ebal with the festive words: "The Lord your God commands you this day to observe... You have affirmed this day that the Lord is your God... And the Lord has affirmed this day that you are His treasured people" (Deut. 26:16–18). Later, he concluded the section saying, "*I make this covenant*, with its sanctions, not with you alone, but both with those who are standing here with us... and with those who are not with us here this day" (29:13–14). But by definition, this covenant was a preparation for the great covenant forged between Gerizim and Ebal, and the ambiguous language of the verse, "These are the terms of the covenant..." (28:69) gives a measure of power to the covenant at the plains of Moab as well. Ibn Ezra's approach also fits the verse in Joshua 8:34: "After that, he read all the words of the Torah, the blessing and the curse, just as is written in the Book of the Torah." The opening of the impressive ceremony was punctuated by the initial proclamation of the twelve "Cursed be" verses, through which each Israelite swore to adhere to commandments that are germane to the private realm – and thus practically unenforceable at the hands of the community. These curses were presented to the nation of Israel as a warning and an oath for each of its members, and the entire nation – all twelve tribes – answered with a great, resounding "Amen."

Why Specifically on Mount Gerizim and Mount Ebal?

Now let us dedicate a few words to the question of why Mount Gerizim and Mount Ebal specifically were chosen as the venue for this event. What is the unique significance of this place? And why was the city of Shechem not mentioned explicitly in the Torah's description of the location? I will present three ideas here that are not mutually exclusive; rather, they complete one another.

---

4. For verses with a similar structure, compare to Deuteronomy 12:2 (and Rashi's commentary) and Amos 9:12 (and Radak's commentary).

The first idea was proposed by Henry Baker Tristram, a Christian scholar who possessed great love and knowledge of the Tanakh. Tristram toured the land and studied its sites, focusing specifically on their flora and fauna, about 155 years ago. He scaled Mount Gerizim, reaching its peak on December 21, 1863. According to Tristram, Mount Gerizim was chosen for the blessing and curse ceremony, and later as the site where Jotham delivered his parable, because of the unique acoustic effect created by the two tall mountains that enclose the Shechem valley. Tristram writes:

> A single voice might be heard by many thousands, shut in and conveyed up and down by the enclosing hills. In the early morning we could not only see from Gerizim a man driving his ass down a path on Mount Ebal, but could hear every word he uttered as he urged it on; and in order to test the matter more certainly, on a subsequent occasion two of our party stationed themselves on opposite sides of the valley, and with perfect ease recited the commandments antiphonally.

I do not know what inspired Tristram's companions to recite the Ten Commandments specifically for this test, but the key point here is the technical appropriateness of the location for its purpose, as Tristram states: "It is impossible to conceive a spot more admirably adapted for the purpose than this one." It is significant that Eusebius, the Greek bishop of Caesarea around 320 CE, believed that Mount Gerizim and Mount Ebal near Shechem are not the actual mountains in question, "because they are too far from one another, so that it is not possible to hear speech from one to the other" (*Onomasticon* 64:13–15). Tristram's "test" and my own personal experience (as well as that of many others) seem to belie this statement.

While Tristram's account is as charming as it is true, it is somewhat difficult to suffice with such a technical explanation for such a portentous choice. I will present here two additional avenues of thought that relate to the connection between the two mountains and the essence of the covenant.

The second idea is my own. Let us recall what we already noted above: the Torah stresses that the blessing and curse ceremony must take place between the two mountains, Gerizim and Ebal and the Torah intentionally refrains from mentioning Shechem by name, apparently in order to

Henry Baker Tristram (1822–1906)

distance the covenant from any connection to the city. While Shechem certainly has its own virtues, the covenant of the blessing and the curse is not connected to those virtues but to those of the two mountains. Nonetheless, Shechem can provide us with a frame of reference for the division of the land into regions. A map of the cities of refuge in the Land of Israel demonstrates that Shechem is located in the central region of the land. The northern city of refuge is Kedesh in Naphtali, the middle city is Shechem, and the southern city is Hebron, and the Torah states, "You shall divide into three parts the territory of the country" (Deut. 19:3). This teaches us that Shechem, located between Mount Gerizim and Mount Ebal, is considered the midpoint of the Land of Israel. From the perspective of road travel as well, one of the branches of the ancient international road bisected the Land of Israel at the valley conveniently located between Mount Gerizim and Mount Ebal. From here, this branch splits off into the national road from Shechem, passing through Shiloh, Bethel, Jerusalem, Bethlehem, Hebron, and Beersheba. Jacob, and apparently Abraham before him, arrived in the land of Canaan via this road. Mount Gerizim and Mount Ebal are very tall mountains; Mount Ebal is 3,084 feet above sea level, while Mount Gerizim is 2,890 feet above sea level. A steep slope from each mountain leads to the valley between the two, about 1,640 feet above sea level. It is noteworthy that Shechem is located exactly at the same distance – 71.5 mile – from both Dan in the north and Beersheba in the south.[5]

The Hebrew verb for forging a covenant is *kerita* (literally, cutting off), and similar verbs serve the same purpose in other languages as well. In two places in the Tanakh, we indeed find that the parties involved in a covenant would cut up the body of a live animal and pass through the pieces. Thus we read regarding the Covenant of the Pieces:

> Bring Me a three-year-old heifer, a three-year-old she-goat, a three-year-old ram, a turtledove and a young bird... He cut them in two, placing each half opposite the other...There appeared a smoking oven and a flaming torch [Rashi: the proxy of the *Divine Presence*, which is fire] that passed between those pieces. (Gen. 15:9–17)

Likewise, in Jeremiah 34:18: "The calf that they cut in two so as to pass between the halves." The meaning of this practice in the context of forging a covenant is perhaps the following statement: We are symbolically connected to each other as one live body. If we violate the terms of the covenant, may the two of us be like these two carcasses. An ancient Aramaic inscription from northern Syria describes an alliance in which a calf was cut in half, and the inscription curses the one who would break the covenant to be cut in half like this calf. It seems to me that Mount Gerizim and Mount Ebal were chosen because this was the place where God, as it were, cut the Land of Israel in two. Between the pieces, the Ark – representing the Divine Presence – stood along

5. I have to thank Yehuda Foist for this note.

with the people of Israel and together forged a covenant. The covenant between God and the people of Israel had already been forged at Sinai, but that was merely a theoretical covenant, established in the wilderness, over a Torah that was neither connected to the Land of Israel nor grounded in reality. In the land of Canaan, the Torah assumed its true form, as it was given "for you to observe in the land that you are about to cross into and occupy" (Deut. 4:14). The Land of Israel is a living body, a land that bestows its bounty upon its faithful children ("The land shall yield its fruit" [Lev. 25:19]), listens closely to the word of God ("Let the earth hear the words I utter!" [Deut. 32:1]), acts as a witness ("I call heaven and earth to witness against you this day" [30:19]) and spews out those that defile it ("Let not the land spew you out for defiling it" [Leviticus 18:28]). Now, the covenant is renewed together with the land itself, between the pieces of the "living body" of the Land of Israel.

Rabbi Uri Sherki of Jerusalem

The third idea was conceived by Rabbi Uri Sherki of Jerusalem. I heard this idea from Rabbi Yisrael Ariel, a teacher at Yeshivat Od Yosef Ḥai in Yitzhar. The yeshiva was situated in the very plot of land purchased by Jacob (Gen. 33:19) in which Joseph's Tomb was later situated (Josh. 24:32) near the mound of ancient Shechem[6] until the riots of September-October 2000. It can be said that the biblical virtue of this site and its vicinity was a central theme in the yeshiva's guiding philosophy. The following is the idea, in brief.

Aerial photograph from the west of Mount Gerizim (right), Mount Ebal (left,) and the valley in which the covenant was forged

The area between Gerizim and Ebal has a distinctive landscape, one that resembles an overturned mountain. The ceremony at Mount Gerizim and Mount Ebal can be seen as a kind of negative image of the revelation at Sinai. At Mount Sinai, the people of Israel stood at the foot of the mountain. The mountain itself was enveloped in thick cloud, smoke, and fire, and God's voice emanated from within the fire, addressing the nation. At this heady juncture, what did the nation do? All the people needed to do was listen. This task was perfectly suited for the

6. For the authenticity of this site and its role in the public discourse in contemporary Israel, see the chapter on *Parashat Vayishlaḥ*.

people who had only recently left Egypt, who now subsisted on manna in the wilderness; all that was asked of them was to listen to the voice of God. Upon entering the land, however, their hierarchy of values was turned on its head. In the Land of Israel, nature took the place of miracles; "You shall gather in your new grain and wine and oil" (Deut. 11:14). God's voice did not emanate from within the fire; rather we had to broadcast God's voice on our own. In the Land of Israel, the divine word did not come from some mountain that towered above us; quite the opposite, God's voice came from within the holy ground itself. The Ark stood in the middle, surrounded by the Levites, in lieu of God's actual voice, the Levites transmitted God's message from within the land, and the nation of Israel stood on the slopes of Mount Gerizim and Mount Ebal on both sides of the valley. Instead of clouds and smoke, there were stones painted by the Israelites themselves with white plaster. The whole ceremony was a metaphor for divine worship in the Land of Israel, a worship firmly rooted in the land's holy soil. Even the very voice of God did not ring out on its own; we are those who have to utter it on our own.

I will close with an addition to this idea that I came to understand through an emotional encounter. In the year 2007, I spent the Shabbat of *Parashat Lekh Lekha* in Elon Moreh – a settlement overlooking ancient Shechem from the east, and whose name is featured in that *parasha* – along with many other like-minded Jewish visitors. In the afternoon, after viewing Mount Gerizim and Mount Ebal from a lookout point and speaking about their importance, I was approached by Yael Lieberman, the widow of Rabbi Hillel Lieberman, who was murdered on his way to Joseph's Tomb during the Arab riots of September 2000. Yael showed me a piece of gold jewelry made of two triangles that she had received as a gift from her husband. Hillel had explained to his wife[7] that the two triangles – one pointing up and the other pointing down – represent Mount Sinai and the valley between Mount Gerizim and Mount Ebal respectively. When combined, the two triangles form the basis for the essence of the covenant between the nation of Israel and God. It is no coincidence that this combination of the upright triangle and the inverted triangle was chosen as the symbol of the nation of Israel: the Star of David.

7. Based on the teachings of Rabbi Sherki as well, as he later communicated to me.

Rabbi Hillel Lieberman *Hy"d* (1964–2000)

For further study:

Ariel, Y. *Tabbur Haaretz: Leshivhah Shel Ir Haberit.* Jerusalem, 1990, 18 [Hebrew].

Artom, E. S. "*Berit.*" In *Encyclopaedia Biblica* 2, col. 347–351 [Hebrew].

Broyde, M. J. and S. S. Weiner. "A Mathematical Analysis of the Division of the Tribes and the Role of the Levites on Grizim and Aval in Deuteronomy 27." *Tradition* 27 (1992): 48–57.

Fitzmyer, J. A. "The Aramaic Inscriptions of Sefire I and II." *JAOS* 81 (1961): 201.

Freeman-Grenville, G. S. P., R. L. Chapman, and J. Tailor. *The Onomasticon by Eusebius of Caesarea.* Jerusalem, 2003, 40–41.

Tristram, H. B. *The Land of Israel, a Journal of Travels with Reference to its Physical History.* London, 1865, 149–150.

Parashat Nitzavim

"That Land"

An Appendix to the Blessings and Curses of *Parashat Ki Tavo*

The opening passage of *Parashat Nitzavim* is a majestic epilogue to *Parashat Ki Tavo*, summarizing and concluding the story of the covenant of the blessing and the curse:

> You stand this day, all of you, before the Lord your God...to enter into the covenant of the Lord your God, which the Lord your God is concluding with you this day, with its sanctions; to the end that He may establish you this day as His people and be your God, as He promised you and as He swore to your fathers... I make this covenant, with its sanctions, not with you alone, but both with those who are standing here with us this day before the Lord our God and with those who are not with us here this day. (Deut. 29:9–14)

Following these verses is a kind of appendix, dealing with individuals and with families:

> Perchance there is among you some man or woman, or some clan or tribe, whose heart is even now turning away from the Lord our God to go and worship the gods of those nations...The Lord will never forgive him.... (29:17–19)

The Torah then apparently goes back to speaking about the nation of Israel in general: "And later generations will ask – the children who succeed you, and foreigners who come from distant lands..." (29:21). Here, the Torah fills in what it left out in the lengthy curse section of *Parashat Ki Tavo*: the curse that will befall the *land* if the nation violates the terms of the covenant: "All its soil devastated by sulfur and salt, beyond sowing and producing, no grass growing in it, just like the upheaval of Sodom and Gomorrah, Admah, and Zeboiim, which the Lord overthrew in His fierce anger" (29:22). Finally, the section ends with the uplifting, unique, mysterious verse: "The secret things belong to the Lord our God, but the things revealed belong to us and to our children forever, that we may follow all the words of this law" (29:28). The next verse begins a new narrative entirely, one that concerns the eventual redemption and return: "When all these things befall you..." (ch. 30).

This Land and That Land

In this conclusion to the blessing and curse section, the expression "that land" appears twice:

> And see the plagues and diseases that the Lord has inflicted upon that land.... All nations will ask, "Why did the Lord do thus to this land? Wherefore that awful wrath?" They will be told, "Because they forsook the covenant that the Lord, God of their fathers, made with them...So the Lord was incensed at that land and brought upon it all the curses recorded in this book. (Deut. 29:21–26).

The nations that ask these questions use the intuitive expression "this land (*haaretz hazot*)" to refer to the Land of Israel, but in the response that they are given, as well as in the Torah's own description of the ravaged land, it is called "that land (*haaretz hahi*)." The expression "this land" has appeared earlier in the Torah, as recently as the beginning of *Parashat Ki Tavo*. When a person brings *bikkurim* (first fruits) during happy times, he stands before God and says, "He brought us to this place and gave us this land, a land flowing with milk and honey" (26:9). Thus, the Land of Israel during its good times is "this land," where the members of its nation eat its fruits, where one is sated by its goodness, and where one goes on to thank God for this bounty. During times of exile, banishment, and desolation, the land is called "that land," a language that implies distance and possibly even revulsion. The land is not here; it is something remote, far from all normal reality.

A Command for the Later Generations

Here we find a remarkable and very fundamental point that is connected to the essence of the Land of Israel and to its ever-changing character throughout history. As Nahmanides emphasized upon viewing the ruins of the land with his own eyes: "You will not find anywhere in the world a land so good and spacious, which was once so developed and is [now] in such a state of ruin" (commentary on Leviticus 26:32). The Talmud states that the nation of Israel is unique in that when they rise, they rise to the stars; but when they fall, they fall to the dust (Megilla 16a). Indeed, the same is true of the Land of Israel: When the nation rises, the land rises along with them to the heavens, and when they fall and are scattered and cast away to distant lands, the land falls as well, sinking into the depths of doom and oblivion.

Here in *Parashat Nitzavim*, the Torah gives a kind of long-distant command to future generations, "the children who succeed you, and foreigners who come from distant lands," to come and witness for themselves the "plagues and diseases that the Lord has inflicted upon that land." The land will be a remote, distant, wretched place, bearing no resemblance to settled areas throughout the world. Visitors who gaze upon the land with plaintive wonder cannot help but ask: "Why did the Lord do thus to this land? Wherefore that awful wrath?"

Mark Twain

I will present here a few select excerpts – some of which may already be familiar to readers – from Mark Twain's book *The Innocents Abroad*, in which he includes a chapter (entitled "Pleasure Excursion to the Holy Land") recounting his visit to the Land of Israel in 1867. Twain, a humorist extraordinaire and an acute observer, sensed that he was facing something that could not be spoken of humorously. When standing in the Hula Valley near Ain Mallaha, a spring without any trees or vegetation in the middle of the wilderness,[1] he writes:

> Stirring scenes like these [i.e., the war between Barak and Sisera and the bravery of Yael] occur in this valley no more. There is not a solitary village throughout its whole extent – not for thirty miles in either direction. There are two or three small clusters of Bedouin tents, but not a single permanent habitation. One may ride ten miles, hereabouts, and not see ten human beings.
>
> To this region one of the prophecies is applied:
>
> "I will bring the land into desolation; and your enemies which dwell therein shall be astonished at it. And I will scatter you among the heathen, and I will draw out a sword after you; and your land shall be desolate and your cities waste."

(L. Lortet, 1880)

The desolated and arid Hula Valley in the nineteenth century

1. This is known today as the Einan Springs or the Naḥal Einan Reserve, a quiet, verdant spot at the foot of Keren Naftali in the Upper Galilee. Notably, a prehistoric settlement was revealed near these springs.

> No man can stand here by deserted Ain Mellahah and say the prophecy has not been fulfilled.

Twain elaborates on the notion of "your enemies which dwell therein shall be astonished (or desolated) at it" in various places in the chapter, including in his description of al-Majdal/Magdala just north of Tiberias:

> Magdala is not a beautiful place. It is thoroughly Syrian, and that is to say that it is thoroughly ugly, and cramped, squalid, uncomfortable, and filthy… The streets of Magdala are any where from three to six feet wide, and reeking with uncleanliness… As we rode into Magdala not a soul was visible. But the ring of the horses' hoofs roused the stupid population, and they all came trooping out – old men and old women, boys and girls, the blind, the crazy, and the crippled, all in ragged, soiled and scanty raiment, and all abject beggars by nature, instinct and education. How the vermin-tortured vagabonds did swarm! How they showed their scars and sores, and piteously pointed to their maimed and crooked limbs, and begged with their pleading eyes for charity...They hung to the horses' tails, clung to their manes and the stirrups… "Howajji, bucksheesh! howajji, bucksheesh! howajji, bucksheesh! bucksheesh! bucksheesh!"

In Jaffa, before Twain boarded his ship and took his leave of the Land of Israel, he summarized:

> Of all the lands there are for dismal scenery, I think Palestine must be the prince. The hills are barren, they are dull of color, they are unpicturesque in shape. The valleys are unsightly deserts fringed with a feeble vegetation that has an expression about it of being sorrowful and despondent. The Dead Sea and the Sea of Galilee sleep in the midst of a vast stretch… wherein the eye rests upon no pleasant tint… It is a hopeless, dreary, heart-broken land… Palestine sits in sackcloth and ashes. Over it broods the spell of a curse that has withered its fields and fettered its energies… desolate and unlovely… Palestine is no more of this work-day world. It is sacred to poetry and tradition – it is dream-land.

Jericho

I will quote one more excerpt, a fascinating passage that is likely less familiar to readers. Perhaps in order to illustrate the stark contrasts that the Land of Israel can reach, from the heavens to the abyss, it is worth examining one the most beautiful locations in the Land of Israel, namely, Jericho.

At the end of the Second Temple period, Jericho was at the pinnacle of its glory. It was home to twelve priestly divisions (Taanit 27a), as well as the winter palaces of the Hasmonean and Herodian kings. Josephus writes in his book *The Jewish War* (IV, 8:3, 466–471):

> [The advantage] of this water is great when it flows even in little quantities. Accordingly, it waters a larger space of ground than any other waters do, and passes along a plain of seventy furlongs [originally: stadia, i.e., about eight miles] long, and twenty broad; wherein it affords nourishment to those most excellent gardens that are thick set with trees. There are in it many sorts of palm trees that are watered by it, different from each other in taste and name; the better sort of them, when they are pressed, yield an excellent kind of honey, not much inferior in sweetness to other honey. This country withal produces honey from bees; it also bears that balsam which is the most precious of all the fruits in that place...cypress trees also, and those that bear myrobalanum; so that he who should pronounce this place to be divine would not be mistaken, wherein is such plenty of trees produced as are very rare, and of the most excellent sort. And indeed, if we speak of those other fruits, it will not be easy to light on any climate in the habitable earth that can well be compared to it, what is here sown comes up in such clusters; the cause of which seems to me to be the warmth of the air, and the fertility of the waters; the warmth calling forth the sprouts, and making them spread, and the moisture making every one of them take root firmly, and supplying that virtue which it stands in need of in summer time.

In short, Jericho is a paradise.

By contrast, it is telling to read a very different description of Jericho, that of Edward Robinson – the most prominent scholar of the Land of Israel in the mid-nineteenth century – from 1838:

> We now returned through the village, which bears in Arabic the name of Erîha, or as it is more commonly pronounced Rîha, a degenerate shoot, both in name and character, of the ancient Jericho. Situated in the midst of this vast plain, it reminded me much of an Egyptian village. The plain is rich, and susceptible of easy tillage and abundant irrigation, with a climate to produce anything. Yet it lies almost desert; and the village is the most miserable and filthy that we saw in Palestine. The houses, or hovels, are merely four walls of stones taken from ancient ruins, and loosely thrown together, with flat roofs of cornstalks or brushwood spread over with gravel. They stand quite irregularly and with large intervals; and each has around it a yard enclosed by a hedge of the dry thorny boughs of the Nŭbk. In many of these

The fertile Hula Valley today

> yards are open sheds with similar roofs; the flocks and herds are brought into them at night, and render them filthy in the extreme...One single solitary palm now timidly rears its head, where once stood the renowned "City of Palm-trees."

Thus, we see that the Land of Israel has the ability both to ascend to the heights of blessing and to plummet to the depths of curse. This fact itself is a historical wonder. How fortunate we are to have merited living in a generation when the land is green and beautiful once more; may it stay this way forever.

For further study:

Robinson, E. and E. Smith. *Biblical Researches in Palestine, Mount Sinai and Arabia Petraea: A Journal of Travels in the Year 1838*, II. London, 1841, 279–280.

Twain, M. *The Innocents Abroad*. Hartford, 1869, 485, 503–505, 606–608.

Parashat Vayelekh – Shuva

Sukka, Redemption, and the Talmudic Principle: "You shall make but not from that which is already made"

In honor of Shabbat Shuva, we will deviate from our usual framework and delve into the world of Jewish thought and homiletics.

Background

Long ago in the annals of Jewish history, it was customary that every Shabbat afternoon, members of the congregation would gather in the beit midrash and the local sage would deliver his weekly *derasha* (Torah lecture). This *derasha* would integrate halakha, Aggada, and current events, weaving these subjects together with verses from that week's *parasha*. *Ḥazal* denounced those who would schedule a meal at the same time as the *derasha* (Gittin 38b), and even prohibited reading certain parts of the Tanakh on Shabbat "because of the neglect of the beit midrash" (Shabbat 115a).[1] These *derashot* had a set format, more or less. One such *derasha* was preserved in the Talmud in its entirety (Shabbat 30a–b). In another case, two talmudic statements were presented together in the series of passages on Ḥanukka, both attributed to the famous *darshan* R. Tanḥum: "If a Ḥanukka lamp is placed above twenty cubits [from the ground] it is unfit, like a sukka and a crossbeam over [the entrance of] an alley"; and "'And the pit was empty; there was no water in it'.... There was no water, but there were snakes and scorpions in it" (21b–22a). These statements appear to be an abridged version or a skeleton of a *derasha* that was delivered on the Shabbat preceding Ḥanukka, and that was connected to the story of Joseph and his brothers in that week's *parasha*. The *Midrash Tanḥuma* and *Midrash Yelamdenu* on the one hand and the *She'iltot* of Rav Aha of Shabha (from Babylonia in the early Gaonic period) on the other are collections of dozens of such eclectic *derashot*.

Over time, the custom gradually fell into near-disuse, and in later generations was (and still is) observed on only two Shabbatot each year: on *Shabbat HaGadol* (the Shabbat immediately preceding Passover) and on *Shabbat Shuva* (between Rosh HaShana and Yom Kippur). The months of Nisan and Tishrei are the two focal points of Jewish life, both in halakha and in Jewish thought. It is the *darshan*'s task to deliver successfully a *derasha* that incorporates both elements of practical halakha regarding the festivals as well as elements that inspire repentance and improving one's behavior in Tishrei and spiritual freedom in Nisan. I will attempt to adhere to this model in the following discussion.

I conceived the idea at the basis of this *derasha* during the period between Rosh HaShana and Yom Kippur in 1984, writing it down in a book margin at the time. I shared the idea with friends on a few occasions, including on *Shabbat Shuva* in 1996 at the ancient Shalom Al Yisrael

1. Rashi explains: "On Shabbat they would deliver a lecture to the laymen, who were preoccupied with their labor throughout the week. Through the lecture, they would teach them the laws of what is prohibited and what is permitted, and it was better for them to listen [to the *derasha*] than to read the sacred writings."

Synagogue in Jericho.[2] An abridged version of this *derasha* was published in the Shabbat insert of *Makor Rishon* in Tishrei 5773 (September 2012).

The Dispute between Rav and Shmuel Regarding the Sukka

We read in Mishna Sukka 1:4:

> If a man trailed upon it [a sukka] vine, or a gourd or ivy, and he covered [it with a valid covering], it is invalid. But if the valid covering exceeded these in quantity, or if one cut them, it is valid.

Rav interprets the mishna according to the simple reading, explaining that one who has already draped a vine, gourd, or ivy over his sukka can render his sukka valid by cutting these creepers, thus disconnecting them from the ground. Shmuel disagrees, maintaining that it is impossible to render such a sukka valid by simply cutting the material, since the Torah states, "You shall hold (*taaseh,* literally 'you shall make') the Feast of Booths" (Deut. 16:13) – implying that one must make a sukka, but not from materials that were already made. Thus, Shmuel is forced to interpret the mishna against its simple meaning and tack on an additional requirement for validating the sukka: "He must shake them." Rav responds, insisting that "their cutting is their [valid] preparation."

This dispute between Rav and Shmuel carries over to cases of tzitzit and lulav as well. In the case of tzitzit, the Torah uses the same verb *laasot*: "To make (*ve'asu*) for themselves fringes" (Num. 15:38). Thus, according to Rav, if one attaches tzitzit to the corners of his garment before the fringes have been separated from one another, and then proceeds to separate them, the tzitzit is valid. Shmuel, however, maintains that the tzitzit is invalid in such a situation. The same is true for the Four Species[3]: If the *hadas* (myrtle) is bound together with the lulav and the *arava* (willow) and the berries of the *hadas* are more numerous

2. This was apparently the only Shabbat that Jews have spent in Jericho since the Oslo Accords until today. The week following this Shabbat marked the beginning of the "Western Wall Tunnel riots" of September 1996.
3. This is only according to the opinion that a lulav must be bound, and that the laws of lulav can be derived from the laws of sukka.

than its leaves (a condition that invalidates it), according to Rav one may pick the berries in order to reduce their number and validate the *hadas*. However, according to Shmuel one must first take apart the entire binding before picking the berries, and then bind the species anew, in order to validate the *hadas*.

What is at the root of this dispute? According to Shmuel, when one needs to "make" something in order to fulfill a mitzva, one's action must be directly focused upon the object in question; an action that affects the state of the object indirectly is not considered "making." By contrast, Rav maintains that even an indirect action can be considered "making."

Despite the general halakhic principle that we follow Rav's position in cases of disputes over ritual law between him and Shmuel,[4] and despite the fact that Rav's position here seems to fit more smoothly with the simple reading of the mishna, the *posekim* ruled in accordance with Shmuel in this case. The reason for this is that a *baraita* supporting Shmuel's position was cited in the Gemara, constituting an unanswered challenge to Rav's position.

The Dispute between Rav and Shmuel Regarding *Geula* and *Teshuva*

Let us move now to another talmudic dispute with a different character entirely from the last one. It is a famous case, found in the tenth chapter of Sanhedrin (97b–98a), dealing with redemption and repentance, and with end times and calculating end times: "Rav said: All the predestined dates [for redemption] have passed, and the matter [now] depends on repentance and good deeds. But Shmuel maintained: It is sufficient for a mourner to keep his [period of] mourning." Rashi offers two different interpretations of Shmuel's position. Let us open with the second: "'It is sufficient for a mourner' – The pain of the exile is sufficient for Israel; they are redeemed even without repentance." In Rashi's first interpretation, he boldly and shockingly maintains that the "mourner" is a metaphor for God Himself:

4. Bekhorot 49b, Nidda 24b.

> It is sufficient that God waits for numerous days [i.e., a long period of time] with His right hand withdrawn [i.e., without coming to Israel's aid]. That is to say, if they do not repent, He does not keep his mourning forever, but certainly puts an end to it.

The Talmud posits that this dispute is parallel to a tannaitic dispute:

> This matter is disputed by *Tanna'im*: R. Eliezer said: If Israel repent, they will be redeemed; if not, they will not be redeemed. R. Yehoshua said to him: If he does not repent, will they not be redeemed?! Rather, the Holy One, blessed be He, will set up a king over them whose decrees shall be as cruel as Haman's, whereby Israel shall engage in repentance.

The Talmud then cites an additional *baraita* in which R. Eliezer and R. Yehoshua quote verses supporting their respective positions in an argument resembling a back-and-forth ping pong match:

> R. Eliezer said: If Israel repent, they will be redeemed, as it is written, "Return, faithless people; I will cure you of backsliding" (Jer. 3:22). R. Yehoshua said to him: But is it not written, "You were sold for no price" – for idolatry – "and shall be redeemed without money" (Is. 52:3) – without repentance and good deeds? R. Eliezer retorted to R. Yehoshua: But is it not written, "Turn back to Me, and I will turn back to you" (Mal. 3:7)? R. Yehoshua rejoined: But is it not written: "Since I have espoused you, I will take you, one from a town and two from a clan, and bring you to Zion" (Jer. 3:14)? R. Eliezer replied: But it is written, "In returning (*shuva*; R. Eliezer interprets this to mean 'repentance') and rest will be your salvation" (Is. 30:15). R. Yehoshua replied: But is it not written, "Thus said the Lord, the Redeemer of Israel, his Holy One, to the despised one, to the abhorred nation, to the slave of rulers: Kings shall see and stand up; nobles, and they shall prostrate themselves" (Is. 49:7)? R. Eliezer countered: But is it not written, "If you return, O Israel – declares the Lord – if you

return to Me" (Jer. 4:1)? R. Yehoshua answered: But it is elsewhere written: "Then I heard the man dressed in linen, who was above the water of the river, swear by the Ever-Living One as he lifted his right hand and left hand to heaven: 'For a time, times, and half a time; and when the breaking of the power of the holy people comes to an end, then shall all these things be fulfilled'" (Dan. 12:7). At this R. Eliezer remained silent.

A Dispute Within the Tanakh?

This passage raises a few questions:

- R. Eliezer quoted four verses supporting his position and R. Yehoshua countered with four verses supporting his own position. In every other dispute of this nature, the Gemara requires that each disputant explain why the verses cited by his opponent do not adequately prove the latter's position or refute his own. By contrast, in this case it seems that each side is merely tallying its supporting verses, as if they were tallying votes in an election. Where is the logic in such an approach?
- The Gemara transitions from the dispute between Rav and Shmuel to that between R. Eliezer and R. Yehoshua with the word *ketana'ei* ("This matter is disputed by *Tanna'im*"). But is this really the case? Indeed, Rav's position is identical to that of R. Eliezer – that Israel must repent in order to be redeemed – but Shmuel's position contains a key difference from that of R. Yehoshua. According to R. Yehoshua, the redemption will come through, and in the wake of, harsh decrees as well as repentance, whereas Shmuel maintained that God will "give in" and redeem Israel even if they have not taken any steps in the direction of repentance![5]
- At the conclusion of the *baraita*, R. Yehoshua emerges victorious, as R. Eliezer accepted his position in the end, having had no answer for the final verse that R. Yehoshua quoted. If so, why

5. See Maharsha; the Yerushalmi takes this issue in another direction, but for our purposes we will remain with the Bavli.

> would Rav, who followed R. Eliezer chronologically, take up his predecessor's position? This position had already been removed from the table, and what is more, it is to the detriment of the nation of Israel, since it demands repentance while Shmuel's position ultimately does not.

The "verse-quoting contest" between R. Eliezer and R. Yehoshua demonstrates that this is no ordinary argument, where each side attempts to establish the truth of the matter by presenting support for its own position and by resolving apparent contradictions. Rather, it seems that this is a case of a dispute within the Tanakh itself. To state what R. Eliezer and R. Yehoshua would not permit themselves to state: Each side to this question seems to have a clear measure of support from the Torah, meaning that there exists an internal dispute between the Torah and itself.

In *Parashat Nitzavim*, which we read before Rosh HaShana, redemption is portrayed as the clear result of repentance:

> When all these things befall you – the blessing and the curse that I have set before you – and you take them to heart amidst the various nations to which the Lord your God has banished you, and you return to the Lord your God, and you and your children heed His command with all your heart and soul, just as I enjoin upon you this day, then the Lord your God will restore your fortunes and take you back in love. He will bring you together again from all the peoples where the Lord your God has scattered you. (Deut. 30:1–3)

In contrast, a different impression arises from the Song of *Haazinu* that appears shortly thereafter:

> To be My vengeance and recompense, at the time that their foot falters. Yea, their day of disaster is near, and destiny rushes upon them. For the Lord will vindicate His people and take revenge for His servants, when He sees that their might is gone, and neither bond nor free is left ... O nations, acclaim His people! For He will

> avenge the blood of His servants, wreak vengeance on His foes, and cleanse the land of His people. (32:35–43)

Nahmanides correctly notes here:

> Behold, this song contains no condition on repentance and worship. Rather, it is a bill of testimony that we will experience disaster but we will survive, and that God will send us furious admonitions but will never eliminate His memory of us. He will return and repent, and will exact vengeance upon our enemies with his great, harsh, and powerful sword.

If so, the Song of *Haazinu* truly supports Shmuel's position (according to both interpretations): "It is sufficient for a mourner to keep his mourning"!

Nevertheless, support for even the intermediate position of R. Yehoshua can be found in the Torah: "When I, in turn, have been hostile to them and have removed them into the land of their enemies, then at last shall their obdurate heart humble itself, and they shall atone for their iniquity" (Lev. 26:41).

God Himself, in all His glory, stands, as it were, at the heart of this debate. The issue touches on a fundamental paradox, and on the question of Israel's role as the chosen people. From a logical perspective, redemption without repentance is, of course, impossible and unjust; God forged a covenant with us stating what will befall us "If you follow My laws" and "If you reject My laws." When we reject God's laws, He casts us out of the land, scattering us across the world amid foreign people and places, bringing upon us all the curses found in the Torah. Can it possibly be that the Torah would suddenly forgo its principles and return us to our land if we do not first mend our ways? And if that is indeed God's intention, why did He put Jewish people throughout the generations through torture and suffering – if He could have restored us to our homeland at any such point in our history?

All of this amounts to a theological "system malfunction." God created the entire world for the sake of Israel – "He fixed the boundaries of peoples in relation to Israel's numbers" (Deut. 32:8). God also gave Israel the sole responsibility to validate the power of His kingship:

> You have affirmed this day that the Lord is your God, that you will walk in His ways, that you will observe His laws and commandments and rules, and that you will obey Him. And the Lord has affirmed this day that you are, as He promised you, His treasured people who shall observe all His commandments, and that He will set you, in fame and renown and glory, high above all the nations that He has made; and that you shall be, as He promised, a holy people to the Lord your God. (26:17–19)

On the other hand, the principle of the freedom of choice looms like an impassable boulder. God is not willing to engage in a chess match with himself, so to speak; He is unable to choose life and prosperity in our stead. The only thing that He can do is request of us, perhaps even beg of us: "Choose life – so that you and your offspring would live" (30:19). As history moves forward and the nation takes itself spiritually from bad to worse, this problem only deepens. If it is indeed true that the world was created with the innate goal of placing Israel at its heart and at its essence, for how many more generations can the realization of this program be postponed?

Returning to the Passage in Sanhedrin

It seems that when the Gemara says *ketana'ei*, it does not mean that Rav and Shmuel are rehashing the dispute between R. Eliezer and R. Yehoshua verbatim. Rav and Shmuel accepted the conclusion of the *baraita* – R. Eliezer remained silent and R. Yehoshua won the debate. Instead of reiterating what was already said, they sharpened the dispute itself, taking its conclusion to the maximum extent.

When I was in elementary school, the principal once visited our classroom on a day when class was canceled for some reason. He posed the following question: Let us say that you are walking in the desert with your good friend, and you are holding a bottle of water in your hands containing only enough water to allow one person to survive. If you attempt to divide the water between the two of you, you will both die. What would you do? The principal paused to allow us to ponder this dilemma for a little while, and then the students began to share their opinions. Since that day in my childhood many years have passed, but if I recall correctly, not one student in our class suggested R. Akiva's opinion on this case, that "your life takes precedence over your fellow's life." It seems to me, as well, that Ben Patura's opinion – "It is better that both should drink and die" (Bava Metzia 62a) – did not have very many supporters either. Some students suggested that one should give the entire quantity of water to his friend, but most proposed various practical solutions to the dilemma: The two friends should each take a few sips of water every half-hour, thus conserving the water effectively and enabling both people to survive; or they should find a cave or a lonely tree and rest in the shade until nightfall, then travel all night so that the cool nighttime air allows them to reach civilization before perishing. The principal happily seized on the opportunity to explain to us the concept of a question that has no easy solution. The case is a thought experiment, he explained. The conditions of the case are absolute and one cannot alter them or maneuver around them: Two people will not come out of this scenario alive – either you will survive, or your friend, or neither of you. The task of the student is to provide an answer to the question in all its nakedness.

In our case, R. Yehoshua provides an answer that is analogous to the answers given by my classmates to the principal. The question is if God will redeem Israel without their repentance, and R. Yehoshua answers by rejecting the premise of the question: somehow, the repentance will come.

Rav and Shmuel are not willing to suffice with such an ambiguous response, and thus demand a clear answer to a very weighty question, which in our generation is alarmingly relevant:

> R. Yehoshua said to him: If he does not repent, will they not be redeemed?! Rather, the Holy One, blessed be He, will set up a king over them whose decrees shall be as cruel as Haman's, whereby Israel shall engage in repentance.

Rav and Shmuel then ask: What if an oppressive enemy arises whose decrees are even crueler than Haman's, an enemy for whom the goal of "to destroy, massacre, and exterminate all the Jews" (Est. 3:13) moves beyond the planning stage? What if the cruelty, torture, and degradation that the nation of Israel suffers at this enemy's hands exceed every imaginable extent? If, after all this, the nation still does not mend its ways, what will happen then? Will they be redeemed or not?

Rav and Shmuel analyze R. Yehoshua's opinion, each according to his own style and methodology. Redemption and repentance are essentially similar concepts, both implying a return to a previous state. The key difference between the two is that repentance is a return that a person undertakes on his own. This can be seen in several biblical verses that feature the word *teshuva* (repentance) or words that share its root: "Then he would return (*teshuvato*) to Ramah, for his home was there" (I Sam. 7:17); "He shall return (*veshav*) to his holding" (Lev. 25:27–28); "He shall go back (*veshav*) to his family and return (*yashuv*) to his ancestral holding" (25:41). *Geula* (redemption), on the other hand, is the same action done by others, as in: "He shall come and redeem (*vega'al*) what his kinsman has sold" (25:25); "Or his uncle or his uncle's son shall redeem him (*yig'alennu*)" (25:49). Since repentance is a person's independent choice, done of his own free will, Rav and Shmuel disputed whether a repentance that comes as a result of oppression and enslavement can be considered an act of true repentance. For Rav, who maintains that "their cutting is their [valid] preparation," even a coerced repentance that results from the trauma of oppression and enslavement is, in the end, still considered a person's own act. Consequently according to Rav, then, R. Yehoshua agrees with R. Eliezer fundamentally that the requirement of repentance can never be waived; a bare minimum of repentance must occur for the redemption to take place. Thus, if Israel does not repent on even the minutest level, they will not be redeemed. However, according to Shmuel, repentance that is induced by coercion, through the oppression of a cruel enemy, is invalid, as it falls under the category of "'You shall make' – but not from that which is made." According to Shmuel's position, R. Yehoshua actually does maintain that the redemption can come in the absence of repentance. When he says in the end that Israel will indeed engage in repentance, he is merely expressing his hope that a unilateral redemption will never be necessary – that neither Israel's disgrace nor God's willingness to overlook their intransigence will reach extreme levels. It follows from this that if somehow, despite everything, Israel does not repent even after experiencing the harshest oppression, God will still redeem them unconditionally. It is clear that this kind redemption is "bought on credit." God certainly does not wish to forgo His principles, as the Talmud states, "If a man says that the Holy One, blessed be He, is lax [in the execution of justice], his life shall be outlawed" (Bava Kama 50a). God redeems His people, and it is as if He says: I cannot talk to dry bones and worn-out rags. First I will resuscitate you, help you regain your health, return you to your land and your language, teach you to carry arms and work the land – and let us both hope that this time you do not let me down again.

Allow me to interrupt the discussion here for a moment and refer the reader to two of Israel's great sages who each presented the two conflicting interpretations of R. Yehoshua's opinion – albeit only through clever hidden clues. The first is Rabbi Saadia Gaon in *The Book of Doctrines and Beliefs* 8:2 (trans. Alexander Altmann):

> When the fixed time is come, and we have not yet repented of our sins, *it would not be fitting that salvation should come to us whilst we are still entangled in our sins.* God exiled us because of our sins, and should He restore us merely because our stay in exile has been prolonged even though we have not returned to Him, and we have not bettered our ways? That would make no sense. Our ancient prophets have, however, handed down to us a tradition, according to which hardships and sufferings will, at the fixed time, come upon us in such overwhelming measure that under their impact we shall be forced to choose the way of repentance, and thus become worthy of redemption. This is what our ancestors said: "If Israel will do penitence, they will be redeemed; if not, the Holy One (blessed be He) will appoint a king whose harsh decrees will be more terrible than those of Haman, whereupon they will do penitence, and then they will be redeemed."

It seems from here that Rabbi Saadia Gaon sided with Rav's interpretation, that the redemption cannot come if Israel does not first repent.

However, there is another edition of Rabbi Saadia's original Arabic text, which Rabbi Yosef Qafiḥ used in his Hebrew translation of the work, in which a few key changes turn this conclusion on its head. First, in the line stating that "it would not be fitting that salvation should come to us while we are still entangled in our sins," the Arabic word meaning "not" was omitted. This omission yields the sentence, "It would be possible that salvation should come to us while we are still entangled in our sins," a complete reversal of the position espoused in the other edition. Second, a reversal of two letters in the original text changes the sentence reading, "That would make no sense" to "That would be with the appearance of the Redeemer." Notably, Rabbi Qafiḥ speculated that Rabbi Saadia had changed his mind and both editions of the text were written by the *Gaon* himself.

The second source that contains hints of both Rav and Shmuel's interpretations is Rashi. My good friend Michael Cohen of Ofra drew my attention (after hearing a lecture given by Rabbi Uri Sherki) to Rashi's commentary on the verse, "When I, in turn, have been hostile to them and have removed them into the land of their enemies, then at last (*o az*) shall their obdurate heart humble itself, and they shall atone for their iniquity" (Lev. 26:41). As we noted above, this verse expresses R. Yehoshua's position almost precisely: God will set up a king over them whose decrees shall be as cruel as Haman's, whereby Israel shall engage in repentance. Rashi interprets the unusual phrase *o az* in two ways:

> It is similar to [the verse] "If, however, it is known (*o noda*) that the ox was in the habit of goring." [Thus, the meaning of this verse is:] *If*, then, [their obdurate heart] shall humble itself. Another meaning is: Perhaps. [Thus, the verse means:] *Perhaps*, then, their obdurate heart shall humble itself.

From a syntactical perspective, according to Rashi's first interpretation the verse contains a conditional statement whose conclusion is found in the following verse: "If, then, their obdurate heart shall humble itself... I will remember in their favor the covenant with the ancients." According to the second interpretation, however, the sentence concludes at the end of verse 41, while verse 42 begins an entirely new statement. Thus, Rashi's first interpretation of this verse follows Rav's interpretation of R. Yehoshua's position: When I have removed them into the land of their enemies, and *if* – and only if – then, their obdurate heart shall humble itself – then I will remember in their favor the covenant with the ancients. But Rashi's second interpretation of the verse follows Shmuel's interpretation of R. Yehoshua's position: I will remove them into the land of their enemies, and I hope that *perhaps*, then, their obdurate heart shall humble itself. But whatever the case may be – "I will remember in their favor the covenant."

What is the Halakha Regarding Redemption and Repentance?

The answer to this question is both fascinating and utterly complicated on a fundamental level. The essence of Rav's very being was the way in which he related to the world of ritual law. Shmuel, on the other hand, was an expert judge; the world of civil law was eminently central in his life. Because of this dichotomy, the unique principle was established that "the halakha follows Rav in ritual law and Shmuel in civil law."[6] But is redemption considered ritual law or civil law?

When relating the story of the redemption from Egypt on Passover, we are instructed to "commence with shame and end with praise," and Rav and Shmuel argue over what is meant by "commence with shame." According to Rav, we begin with, "In the beginning our ancestors were idol worshippers"; and according to Shmuel we begin with, "We were slaves" (Pesaḥim 116a). In other words, Rav maintained that the primary shame of our ancestors was idol worship, which is in the realm of ritual law, while Shmuel maintained that the shame was the physical enslavement, which is in the realm of civil law. What is the accepted halakhic ruling in this case? Since both Rav and Shmuel insist that we follow their respective positions, when relating the Haggada

6. See Rosh (Rabbeinu Asher), Bava Kama 4:4.

on Passover today we follow *both* positions, reciting both "In the beginning our ancestors were idol worshipers" and "We were slaves."

It seems that Rav and Shmuel are similarly divided over the true essence of the ultimate redemption as well. In fact, this is spelled out in the Talmud almost explicitly. "Shmuel said: There is no difference between this world and the days of the Messiah except [that in the latter there will be no] bondage of foreign powers" (Berakhot 34b and others). Rav did not express his view on this matter explicitly, but in the section of the *Musaf* service on Rosh HaShana known as the *Tekiata deRav* ("shofar service of Rav"),[7] the emphasis is undoubtedly on the spiritual: "Therefore, we place our hope in You, Lord our God, that we may soon see the glory of Your power, when You will remove abominations from the earth … when all humanity will call on Your name." Here there is no simple solution as in the question of how to begin the Haggada. It is impossible to both redeem and not redeem simultaneously. God must render a definitive halakhic ruling here and now. Fortunately – perhaps miraculously – we learned that the halakha follows Shmuel's position in the case of "'You shall make' – but not from that which is made" with respect to building a sukka. Based on what we have established here, if the halakha follows Shmuel's position in that case, it necessarily follows his position in the case of redemption as well. In truth, when God set up a king over us whose decrees were crueler than Haman's, it effectively fit both Rav's and Shmuel's interpretations. When we were redeemed without having repented after undergoing such terrible suffering, it was in accordance with Shmuel: "It is sufficient for a mourner to keep his mourning – it is sufficient that God waits for a so many days with His right hand withdrawn." The prophet Ezekiel had prophesied thus thousands of years earlier:

> Therefore I am concerned for My holy name, which the House of Israel have caused to be profaned among the nations to which they have come. Say to the House of Israel: Thus said the Lord God: Not for your sake will I act, O House of Israel, but for My holy name, which you have caused to be profaned among the

7. Y. Rosh HaShana 1:3 (57a) and parallels.

> nations to which you have come. I will sanctify My great name which has been profaned among the nations – among whom you have caused it to be profaned. And the nations shall know that I am the Lord – declares the Lord God – when I manifest My holiness before their eyes through you. I will take you from among the nations and gather you from all the countries, and I will bring you back to your own land. (Ezek. 36:21–24)

For further study:

Sofer, Y. "*Daat Rasag Be'inyan Telut Hage'ula Biteshuva.*" *Morashteinu* 7 (1993): 88–92 [Hebrew].

Zunz, L. *Haderashot BeYisrael.* Edited and revised by H. Albeck. Jerusalem, 1974, 163–197 [Hebrew].

Parashat Haazinu

Mount Nebo: Did Moses Enter the Land of Israel?

Moses' Farewell Speech in *Haazinu* – Not in *Vezot HaBerakha*

Following the lofty song that occupies most of *Parashat Haazinu*, Moses bids farewell to the people of Israel:

> Moses came and recited all the words of this poem ... And when Moses finished reciting all these words to all Israel, he said to them: Take to heart all the words with which I have warned you this day. Enjoin them upon your children, that they may observe faithfully all the terms of this Torah. For this is not a trifling thing for you: It is your very life; through it you shall long endure on the land that you are to possess upon crossing the Jordan. (Deut. 32:44–47)

With that, Moses takes his leave of the nation of Israel. We can see that *Parashat Vezot HaBerakha*, which follows this passage, is formulated very differently, from a stylistic perspective. It does not say "Moses called to the people of Israel and blessed them," but rather, "This is the blessing with which Moses, the man of God, bade the Israelites farewell before he died" (33:1). In light of the general syntactic patterns in the Tanakh, this formulation seems to indicate that the event described in the verse occurred a while previously. The Torah wanted to conclude with a blessing, but the actual relevant blessing had already been given before this point in time.[1] This can be seen from the content as well. The ending of *Parashat Haazinu* is "That very day the Lord spoke to Moses: Ascend these heights of Abarim to Mount Nebo…You may view the land from a distance, but you shall not enter it – the land that I am giving to the Israelite people" (32:48–52). The natural continuation to this passage is clearly found later on, in chapter 34: "Moses went up from the steppes of Moab to Mount Nebo, to the top of Pisgah, opposite Jericho, and the Lord showed him the whole land: Gilead as far as Dan" (34:1). As we have said, the Torah wanted to conclude with a blessing, so it inserted the blessing chapter between God's command to Moses to ascend to Mount Nebo and the story of the ascent itself. Thus, Moses' actual final communication to the people of Israel before departing was the uplifting message at the end of chapter 32, which tied together the themes of the Torah, the national destiny of Israel and the Land of Israel: "For this is not a trifling thing for you: It is your very life; through it you shall long endure on the land that you are to possess upon crossing the Jordan" (32:47).

On the other hand, the introduction of the blessings bestowed upon the tribes of Israel between the command to ascend to Mount Nebo and the ascent itself places a very strong emphasis on this ascent to the mountain. This emphasis removes it from the context of Moses' personal life and places it out in the open, making it part of the inter-generational legacy of the nation of Israel. We will attempt here to understand the true nature of Mount Nebo and the significance of the view from its peak.

The Location of Mount Nebo

The Tanakh makes mention of Mount Nebo, as well as a city called Nebo next to the mountain.[2] The location of Mount Nebo is known;

1. Thus explained Ibn Ezra at the beginning of *Parashat Vayelekh*.
2. The city of Nebo is also mentioned in the Mesha Stele as one of the Reubenite cities. King Mesha of Moab relates that he wiped out all seven thousand of its Israelite inhabitants.

(Courtesy of Erna Covos)

A view from Beth-hoglah near Jericho toward Mount Nebo

an ancient tradition places it on a rocky spur about half a mile above sea level, overlooking the plains of Moab, at a site called Khirbet Siyāgha and at a nearby site called Khirbet Mukhayyaṭ. Many churches, both ancient and recent, have been built there. Remnants written in Samaritan script have been found at the site as well, indicating that even the Samaritans (during the Byzantine period or thereafter) identified this site as the place where Moses bid farewell to his people and looked out upon the Land of Israel. The ancient name "Nebo" has been preserved there by the Arabs in the form *Niba*.[3] In the western part of the spur is a lower peak (2,215 feet above sea level) from which a very steep slope descends in the direction of the plains of Moab (a descent of 1,970 feet over about three miles). Since the mountain is situated slightly west of its neighboring mountain ranges, and dominates the Jordan Rift Valley, its peak makes for a very unique lookout point even for a modern visitor. The fact that Mount Nebo is located in this region is basically evident from

3. This is a territorial name for the northern slope of the mountain, as I personally corroborated on a visit to the site.

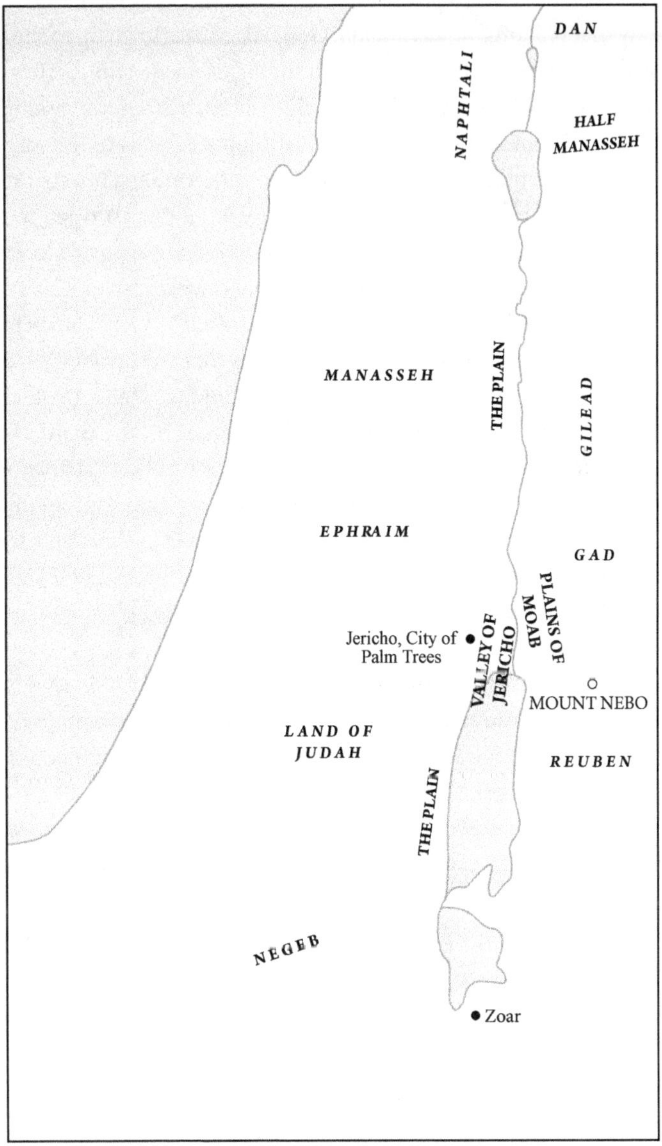

the Tanakh: "the top of Pisgah (literally, 'the summit'), opposite Jericho" (Deut. 34:1). However, even the highest summit in this region (2,630 feet above sea level) is lower than the mountain to its east, which lies between the first peak and Madaba. Furthermore, Ze'ev Erlich notes correctly that in *Parashat Va'etḥanan*, God tells Moses to go up to the top of Pisgah and gaze in all directions, including east (we will discuss the precise meaning of this below). But across the entirety of the mountain accepted as Mount Nebo there is no location with a view to the east. In contrast, the mountain range east of that mountain indeed boasts a view to the east, and thus it seems that this is the summit described in the Torah.[4] It is impossible to see the Western (Mediterranean) Sea from any summit in this region. Erlich explains that the expressions "as far as Dan," "as far as the Western Sea" and "as far as Zoar" (34:1–3) may refer to the boundaries of the geographical regions that Moses viewed, and not necessarily to the maximal extent of his lookout itself.[5] I will comment here further that in the opinion of my father *z"l* the name "Dan" mentioned in this context does not refer to the city of Dan (also known as Laish/Leshem) but to the region that contains all the sources of the Jordan. This region was designated for the tribe of Dan through a tradition from the time of Jacob, as alluded to in Moses' blessing: "Dan is a lion's whelp that leaps forth from Bashan" (Deut. 33:22).[6]

Did Moses Enter the Land of Israel?

Before we discuss the significance of Moses' view from Mount Nebo, I would like to raise a fundamental question that may seem strange at first glance: Did Moses enter the Land of Israel?

Obviously, based on the Torah's account here and in other places, Moses certainly did not enter the land: "You may view the land from a distance, but you shall not enter it" (Deut. 32:52). Moses begged and pleaded, "Let me, I pray, cross over and see the good land on the other side of the Jordan" (3:25), but his plea was not accepted: "But the Lord was wrathful with me on your account and would not listen

4. As I mentioned in the above note, the Arabic name "Niba" refers to a territory, not a geographical point.
5. I heard a similar interpretation from Rabbi Yoel Bin-Nun, in his explanation of Numbers 13:21: "They went up and scouted the land, from the wilderness of Zin to Rehob of Lebo-hamath." They did not necessarily reach Lebo-hamath in practice; rather, it is more reasonable to interpret that this was the general border of the land that they scouted, in line with the set of borders recorded in *Parashat Masei* (Numbers 34).
6. See the chapters on *Parashat Va'era* and *Parashat Matot*.

to me" (3:26). Moses bemoaned his fate: "For I must die in this land; I shall not cross the Jordan. But you will cross and take possession of this good land" (4:22). The view from Mount Nebo served as a kind of consolation to Moses, recognizing the fact that he would not merit entering the land.

On the other hand, Moses' burial place is located in Gadite territory, which is certainly part of the Land of Israel. Moreover, we read in *Parashat Vezot HaBerakha* that Moses praises the tribe of Gad: "He chose for himself the best, for there is the portion of the revered chieftain" (33:21). According to the accepted interpretation, this blessing praises the Gadites for rushing to take possession of this region, where "the revered chieftain" – Moses himself – would ultimately be buried. If so, Moses is indeed buried in the Land of Israel, in the tribal territory of God's chosen people.

So let us ask again: Did Moses enter the Land of Israel or not?

The View from Atop Mount Nebo

> Moses went up from the steppes of Moab to Mount Nebo, to the top of Pisgah, opposite Jericho, and the Lord showed him the whole land: Gilead as far as Dan; all Naphtali; the land of Ephraim and Manasseh; the whole land of Judah as far as the Western Sea; the Negeb; and the Plain – the Valley of Jericho, the city of palm trees – as far as Zoar. And the Lord said to him, "This is the land of which I swore to Abraham, Isaac, and Jacob, 'I will assign it to your offspring.' I have let you see it with your own eyes, but you shall not cross there." (Deut. 34:1–4)

I would like to pose a question here. "And the Lord showed him the whole land: Gilead as far as Dan" – why did God show Moses Gilead in particular? Gilead is located in Transjordan, and Moses had already been there; in fact, if Moses desired, he could stroll through Gilead on his own two feet. So why did God need to show Gilead to Moses from the top of Mount Nebo?

The same question can be asked in relation to the parallel passage in *Parashat Va'etḥanan*: "Go up to the top of Pisgah and gaze about, to the west, the north, the south and the east. Look at it well, for you shall

(David Bjorgen/Wikimedia Commons)

View from Mount Nebo (according to the common tradition) toward the plains of Moab and the Dead Sea

not go across yonder Jordan" (3:27). It is understandable that Moses is asked to look out to the west, north, and south, but can there be any possible reason for Moses to look out to the east?

The solution is that Moses truly did not enter the Land of Israel. In reality, when Moses conquered Transjordan, and when the Gadites and the Reubenites requested, "Do not move us across the Jordan" (Num. 32:5), and when Moses replied angrily, "Are your brothers to go to war while you stay here?!" (32:6) – Transjordan was not part of the land the nation of Israel was required to conquer at the time. At that point, the people of Israel's sights were set on the land between the Jordan and the Mediterranean Sea, and not on Transjordan.

On the other hand, Transjordan was always included in the Promised Land: "From the river of Egypt to the great river, the river Euphrates" (Gen. 15:18); "From the Sea of Suph to the Sea of Philistia, and from the wilderness to the Euphrates" (Ex. 23:31) – but this definition of the Land of Israel was only meant to be realized at a later stage. The guiding principle here is similar to that of the agreement between Moses and the Gadites and Reubenites: Once the Gadites and Reubenites participate in conquering the nuclear, primary Land of Israel alongside the rest of the tribes of Israel, the sanctity of the land will spread to Transjordan as well, as the verse states: "And this land shall be *your holding under the Lord*" (Num. 32:22) – "your holding under the Lord" just like the territories of the remaining tribes.

The matter can be illustrated through an important halakhic example: the cities of refuge. Moses set aside three cities in Transjordan and Joshua set aside three cities in the land of Canaan. *Ḥazal* stated in the Mishna:

> Not until three cities were selected in the Land of Israel did the [first] three cities beyond the Jordan receive fugitives, as ordained, 'Six cities of refuge in all' – [they did not function] until all six could simultaneously afford asylum. (Makkot 2:4)

In other words, when Moses set aside the three cities in Transjordan, it was merely an act of *hekhsher mitzva*, preparation for the actual mitzva of setting aside cities of refuge. The commandment to set aside cities of refuge in Transjordan only became relevant once that region became incorporated into the greater Land of Israel, made up of the territory on both sides of the Jordan.

The same is true regarding the sanctity of the land as a whole. Only once the sanctity of the land began to apply in Cisjordan, and the Gadites and Reubenites participated in conquering this region with the rest of the nation, was it possible for those tribes to return to Transjordan and settle it. Only then could they fulfill the verse, "And this land shall be your holding under the Lord" (Num. 32:22). Note the words of the Psalmist:

> Sihon, king of the Amorites, His steadfast love is eternal; Og, king of Bashan – His steadfast love is eternal; and gave their land as a *heritage,* His steadfast love is eternal; *a heritage to His servant Israel,* His steadfast love is eternal. (Ps. 136:19–22)

Thus, when Moses stood atop Mount Nebo and looked out upon the Chosen Land, God had to show him Gilead as well. The Gilead that Moses had already traveled through and experienced cannot compare to the Gilead of the future, the Gilead that would one day become a heritage to Israel. The Gilead that Moses knew was a mere preview, the faintest foretaste of the sanctified Gilead that would eventually come into existence as it is added to the land of Canaan and began to share in its sanctity. Once it is connected to the land of Canaan, the Gilead becomes a different Gilead entirely. When Moses looked upon Gilead in one sweeping gaze, together with the whole Cisjordan, when he saw the future in his mind's eye – the tribal territories into which the land would be divided (akin to *Ḥazal*'s midrashic reading *yam ha-acharon* – "the Western Sea" – as *yom ha-acharon* – "the end times") – he is able to see Gilead in its true form.

Ultimately, Moses truly did not enter the Land of Israel, was not in the Land of Israel, and was deeply pained that he would not enter the Land of Israel. As he stood atop Mount Nebo, Moses viewed the Land of Israel from afar, knowing that he would not be able to enter. However, after Moses' death, once Joshua and the people of Israel conquered the land and the Gadites and Reubenites went on to settle Gilead, it did not matter that Moses had never reached the Land of Israel – the Land of Israel reached him, its sanctity pouring forth and subsuming Moses and his burial site. Indeed, Moses is now in the Land of Israel.

For further study:

Elitzur, Yehuda and Y. Kiel. *Daat Mikra Bible Atlas*, translated by L. J. Schramm. Jerusalem, 2011, 122–123.

Erlich, Z. H. "*Nevo – Ha'ir Vehahar.*" *Mizraḥ HaYarden Bemabat Yehudi*. Bnei Brak, 1996, 193–213 [Hebrew].

Piccirillo, M. "Mount Nebo." In *The New Encyclopedia of Archaeological Excavations in the Holy Land* 3 (1993): 1110–1118.

Piccirillo, M. and E. Alliata. *Mount Nebo: New Archaeological Excavations 1967–1997*, vols. 1–2. Jerusalem, 1998.

Tronk, Yisrael Yehoshua of Kutna. *Yeshuot Malko, Yoreh De'a* 67 [Hebrew].

Parashat Vezot HaBerakha

Benjamin's Portion

The Borders of Benjamin's Portion

"Of Benjamin he said: Beloved of the Lord, he rests securely beside Him; ever does He protect him, as he rests between His shoulders" (Deut. 33:12).[1] Before we address the inner content of this blessing, let us first review Benjamin's portion in the Land of Israel.

Benjamin's portion is situated "between the Judahites and the Josephites" (Josh. 18:11). It is described in detail in Joshua 18, and its southern and northern borderlines are described again in detail in the description of the borders of Benjamin's tribal neighbors: the northern borderline of Judah (15:5–9) and the southern borderline of Ephraim (16:1–3). The descriptions in Joshua 15 and 16 fit well with the description in Joshua 18. The emerging picture is that Benjamin's portion is a narrow strip between

1. There is some ambiguity, perhaps intentional, in this verse. The verse contains three sentences. In the Hebrew source the word *alav* occurs here twice: in the first and second clauses. In the current translation (taken from NJPS) the first *alav* is understood as related to God ("beside Him"; for *alav* in this sense, compare Num. 2:5), whereas the second one relates to Benjamin (in accordance with the common meaning of *alav*, "upon him"). Both interpretations are feasible in both clauses. Similarly, the third clause might be interpreted as either "as he rests between His shoulders" or "as He rests between his shoulders."

Jerusalem to the south and Bethel to the north, and between the Jordan to the east and the line of mountain slopes to the west.

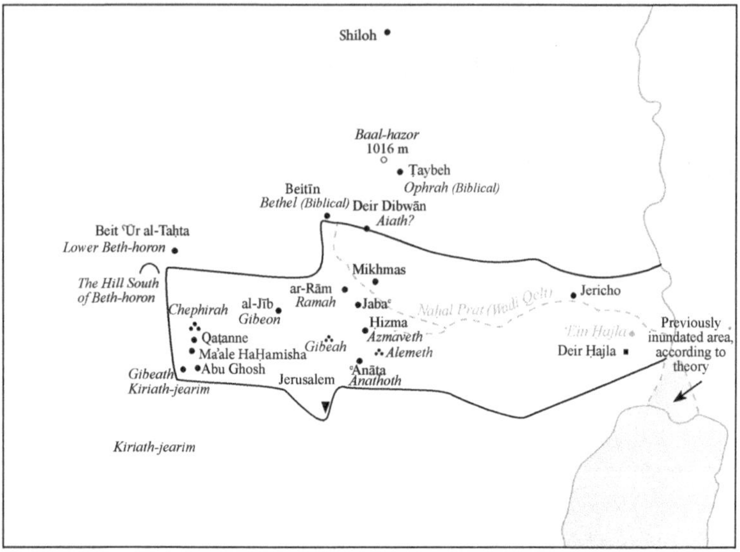

www.zerothkoff.com (Courtesy of Dr. Zev Rothkoff)

"The northern tongue of the Dead Sea, at the southern end of the Jordan" (Josh. 18:19) – the estuary of the Jordan

The northeast corner of the land of Benjamin is "the Jordan near Jericho"; the northwest corner is "the hill south of Lower Beth-horon";[2] the southwest corner is the edge of Kiriath-jearim (a city that belonged to the Judahites); and the southeast corner is "the northern tongue of the Dead Sea, at the southern end of the Jordan" – in other words, the Jordan estuary at the Dead Sea.[3]

The width of Benjamin's portion at its center, from the village of Beitin (within which ancient Bethel has been identified) to Jerusalem, is about ten miles. Its eastern and western sections are narrower, generally about six miles wide or even less. The portion's length is about twenty-six miles. I will make two comments here regarding the course of the borderline:

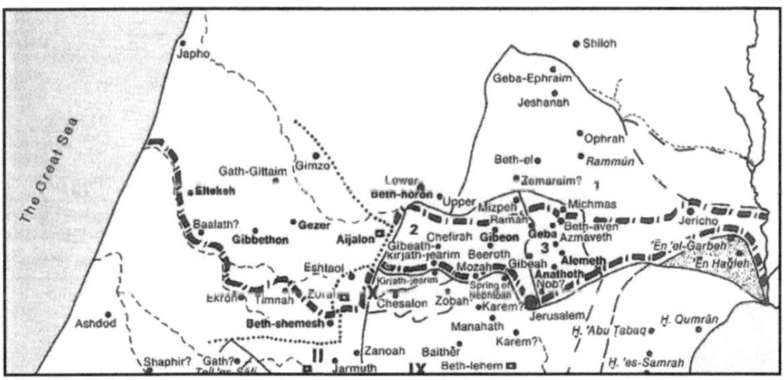

This map was taken from Z. Kallai, *Historical Geography of the Bible*, Jerusalem-Leiden 1986, Map 2. Note the curious twist in the southeast of the territory of Benjamin.

- In historical atlases and biblical maps, the eastern side of Benjamin's southern borderline is generally drawn with a curved line, creating an unusual protuberance. The line begins at the Jordan

2. Today, this site is home to the village of Kharbatha al-Miṣbāḥ. There is no hill in the area that stands out in terms of its dimensions; the verse is conveying that Beth-horon itself is located in Ephraim rather than in Benjamin.
3. The term "tongue of the sea" in biblical geographical terminology refers to an elongated body of water that juts into the land.

estuary and runs north, parallel to the Jordan River, and only turns west after a few miles. The reason for this is that the border must account for Beth-hogla, noted in Joshua 15:6 and 18:19 as the first border point after the "northern tongue of the Sea at the southern end of the Jordan" on the borderline between Judah and Benjamin. Beth-hogla's name was preserved in 'Ein Ḥajla and Deir Ḥajla, about five miles northwest of the Jordan estuary at the Dead Sea.[4] This sharp deviation from the otherwise straight borderline seems unreasonable, but I believe the solution is tied to the question of the water level of the Dead Sea. In my joint research with Professor Amos Frumkin, who investigated the changes in the water level of the Dead Sea over the course of the geological history of the Land of Israel, we claimed that at the time of the land's apportionment the water level of the Dead Sea was significantly higher than it is today – about 1,250 feet below sea level. As a result, the Jordan estuary at the sea was located about 4.5 miles north of where it is today, near 'Ein Ḥajla, such that the borderline was basically straight, without any unusual twists and turns.

- Ophrah, which is enumerated in Joshua 18 in the list of Benjaminite cities and is identified with certainty with the summit of the village of aṭ-Ṭaybeh, is situated about four miles northeast of Beitin (biblical Bethel) – in other words, outside Benjamin's portion. The towering Mount Hazor (also known as Mount Baal-hazor) near aṭ-Ṭaybeh appears to have been located outside Benjamin's portion as well. However, the Tanakh calls it "Baal-hazor near Ephraim" (II Sam. 13:23), meaning apparently that it was a border point between Ephraim and Benjamin. In addition, the language of the verse describing Benjamin's northern border in the area of Bethel seems strange as well: "From Jericho it ascended through the hill country toward Bethel. From Bethel it ran to Luz" (Josh. 16:1–2). The

4. A Greek Orthodox monastery is located today in Deir Ḥajla, as well as an IDF army base and a stubborn settlers' outpost.

aṭ-Ṭaybeh – identified with ancient Ophrah, located four miles northeast of Bethel

difficulty of this description is, quite simply, that Bethel is itself Luz (Gen. 28:19, 35:6, Judges 1:23). Because of these difficulties, my father *z"l* maintained that the northern border of Benjamin was not at Bethel itself, but 4.5 miles farther to the north, at Mount Hazor. This mountain rises 3,333 feet above sea level and is the summit of "the hill country of Bethel." My father suggested that although the word *har* (mountain) is written only once in this verse, it should be understood as if it were written twice. Thus, the verse should be interpreted as follows: "From Jericho it ascended through the hill country to the hills of Bethel. From (the hills of) Bethel it ran to Luz" – meaning that the border ascended from Jericho to the *hills* of Bethel, and from there to the city of Bethel. In order to distinguish between the region known as "the hills of Bethel" and the city of Bethel, the verse chose to call the city by its ancient Canaanite name, "Luz." Thus, it turns out that the northern border of Benjamin was actually located farther north, enough to include even Ophrah.

www.zerothkoff.com (Courtesy of Dr. Zev Rothkoff)

Burj Beitin – the traditional site of Jacob's dream

In my own research on the verse in Joshua, I begged forgiveness of my father *z"l* and preferred a different interpretation: that "Bethel" and "Luz" were two distinct, non-identical locations within the same vicinity. According to the story of Jacob's dream at Bethel (Gen. 28), and in particular the verse, "He named that site Bethel; but previously the name of the city had been Luz" (28:19), we can infer that Luz was the city, while Bethel was the site. In my humble opinion, an analysis of the borderline and its topographical surroundings, with this approach in mind, supports an ancient tradition identifying the site of Jacob's dream with a site called Burj Beitin. This site is located southeast of the village of Beitin, near modern-day Highway 60. As for the deviation of Ophrah from the portion's borders and the subtle indication that there was some kind of de facto border at Baal-hazor, the matter seems to be tied to several other unusual details. The Tanakh states explicitly that some Ephraimite cities were located within the portion of Manasseh (Josh. 16:9, 17:9), and that some Manassite cities were located within the portions of Issachar and Asher to the north (17:11). One clue that some territory in the southern part of Ephraim was seized by Benjaminites can be found in the name "Eretz Yemini" – a strip of land within the hill country of Ephraim, north of Benjamin's portion (I Sam. 9:4; see the chapter on *Parashat Tazria*). Similarly, the Ephraimite cities within Manasseh were called "Eretz Efrayim" (Judges 12:15). A kind of domino effect can be seen here: The Benjaminites apparently encroached on the portion of Ephraim to the north, while the Ephraimites, in turn, encroached on Manasseh, who, in turn, encroached on Issachar and Asher.

The Tribe of Benjamin in Its Portion

When the people of Israel entered the land, Benjamin was an intermediate tribe with respect to its population,[5] but its portion was among the smallest. To be more precise, its portion is exceedingly narrow. As stated above, it is a strip about twenty-six miles long from east to west, about ten miles wide at its widest point, and less than six miles wide on the east and west sides. This portion was made up of four regions:

- on the east, the Jericho oasis, the entirety of which is contained within Benjamin's portion;
- to its west, an arid, desert area that is devoid of settlement;
- the central mountain ridge, the watershed region, and the semi-desert ecotone region a few miles to its east;
- the fertile, mostly flat region in the western part of the portion.

Where were the Benjaminites able to settle? In the area of Jericho there was a destroyed tell that had been included in Joshua's curse over the city and was not rebuilt until the time of Ḥiel of Bethel. In the early Judges period, at a different site within the Jericho oasis, a new city called "the City of Palms" was apparently built, and was first settled by "the descendants of the Kenite, the father-in-law of Moses" (Judges 1:16). Then the city fell to King Eglon of Moab (3:13), and following Ehud's triumph over Eglon the city returned to the hands of the Benjaminites. However, it should be pointed out that even in the time of David, the Jericho region was considered a desolated place (II Sam. 10:5). The desert region west

5. According to the data provided in *Parashat Pinḥas*, Benjamin ranked sixth in population out of the twelve tribes.

of Jericho was not suitable for habitation, and the fertile region to the west then belonged to the Gibeonites, the native Canaanites whose lives the people of Israel spared. The watershed and the semi-desert ecotone strip, which extended 2.5 miles east of the watershed, thus became the regions most crowded with settlements. Despite the poor agricultural conditions – rocky terrain, relatively minimal rain, and only one significant spring (Ein Prat) – this was apparently the most crowded settlement bloc in the entire Land of Israel. This situation continued throughout the biblical period. In Isaiah 10:28–32, thirteen[6] settlements were enumerated: Aiath (Ai), Migron, Michmas, Geba, Ramah, Gibeah of Saul, Bath-gallim, Laish, Anathoth, Madmenah, Gebim, Nob, and Jerusalem. If we include other sources from the Tanakh, additional names can be appended to this list: Bethel, Mizpah, Beth-azmaveth, Alemeth, Zimri, Parah-Perath, Zela/Zelzah. This list amounts to more than twenty settlements in a strip of land about ten miles long and 2.5 miles wide.

On the other hand, according to the account at the end of Judges, the Benjaminite cities were burned and most Benjaminites, along with their wives and children, were killed by their kinsmen at the Battle of Gibeah, leaving only six hundred men to form new families with the daughters of Jabesh-gilead and Shiloh. As both Josephus (*Antiquities* 5:132–174) and *Seder Olam* (ch. 12) interpreted, this incident took place in the early Judges period.[7] The recovery process for the Benjaminites certainly extended well into the Judges period, and toward the end of the period it seems that the land of Benjamin was once again too small for the needs of the Benjaminites.

As we have said, the most fertile section of the portion remained in the hands of the Gibeonites. Because of this, the Benjaminites became the party that suffered the most from the decision to spare the lives of the Gibeonites. In several places, the Tanakh indicates – either explicitly

---

6. The number reaches fourteen if the word *aniya* preceding Anathoth, interpreted by most as an adjective meaning "poor," describing the state of Anathoth, and by others (who read the word as *aniha*) as an instruction to Anathoth to "take up the cry," is understood as an additional settlement called Anijah.

7. This can be inferred from the fact that Phineas son of Eleazar son of Aaron led the warriors, and also from the summarizing words of the section: "Thereupon, the Israelites dispersed, each to his own tribe and clan; everyone departed for his own territory" (Judges 21:24).

www.zerothkoff.com (Courtesy of Dr. Zev Rothkoff)

Al-Jīb – ancient Gibeon

or implicitly – that the Benjaminites, and especially, it seems, the family of Saul's father and of Saul himself, reneged on the oath to leave the Gibeonites unharmed. They raided the Gibeonites, killed many of them, banished many of them and settled in their place in the Gibeon region and in the cities surrounding it: Beeroth, Chephirah, and Kiriath-jearim. Saul's extended family was a family of settlers. They spread out over various places in the land of Benjamin, generally not remaining to settle in their ancestral homes. Saul's great-grandfather earned the moniker "the father of Gibeon," meaning that he was the founder of Israelite settlement in Gibeon. The sin of reneging on the oath to the Gibeonites was considered a grave crime, but as it condemned this behavior, the Tanakh also defended Saul, explaining that his attack on the Gibeonites was "in his zeal for the people of Israel and Judah" (II Sam. 21:2; also see 4:2–3, I Chr. 8:29–40, 9:35–44).

"Beloved of the Lord, He Rests Securely Beside Him; Ever Does He Protect Him, As He Rests Between His Shoulders"

This pithy blessing highlights the fact that Benjamin is defined and characterized by the Divine Presence. This is evidenced by *Ḥazal*'s statement: "The Divine Presence rested [on Israel] only in the portion of Benjamin ... all 'protections' shall be naught elsewhere but in

Benjamin's portion" (Zevaḥim 118b; Y. Megilla 1:11, 72c). This talmudic statement is based on the aggadic assumption that the border between Benjamin and Ephraim ran through Shiloh. This notion, however, does not fit the simple understanding of biblical geography, according to which Shiloh is located in the heart of Ephraim's portion. On the other hand, the statement certainly represents the most faithful expression that we possess of the spirit of Moses' blessing to Benjamin. It is certainly true as well that Gilgal, Nob, Gibeon, Bethel, Kiriath-jearim, and Jerusalem were indeed located in the land of Benjamin. Rabbi Yoel Bin-Nun listed eight facts that demonstrate, in his opinion, that Benjamin's portion was considered "the portion of the Divine Presence," not all of which are equally convincing. Here are all eight facts, in brief:

- The pact with the Gibeonites, who lived in the land of Benjamin, concludes: "That day Joshua made them hewers of wood and drawers of water – as they still are – for the community and for the altar of the Lord, in the place that He would choose" (Josh. 9:27).
- The Gibeonites' harsh demand – "Let seven of his male issue be handed over to us, *and we will impale them* before the Lord in Gibeah of Saul, the chosen of the Lord" (II Sam. 21:6) – testifies to the sanctity of the land of Benjamin in the eyes of the Gibeonites.
- The bloody war following the incident of the concubine at Gibeah, which was accompanied by fasting and sacrifices, the Urim and Thummim and the high priest leading the warriors, demonstrates that the incident was perceived not just as an abomination, but also as a desecration of the sanctity of the land.
- Despite the great importance of Shechem, Shiloh, Hebron, and Beersheba, there was a disproportionate concentration of sites designated for divine worship specifically in Benjamin: in Gilgal, Bethel, Kiriath-jearim, Mizpah, Gibeath-elohim, Nob, Gibeon, and finally Jerusalem.
- While implementing the census that David instructed him to conduct, Yoav skipped over the tribes of Levi and Benjamin, and they are mentioned in this context in the same breath (I Chr. 21:6), indicating that both tribes are considered the portion of the Divine Presence.

- Saul, the Benjaminite king, was an anomalous ruler. He often more closely resembled a religious leader and a man of God: he was chosen with the help of the Urim and Thummim; he brought a burnt-offering at Gilgal; he imposed a *ḥerem* (religious ban) upon the nation; he taught the people the halakhot of blood and religious slaughter; he eliminated the practice of consulting ghosts and familiar spirits; and it might even be added – prophesied with the prophets ("Is Saul too among the prophets?" [I Sam. 10:11]).
- Our verse here, in Moses' blessing (Deut. 33:12), uses the unique terms *ḥofef* ("cover" or "protect") and *shakhen* ("rests").
- When the Ark of God was returned from the territory of the Philistines and struck the men of Beth-shemesh, the latter sent messengers to the inhabitants of Kiriath-jearim, imploring them to take away the Ark (I Sam. 6:21–7:1). The Tanakh does not explain why the men of Kiriath-jearim were better suited to receive the Ark than the men of Beth-shemesh were, and what could possibly have motivated them to put their lives in danger by bringing the Ark into their midst after it had exacted such a heavy toll on both the Philistines and the Israelites. It was simply clear to all at the time that the place where the Ark of God belonged was the land of Benjamin, not Judah. The nation understood this, and sent messengers to the inhabitants of the Benjaminite point closest to Beth-shemesh to take the Ark to their portion. Once the Ark was installed there, the nation finally merited repentance and salvation (7:2–11).

Rabbi Yoel Bin-Nun pointed out another interesting discovery of his: The tribes surrounding Benjamin's portion were the tribal division leaders that surrounded the *Mishkan* in the wilderness – Judah, Dan, Ephraim, and Reuben![8]

8. Admittedly, as a result of unforeseen developments such as the decision of the Reubenites to settle in Transjordan. In addition, the orientation of the tribal portions was flipped with respect to the wilderness orientation, yielding a sort of mirror image of the wilderness encampment scheme.

He Rests Between His Shoulders

It is also worth noting where Benjamin's blessing is found within the order of the tribal blessings. Benjamin is blessed together with Levi, between Judah and Joseph, in accordance with its geographical location. With this in mind, let us note the respective locations of the two Temples. The Temple of the Patriarchs was located in Bethel: "This is none other than the house of God, and that is the gateway to heaven" (Gen. 28:17). The Temple for future generations and for all eternity is located in Jerusalem: "This is my resting-place for all time; here I will dwell, for I desire it" (Ps. 132:14). Both places are in Benjamin's portion, but surprisingly, neither of them is situated in the heart of the portion; rather, both are situated along the portion's borders, the first in the middle of the borderline with the Josephites and the second in the middle of the borderline with Judah. Furthermore, at each of these points, the borderline seems to waver somewhat, as if it were attempting to give the site two names – one holy Israelite name for the part of the site in Benjamin's portion and one "secular" Canaanite name for the part of the site in the neighboring portion. In the case of Bethel, the borderline is

www.zerothkoff.com (Courtesy of Dr. Zev Rothkoff)

Valley of Ben-hinnom; the bare slope to the left is probably "the shoulder of the Jebusites to the south," where the borderline between Benjamin and Judah passes

described on two occasions from east to west. The first description is, "From Bethel it ran to Luz" (Josh. 16:2), and the second description is, "From there the boundary passed on to Luz, to the 'shoulder' (flank) of Luz to the south – that is, Bethel" (18:13). This means that the site of "Bethel" is located southeast of the city of "Luz," with the border running between the two, Bethel in Benjamin and Luz in Ephraim. In the case of Jerusalem it is less explicit. The border runs through En-rogel and the Valley of Ben-hinnom, but the Tanakh stresses that the border abuts on Jerusalem itself, which is in Benjamin: "Along the southern 'shoulder' (flank) of the Jebusites – that is, Jerusalem" (15:8). There are good reasons to assume that this borderline passes between the *city* of Jerusalem that belonged to Benjamin, and the *territory* of Jerusalem, which was part of the allotment of Judah. It seems that the midrashic approach, which places the border within the Temple itself, at the foundation of the altar (Zevaḥim 53b and parallels) only reinforces what the Tanakh itself already states here. Note as well the unique and virtually identical structure of the two verses: "To the *shoulder* of Luz to the south – that is, Bethel" and "Along the *shoulder* of the Jebusites to the south – that is, Jerusalem." It is difficult not to notice an intentional connection here to the expression from Moses' blessing: "He rests between His *shoulders*."

www.zerothkoff.com (Courtesy of Dr. Zev Rothkoff)

Lower Beth-horon

The borderline of Benjamin contains a third example of this same phenomenon as well: Kiriath-jearim, in the southwest corner of Benjamin's portion. Kiriath-jearim has a satellite city known as "Gibeah" or "Gibeath Kiriath(-jearim)." The Tanakh emphasizes that Kiriath-jearim itself is "a city of the Judahites" (18:14), meaning that the borderline runs between the two sites. When the Ark was brought from Beth-shemesh to Kiriath-jearim, it was brought specifically to Gibeah, where Abinadab and his sons were appointed to safeguard it. Against this backdrop, we can now understand well what we mentioned earlier with regard to Lower Beth-horon. The Tanakh went out of its way to describe at great length the northwesternmost point in the land of Benjamin – "the hill south of Lower Beth-horon"; and again, "the hill on the south side of Beth-horon," the purpose apparently being to stress that Beth-horon was not one of the holy sites that the Benjaminite borderline split down the middle, but it was contained entirely within Ephraim.

What is the idea behind all these concepts? First, Benjamin's role within the nation of Israel is connecting. In a theoretical, ideal world, Benjamin's entire portion would consist of one long connecting line, with no width whatsoever. Since we exist in the real world, the portion does contain a minimal width, but the centers of Benjamin's true essence are located on the borderlines with its two powerful neighbors, the two major powers of the nation of Israel: Judah and Joseph. Second, this connection is defined by holiness. The Divine Presence and the sanctity of the location burst out from the place where the tribes of Israel connect to one another.

Benjamin the tribe is a reflection of Benjamin the person. Benjamin the person began his life as the child of Jacob and Rachel's old age. Biologically, Benjamin was the full brother of Joseph, but over the course of the tumultuous events of his early life Judah took him under his wing: "I myself will be surety for him; you may hold me responsible" (Gen. 43:9). Judah's absolute loyalty to Benjamin – "Therefore, please let your servant remain as a slave to my lord instead of the boy... For how can I go back to my father unless the boy is with me?" (44:33–34) – was what renewed and recreated the connection between Jacob's sons and their brother Joseph.

Similarly, the tribe of Benjamin began its existence as part of "the house of Joseph." The distinction between "Judah" and "Israel" was born long before the days of Rehoboam and Jeroboam; it existed from the beginning of the nation of Israel's presence in the Land of Israel (see Josh. 11:16; I Sam. 15:4; II Sam. 19:41–20:2, 24:9). The difference is that in all the early contexts, Benjamin is associated with "Israel"; in the time of Saul, the tribe of Benjamin even produced a king of "Israel." But from the moment that the kingdom split following the death of Solomon, Benjamin transferred to the protection of the tribe of Judah.

It is exceptionally appropriate that the Temple of the Patriarchs was located at Benjamin's original, natural "connection point" with the tribe of Joseph. By contrast, the eternal Temple is located at the acquired connection point with the tribe of Judah, strengthened by the bonds of loyalty and self-sacrifice.

The Model of a Tightly Stretched Tent

The national ideal is a vibrant life in which both of Israel's major powers – Judah and Joseph – must develop the nation and themselves, and each must exert a strong pull in its respective direction. If this mutual pulling is accompanied by a true connection between the two powers, built upon holiness and shared divine worship, it will create, in effect, a tightly stretched tent, where Benjamin represents the sturdy central cord that connects the two sides. If "Benjamin" and all it represents loosens its grip on the two sides, this will create a disastrous schism between Judah and Israel, each disconnected from the Divine Presence and from the other – "There was a continual war between Rehoboam and Jeroboam" (I Kings 14:30). And there is another possibility that is just as bleak: "Benjamin" may remain strong, but the centers of the nation's life force will become extinguished. The tent's cord will remain taut, but the tent itself will still collapse. This situation – where people maintain a lifestyle of ethereal holiness without any connection to reality – has a name: It is called *galut* – exile.

All these ideas are condensed into one short verse: "Of Benjamin he said: Beloved of the Lord, he rests securely beside Him; ever does He protect him, as he rests between His shoulders" (Deut. 33:12).

For further study:

Bin-Nun, Y. "*Naḥalat Binyamin Naḥalat Shekhina.*" In *Lifnei Efrayim UBinyamin UMenasheh.* Jerusalem, 1985, 25–46 [Hebrew].

Dar, S. et al. *Eretz Binyamin: Leket Maamarim Umekorot,* Tel Aviv 1972 [Hebrew].

Elitzur, Yehuda. *Israel and the Bible: Studies in Geography, History and Biblical Thought.* Ramat Gan, 1999, 71–72, 341–347 [Hebrew].

Elitzur, Yoel. "*Burj Beitin – Masoret Umekorah.*" *Shomron UBinyamin* 2, Jerusalem, (1991): 103–111 [Hebrew].

Frumkin, A. and Yoel Elitzur. "The Rise and Fall of the Dead Sea." *Biblical Archaeology Review* 27:6 (2001): 42–50.

Frumkin, A. and Yoel Elitzur. "Historic Dead Sea Level Fluctuations Calibrated with Geological and Archaeological Evidence." *Quaternary Research* 57, (2002): 334–342.

Kallai, Z. *Historical Geography of the Bible.* Jerusalem, 1986, 125–137, 398–404.

Holidays

Rosh HaShana

Shiloh

Rosh HaShana and Shiloh

Let the year and its blessings begin! Some people think that the most appropriate place to celebrate Rosh HaShana and to reach lofty spiritual heights is Ukraine. I believe that the best place to celebrate Rosh HaShana and to reach lofty spiritual heights on that momentous holiday is… Shiloh. Allow me to explain.

The customary Torah reading and *haftara* on the two days of Rosh HaShana express the two exalted aspects of Rosh HaShana. According to Megilla 31a, on the first day of Rosh HaShana we read the section of the Torah beginning "The Lord took note of Sarah" (Gen. 21:1), while the *haftara* recounts the story of Hannah. The next day the Torah reading begins "God put Abraham to the test" (22:1), while the *haftara* ends with, "Ephraim is a dear son to Me" (Jer. 31:19). On the first day of Rosh HaShana the emphasis is on kingship (*malkhiyot*), while on the second day of Rosh HaShana the emphasis is on remembrance (*zikhronot*). On the first day we read the story of Ishmael's expulsion from Abraham's household. Hagar and Ishmael wandered through the wilderness until God decreed that Ishmael would survive the ordeal "where he is," meaning by virtue of his current innocence. God then caused a well of water to present itself before the two wanderers, revitalizing them. The Midrash states:

> Rabbi Yuda son of Rabbi Simon: The ministering angels jumped up to indict [Ishmael], saying before Him, "Master of the World! For a man who will someday kill your children with thirst, you will bring up a well?" He said to them, "Right now, is he righteous or wicked?" They said to Him, "Righteous." He said to them, "I judge a person only [where he is] at that moment." (Genesis Rabba 53)

God's attributes of justice and mercy are not the sole possessions of any particular nation; God judges His world and His creations without bias or prejudice. While it is true that Ishmael needed to be distanced from Isaac, he did not forfeit his right to live.

In the *haftara* of the first day of Rosh HaShana, we read:

> The Lord deals death and gives life, casts down into Sheol and raises up. The Lord makes poor and makes rich; He casts down, He also lifts high. He raises the poor from the dust, lifts up the needy from the dunghill, setting them with nobles, granting them seats of honor. For the pillars of the earth are the Lord's; He has set the world upon them. (I Sam. 2:6–8)

This passage exhibits God's attribute of broad justice, fitting for a day whose theme is kingship.

On the second day, we focus on the concept of remembrance, on Israel's merits, on the intimate and unique connection between God and His chosen people. We read about the Binding of Isaac, about "on the mount of the Lord there is vision," and about the oath that God made:

> Because you have done this and have not withheld your son, your favored one, I will bestow My blessing upon you and make your descendants as numerous as the stars of heaven and the sands on the seashore. (Gen. 22:16–17)

In the *haftara,* we mention the merit of "Rachel weeping for her children." God Himself comforts her: "Restrain your voice from weeping, your eyes from shedding tears" – and the wonderful ending – "Truly, Ephraim is a dear son to Me" (Jer. 31).

The location common to both *haftarot* is Shiloh. At Shiloh, we encounter the direct confluence of *peshat* and reality as we see the same earth and the same scenery as those described in the *haftara* of the first day:

> This man used to go up from his town every year to worship and to offer sacrifice to the Lord of Hosts at Shiloh…The priest Eli was sitting on the seat near the doorpost of the temple of the Lord…She prayed to the Lord, weeping all the while… "Then go in peace, and may the God of Israel grant you what you have asked of Him"…"I am the woman who stood here beside you and prayed to the Lord. It was this boy I prayed for." (I Sam. 1)

The personal, human story of Elkanah and Hannah, of Eli and Samuel, contains no sound and fury, but it does feature the themes of faith, prayer, justice, and mercy. These themes fit well with the setting of the humble *Mishkan*, situated in a moderately hilly landscape that was terraced and well planted.

In Shiloh, we can connect on a deep level to the *haftara* of the second day: "The people who escaped from the sword, found favor in the wilderness; Go to calm him, Israel" (Jer. 31:1). We find ourselves in a place where a large settlement cascades down the slopes of the mountain toward the ancient tell where the Divine Presence dwelled for centuries in the early years of the nation of Israel's existence.

In Shiloh, we turn right and left and see numerous small Israeli settlements and outposts that revitalize the earth. We see countless traditional olive trees, fruit trees, and vineyards that directly recall the vineyards that existed in Shiloh during the period of the Judges. All these are planted and cultivated by people who remain faithful to the nation of Israel, faithful to the earth, and faithful to the God of Israel.

In Shiloh, located in the heights of Ephraim, we can connect to the verse, "For the day is coming when watchmen shall proclaim on the heights of Ephraim: Come, let us go up to Zion, to the Lord our God!" (Jer. 31:5).

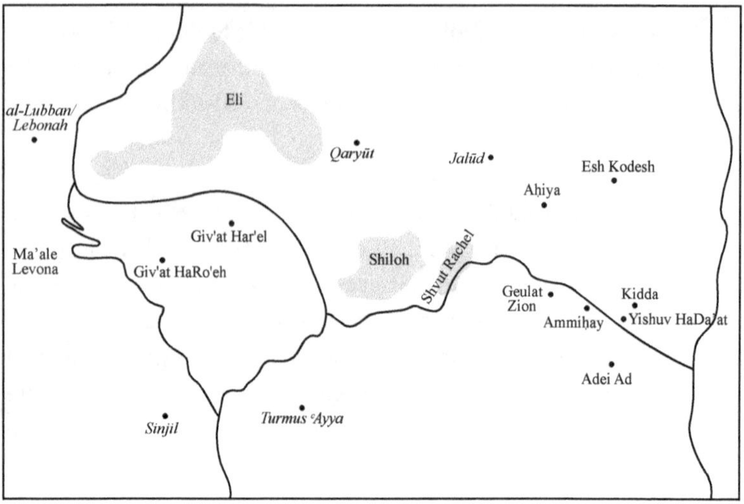

In Shiloh, we connect to the verse:

> Truly, Ephraim is a dear son to Me, the child whom I delight! Whenever I have turned against him, My thoughts would dwell on him still. That is why My heart yearns for him; I will receive him back in love – declares the Lord. (Jer. 31:20)

Where Was the *Mishkan* Located?

In Shiloh, most people are familiar with the tell that is today a well-maintained visitors' site. The tell contains within it archaeological excavations that continue even today at a remarkable pace and scope. Visitors today can enjoy the scenic view from the top of a tower that was erected at the highest point of the tell, as well as a moving audiovisual presentation. Since the site was first excavated ninety years ago by a Danish team, it has been excavated again several times over the last four decades by Israeli teams, and recently also by American archaeologists, leading to many interesting findings. The Arabic name of the tell was Seilun, a preservation of the original ancient Hebrew name. In a Greek inscription written on a mosaic floor found here in recent years, the name of the place was mentioned in the version *Silun*. The Arab villages and ruins adjacent to Shiloh also have ancient Hebrew names: Jalud (mentioned on a legal document from the time of Bar Kokhba as "Galoda of Akrabatta"); Qaryut (likely the place of origin of Judas Iscariot); al-Lubban (Lebonah, mentioned in Judges 21:19); Talfit (in ancient Hebrew probably "row of fine stones" (compare Song. 4:4)); and Jarabe/Ghrabe (= Garab of Bavli Sanhedrin 103b/ ᶜArabo of *Pesikta Rabbati* 29).

At this juncture, it is worth dedicating a few words to the thing that everyone has been searching for in Shiloh: the location of the *Mishkan*. Archaeologists have not found remnants of the *Mishkan*. There are remnants in Shiloh that teach us indirectly about the *Mishkan* in Shiloh. There are prominent remnants of a Canaanite city that was surrounded by a fortified wall, above which were findings typical of the period of Israelite settlement, indicating that the Israelites had settled atop the ruins of the Canaanite city. They spread out beyond the walls of the city, and did not use the massive wall for the purpose of fortification, but instead used the wall and its stones to build houses. Among the various findings were large storage jars ("collar-rim jars") typical of the period of Israelite settlement (Iron I).

Where was the *Mishkan* in Shiloh? We will attempt here to present a fascinating original theory first suggested by Charles Wilson in 1873. More than one hundred years later, without having seen or read Wilson's theory, Rabbi Yoel Bin-Nun raised the same ideas and even developed them somewhat further. The essence of the idea is as follows: When you stand at Tel Shiloh, below you to the north is a kind of terrace that extends from the tell, but is situated outside the walls; below that is a wadi. The entrance to Tel Shiloh in earlier periods was certainly from the south. While the city gate has not yet been discovered, the topography dictates the assumption that this is where the gate was located, since the southern side of Tel Shiloh is the only side that does not feature steep slopes. Thus, it must be that the entrance gate to Shiloh was on the southern side.

Beyond the tell on the northern side, opposite the city gate, there is the terrace mentioned above that protrudes from the tell but is located outside the walls. The terrace is a part of the same mountain range, but distinct from it. Behind the terrace to the north is a deep wadi, followed by a taller mountain behind the wadi.

(The Palestine Exploration Fund)

1866 photograph of Jāmiʿ el-Arbaʿīn – perhaps an ancient synagogue, located south of Tel Shiloh, today adjacent to the Tel Shiloh visitors' center

The interesting thing is that this terrace contains two natural rows of boulders one opposite the other. At some point in history, someone cut through the boulders artificially, creating a straight line pointing inward on the northern wall and a straight line on the opposing wall on the southern side. These two rows of boulders run precisely east-west and the distance between the rows is just less than eighty feet. These unique details bring to mind a biblical association! Eighty feet is about fifty cubits, which is the very width of the *Mishkan*'s enclosure according to the Torah. Recall that the enclosure of the *Mishkan* must be oriented such that the longer side runs from east to west, while the shorter side runs from north to south! *Ḥazal* addressed the fact that the Tanakh calls the *Mishkan* in Shiloh both a *heikhal* (temple) and an *ohel* (tent). This indicates that the *Mishkan* in Shiloh had a kind of intermediate status between the original *Mishkan* in the wilderness, which was made of strips of cloth and wooden planks, and the Temple in Jerusalem, which was a house of cedar and hewn stones. The sages state: "There was no roof there, but there was a structure of stone beneath, and cloths above them. It was [considered] 'the Resting Place'" (Mishna Zevaḥim 12:6). A logical addition to complete this picture would be an enclosure with walls hewn out of stone, in place

(Zev Radovan)

Tel Shiloh before the excavations of recent years, viewed from the west. On the left side, note the northern terrace with the two rocky ranges.

of the walls of the enclosure in the wilderness, which were made of linen hangings.

Placing the location of the *Mishkan* in the northern terrace and outside the city walls would also explain the details of the story of the fiasco at Eben-ezer, recounted in I Samuel 4. We read:

> A Benjaminite ran from the battlefield and reached Shiloh the same day.... The man entered the city to spread the news, and the whole city broke out in a cry. And when Eli heard the sound of the outcry and asked, "What is the meaning of this uproar?" the man rushed over to tell Eli. (I Sam. 4:12–14)

We see from here that the man first arrived in the city; the city then "broke out in a cry"; and only afterward did Eli hear "the sound of the outcry." Where was Eli at the time? We learned in I Samuel 1: "The priest Eli was sitting on the seat near the doorpost of the temple of the Lord" (v. 9), meaning that the *Mishkan* must have been located outside the city, on the side opposite the city's gate.

Let us briefly add one more conceptual perspective. We know that the Torah prohibits planting sacred trees and erecting pillars in the enclosure of the Temple: "You shall not plant an *ashera* – any kind of tree beside the altar of the Lord your God that you may make – or erect a stone pillar; for such the Lord your God detests" (Deut. 16:21–22). Setting up trees and erecting stone pillars were deeply rooted worship rituals among the Canaanites, and were therefore prohibited by the Torah, even though at the time of the Patriarchs these practices had not yet been prohibited. This prohibited pair – the tree and the pillar – are connected to the tall mountains as well, as we learn:

> You must destroy all the sites at which the nations you are to dispossess worshipped their gods, whether on lofty mountains and on hills or under any luxuriant tree. Tear down their altars, smash their pillars, put their *ashera* plants to the fire and cut down the images of their gods, obliterating their name from that site. (Deut. 12:2–3)

It seems that just as the Torah is opposed to a tree, so is it opposed to the perception that the Temple must be situated at the highest possible point. This notion is illustrated well in Jerusalem. The Temple Mount is higher than its immediate vicinity but lower than the mountains in the surrounding area.

In Shiloh as well, we see a similar topographical picture to that of Jerusalem. This terrace, atop which stood the *Mishkan* according to the hypothesis of Wilson and Bin-Nun, is lower than the highest point of the city and lower than the mountain behind it as well. It is a perfect candidate for the location of God's sanctuary.

We can conclude that anyone who merits the opportunity to be in Shiloh on Rosh HaShana can stand in awe of the place, breathing in the exalted air that is full of the sanctity of the Holy Land, together with the glory of Heaven.

For further study:

Bin-Nun, Y. "*Mekomi Asher BeShilo.*" In *Shomron UBinyamin*, edited by Z. Erlich, 102–106. Ofrah, 1987, [Hebrew].

Conder C. R. and H. H. Kitchener. *The Survey of Western Palestine – Memoirs*, II. Samaria, London, 1882, 367–369.

Miron E., H. Ehrlich and Y. Etzion Y. eds. *Shiloh Book*. Beit El, 2016 [Hebrew].

Wilson, C. W. *Palestine Exploration Quarterly Statement* 5. January, 1873, 38.

Yeivin, Z. "Shiloh – Excavation on the Northern Plateau." *Judea and Samaria Research Studies: Proceedings of the Second Annual Meeting* – 1992 (1993), 95–110 [Hebrew].

Yom Kippur

The Temple and Azazel

Two Places in the Chapter of the Yom Kippur Service

Of all the places in the Land of Israel, which one interests us the most on Yom Kippur?

There are two answers to this question. The first is the most important and exalted place of all: the Holy Temple, which housed the Holy of Holies. It was there that the high priest would enter the sanctuary within on Yom Kippur each year to atone for the sins of the people of Israel.

But there is a second place that is the parallel opposite of the Holy of Holies: Azazel – "Azazel in the wilderness" (Lev. 16:10). This parallel opposition on the holiest day of the year is a mysterious dichotomy that commentators and thinkers – including notable *Rishonim* and *Aḥaronim* – have discussed at length. Ibn Ezra hinted at a daring interpretation and Nahmanides (commenting on Leviticus 16:8) deciphered his riddle; indeed, there are many deep insights to glean from the matter. But I would like to discuss Azazel from a geographical perspective.

First, we must remember that Jerusalem was only chosen as the home of the Temple in the time of David and Solomon. Before that, the *Mishkan* was located in other places, but the mitzva of the Yom Kippur service always existed. In other words, if "Azazel

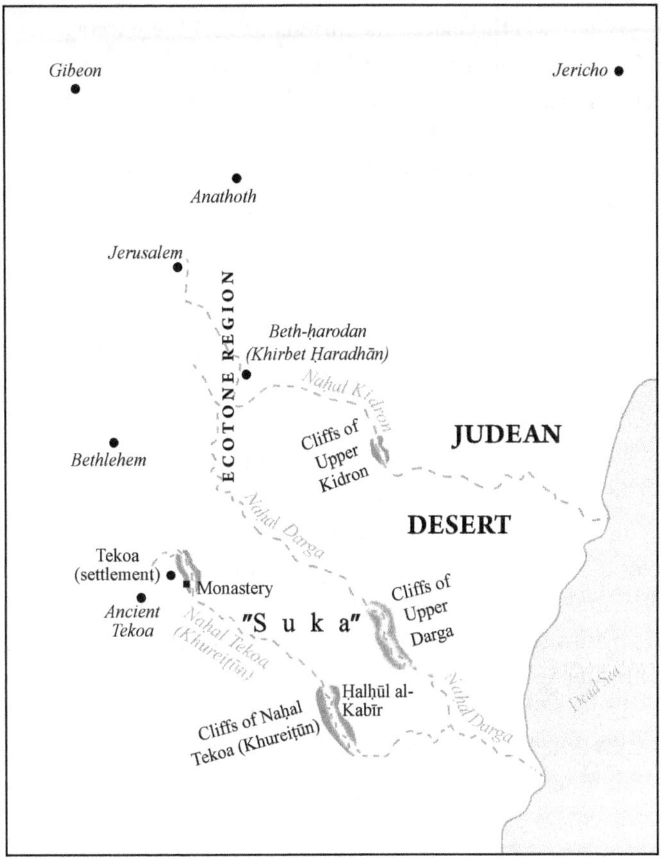

in the wilderness" is an expression with geographical implications (rather than referring to the name of an angel or a demon, as more than a few early and modern authorities thought), it does not necessarily refer to a specific point on the globe. Rather, it is a general name for a desert-like place that contains a precipice from which a goat can be thrown, as it says, "To an inaccessible region (*el eretz gezera*)" (Lev. 16:22). We see from here that the particular location of the precipice where the goat was brought from Jerusalem was not mandated by the Torah. However, since Jerusalem was chosen to be "the site (*hamakom*) that the Lord your God will choose" it had its own Azazel.

Where was this place? The Mishna states: "There were ten booths from Jerusalem up to the *tzok* (lit. "the precipice"), [a distance of] ninety *ris*, seven and a half of which make a *mil*" (Yoma 6:4), meaning that the distance was twelve *mil*. A parallel *baraita* to this mishna is cited in the Tosefta and in the Talmuds in which twelve *mil* is the position advanced by Rabbi Meir, while according to R. Yehuda and R. Yose the distance was only ten *mil*.

The Mil

I have a theory concerning the *mil*, a unit of length used by *Ḥazal*. It is a debatable position, and requires much explanation. I heard the foundations of this theory many years ago from Rabbi Yoel Bin-Nun, and I developed the details through my own analysis. A decade ago, an article by J. J. Ajdler was published that proposed a similar view, but it seems to me that a few details in his study need some correction. We address this issue briefly in the chapter on Ḥanukka and the location of Modi'in. We will dedicate a few words here to the main parts of the theory, while going into greater detail regarding the points that relate to the matter at hand.

In general, it is widely accepted in Jewish literature – in talmudic exegesis, in the halakhic literature of the *Rishonim* and *Aḥaronim*, and even in modern talmudic scholarship – that the *mil* of the *Tanna'im* and *Amora'im* is equivalent to two thousand cubits. In other words, the Jewish *mil* was different from the Roman mile, which was about 4,850 feet (sometimes a bit less). According to Bin-Nun and Ajdler, and in my own humble opinion, it seems that, with all due respect to the *Rishonim*, *Aḥaronim*, and scholars, we can infer from both reasoning and from the sources that *Ḥazal*'s *mil* was actually the same as the Roman mile.

How can we infer this position through reasoning? The word *mil* is a Roman noun, meaning one thousand double paces (an average man can indeed travel a distance of 4,800–4,900 feet in one thousand double paces). It is inconceivable that *Ḥazal* took the Roman word, which was in common use at the time, and gave it a different numerical value. Furthermore, the Romans used milestones on all their paved roads, placing a milestone at every (Roman) mile. The names and titles of the current caesar and governor were engraved or written in color on each milestone. The Jews were obligated to rely on these milestones that the Roman government would erect, as in that time there was no other way to measure distances. They did not have maps, clocks, or speedometers then, nor would anyone have dared erect alternative Jewish markers on the roads if he valued his life.

How can this position be inferred through the sources? There is a positive testimony and a negative testimony supporting this approach. The positive testimony is the accounts of our sages regarding the distances between various places in the Land of Israel, such as from Hammathan to Tiberias, from Tiberias to Sepphoris, from Chezib to the Ladder of Tyre, and from Garab to Shiloh. In general, in almost every case in which we can identify the places mentioned, the distance provided by *Ḥazal* is accurate using the Roman mile – and not the two thousand-cubit measurement. Some of the sources are questionable and require their own discussion. In any case, this is not the place to discuss all these details. Ajdler discussed some of them at length in the article mentioned above, and I hope to make my own additions and corrections to his approach in the future. In the present volume, I focus on two such issues – possibly the most complicated of all: the distance between Modi'in and Jerusalem (in the chapter on Ḥanukka); and the distance between Jerusalem and the *tzok* (in the present discussion).

The negative testimony for our view is the fact that the term *mil* does not appear at all in places where it might have been expected. The concept of *teḥum Shabbat* (the maximum distance that one is permitted to walk outside his settlement on Shabbat) is mentioned countless times in Tractates Shabbat, Eiruvin, and Beitza. The distance there is always defined using the words "two thousand cubits," rather than referring to the *mil*.[1]

1. The extent to which the accepted equation of the *mil* with two thousand cubits has influenced the great Torah sages can be seen in the commentary of Rabbi David HaLevi Segal, the author of *Turei Zahav* (*Taz*), one of the greatest *posekim* of all time. Commenting on the law that residents of a village situated adjacent to a city

Thus, it is reasonable that the Roman mile is identical to the *mil* that *Ḥazal* use in their literature. So how did the incontrovertible assumption that *Ḥazal* used a different *mil* enter our minds in the first place? The primary cause of this phenomenon was the passage from Tractate Yoma (above), as well as a few more solitary statements from rabbinic literature. In addition, there is the fact that the *Rishonim* and *Aḥaronim* – and even some talmudic scholars – were not personally familiar with the Land of Israel, or were not sufficiently immersed in its landscape or its historical geography. The remainder of this discussion will be dedicated to the passage in Yoma and its ramifications for the common understanding of the length of the *mil*.

What Is the *Ris*?

First we must clarify the meaning of the *ris*, and why the Mishna chose to use this unit of length while presenting it parallel to the *mil*, instead of simply using the *mil*. *Ris*, or more accurately, *reis*,[2] is a word of Persian origin, meaning an arena for horse racing. The Persian *reis* is parallel to the Greek word *stadion*, which is generally found in the plural form *stadia* (referring either to a stadium or to the length of the race track). The length of a stadion varied in different places (between 600 and 660 feet) since not all stadia were equal in size. In general, *Ḥazal* used the *mil* when measuring distances along municipal roads, which contained milestones. The *reis* is only mentioned in a few contexts in the Dead Sea Scrolls and in rabbinic literature. Referring to something other than a unit of

"walled from the days of Joshua son of Nun" must similarly read the Book of Esther on the fifteenth of Adar – as long as the distance between the two locales is not greater than one *mil* – the *Taz* states: "The measure of a *mil* is two thousand cubits, and the entirety of Tractate Shabbat is full of this" (*Oraḥ Ḥayim* 688:3; also see his discussion in light of this pronouncement). However, the equation of two thousand cubits and one *mil* does not appear even once in Tractate Shabbat. But when this equation becomes lodged in one's consciousness, it is easy to unwittingly switch the terms, thinking that he read the word *mil* instead of "two thousand cubits." (This impreciseness of the *Taz* was discerned already by Rabbi Reuven Margaliot in 1954; I am indebted to Rabbi Yisrael Ariel of Yitzhar for this note).

2. The word is punctuated רֵיס with a *tzerei* in the most reliable manuscripts of the Mishna, and similarly רֵיסָא in the good testimonies of the *Targumim*.

measure, it is found on three occasions: once in the Midrash – "The beit midrash of R. Eliezer was shaped like an arena (*kemin reis*)" (Song of Songs Rabba 1:1); once in *Targum Onkelos*, translating the expression *emek hamelekh* (Gen. 14:17) – "The king's arena (*beit reisa demalka*)"; and once in *Targum Yonatan*, translating the expression *shaar hasusim* (Jer. 31:39) – "The Gate of the King's Arena (*tera' beit reisa demalka*)." In all other instances the word *reis* refers to a unit of distance, always in cases of distances across open spaces, rather than along paved roads. One of these instances is our case, in which the person entrusted with bringing the goat to the wilderness would pass through wadis and mountains, most of the way in an uninhabited area, with no official roads or milestones. One of the characteristics of the use of the *reis* or the stadia is the use of either numbers smaller than ten or round numbers. We find this, for instance, in the writings of Josephus. Josephus always used stadia and not miles, since in his time the Roman road system was not yet developed in the Land of Israel.[3]

Where Was the *Tzok* from Which the Goat Was Thrown, and How Does This Affect the Length of a *Mil*?

The Mishna refers to Azazel – the place where the goat would be sent and thrown during the Temple period – as *tzok* or *tzuk*,[4] generally with the definite article: "the *tzok*." The word *tzok/tzuk* is unique to the Hebrew of the Second Temple period and to rabbinic literature. It is mentioned twice in the Copper Scroll from Qumran: "the mouth of the *tzok* of the Qidron" and "the mouth of the *tzok* of Beth-Tamar." In rabbinic literature, aside from the context of the scapegoat, the word *tzok/tzuk* is also found in the Mishna: "If it ascended to the top of *tzukim* and then fell down, it is an unavoidable accident; but if he took it up to the top of *tzukim* and it fell and died, it is no unavoidable

3. I am indebted to Professers Chaim Ben-David and Moshe Fisher, who clarified this point to me.
4. The vocalization of this word in most punctuated manuscripts and in the Yemenite traditional pronunciation is with an ō vowel, although there is also attestation for an ū vowel. However, it is noteworthy that there was no clear-cut distinction between ō and ū in the Land of Israel during the first millenium CE; see the sources cited in the bibliography below.

accident" (Bava Metzia 7:10, cited in Bava Metzia 36b; see also parallel passage in Tosefta Bava Metzia 8:15). The word *tzok/tzuk* is used to refer to the place where the scapegoat was thrown to its death on Yom Kippur in dozens of the well-known *piyutim* that focused on the Yom Kippur service. One of the versions of the Jerusalem *Targum* (MS *Neofiti* margin) translates the expression "to Azazel in the wilderness" as "to the wilderness of *Tzok* – to Azazel."

The location of this *tzok/tzuk* was apparently southeast of Jerusalem. The well-known researcher of the historical geography of the Land of Israel, Gustaf Dalman, called attention to a Christian source – *The Life of Chariton*. Chariton lived in the fourth century CE and was the father of the ascetic movement in the Judean desert. *The Life of Chariton* was written in Greek by an anonymous ascetic between the years 560 and 614 CE. The third and final monastery that Chariton constructed, in which he lived for several years, is described in *The Life of Chariton* as follows:

> And he went to a different part of the desert, to a place approximately fourteen stadia from Tekoa (Thekō), which was the name of a certain possession (*ktēma* in Greek; the residents of Tekoa were apparently sharecroppers who worked the land for its wealthy owners)...Thus Chariton founded in this place as well a holy *laura* (a primary type of monastery for hermits, usually located in a craggy landscape). This *laura* is called Suka (Σουκα) by some, who claim to use the Syriac language, while others call it in Greek "the New Laura."

Fourteen stadia are approximately 8,500 feet. The ruins of the monastery, along with the small spring nearby and the "hanging cave" where Chariton himself lived, are well known today and have been studied from an archaeological perspective. They are located below the modern Jewish settlement of Tekoa and about nine thousand feet northeast of ancient Tekoa on the cliffs of Naḥal Tekoa (Wadi Khureitun).

Dalman believed that Suka (Σουκα in the Greek source) is actually *tzuka* – the *tzuk*, the place where the goat was thrown – whose name was preserved in local tradition since the time of the Temple. He speculates that this was a territorial name that related to the higher, craggy areas of Naḥal Tekoa and Naḥal Dragot, citing other Christian sources on the ascetic movement in the Judean desert that mention the names of two additional regions in the Judean desert. The vicinity of the monastery itself, located today by the section of the wadi between the settlements of Tekoa and Nokdim, is not particularly desert-like. Thus, it would seem that the goat would be thrown from cliffs farther to the east in the same region.

Based on this, the road from Jerusalem to the *tzok/tzuk* must have run from the northwest to the southeast. This conclusion has importance that transcends all topographical questions. The Mishna relates that there were ten booths (*sukkot*) along this road, and that the nobility of Jerusalem would accompany the "designated man" up to the first booth, and then from booth to booth – each time traveling the maximum distance permitted under the laws of *teḥum Shabbat*. This would seem to be an explicit proof that a *mil* is two thousand cubits. However, the distance from Jerusalem to the estimated location of the *tzok/tzuk* is greater than 50,000 feet, which is a close approximation of 10–12 *mils* only when a *mil* is defined as one Roman mile, and not when it is defined as two thousand cubits.

It seems that the solution is as follows. According to the halakha, the distance of *teḥum Shabbat* is not measured in a circle, but in a square oriented according to the cardinal directions. Thus, if one walks to the north or to the east, he is permitted to travel up to two thousand cubits, but if one walks in a diagonal direction, such as northeast or southeast – he is permitted up to the distance of the diagonal of a 2,000 x 2,000 cubit square (Eiruvin 55a; Maimonides, *Hilkhot Shabbat* 28:7; *Shulḥan Arukh, Oraḥ Ḥayim* 398:3). Thus, it turns out that the *teḥum Shabbat* of those accompanying the designated man was not two thousand cubits but more than 2,800 cubits ($2{,}000 \times \sqrt{2}$),[5] a distance very close to one Roman mile.

5. The Talmud states: "Every cubit in the side of a square corresponds to one and two fifths of a cubit in its diagonal" (Eiruvin 57a; see *Tosafot* there). When the dimensions in question are larger, we find that the sages were more precise in their calculations: The sages evaluated $50 \times \sqrt{2}$ as "seventy cubits and a fraction," and that fraction was evaluated as close to 2/3 or 5/7 of a cubit (Eiruvin 23a–b, 57a).

On the road to the *tzok/tzuk*, at a distance of three *mils* from Jerusalem, there is another place mentioned in the Mishna (Yoma 6:8), though the traditions differ regarding its precise name. The printed versions read "*byt ḥrwrw*"; the most reliable manuscripts of the Mishna read "*byt ḥrwrw*"; Maimonides, the Mishna in the Yerushalmi, and a manuscript from the Vatican library read "Beth-horon"; and other versions abound. It seems that the best reading is "*byt ḥrwdn,*" since we are familiar with a place that bears a similar name in an appropriate location – south of Abu Dis, about three Roman miles from Jerusalem. This site is called Khirbet Ḥaradhān. I visited there and ascertained from local Arabs that the name of the site is actually pronounced in this way.[6] At this place, the landscape begins to to be defined as "desert." The moment the goat reached this point, the high priest would be able to continue his service. The designated man should continue accompanying the goat until reaching the place where he should fulfill the mitzva of throwing the goat from the precipice (an element of the mitzva that is not absolutely necessary; the main part of the obligation is that he reach the wilderness). A distance of ten *mils* (according to R. Yehuda and R. Yose) fits with the cliffs of Naḥal Kidron in the vicinity of the Mar Saba monastery, while a distance of twelve *mils* (according to R. Meir) fits with the cliffs of upper Naḥal Dragot.

A tradition identifying the *tzok* with a location in the upper Naḥal Dragot region apparently continued to exist until the time of Rabbi Ishtori Haparḥi, about seven hundred years ago. He writes: "From Jerusalem to Azazel is [a journey of] about three hours, and Ḥalḥūl and Tekoa are near there." The "Ḥalḥūl" that he mentions here is not the well-known city of Ḥalḥūl located north of Hebron, but a desert-like region known on today's maps as Ḥalḥūl al-Kabir, about six miles southeast of Tekoa. The maps note the location of Wadi Ḥalḥūl in this region as well, between Naḥal Darga and Naḥal Tekoa (Khureitun). From the language used by Rabbi Ishtori Haparḥi, it seems that he was relating an eyewitness account rather than some kind of inference made on his own.

6. The name "Ḥarodan" is also mentioned in an ancient *ketuba* that was discovered in the Judean desert.

Could the Temple Have Been in Tel Aviv?

(Zev Radovan)

The two opposite parallels of Yom Kippur: the Temple Mount (above) and the cliffs of the wilderness (below). Pictured here are the cliffs of Nahal Kidron, near Mar Saba – probably the site of Azazel according to R. Yehuda and R. Yose.

I would like to conclude by presenting a novel understanding of the connection between the Temple and the wilderness. In the chapter on *Parashat Re'eh,* we spoke about the term *hamakom* ("the place"). We determined that, in reality, according to the Torah, "the place (*hamakom*) that the Lord will choose" is not necessarily Jerusalem. As the *Sifrei Zuta* states, "the land of Canaan is suitable as a home for the Divine Presence, while Transjordan is not suitable as a home for the Divine Presence" (*Sifrei Zuta, Naso,* 228). In other words, every place in the western part of the Land of Israel – in Cisjordan – can be "the place that the Lord will choose." It was the prophets who revealed that just as God was already planning to choose David and his descendants as kings of Israel, He was also already planning to choose Jerusalem: "This is My resting-place for all time" (Ps. 132:14). From the present discussion, we learn that every version of "the place that the Lord will choose" always had its own Azazel attached to it. When the *Mishkan* was in Shiloh, the scapegoat was certainly thrown from a different place, somewhere in the arid cliffs above the Jordan Rift Valley.

At this juncture, an interesting point arises. In principle, until Jerusalem was chosen the entire Land of Israel was actually "suitable as a home for the Divine Presence" as the place of the *Mishkan* or of the Temple, but not all of the land was suitable in practice. For example, I would claim that places like Tel Aviv, Haifa, Bnei Brak, and Tiberias are not appropriate places. Why? Because the place of the *Mishkan* or the Temple must be located within a day's walking distance of the desert. What this means is that places that are not close to a desert area cannot host the Divine Presence. The Divine Presence requires a wilderness in its close vicinity! It seems that this notion is connected to the choice of the Land of Israel that we addressed in the chapters on *Parashat Ekev* and *Parashat Nitzavim.* The Land of Israel, in its essence, is a land that experiences both extreme blooming and extreme desert conditions. Thus, the Temple – the heart of the Land of Israel – must be located in a place that is not desert-like but is close to the desert, near the border between the fertile and the desolate.

In a historic moment described in Jeremiah 28, two people representing these two starkly contrasting landscapes on either side of Jerusalem stood together in the Temple. These two people were Hananiah son of Azzur, the prophet from Gibeon, and Jeremiah, the prophet from Anathoth. Gibeon is located just a few miles northwest of Jerusalem, in a region that receives abundant rainfall, on a hill encircled by springs and surrounded by a fertile valley. In contrast, Anathoth is located a few miles northeast of Jerusalem, in the semi-desert ecotone region that is reflected in all the prophecies of Jeremiah, who lived there. When Hananiah, the false prophet, came to the house of God, it was as if the false promises that he uttered reflected the serene landscape of his home city, whereas the prophecy of Jeremiah, the true prophet, reflected the harsh nature of his own. Perhaps it was specifically because of Jeremiah's personal connection to the unforgiving desert that there are no prophecies of consolation more stirring and uplifting than those few prophecies of consolation in the Book of Jeremiah.

In the Holy Temple – the most sacred place in the world – and on Yom Kippur – the epicenter and the quintessence of the entire year ("'In due time they were formed, to the very last one of them' [Ps. 139:16] – this is Yom Kippur" [*Pesikta Rabbati* 23 and parallels]) – the day's service centers on the concept of "One lot marked for the Lord and one lot marked for Azazel" (Lev. 16:8).

This is how the fundamental principles of the Torah and of the faith of Israel are actualized – "See, this day I set before you blessing and curse" (Deut. 11:26). May it be God's will that we merit the blessing.

For further study:

Ajdler, J. J. "Talmudic Metrology I: The Mile as a Unit of Length." *BDD* 19 (2008): 55–83.

Avi-Yonah, M. *Historical Geography of Palestine*. Jerusalem, 1984, 104 [Hebrew].

Ben-Yehuda, E. *A Complete Dictionary of Ancient and Modern Hebrew*. 5431, 6575–6576 [Hebrew].

Dalman, G. *Sacred Sites and Ways*. Translated by P. P. Levertoff. London 1935, 95–96.

Di Segni, L. "The Life of Chariton." In *Ascetic Behavior in Greco-Roman Antiquity: A Source Book*, edited by V. L. Wimbush, 410. Minneapolis, 1990.

Elitzur, Yoel. *Ancient Place Names in the Holy Land: Preservation and History*. Jerusalem and Winona Lake, 2004, 234–239.

Fischer, M., B. Isaac, and I. Roll. *Roman Roads in Judaea II. The Jaffa-Jerusalem Roads* (British Archaeological Reports, International Series, No. 628), Oxford, 1996, 329–330.

Hirschfeld, Y. "Life of Chariton in Light of Archeological Research." In *Ascetic Behavior in Greco-Roman Antiquity: A Source Book*, edited by V. L. Wimbush, 439–446. Minneapolis, 1990.

Haparḥi, Ishtori. *Kaftor Vaferaḥ*. Lunz ed. Jerusalem, 1897, 299 [Hebrew].

Margaliot, R. *He'arot al HaShulḥan Arukh veNosei Kelav: Oraḥ Ḥayim*. Tel Aviv, 5714 (1954).

Tsafrir, Y., L. Di Segni, and J. Green. *Tabula Imperii Romani Iudaea Palaestina: Eretz Israel in the Hellenistic, Roman and Byzantine Periods*. Jerusalem, 1994, 236.

Yeivin, I. *The Hebrew Language Tradition as Reflected in the Babylonian Vocalisation*. Jerusalem, 1985, 760 [Hebrew].

Sukkot

Kaarava

Zechariah's Prophecy and the Essence of Sukkot

The Jewish festivals possess a dual identity: They are partly global, relevant to all of mankind, and partly exclusive, relevant to the people of Israel alone. The global side of the festivals is rooted in nature, while the other side is intrinsically connected to the history of the nation of Israel. Passover is the Festival of Spring, of the blossoming and rejuvenation of the natural world. At the same time, it celebrates the rejuvenation of the nation of Israel, the pivotal transition from the darkness of enslavement to complete freedom. Shavuot marks the wheat harvest on the calendar and the beginning of the fruit season, while in terms of our national history it is a celebration of the Giving of the Torah and the promise of "But you shall be to Me a kingdom of priests and a holy nation" (Ex. 19:6). What about the festival of Sukkot? We are familiar with the natural side of the festival, the joyous celebration as we gather the summer harvest and bring it into our homes: "And the Feast of the Ingathering at the end of the year, when you gather in the results of your work from the field" (23:16). What is the side of the festival that pertains to the nation of Israel and its history? Of course, the verse, "I made the Israelite people live in booths" (Lev. 23:43) is not relevant to this matter at all, as the verse does not refer to any particular date in the month of Tishrei, but rather to the overall experience of the nation of Israel. The answer to the question is provided by the prophet Zechariah, in a prophecy that we read as the *haftara* on the first day of Sukkot. Zechariah reveals to us that according to the divine plan, there will be a great war at the end of days. In this war, God will fight against the nations, and the wicked will be defeated at the gates of Jerusalem. Following this, the prophet states: "All who survive of all those nations that came up against Jerusalem shall make a pilgrimage year by year to bow low to the King Lord of Hosts and to celebrate the Feast of Booths" – Sukkot (Zech. 14:16). The prophet seems to be alluding here to the notion that this war will be "the war of the festival of Sukkot." We find here the missing piece of the puzzle, the national historical event that parallels the natural aspect of the festival. In addition to the agricultural ingathering of the harvest on Sukkot, we have a national ingathering as well, redemption for a nation that has finally ended the saga of suffering and wandering. Henceforth, the nation of Israel will dwell safely and securely in its national homeland.

"Then the Whole Country Will Become *KaArava*"

I would like to relate to a minor point in Zechariah's prophecy, a linguistic point of geographical significance. The prophet speaks of changes that will affect the natural world as a result of the great war: the Mount of Olives will split, creating a huge gorge, fresh water shall flow from Jerusalem, and so on. Then comes a unique verse: "Then the whole country will become *kaarava*...but [Jerusalem] shall perch high up where it is, and shall be inhabited" (Zech. 14:10). What is the meaning of this verse? It seems to be conveying that Jerusalem will be lifted up above all its surroundings.

The linguistic issue that I would like to clarify here does not concern a name, a word, a letter, or even a whole vowel point. The issue concerns half of a vowel point, or more precisely, whether the point beneath the first letter in the word *kaarava* is a *kamatz* (כָּעֲרָבָה) or a *pataḥ* (כַּעֲרָבָה). Most accurate versions of the Tanakh print the word with a

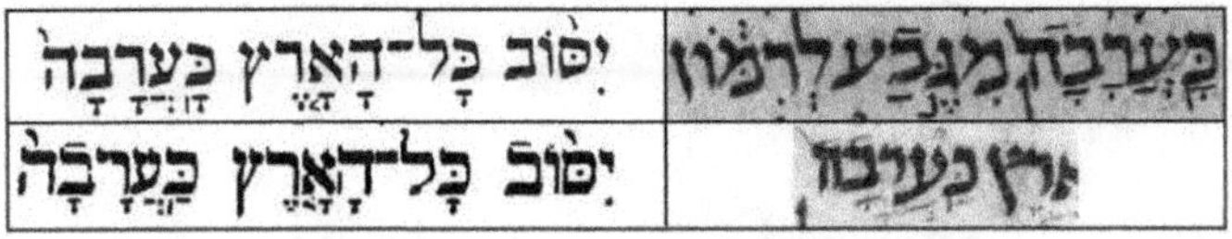

Kaarava in various printings; the top two versions read כָּעֲרָבָה, with a *kamatz*, while the bottom two versions read כַּעֲרָבָה, with a *pataḥ*. Clockwise from top-left: Koren Bible (courtesy of Koren Publishing House); Keter Aram Zova – the Aleppo Codex (courtesy of Machon Ben Zvi and Ardon Bar-Hama); MS T-S A16.4 from the Cairo Geniza (Cambridge Library); D. Ginzburg Bible, London, 1906.

kamatz. Some older printings and a few manuscripts render the word with a *pataḥ*.

What Is the Difference between *Arava* and *HaArava*?

What significance can there possibly be in such a seemingly miniscule distinction? As it turns out, even this tiny change in one diacritical mark can affect the deeper meaning of the entire message of the verse. First, a few words of background on prepositional prefixes in Hebrew. When the prefix letters *beit*, *kaf*, and *lamed* are followed by the definite article, the letter *heh* is dropped and the prefix letter receives the vowel point of the *heh* (generally a *pataḥ* followed by a *dagesh*). When the prefix is not followed by the definite article, it generally receives a *shva*. When the word *arava* – which begins with the guttural letter *ayin* punctuated with a *ḥataf pataḥ* (עֲרָבָה) – is preceded by the definite article, it undergoes compensatory lengthening, becoming *haarava* with a *kamatz* (הָעֲרָבָה). When a preposition is added – *baarava*, *kaarava* or *laarava* – the prefix letter *beit*, *kaf*, or *lamed* receives the *kamatz* of the definite article *heh* (בָּעֲרָבָה, כָּעֲרָבָה, לָעֲרָבָה). However, in the word's indefinite form, the prefix letter does not receive a *shva* as in most other cases (due to the presence of the *ḥataf pataḥ* following it). Instead, it receives a *pataḥ*, yielding *vaarava*, *baarava*, *kaarava*, and *laarava* (וַעֲרָבָה, בַּעֲרָבָה, כַּעֲרָבָה, לַעֲרָבָה).

Why does all this matter? If one were to open a Bible concordance to view the various instances of the word *arava* in the Tanakh, one would encounter an interesting phenomenon. It turns out that throughout the Tanakh, the word's usage in poetic sections is distinctly different from its usage in prose sections. This is not the first time we have highlighted this kind of distinction; we similarly noted in the chapter on *Parashat*

(Courtesy of Dr. Zev Rothkoff)

The fertile "Negev Kinerot," south of the Sea of Galilee – part of the biblical Arabah

Shofetim two different usages of the term *naḥal* in biblical poetry and prose. Indeed, the same dichotomy exists in the case of *arava*. It is easy to see that in every poetic, literary usage of the word *arava*, the meaning is "wilderness" or "desolation." In addition, the word generally appears without the definite article, as in the following verses: "Arid desert shall be glad, wilderness (*arava*) shall rejoice and shall blossom like a rose" (Is. 35:1); "who led us through the wilderness, a land of deserts (*arava*) and pits, a land of drought and darkness, a land no man had traversed, where no human being had dwelt" (Jer. 2:6); "Her towns are a desolation, a dry land, and a wilderness (*vaarava*)" (51:43). In contrast, in prose sections throughout the Tanakh the situation is quite different. There, the word consistently refers to the name of a region in the Land of Israel, and thus it always appears with the definite article: *Ha-Arava*.[1]

Where is this region? Based on the lists of regions in the Land of Israel that appear once in Deuteronomy and seven times in the Book

1. This follows the Hebrew principle that names of regions in the Land of Israel always use the definite article, as in "the Negeb"; "the Shephelah"; "the Sharon"; "the Galilee"; "the Lebanon"; "the Bashan."

(Courtesy of Dr. Zev Rothkoff)

The region of the sources of the Jordan River (view from Mt. Hermon) – the northern part of the biblical Arabah

of Joshua – such as, "In the Arabah, the hill country, the Shephelah, the Negeb, the seacoast" (Deut. 1:7) and "Joshua conquered the whole of this land: the hill country, the Negeb, the whole land of Goshen, the Shephelah, the Arabah" (Josh. 11:16) – it seems that the Arabah is the Jordan Rift Valley and the Dead Sea. This is sometimes written explicitly, as in the verse, "And the Arabah and the Jordan with its environs from Chinnereth down to the sea of the Arabah, the Dead Sea" (Deut. 3:17). In another place, the word *Ha-Arava* is mentioned in relation to Elath and the Sea of Suph: "We then moved on, away from our kinsmen, the descendants of Esau, who live in Seir, away from the road of the Arabah, away from Elath and Ezion-geber" (2:8). However, we encounter the Arabah in the northern part of the Land of Israel as well. King Jabin of Hazor calls to arms "the other kings in the north – in the hill country, in the Arabah, south of Chinnereth, in the lowlands and in the district of Dor on the west" (Josh. 11:2), meaning that there is a region called "the Arabah" in the north – a green, fertile region – as well. What can all these regions that the Tanakh calls "the Arabah" possibly have in common?

Apparently, all these regions are found within what is known today as the Great Rift Valley, and the Arabah is the name of the long

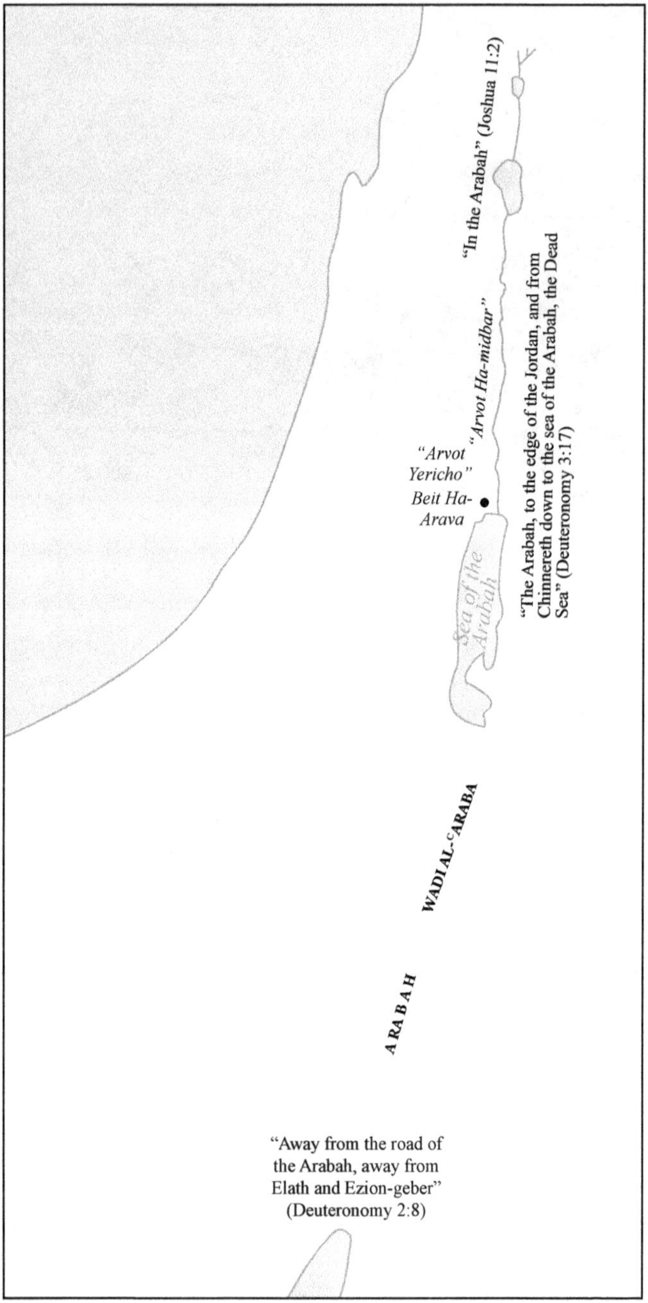
"In the Arabah" (Joshua 11:2)
"Arvot Ha-midbar"
"Arvot Yericho"
Beit Ha-Arava
Sea of the Arabah
"The Arabah, to the edge of the Jordan, and from Chinnereth down to the sea of the Arabah, the Dead Sea" (Deuteronomy 3:17)
WADI AL-ᶜARABA
ARABAH
"Away from the road of the Arabah, away from Elath and Ezion-geber" (Deuteronomy 2:8)

valley between Transjordan and Cisjordan, running from the sources of the Jordan all the way to Eilat. Several biblical expressions containing the term *arava* or *aravot* also refer to locations within that same rift, including *Arvot Mo'av*; *Arvot Yericho*; *Arvot Ha-Yarden* and, of course, *Yam Ha-Arava* (the sea of the Arabah, meaning the Dead Sea); and the old/new settlement *Beit Ha-Arava* to its north. The instances of these

www.zerothkoff.com (Courtesy of Dr. Zev Rothkoff)

The southern Arabah, near Eilat

place-names in the Tanakh are all found in section of biblical prose, and they all are definite as well.[2]

The region known today as the Arava (preserved also in Arabic as Wadi 'Araba) is in fact one part of the biblical region called the Arabah.

How did two different meanings for the same concept develop in Biblical Hebrew? We will probably never be able to answer this question, which relates to a very ancient period in the history of the Hebrew language. It may be that at first, the name referred to any region resembling the southern Dead Sea region – a region both very arid and very flat[3] – and then each of these two features became the defining characteristic of *arava* in different linguistic contexts.

Returning to the Verse in Zechariah

If the word *kaarava* were vowelized with a *pataḥ* (כַּערבה), the meaning of the verse would be that the entire land would become like an *arava* – like a desolate wilderness. If that were the case, the verse would completely negate the message of the rest of the chapter, a prophecy of consolation promising that "fresh water shall flow from Jerusalem, part of it to the Eastern Sea and part to the Western Sea, throughout the summer and winter" (Zech. 14:8).

But the proper vowelization is with a *kamatz* (כָּעֲרָבָה) – meaning "like the Arabah." In other words, the entire region surrounding Jerusalem will become completely flat, like the Arabah, and Jerusalem will perch high above it all. This is a prophecy similar in its message to that of the Book of Isaiah: "Let the rugged ground become level and the ridges become a plain. The Presence of the Lord shall appear" (Is. 40:4–5). I am not sure if the prophet was describing an actual geological phenomenon in this verse. Azaria Alon *z"l*, one of the founders of the Society for the Protection of Nature in Israel, once quipped in a radio interview that he hoped the prophets who predicted that the deserts will transform into habitable land only meant this theoretically

2. A construct state is definite whenever the compositional morpheme is definite (such as *beit yosef* or *beit hamelekh*).
3. Such a usage can be found in Job 39:6: "Whose home I have made the wilderness (*arava*), the salt land his dwelling place."

www.zerothkoff.com (Courtesy of Dr. Zev Rothkoff)

A typical view of the Jordan Rift Valley between the Sea of Galilee and the Dead Sea in its middle and southern parts – the biblical Arvot HaYarden

and symbolically – because if not, the Society would no longer be able to conduct their desert tours. In the same vein, we are permitted to hope that our prophets did not intend for Israel to transform into the Netherlands, famous for its low and flat geography. In any case, what is clear from the verse in Zechariah is that Jerusalem will be lifted up as a model for all to see, a symbol of redemption for the people of Israel and for the world as a whole.

For further study:

Elitzur, Yehuda, and Y. Kiel. *Daat Mikra Bible Atlas*. Translated by L. J. Schramm. Jerusalem, 2011, 5.

Press, I. *Meḥkarim Biyedi'at Haaretz Vetopografiya Mikra'it*. Jerusalem, 1961, 223–224 [Hebrew].

Simons, J. *The Geographical and Topographical Texts of the Old Testament*. Leiden, 1959, 49–50.

Targumim and commentators on Zechariah 14:10.

Tosefta Sota 11:14 (Lieberman ed. 222–223).

Shabbat Ḥol HaMoed Sukkot

What Are Sukkot and Why Do We Live in Them?

What Were the Original Sukkot and Why Do We Live in Them?
The answer to the question seems to depend on whom you ask. If we ask the *darshan* – the homilist – he will respond that the sukkot represent the clouds of glory, and we live in them on Sukkot because "I made the people of Israel live in sukkot when I brought them out of the land of Egypt" (Lev. 23:43), as Onkelos translates, "I made the people of Israel live in the shade of the clouds."

If we ask the *pashtan* – the realist – he will say that the people of Israel lived in literal sukkot, or booths, when they wandered through the wilderness. The *pashtan* may even criticize the *darshan* for not considering the simple reading of the verse sufficiently dignified for him to accept; why must he feel obligated to add a supernatural interpretation on top of that? Meanwhile, the *darshan* will accuse the *pashtan* of shallowness: If the verse does not refer to something lofty and divine, then why was it important to note what kind of dwellings the people of Israel used?

There is a well-known dispute between R. Eliezer and R. Akiva on the matter: "These were clouds of glory – so said R. Eliezer. R. Akiva said: They made for themselves real booths" (Sukka 11b). In *Mekhilta DeRabbi Yishmael* (on the verse, "The Israelites journeyed from Raamses to Succoth" [Ex. 12:37]) and *Torat Kohanim*, the proponents of these two views are reversed: R. Akiva said that sukkot are clouds of glory, while R. Eliezer claimed that they were actual booths. *Mekhilta DeRashbi* on *Parashat Bo* shares the Talmud Bavli's version, while on *Parashat Beshallaḥ* it has the version of the halakhic midrashim.

The Jewish *Targumim* – Onkelos, the Jerusalem *Targum* (Genizah fragment and MS *Neofiti*) and *Targum Pseudo-Jonathan* – translate the word as "clouds of glory." On the other hand, the Septuagint, the Peshitta, the Vulgate, and the Samaritan Targum translate it as actual booths.

From that point on in history there has been a divergence among the interpretations, like parallel lines that will never meet. In the traditional beit midrash setting, the sages – including Rabbi Saadia Gaon, Rashi, Ḥizkuni, Nahmanides, the Zohar, and various homiletic and hasidic works – have consistently interpreted *sukkot* as clouds of glory. The same is true even in halakhic literature. Rabbeinu Yaakov, known as *Baal Haturim*, opens his "Laws of Sukka" with the following:

> "You shall live in sukkot seven days … in order that future generations may know that I made the people of Israel live in sukkot when I brought them out." The ṣukkot in which the verse states that God made them live are clouds of glory in which [God] enveloped them, so that hot wind and sun would not strike them. (*Tur, Oraḥ Ḥayim* 625)

Echoing this position, Rabbi Yosef Karo states there: "You shall live in sukkot seven days … that I made the people of Israel live in sukkot. These are clouds of glory in which [God] enveloped them, so that hot wind and sun would not strike them" (*Shulḥan Arukh, Oraḥ Ḥayim* 625). In his commentary *Maḥatzit Hashekel*, Rabbi Shmuel HaLevi Kelin (1724–1806) writes that in general, it is not appropriate to render halakhic rulings on questions of biblical interpretation. Here, however, since the Torah specifically commanded "in order that future generations may know," it is incumbent on the halakhic *posekim* to rule on the matter, thus determining what it is that future generations must "know" and what a person's intentions should be when fulfilling the mitzva.

In contrast to the prevailing traditional approach is the opinion of the *pashtanim* Rashbam and Ibn Ezra, along with most of the later translators and commentators and virtually all the non-Jewish exegetical literature. All the members of this group are certain that the sukkot described in the verse are actual booths.

A Few Questions to Ask Ourselves

- In what kind of dwellings did the people of Israel live in the wilderness? The people of Israel's wanderings through the wilderness from the time of the Exodus from Egypt until Moses' death in the plains of Moab are described at length throughout the books of Exodus, Numbers, and Deuteronomy. We find that they generally lived in *ohalim* ("tents"; for a few examples, see Ex. 16:16; 33:8–10; Num. 16:26–27, 24:5), or as they are occasionally called, *mishkanim* ("abodes"; see Num. 16:24, 27; 24:5). Sukkot are not mentioned throughout the narrative of the people of Israel's journey through the wilderness even once!
- Why is there no connection between the reason for celebrating the festival and the festival's date? If our sukkot serve as a remembrance of the Exodus, why were we not commanded to live in sukkot on Passover, which occurs at the time of year we left Egypt?
- What is the source of the explanation of "in order that future generations may know"? The festivals are enumerated in full or partial lists five times in the Torah: twice briefly in Exodus, once in Leviticus, once in Numbers, and once in Deuteronomy. All three festivals are enumerated in each of the five places. In the two brief overviews of the festivals in Exodus, the festival of Sukkot is known as "the Festival of the Ingathering" (Exodus 23:16; 34:22). In Numbers 29:12–38, the festival is called only "a festival of the Lord." It is described at length (including the eighth day), and the only mitzvot mentioned are the unique *musaf* offerings of

the festival and the prohibition on ordinary work (*melekhet avoda*) on the first and eighth days. Only in two of the five lists – in Leviticus 23:33–44 and in Deuteronomy 16:13–15 – is the festival called "the Festival of Sukkot," and only in Leviticus is the mitzva of living in the sukka mentioned explicitly! In Deuteronomy, the festival is indeed called "the Festival of Sukkot,"[1] but only two mitzvot are mentioned there: the mitzva to rejoice "with your son and daughter, your male and female slave, the Levite, the stranger, the fatherless, and the widow in your communities"; and the mitzva to hold a festival for the Lord in the place that the Lord will choose.

Thus, we are left only with Leviticus. Let us carefully examine the situation. It is easy to see that the passage dealing with the festival of Sukkot is divided here into two parts: one part in its proper place within the passage that discusses all the festivals, and the other part as a kind of addendum. I will not attempt here to deal with the question of why the passage is structured in this way. Instead, I will focus on the manner in which the festival is depicted in the two descriptions contained in the passage. Like in Numbers and Deuteronomy, in the first section (Lev. 23:33–36), an integral part of the passage of the festivals in general, the festival is called "the Festival of Sukkot." However, the mitzva of sukka is not mentioned; the mitzvot of the festival that are mentioned are the prohibition on work on the first and eighth day and the mitzva to bring offerings for seven days. Then come the verses that conclude the entire passage of the festivals:

> Those are the set times of the Lord that you shall celebrate as sacred occasions, bringing offerings by fire to the Lord… apart from the Sabbaths of the Lord, and apart from your gifts and from all your votive offerings and from all your freewill offerings that you give to the Lord. (23:37–38)

---

1. Deuteronomy also alludes to the name "the Festival of the Ingathering" in the words "after the ingathering from your threshing floor and your winepress."

At the end appears an appendix, a kind of postscript:

> Mark, on the fifteenth day of the seventh month, when you have gathered in the yield of your land, you shall observe the festival of the Lord seven days: a rest on the first day and a rest on the eighth day. On the first day you shall take the product of *hadar* trees, branches of palm trees, boughs of leafy trees, and willows of the brook, and you shall rejoice before the Lord your God seven days. You shall observe it as a festival of the Lord for seven days in the year; you shall observe it in the seventh month as a law for all time, throughout the ages. You shall live in sukkot seven days; all citizens in Israel shall live in sukkot, in order that future generations may know that I made the people of Israel live in sukkot when I brought them out of the land of Egypt, I the Lord your God. (23:39–43)

What comes out of all this? It seems that the only place in the Torah that explicitly describes the festival of Sukkot as we know it – the festival when we are commanded to live in the sukka and take the Four Species, along with the explanation, "in order that future generations may know that I made the people of Israel live in sukkot" – is the appendix of only one of the five festivals passages in the Torah. Why did the Torah only reveal the most important concept of the festival – "that I made the people of Israel live in sukkot" – in the closing lines of the appendix of one out of five passages?

When the Tanakh Provides a Reason

The questions we have raised here strongly bring to mind the questions we asked regarding the approach to naming people and places in the Tanakh (in the chapter on *Parashat Vayetzeh*). We saw there that the explanations given in the Tanakh for names are almost always artificial. When the name of a person or place in the Tanakh is given together with an explicit explanation, there generally exists another, simpler explanation. There are times when the text provides two different explanations for the same name, times when the same name is "given" twice or even three times, times when the text states explicitly that the name existed before it was "given" in a particular instance, and times when we find that the same name was given to a different person or place without an accompanying explanation. Our conclusion was that in most cases, the names predated their explanations. When a person or place is named for a specified reason, it does not mean that this was when the name itself was created, but only when it was given a new interpretation to reflect the events of the time.

This idea can serve as an effective general explanation for any case in which the Tanakh provides a reason for a certain statement. When the Tanakh gives a reason for something, our point of departure must be the understanding that this reason represents a kind of second-level explanation, rather than a primary explanation.

Let us introduce another similar example. Why do we eat matza on Passover? Every child knows the answer to this question: Because our ancestors did not allow their dough time to rise, as the Torah says:

> And they baked unleavened cakes of the dough that they had taken out of Egypt, for it was not leavened, since they had been driven out of Egypt and could not delay; nor had they prepared any provisions for themselves. (Ex. 12:39)

This explanation is found in an explicit verse, but it seems artificial; can it truly be that each of the 600,000 people who left Egypt began to knead their dough at precisely the same moment, such that none of the dough was able to rise? Furthermore, did they all travel with "their kneading bowls wrapped in their cloaks upon their shoulders" (12:34)? And apart from this, there is also a mitzva involving matza that pertains to the entire Temple service – "all meal offerings must be offered unleavened" (Menaḥot 5:1) – as well as the prohibition of "It shall not be baked with leaven" (Lev. 6:10). What, then, is the reason we use matza in the Temple? In addition, making matza was clearly not a novelty at the time of the Exodus, as the Torah records that Abraham and Lot baked matza for their guests! And the ultimate question: How can the mitzva of matza and the prohibition of *ḥametz* be a mere consequence of some circumstances that took place during the Exodus, if they had been already commanded to bake matza and that "no leavened bread shall be found with you" before then – in the passage of "This month shall mark for you…" (Ex. 12:2)?

The Mishna in Ḥullin 7 provides the key to understanding this matter. The chapter deals with the prohibition of eating an animal's sciatic nerve. The final mishna presents a dispute between R. Yehuda and the sages:

> It applies to pure animals but not to impure. R. Yehuda says: Even to impure animals. R. Yehuda argued, was not the sciatic nerve prohibited from the time of the sons of Jacob, and at that time impure animals were still permitted to them? They replied: This law was ordained at Sinai but was written in its proper place.

According to the sages, whose opinion the halakha follows in practice, one can only violate the prohibition of eating the sciatic nerve if it belonged to a pure animal. According to R. Yehuda, the prohibition applies even if one ate the sciatic nerve of a camel or a donkey. In such a case, he violates two prohibitions: the prohibition of eating an impure animal and the prohibition of eating the sciatic nerve.

The prohibition of eating the sciatic nerve and its connection to the struggle between Jacob and the angel raises questions once again. It is not clear why one is prohibited to eat a certain nerve in a cow's leg merely because the angel touched Jacob's thigh during their struggle. Furthermore, the story of the struggle itself, which gave rise to the prohibition of eating the sciatic nerve, does not actually mention the sciatic nerve – it only refers to Jacob's hip socket! The dispute in the Mishna clarifies the matter. R. Yehuda's claim seems to be justified: If the prohibition of eating the sciatic nerve originated in the time of the sons of Jacob, then it should include impure animals as well. The sages respond that while the law was ordained at Sinai, it was written in its proper place. In other words, the prohibition of eating the sciatic nerve is simply one of the many food-related prohibitions in the Torah, like the prohibitions of eating *ḥelev* (certain kinds of animal fat) and blood, or eating a pig or a camel. The Torah would have prohibited the sciatic nerve even if the incident with Jacob and the angel had not transpired, but the Torah chose to link the prohibition to the story of Jacob and the angel in order to create a homiletic connection between the experiences of the nation's Patriarchs and the mitzvot that the nation is obligated to fulfill.

Thus, in the cases that we have discussed, as well as in all similar cases, the explanations given in the text cannot be considered *peshat*. These verses have no *peshat*. Rather, they take a homiletic approach in their explanations, and leave the simple explanation unsaid, perhaps for us to attempt to understand it on our own. Ironically, the *peshat* is actually the explanation provided by the *darshanim*. We eat matza during the seven days of the Festival of Freedom, first of all because it represents simplicity, new beginnings, and humility, flour and water – "man may live on anything that the Lord decrees" (Deut 8:3); "Remember that it is the Lord your God who gives you the power to get wealth" (8:18). It seems that the matzot of the Passover offering also contain the aspects of a meal offering that accompanies the consumption of meat from a holy offering and the exclusion of all leaven and honey from the Sanctuary and from the offerings brought therein (a law that is itself perhaps connected to simplicity and modesty before God). On the level of homiletic connection, the Torah says: Lo and behold – the turn of events during the actual Exodus led to a point when the nation, or many of its members, left Egypt with nothing but matzot on their shoulders.

(Meir Rotter)

Guard hut in Wadi Jinān

What about Sukkot? First of all, it should be noted again that the term "sukkot" was not mentioned at all in the description of the people of Israel's journey through the wilderness. In other words, the word's point of origin is actually the sukka that we live in on the festival of Sukkot. The use of the word to describe our ancestors' tents represents an artificial, homiletic usage that stems from our own sukkot. Why do we live in sukkot? During the summer, which is the threshing season, followed by the summer fruit harvest, people would generally live in guard huts or booths near their threshing floors and vineyards. The Torah commands us to preserve the atmosphere of the outdoors and the simple life until the harvest, and to celebrate the end of the agricultural year in a simple manner, to remember God and to avoid the mindset of "My own power and the might of my own hand have won this wealth for me" (Deut. 8:17; see Rashbam on Lev. 23:43). Just as when we bring the *bikkurim* (first fruits) offering our recitation begins with the shame of "My father was a fugitive Aramean" (26:5) and conclude with the praise and thanksgiving of "He brought us to this place and gave us this land, a land flowing with milk and honey" (26:9), the same is true of the Festival of the Ingathering. We are commanded to remember God who redeemed us from Egypt, led us through the wilderness and gave us the power to become wealthy. And since the Torah has been focused on the concept of the sukka here, it uses a homiletic, somewhat artificial connection, explaining that it is "in order that future generations may know that I made the people of Israel live in sukkot when I brought them out of the land of Egypt." In other words, during the Exodus from Egypt, when you possessed nothing, I housed you in structures that, in midrashic language, can be called sukkot. And since, as we explained, this verse exists outside the realm of *peshat*, and indeed, represents *derash* in the most basic sense, there is no reason to favor one explanation over the other. It may be that the dispute between R. Eliezer and R. Akiva is not exegetical but ideological: R. Eliezer believes that the redemption must come by way of divine intervention – through the clouds of glory; while R. Akiva, Bar Kokhba's greatest supporter, believes that the redemption and the Divine Presence must be achieved through actual booths, which one builds with his own two hands that toil in the threshing floor or in the winepress.[2]

2. I heard this latter view from Rabbi Yoel Bin-Nun.

Etiology

The world of modern biblical criticism is well aware of what we have presented here and of our analysis of the Torah's approach to naming, presented in the chapter on *Parashat Vayetzeh*. This approach is known as etiology, or the study of causation (from the Greek *aitia* – "cause" – and *-logia* – "study of"). The problem is that scholars, in their criticism, view biblical etiology as a characteristic of primitive folkloric thinking. They maintain that people from the biblical period were utterly naïve, lacking the ability of logical analysis. In the view of modern scholars, these people truly believed that the name "Gilgal" was created when the people of Israel were circumcised, and they really believed that the original reason they ate matza on Passover was that their ancestors had not given their dough time to rise. Many scholars even expand this approach, applying it to the biblical narrative in general, maintaining, for example, that the conquest stories in the Book of Joshua originated in myths that were created in order to explain the existence of an uninhabited tell in Jericho, a large heap of stones in the valley of Achor and five trees at the entrance to a sealed cave in Makkedah.

It seems that the primitive and naive ones are those scholars themselves. We can demonstrate from the biblical text itself that while the people of the biblical period loved to engage in linguistic homiletics and etiological explanations, they knew quite well how to distinguish between them and the simple elements of cause and effect. When Esau cries out bitterly, "Was he, then, named Jacob that he might supplant me (*vaye'akveni*) these two times? First he took away my birthright and now he has taken away my blessing!" (Gen. 27:36), his purpose was not to provide the "true" explanation for Jacob's name. He and those who heard his declaration understood that this was merely a defiant, personal statement formulated as a name interpretation. When the verse states: "And Mizpah, because he said, 'May the Lord watch (*yitzef*) between you and me'" (31:49), even without stating explicitly, "That is why the place was called Mizpah," it is clear that the verse's intention is to create a homiletic connection rather than an actual "true" explanation.

It is worth turning our attention to a few cases in which a verse's etiological explanation is actually meant to be ironic. In the culture of the biblical period, everyone knew that the name "Babel" (בבל) derived from the term *bāb-ili*, meaning "Gate of God." The name was written as "Bab-el" (בבאל) in sources as late as Aramaic documents from the Persian period. When the Torah interprets that Babel was given its name "because there the Lord confounded (*balal*) the speech of the whole earth" (11:9), it was clear to every reader from the ancient periods that this was a case of irony. The Torah uses this etiological technique to argue against the pagan Babylonian belief systems of the time, saying, in essence: You think that Babel is the gate of the gods, the nexus between heaven and earth; but in truth your belief is no more than a confused mess.

A similar, yet more extreme example can be found in the concluding words of the story of the Philistine god Dagon in the Book of Samuel. After the Philistines brought the Ark of God into the temple of Dagon in Ashdod, they found their god lying face down on the ground, with its head and both hands cut off. The verse states: "That is why, to this day, the priests of Dagon and all who enter the temple of Dagon do not tread on the threshold of Dagon in Ashdod" (I Sam. 5:5). The entire purpose of this verse is to serve as a literary joke. Stepping over the threshold of the temple was an established custom of all pagan worship during the biblical period, as we know from various sources and as we read in Zephaniah:

> And I will wipe out from this place every vestige of Baal, and the name of the priestlings along with the priests; and those who bow down on the roofs to the host of heaven…I will punish the officials and the king's sons, and all who don a foreign vestment. I will also punish on that day everyone who steps over the threshold. (Zeph. 1:4–9)

When the Book of Samuel emphasizes that "That is why, to this day, the priests of Dagon and all who enter the temple of Dagon do not tread on the threshold of Dagon in Ashdod," this is a prime example of "poking fun at idolatry" (a practice that *Ḥazal* expressly permit in Megilla 25b). The priests of Dagon certainly do not believe that their god fell, hands severed, onto the threshold of its temple, and the custom of stepping over the threshold was not unique to them. The verse here is mocking them through the use of an etiological formulation: it is good that they do not step on the threshold of their god's house, since that is where its severed head and hands were found.

We find other instances of this "winking" etiology in the *aggadot* of *Ḥazal*. One example is the *aggada* about the two celestial luminaries that were originally created equal in size. When the moon then complained to God that "two kings cannot use one crown," God responded: "Go and diminish yourself" (Ḥullin 60b and parallels). In the same vein, we read in Genesis Rabba: "When iron was created, the trees began to tremble. [The iron] said to them, 'Why do you tremble? Let none of your wood enter me, and not one of you shall be harmed'" (Genesis Rabba 5:10). These *aggadot* and their like express moral concepts through the vehicle of etiological mythology.

A Word on the Ideology behind the Etiology

Toward the end of the chapter on *Parashat Vayetzeh*, I explained that the Torah's general approach is not to raze the old world to the ground, uproot its foundations, and build a new world in its place. Rather, the Torah's approach is to sustain and sanctify the existing world through the sanctity of Israel, the Land of Israel, and the mitzvot. To this end, it should come as no surprise that the Torah refrains from changing the names of people and places that were given through a natural linguistic process and reflected the development of nations and the lives of their members, instead preferring to inject new meaning within these names. This observation can be expanded and applied to other areas as well.

I would like to relate a short story. My teacher, Rabbi Chaim Yaakov Goldwicht, *z"l* (1924–1995), *rosh yeshiva* of Yeshivat Kerem B'Yavneh, struggled for many years with a chronic heart disease. Following the advice of his doctors, Rabbi Goldwicht would occasionally travel to the Swiss Alps to breathe the mountain air. In one of his talks, Rabbi Goldwicht recounted that on one wintry Shabbat he sat in his hotel, which was perched near a mountaintop, along with another Jew – a Torah scholar who happened to be staying in the same hotel. The two of them looked out through a large glass window at the snowy mountains above and a blue lake and green forest below. Rabbi Goldwicht related: "The two of us spent Shabbat alone, amid Torah, singing, and festive meals, and the incredible landscape inspired and uplifted us.

"In the afternoon, when it came time for *seuda shelishit*, my Shabbat partner said to me, 'I have a question for God. Why did He create this amazing place so far away from the Land of Israel, in the midst of blundering people who lack the heart to feel it and to understand it?'

I answered him, 'God knew perfectly well that on one wintry Shabbat, two Jews from the Land of Israel would find themselves in this location; and that the sheer power and beauty of the place would allow them to attain great levels of sanctity. Perhaps it was for the sake of this very Shabbat that this place was created!'"

It seems to me that a similar approach often underpins instances of etiology in the Tanakh. It is as if the text defies the low perspective of reality when it states, "He built a house for himself and made stalls (*sukkot*) for his cattle; that is why the place was called Succoth" (Gen. 33:17). Linguists and historians will give you scholarly – and accurate – explanations for why the place was actually called Succoth, but the Torah takes a different approach entirely. The Torah points its finger at the moment when Jacob, father of the chosen people, passed through this place, declaring, "From my perspective, that is why the place was called Succoth."

When an unusual event occurs that creates an additional connection between a place and its name, or between a mitzva and the history of the nation that is tied to that mitzva, that event constitutes a kind of sign that this thing was created for this very moment. It is true, for example, in the case of the dough that was not given time to rise, which shows that the essence of the moment is connected to matzot.

Let us pay attention to the only two Aramaic words in the Torah: Yegar-sahadutha. Why does the Torah contain these two foreign words? The Torah relates that Jacob and Laban met in the hill country of Gilead. After arguing with each other over several issues, they collected stones and made a mound, testifying to the pact forged between them. Laban, using his own language, called the site Yegar-sahadutha, an expression that does not contain any additional meaning. But when Jacob translated this expression into the Holy Tongue, the consequence was Gal-ed (גַּלְעֵד), a name whose letters are identical to those of the place's original name: Gilead (גִּלְעָד). It was like a heavenly sign that at the dawn of time, that place was created for that very moment.

This idea is similar to the role of the servants in the story of the Binding of Isaac. The servants are mentioned only in order to provide a contrasting background to the exalted, transcendent state that Abraham and Isaac reached. (The servants also walked for three days; they also saw the firestone and the wood, and perhaps even the ram caught in the thicket. But at the moment of truth they stayed behind "with the ass.") Here as well, Laban is portrayed as the stereotypical "normal" person: nothing special happens to him; there is no connection formed between the place and the incident. In contrast, for Jacob it is as if the place were created for his sake alone.

For further study:

Ashbel, D. "*Ki Basukkot Yashevu Avoteikhem Betzeitam MiMitzrayim.*" *Beit Mikra* 29 (1967): 100–104 [Hebrew].

Elitzur, Yehuda. "*Midgal Bavel Vesulam Yaakov.*" *Israel and the Bible*. Ramat-Gan, 2000, 44–48 [Hebrew].

Elitzur, Yehuda, "*Aron Hashem Be'eretz Pelishtim.*" *Israel and the Bible*, Ramat-Gan, 2000, 89–95 [Hebrew].

Kaufmann, Y. "Criticism of the Aetiological Interpretation." *The Biblical Account of the Conquest of Palestine*. Jerusalem, 1953, 70–74.

Loewenstamm, S. "Etiology." *Encyclopaedia Biblica* 1, 258–259 [Hebrew].

Long, B. O. *The Problem of Etiological Narrative in the Old Testament*. Berlin, 1968.

Pesaḥ

Gilgal

The Starting Point for the Nation of Israel in the Land of Israel

In the *haftara* for the first day of Pesaḥ, we read about Gilgal.

Every book in the Tanakh presents the reader with a different atmosphere. The Book of Exodus transports the reader into the atmosphere of Egypt, allowing him to experience the plagues, the Egyptian gods, the fear and excitement of the night when the Egyptian firstborn were struck down, and the great revolution of the Exodus itself. The Book of Kings brings the reader to an atmosphere of kings and prophets, hardships and complications, rebellions and assassinations, Judah and Israel, and an endless struggle against Aram and Assyria.

The atmosphere of the Book of Joshua is one of liberation, of open skies, sunshine, simple, sincere faith, and new beginnings, as the nation of Israel enters the Land of Israel. The landscape of Gilgal perhaps represents a perfect characterization of the atmosphere of the entire Book of Joshua.

The people of Israel crossed the Jordan on the tenth of Nisan and encamped in Gilgal. There, we read that "At that time the Lord said to Joshua, 'Make flint knives and proceed with a second circumcision of the Israelites'" (Josh. 5:2). And it was in Gilgal, in the steppes of Jericho, that they brought the Passover offering: "The Israelites offered the Passover offering... in the steppes of Jericho. On the day after the Passover offering, on that very day, they ate of the produce of the country, unleavened bread and parched grain" (5:10–11). It was here that the people of Israel became a nation living in its own homeland. It was here that the *Mishkan* and the Ark of the Covenant resided throughout the period of the conquest and allotment of the land, until they moved to Shiloh.

In Gilgal, the people of Israel set up the twelve stones they had taken from the Jordan. Just as the night of Passover is the *time* for "And you shall explain to your son" (Ex. 13:8), Gilgal is the *place* for "And you shall explain to your son":

> [Joshua] charged the Israelites as follows: "In time to come, when your children ask their fathers, 'What is the meaning of these stones?' tell your children: 'Here the Israelites crossed the Jordan on dry land.' For the Lord your God dried up the waters of the Jordan before you until you crossed over, as the Lord your

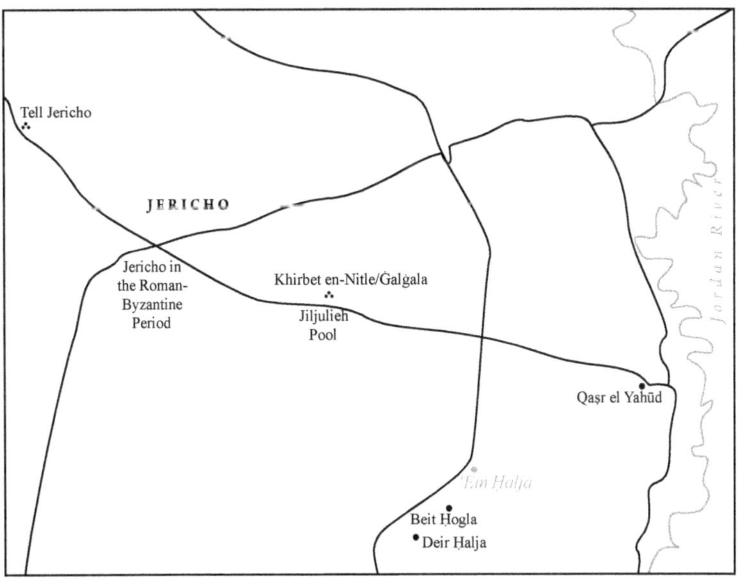

> God did to the Red Sea when He dried it up before us until we crossed over. Thus all the peoples of the earth shall know how mighty is the hand of the Lord, and you shall fear the Lord your God always." (Josh. 4:21–24)

Where Is Gilgal?

Based on the geographical context, it is clear that Gilgal is situated between the Jordan and Jericho. But the verse provides a more precise description of Gilgal's location: "The people came up from the Jordan on the tenth day of the first month, and encamped at Gilgal on the edge of the eastern portion of Jericho" (Josh. 4:19). It is worth paying close attention to the formulation. The verse does not say "east of Jericho" but "on the edge of the eastern portion of Jericho (*biktzeh mizraḥ Yeriḥo*)." In other words, "Jericho" refers here to the entire large territorial area watered by the springs of Jericho. Gilgal can be found on the eastern part of this territorial area. It seems that Gilgal is not the name of a settlement here (it is never mentioned in any list of cities) but of a region.[1] We learn from our chapter in Joshua that Gilgal refers to a large region that could accommodate the sizeable population of the people of Israel at the time – 600,000 men, not including children.

Traditions regarding the twelve stones of Gilgal have existed for many years. Josephus wrote (*Antiquities* 5:20) that the place where the nation encamped and set up the stones that the people had taken from the Jordan is located a distance of fifty stadia from the Jordan and ten stadia from Jericho.[2]

We read in a *baraita*: "R. Yehuda said: Abba Ḥalafta, R. Elazar b. Mathia and Hananiah b. Ḥachinai (sages of the Yavne generation) stood upon these stones and estimated that each was equal to about forty *se'ah*"

1. In my opinion, following my teacher and father *z"l*, the original meaning of Gilgal was "plain." An article in which I give reasons for this approach was published recently; see the reference list at the end of the chapter.
2. Josephus claimed that Joshua built a stone altar there and offered sacrifices on it, a tradition not supported in any other source.

(Sota 34a[3]). Forty *se'ah* was not an imaginary measurement, nor is the story in the *baraita* of the sort that is prone to extreme exaggeration. The volume of a cubic stone that is slightly less than thirty inches long on each side is approximately forty *se'ah*. This means that the stones reported by the sages were large but not enormous, keeping in mind that these were natural stones.

(Zev Radovan)

Gilgal in the Madaba Map: a tile-roofed church with twelve stones and the caption ΓΑΛΓΑΛΑΔWΔΕΚΑΛΙΘΟΝ – "Galgala, which is also the twelve stones"

This tradition, of which the *Tanna'im* were aware, was then transmitted to the early Christian pilgrims, who certainly attested to the same tradition. The first of these pilgrims was known as the "Pilgrim of Bordeaux" (333 CE, about two hundred years after the period of the three *Tanna'im* who "stood upon these stones"). The Pilgrim writes (in Latin) that the twelve stones can be seen in the vicinity of Jericho.

3. Also see Tosefta Sota 8:3 and Y. Sota 7:5. Abba Ḥalafta was R. Yosi's father. He was usually called Abba Ḥalafta, meaning "my father Ḥalafta," by R. Yosi, while others called him Rabbi Ḥalafta. Here, however, according to the most reliable testimonies, it was R. Yehuda who referred to him using the title "Abba," which should be interpreted as an honorific title in this case.

Eusebius of Caesarea, a contemporary of the Pilgrim of Bordeaux, writes in his *Onomasticon* that Gilgal is pointed out in a deserted place two Roman miles east of Jericho, and that the people at the time considered it a holy place. Two hundred years later, the Madaba Map (sixth century CE, according to the accepted dating) shows an illustration of a church with a pitched tiled roof located between Jericho and the Jordan. Attached to the building, twelve stones can be seen, arranged in two rows, each of six stones put one on top of the other, and above this structure is the Greek inscription: ΓΑΛΓΑΛΑ ΤΟ ΚΑΙ ΔWΔΕΚΑΛΙΘΟΝ (*galgala to kai dodekalithon*) – "Galgala, which is also [the place of] the twelve stones."

The information provided by the Christian sources allows us to identify with confidence the place that they describe. Two Roman miles is slightly less than two standard modern miles. And indeed, about 1.7 miles east of Byzantine Jericho (located in the area of the market of modern Jericho) between the old Roman road that led to the Jordan and the modern highway that runs parallel to it about a third of a mile to its south, we find an ancient site that is clearly the place that the sources describe. The Arabs call the place Khirbet en-Nitle, but interestingly, there are reliable testimonies from the nineteenth and twentieth centuries regarding the preservation of the name Gilgal in this region, in two different versions. The first version is *ġalġala*, another name for that same ruin, and the second version is *jaljul* or *jiljulieh*, another name for the ruin or for the area surrounding it, or according to the testimony of Claude Conder in the Palestine Exploration Fund (PEF) survey, for the name of a rectangular pool that was located southeast of the site. There have been several known cases of Arab preservation of an ancient name in two different versions. The reason for this may be that there were two different populations. In our case, we may speculate that there were Hebrew or Aramaic speakers on one side and Greek speakers on the other side. In late Greek, for about the past 1,500 years, the letter *gamma* is pronounced as [ġ] (the voiced velar fricative), such that the word "Galgala" sounds like *ġalġala*. It was not difficult for the Arabs to accept a word with such a pronunciation, since the root *ġalġal* is known in Arabic, meaning to deepen, permeate, or suffuse.

What Can We Find in Khirbet en-Nitle?

The most prominent feature here is the remnants of a Byzantine church. Particularly prominent in the area are fragments of a red-tiled roof scattered throughout the area, which are apparently pieces of the roof that was illustrated on the Madaba Map. And what about the stones? Indeed, many stones – both large and small – can be found at the site. Some of these stones may have come from the traditional twelve stones that we have been seeking.

To our great sorrow, control of this invaluable site, along with Jericho itself, including Tell Jericho (Tell as-Sulṭān), Elisha Spring ('Ein as-Sulṭān), and the ancient Shalom Al Yisrael Synagogue, was given over to the Palestinian Authority, and Jews do not usually visit this vicinity. On the road bypassing Jericho, about a mile north of the Beit Hogla outpost and the Mul Nevo army base, one crosses the old highway path that formerly ran from Jericho to the King Abdullah Bridge at the point about a mile east of the ruins of Gilgal. A helpful landmark for finding this point is a small rise on the left side of the highway containing several tall trees.

I have visited Khirbet en-Nitle – Gilgal – many times in the past. Not long ago I visited again and found that the Palestinian Authority

(Donia Al-Watan)

The large tamarisk in Gilgal

had marked the site with a sign in Arabic and English: Shajarat an-Nitla ("the Tree of Nitla"). Aside from the archaeological remnants, the site is also quite beautiful. Its surroundings are open and verdant, and in the center stands a tall, spreading tamarisk tree (the Tree of Nitle).[4] The foot of this tree is a perfect spot to rest, as well as to celebrate on Ḥol HaMoed. We did just this on several occasions in the past. During the month of Nisan, the springtime sun rising above this tree symbolizes the early days following the arrival of the nation of Israel in its land: "I fell in love with Israel when he was still a child" (Hos. 11:1).

For further study:

Avi-Yonah, M. *The Madaba Mosaic Map: with Introduction and Commentary.* Jerusalem, 1954, 36–37.

Bernard, J. H. *Theodosius* (Palestine Pilgrims' Text Society). London, 1893, 7.

Conder, C. R., and H. H. Kitchener. *The Survey of Western Palestine,* III. London, 1883, 173, 191.

Elitzur, Yoel. *Ancient Place Names in the Holy Land.* Jerusalem-Winona Lake, 2004, 146, 359.

Elitzur, Yoel. "The Meaning of Gilgal." *Revue Biblique* 126 (2019), 321–343.

Freeman-Grenville, G. S. P., R. L. Chapman III, and J. E. Taylor. *The Onomasticon of Eusebius of Caesarea.* Jerusalem, 2003, 41.

Limor, O. *Holy Land Travels: Christian Pilgrims in Late Antiquity,* Jerusalem, 1998, 35, 149, 175, 227 [Hebrew].

Piccirillo, M., and E. Alliata. *The Madaba Map Centenary.* Jerusalem, 1999, 52.

Stewart, A. *The Pilgrimage of the Holy Paula by St. Jerome* (Palestine Pilgrims' Text Society). London, 1896, 12.

Wilkinson, J. *Egeria's Travels to the Holy Land.* Jerusalem, 1981, 161.

4. In the PEF survey and map it was called "Shejeret el Ithleh." The Arabic word *'athleh* is the etymological parallel of the Hebrew *eshel,* meaning "tamarisk." Perhaps the current *nitle* was developed from this name.

Shabbat Ḥol HaMoed Pesaḥ

Aviv and Tel Aviv

In honor of *Ḥag HaAviv* and *Ḥodesh HaAviv*, we will now discuss the word *aviv* and one geographical name that contains it: "Tel Aviv."

Aviv

Spring is a wonderful time of year. But the Tanakh does not use the word *aviv* on its own to refer to the spring season, as we do in Modern Hebrew, instead using only the phrase *Ḥodesh HaAviv*: "Observe *Ḥodesh HaAviv* and offer a Passover sacrifice to the Lord your God, for it was in *Ḥodesh HaAviv*, at night, that the Lord your God freed you from Egypt" (Deut. 16:1). *Aviv* is a very real agricultural term, meaning the grain that no longer consists of soft grass as it does in the winter, but is not yet yellow and dry as it is in the summer. As we read in *Parashat Bo*: "Now the flax and barley were ruined, for the barley was in the ear (*aviv*) and the flax was in bud" (Ex. 9:31). *Ḥazal* used this word to mean the same thing; thus we read in the Mishna: "If it has produced blades, he must turn the soil; if it is in the ear (*aviv*), he must beat them out; if it has grown into corn, it must be burned" (Kilayim 5:7). A similar word to *aviv* is **ev*, which is found twice in the Tanakh: "To see the budding of the vale (*be'ibbei hanaḥal*)" (Song. 6:11); and "While still tender (*be'ibbo*), not yet plucked, it would wither before any other grass" (Job 8:12). This word has parallels in Akkadian and in Arabic. In Akkadian we find the word *abbu*, meaning swamp, and in archaic Arabic we find the word *abbu*, which refers to plants for grazing in swamps and meadows. Based on these parallels, Eliezer Ben-Yehuda suggested that perhaps in Hebrew as well, the singular form of the words *ibbei* and *ibbo* was **av*. If so, the change in the word's first vowel would be similar to the words *pat* and *tzad*, which become *pitto* and *tziddo*, respectively, in their possessive forms.

We should mention that, in contrast to the way it appears at first glance, there is apparently no connection between the Hebrew **ev* and the Aramaic *ibba*, which Onkelos and Jonathan frequently use to translate the word *peri* ("fruit") when it appears in the Tanakh.[1] This Aramaic word appears three times in Daniel 4 in the form *inba*, and is apparently the cognate of the Akkadian word *inbu* ("fruit"). Akkadian also features the verb *enēbu*, meaning "to carry fruit." Another seemingly similar Aramaic word that has a completely different etymological background is *aba*, meaning "forest" in the Aramaic of the Talmud Bavli.[2] This word is parallel to the Arabic word *ġāba* and the Syriac word ᶜava, both of which also mean "forest."[3] The Bavli's Aramaic had a strong tendency to omit guttural letters, rendering the word as *aba* with an *aleph* rather than an *ayin*.

Tel Aviv Today

The Tel Aviv-Yafo metropolis, which today boasts over 410,000 residents and close to 3.5 million people including the satellite cities in its greater metropolitan area, began as "Ahuzat Bayit," founded in April 1909 on the sand dunes north of Yafo. A year after the establishment of Ahuzat Bayit, it was decided to name the new city Tel Aviv, which was the title

1. We also find this word in the Talmud Bavli in Ḥullin 67b.
2. For example: "Thus the proverb runs, 'From the very forest (*aba*) itself comes the [handle of the] axe [that fells it]" (Sanhedrin 39b).
3. The Peshitta, the Syriac translation of the Bible, uses the word *ʿava* (with an *ayin*) in its translation of the verse, "A man goes with his neighbor into a grove" (Deut. 19:5).

of the Hebrew version of Theodor Herzl's novel *Altneuland*. Herzl published *Altneuland* in German in Leipzig in 1902, at the age of forty-two. This was seven years after the verdict in the Dreyfus case that shaped Herzl's identity as a Zionist, and two years before his untimely death. *Altneuland* made a great impression on the Jewish world, and in the very same year the book was translated into Yiddish by Isidor Elyashev and into Hebrew by Naḥum Sokolow. The inspiration for the name "*Altneuland*," which means "Old-New-Land," came to Herzl from the famos *Altneuschul* synagogue in Prague . According to tradition, this synagogue contained a building stone from Jerusalem that would one day be returned to its source. Naḥum Sokolow, a journalist, author, and public figure, was about the same age as Herzl, and was taken by Zionism fever. After Herzl's death, Sokolow was appointed in his place as the secretary-general of the World Zionist Congress and was eventually elected president of that body. He worked for many years on behalf of the Zionist movement, though, like many of his contemporaries, did

(Zev Radovan)

Tel Aviv in its early years

so from outside the Land of Israel.[4] The name "Tel Aviv" is explained as follows in Sokolow's novel:

> And Friedrich whispered: "Tel Aviv!"
>
> "Indeed so! You aimed well. This was an everlasting ruin, a hill of ancient ruins, and now it is a hill of spring (*tel aviv*) and life. We established a new state on our old land."

Tel Aviv and Similar Names in the Tanakh

In Zev Vilnay's *Ariel* encyclopedia of the Land of Israel (Vol. 8, 1980), there are twenty modern place-names in the form Tel-X. These include: one city (Tel Aviv); seven existing Jewish settlements (Tel Yosef, Tel Yitzhak, Tel Litwinsky, Tel Mond, Tel Adashim, Tel Tzur in the Sharon plain, and Tel Katzir); two abandoned Jewish settlements (Tel Hai and Tel Tzur in the Carmel region); one Bedouin settlement (Tel Sheva); six neighborhoods (Tel Or, Tel Arza, Tel Asher, Tel Binyamin, Tel Baruch, and Tel Giborim); two neighborhoods that were swallowed up by their surrounding areas and whose names have been forgotten (Tel Hayim and Tel Yehuda); and one hospital (Tel HaShomer). In addition there was one Tel-X name that existed six months – Tel Amal, the first settlement of the Tower and Stockade campaign, established in December 1936, renamed as Nir David in May 1937. To date some changes have occurred[5] and a new settlement of the same kind, namely Tel Te'omim south of Beit She'an, was founded.

In ancient times, however, this kind of name was almost non-existent in the Land of Israel. In biblical periods it was not known at all. In post-biblical sources the only name of this type that is known is Tel Arza (Mishna Yevamot 16:7).

4. Sokolow died in London in 1936; his remains were brought to Israel in 1956 and reinterred next to Herzl's tomb.
5. Tel Tzur of the Sharon became a neighborhood in Even Yehuda, the terrıtoty of Tel Lituinski was divided between Tel HaShomer hospital, Tel HaShomer army camp, and Kiryat Krinitzi neighborhood of Ramat Gan, and Tel HaShomer hospital later received the name Sheba Medical Center.

In the Tanakh we find three place-names in the form Tel-X – Tel Abib (Ezek. 3:15), Tel-melah, and Tel-harsha (Ezra 2:59 and Neh. 7:61) – all three of which are in Babylonia. Names of this type were apparently common in Mesopotamia at the time. In the list of place-names mentioned in Assyrian sources collected by Finnish Assyriologist Simo Parpola there appear twenty-four names in the form Til-X, and in the list of names from Babylonian sources collected by Ran Zadok there appear twenty-one such names. The three names from the Tanakh mentioned above are not mentioned in Assyrian and Babylonian sources, but one of the twenty-four names from Assyrian sources is perhaps mentioned in the Tanakh in a slightly different version. The name in question is Til-Aššūr, mentioned in three royal inscriptions of Tiglat Pileser III (744–727 BCE) and in three inscriptions of Esarhaddon (680–669 BCE). It has been suggested that this Assyrian name should be identified with Telassar, a place mentioned in the Ravshakeh's speech opposite the walls of Jerusalem (II Kings 19:12, Is. 37:12). It has even been speculated that the biblical version of the name is actually the original name, while the Assyrian sources adjusted it to the more common formula, Til-X.

Tel Abib: The City of Judean Exiles in Babylonia

The Book of Ezekiel begins with the vision of the chariot revealed to the prophet Ezekiel "in the community of exiles by the Chebar Canal" (Ezek. 1:1). After this revelation, Ezekiel travels to "the exile community that dwelled in Tel Abib by the Chebar Canal" (3:15), where he seems to have continued to dwell with the exiles. The Chebar Canal is mentioned in the form *nâr Kabâru* in Babylonian documents of that period, and in the Persian Period in the archives of the Murashu family of Nippur, which was located about forty-five miles southeast of the city of Babylon (about ninety miles south of Baghdad). The Chebar Canal was a large, artificial stream that ran from the Euphrates River north of Babylon and returned to flow back into the Euphrates about seventy miles farther south. The canal split into secondary canals and watered a large stretch of land east of the Euphrates. The Chebar Canal flowed through Nippur, which was located in the region where the Judean exiles settled. In recent years,

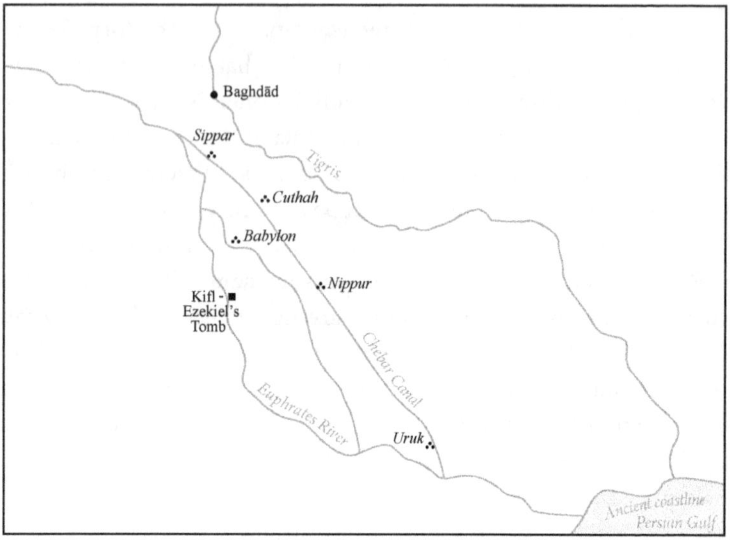

documents have been found in Babylonia that mention "the city of the people of Judea," and in a shortened version, "the city of Judea."[6] This place may have been another city of Judean exiles, and possibly even Tel Abib itself.

It is noteworthy that an ancient tradition identifies a site on the banks of the Euphrates River, west of the remains of Nippur, as the tomb of the prophet Ezekiel. The place is called Kifl and contains an impressive, fortified site, featuring two towers and about two hundred stores that used to be owned by Jews. The place is mentioned as early as in the geonic literature. Two of the first and most famous Jewish travelers of the Middle Ages, Rabbi Benjamin of Tudela and Rabbi Petaḥiah of Regensburg, who visited the site between 1170 and 1180, described it in detail and with great admiration. Iraqi Jews would visit the site and fill it and its surrounding area with large crowds of people on the Jewish festivals.[7] The place was also home to clay tiles on which the verses of the Book of Ezekiel were engraved. Starting from 1937 until the decade

6. For more details and references, see the chapter on *Parashat Kedoshim.*
7. During the Middle Ages this occurred primarily on Sukkot and in the modern period on Shavuot.

Ezekiel's Tomb by the Euphrates River

following the establishment of the State of Israel, these tiles were dismantled. Some pieces reached Israel and were handed over to the president of Israel at the time, Yitzḥak Ben-Zvi; they can be viewed today at the Ben-Zvi Institute (Yad Ben-Zvi). Following the Gulf War, Jewish groups from Israel and from around the world returned to visit the site once more, and it became clear that anti-Semitic Arabs had damaged the Hebrew inscriptions at the site.

The Linguistic Background of the Name of the Babylonian Tel Abib

The word *aviv* and the name Tel Abib do not carry any meaning in Akkadian, the language of Babylonia, but there is a famous and important expression in Akkadian similar in its form to *aviv*: *abūbu*, meaning "the deluge." The expression is used in the same contexts in which the word *mabbul* is used in Hebrew, primarily as a name for the cosmic event of the destruction of the world in the early days of humanity, through a divinely ordained flood. Here and there, however, it is also a name for an exceptionally devastating rainstorm. Two unique linguistic expressions sometimes include the word *abūbu*. The first is *lām abūbi*, meaning "before the deluge," used to refer to something that is primordially ancient.[8] The second expression is *til abūbi*, meaning "a hill of ruins made by the flood," or in other words, an everlasting ruin, a place that is eternally destroyed and desolate. The expression is generally mentioned in victory inscriptions that describe the conquest and destruction of cities and lands, and sometimes in the formulations of curses for those who would break a pact. Modern scholars have connected the biblical "Tel Abib" to this expression, maintaining that the exiles were resettled in a ruined tell called *Til Abūbi*. Some scholars suggested emending the text of the verse from "Tel Abib" to "Tel Abub," while others posited that "Tel Abib" was a euphemism: The exiles changed the name of the site from one with negative connotations to a more pleasant-sounding Hebrew name. The difficulty with these theories is that in all the Babylonian and Assyrian literature there is not one mention of an actual place described as a "*til abūbi*," nor is there any hint that a place called Til Abūbi actually exists. The phrase is always used as literary imagery for cases of extreme destruction, similar to the Hebrew phrase *tel olam* ("an everlasting ruin"; see Deut. 13:17). The *Chicago Assyrian Dictionary* cites eight sources that mention *til abūbi*. In seven of them, the full expression is *kīma til abūbi*, meaning, "like hills of ruins," and in the eighth the expression is *māssu ana til abūbi litēr*, meaning, "may (Adad) turn his land into hills of ruins."

It seems to me that we will be able to understand the matter once we delve into the world of Ezekiel, his contemporaries, and his geographical setting. Tel Abib by the Chebar Canal in Babylonia was a city of Judean exiles who arrived in Babylonia during the exile of Yehoyachin. Ezekiel, who arrived in Babylonia with them, saw divine visions and was chosen as a prophet by the Chebar Canal, on the fifth day of the fourth month, during the fifth year of the exile of King Yehoyachin

8. Professor Chaim Cohen, *z"l*, of Ben-Gurion University in Beersheba suggested using this expression to interpret the verse, "The Lord sat enthroned at the Flood (*lammabbūl*); the Lord sits enthroned, king forever" (Ps. 29:10). In his view the Hebrew here imitates the Akkadian phrase to mean that God sits on His royal throne forever; from everlasting to everlasting: "Your throne stands firm from of old; from eternity You have existed" (93:2).

(Ezek. 1:1–2) – six years before the destruction of Jerusalem (592 BCE). Immediately after the revelation by the Chebar Canal, the prophet says:

> A spirit seized me and carried me away. I went in bitterness, in the fury of my spirit, while the hand of the Lord was strong upon me. And I came to the exile community that dwelt in Tel Abib... and for seven days I sat there stunned among them. (3:14–15).

Ezekiel's prophetic career continues for at least twenty-two years (compare to Ezekiel 29:17), and the next dated prophecy comes to him in his home in Tel Abib on the fifth of Elul, one year after the first revelation (8:1).

In the summer of 2005, my friends – and I alongside them – suffered the difficult experience of destruction, as well as a kind of exile: Israel's dismantlement of the communities of Gush Katif. What we experienced was not nearly as grievous as what our ancestors experienced in the time of Ezekiel, but the last two weeks that I spent in Kfar Darom with its residents, and the tears on the day of the expulsion are things that one who experienced them remembers anew every day of his life. "Like a sparrow wandering from its nest is a man who wanders from his home" (Prov. 27:8). Even today, when I happen to meet one of the evictees, our conversation is different from the conversation I might have with any past friend or acquaintance. Simple small talk like "How are you?" and "How's it going?" takes on new, loaded significance.

When I read about Tel Abib by the Chebar Canal in the Book of Ezekiel today, it is no longer simply "the city of Judean exiles" as it says in the commentaries or in encyclopedias. These were people torn by brute force from their lives and from their homes in Jerusalem or in Judea, shackled in chains and shipped off to a foreign, distant land so different in its landscape, language, and climate from their own. Even if these people later managed to maintain reasonable, civil relationships with the Babylonian authorities, they can never be the same people they once were. Five years after the initial trauma, Tel Abib by the Chebar Canal is a settlement under construction. The settlement that they are building or that the authority is building for them is a settlement of uprooted people, devoid of the usual joy and delight of building. Today

I understand that "I sat there stunned among them" has a dual meaning: It describes both Ezekiel and the people around him.

It is easy to understand how the people there lapsed into apathy and despair. It is also easy to understand the feelings that the false prophets – Aḥav son of Kolaiah, Tzidkiyahu son of Maaseiah and Shemaiah the Nehelamite (Jer. 29:21–32) – sowed among the people, promising the nation that the awful nightmare was about to end, and that in a short time they would all joyfully return to Judea and Jerusalem. It seems to be no coincidence that only after a year in Tel Abib does the Tanakh mention that the prophet lived in a house. Indeed, it is logical to presume that the settlement, during its construction, was made up of tents or temporary huts, and that it took some time until the first real houses appeared. Ezekiel and the elders of Judea who "were sitting before [him]" (Ezek. 8:1, 14:1) were certainly among the people who agreed to take the reasonable and responsible albeit unexciting path, as Jeremiah encouraged them to do in his letter:

> Thus said the Lord of Hosts, the God of Israel, to the whole community that I exiled from Jerusalem to Babylon: Build houses and live in them, plant gardens and eat their fruit. Take wives and beget sons and daughters ... Multiply there, do not decrease. And seek the welfare of the city to which I have exiled you and pray to the Lord in its behalf; for in its prosperity you shall prosper. (Jer. 29:4–7)

This is not an easy task: to build without the delight of creation, to know that "It will be a long time" (29:28), to accept the decree of Babylonian exile that could be – and indeed was – not particularly harsh. The exile lacked the curses, destruction, bloodshed, famine, and pestilence described in the Torah's admonition, but it was still a full-fledged exile.

It may be that the Hebrew name adapted to the Babylonian setting – "Tel Abib" – was born of this prophetic approach. I will permit myself to speculate that at least from a linguistic and literary perspective, the rationale behind the Hebrew name "Tel Abib," given by exiles from Jerusalem in the sixth century BCE, was not too far from the idea that inspired Naḥum Sokolow in the early twentieth century CE. Perhaps they too considered the integration of *tel*, symbolizing the destruction, with *aviv*, symbolizing the new – albeit slow – growth. I believe that the Babylonian-Assyrian expression *til abūbi* is certainly the key to the background of name "Tel Abib" that the exiles gave to their settlement. However, this was not the true name of the place, but rather a literary concept. When they chose to give the name Tel Abib to the city of exiles that they built, it was as if they were defying the original Akkadian expression by presenting in its place a Hebrew expression so similar to it in linguistic structure and yet so different from it in its contextual meaning. The exiles were declaring to themselves and to others: We will not allow ourselves to become mired here out of apathy caused by the destruction of our former lives. Neither will we entertain delusions of a sudden return to our homeland on the wings of eagles. We will develop ourselves slowly but surely, like the stalks of grain that are still green in the springtime, until the conditions are ripe for us to return home, to the Land of Israel.

For further study:

Ben-Yehuda, E. *A Complete Dictionary of Ancient and Modern Hebrew*, 7 [Hebrew].

Cohen, C. "Tel Aviv." In *Sha'are Lashon* 1, edited by A. Maman, S. E. Fassberg, and Y. Breuer, 30–32. Jerusalem, 2007 [Hebrew].

Cohen, C. "The Lord Sat Enthroned Before the Flood (Ps. 29:10): A New Interpretation." *Leshonenu* 53 (1990): 193–201 [Hebrew].

Cook, G. A. *The Book of Ezekiel* (ICC). Edinburgh, 1967, 42–43.

Gelb I. J. et al. (eds.). *The Assyrian Dictionary*, A/1, sv *abūbu*. Chicago, 1964, 77–78.

Kaufman, S. A. *The Akkadian Influences on Aramaic*. Chicago, 1974, 58–59.

Kobayashi, Y. "Tel Abib." In *The Anchor Bible Dictionary*, 6, 344.

Parpola, S. *Neo-Assyrian Toponyms*. Neukirchen-Vluyn, 1970, 352–356.

Sokolow, N. *Tel Aviv: A Story by Theodor Herzl. Translated into Hebrew by N. S.* Warsaw, The Russian Zionist Organization, 1902 [Hebrew].

Zadok, R. *Geographical Names According to Neo- and Late-Babylonian Texts*. (RGTC 8), Wiesbaden, 1985, 308–313.

Zadok, R. *The Nippur Region during the Late Assyrian, Chaldaean and Achaemenian Periods, Chiefly according to Written Sources. IOS* 8: 266–332.

Zadok, R. "Tel Abib"; "Telassar." In *Encyclopaedia Biblica* 8, 568 [Hebrew].

Wikipedia entries: "*Altneuland*"; "Nahum Sokolow"; "Ezekiel's Tomb"; "Tel Aviv."

Seventh Day of Pesaḥ

The Sea of Suph

We will now discuss the Sea of Suph, where an unprecedented and unequaled miracle took place, and whose shores first heard the jubilant sound of the Song at the Sea: "I will sing to the Lord, for He has triumphed gloriously" (Exodus 15:1).

The Red Sea

We all know that the Sea of Suph is the body of water we know today as "the Red Sea." Do not believe the fictitious explanation for this name that one hears frequently from tour guides and others easily taken by false etymologies, that the source of the name "the Red Sea" is a misspelling of the English translation of *Yam Suf* – "Reed Sea." The name "the Red Sea" originated from the Greek *Erythra Thalassa,* which became the Latin *Mare Rubrum* and the Aramaic *Yamma Samoka* (as appears in the Dead Sea Scrolls). The name then migrated to all the European languages. Herodotus mentions this name already in the middle of the fifth century BCE, and the translators who authored the Septuagint used the name in the middle of the third century BCE as the established translation for *Yam Suf.* In ancient sources, the name refers occasionally to the Persian Gulf or even to the Indian Ocean. The source of the name is not clear, though it may be that it derives from the mountains of red granite in its vicinity. We will suffice by saying that English and many other languages refer to the Sea of Suph as "the Red Sea."

(Wellcome Images)

Lithograph of Suez and the Gulf of Suez, 1849

The Scholarly View Placing the Sea of Suph in a Northern Lake

In Modern Hebrew, Yam Suf also refers to the Red Sea, and specifically to its two gulfs on either coast of the Sinai Peninsula: the Gulf of Eilat and the Gulf of Suez (in Arabic *Suways*). However, if we look at encyclopedias, historical atlases, or various modern commentators, we are in for a surprise. Most modern scholars identify the Sea of Suph – where the people of Israel crossed – as one of various bodies of water other than the Red Sea itself. Most label one of the two so-called Bitter Lakes, which are today combined in the Suez Canal as "the Sea of Suph," while others choose Lake Manzala, close to the Mediterranean Sea, near Port Said. Still others strayed even farther away from the Red Sea, preferring Lake

Bardawil (Herodotus' "Serbonian Bog") within the Mediterranean Sea in northern Sinai.[1]

Are the Scholars Right?

If we follow the occurrences of the name "the Sea of Suph" in the Tanakh, it is easy to conclude that the biblical Sea of Suph indeed refers to both gulfs of the Red Sea. Particularly interesting in this regard is Rashi's commentary on *Parashat Bo*. Rashi, who lived more than nine hundred years ago, never visited the Land of Israel and seemingly did not use maps either. The only materials at his disposal were the Tanakh and the literature of *Ḥazal*. The visual appearance of the Sea of Suph as we know it – a sea bifurcated into two long, narrow gulfs, one on the east and one on the west, reaching Egypt – is highly unusual and difficult to guess without prior knowledge of it. But Rashi, using only the texts available to him, appears to have guessed correctly: "I believe that the Sea of Suph was partly in the west, opposite the entire southern boundary, and also east of the Land of Israel" (Rashi, Ex. 10:19). We will list a few of the sources that prove this (based on Rashi, with certain differences). The most prominent source, which demonstrates clearly that the entire Gulf of Suez is called "the Sea of Suph" is the story of the plague of locusts: "And when morning came, the east wind had brought the locusts. Locusts invaded *all the land of Egypt* and settled within *all the territory of Egypt*" (Ex. 10:13–14). Ancient Egypt was a strip of land a few dozen miles wide concentrated along the entire length of the Nile River (the northern region was much wider because of the many branches of the Nile Delta). The Torah states that the locusts reached Egypt by way of an "east wind,"[2] and they "settled within all the territory of Egypt." After Moses pleaded with God on behalf of Pharaoh, the locusts left by way of a west wind: "The Lord caused a shift to a very strong west wind, which lifted the locusts and hurled them into the Sea of Suph; not a single locust remained in all the territory of Egypt" (10:19). The verse indicates that

---

1. The former Israeli military settlement of Naḥal Yam was established immediately after the Six-Day War on the shore of this lake, and its residents supported themselves by fishing there. In 1970 a popular song praising Naḥal Yam was composed. It was settled in 1973 but evacuated in 1974 and then handed over to Egypt in 1980.
2. According to Cassuto, the locusts came from the direction of Sudan. He explains that the phrase *ruaḥ kadim* throughout the Tanakh refers to a strong, dry wind and not necessarily an eastern wind.

a west wind "thrust the locusts into the Sea of Suph, which was opposite it" (Rashi), demonstrating that just as Egypt was a kind of long strip running from south to north, the Sea of Suph was similarly a long strip running from south to north, east of Egypt. On the other hand, one can cite other verses that seem to indicate that the Sea of Suph is located southeast of the Land of Israel: "I will set your borders from the Sea of Suph to the Sea of Philistia" (23:31); "They set out from Mount Hor by way of the Sea of Suph to skirt the land of Edom" (Num. 21:4); "King Solomon also built a fleet of ships at Ezion-geber, which is near Eloth on the shore of the Sea of Suph in the land of Edom" (I Kings 9:26). The meaning seems clear: The biblical Sea of Suph refers to the two gulfs of the Red Sea.

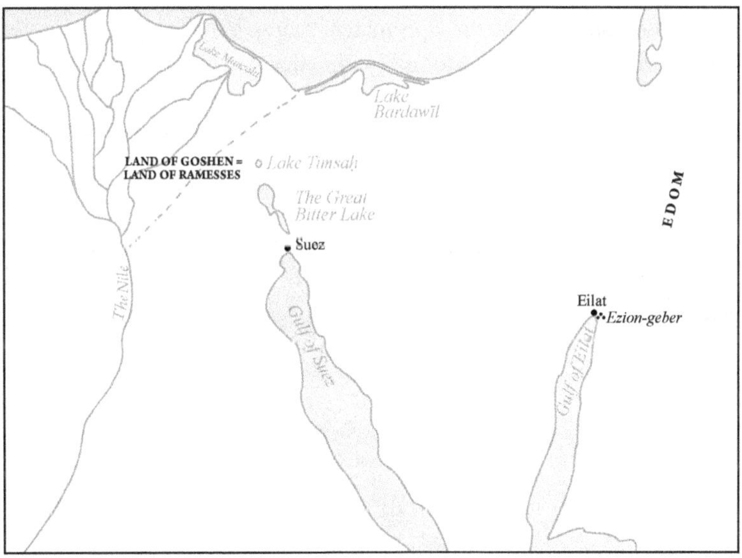

Why Did the Scholars Move the Sea of Suph North?

There are two answers to this question, one geographical-historical and one linguistic. The geographical-historical reason is the scholars' desire to find a place that would provide a natural explanation for the miracle of the Splitting of the Sea (or "the creation myth of the Splitting of the Sea," as Bible critics would say). We will not address the topic of miracles and nature in Jewish thought and throughout the Tanakh in this framework. We will merely note that, at least in our case, the desire to find a natural explanation for the Splitting of the Sea is justified; such an explanation is even implied in the biblical text itself. The Torah speaks of a powerful east wind that blew for many long hours preceding the Splitting of the Sea, and hints at the fact that the water returned to its place only gradually, in stages. First, the ground became muddy and the wheels of the Egyptian chariots became stuck in it, causing them to become dislodged from their axles. At this stage, the Egyptians attempted to return toward Egypt, at which point the water returned and engulfed them and their chariots. Various scholars considered the marshy swamps near the northern lakes as an appropriate location for the drowning of the Egyptians, and some scholars believed that in those lakes there was likely to be greater differences in water level between high and low tides. Others explained alternatively that the strong wind created sandstorms that could transport whole dunes into the lakes. The most prominent example of such phenomena is Lake Bardawil, a shallow lake located within the Mediterranean Sea. On the northern boundary between the lake and the deep waters of the sea is a strip of land that appears during low tide and is covered by water during high tide.

The linguistic reason is the desire to understand the name "Sea of Suph," in Hebrew and possibly in Egyptian as well.[3] The Hebrew *suf* refers to the sedge, papyrus, reed or the like, a freshwater plant that grows

The Great Bitter Lake

3. In classical Egyptian, the word *swt* is equivalent to the Hebrew *suf* (the last letter may not be part of the root). In later Egyptian the word is *ṯwfy*.

on the banks of the Nile. The Red Sea is a salty sea and thus no sedge or similar plant can grow on its shores. By contrast, sedge are common on the shores of the Bitter Lakes, as well as in Egypt and in the Northern Sinai Peninsula, due to the high groundwater there.

Because of these two perspectives, scholars saw fit to move the Sea of Suph northward. From the etymological perspective, one may claim that the name indeed at first referred to the northern lakes, but its usage later spread to the salty sea south of the lakes as well, and the meaning of the name was forgotten.[4] However, the burden of proof lies with one who would make such a claim. From the perspective of the Torah's narrative, scholars have had the most difficulty grappling with the verse teaching us that "God did not lead them by way of the land of the Philistines, although it was nearer… So God led the people roundabout, by way of the wilderness at the Sea of Suph" (Ex. 13:17–18). The Bitter Lakes, and even more so the lakes adjacent to and within the Mediterranean Sea, are "by way of the land of the Philistines," the shortest route from Egypt to Canaan – not "by way of the wilderness." The scholars attempted to resolve this problem in various ways, both exegetical and critical, and I will not review them here.

In my opinion, this is a typical case of hard data against speculation. In every place where the information found in the Tanakh is clear, the biblical Sea of Suph is the Red Sea. Etymological speculations and scientific reconstructions of miraculous events cannot simply brush away hard data. We may be able to explain the Splitting of the Sea or we may not; we may succeed in understanding the etymological background of the word *suf* or we may not (do we understand the names "Sinai," "Zin," "Alush," "Amalek," and many others?). But the explicit facts arising from the words of the Tanakh in other prominent places must form the basis for our conclusions.

Where Did the Splitting of the Sea Take Place?

In order to understand the geographical location of the Splitting of the Sea, it is worth mentioning the name Etham, "which is on the edge of

4. This would be similar to the name "the Red Sea," which grew to include the Indian Ocean and the Persian Gulf in various sources, or "Africa," which once referred to North Africa alone, and now refers to the entire continent.

the wilderness," where Israel encamped before the Splitting of the Sea. From there the people traveled to Pi-hahiroth, Migdol, and Baal-zephon, until they finally marched into the sea on dry ground. In the list of the marches of the people of Israel in Numbers 33, it says that *after* they crossed the sea "they made a three-day journey in the wilderness of Etham and encamped at Marah." These combined pieces of information demonstrate that Etham was located on the edge of the Sea of Suph, on the border between "the wilderness" and "the land,"[5] apparently in the place where the modern-day city of Suez is situated. This demonstrates that the Splitting of the Sea took place just south of Suez.

One attempt to explain the miracle scientifically in this location was made by a hydrologist named Moshe Dayan (no relation to the famous general). Dayan examined the data regarding the sea in the period preceding the construction of the Suez Canal, according to maps and diagrams that the canal's excavators used in the mid-nineteenth century. He came to the conclusion that the area contained a raised terrace that could become exposed for a certain amount of time under extreme conditions of both low tide and strong winds, and then become inundated with large amounts of water immediately thereafter. One of the early preparations that the members of Ferdinand de Lesseps' delegation undertook prior to excavating the Suez Canal was to inspect the tidal range (the difference between the high tide and the low tide) in the various bodies of water that the canal would connect. The tidal range in the Bitter Lakes was 0.66 meters; in the Mediterranean Sea it was 1.10 meters; but in the Gulf of Suez it was 3.24 meters!

In conclusion, whether or not we are convinced by the veracity of Moshe Dayan's analysis, the Sea of Suph is indeed the Red Sea, and not any lake to its north or on the shores of the Mediterranean Sea. The people of Israel crossed the sea near the northern edge of the Gulf of Suez. Blessed is He who performed miracles for our ancestors in this place!

For further study:

Aharoni, Y. *The Land of the Bible: A Historical Geography*. Translated and edited by A. F. Rainey. Pennsylvania, 1979, 196–197.

5. See Ex. 8:21–23 to compare the Torah's usage of these two terms.

Cassuto, U. *A Commentary on the Book of Exodus*. Translated by I. Abrahams. Jerusalem, 1974, 127.

Cohen, C. "*Musagim Geografiyim Bemivḥan Ha'etimologiya Vehaheksher (Mishi'urei Dr. Yoel Elitzur).*" *Maaliot* (1995): 158–167 [Hebrew].

Dayan, M. "The Dividing of the Red Sea According to Natural Sciences." *Beit Mikra* 73 (1978): 162–176 [Hebrew].

Kitchen, K. A. *The Reliability of the Old Testament*. Michigan-Cambridge, 2003, 259, 261–263.

Lambdin, T. O. "Egyptian Loan Words in the Old Testament." *JAOS* 73 (1953): 153.

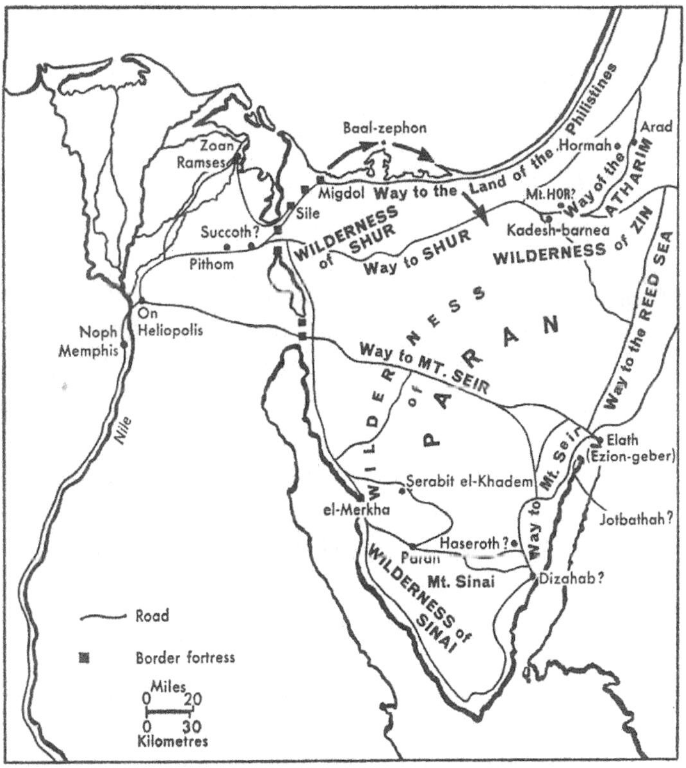

(Westminster Press Philadelphia)

The route of the Exodus according to the revised edition of Yohanan Aharoni's *The Land of the Bible*, translated from the Hebrew and edited by A. F. Rainey (1979), p. 197. The map is not definitive about the route, but gives priority to the northern route along the Mediterranean Sea. This northern route was the only option in Aharoni's first Hebrew edition.

Shavuot

Sinai

"On the third new moon after the Israelites had gone forth from the land of Egypt, on that very day, they entered the wilderness of Sinai ... Israel encamped there in front of the mountain" (Ex. 19:1–2). At Sinai we encamped as one man, with one heart. At Sinai, we heard the voice of God speaking from out of the fire. At Sinai, we made the golden calf – but also the *Mishkan*. At Sinai, we became a nation, with chieftains, flags, Levites, and priests. Sinai is the setting for half of the Book of Exodus, all of the Book of Leviticus, and a third of the Book of Numbers. The nation of Israel stayed in Sinai for almost a year, a year in which it acquired its eternal, unchanging identity.

Where is Mount Sinai? The number of different views on this matter is almost equal to the number of scholars who tackled the question. Menashe Har-el, in his book *The Sinai Journeys*, first published in Hebrew in 1968, listed twelve different views regarding the location of the mountain, and in the decades since the book's publication, even more suggestions have been proposed. Mount Sinai has been identified with almost every significant peak in the Sinai Peninsula. After the Sinai Peninsula was handed over to Egypt, one scholar even identified

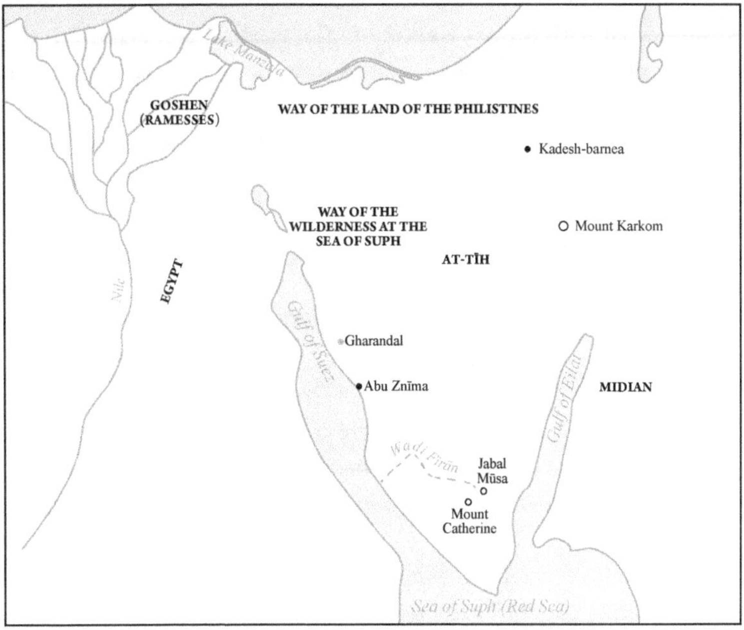

(Zev Radovan)

Mount Karkom, south of Makhtesh Ramon – "Mount Sinai" according to Prof. Emmanuel Anati

Mount Sinai with Mount Karkom in the western Negev, within the borders of the state of Israel – quite a convenience for Israeli visitors. Some identified Mount Sinai in Midian, east of the Gulf of Eilat, and some went so far as to identify it in northern Transjordan or even in the depths of the Arabian Peninsula.

Is There a Way to Determine Which View Is the Right One?

In my opinion, there is.

What do we know from the Tanakh about the wilderness of Sinai and Mount Sinai? The meaning of the name Sinai is actually not clear to us, but the location's other name – Horeb – indicates an arid region. The verses teach us that the region contains rocks and boulders, from which God – through the hand of Moses – drew water for Israel: "I will be standing there before you on the rock at Horeb. Strike the rock and water will issue from it" (Ex. 17:6). It seems that a verse in Deuteronomy describes the very same incident: "Who brought forth water for you from the flinty rock" (Deut. 8:15). This outpouring of water was not a one-time event. The water continued to flow long after Moses struck the rock, and it was mentioned later in connection to the sin of the Golden Calf: "He strewed it upon the water" (Ex. 32:20); and in the account in Deuteronomy: "I threw its dust into the brook that comes down from the mountain" (9:21). At the foot of the mountain there must have been room for a large encampment. One of the rabbinic *aggadot* (Sota 5a; *Midrash Tehillim* 68) presents Mount Sinai as a hill that is not particularly tall. Indeed, it was because of its humility that it merited serving as the setting for the Giving of the Torah, instead of other towering peaks like Tabor and Hermon. However, it is far from certain if this *aggada* was speaking of an actual geographical identification; it is more likely that the details of the *aggada* remain in the realm of ideas and moral lessons.

Finding Sinai

The biblical text provides a few clues as to the location of Sinai. The people of Israel reached the wilderness of Sinai a month and a half after leaving Egypt, taking a discontinuous path with several stops along the way. The Torah reports: "It is eleven days from Horeb to Kadesh-barnea by the Mount Seir route" (Deut. 1:2), and the prophet Elijah walked forty days and forty nights from the wilderness of Beer-sheba "as far as the mountain of God at Horeb" (I Kings 19:8). However, the most basic piece of geographical information in the Torah regarding Sinai is its location between Midian and Egypt. Moses traveled there initially from Midian, when he led his flock far from his normal grazing area.[1] Moses passed through this place again when he later returned from Midian to Egypt. On that occasion, God sent Aaron to meet him: "He went and met him at the mountain of God, and he kissed him" (Ex. 4:27).

Sinai's location between Midian (whose identity has been established as the eastern coast of the Gulf of Eilat, in our context the northern part of this region) and Egypt allows us to reject outright all the views that place it outside the Sinai Peninsula. Even within the Sinai Peninsula, there are vast regions in which Mount Sinai could not possibly be located.

First of all, the reader should beware of being misled by the modern name "the Sinai Peninsula." In biblical terminology, Sinai was only one of several wildernesses in this huge space, and by no means the largest among them.[2] From a geographical perspective, the Sinai Peninsula is made up, broadly speaking, of three major sections:

- The northern section close to the Mediterranean Sea is not very arid. It has relatively high groundwater levels, numerous dune fields and, here and there, settlements and the remnants of ancient settlements.

1. "He drove the flock *aḥar hamidbar*" (Ex. 3:1). According to Radak, Shadal, Cassuto, and some modern translators, *midbar* here means "pasture" (cf. Aramaic DBR, "to guide"; *Ḥazal's dabbar,* "leader"; and the use of *midbar* in Gen. 37:22, II Sam. 17:29, and Mishna Beitza 5:7, as well as *haddavero* in Micah 2:12). Other translations of *aḥar hamidbar* have included: "to the far side of the desert"; "to the backside of the desert"; "to the west side of the desert"; "to the inner parts of the desert"; "to the edge of the desert"; and "to the farthest side of the desert."
2. See the chapter on *Parashat Behaalotekha* for a detailed examination of the various wildernesses. In this discussion we will only mention briefly what is necessary for the context here.

- The central section, known in Arabic as *at-Tīh*, is an absolute desert, mostly flat and large in area – almost 7.5 million acres with virtually no signs of life.
- The southern section is a region whose center contains an exceptionally tall massif with lofty granite mountains reaching up to 8,500 feet above sea level.

The northern section of the Sinai Peninsula is known in the Tanakh as the wilderness of Shur. It is mentioned in the Book of Genesis in connection to the Patriarchs and their settlement in the western Negeb; in the description of the settlement patterns of the Ishmaelites; and in Exodus as the wilderness that the people of Israel entered after they crossed the Sea of Suph.

The large, dry central section is known in the Tanakh as the wilderness of Paran. It was this wilderness that the people of Israel entered after leaving the wilderness of Sinai, and it was there that they wandered until reaching Kadesh-barnea, at the edge of the land of Canaan (Num. 11–12). In the eastern section of the northern part of this wilderness, around Kadesh-barnea, was the wilderness of Zin.

Mount Catherine, the highest mountain in the entire Sinai Peninsula, with the ancient monastery at its foot

(C. W. Wilson, *Picturesque Palestine, Sinai and Egypt*, London, 1881–1884)

Jabal Musa, view from the south

The remaining section, the tall, southern part of the peninsula, is apparently where the wilderness of Sinai and Mount Sinai can be found. From ancient times, the Christian tradition has identified Mount Sinai in Jabal Musa (lit. "Moses' Mountain"), one of the highest peaks in the Sinai Massif. A famous monastery was built not far from there, at the foot of Mount Catherine, the highest peak in the entire region. It is worth according a measure of respect to the Christian traditions of identification from the period of early Christianity. The traditions from this period are often based on Jewish traditions, and it is not inconceivable that the source of this tradition predates Christianity.

An examination of various parts of the Torah can reaffirm this fundamental outlook, without necessarily committing to one particular peak or another. In *Parashat Beshallaḥ*, the Torah emphasizes that "God did not lead them by way of the land of the Philistines...God led the people roundabout, by way of the wilderness at the Sea of Suph" (Ex. 13:17–18). The southern section of the peninsula is a wilderness flanked on its right and on its left by the two gulfs of the Sea of Suph.

Elim and "the Sea of Suph"

Moreover, my father and teacher *z"l* emphasized in this context a verse that usually attracts little attention. In the list of the marches of the people of Israel in the wilderness in Numbers 33, the Torah enumerates the places where the people of Israel encamped after crossing through the sea: Marah, Elim, the Sea of Suph, the wilderness of Sin, Dophkah, Alush, Rephidim, and the wilderness of Sinai. This list is parallel to the list in Exodus but adds several stations not mentioned in the latter. The surprise here is the Sea of Suph: "They set out from Elim and encamped by the Sea of Suph" (Num. 33:10). Why would the people of Israel return to the Sea of Suph after having crossed the sea long ago? We are forced to conclude, therefore, that after Israel crossed the sea and emerged into the wilderness, they needed to return

(Picturesque Palestine, Sinai and Egypt)

Ras Abu Znima; the mountains reach the sea and the caravan route passes through the seashore.

to encamp by the Sea of Suph – not on the Egyptian side of the sea but on the Sinaitic side. We see from this that the direction of their movement was from the north to the south, parallel to the length of the Gulf of Suez, until they reached an area where the tall mountains draw so close to the sea that they had no choice but to return to traveling along the shoreline. We are familiar with these details from the reality on the ground.

Even today, the road that runs north-south on the western side of the Sinai Peninsula must run along the shoreline at a point known today as Abu Znīma. This point, located about seventy-five miles south of Suez and about sixty miles northwest of Mount Catherine, is presumably "the Sea of Suph" to which the verse refers. Elim, the point before the Sea of Suph, is, according to the verses, a large desert oasis containing "twelve springs and seventy palm trees." This station, where the people of Israel encamped, also has an excellent identification. It is known today as Gharandal, and it contains very high groundwater levels. The surrounding area contains large palm

(www.efratnakash.com)

The oasis of Gharandal in the western part of the Sinai Peninsula; "Twelve springs and seventy palm trees"; most probably the biblical Elim

groves growing above the high groundwater, which occasionally rises above ground. Residents of this region often draw water from the ground by digging small wells about seven feet deep.[3] I remember this area well from the years when Israel controlled Sinai following the Six-Day War. During that period, it was common practice for all those passing through Gharandal to buy bottles of cola from the Bedouins who lived there.

Sure enough, the accounts of early pilgrims describing the place highlight these same typical characteristics, identifying it with the biblical Elim as well. Note the details in the following description (translated from the original Latin), from a twelfth-century copy of an early Christian source, *Egeria's Travels,* originally written in the fourth century CE:

> Then you reach Arandara, the Arandara which was called Helim. There is a stream there, and, though it dries up from time to time, there is water to be had from its bed or from near the bank. In that place there is plenty of grass and a great many palm trees, and all the way from Sur, where we crossed the Red Sea, there is no place as pleasant as this, or with such good plentiful water. The next staging-post from there is beside the sea.

The massif in southern Sinai also fits the Torah's descriptions of "the flinty rock" and "the brook that comes down from the mountain." A flowing stream is certainly a rarity in the desert, but such a stream exists on the Sinai Massif. There, in the vicinity of the Mount Sinai of the Christian tradition, we find Wadi Firān, which contains a constant flow of water. In all likelihood, it was against the backdrop of these majestic landscapes that we received the Torah.

---

3. The Torah's phrase *einot mayim* probably refers to artificial wells. Compare to: "An angel of the Lord found her by a spring of water (*ein hamayim*) in the wilderness… Therefore the well was called Beer-lahai-roi" (Gen. 16:7, 14); "He made the camels kneel down by the well outside the city… Here I stand by the spring of water (*ein hamayim*)" (24:11, 13).

(Picturesque Palestine, Sinai and Egypt)

Wadi Firan and Jabal Sirbal: a combination of rocky flints, arid environment, and flowing water

For further study:

Anati E. et al. "Where is Mt. Sinai?" *Biblical Archaeology Review* 11 (1985).
Elitzur Yehuda, and Y. Kiel. *Daat Mikra Bible Atlas*. Translated by L. J. Schramm. Jerusalem, 2011, 96–97.
Har-el, M. *The Sinai Journeys: The Route of the Exodus*. San Diego, 1983.
Har-el, M. "*Sinai, Mount Sinai*." In *Encyclopaedia Biblica* 5, col. 1020–1022 [Hebrew].
Ilan, Z. "*Ha'im Efshar SheHar Sinai Hu Serabit el-Khadim?*" *Beit Mikra* 24 (1979): 278–282 [Hebrew].
Kimchi, D. *Sefer Hashorashim*. Edited by J. H. R. Biesenthal and F. Lebrecht. Berlin, 1847, 135.
[http://www.daat.ac.il/daat/vl/radak/radak01.pdf]
Stewart, A. *Antoninus Martyr* (PPTS 2). London, 1896, paragraphs 37 40.
Wilkinson, J. *Egeria's Travels to the Holy Land*. Jerusalem-Warminster, 1981, 91–100, 208.

Subject Index

Subject Index

Source Index

BIBLE

Source Index

ANCIENT TRANSLATIONS

Septuagint

SOURCES FROM BIBLICAL PERIODS

APOCRYPHA

DEAD SEA SCROLLS

JOSEPHUS

RABBINIC SOURCES

Mishna

Tosefta

EARLY CHRISTIAN SOURCES

MEDIEVAL JEWISH SOURCES

The fonts used in this book are from the Arno family

Maggid Books
The best of contemporary Jewish thought from
Koren Publishers Jerusalem Ltd.